WILLY BRANDT

Klaus Harpprecht

WILLY BRANDT
Portrait and Self-Portrait

Translated by Hank Keller

Abelard-Schuman · London

First published in Great Britain in 1972 by
Abelard-Schuman Limited
Copyright © 1971 by Nash Publishing
Originally published in German under the title of
Willy Brandt, Portrat und Selbstportrat
by Kindler Verlag, Munich

ISBN 0 200 71947 5

Printed in Great Britain

Abelard-Schuman Limited,   Abelard-Schuman Limited,
158 Buckingham Palace Road, 24 Market Square,
London, S.W.1   Aylesbury, Bucks.

Contents

PREFACE

To the Honorable
Federal Chancellor:

To the honorable Federal Chancellor:

Dear Mr. Brandt:

I shun the formality of a preface. New Year's Day, as I write these lines, seems an auspicious occasion to wish you courage and perseverance in your difficult task. No one knows—not even you—how long this coalition of Social and Liberal Democrats will last. For your colleagues, on whose votes in Parliament you depend, it is a question of survival which can only be assured through the firmness of Walter Scheel's stance. The reactionary resistance will stir up (more effectively than Erich Mendes' braggadocio can convey) that Levantine phony in Prussian disguise who has confused the quality of respectability with the ordinary bourgeois quality of his life.

As I know you, you have the capacity to discriminate very precisely between reactionary and conservative behavior. These days, *conservative* means to accept the necessity of social development; preservation can only be attained through progress. The partners in your coalition will have to grasp that, as will the opposition, whose function is crucial to the existence of the State.

Unless all is delusion, German democracy began to function in earnest on September 28. Your government is subject to the laws of a rationality which has the mission of confronting your fellow citizens with Truth.

It is now pointless to want to "overcome" the so-called "past." Now it is important to master the present—and thereby, the past.

America, France, Great Britain, Poland, Russia—these outside forces told us that the Social-Liberal Coalition meant the end of the postwar era. Perhaps. You, your ministers and parliamentary party groups have, in fact, the duty of writing "finis" to that evil heritage. That can mean to forgive, yes, but certainly not to forget.

You have the task—and the opportunity—to free us Germans from the deception that has beclouded our view for two decades. In other words, you can bring to the attention of our people those realities that the year 1945 brought into being. Even if you should fail as Chancellor (and the coalition's slim majority may consign you to that fate), then you still would have accomplished the crucial, if you speak to us of what has been hushed up for two decades:

First: The partition of Europe, manifested with antihuman ferocity through the Big Fence and the Berlin Wall, is the result of the Nazi venture—the imperialistic ambition to catch up to the world powers. Through this, we brought unending sorrow to our neighbor nations and upon Germany. Now we must bear the consequences and the sorrow.

Second: Within your generation, no German national state will be reestablished. You courageously hinted as much in an interview. Herbert Wehner said it. The word "reunification" must be deleted. For twenty years it has been kept secret from the German people that the results of the year 1945 are not going to be rectified, even through an alliance of men of strength and good will.

Third: Konrad Adenauer was definitely aware of this truth, but never dared speak it out. You must do it. That is your historical mission, even if you and your colleagues must pay dearly for it.

Fourth: You must impress upon the conscience of a majority of the Germans that there is no returning to pre-1945 times. That means that both German States are, in fact, realities. This does not imply any approval of the moral qualities of the other Germany. It is a regime of terror and of totalitarianism. But it exists. You must say to the refugees that they cannot go back to Silesia, to Pomerania, East Prussia, or West Prussia. Others have made these their homelands. And if the saying "Recht auf Heimat" holds true, then these millions of displaced persons have long since acquired their "rights" in the Federal Republic.

Fifth: You must use that energy which is native to you to shape that Europe which is threatening trauma if it remains only a verbal profession and the unripe dream of youth. This Europe is the task of this century. As third or fourth force, it will serve as a moderating influence on the conflict of the three mighty empires.

Sixth: The integration of Western Europe is a prerequisite for an approach to our Eastern European neighbors.

Seventh: You must now make up for what the Kiesinger, Erhard and Adenauer regimes missed: Harmonious coordination of our Eastern policy with our near neighbors, and above all, with France. You will not be taken in by the alternative —which presents itself also for Paris—that you must choose between an *entendu* with Moscow or the erection of a ring of "satellites." An understanding with Prague, Warsaw and East

Berlin will not be possible without harmonizing our relations with the Soviet Union—which are susceptible of being reconciled with the interests of our allies in Washington, Paris and London. Neither for France nor for us can there be a new "cordon sanitaire."

Eighth: These are not signposts to a popular policy. It may be that the Social Democrats will again have the job of clearing up the balance sheet of German history. Don't count on any thanks. You are not dependent on the applause of the majority. Retain that self-confidence you demonstrated on election night. Even if you only show a new parliamentary majority the way, you have accomplished your job. There is a measure of reason which even the opposition must respect. You and your friends have to set the guidelines.

Ninth: This book is intended to prove nothing other than your statement that a good German cannot be a nationalist. It contains, in addition to a profile by Rolf Zundel which appeared in *Zeit,* a discussion which I hope will be taken as sincerely as it was conducted. In addition, it contains excerpts from your earlier works which we sought to put into concise form.

Tenth: Through "Portrait" and "Self-Portrait," it will be shown that the date of September 28, 1969 was, in fact, a turning point in German history, no matter how long you —depending on good or bad luck—remain head of government. The date will not be rectified. It can mark the German decision to become a republic in which conservative and progressive elements have equal shares.

That could mean that we are finally at one with our country; that we have decided to be happy with ourselves and with our neighbors.

With heartfelt good wishes, your devoted,

Klaus Harpprecht

WILLY BRANDT

I. PORTRAIT

The New Chancellor

There was no trace of his resounding triumph. Willy Brandt, elected Chancellor of the Federal Republic by 251 votes, eschewed any ostentatious victory gestures. But one scene will not soon be forgotten—Brandt and Wehner, silent, arm-in-arm—the two men who probably contributed most to the election of a Social Democrat as Chancellor of the Federal Republic.

"Anyone who has a sense of history," said Willy Brandt when he became Bonn's foreign minister, "cannot easily ignore the fact that a man of my political persuasion could have become foreign minister of Germany." This statement is even more strikingly valid for the powerful post of Chancellor. Not only his political affiliation, but also the personal and political destiny of this man were such that he was long considered a "maverick" by the inner circles of German politics. The mere fact of being a Social Democrat was long sufficient to bar him from consideration as government timber. His origins—son of an unwed salesgirl, brought up in a humble working-class home—were apt to arouse against him, the prejudices of "polite society." "He can't help it, poor fellow," ran the falsely sympathetic pronouncement, "but . . ." No need to finish the sentence—the unspoken condemnation hung in the air.

And, of course, there was the matter of fleeing the country. As a young man, Brandt had had to escape from his fatherland, in the night and the fog, to elude the clutches of the Nazis. He took refuge in neutral Sweden to avoid being crushed by the Third Reich's war machine. After the war he returned, but his political rise was shadowed by character assassination and besmirched by whispering campaigns. That this very man should now have become Chancellor indicates a historic landmark.

Brandt fought long and hard to batter down the walls of prejudice. When he first became SPD candidate for the office of Chancellor—in 1960, at the Party Congress in Hannover —he himself raised the matter of his flight from the country and laid bare his entire life. The disclosure was little help to him. The attacks continued. Even as late as September, 1965, after the election, he acknowledged, "I must admit I haven't come out of this campaign unscathed." No Social Democrat except Herbert Wehner had to swallow more insults. The astounding thing is that all this didn't make him bitter, mean or scornful of his fellow men.

Today he is no longer driven by the need to vindicate himself—to be understood and accepted no matter what. For this very reason, he has become a free man. Shortly before his election to the highest office in the Republic, he told foreign journalists that he could only conceive of himself as Chancellor of a liberated country, not of a conquered one. That is a statement which no Chancellor before him ever made—probably no other could have made it. A liberated country? If a man like Brandt has become Chancellor—if his past is no longer thrown back at him, but only his qualifications for the job are what count—if this historical changeover has been so undramatically accomplished, then we have concrete evidence that the Federal Republic has indeed become more free and more mature.

Brandt's development is interwoven in a most remarkable fashion with the history of the Social Democratic movement in the Federal Republic. Brandt was, so to speak, cast up by the waves of popular democracy as exemplifying the positive aspects of the Party. This was not the least of the reasons why it was so difficult for him to find his political identity; to bring himself and his role into harmony.

Brandt has long been the darling of the press. Young, dynamic, modern, untrammeled by traditional SPD complexes, he was a shining figure against the grey backdrop of Party functionaries. He was one of the reformers long before the new program was ratified at Godesberg. When the SPD abruptly rejected Adenauer's European policy, Brandt was one of the Berlin Social Democrats who differed with the official Party line because he believed Adenauer's policy, despite all its shortcomings, was a step forward toward an outline of European cooperation.

The Berlin Social Democrats surrounding Reuter took a less negative view of Adenauer's Alliance policy than did their colleagues in West Germany proper. Part of this picture, too, is the fact that Brandt had long been labeled a Social Democrat who was usually friendly toward the military. Also, he seemed burdened with far fewer ideological scruples than many of his colleagues. Unimpressed by the weight of German history, he expressed himself thusly: "If you don't know how to utilize military force, it will wipe you out."

Berlin offered Brandt a favorable starting position. The mayor of a city in which the political rules were different from those of the Federal Republic—where the trump card was community spirit—he appeared as the big, congenial "outsider." Berlin was a symbol, and Willy Brandt learned quickly. He dealt on an equal plane with the leading statesmen of the Western world; acquired international expertise entirely different from that of the tough, crafty old Chancellor on the Rhine. He was neither a simple Party worker like Ollenhauer, nor entangled in Party squabbles. Wherever Brandt appeared, people liked him.

The SPD sought to exploit Brandt's popularity. Under the leadership of Wehner, (during the Godesberg Program) the Party sundered the chains which had bound them to the past, and began to promote a personal "new look" for Brandt. (Like many of the earlier reformers, he had played only a modest role in launching the new program—the man of the hour was Herbert Wehner.)

The use of the American term "new look" was no accident. Kennedy, the newly elected American President, was at that time the idol of all who yearned to break out of the rigid, stifling, domestic and foreign policies. Willy Brandt became their German prophet.

The SPD chose him as candidate for the office of Chancellor. Many of the old Party veterans weren't exactly pleased about this concession to public taste; even Herbert Wehner was at that time among the skeptical.

In retrospect, the proportions of the experiment become meaningful. All the honest enthusiasm for Brandt couldn't conceal the fact that he, who had only recently come in third for the Party directorate, was being propped up by the Party. And, in retrospect, it also becomes clear that these maneuvers thrust the candidate into a crisis situation. It wasn't that

Brandt had done a bad job—just the sheer physical achievement of having made his swing throughout Germany was
admirable. And those who later shuddered at the memory of
"Smiling Willy" and his progressive tune, at the same time
had to agree it was amazing that Brandt, though exploited for
Party purposes as the very model of a German Kennedy, had
still won more than superficial liking. Many sensed that
behind the slick P.R. veneer there was honor, strength, and
political know-how.

Years later, during the 1965 election campaign, Brandt was
no longer the congenial "outsider" whose personal popularity
far exceeded that of the Party. He had become identified
with the Party; the SPD had chosen him as successor to
Ollenhauer as Party leader. The communal watchwords were
no longer alternatives, for Ludwig Erhard had preempted
these slogans and made them his own in a voice which rang
with utter conviction and rallied all "virtuous, upright
burghers" around him. The SPD election campaign had to fly
on a broken wing. Brandt was no longer such a "drawing
card." The Social Democrat election strategists pondered
how they could avoid a direct confrontation with Ludwig
Erhard. Although the SPD did gain votes, even this time,
Willy Brandt lost the election. He announced he was returning to Berlin and would never again run for the office of
Chancellor of the Federal Republic. Brandt renounced his
seat in Parliament and the opportunity to become leader of
the opposition. Scornfully, Gunter Gaus wrote: "Brandt
hasn't worn out the mantle of candidate—he has merely
declared that it's now a rental jacket available for hire!"
Many believed that Brandt's decline had begun. How could
he really lead the Party from Berlin? Wasn't Herbert Wehner
master of the Party? Weren't Helmut Schmidt and Fritz Erler
leaders of the powerful opposition in the Parliament? Brandt

was threatened with the danger of becoming the Hindenberg of the SPD—a "Party President"—honored and beloved, but without the power and the determination to lead the tradition-rich Party.

Brandt withdrew (into himself, say his friends) to work things out. Explanations have been offered as to why he underwent a change, became more composed, yet more vigorous. One version holds that he came to grips with his past and was able to view it more objectively. Another story is that once, during a nervous cardiac-digestive attack, he thought himself at death's door and in the course of his encounter with the Absolute, realized the relatively of human existence. These tales could well be true—but they are indications of Brandt's marked ability to learn and to grow.

A young companion of Brandt's once said of him (in rather impertinent boxing jargon): "He's the biggest 'catcher' we've got. He can take more punishment than anyone." Naturally that doesn't mean he stoically absorbed endless blows without showing any effect. Brandt did show the effects—seldom openly; more often he dealt with his feelings internally. His friends recall many times when, brooding, head bowed, unresponsive, he ate his heart out over a defeat. But he always came back into the ring. Barely a year after he, grey-faced and weary-voiced, renounced his aspirations for the Chancellorship, he was reelected Party chairman by a vote of 324-2. And the reason was not only old Social Democrat loyalty; there was suddenly no more doubt within the SPD: "Brandt is our man!"

The Party chairman had allowed himself to be pressured into the Grand Coalition. Once again he seemed hesitant and indecisive. But in the government he soon found his place, and after a while, even the CDU realized that the Social Democrats didn't go against Willy Brandt's wishes on any important decisions. In the election campaign, he played it lordly and distant. He acted as though "popularity" had become a foreign word to him. And since election day, many of his friends say: "This is an entirely new Brandt! He reached out and grasped for power without ever looking to the right or left. We've never seen him so sure of himself. He's gotten rid of all the 'psychic' garbage."

In any event, it is certain that the stereotype of vacillating Brandt—the "Kiesinger of the SPD" which was often applied even by friends of the Party, was a rather useless cliché. Throughout the Fifties, by hard work and unrelenting trench warfare, Brandt captured for himself district after district of the Berlin SPD. Had he still been the same vacillating Brandt, he would, instead, have quickly thrown up his hands.

After the Hungarian uprising, Berlin was convulsed with shock and indignation. A crowd of demonstrators marched to the Brandenburg Gate, where the Volkspolizei (the People's Police of the East) awaited them with carbines at the ready. A clash, whose consequences could not be predicted, seemed almost inevitable until Brandt appeared, speaking through the loudspeaker of a police car. He addressed the demonstrators and convinced the furious mob to retreat. And when Krushchev delivered his Berlin ultimatum, it was Brandt who, without consulting the Bonn government's allies, rejected the ultimatum as unacceptable. Again, during the Cuban missile crisis, Brandt, unilaterally, at his own risk, wired President Kennedy not to let himself be blackmailed over the Berlin question.

In many extreme situations, Brandt demonstrated that he could be a cold, tough and decisive negotiator. Only once did he fail to seize his opportunity during a crisis. In January 1963, when Krushchev invited the mayor to a meeting in East Berlin, Brandt gave in to the threats of Amrehns that he would cause the Grand Coalition to collapse if he accepted the invitation. As it happened, the coalition fell apart shortly thereafter anyway.

Granted, a politician must be on the job not only in exceptional situations. Success is a day-by-day achievement. And Brandt is undoubtedly not the man to force decisions. In many instances, Party friends reproached him for not having taken a clear enough stand; not having made rapid enough decisions. The best-known instance of such behavior was the debate over the Emergency Decrees. The SPD was agonized about them; Helmut Schmidt beat his brains out over them; Brandt kept silent. Only during the last reading of the decrees did Brandt at last speak out—and suddenly it was he who enabled the Party to regain its unity.

What characterizes Brandt is not that he is hesitant to make decisions, but the careful, economical use of his leadership authority. Precisely because he is the uncontested symbol of Party unity, he is very careful not to dissipate his authority. To be sure, it is true that many sessions over which he presides end inconclusively, but not because he has no opinion on the matter under discussion. He is a master of the art of letting things develop; of giving almost imperceptible little nudges in the direction he wants, but in many cases he waits until the decision has matured of itself—and sometimes he waits a very long time. Another factor might be that he is a man who believes in discussion; in persuasion. He is very much aware of the liberal process of opinion formation, particularly because in this way stable decisions are reached, backed by a solid majority. This leadership technique is far from starry-eyed idealistic liberalism; it is strictly controlled. Brandt knows at all times how to manipulate people. For example, he sends a trusted associate in to get the lay of the land, by stimulating discussion of certain issues. Then the associate causes the discussion to be dropped, as though for the time being it isn't so important; then Brandt sends a second emissary into battle, who restimulates the discussion; it develops . . . and then he himself moves in, bringing it to fruition. That indicates mastery and cool calculation. "He is much more cunning than many realize," said one of his friends, with almost unwilling admiration. Somewhat more elegantly expressed: Brandt is a man who wields power subtly—not out of weakness, but out of the objective realization, born of experience, that this kind of power is more enduring.

Precisely because he wields his authority sparingly, he has become known as the "peacemaker"; his opinion counts in critical situations. During many past negotiations, the simple fact of Brandt's presence is sufficient to bring squabblers to compromise. When necessary, he becomes explicit, and then the word quickly gets around: "Brandt has lowered the boom!" The discussion over the appointment of Leussink, the new Science Minister, which was so hotly debated in the Party, finally ended with the awareness that "Willy wants it."

Another indication of Brandt's ability to "utilize" people can be seen in his appointment of Horst Ehmke as minister in the Chancellor's Office. Ehmke is not only an excellent constitutional lawyer, a hard worker and a good organizer—qualities which are indispensable in that office—he is the type who rolls up his sleeves and bulls his way through. That the Chancellor should very deliberately have brought in such a man as his assistant indicates his matter-of-fact, almost self-assured assessment of his limitations. This arrangement allows him to participate actively only on the most decisive questions. And, at a higher level, he continues, unchallenged to play his role of peacemaker; symbol of Party unity. If the Chancellor in question were not Willy Brandt, this system would seem a Machiavellian piece of work.

Brandt, of course, can hardly be suspected of having

Machiavellian tendencies. That he has never openly made a derogatory statement about a Party friend could be calculated behavior, but that he should never completely drop colleagues, even when he is not satisfied with their performance, can't be explained away as calculation. Personal loyalty is very important to him. Here, perhaps, can be detected a second weakness: He hasn't always made the most felicitous choices of associates, and he retained many of them even when the Party itself would long since have kicked them out. This failing is the counterpart of a remarkable quality: Brandt embodies in a most exemplary fashion that solidarity which is so much spoken of in the SPD, and which is perhaps still the most outstanding characteristic of that Party. So often he consoled colleagues who, during Party meetings, had to swallow defeats. And no one knows better than he, how through intuitive management, to awaken in his associates a community feeling, and instill in them a sense of solidarity. Brandt is not a man without failings—how could he be? But what sets him apart from others is the sure mastery of those weaknesses; he has made more of them than others have of their talents.

The only kind of person who could carry off such a coup is one who is honest with himself—free of pretensions and greedy ambitions; one who has learned to keep his eye on the ball; not to let personal problems distract him from the realities—in short, one who no longer takes himself quite so seriously. So that, when one of his friends asked what the real motivation was behind his actions, he gave the remarkable answer: "I want to help." (A motive, incidentally, that links him with the far more irascible Herbert Wehner.)

So it follows that "internal reconciliation" should be the perpetually recurring theme of his speeches—a lessening of tensions among the political parties. "Bebel and Bismark together are the only ones who convey the historical portrait of the Reich." In 1966 at the SPD Congress in Dortmund, he made what is for him a thoroughly typical remark: "No people can long survive without losing their inner equilibrium—without faltering in the hour of internal or external crisis, if they cannot approve of their fatherland. We Germans must not forget history, but we cannot eternally run around with a sense of guilt." This is how he translated his desire to help into the political-historical realm: Help in the search for a national identity.

Brandt's statement on the role of Germany in the world would almost represent the man himself: "National self-awareness is something other than arrogance and overestimation of one's own worth as compared with that of other people. It is based on a sure evaluation of one's own strengths, achievements, and virtues—one's own limitations." Brandt no longer considers himself an undervalued man, and he will not be the Chancellor of an undervalued nation.

There are probably politicians who write more brilliantly (his prose is often mediocre) and what he does have to say is often dissipated in far too many explanations, statements of position, and interviews. There are more exciting leaders than he—quicker to catch fire and to inspire others. But there is no one who embodies quiet strength more perfectly than he.

At the Shaumburg Palace

CONVERSATION BETWEEN WILLY BRANDT
AND KLAUS HARPPRECHT

KH: Mr. Chancellor, the office of Chancellor is undoubtedly a historic commitment. When you moved into the Shaumburg Palace, did you feel yourself in the presence of history?—the hem of the mantle of history, as it were, to quote Bismark?

WB: No, not when I moved into the house. In the weeks between the national election and the election for Chancellor, I got over that. In this connection, I must tell you something awful. The morning of the election, I was already signing postcards which had been printed in anticipation of the forthcoming election because I was quite sure that I would be elected. I had, during the intervening weeks, thought through what the task required. Then two or three weeks went by, until I sensed what the office really signified and that it was going to take a lot to do the job.

KH: You said you were sure of your election. That couldn't have been just a matter of election results. It presupposes a certain inner sureness—the sureness of a determination to predict the decisive moment.

WB: That presupposes that I did not want to become anything more—or rather that I had no further personal political ambitions in the narrow sense. The year 1965 was a landmark for me and it was most salutary. Since then, the decisions I have had to make have been simpler, for they no longer deal in terms of others' expectations of me—of what I should be—but rather of what *I* want. No matter how close the election results were, the crucial aspect was that I wanted the victory, not necessarily that I won it. They went together—because I wanted it, I would get it.

KH: In Germany (at least among the observant) and also abroad—the election is perceived as a truly historic landmark, particularly in view of the often changing and not always felicitous history of the Social Democrats—a party which, nevertheless, has a century-old tradition.

WB: I haven't given as much thought as have others to the fact that, it has been 39 years since a Social Democrat was Chancellor. I looked more at the total historical continuum. My connection is rather with Bebel than, with all due respect, Hermann Muller. I now perceive the opportunity, which unfortunately did not exist under the Weimar Republic, to create the great reconciliation of which Bebel has spoken. What counts is to fashion a fatherland of love and justice to the extent that such can be realized on this earth. That differs from what was attempted under Weimar.

KH: The Weimar Republic was shorter lived than this republic. . .

WB: We keep forgetting that. Right!

KH: . . . The Federal Republic, which is twenty years old and can be presumed to continue for a long time. Aren't you grateful also, to the men of other parties who helped stamp the character of this republic? We know the merits of Kurt Schumacher and Erler, but we also know that your opponents are worthy—for example Konrad Adenauer and in the economic sphere, Ludwig Erhard. Do you see continuity there as well?

WB: Well, in the case of Schumacher, I must observe that he could no longer demonstrate what he would have wanted to accomplish had he become head of the Government. This is, by the way, true for Erler as well, in another sense. But there is no doubt whatsoever that Adenauer accomplished infinitely much—in view of what we had left in 1945. Much that could initially have been interpreted as opportunism was, in fact, a very conscious determination to gain perspective—the readiness to give the new generation—new generations!—their chance. Just to make it perfectly clear in this conversation, even Adenauer's much heralded European orientation wasn't really as controversial as it might have seemed in the previous 50 years. In those times, discussions and efforts were not carried right through to the end. What, in fact, might have come about had we had more exact knowledge of certain factors? In any case, we must say this, too, of Erhard: Though he was right to set free the independent forces of economic activity, he did not test what a stronger combination of free enterprise and collective economic activity might have achieved. But it's good that these foundations were laid.

WB: During the last session of Parliament—the fifth one—working together, with a broad base of support and with very little opposition, we passed a law on growth and stability. Many economists consider it the most up-to-date tax statute of modern economics in the Western world.

KH: This was, no doubt, a positive expression of what the former Opposition Party—the Social Democrats—and the Administration Party have learned together, and have managed to translate into a common policy within the Grand Coalition. They alluded to the European components of Adenauer's policy. Wasn't there a certain antagonism within the Social Democratic Party—namely the contradiction between the emphatically European oriented Social Democrats and the former—I put this in quotes—"national social" designed course of Kurt Schumacher? You dealt with this in your books—not uncritically. . .

WB: In 1950, at the Hamburg Party Congress of the SPD, I did not vote for the party directorate's resolution, making clear their opposition to joining the council of Europe—and that didn't improve my relations with Schumacher at the time. I must, however, point out that I was not very consistent, for I didn't vote "No"; only two or three delegates did. I was one of the scant dozen who abstained. I don't know whether one should call Schumacher "social national." It's certain that Schumacher, despite his many achievements, knows too little of the world in which we live. We must not forget that in his youth—before 1963—he had seen very little of the world of our neighbors.

KH: Though he was born in West Prussia, he was a member of the Wurttemberg State Parliament.

WB: And then a member of the national Parliament. He spent ten out of the twelve Nazi years in concentration camps and prisons. He is afraid his party—the democratic Left— might still be tarred with the odious label of "national unreliability."

KH: With the slogan "comrades without a country."

WB: That was Bebel—that was the Kaiser's Reich—the next one was an empty phrase from the "politics of renunciation." You still hear it today occasionally. Of course it's no longer taken so seriously. That was Weimar—that was Versailles—that was the burden of Versailles which they took upon themselves . . . Schumacher wanted to take the wind out of the sails of a perilous nationalism. That's what it was about. But he had no doubts as to the indispensability of German-French reconciliation, which Social Democrats had been working toward for decades. He found himself in agreement with Adenauer, for Schumacher believed that there was more to be gained by a debate among the powers, directed toward a general solution of the German question.

KH: You used the slogan of the politicians of renunciation and accommodation. In your election campaign, I noticed that you often mentioned two former German foreign ministers, Rathenau and Stresemann, who sought to pursue a policy of reason and conciliation with East and West. Both, in their way, were shrewd. Do you consider yourself the heir and executor of his policy, which could now have a chance of succeeding—namely, a rational conciliation between our friends and allies in the West and between our neighbors to the East, who after all, *are* our neighbors too?

WB: There are two factors here. You alluded to the election campaign. I said we have it easier than before, but the task is also more far-reaching. It is easier because we do—despite some nationalistic discord—feel that the majority of our citizens better understand a policy of conciliation—of friendship with the West and accommodation with the East. But the task is greater. I don't say that to belittle the efforts made during the Weimar Republic. Stresemann wore himself out for many years in the struggle over membership in the United Nations. Today we are confronted with questions of equal importance—but several other important problems are keeping us busy at the same time. After World War I, the situation was simpler—the tempo, above all, was not so hectic as it is today. But there is a continuity, before all else, when the proposition is advanced that we could again become wanderers between two worlds. We belong to the West, and try to reach an accommodation with the East. That is important. We are anchored in the West, and with our Western partners, we endeavour to reach an accommodation, a reconciliation, a friendship with our Eastern neighbors—not because we think we are a world political giant who can march back and forth between both camps. We don't pursue that illusion. We intend—through our trustworthiness as allies—to show our desire for a policy of peace.

KH: This formulation certainly embraces many of Adenauer's foreign policy insights. Could you have imagined that Konrad Adenauer—and there is supporting evidence to this effect—might have considered you as a possible successor? I know you and he had many political quarrels.

WB: We also got along very well sometimes.

KH: I always had the feeling that basically, Adenauer rather liked you, despite all the political opposition.

WB: How much, I don't know. We met often during my term as mayor of Berlin and afterwards as well. I spoke with him several times while I was foreign minister, too. Once, in October 1962, we had a very thorough going session. I spent a whole day with him at Cadenabbia, and there I particularly sensed, as I had during other conversations, that we could see eye to eye. But today, in practical politics, I find many solutions other than those he gave. That doesn't mean that if he were still here among us today, he might not see many things differently, too. I'll give you an example. Before the government of the Grand Coalition was formed, we had a thorough discussion. That was in 1966. He told me I ought to work with him, for great mistakes had been made in our relations with the Soviet Union. That interested me. He recollected very accurately the events of his own administration—certainly not everything, but particularly those which fitted into the development of the thesis he wished to sustain. He was, by the way, quite convinced that the Soviet Ambassador had been improperly treated.

KH: That was after the CDU Party Congress where Adenauer astounded the delegates by taking the position that the Soviet Union was a peaceful power.

WB: It could also have been shortly before that. In any case, I was astonished at the firmness of his assertion. Of course I couldn't agree—even though I wasn't foreign minister as yet—with his unilateral, negative opinion of the foreign ministry for not having developed as it should have.

KH: In all German history, there were only two figures who correspond to the public's image of what a Chancellor should be. One is Adenauer, the other is Bismarck. Doubtless Adenauer had a problematical relationship to Bismarck's historical accomplishments. Nevertheless, he was in the Sachsenwald in Friedrichsruh, and there, rather intelligently by the way, meditated upon Bismarck's place in history. How do you view Bismarck—this man who formulated the laws against Socialists and had them passed in the Reichstag?

WB: I don't know whether Adenauer also traveled from Cologne to Friedrichsruh as a young man. As a youngster, I was there a number of times. I didn't have to make up for that. Why shouldn't I go there? I'm not from Prussia, but from what was then the Hanseatic State, Lubeck. But I believe I have a healthy respect for Bismarck's achievements.

KH: Do you feel that his German nationalism, his "small Germany" national state concept, was the only possible historical solution for his era?

WB: . . . which gives reason for reflection, like so many other historical decisions. The alternative wasn't seriously attempted; other methods that might have been employed showed no tangible result. His foreign policy, considered overall, was grandiose and successful. He was unbelievably gifted in domestic politics—anything but a narrow Party man. He was never that. You can't blame him for not having understood what the labor movement meant.

KH: Was his encounter with Lassalle just an episode, or was it, according to your interpretation, seriously intended?

WB: No, that was an attempt to consolidate the Prussian position by means of a plebiscite. But that, too, was significant.

KH: I suppose, Mr. Chancellor, that you approve the federative basis of our country. Bismarck's national state was, in theory and concept, federative; however, it inclined more and more toward a strong central state.

WB: Prussia was too big. The Reich, as originally conceived, was greater Prussia. Prussia dominated in the parliament, even though during the Weimar Republic, each state had its own vote. Prussia really dominated excessively. By that I don't mean to convey a totally negative judgment on Prussia. Prussia was better than its reputation. They brought many good qualities and accomplishments to our country. Only, the structure of the country is basically different today. As far as the problem of federalism is concerned, I don't know what solutions we will arrive at. I only see the necessity for working more closely together, above all in the general areas of education and science, for the next few years will decide whether we will be able to manage under the present system of responsibilities. I very much hope that a cooperative federalism will succeed, because if not, I foresee an increasing demand to vest more responsibility in the federal government instead of leaving it in the hands of the states. I would prefer that we not return to a strong central government.

KH: For a good thousand years, Central Europe was organized according to a federative concept. This principle of federalism collapsed in the aftermath of Bismarck's politics, and according to the inexorable laws of the development of national states. Would you agree that a Central European federal system could be the model for a greater Europe?

WB: If we want to develop this concept further, we must proceed with care. We could get into trouble by interfering with the affairs of our French neighbors, who have not yet, to this very day, renounced the basic characteristics of the Napoleonic empire. I believe, in fact, that our future lies in a federated Europe. And the better we build our part of Europe, the easier it will be for us or for the next generation to work out a greater European order. This seems clear to me: Whatever took place in the other part of Europe—I think above all of the frightful setback of 1968 in Czechoslovakia—federal cooperation is a problem that they were not able to solve, even there. A trail has been laid, and can no longer be effaced. And the desire—the striving toward individual responsibility of surrounding national and regional areas will always break through. These are points of contact between the various parts of Europe.

KH: Mr. Chancellor, for better or for worse, the history of Social Democracy is associated with Prussia. For a while, it even defined the shape of Prussia. I think of the period when Otto Braun was governor of Prussia. At that time a change took place. The decisive element is the Godesberg Program. In your party, who intellectually prepared the Godesberg Program? Was it you? Was it Fritz Erler? Was it Herbert Wehner?

WB: It was no single one. I wasn't able to work on it very much because I was a member of another program committee. I remember the last meeting of the party directorate before the Godesberg Program. I discussed with my friend Klaus Schutz, currently mayor of Berlin, what suggestions I should contribute. I carried through these suggestions, as far as I can remember. No, you can't give the credit to any one of them. This was a task on which many worked together. I would, along with Erler and Wehner, whom you mentioned, also cite Adolf Arndt, who was a strong driving force that year. I would name Eichler; also Gustav Heinemann, a new man in our Party, who concerned himself most of all with a better understanding between Church and State. At the Godesberg Party Congress, against a much stronger minority than might appear from the final vote, he established cooperative relationships between Church and states—and was commended therefor.

KH: Isn't this altered attitude toward the Church one of the decisive changes, if you will, in the philosophy of Social Democracy?

WB: Though I don't want to underestimate the magnitude of the Church's task, this is really only a secondary chapter. In the early days of the labor movement, or socialist movement, they thought themselves in posses-

27

sion of the eternal verities. It wasn't at Godesberg that they first lost their illusions, either. The concept of "Kirchen-Ersatz"—the idea that one could decide one's own philosophy, has always encountered opposition. It was already running into trouble before the First World War. During Weimar, the idea became relevant. For the first time, consistently at Godesberg, conclusions were drawn from what Schumacher had formulated immediately after the Second World War. In a party of this type, someone who draws his inspiration from the economic or sociological theories of Marx, should have his place just as well as someone inspired by the Sermon on the Mount or Kant's Categorical Imperative.

KH: Was there an atheistic period in your life?

WB: Not atheistic, but anti-clerical. In my youth—my early youth—the Protestant church seemed a link between throne and altar. But during the Weimar Republic it was, rather, a link with German nationalism. But this view of the Church changed during my Scandinavian period—especially in Norway—before World War II, through the realization that the Church is not constrained to follow any dominating orientation.

KH: But you did have personal faith?

WB: Yes, I did, even if it was fluctuating and never quite fitted into established forms. But I have no problems getting along in my church.

KH: . . . A church that has again become a forum for dialogue.

WB: That's right.

KH: Mr. Brandt, you didn't exactly have an easy time of it in your party. I remember the Stuttgart Party Congress.

WB: And Munich before that! And Berlin!

KH: What was the origin of your friends' and colleagues' mistrust, which so long prevented you from rising to the Party's leadership—not just you, but Fritz Erler too? After all, you and he were elected to the party directorate together.

WB: I believe he was elected two years before me. He was already in the leadership in Munich, in 1956. I only got in in 1958, in Stuttgart. In 1954, we both struck out in Berlin. Thinking back, it wasn't all that bad. Of course that's easily said from the viewpoint of a man who has leaped the hurdles. It is not without reason that a party—not just a party machine—is suspicious. I was sixteen when I joined the Party. I withdrew from it. And then I returned and demanded reforms. Even when I was sixteen I pushed for reforms—different ones from today's. Only now has the party directorate agreed to accept sixteen-year-olds.

KH: At your suggestion?

WB: Upon my recommendation. Nowhere do the regulations specify at what age one can join. But until now, almost all districts of the SPD accepted youngsters only at age eighteen. Now they have been instructed to accept youths of sixteen. Because if they are going to vote in the next election at eighteen, they should, if they wish, be able to participate in party activities at sixteen.

I joined the party at sixteen, but before I was eighteen, I was already out—oriented to the Left of the SPD. While I was abroad, I again became a Social Democrat. My path was not typical of most; much more typical of the majority of my countrymen. I left Germany at a young age. Hitler took my citizenship away from me. I became a Norwegian. All that deviated greatly from the norm. And besides, I had gained a high degree of independence. I made that clear to all concerned, including Kurt Schumacher, and that was probably why, somewhat later, I was elected to the directorate of the party.

All in all, it did me no harm, except for one thing: Now I sometimes wonder . . . I, a man of fifty-five—it is certainly good that I managed to store up many experiences. At thirty or thirty-five, one hasn't the experience, but more energy. I sincerely believe that in this country we wait too long before men and women can assume really important political responsibilities. The increased experience that they contribute when they are past fifty, is purchased with a goodly share (I don't exactly want to call it resignation) of compromise with all possible difficulties. For myself, I don't think of it as resignation. But herein lies part of our conflict with the younger generation. They feel that the old and the middle-aged might already have made so many compromises with their equals, with life and with the world, that they can no longer confront the new tasks of today without preconceptions.

KH: No doubt the conflict will become more acute in the next few years—in the next decade. If I'm not mistaken, the younger generation will push ahead still more drastically. But as far as energy is concerned, you showed no lack of it in your statement on election night. You showed decisiveness. Perhaps your relationship to the younger generation, with whom you get along better than other German politicians, can be explained by the fact that you, yourself, had a rebellious youth?

WB: Yes.

KH: At that time, you lived in deliberate opposition to the majority of our citizens. You chose this contrast. You had the courage and the will to resist. Is that why young people understand you better?

WB: That's one reason. Only I chose to oppose the weak, in my opinion—at least Weimar politics. Now I hesitate a little to repeat that without reservations. Weimar is sometimes slandered when it should be praised. My opposition has to be viewed in two stages: One, against a Weimar Republic which could not lead us to a solution; and subsequently, my resistence to the regime that followed the collapse.

KH: Do you believe that the Germans today are immune to those nationalistic temptations which led to the collapse of the Weimar Republic?

WB: More today than in those times. But I must tell you frankly that I was worried in 1966. As soon as we had a recession—not even a crisis, but only a small setback in the economy—we noticed, incidentally, *before* the Grand Coalition, which some later blamed, the growing popularity of an extremely nationalistic group in two such different federal states as Bavaria and Hesse. One state was governed by the CSU, the other by the SPD—sociologically completely diverse. That means the fault did not lie with the individual characteristics of the state. That gave me food for thought. Still, I do not believe that we were or are seriously endangered. However, we must make it clear that we have not yet been faced with the need to defend this state, this democratic order, against the kind of danger that existed after the First World War. Of course we have today, thanks to advanced insights and technology, especially in economics, a much better chance to avert an economic crisis. The possibility of preventing economic crises is better. Perhaps that is why we will not have to put this unfortunate experience to the test again. But I wouldn't be too sure about that.

KH: What do you think of the attempts by groups such as the NPD to move to the Right of the Nationalists?

WB: Not much. I prefer an honest exposition of our problems and a sensible solution of such economic and social problems as might become fertile soil for nationalism.

KH: If I have observed correctly, the increase of extremist nationalism diminished when a new authority appeared in Bonn in the form of the Grand Coalition.

WB: There was a setback in the development in Baden-Württemberg. To this day, I can't understand what happened, in of all places, Baden-Württemberg in the spring of '68. With the exception of this case, you're right.

KH: To what do you owe your personal authority, which is unchallenged in your Party, as far as I can tell? That must have something to do with your personal strength of character. You don't project a father image, like Konrad Adenauer. You're too young for that; that doesn't match your temperament. Certainly you're not a man inclined toward dictatorial decisions. What is the root of your authority?

WB: That's for others to answer. I can't do that myself. What I could contribute to an answer is: I try to listen, not only to the young, but also to my associates in the Party. I also try to consider differing opinions and finally to find a common denominator of convictions. That must be it. And I believe that my Party basically realizes that I don't want to steamroller anybody. On the other hand, when I feel that a cause is just, I support it wholeheartedly. I have been forced to do that, thank God, only on occasion. There were situations in which I later realized I had overstepped my limits. But my relationship of trust with my Party didn't suffer from it. At the last Party convention, the extraordinary session in Bad Godesberg, I said that I couldn't take the responsibility for a resolution which had already been passed; it was subsequently altered. After that, I had a guilty conscience and apologized, which of course didn't change the revised resolution. I mention this as an example. I believe the Party feels I treat it fairly.

KH: What is your relationship to power? For Germans, and especially for German intellectuals, power is no normal, natural phenomenon; to them power is evil.

WB: You have to talk to my wife about that. In the early fifties, before I became mayor of Berlin, she looked at me in horror when I said I wanted power. She considered this something quite evil and had a hard time accepting it. Now she has long understood what I really meant. One seeks influence in a democratic state in order to accomplish something reasonable. That alone counts.

KH: Mr. Chancellor, by chance I saw some of your hand-written notes. Your handwriting surprised me. I'm not a

33

graphologist, and my opinion on the quasi-science of graphology is not entirely favorable. But I noticed the artistic traits of your handwriting, which show a basic contradiction with the matter-of-fact quality of your public appearances. Are you intensely drawn to music?

WB: When I was little, I liked military music, and I played in a mandolin orchestra. That was a part of the labor movement. I grew up in an era when—and that is also a thing of Weimar—there existed not only labor sports, but also labor stamp collectors and labor mandolin players. But I didn't really come into contact with music until the year 1936 in Berlin, when I lived there illegally for half a year. I was, after all, twenty-two years old. I went quite regularly to the Philharmonic concerts. There, a new world opened up for me. But I still have considerable difficulty understanding modern music— my wife does not.

KH: And what is your feeling for literature? I know, or I think I know, that you, unlike your predecessor in office, have written little poetry, or at least have not published any poems. What kind of literature do you prefer?

WB: Beside my bed and near my desk there are the books I would like to read, and then keep stored away. I only read modern literature during vacations. I read Gunter Grass Saturday night and Sunday morning. Aside from that, old and new biographies, and history—above all, modern history. Not only the recent works that arrive on my desk, but also what I seek out on my bookshelves.

KH: Is there a poet of the past—a so-called classical poet, or perhaps a romantic poet, of whom you are particularly fond?

WB: I decided I wouldn't want to choose in the various areas. That also pertains to the question: Which statesman do I most admire? I would say none.

KH: Thank God I didn't ask that. To get back to your experiences of 1936, when you lived illegally for half a year in Berlin as an organizer of resistance groups. . . Did you manage at that time to keep the respect of your fellow citizens?

WB: Yes, I was in touch with a group of political friends, young and old; only a few each day, but collectively there were many. I had a wonderful landlady, and I met many people; for example in the Prussian State Library where I worked during that period. I would never have become familiar with Nazi literature if I hadn't made a daily pilgrimage there to read my way through, Hitler's *Mein Kampf*—which I hadn't read either—to . . . I don't know . . . to Darré, the so-called "Reich's Bauerführer" (peasant leader), difficult as it was. There, among the librarians and in many other groups, I found no reason not to identify with my fellow citizens, especially in Berlin—this vast Berlin, where it was easier for me than in a smaller city.

KH: It may have been easier in Berlin. But you still took a great risk. If the Gestapo had caught you, it would have cost you a few years in the penitentiary, maybe your life. . .

WB: More than a few years of penitentiary!

35

KH: Were you afraid?

WB: Yes. It's like this. Earlier, I had returned to Germany once, and I shall never forget when I entered the country at Warnemünde with false papers, and saw a man among the customs officers who had gone to school with me in Lübeck... He could have denounced me. But he didn't.

KH: That you went to Berlin seems to mean (I ask this) that you have strong ties to this country, which survived the time when you owed allegiance to the Norwegian nation. What binds you to Germany and the Germans?

WB: I always considered Hitler a traitor to the nation. Not just because of the rubble he left behind. Perhaps I would not always have said it like this. What person knows for certain what he was thinking thirty years ago? To me, Nazism was not only treason to the nation, but also treason to Europe. What binds me is the language, the culture; also the potential of this nation, whose defeat was more severe than that of others, partially through its own fault—but which, therefore, has more possibility of doing something for itself and for others, if it so desires.

KH: Have you always felt responsible for German problems?

WB: Yes, also during the time when I was not a citizen because they didn't want me to be one. Trygve Lie, who later became the first Secretary General of the United Nations, wrote to a mutual friend (I was still in Sweden): "Brandt also serves as an example that blood is thicker than water." At the time, I was hurt. Trygve Lie said this because, during discussions in an inter-

36

national group, I emphatically pointed out that one couldn't condemn the German people collectively for the crimes of the Nazi leadership.

KH: Is there a certain logic to the fact that, two decades after Chancellor Konrad Adenauer, who was a man of "inward migration," now a man of "outward migration" represents Germany?

WB: I said it on election night and I repeat it: Now Hitler has finally lost the war.

Moderation and Value

To really get to know the Chancellor, you should spend a day walking around Lübeck with him. At the proper time, you should accompany him to one of those small restaurants where the tables do not have plastic cloths, but only plain, scrubbed wood. The innkeeper pronounces the "st" peculiar to Northern Germany, with that apple-cheeked good nature which can still be found in Central Europe, if one is lucky.

You should talk with him about his childhood, certainly a difficult one; about his mother, who was buried in 1969 without ostentation. No cameras, no reporters, no State ceremony. Only her son and a few relatives.

And over a second bottle of wine, you would recall that the French, before World War I, used to store their great wines from Bordeaux and Burgundy in the wine cellars of the Hanseatic towns—Bremen, Hamburg, Lübeck, Svenemunde, Danzig—in order to allow them to age in the climate of the Baltic Sea. Long ago, when Europe was still European—when one could travel without passport or visa from Berlin to Paris—certainly a Europe of states, or, in the words of the old gentleman from Colombey les deux Eglises, "a Europe of Fatherlands."

After a spicy beefsteak tartar, a glance through a handy pocket edition of Thomas Mann's *Buddenbrooks;* and then you might inquire whether the world of the senators and their ladies was alien to the boy from Lübeck, Willy Brandt. Had he read the book? When, and with what feelings? Did he look up to, or disdain the aristocracy of grain and fish dealers? Did he perhaps secretly admire the world of the patricians? Did he, son of a poor woman, feel rejected during his high school years, even though he was, according to his teachers, one of the more gifted students? Did he wear the blue Socialist Youth shirt to school out of spite? Was it over sensitivity, brought about by social or personal circumstances, that caused him to force his bourgeois schoolmates into discussions that didn't interest them, because they preferred to withdraw into the security of their bourgeois homes—homes whose foundations were already undermined long before they were completely destroyed during the wartime bombings? One might ask him whether, at sixteen or seventeen, he had a presentiment concerning the crumbling—the destruction—of his country. Wouldn't it have been a belated satisfaction, had he accepted the offer, to become mayor of his home town, after his return?

He passed his school examinations brilliantly, but the tests of maturity demanded of him were surely more difficult.

It is most unusual for a nineteen-year-old to decide to leave his country and his people because they have succumbed to a barbarous totalitarian dictatorship. It's rare that a youth—the antiquated term is permissible here—should flee through night and fog aboard a fishing boat, into an uncertain future.

He viewed his departure as a Leftist radical protest against the conformity which eventually suffocated the sense of justice and liberty, even in the Labor party. He withdrew from a society of turncoats and fellow travelers. He was very well aware that, under social and political pressures, too many of his comrades decided all too easily to become Party members. He had no reason to rely on the dependability of the Resistance. He had withdrawn from the Social Democratic Party, and his mentor, Dr. Julius Leber. The radical element in his decision was its own justification, not merely that of youth. The SPD as it existed in those years did not manifest the energy necessary to ward off dictatorship. The courageous rejection of the Enabling Act in the Reichstag was a proof of decency, and at the same time an admission that it was too late.

In that quiet little restaurant, left in privacy by the innkeeper, you might discuss with Chancellor Brandt whether a democracy could exist without democrats. That was the trauma of Weimar. A social republic needs radicalism just as much as the desire for moderation. A balance cannot be achieved without the angry demands of the young and the inclination toward compromise of the old. Thus is civic spirit developed and the use of the word "developed" is not fortuitous. It means shaping through compromise, across the generation gap. This alone is the correct concept of development, which can only come from reconciliation of the intellectual and the economic differences in a society. Therefrom arises the concept of "citizenship," far above the stodgy, conventional view. "I Want to Be a Citizen" was the title of Professor Sternberger's brilliant essay. He cited Mommsen, among the 19th-century historians, the enlightened one. Yet he influenced the consciousness of his fellow citizens less than the national-liberal, ultimately nationalistic Treitschke, who, though from Saxony, tried to pass himself off as a Prussian—a procedure which had grotesque repercussions, for when Ulbricht entered Berlin, Saxony did, in effect, conquer Prussia. Count Brühl has been wearing a goatee since 1945. There also, may be recognized a dialectical ruse of history. Almost two hundred years later, the Seven Years War and the Peace Treaty of Hubertusberg were rewritten.

The nineteen-year-old emigrant from the Hanseatic town of Lübeck certainly considered himself anti-bourgeois. His baptismal name was Frahm. Now he took the name Brandt— and he himself would have to explain whether in choosing this name, there wasn't an unconscious desire to protest—not a death wish in the Freudian sense, but a positive achievement. Not a wish to see the world in flames and destruction, but rather to light the way, to the clarity of enlightenment.

Rebellion and enlightenment are concepts of our European history of the past two centuries. A drive toward true citizenship was at work through anti-bourgeois actions. Readiness for revolution paved the way for evolution. Brandt, thanks to his Scandinavian experience, is a classic example of this process. He who is now the pilot of our destiny, learned long ago that revolution is first of all a plunge into the uncertain, the unknown—into depths of history from which no one can pull himself out by the scruff of the neck, like Baron Münchhausen.

His early maturity gave him the insight that transitional periods are more meaningful than sharply dramatic breaks, which appear as historical quotation marks and exclamation points. That is probably the secret of good politics in general—a feeling for transitions; the sensitive evaluation of words. Coexistence, for example, meant to the Kremlin leaders, even after Stalin's era, nothing more than consolidation of the power relationships bequeathed by the dictator.

Coexistence changed its meaning in the period after Stalin's death, the revolt of the East Berlin workers, the Hungarian rebellion, and that of Czechoslovakia. Europeans, whether Poles, Hungarians, Germans, Czechs or Slovaks, remembered that they were all interdependent. In other words, that a united greater Europe really exists. A Europe which is inconceivable without Germany—a Europe which could fail because of Germany's ideological division, or could flourish under the positive design of a new and differently conceived coexistence. A Europe that, if this grand design were given a chance, would force the Soviet Union to decide whether or not it wants to consider itself a European power.

Here is the fateful issue facing this continent. The question is not to separate the great Russian empire from the dependent peoples of Eastern Europe. Europe, stretching to the Urals, is a reality, but not as defined by Hallstein, "legalistic translator of Adenauer's world view." The alternative—a German decision in favor of either Moscow or Warsaw, or even East Berlin or the Big Red Brother, is no longer viable. The French have understood that, thanks to their heritage of reason and enlightenment. Kiesinger seemed to have made himself the ambassador of reason under the auspices of the Grand Coalition. But in this regard, we were deceived by him. And he deceived himself in judging existing realities, and in the ability of the Germans to recognize these realities. He was like Empress Maria Theresa, with no hope of a pact with Madame Pompadour, or a Russian Elizabeth. He was no Frederick the Second, either.

These, and other matters, you could discuss at the Lübeck Inn. You could hold up to this man, who does not deprecate his fatherland, the mirror of liberal and European intellect which once characterized his native land.

"Morton," to quote *Buddenbrooks,* "spoke with naive and

good-natured indignation: 'We, the bourgeoisie, the third class as we have been called up to now, we want there to be only an aristocracy of merit; we no longer recognize the lazy nobility; we abjure the existing hierarchy of class. . . We want all people to be free and equal, and that none be subject to any one person, but that all be submissive to the law. There shall be no more privileges and no more despotism. All shall be children of the state, having equal rights, and as there no longer exists an intermediary between the layman and God, so the citizen shall stand in a direct relationship with the states. We want freedom of the press, freedom of trade and commerce. . . We want all people to be able to compete with each other without privileges, for the rewards of profit. But we are subjugated and suppressed. . . No truth that does not agree with the existing order of things may be written down or taught . . . do you understand? Truth is suppressed; it cannot be spoken out. And why? To please an idiotic, obsolete, decaying state, which as everyone knows, will sooner or later be gotten rid of. I don't think you comprehend this meanness! Power—raw, coarse, transitory police power, totally without understanding of the intellectual and the new. . .' "

Did he remember reading *Buddenbrooks* when he wrote, years ago, that he considered Germany, after the surrender, not a defeated land, but a liberated one. Was it as the spiritual heir of Thomas Mann that he remarked, after his election as Chancellor—drily, yet with feeling—that Hitler had now definitely lost the Second World War?

The defeat of a power, the collapse of a society, are certainly not the conventional prerequisites for freedom, nor do they offer the best prospects for democracy. We experienced that under the first German Republic—Weimar. Kurt Schumacher feared just this "policy of resignation and compliance" which doomed fourteen years of German history begun by Ebert and ended by Hindenberg. Schumacher, tense and alert, tried to fashion nation and society differently from the perversion called National Socialism which had become the nightmare of Europe and the terror of the world. Marked by ten years of concentration camp imprisonment, he appealed to the self-confidence of a defeated Germany, not to forget, not to lose its national determination. He conceived the new Social Democracy as the national homeland, even as the avant-garde of patriotism, the only one capable of withstanding the new totalitarian clutches of the Left. With that, he doubtless laid the groundwork for the stability of the second German experiment with the republican form of government.

It must not be forgotten that Schumacher created the basis for the construction of a true and real democracy in West Germany and in West Berlin by his icy refusal of Communist offers of alliance, and his tough resistance to compulsory alliance with a "closed" party of the Left—"closed" in every sense of the word.

The part played by homeward returning young Brandt in that decision has been noted. Not to be underestimated or belittled, however, is the courage of those old and true comrades, Neumann's "Keulen-Riege" (club-squad)—the nucleus of the labor union liberal front; although in the course of the years, they became elements of reaction against the reformation of the Left—against liberalization of social democracy, against the transformation of the "Workers' Party" into the "People's Party." Brandt calculated the price of hope more exactly than Schumacher, whose view of the lessons of history was inadequate, too restrained, too frightened, too narrow.

For that reason, he lost by one vote when the first Parliament had to decide the administration of power. That vote was the vote of Konrad Adenauer of the Rhineland, who voted for himself, and who understood, with calm instinct, that one had to consider Europe if one wanted a nation. Brandt has rightly commented that subsequent developments bore out Konrad Adenauer's insight that a rebirth of small German nation-states is no longer feasible—that a grander concept must be envisioned if we are to achieve, with luck, that balance of power which will give us peace in the last decades of this century.

The chief of this reborn Social Democracy allowed himself to be greatly misled by the trauma of Weimar. Schumacher's angry epithet "chancellor of the Allies" delivered during the debates on the Petersberg Pact, will be deemed by historians to be a commendation. To have a chance for survival, Western Germany needed an alliance with its enemies of yesterday. Above all, it needed a partnership with its neighbor, France, Great Britain and with the United States, the policeman of the Western world.

In Berlin this was recognized more clearly than in Bonn. The confirmation of this theory was twofold: First, Social Democracy withdrew from its compulsory pact with those Germans who were executing Moscow's strategy. Second, confirmation was in the realistic views of Ernst Reuter, who realized more clearly than Kurt Schumacher that the German Republic had to rely on the victors, the occupiers, and finally upon its allies. For Berlin, it was a question of life or death. It could not have endured the blockade if Washington, London and Paris had not accepted the German Republic as a partner before it really existed.

Old Adenauer, who busied himself with plans for a sensible West German constitution, certainly would not have placed the fate of the people of the Rhineland, Westphalia,

Württemberg and Baden in the balance with the former
German capital. What he had in mind from the beginning was
a West European federation. He said and thought that
Germany's path should no longer branch off from that of its
Western neighbors. He certainly did not waste any sentiment
on Eastern Germany—not through lack of sympathy with the
Protestant world—that would be an unworthy insinuation.
After all, he was president of the Prussian Council of State
during Weimar, and did his duty loyally. His closest—perhaps
his only friend—Pferdmenges, the banker, was a strict Protestant. It must be remembered that Adenauer took a pragmatic
attitude toward relations with Catholic Poland. In his political judgments, he did not bow to the authority of ideologies,
so to speak. The religious believer is also free. He considered
the future German order a design for a future Europe. What
was called his "Western" concept—the return to a Lorrainian
core of a European community, was nothing less than the
beginnings of an agreement aimed toward the organization of
all Europe. It should not be forgotten that Adenauer also
spoke of a potential confederation of the two German states
and we should remember that he did not consider a German-
Polish condominium impossible.

These reminiscences are not only historical but topical
notes. Ernst Reuter would have, I assume, underwritten every
maxim of the principles of Adenauer's German policy. The
conflict between the two men is one of the tragedies of
history—a tragedy, incidentally, with its own humorous over-
tones. The Conservative Catholic petit bourgeois from
Cologne, who worked his way up to a position of importance, and the Protestant, reared in the climate of German
idealism, were of the same opinion as regards the basic design
for German politics. Their differing intellectual characters
were the source of the misunderstandings: One was the solid

son of a solid family, whose career was an outstanding success: Government official, mayor, outlaw for twelve black years because of his civic spirit, organizer of a political group which he ruled with that same self-assurance which later led him to the Chancellorship. The other was Ernst Reuter, son of a conservative Protestant family, youthful rebel, Communist, reformed Social Democrat, mayor of Magdeburg, refugee, restless returnee after long years of Turkish asylum; despite his intellectuality, hero of proletarian masses who used to assemble at his call in the Square of the Republic —and a European as good and as determined as Konrad Adenauer, his opponent from the Rhineland. Yet no agreement was reached between these decisive European figures, despite the similarity of their ambitions and aims. The "European attitude" was inherited tradition to the conservative from Cologne. But Reuter, a Red from Prussia, attained it through the struggles of a radical youth and the hardships of exile.

This allusion to the great contemporaries who showed Germany the way after the Second World War, is basic to an understanding of how Willy Brandt's political character was formed.

Kurt Schmacher had asked Brandt to represent Berlin's interests in the governing body of the SPD. He convinced him, reinforcing Brandt's own decision, that he should doff his Norwegian uniform and again take out a German passport—at a time when German citizenship seemed the least desirable to a young man who wanted success in life. His relations with Schumacher were not harmonious, as we know. Resistance clashed with obstinacy. Brandt, as he himself says, respected the severity and refusal to compromise by the Party's head, who, during his years of totalitarian sufferings, sustained incurable psychic wounds; and above all, never had the opportunity to see Germany's problems from a distance, as though through binoculars. He hardly knew our European neighbors.

The concentration camps to which he had been exiled for years, were undoubtedly also a rallying point for intellectual concentration, which was far from the intention of their ignoble founders. They, too, had their European elements. The persecuted Germans existed in involuntary, but harmonious company, with comrades of the French, Belgian, Czechoslovakian, and Russian Resistance against the dictator who sought to conquer Europe.

But still, there is a difference—seeing the results and the inevitability of events from inside Buchenwald and Sachsenhausen—or analyzing them from the point of view of one who stood guard outside. The view from across the fence was the more precise.

Brandt observed the complexity of Germany's problems from the outside, and he knew well that it was twofold: the problem of intra-German relations and the problem of relating to their neighbors. He returned with the insight—and his writings from the time of his emigration prove this—that there can be only a European answer to the German question. That was the basis of his agreement with Ernst Reuter, who almost became his substitute father. Reuter, the man with the beret, tried to cast a spell once more over the idealistic feelings of our people with an ardor no longer acceptable today. He probably pulled out of his pockets a little too quickly his Goethe, his Schiller, his Hölderlin, his Hegel, his Heine and his Marx. Richard Löwenthal, in a biography of the mayor which he co-authored with Willy Brandt, makes exactly the same comment in the last chapter dealing with the days preceding Reuter's death: German idealism which brought the world some happiness, but more tragedy, represented for Ernest Reuter the expression of a civic desire for freedom which endured for two decades. He taught the Germans to understand that they are not condemned to be subjects of changing regimes, but rather administrators of their own fate—citizens who must defend their inherited rights, but also the rights they fought for. Here the progressive program of a follower of Kant's later works came in contact with the conservative instinct of a Rheinish Catholic. Both, Reuter and Adenauer, Germans and Europeans at the same time, respected each other, but they did not go easy on each other.

It must also be noted that both are guilty of that "life deceit" as Ibsen put it, of our people, which is called "reunification." Central Europe had been federally organized for a thousand years. It had attained unity when possible, only in multiplicity. The old gentleman of Rhondorf was very conscious of that. But he was not able—overestimating the emotional attachment of a majority of the voters to the nation-state concept—to tell the people a second truth: it was the man from Braunau who handed Germany over to its partition. He spoke of liberty being more valuable than unity. But he refused to tell the people—with merciless clarity—in the West as in the East—that Bismarck's plan for a united "small-Germany" had failed because it did not take advantage of the opportunity for a federated "great Germany" in the 19th century—because, on the battlefield of Königgrätz, it buried hopes for a real balance in Continental Europe— along with a few thousand dead. The grand old man wanted to correct history. But he surrendered, for the sake of expediency, to that historic lie which sought to convince the German people that the dividing point of 1945 could be reversed. He never told us the truth, which he knew. Reuter's passion for a united Germany contributed to distract us from reality.

The question might have been posed as to whether our European neighbors could tolerate the centralized power of a nation of 90 million people in its midst. Wasn't this, in fact, the decisive argument against reunification?—the deep-rooted fear of the astonishing vitality of a people that had rarely known how to demonstrate its economic and military power in the form of calm, relaxed strength—that again and again had intimidated its neighbors with a type of energy more neurotic than normal.

Brandt's instinct for reality was more exact than that of his mentor, Reuter. He recognized at the right time that the division of Europe—the separation of people by the Big Fence, demands of us also the ability to conceptualize a greater Europe. He recognized just as readily as the old man in the Palais Schaumburg, the necessity for good neighborly relations with France, the Benelux States, Great Britain, and Scandinavia. De Gaulle's national ambitions did not deter Brandt from seeking direct contact with him, not through Francophile sentiments, but because he took the time and trouble to figure out that entry into a greater Europe can only be gained with France and never against France.

The author of this essay was not privy to the conversations between the mayor of Berlin and Chancellor Adenauer about the concept of Europe. He is certain that the difference of opinion was minimal. Here the ideas of the man of "inner migration" who had learned to view Europe from his involuntary retirement in Rhineland isolation, touched the experiences of the man of "outer migration."

Konrad Adenauer and Willy Brandt. Citizen met citizen. They respected each other in their own way, if appearances don't deceive. They had confronted each other in bitter election campaigns. The old man from Rhöndorf did not shrink from using unfair tactics. In his election campaign, he brought up Mother Frahm, the Spanish Civil War, the

Norwegian uniform. Nevertheless, I am of the opinion that Brandt was the only younger political adversary whom Konrad Adenauer respected and because of that, he attacked him with a severity that ill becomes his reputation. More important, he had recognized the competition: the successor. With his attacks against Ludwig Erhardt, Adenauer, as it were, advanced the Grand Coalition. He had a fine feel for the quality of characters.

The Old Man himself had set the stage for the Big Two pact. In those talks with Herbert Wehner, thanks to the intervention of Baron von und zu Guttenberg, the silent coalition between the former member of the Politburo of the KPD and the Franconian baron had, by that time, long been formed. Political calculation and personal liking met in the two men, both of whom had managed definitively to transcend their diverse origins. Konrad Adenauer had no more gone easy on Wehner than Franz Josef Strauss had on his Party friend, Guttenberg. But he distrusted more, and with good reason, the Free Democrats who were led by Erich Mende from Upper Silesia, whom Adenauer considered a Levantine disguised as a Prussian—intelligent and vain, certainly not reliable. He forsaw the failure of Ludwig Erhard.

He also knew that Kurt George Kiesinger was not predestined to administer his political heritage. To tell the truth, he did not trust him very much, and showed it on several occasions. Doubtless he underestimated the qualities of the Catholic South Swabian—his quick intelligence, his feminine energy, his charm, the effect he produced on the public. And yet he gauged, fairly and realistically, his indecisiveness, just as with Ludwig Erhard.

The Old Man took Brandt seriously. The burgher from Cologne met the Hanseat from Lübeck who, through a quirk of history had become a Norwegian by necessity. One should listen with a sharp ear to the secret language of historical interrelationships; one should try to decipher the code. The Hanseatic League ruled the area between the lower Rhine and Riga in the sixteenth and seventeenth centuries. It included settlements in Holland, Great Britain and Scandinavia. Its political might crumbled under the onslaught of the awakened energies of nation-state interests. Still, that heritage could produce a mentality capable of creating a design for Europe. The Catholic from Cologne, Adenauer, was to have as much part in that plan as the Protestant from Lübeck, Brandt.

That area of Europe influenced by the Hanseatic League included London and Rotterdam, Oslo and Stockholm. It might also be said to include Danzig, which has not lost its personality because it is now called Gdansk; on the contrary, it demonstrates to its new Polish citizens that drive toward European membership as clearly as did restoration of the Gothic and Baroque sections of Warsaw. Through this restoration, and by the reconstruction of Bresla, Poland declared itself for a European future, at least as far as architecture is concerned. Poland is still, and probably for decades ahead, will remain imprisoned in a geographical jail between Moscow and Pankow, cooped up behind the electric fences of the high tension fields which can be dismantled only when the Kremlin regime understands that Europe—all of it—is a reality. A reality that guarantees the right to their own national personality also to Czechs, Hungarians, Bulgarians and Greeks. Not the "Third Force" of which de Gaulle and others might have dreamed, for it has long since been established in the Far East, but a Fourth Force, which might give new meaning to the ancient catch phrase "balance of power." Adenauer barely skirted the temptations and opportunities of that concept. Willy Brandt recognized them. He is serious, if we correctly evaluate his first ventures into foreign policy, about "Europe for the Europeans"—slogan first sounded forth in Paris with a little too much pathos. But which Europe? Can a bridge be built between the "Carolignian" design of the West and the conception held by their Nordic Protestant partners?

The wise Richard Löwenthal, professor at the Free University of Berlin, has long pondered on the differences between the Catholic, Mediterranean South and the Protestant North. In the South, he sees feudalism still rampant, with all its blemishes and excesses; the contrasting movement of a two-faceted proletariat, one rural and the other industrial; the continuing inability to compromise for the sake of social harmony. In the North of Europe he identifies the grasping for equalization of social classes—yes, the urge to eliminate class consciousness—the desire to shape a democracy which would not be defined by the letter of a constitution, but only by the solidarity of its citizens, by the balance of property relationships, and by the fair fight for power in the state. Löwenthal owes it to us to write a book setting forth the proof that an accommodation between the early Mediterranean republics and the Northern European concept of citizen communities might yet be conceivable and possible.

It is worthwhile to create such a bond between Ferrara and Flensburg. Common economic interests exist. Religious differences can no longer be barriers, for Christians who take their faith seriously have realized in the past decade, especially after the Vatican council, that Catholicism cannot avoid a reformation, and that Protestantism can no longer evade the task of setting its own house in order. Thus, North and South can unite in a new understanding of the universality of faith, to perform this difficult task. In this sense, too, we can conceive of Europe as challenge and accomplishment.

The definitive transfer of power from Konrad Adenauer to Willy Brandt (little needs to be said of the Erhard and Kiesinger intervals) seems to herald the possibility of developing a European civic spirit—a European middle class. It should be noted that basic public-spiritedness permitted the "changing of the guard" in Bonn to take place with courtesy and democratic matter-of-factness. The Rhineland Catholic and South German element had dominated in the first two decades, the highest offices in the Republic, now held by Protestants. This may be a change of climate, but it only illustrates the candor of a society that is tired of living in the stuffy atmosphere of "proportional representation" and the "hymnbook" way of thinking—a society that seriously aspires to freedom and daily independence. Representatives of the new concept of European citizenship were Robert Schumann, Alcide de Gaspari, and Konrad Adenauer. Winston Churchill, too, even though he could not (nor could his successors), vanquish the schizophrenic position of England, torn between solidarity with the Continent and its special relationship to the United States.

The European reach had widened. The Germans recognized Poland, Czechoslovakia, Hungary and also the Soviet Union as their neighbors, and also recognized what they owed those countries. This indicates that we are in the process of recognizing ourselves as the focal point of the elements composing Europe—that we are the nexus where Germanic, Celtic, Slavic and Jewish influences flowed into each other, fighting each other, capable of destruction and self-destruction in the worst moment of our history.

The Chancellor's features portray a Germany which can make peace with itself. One must examine closely the high, broad cheekbones, steep eyebrows, narrow blue-grey eyes, high forehead, strong jaw, sparse hair with the rebellious forelock that is a problem for his barber. Slavic and Nordic elements are united in this face. All in all, he is truly a German. Add to this the square-built body, the emphatic control of his movements, the precision of his walk, and the conventional clothes, grey or dark blue, tailor-made, always just a shade less than elegant. He cares little for style. (Neither did de Gaulle obey the dictates of fashion, with his paunchy double-breasted suits.)

Willy Brandt hates diplomatic pomp. But the necessity of appearing in evening dress with ribbons and decorations over the white waistcoat, does not bother him in the least. His predecessor in the job of Party President of the SPD, the "old-shoe" type of German socialist, Erich Ollenhauer, all his life refused to wear black tie. Brandt is tolerant enough to follow the rules of etiquette and just as ready to drink a beer and a schnapps with workers at a corner pub, at night after an official state reception. He is, in any situation, a citizen among citizens, the same at a reception by the Queen of England as at the White House. He is the same, whether inviting journalists to his home in the evening, or talking to his rebellious sons, or with his chauffeur. He has never lost the ability to speak to the workers in their own language. From the yellowed *cahiers* of the 1848 bourgeois revolution, comes the concept of a "people's man." If there is a formula for the success of citizen Brandt, it is this: He was indeed always a man of the people—the German and the Scandinavian—all in all, the European people.

In this way he sought the path to power. His party did not make it easy for him. The beginnings in Berlin were difficult enough. He had the stamina to work, to debate his way during long years from one Social Democratic precinct in Moabit and Südende to the next one in Fronau and Tegel, until he gained the confidence of his comrades—until he had West Berlin on his side against the resistance of the old-line Party functionaries—until he forced the "club-squad" of entrenched bureaucrats to its knees. Until he was accepted as heir to Ernst Reuter. Until, after two vain attempts, he won membership in the party directorate, after a stubborn battle with his entrenched opponents who could not admit that their "Reform Party" itself needed reform.

Many clear-sighted individuals foresaw, a decade and a half ago, that this man was destined one day to lead the country. The measure of the man was in his defeats. The sensitivity of his reactions, the tears he shed when he was rejected a second time by his comrades—and at the same time, the tenacity to try again. This mixture of sensitivity and toughness bought him the authority he commands today. That he suffered defeats, that he admitted them to himself and to the public—this, ultimately, sets upon him the seal of honesty which earned him the mandate of leadership at the Dortmund Party Congress which must be deemed a turning point in the history of Social Democracy—that same mandate he had renounced on election night, November 19, 1965.

Out of this readiness to accept renunciation, retreat, and resignation, grew the quality of his power. Then, in Dortmund, he won the party's respect, so long denied him. The delegates, whatever their intellectual capacity, felt that the man confronting them was sure of his inner freedom—no longer prisoner of the public relations clan who sought to present him to the public as the new German Kennedy—no longer dependent on the rusty party machinery—no longer his own advocate, constrained to justify his origins, his flight and his emigration—no longer the representative of the "men without a country," but rather the calm administrator of a mandate to set new goals for his party and his people.

Only incidentally does he number himself among the insti-
gators of the "Godesberg Program" which the Social
Democratic Party confronted after a hundred years of existence in conformity with the customs of a capitalistic society
in its later stages. Other minds may have contributed more.
He himself cites Heinemann and Adolf Arndt, and especially
Herbert Wehner, who realized that reconciling power and
intellect was a harsh, pressing, day-to-day political job, to be
accomplished by relentless manipulation of the party machinery which he knew so well how to steer. Brandt would not
hesitate to call him the leader of the reform. But Wehner
would certainly admit truthfully that the new party structure
could never have been achieved without the citizen of
Lübeck, for he represented what the Germans demanded—
that will for continuity which does not inhibit the drive
toward social reform, but in fact stimulates it—that is the
continuity of integrity. One could discuss the psychological
complexity of the relationship between Wehner and Brandt—
most felicitously with both present (as well as another,
Günter Gaus). On the one hand, you have the liberal rational-
ist, formed by the Scandinavian school of reason, of social
conservative adjustment. On the other hand, you have the
bitter experience of the Communist resistance; of Stalinist
terror; of those nights in the Hotel Luxor in Moscow, dreading footsteps in the hall at 2:00 or 4:00 A.M.; the painful
farewell to an ideology that proved no substitute for religion;
then Sweden, jail, and finally return to Germany.

Both Brandt and Wehner were exiles. Only they suffered
that fate a good decade earlier than 11 million Germans.
Both have come home. That demonstrates a solidarity with
German destiny that is more impressive than the nationalistic
fervor of fellow travelers. They risked their lives in the fight
against the totalitarian regime of the man from Braunau. For

this reason they scorn the arrogance of any scheme which could sentence a whole people to destruction—which could send millions upon millions to their death, whether in Stalingrad or Auschwitz. There is no such thing as gradations of criminality. The Germans who were sent under Russian guns were just as much sinned against as the Russian prisoners who were allowed to starve, or the Jews herded into the gas chambers. Wehner and Brandt are symbols of a patriotism which rejects any sympathy with murderers of the fatherland and of Europe.

That is how Brandt earned the right to remark, after the Chancellor's election, that now Hitler had really lost the war. It is indeed so. Another truth has been made manifest— decency. This is doubtless a bourgeois concept, but, wonder of wonders in this age, still not threadbare . . . violated a thousand times, but a hundred times sustained and preserved. The Germans seem (and this is no illusion) to have resuscitated this virtue. But is it in fact a virtue and not, more realistically evaluated, the basic law of human coexistence?

The propriety of that "inner and outer emigration"—that flight abroad and imprisonment at home—but also that decency which revealed itself in civic readiness to help in protecting the persecuted during air-raid nights, in the chaos of collapse—these form the bases for that clause in the government's statement that the process of democratization has just begun. It is a decisive rejection of the fellow travelers' irresponsibility, which Brandt did not condemn too harshly, because he accepted the necessity of compromise sooner and more realistically than many a belated Robespierre. He even recognizes the right to cowardice, for he knows what fear is and doesn't deny it. Where there is no fear, there is no bravery. He is not the man to think himself the judge of history. He considers himself a witness. That is why he can say, with the ring of authority, that he never lost his respect for the German people. He was free to state this matter-of-factly, precisely because he had dared to live for half a year, with a falsified passport in our country. Discovery, he rightly says, would have cost him more than just a few years of jail—very possibly his life. He doesn't talk much about that, and if he does, only to call attention to the solidarity demonstrated by many a citizen—for example, when he reentered the country from Scandinavia—the customs agent who recognized him as a schoolmate and kept his mouth shut.

Brandt is accused of having escaped Germany's fate by fleeing first to Norway and then to Sweden. His illegal stay in Berlin proves the opposite, as do his writings during the exile. Not for one moment did he cease to feel responsible for Germany, despite its yielding to the grotesque error of Nazism. He defended a people and a country that had been dragged into the abyss by slave drivers and executioners. He even inveighed with the requisite sharpness against the prophets of reverse racism, as can be discerned from his polemic against the ideology of Fansardism.

The young revolutionary practiced Scandinavian precepts of egalitarianism. He renounced arrogance and discovered moderation. Berlin, during the tempests of the Cold War, gave him an opportunity to demonstrate this virtue—and it is a virtue. For example, that dramatic night after the failure of the Hungarian Revolution in October 1956, when he was able to prevent a galvanized mob from attacking the Brandenburg Gate.

He is a man of crises, of challenges, which he meets with stupendous self-assurance, perhaps just because he is not one for theatrical gestures. At that time in Berlin, he calmly forestalled the escalation of a conflict which could have led to a fatal confrontation of world powers. But today, he no longer needs alarums and crises to demonstrate his energy, quietly yet efficiently. He has grown accustomed to the daily routine of work. He reads important documents. He listens to discussions. He does not think the federal Chancellor should be a national chatterbox. He performs his duties with a discipline that permits him more freedom than the sloppiness of his predecessors. For example, the night of his election, he opened the doors of his home on Bonn's Venusberg to his neighbors, his sons' hippie friends, prominent personalities, and chauffeurs.

Perhaps in those hours the social climate of the Federal Republic changed. Bourgeoisie becomes, if the experiment succeeds, citizenship. Not only had the barriers of protocol fallen, but even more importantly, the psychological barriers fell too. Under the leadership of a man who chose freedom when he was young and who fought for it in Germany, in Scandinavia, in Spain, and again in Germany, we have become more free. No longer are we prisoners of our guilty conscience and the distrust of the world. We are citizens of a State which bases its authority on the renunciation of authoritarianism.

The same holds true for the Opposition, which, if Rainer Barzel is to be believed, understood well that the Christian Democratic Union must now undergo its test of maturity— must consolidate and concentrate, for it is indispensable to the State—to the vitality of democracy. The opposition must learn that power is not the only magical goal of politics, but that *control* of power is equally important. It takes practice, and it takes respect for moderation and value.

Moderation and Value was the title of a magazine which Thomas Mann, son of Lübeck aristocrats, edited during his Swiss exile. It was published by his son Golo and by

Ferdinand Lion—very Hanseatic and democratic combination of concepts. The family of Chancellor Brandt surely had no social relations with the senators and kingly merchants who moved in the world of *Buddenbrooks*. But young Brandt, I am sure, could have gotten on well with Heinrich and Thomas Mann, two brothers long estranged and finally reconciled, sharing basic republican opinions. "The bad Germany is the good gone wrong; the good in misfortune, in guilt and transition," read the manuscript of a speech Thomas Mann gave in Los Angeles in May of 1945. "It is in me too," he added.

Brandt would not disagree with this insight. Identity is the index to character. The Lübeck brothers, Heinrich and Thomas Mann, cultivated it as assiduously as the stepson of their city, who now governs Western Germany. They, no more than Schumacher or Adenauer, ever lost their discriminating love for country and people.

It is uncomfortable for us Germans to give equal importance to criticism and love. One does not exclude the other, but rather stipulates it: The first is Moderation, the second is Value.

II. SELF-PORTRAIT

My Road to Berlin

CONFETTI IN NEW YORK

A hard, cold rain swept angrily around the street corners; it whipped the walls of the buildings which, smooth and unassailable like the ramparts of a huge fortress, mocked its fury. It stung the faces of the people like a thousand needles. They pressed themselves against the walls, seeking protection under umbrellas and marquees. It was a poor protection; against this kind of rain, there was no defense, but the people did not budge. Four and five rows deep, they stood along the edge of the sidewalks on both sides of the street—men and women, young and old, workers, office girls, executives. They yelled, clapped, many waved small flags: thick red horizontal stripes and a broad white stripe in the middle showing a bear standing on its hind legs—the coat of arms of the city of Berlin.

Most of the windows of the thirty- and forty-story buildings were open; heads and faces formed bright spots in the gray curtain of rain. The rain turned to snow. It fell from all the windows—a colored snow, like confetti: it was snowing paper. Presently the narrow gorge of lower Broadway was covered with a thick layer of paper scraps.

It was noon, February 10, 1959. Slowly I drove along Broadway toward City Hall. I stood in the open car, but I felt no cold; I hardly noticed the rain. Forms and figures mixed and dissolved. My eyes focused on some patches of color: the flags on the street poles and lampposts—the red-white-blue of the star-spangled banner, the black-red-gold of the German Federal Republic, the red-white of the city of Berlin. The applause of the crowd was like ocean surf. Shouts rose above the noise: "Hi, Willy!" "Good luck, Willy!"

In front of Trinity Church my eyes fell upon an elderly man. Bareheaded, without a topcoat, he stood on one of the steps; judging from the expensive cut of his suit, he might have been a banker or broker. Now he raised his umbrella, and waving it, he shouted in a thin voice: "Hurrah for West Berlin!" Those around him joined in—a group of laborers in their overalls, dripping wet, some Negro construction workers, tin hats on their heads, their faces like polished ebony, their voices deep and resonant: "Hurrah for West Berlin!"

No, I felt neither cold nor rain. I felt quite warm, sheltered, as if I were not driving through the strange streets of New York but through my own Berlin.

I do not know how many of the New Yorkers who greeted me so enthusiastically understood the example and the lesson of Berlin fully and clearly. Nevertheless, I would like to believe they all felt that what united them with Berlin was more than expediency.

New Yorkers seemed to me very much like Berliners. They have the same instinctive aversion for bombast and pomp; they have natural wit, a refreshing irreverence which is never a sign of envy or enmity, but the natural way to make one feel a friend among friends: "Good boy, Willy!" "Good luck, Willy!" "Mach's gut Willy!" Berliners and New Yorkers speak the same language.

I am not a Berliner. I was born in Lübeck; I spent many years in foreign countries, a critical period of my life in Norway and Sweden. It was only after the end of the war that I became a Berliner. But since my early youth I have been devoted to what Berlin stands for today. And it was not accidental that I returned to Berlin in 1948. The decision to link my fate with the fate of Berlin was as well considered as it was inevitable.

Norway, where I had fled in 1933, meant more to me than an asylum. It was my second home. In 1940, Hitler robbed me of my home the second time. I worked for a free Norway and a democratic Germany. When I made up my mind to devote all my energies to the reconstruction of Germany, I did not choose Germany in preference to Norway—I chose a future upon whose realization the fate of all of us depends—not only Germany's or Norway's.

How I reached that decision and why I became a Berliner, is the story of my life. Or rather, two stories: mine and Berlin's. They cannot be separated from each other.

LÜBECK

Of the boy Herbert Ernst Karl Frahm, I have only a vague recollection. I know that he was born in Lübeck just before Christmas 1913, on December 18. The mother was very young, a salesgirl in a cooperative store. He never knew his father, not even who his father was. And he did not want to know. He bore the name of the mother; the father was never mentioned at home.

Home was a modest worker's flat, one room and a kitchen, but to him it was not a home. Since the mother could take care of him only after working hours, he was, during the first years of his life, left all day long in the charge of a woman who lived not far from where the mother was employed. He was often alone, left to himself for many hours. He had practically no playmates.

When Herbert was four or five years old the war entered his life for the first time. The war appeared in the shape of a man in muddy soldier's coat. The man smelled of sweat, wet leather, powder and oil. The odor fascinated Herbert, as did the rough cloth of the heavy coat, the leather belt, the long bayonet. He climbed quickly on the lap of the man whom he called "Papa." He let himself be kissed; the bristly beard tickled him. He liked the soldier from the very beginning. From then on the three lived together and the little apartment became a home.

But not for long. "Papa," who was the widowed grandfather, remarried. Herbert went to live with him and his wife, whom he called aunt. He didn't like her too much.

To Grandfather, on the other hand, he became very much attached. This was a simple honest man and an excellent storyteller. He could answer all questions and answered them gladly. Mother visited them once or twice a week. She tried to spoil the boy within the limits of her modest means.

Grandfather had grown up in the country, as a laborer on one of the big estates of a famous count in Mecklenburg. Grandfather's father had still been treated like a bondsman and had been whipped more than once. Corporal punishment was given even for a slight offense. Grandfather, however, revolted against the landlord's rule.

Until then it was the custom that just before an election to the Parliament the landlords had brandy distributed among the laborers. On election day the men had to come to the house of the overseer. There in the living room a big soup tureen stood in the middle of a table. The men passed in front of the overseer, who sat behind the table and took down their names. They had to put their ballots into the tureen, one on top of the other. Thus, the landlord could easily ascertain later how each laborer had voted.

When Grandfather approached the table he overturned the tureen, as if by accident. The ballots scattered; the overseer fumed and cursed, but there was nothing he could do. He could not find out which ballot belonged to which worker. Grandfather had outwitted him, for he was a follower of August Bebel, the leader of the Socialists, one of the first party members in the village.

Later Grandfather moved into town and became a worker in a factory. After the war he found employment in the Lübeck Draeger Works. He was a truck driver.

A few years later Herbert had probably the strongest experience of his childhood.

The workers in Lübeck went on strike. The strike led to a general lockout. Those were bad days.

Herbert was eight or nine years old, old enough to understand the difference between rich and poor. He knew that he belonged to the poor, that there was much that was beyond his reach. But real misery he had not yet known. Now suddenly hunger was standing in the kitchen, like an evil landlord.

"Are you hungry, my boy?"

Herbert had stopped in front of a bakery and was staring

longingly at the bread and the rolls. Never before had they seemed so crisp. The smell from the shop made him slightly dizzy. In confusion he turned around.

The boy immediately recognized the gentleman who had spoken to him. He was the "Herr Attorney General," one of the directors of the Draeger Works.

Herbert swallowed with difficulty. Then he nodded.

Whereupon the director took him by the hand, led him into the store, bought two loaves of bread, and gave them to him. "Here you are, my boy," he said.

Herbert turned on his heels and ran as fast as he could. He was afraid the gentleman might change his mind and take the bread away from him.

He arrived at home out of breath. And breathlessly he told his grandfather of the unexpected luck.

Grandfather became very serious. "Take the bread back!" he said. "At once."

Herbert did not understand. "Back...? The Herr Attorney General gave them to me."

"Gave them...! A striker accepts no gifts from his employer. We will not let ourselves be bribed by our enemy. We are no beggers, to whom one throws alms. We ask for our right, not for gifts. Take back the bread, immediately."

Never before had Herbert seen his grandfather so hard and so angry. Great was his confusion, yet still greater his shame. Should he not have known? He had listened carefully to the discussions at home between Grandfather and his relatives and fellow workers. Now, of course, he could do nothing but carry out the order. In fact, it was more than an ordinary order; it was rather a mission which Grandfather entrusted to him. He felt like a soldier who was sent with a message into the camp of the enemy.

Proudly he marched back to the bakery, haughtily he put

the bread on the counter. "Here—we don't want it!" he shouted. The triumph he felt made him forget even the hunger. This childhood experience strengthened the bond between Herbert and his grandfather.

Herbert was a good student, the best in his class. He learned easily, he was an avid reader. But he liked even more to listen to Grandfather's tales about the war and about the future when there would be no wars, about the misery in the country and how the Social Democrats would end all misery forever.

Like his schoolmates, Herbert found his heroes in the world of fairy tales and legends. However, unlike most of his friends, he had heroes of his own: August Bebel and Ferdinand Lassalle, the leaders of the new Social Democratic party.

To Grandfather socialism was more than a political program; it was rather a kind of religion. It would make all men brothers, eliminate all injustice from the world, even the money would disappear. Herbert never tired of listening to these prophecies, and his heart beat faster when Grandfather started to sing the revolutionary songs of the workers, the "Marseillaise," and the "March of the Socialists."

Those were hectic years. It was said the Social Democrats were in power—but did they really have power? Their leader, Fritz Ebert, was president of the Republic—but mostly the will of the other parties prevailed. Grandfather and his friends always spoke about the danger that the clock of history might soon be turned back. This fear they never lost.

In 1920 the Kapp Putsch, a reactionary coup of the military in Berlin, was crushed by a general strike of the workers.

In 1921 the Communists staged a coup. It too was unsuccessful.

In 1922, after the assassination of Walter Rathenau, Foreign Minister of the Republic, the pent up wrath of the workers exploded in huge demonstrations.

At one of these occasions the workers of Lübeck disarmed, interned the police and formed a militia. Grandfather was on duty in one of the police stations as a clerk behind the desk, a red badge around his arm. Herbert was permitted to take Grandfather his lunch.

He found Grandfather and his comrades in great excitement. A republican guard had caught a man who had answered the call of nature at a street corner. The man was a worker! How could he behave so lowly! At once the punishment was meted out—a sound thrashing on his behind. That would teach him to remember proletarian dignity and republican discipline.

In 1923 the inflation reached its climax. The ten-year-old boy did not understand its causes. This strange word "inflation" that everyone used—the way the words "war" and "revolution" were still used—acquired a concrete meaning when you had to buy your provisions immediately after you had received your pay check, since the next day the money had lost its value. When the new mark was introduced, the pupils were asked to collect all the old paper money and bring it to school. Big laundry baskets full of bank notes were brought. For each ten billion marks the collector got a candy stick. It cost a pfennig in the new money.

When he was thirteen, Herbert, in recognition of his good marks, was admitted to a Realschule (high school). He was granted a scholarship. The following year he entered the Johanneum, a senior high school of great reputation.

At that time his mother married. Her husband was a tall, sturdy, warmhearted bricklayer who hailed from Mecklenburg and was a Social Democrat like the grandfather. Herbert called him uncle.

72

It was in those days that Herbert heard for the first time the name of a man who was allegedly his father. The name sounded Swedish or Danish or Norwegian. The boy was not interested. Or was he?

I don't know. I remember no more than the few episodes just described. An opaque veil hangs over those years, gray as the fog over the port of Lübeck. . . Figures and faces are like shadows—they rise to the surface and disappear again, like flotsam on the waves of the northern sea.

It is hard for me to believe that the boy Herbert Frahm was—I myself.

POLITICAL PUBERTY

Already, at fourteen, I had written little pieces for the local Social Democratic paper, the *Volksboten* (the People's Messenger). I won a prize, a copy of Fenimore Cooper's *Leatherstocking Tales*. Encouraged by this success, I tried my hand at short features and little essays.

Little as I was paid for my literary efforts, this was the first money I had earned.

I joined the Socialist Youth by necessity, as it were. Mother, her husband, and Grandfather were all active members of the Social Democratic party and of the trade unions. I was born into socialism, so to speak. But that doesn't mean I was spared troubles and errors trying to find my own place in the socialist organization.

The youth movement attracted me primarily on account of its romanticism. It meant hiking and camping, close comradeship. We went on long hikes, visited the North Sea and the Baltic. We spent a summer on an island near Andernach on the Rhine, where the "Falcons" had a camp.

The youth movement was good training. I showed a certain gift for organization, I was a good speaker, and already at sixteen I was given a responsible position. Temporarily I was president of the organization in my district.

In 1930 I was admitted to the Social Democratic party as a regular member. I was not yet seventeen, and to become a member one had to be at least eighteen years old. An exception was made in the case of the "contributing editor" of the *Volksboten.* Julius Leber was my sponsor.

Julius Leber was editor-in-chief of the *Volksboten,* the uncontested leader of the Lübeck Social Democrats and deputy to the Reichstag. He was an unusually effective speaker, with the bearing of a Roman Tribune.

He was an intellectual, yet the little people, the workers, regarded him as one of their own. He expressed what they felt at heart, and had an unerring instinct for their aspirations and hopes. He had their confidence, for they felt rightly: Here was a man who knew what he wanted and wanted it passionately. Here was a man who never compromised, not a fanatic, but a real fighter.

His experience at the front had formed him. He was convinced that personality, strong will, and strong hearts had more weight than the dead apparatus of a political party. This point of view brought him in conflict with the bureaucrats of his party. He reproached the leaders for stifling the creative energies of the youth; he called them "captives of outdated formulas and slogans."

With equal determination he fought against the radicals who in pursuing their socialist goals declared democracy "old hat" not worth defending. As internationalists they equated love of one's country with shallow nationalism. Leber criticized the weaknesses of the Weimar Republic but vigorously upheld the thesis that "socialism without democracy was inconceivable."

Since he endorsed the Republic, represented democratic honesty, fought those who "live from hand to mouth by endemic idealism" he was called a "Rightist."

The Left accused him of betraying the principles of the class struggle. He wanted the Social Democratic party to be "a home for the youth of the middle class who in the war had lost its way and was searching for a new fatherland." Not only the Left scoffed at this strange socialist who was traveling his own special road to socialism.

We members of the Socialist Youth were, naturally, "Leftists." But that did not affect my personal relationship with Leber. In retrospect, it seemed to me as though I, who grew up without a father, stood in the same relationship to him as a son to his father.

In the fall of 1931, Nazis and German Nationalists, storm troopers and Stahlhelm (steel helmet), a reactionary veterans' organization, united in the "Harzburger Front." The followers of Hitler hoped to overthrow the hated Social Democratic government of Prussia. But in spite of their alliance with the Conservatives and though supported by the Communists, their referendum, aimed at the dissolution of the Prussian assembly, failed. Now the most reactionary circles— the rich landowners and industrialists; financiers and officers; Schacht, the Minister of Finance; and the head of the German Army—thought the moment opportune for "direct action." The answer of the Social Democrats to that threat was the formation of the "Eiserne Front" (iron front), a concentration of different workers' sports organizations and of the Reichsbanner, a democratic veterans' association and factory "Hammerschaften."

At the very same time the left-wing, Social Democrats, broke with the party; disciplinarian measures of the leadership provoked the split. A few deputies, a number of active party locals, especially in Saxony, and last but not least, a great part of the Socialist youth, formed a new Socialist Workers party.

In Lübeck only a small number of older Social Democrats, but many young comrades joined the new party. Leber tried to prevent me from following them. Was I completely mad? he asked. This time he lost his superior calm, which until then he had always shown in our personal discussions. The new party was an association of cripples, he asserted. They wanted to be revolutionary? They were impotents who, conscious of their physical and intellectual incapacities, escaped into radicalism. "In spite of your youth you can appreciate a good book, a good drink, the favors of a beautiful girl. You are quite normal, you don't belong to that band of sectarians."

I thought Leber unjust and protested more violently than I had ever dared before. We separated in bitterness.

I left the Social Democratic party. The direct consequences were hard on me. I suffered from my break with Leber. I could also no longer work on the *Volksboten*. The income from my other journalistic endeavors was minimal.

This was not the only material disadvantage of my joining the new party. I had planned to go to the university; Leber had offered to help finance my studies. That was now out of the question.

I could not complain about a lack of work. The new party made me, in spite of my youth, a political instructor. As organizer and speaker I was on the go day and night. But all my work was honorary. How should I earn my living?

I took a job with a firm of ship brokers in Lübeck. There I came in close contact with people who later proved useful to me--sailors, fishermen, longshoremen. I made good friends with the Scandinavian "clients." Between my political activity in the evening and my work for the firm during the day, I found no time for meditation and self-pity. That was good. My life was hard, but I felt strong enough to master it.

On February 1, 1933, two days after Hitler was appointed Chancellor, Julius Leber was arrested.

On his way home from a session with some friends he was held up by a band of storm troopers. The comrades of the "Reichsbanner" who accompanied him as his bodyguard, offered fierce resistance. Leber was severely injured; with a cut nasal bone, he was carried off. One of the assailants was killed in this fight. Although he and his friends had acted in self-defense and in spite of his immunity as a member of the Reichstag, Leber was imprisoned.

The workers of Lübeck were highly incensed. In every factory they met and demanded the proclamation of a general strike in order to enforce Leber's release.

I was a member of a delegation that was to present those demands to the chairman of the local branch of the Free Trade Unions. When we put our resolution on his table he refused even to read it and asked us to take it back at once. Did we not know that according to the last decrees strikes were strictly forbidden, against the law?

In the next two weeks I hardly went to bed. The fire of resistance had to be kindled. I thought—and I was right in this assumption—that there must be many more workers in other towns and cities who felt as we did. A one hour protest strike for Leber's release was carried out.

Then, on the nineteenth of February, Lübeck saw one of the most powerful demonstrations in the history of the city. Fifteen thousand people gathered on the Burgfeld. The threats of the new rulers could not frighten them, the icy cold did not scare them away.

At the intercession of his wife, Leber was released from

prison hospital for a few days. He was allowed to attend the meeting on the Burgfeld.

When he appeared on the platform with a bandaged head, unbroken, unbent, he shouted only a single word: "Freedom!"

It was the last time I saw Leber.

FLIGHT

Nine days later, the twenty-eighth of February, was the day of the Reichstag fire. But in spite of swindle and terror, the elections of March 5 did not give Hitler the majority he had hoped for.

On the following Sunday a national convention of our left socialist group was to be held in Dresden. We were already "illegal." To escape the police I had to conceal my identity. My not very ingeniously chosen disguise consisted of a colored student's cap. I traveled under my party name of Willy Brandt.

I had been warned of my imminent arrest and had to expect the worst because of local occurrences. It was impossible for me to hide in another German town, for I had no profession which could cover my political activity; and no way to earn my livelihood in Germany.

As much as I was tempted by the great adventure, it was not easy for me to say good-bye to Lübeck.

First I went to nearby Travemuende, where a hiding place had been arranged in a fisherman's house. Even here my escape came within a hair of failing.

I was careless enough to accompany the fisherman to a bar for a glass of beer. There I ran into a former comrade who had deserted to the new masters and who obviously knew at once what my intentions were. To turn around and run away was out of the question. I behaved as if I had not the slightest cause for fear, greeted the man very warmly, and stood at the counter with him for a few minutes. Those were long and anxious minutes I spent in the bar.

When I left, I didn't know whether he would follow me, call the police, betray me.

At midnight I breathed more freely when the fisherman took me to his boat. It was a small cutter, equipped with motor and sails. I found a hiding place behind boxes and cordage. The customs inspector did not find me.

At early dawn we set sail—direction Roedbyhavn, a little town on the Danish island, Lolland.

It was the worst journey of my life. The weather was awful, the seasickness was almost unbearable.

When we landed I could hardly stand on my feet. A few cups of strong coffee, to which my friend had added a large dose of brandy, brought me back to life.

Thus I landed in the free world with a briefcase and one hundred marks.

As soon as I arrived in Oslo I paid a call on Finn Moe. He was the foreign editor of the *Arbeiterbladet*, the organ of the Norwegian Labor party, and experienced politician, human and eager to help a comrade in need. After the war he became Norway's representative in the United Nations and chairman of the Foreign Affairs Committee of the Storting.

Thanks to his intervention I was granted a small monthly allowance. It came out of a special fund which the Norwegian trade unions had established for the purpose of aiding needy comrades in their own country. Since I volunteered for some clerical work in the secretariat, I got the double rate—thirty kronen a week and an additional allowance for my rent. My life was very modest, but I found it not at all harsh or depressing.

Within a few months I was able to forego any further financial aid. I had taken up my journalistic career; my articles, distributed to a few dozen papers, and the features I wrote for the trade-union magazines provided an income large enough to make my material existence secure.

Very soon I decided that I didn't want to be a refugee. I was chairman of the Refugee Federation. Much as I was concerned with the sorrows and troubles of my companions in misfortune, I realized the necessity of taking roots again; I did not want to be an outsider. My youth had something to do with this decision. I could not and would not perpetually look to the past. I refused to live in a spiritual and political isolation.

I tried earnestly to keep in close touch with Germany; at the same time I deemed it equally important to take roots in the political life of Norway as quickly as possible. In my case it meant active collaboration with the Labor party, primarily with its Youth Federation. That was impossible without a sound knowledge of the Norwegian language. I could already read it. A few weeks later I could speak it well enough to make myself understood. And a few months after my arrival I made my first public speech in Norwegian. Soon I mastered it as if it were my mother language.

ACTION FOR GERMANY—FROM ABROAD

How could we help our friends in Germany? This question occupied us political refugees incessantly; it gave me many a sleepless night. We tried not to lose our personal and political contacts with our native country. We met as often as possible with our German comrades, exchanged ideas, and comforted each other. I participated in many such meetings. Copenhagen was a good place for conferences with friends from Lubeck and other parts of northern Germany. We also utilized "illegal" correspondence, with cover addresses, invisible ink, more or less clever arrangements to conceal the real meaning of a letter from the censor.

We manufactured "illegal" newspapers and pamphlets and smuggled them across the border; unfortunately only a small number of our publications reached their destination, even though we employed all the well-tried dodges: the suitcase with a false bottom, the "filled" binding of a book.

I remember, for instance, a trial that was held at the end of 1934; the underground leaders of the Socialist Workers party—among them my friends Max Koehler and Stefan Szende—were the defendants. They had to expect heavy penalties, probably a death sentence.

We tried everything to save them. The Berlin authorities were deluged with protests. In Norway we mobilized a number of high judges and lawyers, among them the future mayor of Oslo, Brynjulf Bull, who signed a petition. It was read in the courtroom during the trial, and the German judges mistook it for an official intervention of the Norwegian lawyers' association. The Attorney General fumed against "these gentlemen who call themselves lawyers," but it proved effective. Our friends were fortunate enough to find judges who at that time still could not escape the weight of international opinion, and were still not completely under the thumb of the Nazis, though they were certainly not in sympathy with the "Socialist traitors." The trial ended with relatively light sentences. And thanks to the pressure of our campaign and the presence of observers from abroad, the defendants even had the chance to refute the minutes of the preliminary investigation and actually expose in the court-room the marks of the beatings they had endured in the Gestapo headquarters.

Another case of worldwide importance which we were able to influence from Oslo was that of the noble pacifist, Carl von Ossietzky, editor of the *Weltbühne* which we youngsters eagerly read. Because of his totally uncompromising stance against the secret rearmament, he had already had numerous clashes with the law before 1933. He was one of the first to be arrested on the night of the Reichstag fire.

He spent many years in different concentration camps. It was a miracle that he, a feeble and sick man, could survive those years at all. At last, in 1936, he was, by then suffering from an incurable disease, transferred to a Berlin hospital. In the meantime the "Ossietzky Case" had gained worldwide attention.

I don't think I can agree with every article Ossietzky wrote in the *Weltbühne* prior to 1933; yet I am proud that I was able to take an active part in the effort to obtain the Nobel Peace Prize for this victim of Hitler, this courageous anti-militarist, the "first gentleman of the German press."

The idea originated in 1934 among some of Ossietzky's friends in Strasbourg. It was well received by our Norwegian friends. But it was too late to submit Ossietzky's name to the committee which had to choose the winner for that year.

The following year many more famous personalities came to our support such as former prize winners and professors of philosophy and international law. However, in 1935 no Peace Prize was given. In 1936 nearly one thousand people of international renown and fame nominated Ossietzky. In Switzerland, a hundred twenty-four parlimentarians supported his nomination. It was partially due to my hard work that sixty-nine members of the Norwegian Storting and fifty-nine deputies of the Swedish Ritsdag signed a formal petition of his behalf.

On November 23, 1936 came the long awaited decision. The five man committee gave Carl von Ossietzky the Nobel Peace Prize for 1936.

Hitler had suffered a heavy moral defeat. He was so furious that he issued a special order: henceforth no German citizen would "ever" be permitted to accept a Nobel Prize.

When I was informed about the successful outcome of our campaign, in November 1936, I was no longer in Oslo. I heard about it in Berlin.

THE "OTHER" GERMANY

In the summer of 1936 I received a letter from our Paris committee. I was to take charge of our "Organization Metro"—Metro stood for Berlin. To see Germany again—that was, of course, a very exciting prospect. I realized the grave danger involved, but it would have never occurred to me to take the risk as an excuse for saying no.

In Oslo we had a friend who was an expert in the manufacture of the necessary travel papers. He did it for the good of the cause and would have never accepted a single penny for his work.

Usually I traveled with a Norwegian "passport for foreigners." It was a paper that looked like the real thing, especially if you put it into a nice cover. But it did not impress the German border guards. A fellow student helped me out. He was of my age and lent me his own passport. Our expert exchanged the picture of my friend with mine; I memorized his personal data and practiced his signature until the copy looked exactly like the original.

First I went to Paris to discuss in detail my Berlin assignment. The meeting with my comrades had a sobering effect on me. Here I was ready to risk my life—like my friends in Germany whom I was going to see in a couple of days—but in Paris there was continual quarreling and wrangling, a rather unpleasant refugee atmosphere.

In the sleeper to Berlin I had already eradicated the last days in Paris from my memory. All my thoughts were concentrated on the task that awaited me in Berlin.

The day after my arrival, I went as agreed upon, to the Wertheim Department Store where I was to meet the man who would put me in contact with my Berlin comrades. He was there. And immediately I felt no longer strange and lost. To know that in this city, in spite of all the swastika flags and the parading brownshirts, I had many friends who shared my fate and stood behind me giving me a feeling of comfort and security. My party still had a couple of hundred members in Berlin. They were organized in groups of five. And we were only one of many resistance groups in the German underground.

I found a furnished room at the corner of Kurfurstendamm and Joachimsthaler Strasse. The landlady, a nice middle-aged woman, did not conceal her contempt for the new masters. Nevertheless, I dared not betray my real sentiments. I was afraid to let myself be drawn into political discussions and tried to give the impression of a naive student, full of admiration for German science and culture. I had known such youngsters in Oslo and was sure I would not find it difficult to play this part convincingly.

I had not counted on meeting in person such a Norweigian here in Berlin. And this one was not only naive but in open sympathy with the Nazis.

When a few days after my arrival I visited the Reichsbank

to arrange for the transfer of my "student marks"—foreign currency that was used for studies in Germany was exchanged at a higher rate. The official had good news for me: A countryman of mine, a student like myself, had just been to see him about the same matter. "Here he is!" the official interrupted himself and called to a young man with whom I was forced to start chatting.

"My countryman" was very happy to make my acquaintance; I was much less pleased. He immediately bombarded me with questions about my Norwegian home town, about the school I had attended; he wanted to find out if we had mutual friends. I was sure that the Norwegian I spoke was above suspicion but afraid that in answering the questions I might give myself away. And there was no chance to get rid of him without giving him my address. He actually came to see me two days later, insisting that I should join a group of Norwegian Nazi students. But I had no time.

Every morning I went like a good student to the library of the university. Systematically I waded through the Nazi literature—even *Mein Kampf* didn't scare me. Until then I had tasted only certain excerpts. Now I had to swallow the whole indigestible dish: I read the Hitler bible from beginning to end. A heroic accomplishment, I think, even more so since I also had to find my way through the ideological jungle of Rosenberg and other Nazi "ideologists."

This was the fall of 1936. Those were the months when Hitler's foreign policy dumbfounded and paralyzed the world at large and forced upon his opponents inside the Reich the feeling that the progress of Nazism was irresistible, and that resistance, if not senseless, was in any case past all hope.

While he reintroduced universal compulsory military service, the occupation of the demilitarized Rhineland, the bold abrogation of international agreements—opponents of

Hitler, among them high officers in the general staff of the Wehrmacht, had still hoped the Western powers would block the dictator's way and force him to retreat.

How could we, under these conditions, keep the spirit of resistance alive? That was the question which occupied us most. In the big factories there were still cadres of trustworthy comrades. We wondered how certain quasi-legal kinds of opposition could be developed.

Berlin mirrored the megalomania of the dictator. The Olympic games had attracted tens of thousands of foreigners. They were duly impressed by the propaganda of Goebbels. It was difficult not to be overwhelmed by it, for wherever you looked you saw the successes of Nazism confirmed in the smiling faces of the young people, in the new monumental buildings, in the economic boom. Berlin offered magnificent scenery for a spectacle that took the breath of the world away.

Not a single dissenting voice disturbed the jubilation, for the cries from the concentration camps and the death rattle of the tortured victims did not reach the stadium—not even the Kurfurstendamm. In Wedding, in Neukolln, in the suburbs where the workers lived, we heard at least their faint echo. Out there was the "other Berlin."

Soon I had adapted myself to the life of an "illegal" person: I called myself "Martin"; it was a perpetual pretense and disguise, the necessity of always hiding your true feelings, the mistrust that makes you fear in every chance acquaintance an informer and in every former comrade a traitor, the organization of "contacts" and secret meetings— my head was full of figures and code words, and they pursued me into my sleep.

One day my landlady greeted me with the information I should appear at once at the next police station and bring my passport with me. Was I suspected? Had anyone denounced me? I decided that any hesitation to comply with this request, any sign of fear could only aggravate my situation. I went to the police.

It was a false alarm. My passport was returned to me a few days later. It was to successfully withstand the critical case of other police officials.

Another day I was sitting in a cafe in the Friedrichstrasse when I recognized an old friend of mine from Lübeck at the next table. He too had seen me. A faint smile passed quickly over his face. I wanted to greet him but I did not dare. I knew he had spent some time in a concentration camp. Was he still being shadowed? And what if he should now come over to me. . . ?

By that time his face had again assumed an indifferent expression; he turned his head away. I understood, paid quickly, and left the cafe in a hurry.

There were many such little incidents. They kept my nerves under steady tension.

IN THE SPANISH CROSSFIRE

When I went to Spain in February 1937, the Civil War was eight months old. In a few months the revolution had turned into a war of foreign powers against the Spanish people.

I saw the great dangers that confronted the Republic, and these dangers threatened freedom not only from the side of Franco and his German and Italian allies but from the ranks of the Loyalists. As a member of the terribly beaten German labor movement I thought it my duty not to flatter my Spanish comrades but to speak to them frankly and on the other hand, to draw the proper lessons from the Spanish events for our own future struggle. "We have to help our Spanish comrades," I wrote to Oslo, "but in order to help we must have the courage to criticize."

With this task before my eyes I had gone to Spain as a correspondent for Scandinavian newspapers and as a trusted delegate of my political friends in exile.

The five months I spent in Spain were full of the most contradictory impressions and of important experiences which were to be significant in my future political dealings.

The confusion and the propinquity of human grandeur and human pettiness—under the existing circumstances I could not expect much else. Revolutions are not the solemn spectacle their official bards make them out to be.

Over and over again I was deeply moved by the examples of heroic self-sacrifice and by an idealism which forced even a cynic to admire the dignity and magnanimity of the common man, of a little peasant, of a poor working woman. The Spanish people won my unlimited love.

On the other hand, the confusion in the republican camp, the naivete and political ignorance of the revolutionary leaders drove me to despair.

The crisis in the republican camp reached its climax in Barcelona that fateful first week of May 1937. The bloody clashes between the Communists and the Socialists were followed by a Communist crusade of vengeance against their opponents among the revolutionary workers.

In a pamphlet written under the fresh impression of those tragic events I tried to explain the double character of the war: "On the one hand it was a struggle for a new social order, on the other hand a national insurrection against the Fascist invaders. The left-wing Socialists had as their main—if not the only goal—the social revolution, the Communists acted exclusively as auxiliaries of Moscow. And Stalin was, no doubt, interested in defeating Franco, but he was not at all willing to let the Spanish people decide for themselves about their own future."

After I published a critical brochure, the Communists called me not merely a "Social Fascist" as the Social Democrats had called Stalin during the ultra left era, they also dubbed me "Franco Agent" and "Gestapo spy."

Comrades and friends from many countries, who had followed my activity in Spain, had to vouch for me and to testify that I had always worked in the interest of a sincere collaboration of all anti-fascist and groups—regardless of the accusations that were hurled against me from different sides.

In Berlin, later, a political opponent asserted that I had participated in the Spanish Civil War as a "Red Front Fighter" and as a member of the "International Brigade." Well, I would not be ashamed if I—like some of my friends at the Aragon front—had defended with arms the cause of the legal Spanish Republic and European democracy. However, my activity was limited to political and literary work; later, after my return to Oslo, I was engaged in humanitarian efforts on behalf of the suffering Spanish people.

It is of great importance to me to acknowledge here and now all that I said and did in the year of 1937 on behalf of the Spanish Loyalists; I have never wavered in my sympathy for the great Spanish people, sorely afflicted for centuries. Indeed, the truth was not so simple as we thought in those days; both sides were guilty of many crimes. But there can be no doubt that the resistance against the fascist insurrection was legal and justified. The Western powers would have acted more wisely if they had not let the Spanish Republic fall under the influence of the Soviets and if they had not allowed democracy to bleed to death. A different outcome of the Spanish Civil War would have certainly weakened the position of Hitler and Mussolini, and maybe prevented World War II.

THE POPULAR FRONT—AN ILLUSION

In the Fall of 1938, my friend Boris Goldenberg and I once more attended a popular front congress. It was held in the Hotel Lutetia in Paris.

The noted author Heinrich Mann, Thomas Mann's older brother, served as a figurehead for this enterprise. I had read some of his novels and short stories, but with the exception of his *Der Untertan (The Subject)* a great satirical, even prophetic novel, that had a great influence on my generation, his books left me rather cold. That was probably my fault. I found Heinrich Mann's novels too "artificial," masterful in style and language but without relation to the problems in which I was interested. This, however, did not diminish my admiration for his sincerity and humaneness.

I was all the more depressed when I saw how the Communist wire pullers of the congress abused the political naivete of the novelist for their own aims. Many of the "independent" and "democratic" speakers were known to me as Communist functionaries.

I had the occasion for only a very short private talk with Heinrich Mann. I was deeply touched by the sincere and genuine grief of the writer for his beloved Germany. A citizen of the world, world famous, rooted in the culture and the spirit of France, one of the keenest critics of the German people, he was probably the most German among the German refugees. He, like myself, hailed from Lübeck. That brought us close together. Hitler, the war danger, the rising tide of barbarism—he summarized his sorrow in one sentence: "We will never see our Lübeck again." In his case that was unfortunately true.

The debacle of Munich, the surrender of the Western governments, the ardent wish to unite all anti-fascist forces against Hitler and the coming war made the appeals for unity very attractive even to those who could not believe at all in the Soviet Union's selfless love for peace. Willy Muenzenberg was the driving force behind the efforts to bring about a close collaboration between the different groups of refugees. And again the Communists did more than their most bitter enemies could do to make that collaboration impossible.

Muenzenberg, who in spite of his long membership in the party had kept a certain measure of intellectual independence and whose unusual gift for organization and political acumen even his opponents recognized, lost the confidence of the Comintern. He had been a friend of most of the executed old Bolsheviks, therefore especially suspect to Stalin. Walter Ulbricht, prototype of the single-minded party hack, took over. He was always ready and willing to obey faithfully every order from Moscow. With him no human or political relationship was possible.

Muenzenberg, a strange combination of an old revolutionary and a modern businessman, broke openly with the Communists. Two years later he paid, like many others, with his life for this act of independence. On his flight from a French concentration camp he met his death near the Spanish border. How he was murdered and by whom was never established.

INCURSION OF REALITY

The first months of the war had an aura of unreality. They were like the white nights of the late summer high up in the north: The nerves are tense, you are in a strange state of agitation, the restlessness is like a poison in your blood, and at the same time you feel paralyzed, helpless in the grip of a dull fatalism.

Every morning I went to a small office that I had set up; I

gave lectures, wrote articles—and still a great many letters. I also worked on a book, a dissertation on the war aims. It was based on the certain assumption that the democracies would be victorious, and I tried to penetrate through the fog of slogans to the real problems which would confront Europe after the downfall of the dictators.

Unreal was the war in the west, this "drôle de guerre," not at all droll, but almost grotesque in its paradox. Real was Hitler's lightning victory over Poland, the partition of the unfortunate country between the brown and the red dictators. Real was the Soviet invasion of Finland.

Unreal was the Christmas party with Norwegian friends, radical intellectuals, in a ski hut high up in the mountains; unreal the pacifist ideas they expounded. A few months later the same men were fighters of the resistance.

Real was the harmony, the great quiet and perfect peace which we experienced amidst ice and snow during our Easter vacation of 1940; how far away, here in the mountain retreat of our friends the Lange family, seemed the war, how petty the pretense and the quarreling of human beings. Yet, this thought—was it not self-deceptive, unreal, this feeling of solitude and rapture?

We had been back from our vacation only a few days when on April 8 the reality hit Norway like a hurricane.

The first news in the afternoon papers seemed more mysterious than alarming.

One hundred warships had passed through the Danish straits heading north. What did it mean?

In the afternoon we were told that the Hamburg liner "Rio de Janeiro" had been sunk off the Norwegian south coast by a Polish U-boat. The ship had carried soldiers and horses. A few soldiers were rescued and brought to shore. At their interrogation they declared Bergen had been their port of destination.

The Oslo government was determined to do everything to maintain Norway's neutrality and not to give Germany a cause for intervention. Professor Koht and the majority of the members of the government were convinced such a policy was in the best interest of Germany; in their opinion the neutrality was not threatened by Hitler but by the Allies. A German attack could only be the result of Allied "provocation." To exclude such a contingency the government decided to raise a firm protest against the British and French notes.

The same evening, and in spite of the alarming news, the high command of the Norwegian Army clung stubbornly to the opinion that the German naval action was directed against Denmark, the Shetland Islands or the Faeros, certainly not against Norway. The contrary statements of the shipwrecked soldiers from the "Rio de Janeiro" were dismissed as a mere ruse. The government, moreover, did not order the mobilization of the weak military forces. Only the shore defenses were put on the alert. In the evening the beacon fires were extinguished.

That evening of April 8, I addressed a meeting of German friends and declared we might expect an attack on Oslo probably the next day.

I had just received the first author's copy of my new book. I took it home proudly. I did not imagine that a few weeks later my publisher, on the orders of the Gestapo, would have to destroy the whole edition.

The next morning I was awakened by the insistent but very soft ringing of my telephone. A friend told me in great excitement that for two hours he had tried to reach me without success; the line had been out of order. German warships had penetrated the Oslo fjord; German invasion troops had landed at different places along the coast.

A few minutes later we were on our way. First, we went to

the Sewerins', a doctor's family, good friends of ours. There I was told to drive immediately to a certain place in a suburb of Oslo.

Thousands like us left the city—escaping from harsh reality into an uncertain future.

On April 9 the members of the Storting assembled in Hamar, approximately eighty miles north of Oslo. The foreign minister informed them of the latest developments. In the midst of his report the news arrived that a German unit was approaching the town. The deputies had to continue their flight. They moved to the town of Elverum.

We arrived there late in the evening. We were told that a few hours before, the Storting in its last session had decided to cast a special vote of confidence for the government. To strengthen the national unity, representatives of the non-socialist parties entered the cabinet.

Since the German minister suggested further negotiations, the Storting appointed a delegation which consisted of the foreign minister and three deputies. It was felt that no attempt ought to be left untried in order to arrive at a last minute, peaceful solution of the conflict.

During the nights of April 9-10, a German unit tried to reach Elverum. The intention was probably to prevent further deliberations of the Storting, to take the King and the members of government prisoners, or to chase them at least across the border into Sweden.

This attempt was thwarted by Colonel Otto Ruge, who in a great hurry improvised a line of defense with officers and volunteers. We ourselves had passed that position; we had to leave our car there, and drove then in a truck toward Nybergsund, a little town near the Swedish border, where the King and the government had already established themselves.

On our way we were passed by a car with the then Minister

of Supplies and later UN Secretary-General Trygve Lie; he advised us at what spot we could, if necessary, cross the Swedish border. After the German advance had been checked the necessity did not arise.

On April 10, King Haakon drove to Elverum and received the German minister. The latter stated that the Führer not only insisted on the acceptance of his demands of the previous day but had added a few more "requests." It was Hitler's will that a new government be formed in which he could have confidence. Vidkun Quisling was to become the new prime minister.

The King replied that he had to conform to the constitution and the law. He could not appoint a government which did not have the confidence of the people. However, as a constitutional monarch he was willing to put Hitler's demands before his ministers.

In a session with the government and the members of the Storting the King explained his position: he saw clearly the terrible dangers that threatened Norway. The government ought to make a decision without regard to his person. In case they wanted to accept the German demands, he for his part would take the consequences and resign.

Again the government decided to reject Germany's ultimatum. The next day came Hitler's answer. It was given by the Luftwaffe. Elverum and Nybergsund were subjected to a heavy bombardment. As if by miracle the King and the government escaped with their lives.

The confusion was terrible. That evening, after the bombardment, I found in a hotel room a few forgotten valises with important papers. I helped take them to the police station for safekeeping.

The spiritual chaos was no less frightening. That night, together with a high official, I was quartered with a peasant.

A few months before I had had a rather lively political discussion with the gentleman, since he declared we ought to appreciate Hitler's accomplishments and meet him halfway. Now he put all the blame on the Versailles Treaty—it had not been harsh enough and was, therefore, responsible for our present misery.

The realization of my helplessness, of how difficult it was in times like those to make oneself understood even by men of good will, kept me awake for long hours. Not till dawn did I fall asleep from exhaustion.

Since the war could no longer be stopped, my friends sought refuge in the interior of the country. And what should I do? Escape to Sweden? But did I have the right to abandon my Norwegian friends? And besides, was it so certain that Sweden would not be attacked and occupied also? I decided to stay, and drove back to Hamar and from there north to Lillehammer, where I knew my colleagues from the Peoples' Aid had gone. We immediately went to work.

First we decided to collect woolen blankets and bandages and thus help to alleviate the most urgent need behind the front.

CAPTIVITY

I was a civilian. In the Norwegian war I had carried no arms. But that could not save me from the vengeance of the Gestapo. In 1938, Hitler had taken away my citizenship. The following year I had applied for my naturalization in Norway. Trygve Lie, then Minister of Justice, had informed me that I could expect my papers in half a year.

Then, after May 1, I found myself in a valley north of Aandalsness—an expatriate German and a stateless Norwegian. The valley had only one access. And this was blocked. My friends and I deliberated whether we should try to escape on skis over the mountains, but we had to abandon the plan because it promised no chance of success. Instead it was decided to put me into a Norwegian uniform. As one of thousands of Norwegian soldiers I could hope to be treated as a prisoner of war, and probably I would soon be released. As a civilian, on the other hand, I had to expect the worst, once my true identity was established.

I threw all my papers away and put on the uniform. It did not fit too well, the pants were too short, the jacket was much too wide, but nobody could find fault with my Norwegian pronunciation. Together with a few hundred other soldiers I was taken to Dovre, where the former school served as a prisoner of war camp.

Those were depressing days and weeks. The debacle, Hitler's victories in East, North and West seemed to secure his power for many years to come. The future was without hope. What could I expect? I let my life pass before my eyes and decided with all the superiority of my twenty-six years that it had been a failure.

But over and over again the wonderful comradeship of the young Norwegians among whom I lived restored my spirit.

The four weeks in the camp of Dovre offered me an opportunity for personal contact with German youth that had reached manhood under the Nazis.

The guards were mainly Rhinelanders. It had been impressed upon the German soldiers to treat the Norwegians with respect; since the latter were "purebred Aryans" it should be very easy to win them over to Nazism. Nothing but blindness and vicious propaganda and turned them into enemies of the new Germany. Now tragic that many of the "liberators" did not realize that the real blind were they themselves.

I could also easily see that to many of the young German soldiers Nazism was still something extraneous—an elementary force which one did better not to resist. If you wanted to have nothing to do with it, the best way was to retreat into a private world and concentrate thoughts and hopes on the marriage you planned after victory was won, on the new furniture you had promised your fiancee.

To show his good will the commander of the camp granted us privileges which ordinary prisoners of war usually are not entitled to. We were allowed to visit, in the company of our guard, the nearby farms to buy some food. And while in a backroom we listened to the London radio and enjoyed a free chat with the farmer, our guard sat outside on the doorstep and enjoyed the milk and a piece of sausage, which the farmer's wife served him at our request.

This superficial harmony was broken on May 17.

For already, the week before, an incident had occurred. During a discussion in the schoolyard the flight of the King was mentioned, and a non-commissioned officer accused the King of cowardice. I replied calmly, "If King Haakon is a coward, then Hitler is a coward too."

The sergeant stared at me, more terrified than outraged. He could not comprehend how somebody—on top of it, a prisoner—dared offend the Führer in public. He turned red; for a moment he was speechless. His helplessness was almost comical. Then he summoned an officer and exploded: "You dare call our Führer a coward!"

I remained calm. "I have said: If the King of Norway should be considered a coward, then Hitler is one too. If you take back your insult, we are even."

The officer frowned, took the sergeant aside, and advised him to leave the "hysterical youngster" alone. From then on

I was regarded as a student who could speak German quite well but who otherwise was a little mad.

THE SECOND FLIGHT

In the beginning of June we were released from the camp. I was permitted to return to my "hometown." As soon as I was on the train to Oslo I went to the lavatory, put on my trench coat, and put the military cap in my knapsack. Now I looked like a civilian again. Without difficulty I arrived in Oslo.

Of course I could not go home, nor was it advisable to show up in the city, for the Gestapo would be all too glad to catch me.

At the camp, friends had given me the address of an apartment in a suburb of Oslo where I would be safe. I was heading there now.

In the following weeks I lived the life of a hermit in a secluded summer house on the Oslo fjord which a colleague from the People's Aid had placed at my disposal.

A few friends knew where I was hiding and they sometimes visited me.

As a result of our long talks and deliberations it was decided that I should leave Norway. I could not hope to find a safe hiding place anywhere but in a remote corner of the country. Since I was well known, I could easily be recognized and thus jeopardize my collaborators. I surely did not like the idea of remaining idle. My friends suggested that I go to Sweden, where I could work as a journalist—also for the cause of a free Norway.

In July I started on my flight. A good piece of the way I

traveled by car, then I took a train, the last distance I covered on foot. The third day I reached a farm near the Swedish border. The farmer, a Norwegian reserve officer, knew the surroundings intimately and was well acquainted with the conditions at the border; he put me on the right path, and after a long march, eluding the German patrols, I crossed the border without being noticed.

On Swedish soil I reported to the first military post. The next morning I was taken over by the police and brought to Charlottenberg, where I was interned in a house near the railway station. August Spangberg, a deputy of the Riksdag, whom I had met during the street battles in Barcelona in 1937, came to see me and bailed me out. Via a rather comfortable refugee camp, an old castle where Ernest Paul, the secretary of the Sudetic-German Socialist party, took care of us—I reached Stockholm as a free man.

There I learned shortly afterward that the Norwegian government in exile had approved my citizenship. Now I was a twofold immigrant: A German who had fled to Norway and a Norwegian who had escaped to Sweden.

CONTACT WITH THE RESISTANCE

To maintain our relations with Germany—with the "other" the true Germany—proved in the course of the years more and more difficult. The contacts with our friends in the other refugee centers especially England and America suffered from postal and other technical obstacles.

Yet, through Swedish correspondents, business men, representatives of the Church, also occasionally through government officials, we were much better informed about Germany than our friends in London or New York. We were nearer to things at home, and could sometimes transmit a greeting or receive some sign of life. My friend August Enderle, acting as a liaison man of the International Federation of Transport Workers, tried not without success to organize a system of underground communication with German sailors; till the end of the war, for instance, he regularly kept in touch with a group in Bremen. We had not only sources of information inside Germany but could also rely on trusted persons in many cities who were able to help us in our efforts to save friends in need and danger.

In these endeavors we could always count upon the assistance of Swedish organizations—both private and official. Several times we managed to smuggle forged papers, even ration cards into Germany; without them our comrades, always on the move, always hiding, would not have been able to buy food or to elude the control of the Gestapo. Thanks to Swedish intervention, Leon Blum and the Dutch party leader Koos Vorrink, deported after the occupation of their countries to a German concentration camp, survived this terrible period. During the war Einar Gerhardsen was transferred from Sachsenhausen to the less dangerous camp of Grini, near Oslo.

My acquaintance with a German businessman, who had his residence in Oslo and later fled to Stockholm, was of particular consequence to me. In the second half of the war he put me in contact with outstanding people of the domestic German resistance. One evening he introduced me to Theodor Steltzer, who as head of the German military transport office was attached to General von Falkenhorst's staff in Oslo. Steltzer belonged to the "Kreisauer Circle," a group in which Count Helmuth von Moltke was the dominant figure. He, just as von Moltke, did not approve of the plan for the assassination of Hitler which the other members strongly advocated; he supported the resistance, however, with exemplary courage, regardless of personal danger. From the first he told me that he did not intend to discuss anything that would bring him into conflict with his conscience and honor as an officer—a request which I, of course, respected—but he made no secret of his real feelings and of his close relations with the Norwegian Church. I knew that more than once he had done his best to alleviate some of the hardships and abuses of the occupation.

After the attempt on Hitler's life, the twentieth of July, he was arrested and sentenced to death, the intervention of influential Scandinavian circles saved him from execution. After the war this noble and upright man became one of the founders of the Christian Democratic Union in Berlin and later the first premier of Schleswig-Holstein.

Stelzer gave me an insight into the thoughts and plans of the leaders of the opposition and of their ideas about the new Germany that were to emerge on the "day after." This was the first time that I heard again about Julius Leber and the important position he held among the conspirators in Berlin. I was very thankful to Steltzer for his information and asked him to give Leber my regards and to tell him about my work.

In June 1944 I again received news from Julius Leber. I was visited by a man from Berlin who aside from greetings brought me also an urgent request from my former mentor. This man was Adam von Trott zu Solz.

Adam von Trott, although counselor of the legation in the foreign office, was a convinced enemy of Nazism. As the son of a Prussian minister of education, he had spent the years of his early youth in foreign countries; he had studied as a Cecil Rhodes scholar in Oxford and had lived for a long time in Peiping and Washington. His vast knowledge, his intellectual curiosity, and his liberal, in the best sense of the word,

European background opened for him everywhere the doors of the outstanding personalities of public life and of leading statesmen.

From the start he foresaw the catastrophe into which Hitler's war would drag Germany and the world, and tried to prevent it. In July 1939 he had a long interview with Neville Chamberlain and Lord Halifax. He urged them to take a firm and unyielding stand against the Third Reich.

After the outbreak of the war he took advantage of a visit to America, where he had been invited to a conference, to submit a memorandum to President Roosevelt. He tried to convince the President that the opposition in Germany deserved confidence and support. The identification of all Germans with the Nazi leaders, the demand for unconditional surrender must have driven great parts of the German people right into Hitler's arms and made the fight extremely difficult for the opposition.

Von Trott's arguments met with no response in Washington. He had to return to Germany empty-handed. Yet he refused to be discouraged and continued in his efforts. Because of his personal contacts in England and America, and thanks to his position which permitted him frequent travels abroad, he was an excellent liaison man between the German center of resistance and its friends in the other countries.

He too was in close touch with the Kreisauer Circle around Count von Moltke, with Count Stauffenberg, Count York von Wartenburg, and Colonel-General Ludwig Beck. They all agreed that the dictatorship could not be overthrown by a mere officers' revolt and that the resistance had to be organized on the widest basis possible. Therefore, they had formed an alliance with political personalities "from the Right to the Left" and with representatives of the labor movement. Among them the most prominent were Wilhelm Leuschner, the former Minister of Interior of Hesse and Vice Chairman of the Trade Union Federation, and Dr. Julius Leber. Carlo Mierendorff and Theodor Hauback, Adolf Reichwein and Ludwig Schwamb. Gustav Dahrendorf and Emil Henk were leaders among the German Resistance.

Leber had spent four years in different prisons and concentration camps when he was finally released in 1937. He was still closely watched and frequently summoned to the Gestapo for long and vexatious interrogations. But this did not prevent him from assuming a leading part in the resistance movement. To cover his political activities he established himself as a coal merchant. Later, on the occasion of the fifth anniversary of Leber's death, President Theodor Heuss recalled those years of the underground struggle: "The two small rooms in the shabby little house, near the Schoeneberg railroad station, between coal heaps of the firm Bruno Meier & Sons, were a real den of conspirators. From time to time the doorbell would ring, and Leber had to rush to the anteroom to put a customer off. But in the back room, on wobbly chairs, political passion had its home, scornful hatred, and ardent love."

When Adam von Trott came to see me in Stockholm, the men of the resistance were just making the last preparations for the coup d'etat. The "coal merchant" was in the center of the action; he was a good friend of Count Stauffenberg, who finally took it upon himself to start the overthrow of the Nazi regime by the assassination of Hitler.

At first I had received the information about the intended action with considerable skepticism. Like most of my friends, I had no great faith in the political and revolutionary determination of the high and highest officers. Ernst Reuter had expressed exactly what I, too, thought and felt, in a talk with his colleague Karl Friedrich Goerdeler, the former mayor of Leipzig.

Goerdeler, chosen to be the Chancellor in the temporary government that was to be formed after the fall of Hitler, had visited Reuter in Ankara to inform him about the plans of the conspirators. He could not dispel Reuter's doubts. "I don't know your generals," Reuter said, "but I cannot believe that the generals will overthrow the man who after all is nothing but their own creation."

Von Trott's visit did much to make me change my mind. He told me, for instance, about a recent remark of General Beck. When some generals at the Western Front declared it did not make sense any longer to overthrow Hitler because the Western Allies in a couple of months would break through the front anyhow, Beck replied: "I want the history books of the future to record, 'and yet, there still were men!' "

The young officers around Stauffenberg and the progressive men of the Kreisauer Circle were rather critical of Goerdeler, who all his life had been an avowed German nationalist. To them he seemed too strongly rooted in the conceptions and ideas of the past. They would have preferred Leber as head of the new government. Even Colonel-General Beck, the presumptive head of state, was not unwilling to accept Leber instead of Goerdeler.

But Leber refused. In his opinion the Social Democrats must accept only as a last resort the main responsibility for the liquidation of a war which from the beginning to the end they had tried to prevent at great sacrifices.

Some of my closer political friends regarded Leber's alliance with the officers and conservatives as wrong and dangerous. They were afraid that the "Right-Wing Social Democrats" might let themselves be used as a facade for reactionary forces.

I contradicted them vehemently. The formulas of the time before Hitler seemed to me out of date.

Von Trott was hardly back in Berlin, when the conspirators were hit by a terrible blow. On the Fourth of July, Leber was arrested!

It was a bad omen for the planned action. "It signaled the tragic turning point of the drama whose climax came on the twentieth of July," as Theodor Heuss later described this blow.

The tortures Leber and his friends had to endure were horrible; the martyrdom of their execution was the more tragic, as it was utterly senseless. On January 5, 1945, Leber was executed. Not quite four months later he could have been a free man.

The commission which Julius Leber had asked me to undertake was now pointless. The example of his deed and of his end spoke to me in the course of the next months with ever growing clarity and urgency.

This message of the deceased, more than anything else, prompted me to dedicate my life to the reconstruction of a new Germany: in the spirit of the men of the twentieth of July.

The decision was not made easy for me.

RETURN

With the end of the war the refugees had to face the question of whether they should stay in their countries of asylum or return to their old homes. Those, who in the intervening years had been able to find a new position in exile, whose boys and girls were going to school there and understood the foreign language better than that of their parents, now realized that the country of their children had greater claims on them than the country of their parents.

Others felt that the horrible persecutions which they had endured were a fathomless abyss, separating them from Germany forever. The memories of the past were stronger than their hope for the future.

But to the politically conscious the return to the liberated mother country seemed a point of duty as well as of political opportuneness—though some Allied authorities seemed not to understand this.

My case was different. My Norwegian passport was to me more than just a useful travel document; my Norwegian citizenship was to me more than a mere formality. Consequently, I felt certain obligations which I could not simply shake off.

In October 1945, I came back to Germany for the first time. The Norwegian Social Democratic party press sent me to Nuremberg to report on the trials of the war criminals.

I flew in an American plane from Oslo to Copenhagen, and from there on to Bremen.

Prostrate Germany was like one of those horrible visions that sometimes overcomes us on the verge between sleep and waking—more real than any reality, and at the same time there nests in a remote nook of the brain the conviction that one is but dreaming, and instantly the ghastly dream will disappear.

But the surrealist vision of the destroyed cities, the bombed and burnt-out houses, up and down the streets, the debris-covered fields, the mountains of rubble and rubbish, between which human beings crawled about in the dark like hungry rats, the merciless cold, the unspeakable misery—no, one could not shake off this vision; with every minute it became more urgent, there was nothing beside it, it encompassed heaven and earth.

Of course, I had been prepared for such a sight; I had

many arguments ready which conclusively proved why it had to be so and not otherwise. Yet the raw nerves, the throbbing heart could not be quieted.

Nobody reproached me, nobody brought up the argument that abroad I had had a better life. Yet, I had to admit to myself that my lot had been a much easier one. Certainly, in exile I had not rested on a bed of roses, but through my own work I had made a living, I had had the chance to learn and to widen my horizon, I had overcome these years of terror sound of body and mind.

I was most deeply affected by our conversations about the extermination camps and the mass executions behind the front. Some of my friends pretended to know less about it than they actually did. But why? They were above suspicion; they themselves had been victims of the tyranny. Now one could see the fatal psychological effects of the thesis of the collective guilt. Horrified at the charge that "every German was a murderer" and conscious of the fact that they would not have been able to prevent these foul deeds even at the risk of their lives, these friends took refuge behind paltry excuses and tried to minimize to themselves the actual extent of the crimes.

At that time I did not meet anybody in Germany who would have declared his solidarity with the chief defendents in Nuremberg. But I met many who asked why they had not "cut it short" and hanged the criminals without much ado. There were others who would have preferred to see the Nazi leaders tried by a German court; the representatives of the "other Germany" should have been authorized to prosecute and administer justice themselves. But even among those hundreds of correspondents who were permitted to attend the sessions there were only a few Germans. As if among all the Nazi crimes the gravest had not been the one against the

German people; as if it did not matter how the Germans would accept the evidence presented at Nuremberg.

More serious was the complaint that the International Tribunal did not administer justice impartially. This objection could not be dismissed out of hand, because the Soviets were sitting in judgment, too, and pretended to represent the perfect constitutional state. This hypocrisy was grist to the mill of the cynics, who could declare the Nazi leaders had not been executed because they had started a criminal war, but because they had lost it

From many an observation, from talks with many people, and the reports I gathered, it became obvious to me that it would be more than difficult to build a new German democracy on ruins, on hate and military bureaucratic folly.

In February 1946, I met Kurt Schumacher. We met near Frankfort, although his home was in Hanover, where for months he had been busy with the reorganization of the Social Democratic party. At that time he was more than a party leader; he was a symbol of the suffering and sorely afflicted Germany and the representative of a new national consciousness.

If one wanted to reduce Kurt Schumacher's personality to a short formula one had to say: The dominating feature of character and the strongest impulse of his life and work was his extraordinary willpower. I have met many a man in my life who possessed great energy; in extraordinary times such as ours, statesmen need this quality in a high degree; yet I could hardly name another man who had Kurt Schumacher's strength of will.

He came back from a concentration camp as a cripple, doomed to death. He had lost his right arm in World War I; soon his left leg, too, had to be amputated. His life in these last years was a slow descent into death. His body was dying piece by piece; he was dying alive, as it were. But Schumacher seemed not to take notice of his physical decline.

He had proposed to himself one task, and he was obsessed with it. The Social Democratic party, which Hitler had destroyed, whose leaders had either been executed or forced to flee, the property of which—houses, newspapers, libraries, funds—had been stolen by the Nazis, whose members, provided they had not fallen on the fronts of war or resistance, could keep up their political contacts only in small groups and circles—this party was to be revived, greater and more powerful than before Hitler; it was to become the party of national deliverance and assume leadership. It was to use its power to blot out the mistakes of the past. He knew that only a few years were left to him to complete this task; he realized more clearly than others that especially the first years of the occupation would make the reorganization of an independent party twice as difficult, but he did not shrink. He would just have to work twice as fast and twice as hard and drive his colleagues and himself thrice as hard.

Schumacher had already become a national figure, when Mr. Konrad Adenauer, the mayor of Cologne, was still little known. Schumacher's party seemed to have the best chance to become the moving force behind the reconstruction of Germany.

It shall not be denied that Kurt Schumacher was a rather difficult person. Like many others, I, too, did not find it easy to work with him. His authoritarian attitude, the almost fanatical tenacity with which he clung to his decisions, his way of overemphasizing national points of view—no, I could not say that we were kindred souls. But this did not impair my deep respect for him.

Schumacher was in a precarious position. To the Russians

he was the Number One enemy, for by rejecting any compromise with the Communists he thwarted their "united
front" strategy, barred their way to the west of Germany,
and laid the foundation for their defeat in Berlin. The
Western authorities disapproved of Schumacher for other
reasons. For the Americans he was "too socialistic," for the
English he was "too agressive," for the French "too
German." They all found that he was "too independent."

Schumacher refused to orient his party according to the
views of Washington, London, or Paris. He had only one
guiding star: a free Social Democratic movement in a free
democratic Germany.

HOMEWARD BOUND

But meanwhile Halvard Lange had asked me whether I
would like to go to the Norwegian embassy in Paris as a press
attaché. This assignment would open the door to a diplomatic career which, as Lange said, would offer me an opportunity to serve usefully my second home—Norway. Such an
idea had never occurred to me, but I did not dislike it.

When I looked up Lange to discuss with him the details of
my assignment, he surprised me with the news that he and
Gerhardsen had changed their minds; I was not to go to Paris
but—to Berlin. The Norwegian government wanted a man
there who was thoroughly familiar with the conditions in
Germany and could keep them correctly informed about the
political development. I would get the title of a press attaché,
and, since I would be attached to the military mission at the
Allied Control Council, the rank of a major.

Berlin—this decided the issue. Without hesitation I
accepted the offer.

So after many detours fate had yet brought me back to Berlin. At Christmas I set off, with a Norwegian diplomatic passport in my pocket.

Almost at the same time—only a few weeks before—another emigrant returned to Berlin. I came from the north, he from the southeast, from Turkey: Ernst Reuter. Here in Berlin our paths were soon to cross.

Berlin in winter, 1946: craters, caves, mountains of rubble, debris-covered fields, ruins which hardly allowed one to imagine that once they had been houses; cables and water pipes projecting from the ground like the mangled bowels of antediluvian monsters, no fuel, no light, every little garden a graveyard, and above all this, like an immovable cloud, the stink of putrefaction.

In this no man's land on the edge of the world there lived human beings. Their lives were a daily struggle for a handful of potatoes, a loaf of bread, a few lumps of coal, some cigarettes. Many only went to work from sheer habit, or to get somewhat higher—though still completely insufficient rations.

Berlin had ceased to be the capital, and therefore one half of the population had lost their means of existence. The other half lost their jobs, when seventy-five per cent of the still undamaged machines and industrial plants were dismantled by the Russians and carried off to the Soviet Union. In the beginning of January many of the factories which slowly had resumed production had to shut down again. For want of coal they had worked on a part-time basis—now there was not even enough coal for that. There was no material to repair even the slightest war damages. The clearing of the roads from rubble and debris had to be suspended also. Many women were employed in this work. Since machines were lacking, they removed the ruins with their bare hands, stone by stone. Presently their arms and hands failed them.

For a new terror gripped the city—an icy cold. In the streets it attacked the people like a wild beast, drove them into their houses, but they found no protection there either. The windows had no panes; they were nailed up with boards and pasteboard. The walls and ceilings were full of cracks and holes; one covered them with paper and rags. People heated their rooms with benches from the public parks, cut down the trees in the Grunewald, even burned up their own furniture.

This was the city to which Ernst Reuter returned.

BETWEEN REUTER AND SCHUMACHER

I first met him in Annedore Leber's little house in Zehlendorf. Amidst an icy desert of destruction this was an oasis of kindness and warmheartedness; here German and Allied friends would meet; here reigned an atmosphere of solidarity and humanism.

The heavy man with his big skull gave one the impression of an old tree which had braved many storms, and under which one would like to seek protection, and rest. He looked tired, his hair was thin, his face lined with deep wrinkles, but his eyes were young, and a half-wise, half-roguish smile played around his mouth.

He was full of admiration for this city, and called it "remarkably thrilling—the people more openminded than anywhere in Germany." His praise was without pathos, but he spoke with great seriousness, even when a slight undertone of irony was discernible in his reflections on the weary negotiations with the occupation powers.

Quite early, he already feared that the Western Powers would let the Soviets impose their will.

Like Kurt Schumacher, whom he had only recently come to know better and with whom he hoped to establish a fruitful cooperation, Ernst Reuter desired a renewed democracy, not a mere restoration of the Social Democratic Party. He emphasized more strongly than Schumacher, that the power of the party bureaucracy must never be put above the intellectual and moral aspirations of the individual. The party must do more than defend the workers' material interests, it must become a popular movement, must speak for the middle class and especially for the intellectuals, who were longing for a revival of the social order.

Each time he spoke of freedom and democracy his words had no hint of the common sound of clichés and rally speeches. He did not bray them out; he used them carefully, pensively. To the objection, particularly frequent in hard times, that people cannot live on freedom, he used to answer:

"Well, fish do not live on water either, but in it. Man does not live on freedom, but he can only live in freedom. Without freedom people eventually suffocate in a soulless technological machinery. They become ants in a huge mass of ants. Spiritual death will be followed by physical death and the destruction of everything that makes life worth living."

One could hardly imagine two men of greater contrast than Kurt Schumacher and Ernst Reuter. On one side the man of fanatical will, completely absorbed in his ideas. On the other side the prototype of a humanist, who, though he never compromises in the pursuit of his ideals, also never forgets that all human toil is ephemeral.

Where Schumacher stormed and protested, Reuter sought to win the confidence of his Allied partners and to make them better understand the situation of Berlin and Germany.

Both were resolute in the defense of their political independence, but one felt that Reuter had gathered experience in foreign countries, whereas Schumacher was constantly tormented by the thought that the German Left might once more be accused of weakness and lack of patriotism. Both combined their strict rejection of communism with the conviction that Germany had nothing to gain from playing the four great powers off against each other. Reuter, who loved the Russian people as much as he detested the Stalin regime, wanted no conflict with the Soviets; neither side should have the feeling that the Berliners wanted to fish in troubled waters.

It was not that Schumacher was a "nationalist" and Reuter an "internationalist." Both were—both.

It was not that the one was harder or stronger than the other; one was detached, the other more impetuous—here the man of thought, there a man of action. What most distinguished Reuter from Schumacher was the complexity of his character: he was an intellectual in the good sense of the last century, which had sought a synthesis of thought and action. As a follower of Kant, he rejected the idea that man is but a product of his environment; as a socialist, he knew that, nevertheless, man can only fully develop his personality if conditions that infringe upon the right and dignity of man are abolished.

No doubt, I did not always share Reuter's views of Germany and the political tasks of the day. But from the first moment, I felt that Reuter and I understood each other very well. When I was a young man I never felt that the difference of twenty years in our age alienated me from Julius Leber; that difference did not matter in my relationship with Ernst Reuter either.

No, he was not an "old man." Though he always turned to

the classics when he was in need of courage and faith, and in the gravest crises sought comfort in Homer and Goethe—or rather just because he was accustomed to adopting a lofty standpoint toward life—he remained young at heart and young in spirit. This made him a comrade of the seekers and strugglers. We came from completely different social environments, but we did not only have the same aim, we also traveled the same road, for we had in the political firmament and in the world of the spirit the same stars by which we steered our course.

At the end of the year of 1947, I took a step, which since the end of the war I had considered again and again and yet put off: to become active again in the politics of my destroyed mother country.

I gave up my Norwegian citizenship—and the advantages, economic and personal, which I derived from my status as a Norwegian diplomat. I applied for my renaturalization in Germany. The immediate cause of this decision was a suggestion of Kurt Schumacher.

The suggestion, which had been thoroughly discussed at one of my visits to Hanover, amounted to the proposition that I take over the Berlin liaison office of the executive committee of the Social Democrats. It was not alone and not even primarily my task to maintain contacts with the party organization in Berlin and with friends in the Soviet Zone; but first of all I was to deal with the top ranking officials of the Allied powers who at that time were still in Berlin.

Here a post was offered me in which I could help to win understanding and support for an intelligent policy toward Germany. And also the opportunity to work closely with the party in Berlin. The time seemed to have come when I could do more for democracy and peace as a German in Germany than in my last position.

The adjudication of my German citizenship followed some months later. If I had waited a little longer it would not have been necessary to apply for my renaturalization at all, for according to the constitution of the Federal Republic I would have received it automatically. Since I was born in Lübeck, I was naturalized in Kiel. The document listed both my names—the one which I had borne at my birth and the other which I had used in my political activity since I was nineteen years of age; the formal change of my name was licensed by the president of the police in Berlin. As Willy Brandt I had escaped from the Hitler Reich; as Willy Brandt I had worked in exile and returned to Berlin—therefore I wanted it to be my official name in Germany from now on.

Thus I entered the new—and as I was convinced—decisive phase of my life; but not alone. Ruth stayed in Berlin, at my side. A Norwegian parson married us. We moved into a little house in Hallensee.

BERLIN BLOCKADE

The Soviets proclaimed the blockade of Berlin on the pretext that the streets were temporarily impassable and that near Magdeburg a bridge had to be repaired. Railway traffic, Autobahn, highways, and waterways from and to the West were blocked. Only the three air corridors, each thirty kilometers wide, remained open. The magazines of the municipal council, located in the East sectors, could no longer be used for the supply of the West sectors. Even the supply of medicine for sick persons and milk for little babies was stopped. Two million West Berliners were to be starved into capitulation.

Among the chiefs of the Western Military Administration,

General Clay realized most clearly the danger of retreat and pleaded in a most determined manner for energetic counter-measures. He suggested in Washington that the blockade should be broken by an American military train. He thought it unlikely that the Russians would use force to stop the train. He was convinced that the Soviet Union did not want a war but that they hoped the Western powers, from fear of a war, would abandon their positions. It is less known that Aneurin Beven, then a member of the British cabinet, pleaded also for the same determined action.

Washington and London, however, considered the risk too great. It was decided to hold Berlin and to supply by air the occupation troops—and as far as possible the Berlin popula-tion—with the most urgent necessities of life.

Nobody knew how long and to what extent the city could be supplied in this manner. Clay himself at first counted on a daily capacity of five hundred to seven hundred tons, and hoped to be able to carry on the operation for three to six weeks "until the situation would somehow be clarified." Thus, on June 26, thirty-two twin-engined Dakotas were put into action for the flight to Berlin. They brought medicine, some important foodstuffs, and mail for the civilian popula-tion.

Four weeks later Clay reported to Washington that Berlin could be held for an unlimited time if sufficient airplanes were available. At that time the American and British planes flew an average of fifteen hundred tons daily to Berlin. An extraordinary achievement, though not at all sufficient to secure the existence of the civilian population. And what would happen in the coming winter when people not only needed foodstuffs, raw material and fuel for the industry, but when they would also have to somehow cope with the cold? Could one subject the Berliners to such a severe test? Would they be willing to take upon themselves still greater pri-vations? The decision of the Western occupation powers depended on the answer to this question, as a last resort.

The answer of the Berliners was given to the Americans by Ernst Reuter.

At the end of June, I accompanied him to a conference with some gentlemen of the American administration. They tried to encourage us—perhaps it would yet be possible to supply Berlin. Reuter smiled skeptically. He could not quite believe it. But he told them—and he spoke without any sharpness, "We shall in any case continue on our way. Do what you are able to do; we shall do what we feel to be our duty." Berlin would make all necessary sacrifices and offer resistance—come what may.

The gentlemen were visibly impressed. They had perhaps expected to hear complaints, reproaches, conditions; instead they heard quite another sound. A European politician declared that he was ready to assume a hard task without making its achievement dependent on equivalent American services—not even on a financial support.

Reuter's frankness and his firm unshakable attitude won Clay's sympathy. At first the general had clearly given him the cold shoulder. By the way, this was mutual. Reuter also, had at first a rather critical attitude toward Clay. The southerner, brought up on the ideas of American federalism, thought Reuter too authoritarian, too centristic; it may not have been easy for Clay to free himself on the prejudice that sees a "Red" in every Social Democrat. Reuter, on the other hand, believed that an American general could hardly under-stand the European conditions, and the position of the German democrats in particular. He definitely refused to be considered an instrument of American policy, or of any other foreign government. Nevertheless, in the course of this crucial year the two men formed a close partnership which secured the victory in the struggle for Berlin.

The efficiency of the airlift surpassed the highest expectations. The organization of the operation, the technical achievements of the flyers and the ground crew, the exact cooperation of all nine air bases in western Germany with the airports in Berlin—all that bordered upon the fantastic.

The Berliners couldn't have held their ground without the airlift—but the airlift would have been senseless without the courage of the Berliners; without the determination shown by the civilian population.

It was, however, not the astonishing "normalcy" of those months that impressed me most. It was the simple manner in which the Berliners demonstrated their allegiance to common basic values; their knowledge that they stood for each other and could rely on each other; the determination they manifested in the defense of justice and freedom of speech and press; their acceptance of individual responsibility. All that reminded me of the admirable resistance the Norwegians had offered nine years before against all attempts to break their will and their spirit. As I felt then that Norway had never been greater than in the time of its hardest distress—just so I experienced now the real greatness of Berlin.

Ernst Reuter, in his quality as "elected but not confirmed chief Burgermeister" was the soul of the Berlin resistance. He gave the decisive watchword.

At the beginning of the blockade in a mass demonstration before 80,000 men, he had formulated the order of the day:

"With all means at our disposal we shall fight those who want to turn us into slaves and helots of a party. We have lived under such a slavery in the days of Adolf Hitler. We have had enough of that. We want no return of such times. We know all too well that we are an unarmed, defeated nation, and in fact, a defenseless nation, too. Our strength does not lie in the external power, we are deprived of that. Our strength lies, indeed, only in the fact we represent a good and just cause. . . ."

BERLIN AND BONN

When I visited Copenhagen, at the beginning of April 1949, I predicted in a lecture the early end of the blockade. I did not know about the discussions between American delegate Jessup and Soviet ambassador Malik, but a turn was in the air. Stalin himself had hinted at it.

On May 12 the "traffic restrictions"—as the Soviets called their blockade—were lifted. As Reuter said, the Berliners could celebrate "the most beautiful May since 1945."

They celebrated it in a new spirit. It was more than a mere enthusiasm about the end of pressure and privations—the experience of the resistance had given the Berliners the consciousness of their close solidarity with the democratic nations. The relation between them and the victors of yesterday had fundamentally changed. They now felt like partners and no longer like mere pawns in the hands of the great powers. From this feeling, by realizing the important contribution that they had made to the defense of the West, they derived a new self-confidence and new courage. That, not only had a bearing on the situation in Berlin but also an important influence on the development in West Germany. Berlin was, as Reuter said, the shield behind which the consolidation in the free part of Germany could take place.

The Social Democrats heavily stressed the temporary character of the political reorganization in West Germany so that the possibility of merging the four occupation zones into a single German state remained open.

Konrad Adenauer was at that time and later, less interested

in emphasizing the temporary character of the West German state. He seemed to support the federalistic ideas which were advocated by the French and the Americans. Only much later did he occasionally admit that, in fact, he owed a debt of gratitude to the Social Democrats and the British for having insisted on a strong and firm structure of the German Republic which was essential for its stability.

While the Social Democrats stressed the provisional arrangement of the Federal Republic, they did not want to weaken the executive; on the contrary, they were in favor of strengthening the position of the future Chancellor. To avoid the eternal parliamentarian crises of the Weimar Republic the constitution provided that the Chancellor, once elected, could not be overthrown except by a "constructive" vote of no confidence, at the same time agreeing by majority vote on his successor.

This was the only important point which Kurt Schumacher and Konrad Adenauer could agree, for both prepared themselves to assume the office of the Chancellor.

We Berliners were in a peculiar position. On the one hand, we were the most energetic supporters of a quick and positive conclusion of the deliberations in Bonn. On the other hand, we were the stepchildren of the constitution. The Allies decreed that we could only have a restricted number of representatives in the Parliament, and those were not to be elected directly and had only a limited vote.

The Western Powers argued that this decision was determined by the Four Power agreement on Berlin. The men around Adenauer were all too ready to accept the Allied demands. They were afraid of the Social Democratic votes of Berlin. That's what Allied officials who were in the know told me. And after all, it was not surprising that a man like Konrad Adenauer, with his character and his background, did not feel too strongly about the problem of the German East—and for him the "East" began at the Elbe.

Reuter could never suppress the suspicion that Adenauer's preoccupation with his West German concept did not leave him much interest or sympathy for the restoration of Germany's unity. Reuter felt that the President of the Parliamentarian Council and later Chancellor did little to unite the part of free Germany beyond the Russian Zone as firmly as possible with the Federal Republic—and that part was West Berlin.

In 1949 my work as a liaison man of the Social Democratic executive committee underwent a considerable change. Many Allied authorities moved to Frankfort or Bonn. My contacts with high Allied officials, originally my main task, lost their importance. In addition, my relations with Schumacher were not as good as before. He had the impression that I, instead of representing the Executive, had become "Reuter's man." Plotters and schemers, to be found in every party organization, tried to create distrust between us. They hoped to maneuver Reuter and myself into an open conflict with the party leader.

The elections in August 1949 were a bitter disappointment to me and to my party friends. The Christian Democrats won by a narrow margin. With a majority of one—probably his own vote—Konrad Adenauer was elected Chancellor. With the Free Democrats and the so-called German Party, he had quite an effective majority in the Parliament.

When in September the Parliament convened in Bonn, it became evident how deep the gulf between the two great parties was. And it became deeper and deeper.

This was mainly the result of the strained relationship between the two leading politicians. They were as strange to each other as only a man from the Rhineland and a West

Prussian could be. Yet, after the death of Schumacher, Adenauer still stuck to the old military rule to pursue relentlessly the defeated enemy and to destroy him if possible. He didn't even hesitate to use defamation.

At the Frankfurt Economic Council, the pre-Parliament for the three Western Zones, they had refused to serve on the executive committee. They had often miscalculated future economic development, and had expected a serious recession. In fact, everything was looking up. To a certain extent the Social Democrats had to blame themselves for their plight. A simple and clear program of reconstruction and liberty was needed. My Social Democratic friends tried to do too much and squandered their efforts. The conservative forces, which after a short "socialistic" interlude assumed the leadership of the Christian Democrats, used mainly three arguments. They identified the plan mad Left with the loathsome government controlled economy from which the people had only recently been freed; they presented themselves as trustees of everything respectable—from the Church to the Allied military governors; and they associated the democratic Left with the conditions in the Communist realm.

That was unfair and ungrateful, but effective. The distortion of the Socialist idea in the East was grist to the mill of the Rightists—it compromised their opponents, at least in the eyes of many who had not yet started to think for themselves.

I remarked in a speech given in May 1949: "Early in the labor movement, it may have been important to combine the visionary with the realistic. Our generation must base its actions on a synthesis of sober knowledge and determined will. We must realize that over a lengthy period of time and in a larger context there is never just one possibility.

"First of all, it is up to us to make certain that the State of the future does not become a prison State. We are not the first to recognize the primary importance of the fight for basic human and political rights. Democracy for us, is not a question of expediency but of morality."

Ernst Reuter was a warning and a clear example that performance—even recognized and successful performance—is not enough to achieve influence in a big and tightly organized party organization. He spent an excessive part of his strength in perpetual guerrilla warfare against members of his own party.

Party work was not Reuter's forte. In addition, his relationship with Schumacher was not the best, and the chairman of the Berlin Social Democratic party organization, instead of giving him his loyal support, often adopted the attitude of a hostile rival. This was the result of the conflicting characters of these two men, rather than differences of opinion about the political problems of the day.

In the elections for the new House of Representatives the Social Democrats lost—in comparison to December 1948—200,000 votes; the two other parties together had a majority of five seats. The result expressed the attraction which the federal government and the prosperity in West Germany held for the general public. In addition, the Berliners could not always follow the Social Democratic opposition in the "Bundestag." But this did not mean that they were turning away from Reuter. Most of the Berliners wanted him to continue to govern the city. In a personal election he would have won a tremendous victory.

It was quite different as far as his own party was concerned. Some blamed Reuter for the defeat and declared that it had been brought about by the cooperation with the other democratic parties which Reuter advocated. There followed protracted discussions as to whether the new Senate should be formed again on the basis of a coalition. And after that had been decided, there started long and bitter quarrels about our relationship with Bonn and about the incorporation of Berlin into the legislative federal system. In this question Schumacher and the party executive committee unequivocally supported the "Reuter line."

But aside from this question there existed open and hidden conflicts. The Social Democratic leaders in Bonn were in violent opposition to Adenauer, who would have made it difficult for even the most conciliatory and clever antagonist to create an atmosphere conducive to a fruitful cooperation. In Berlin, on the other hand, we had to be interested in amicably settling our difference with Adenauer's party friends.

GOAL: EUROPE

In Bonn the Social Democrats felt slighted by the Allies, who always sided with the government. They reacted with a certain mistrust against the ambassadors and the governments of the Western powers. In Berlin, under the direct threat of the Communists, we realized the necessity of keeping our position in the Western camp. And last but not least, we knew how important it was to have the United States on our side.

The conflicting points of view became especially apparent when, at the Hamburg Party Congress in the spring of 1950, the majority of the Berlin delegation openly adopted a position contrary to that of the Bonn Executive Committee. In question was the entrance of the Federal Republic into the Council of Europe; also the Schuman Plan.

Germany was to be an associate member only; by voting

"no" Schumacher hoped to gain a status of equality and to prevent the definite separation of the Saar territory. The Montan union which the Schuman Plan had as its objective seemed dangerous to Schumacher because he thought it might lead to a supranational trust. In general he was afraid that by this development the basis was laid for a Catholic conservative little Europe and that hence, the Federal Republic might be diverted from its main task—the reunification of Germany. It cannot be denied that some of these fears later proved justified.

In 1950, I was among the critics of the official line of my party, for I thought that in spite of all deficiencies, the new forms of a European cooperation were a step forward—a step in the right direction. Together with many of my Berlin friends I feared that an intransigent attitude might isolate us in the Western community and deprive us our influence. Even the arguments of my good and esteemed friend, Carlo Schmid, who presented Schumacher's thesis very effectively at a meeting of the Berlin functionaries, could not convince us.

It was different when, in the fall of 1950, the question of Germany's rearmament became the central theme of our political discussions. In consideration of the war in Korea, Adenauer had offered a contribution to the defense of the Western community without asking Parliament or even his own colleagues in the government. On this question—and this has since been forgotten by friend and foe—Schumacher took anything but a "negative" line. He went even beyond the position Adenauer took at the time. He asked that first the Allies strengthen their own military position in Germany. The Western defense ought to be established as far eastward as possible. The German defense contribution was to be made dependent on the granting of full equality—equal risks—equal obligations.

Schumacher had only the conditional support of his own party. Many heard only his objections, did not understand, or did not accept his basic attitude. The Social Democratic position in regard to the defense of the country remained for many years unclear and contradictory.

Along with my friend Fritz Erler, who, as a member of Parliament, had undertaken the thankless job of acting as the Social Democratic spokesman in all military matters, I was labeled an especially "militaristic" Socialist. In fact, we were only concerned about the relationship between labor and the state, including its armed forces; we knew that either you lick the army problem or it licks *you.*

I will not deny that the procedure followed with regard to German rearmament startled and alarmed me. Only a few short years before, when the Federal Republic was formed, it had been solemnly proclaimed that Germany would never again rearm. It was strictly forbidden to wear even the shabby remains of an old Army uniform. And now suddenly the signals change. Fortunately they evoked no military enthusiasm. Our friends abroad were positively horrified at the reaction of the Germans, who were not at all eager to take up arms again as they were now expected to do. But this was better than if great enthusiasm had been evoked for the military.

In August 1952, Kurt Schumacher died. That was a heavy blow to the Party—a grave loss for Germany. Many of his opponents even admitted it. In spite of all the criticism that his autocratic leadership and some of his decisions deserved the integrity, will power and idealism of Schumacher were great assets to the Federal Republic and the German people

The previous spring Schumacher had again called on me

for advice and cooperation. He had also not opposed my candidacy for the Berlin Party chairmanship. In August 1952 I was on vacation in the mountains of Norway. Only a few weeks earlier I had had a long conversation with the party leader. Did he feel the end approaching? A strange, almost pathetic contradiction manifested itself in his statements.

On the one hand, he criticized the stubbornness of a certain type of party functionary and demanded greater intellectual independence. He spoke of the importance of winning over the youth, bringing out those representatives of the "Hitler Youth Generation" at the next parliamentary elections. On the other hand he expressed doubts as to whether the Party would follow him on the path of renovation; he also defended the yes men who always agreed with everything he said.

I had the impression that he himself was aware of these contradictions and that he suffered from them. All the greater was my grief when I received the news of his death.

JUNE 17, 1953

In our fast moving times, the memory of even important political occurrences does not last long, particularly since, in the last few decades we have been swamped with historical events. Many of them have been called "turning points in history," although they were by no means so decisive as the exaggerating chroniclers of our era chose to depict them. To attract the attention of the public, every election, every speech, every conference of the foreign ministers is called "historical"—an inflation of big words which has contributed substantially to making people indifferent even to really important events.

And yet we are not guilty of rhetorical exaggeration if we say today that the seventeenth of June, 1953, is a historical date. This day, as well as the twentieth of July, 1944, has given us the right to call Berlin the capital of resistance.

The uprising of the people in East Berlin and the Soviet Zone was more than an explosion of despair—it was of international significance. This was recognized even more quickly and clearly outside Germany than in certain circles of the Federal Republic.

On the other hand, what was often overlooked abroad was the dual nature of the rebellion. It expressed not only the yearning for *national* freedom but also for *social* liberation. The workers—and they were the vanguard and the main body of the insurgents—rebelled against a system that had disguised slavery under the shabby cloak of an abused, so-called "socialism."

The unmasking of communism as the enemy of the weak, of the helpless, of the workers, whose advocate and guardian it had always claimed to be, had consequences which no countermeasures of the Kremlin could undo. Those consequences strongly influenced the political development in the countries under Soviet rule. While still under the influence of those events, I wrote a pamphlet entitled *Worker and Nation.*

On the afternoon of this June 16, the East Sector of Berlin presented a most unusual appearance. Large groups of people gathered at all the street corners in discussions. Functionaries of the SED (Communist Unity Party) who had been sent out to round up the workers were laughed at, and some were beaten up.

During the night of June 17, the general strike began.

On the morning of June 17, ten thousand people marched to the administration sector. They broke through police barricades. From the suburbs of the East sector, new columns of workers arrived continuously. They carried black-red-gold flags, some adorned with flowers, and signs bearing the inscription "Free Elections."

The workers had set out just as they were—some wearing wooden shoes, some bare-chested, their protective goggles pushed up on their foreheads, many carrying pokers and other tools.

Some 100,000 people had by now gathered in the Leipziger Strasse. In addition to strong police forces, Soviet troops had marched in to protect the government buildings. But the workers would not let themselves be intimidated. Again and again the Berlin wit erupted: "Ulbricht, Pieck and Grotewohl, soon we'll put you in the hole!" "We do not need a norm; today we are in form." "Get rid of Grotewohl and Ulbricht; then the strike will end!"

The agitation grew from minute to minute. A group of demonstrators tore down the red flag of the occupation power from the Brandenburg Gate, and in its place, hoisted the black-red-gold flag. About 50,000 workers assembled in the Lustgarten. Riots broke out all over East Berlin at the same time. The central office of the SED was besieged by a huge mob; eventually it was relieved by tanks. An SED building was stormed. Overturned police cars burned in front of police headquarters. The propanganda kiosks and sales stalls of the state-owned commercial organization, HO, were demolished.

Already during the morning hours, Russian armored cars had appeared in the streets. During the day, two armored divisions were concentrated. At noon, stronger tank units intervened. The workers greeted them with the song "Bruder zur Sonne, zur Freiheit" (Brothers—to the Sun—to Freedom) —a melody well known to the Russians.

Then the first shots rang out. But while youths and women

turned to flee, the workers linked arms and advanced against the fire of the troops. Here and there the ranks of the workers wavered—some were hit by bullets and had to be carried away—but the main body stood like a solid wall.

At 11:30, the Soviet Commandant proclaimed a state of siege.

Still the crowds did not disperse. They held their ground. Workers continued to stream into the city from the suburbs. Not until evening was there calm. Behind units of the Volkspolizei (the People's Police) and the Soviet infantry, tanks had rumbled in along the borders of the Russian Sector. They took care of "peace and order."

The overt intervention of Soviet forces made it clear to the East Berliners that further action was hopeless. It was impossible to continue the general strike under the state of martial law. And yet two days passed until the workers returned to their factories.

The news of the Berlin uprising spread throughout the Soviet Zone like lightning. On June 17 and on the following days, riots, strikes and demonstrations broke out in two hundred and seventy-two towns and communities. Grotewohl declared before the Central Committee of the SED that "only" about 300,000 workers had taken part in the strike. In reality, it was a mighty popular revolt, especially in the industrial centers of Saxony and Thuringia, the traditional strongholds of the German labor movement.

The 17th of June was characterized by the fact that the workers' strike widely assumed the nature of a popular uprising. People were not only rebelling against inadequate wages—they wanted freedom. Following the pattern of all great revolutions, the fury of the crowd was directed against prisons and jails. Many were stormed, and several thousand prisoners were freed.

The number of victims has never been precisely ascertained, but it became known that sixteen death sentences were pronounced by Soviet court-martials. According to reliable estimates, no less than 4,000 people were arrested in East Berlin, and 16,000 in the entire Zone. The majority were soon released, but thousands remained in the penitentiaries of Central Germany.

Yet it would be wrong to say that the 17th of June was futile. The immediate aim of the East Berlin construction workers was realized; the work norms were reduced. The economic and social demands of the workers received some consideration in the ensuing months. Travel between the two parts of Germany was eased to some extent; a few years later, however, an inhuman passport law nullified these improvements.

On July 1, 1953, the Parliament in Bonn decided to proclaim the 17th of July as "Germany Unity Day." Unfortunately, to many in West Germany it has become nothing more than an additional holiday. At that time I made a speech in Parliament which many criticized as too harsh. Yet I was motivated only by my passionate desire not to leave our countrymen in the Zone all alone.

First, I pointed out that the people's uprising in East Berlin and in the Soviet Zone had been brought about by those workers who could by no means be regarded as an indistinguishable mass without a clearly formed will of their own. "These workers have proved themselves in the forefront of the fight for unity in freedom—not only as fellow combatants, but as leaders. As in all great revolutionary crises, they have combined the struggle for their immediate economic and social demands with the interests of the whole nation, and have raised the fight for unity—the central desire of our nation—to a higher plane.

"Anyone who still questions the democratic and national reliability of the German labor movement takes upon himself the responsibility for a further division of our people."

SIGNS OF CHANGE

Many in the Zone had misunderstood the attitude of the Western Powers and Adenauer's slogan "The Policy of Strength." They hoped they would receive military assistance. This was a tragic misunderstanding.

The Soviet government was, after the death of Stalin, in a state of crisis. An attempt should have been made to take advantage of this; to strengthen the position of the West in Berlin; to lighten the burden of the subjugated peoples of Eastern Germany. The Soviet occupation positions far into Europe could have been made the subject of serious negotiations. But the Allies seemed primarily determined to prove that they were in no way responsible for the East German rebellion. By their political passivity, they left the field to the Soviet government.

The events in the German East Zone in 1953 were to become the precedent for the Hungarian tragedy three years later: a courageous uprising of the population, merciless intervention of the Soviets, inability of the West to take action.

A man like Ernst Reuter was shocked at the German people's lack of readiness to make sacrifices, and at the attempts of many to push aside difficult decisions and their obligations toward the community in order to indulge undisturbed in the—generally rather modest—pleasures offered by economic prosperity. He had asked that we should be ready to give the shirt off our backs to win back freedom for the people of the Zone. But this did not fit in with the mood of a populace which was glad they at last had a couple of shirts in their own wardrobes again.

The group of us around Ernst Reuter openly, and in general justly, discussed the mistakes and weaknesses which had led to the defeat of the Social Democratic party in the general elections. There was no lack of criticism of our maneuvers. I, too, was numbered among the "reformers."

Ernst Reuter was bitter; he had hoped for a change of course in Bonn, and had counted on the possibility of infusing new impulses into German politics. We did not know then how much his health was affected; how much his heart had suffered. He never complained; never consulted a doctor. His best friends did not guess how sick he was. So his death came quite unexpectedly.

On that 29th of September, I was at home, at my desk. A telephone call came from Oslo. The Norwegian government organ was asking me to dictate an obituary on Reuter.

In that first instant I did not understand what they meant. Reuter dead? I could not believe it. Fifteen minutes later I was in Reuter's little house in the Bülowstrasse.

As I walked home, benumbed and troubled, I saw an unforgettable sight. In every apartment, in every street I passed, candles were suddenly burning in the windows. No one had called upon the people for such a demonstration. The general feeling of personal grief sought an outlet. And so people remembered that Reuter himself had asked them the Christmas before to put candles in the windows as a greeting to the prisoners far away—as a pledge of faith and solidarity with all those persons who were dearest to each of them, and whom they did not want to forget.

When, on October 1st, at a huge rally in the square later to be named after Ernst Reuter, we Social Democrats of Berlin bade farewell to Germany's great son, I said:

"Berlin is weeping for its protagonist in the fight for its

own rights and for the freedom of all. Not only the younger generation mourns the Father of the People. You have been at the same time our teacher, our advisor, and our good friend.

"You were master of the rare art of rendering complicated problems simple without ever becoming banal. Your words were always unpretentious, impressive, humane. You could speak to university professors as well as to workers.

"You never doubted the victory of Freedom. Therefore you were able to inspire those who worked with you—the whole population, but most of all the young people—with hope and confidence. Sometimes you were called 'too much of an optimist.' What would have become of our Berlin without the stubborn will and the faith that moves mountains?"

With my friend Richard Löwenthal, who had acquired English nationality and had become political editor of the London *Observer*, I undertook the task of describing Ernst Reuter's life in a political biography which appeared in 1957. It certainly did not become a best seller, but through this work I learned a great deal for my own activities.

Abroad

BALANCE SHEET—1945

*[19] In the years following 1933, the main preoccupation of the German Opposition was: After Hitler, what? Since September 1, 1939, the theme has been: After the war, what?

From the first day on, I followed European and international discussions on war and peace goals. I wrote articles and speeches, and finally wrote a book, the first copy of which lay on my desk the day before the occupation of Norway.

During the ensuing years, the topic of war and peace objectives gripped me relentlessly. During the years in Stockholm (1940-45), I commented on them in newspapers, magazines and speeches to study groups. I participated in interesting discussions with international workers' groups and we published laboriously formulated texts. I soon took it upon myself to work at the topic more systematically and more thoroughly. That is why the preface of the book which

---

*The numbers in brackets refer to sources listed on page 301.

was published in Stockholm and Helsinki early in 1944, entitled "After the Victory," noted that the book had actually been created as a by-product of an intensive study of postwar problems, and that it was not my intention to "increase by one more number, the private plans on how to save the world."

There will be no discussion here about the problems of a young man who came in conflict with the German state, when it was enormously powerful, and who returned to Germany after it had been destroyed. Neither will we mention the German refugees' struggle for existence during the Hitler regime. My material existence was—after a difficult start—more secure than that of many others. I was able, through skill and luck, to escape mortal danger. Here, I just want to make two things clear:

I have never tried, insofar as it has been possible, to be taken in by narrow interpretations, especially after too brief exposure to conflicting views. And I have equally sought to steer clear of those emotions and exaggerations which accompany any war, and which must have played a dominant role in considering the excesses committed by the Nazis. I was determined to think above and beyond the events of the war, and to raise my voice for as just a peace as possible.

Still, I was a young German who left his country at nineteen; whose citizenship had been revoked by his country, gratefully accepted Norwegian citizenship—who, as he wrote on peace objectives, had more on his mind than a fatherland—who considered himself a European.

NEVER AGAIN WAR

In 1918, when the soldiers returned from the trenches to their starving wives and children, all had the same desire:

Never again war. And yet, a new world war erupted within one generation, and threatened to set the whole world on fire.

People of various countries, victims of this new war, ask what is behind this conflict of the great powers and what are they really fighting for? Seldom, however, do they get an honest answer.

In contrast to the World War of 1914, the governments of 1939 found it necessary to discuss the objectives for which they were going to war. Much remained unsaid, and how much of what was said is true, nobody knows. But the fact that governments, even at a war's early stages, and using all possible modern propaganda devices, try to present themselves as the most reliable guardians of people's rights, of a just peace, and a positive new order after the war, illustrates that consideration for those at the front and behind the lines—consideration for the general populace—is more important than it was last time.

In the somber atmosphere after the outbreak of this new Great War, there is a very significant ray of light—people have not been carried away by war psychosis and chauvinistic frenzy, but increasingly ask what can lead them out of this misery, and how can the basis for a secure and permanent peace be laid? Certainly, changes in the structure and intensity of the war can also change this expression of popular feeling. A ray of light early in the war can be snuffed out later in the darkness of a great conflict: But no power on earth can prevent that question from being asked again, and people from trying to look beyond superficial symptoms to trace the root causes of the European and international crisis.

Today, few in Europe believe that one only has to trace back to where this war started, or the last war ended. The wheel of history cannot long be reversed without serious consequences. The way back leads to new wars. The future of mankind depends on whether we honestly succeed in vanquishing the barbarity of the Thirty Years' War.

All countries and all peoples—the whole world and mankind—need a permanent peace founded on trust and justice. We need a true peace of nations, to solve problems from an interstate, European, and international point of view. Such a peace cannot be a gift bestowed by a few great men. The "great" men who took it upon themselves to act for the people only led them into misery and war. A peace of nations is not only peace *for* the nations, but just as much peace *by* the nations. They cannot trust dictators who promise them a "new Europe," nor can they trust new Wilsons who are unable to create the "new world" of which they speak. Conditions for a new peace must be created within the individual countries. There, the question is whether the people support those forces which work toward historical progress, or whether they follow those who work toward Europe's destruction and the victory of barbarism. To fight for the new peace means to fight against reaction and oppression in every single country. Work toward a new national social order lays the groundwork for a new Europe and a new world.

FOR A JUST PEACE
(EXCERPTS FROM LETTERS)

[2] Of course Germany carries the main responsibility for this war, but I still cannot admit that *only* Germany is guilty. The others have their share of responsibility for the last peace, for the fact that Hitler rose to power in Germany and was able to build his war machine. Of course the Germans are responsible for having let Hitler come to power, but the other

nations are certainly responsible, too, for the pro-Hitler policies of Chamberlain and Co. If, as some say now, the entire German population had consisted of Nazis, then Hitler surely would not have needed to rule with terror, Gestapo and concentration camps. We must clearly understand that the vacillating policies of the Western Powers constituted one of the decisive reasons for the fact that today there exists in Germany no active political opposition. The people stopped believing that there was any power capable of stopping Nazism. Remarks by anti-Nazi soldiers in Norway definitely bear out this observation. Others point out that a German collapse would only make things worse for the Germans than they already have it, and that German workers would suffer the most from a capitulation. Hitler's appeal to fear gives him an even stronger influence on certain elements of the German working class.

These are the premises from which Nazi propaganda can be defeated: First, the principle of national self-determination shall be valid for a democratic Germany, and second, while Germany shall contribute to the reconstruction of Europe, it will not be left to starve, but will be given the means of developing within the framework of a more comprehensive international organization. It should be understood in England that a policy of humiliation and occupation could be the surest way to lead the Germans into a firm alliance with the Bolsheviks. In spite of my respect for the bravery of the Russians in the war, I do not consider it desirable to have a Bolshevik regime embrace all of East and Central Europe, including Germany. . .

[3] You point to the fact that a democratic revolution in Germany would speed up the healing process. Clearly it would become much easier to vanquish the strong hatred and the justifiable distrust for everything that is German and was

created by the imperialist, militarist, Nazi forces in Germany socicty—forces which during nine years of Nazi rule claimed as many victims and martyrs from among the German people, as now among nations that today feel the Prussian boot. But aspirations toward future democratic development in Germany require that current policy be directed toward strengthening as much as possible the democratic and peace-loving forces among the German people. In addition to the guarantees of the Atlantic Charter that conquered nations would be aided in material reconstruction, it is necessary to specify clearly that the German people, once they have overthrown the Nazi dictatorship, will be accorded basically the same right of self-determination as any other nation.

[4] It has been proven before that a war can be won by the military, but be lost politically. Real victory has not been achieved until guarantees have been furnished that the inter-vening events will not be repeated. The peace goal of the United Nations must be to create conditions which will prevent a third World War.

[5] The wounds of the war can heal; the worst material misery can be conquered; the hatred of nations for each other can cool off—before the task of writing peace treaties is finished. It would not be satisfactory to deal with govern-ments, no matter on what side of the treaty table they sit, that do not speak for their people. It cannot be determined who has the right to represent a country until that nation has regained its calm after the initial period of upheaval.

At Versailles, Germany was sentenced to pay damages because it was responsible for the war. The reparations took on a punitive character. This time, the question of who was guilty of starting the war will be much less debatable than last time. But we wonder if those truly responsible will be made to pay. Even if we take the point of view that all

Germans, including inmates of concentration camps, are responsible for Nazi policies, it is still debatable whether such responsibility also applies to children and to generations as yet unborn.

Adherence to this basic principle means that reparations can play only a secondary role. If they must be employed, they should not take the form of punitive measures, but should become components of a unified European reconstruction policy. As important as economic adjustments may be, emphasis must be on the positive, taking full advantage of the tremendously increased production potential of industry and agriculture. This will lessen the time required to repair the material damage done by the war.

PERSPECTIVES FOR A EUROPEAN FEDERATION

[1] All projects for improving relations between the countries of Eastern Europe fail to deal with the important question of the future relations between Germany and her neighbors to the East. There are many arguments in favor of a federative union of Germany and these countries. This Central and Eastern European group has strong common economic interests. Trade conditions would be considerably improved if Germany and the Eastern European countries under discussion could take their places in a federative organization. The solution of the minority problem would then also become much easier. With common basic national laws for such a United Federation, there would be no reason for separate countries to use and abuse "their" minority on the other side of the border.

[5] The case of Germany and Poland perfectly illustrates the necessity of easing international regulations by "loosening

up" the borders. Against it can be said that it will be difficult for a while—but fortunately not forever—to reconcile the points of view even of a democratic Poland and an anti-Nazi Germany.

In a discussion about borders, two principal tendencies stand in opposition. On the one hand, the emerging realization that the old idea of national sovereignty has to be modified. On the other hand, nationalistic feeling, heightened by war and occupation. In the fight against Nazism, nationalism was a very important and positive element. In the task of European reconstruction, it could become a very negative factor.

[1] Because of the way ethnic groups are mixed, especially in Central Europe, it is impossible to draw completely fair lines. The minority problem cannot be eliminated. No matter what adjustments are made to present borders, there will always remain considerable minorities on the other side of the border. The problem is, then, how minority rights can be protected.

Dictatorships favor forced resettlement. The South Tyroleans have no voice in the land that their forefathers have cultivated for hundreds of years. The Germans in the Baltic countries were ordered "home to the Reich." Millions of Poles are being forcibly resettled... The most natural solution to these problems would be a European Federation. The constitution of a united states of Europe could confer common basic rights on all citizens, independent of language, race or religion. Common organizations to serve the national and cultural needs of the various nations could be set up for these united states. A federative order in Central Europe could solve this problem, even if a broader federation for all of Europe might not as yet be feasible.

Only a unanimous European solution can eradicate the old

conflict between the national security interests of a country and continued progress in economic and cultural development in all of Europe. The subordination of national sovereignty to common European interests need not endanger the liberty and independence of the individual nations. The demand for European unity includes negation of the primitive concept that one's own safety can only be maintained by fighting others. A much solider security is between people who take into consideration the right to live, and the life interests of all nations.

DEMOCRACY CANNOT BE RATIONED

[5] Many European and American democrats think that the future will differentiate between culture-nation and state-nation. If the Alsations are good Frenchmen, as they have shown again in this war, even though they speak a German dialect, and if a German Swiss thinks Swiss despite his ties with German culture, why, then, should it be impossible for a Sudeten German to become a good Czechoslovakian citizen, even though he maintains his cultural, and national characteristics? Certainly, Hitler's slogan about the uniting of all Germans was very seductive, but the war did not start on that account. The roots of international conflicts lie deeper. And Hitler's attraction was not limited to just the German speaking people outside Germany's borders. Austrian Social Democrats, for example, were less inclined to hearken to the siren's song from Berlin, than were certain lords and labor-pacifists.

After this war, two important facts can no longer be ignored. Disarmament of the defeated countries is no guarantee that there will not be conflict between those countries which retain their military establishments. Once such a situation arises, the opponents will be interested to win over the nations that originally cooperated to demilitarize. That means they will be interested to see those nations attain new military power. Continued reliance on the concept of sovereign states implies that each of them will try to command respect through military power. Permanent occupation is a theoretical possibility to prevent this from becoming legitimatized in the defeated countries. Prerequisite for such a continual state of occupation, however, is enduring unity of interests among the occupation forces. It is not known whether this condition will be met. That is why timely regulation of the armaments problem is so important.

The democratic points of view can be sidetracked for a while. Nevertheless, the central problem of the postwar era remains the realization of the objectives announced at the beginning of the war: First, to rebuild and strengthen elementary human rights and respect for law. Second, to carry over basic rules of freedom and equality from the political to the economic sphere. Third, to bring the rules of international coexistence into harmony with the laws governing domestic relations in each civilized commonwealth.

Those who fight in occupied Europe have proven innumerable times, that for them, there exist higher values than transient material gain. To them, freedom is more than an empty word. The will to win freedom has created a fighting humanism. The battle of machines has underlined the significance of human effort. The new democracy must take over this fighting humanism. But that will not be enough. Freedom must be broadened and strengthened. Democracy can no longer be rationed. It must be valid in all areas of social life and in the relationship between people and states.

[6] My opinion regarding orientation to East or to West is

that Germany cannot rise again and cannot maintain her position unless we reach an accommodation with the East as well as the West. To concentrate on one of the power blocks foredooms that policy. It is clear that a socialistic movement cannot be neutral in questions of democracy, but it must go without saying that it has to keep its independence vis-à-vis the large factors in the international power game.

LIBERATION—NOT SUBJUGATION

[7] German democrats who choose the road of honest co-operation need not, on that account, renounce their own goals and interests. They do not have to renounce the right to protest against misunderstandings and distortions. German anti-Nazism chose the road of cooperation and in so doing, did not incur loss of principles, self-humiliation, or servility. Men who are serious about the reconstruction of a Germany that is free within and peaceful without, cannot be content with the role of a lackey. After the unconditional surrender of the regime, they cannot favor unconditional adaptation. They cannot promise to sign *each* paper that is presented to them. The basis of their desire for cooperation is the realization of existing, all-important, mutual interests. . .

But how can one visualize a German policy that is neither geared toward "revenge" nor aimed toward confident cooperation with the Soviets? That is not the same as a one-sided "Eastward orientation." But it is also irreconcilable with a one-sided "Westward orientation." Hitler's Germany was defeated by a coalition of the big Allied powers. Germany is occupied by those Allied powers. It can only emerge from this crisis as a homogeneous nation if the reconstruction is carried out in agreement with and in cooperation with "East as well as West." Any one-sided solution only represents an attempt to change the balance in favor of one of the partners. Each such attempt only arouses the suspicions of the other partner. That contributes toward stabilizing the Zone borders and making Germany a colonial territory. At the worst, it can lead to making the Elbe Line the starting point of a new military conflict, many times more terrible than the one we just lived through.

I know very well that considerable groups abroad are extremely skeptical concerning attempts to unify Germany across Zone borders. Such attempts are considered a new potential threat to peace. But if they are carried out by reliable anti-Nazi forces, and with proper foreign policy orientation, they are something completely different, namely, a decisive *contribution toward safeguarding peace.* It is certainly no particularly sure and satisfactory solution to have Great Power colonies right in the middle of the continent. As long as this situation prevails, there cannot exist a basis for a truly European policy.

One cannot demand that the unconditional surrender of the Nazis shall be followed by the undignified subjugation of the anti-Nazis. In the interests of Europe as much as of Germany, tendencies that lead to spiritual subjugation must be resisted. The point is to give European youth growing up in Germany a new ideal for which they can work. German Europeans and world citizens have not been very lucky in the past. That is no reason not to carry on their task... The Nazis tried to Germanize Europe in their way. Now we have to "Europeanize" Germany.

OPPOSITION IN CONFLICT

[20] Why did I leave Lübeck, where I went to work as unsalaried assistant at a ship brokerage firm after receiving

my high school diploma at the Johanneum in early 1932? I withdrew from difficulties which had to do with an arrest for political reasons and would have had unfortunate local repercussions. Besides, my close political friends in Berlin had ordered me to establish in Oslo one of the bases for our work abroad, after the original emissary was arrested on the Isle of Fehmarn when he tried to leave the country.

"Close political friends" mean the illegal national leadership of the SAP (Socialist Workers' Party). Like many other young Social Democrats, I had joined this group at the end of 1931, when it split off from the official Social Democratic Party as a "Left wing" opposition group. The schism representated to us a revolt against a weak, powerless policy of compromise. This group, which had imposing organizations in Saxony and Silesia, was joined by smaller groups—for example, at the beginning of 1932, by a splinter group of the "Right wing" Communists, which had been excluded from the KPD (German Communist Party) a few years before.

Even though they were the result of a split, the SAP still held to the slogan "Undivided Front." I, too, was convinced at the time that the Social Democrats, Communists, and in-between groups were actually part of one and the same Socialist movement, and that it must be possible to block Nazism if the entire labor movement would erect a cohesive wall against it.

After the victory of Nazism, the Left socialist criticism of the "reformist" errors of the SPD and the "ultra-left" errors of the KPD, seemed largely justified. With a certain self-righteousness and presumption, the SAP developed the bold theory that it constituted the nucleus of the "new" party of the German Left. This Left socialism was also interpreted then in Party idiom as "truly communistic"; "truly" was supposed to express two concepts: point of contact with the theoretical basis of the modern labor movement (Communist

Manifesto of Marx and Engels); and differentiation from Communist practice of calling all those holding different opinions "social fascist" and from the undemocratic organizational practices of the KPD, including their dependence on Moscow. . .

There is no doubt that in my early twenties, thinking I knew more than I really did—I was a bit of a political dilettante. This carried over into my first years in Norway too. In Norwegian, my political mode of expression became clear more rapidly than in German language correspondence with friends from home.

A certain immaturity among the German opposition abroad was not only the result of my closest adherents' characteristics, but also affected other circles, so that the exile groups were called, with bitter irony, "lower life forms," who "multiply by division." Considering the exigencies of the time, the flaws mainly showed up in that the different groups and orientations could not form a halfway decent representation of German opposition abroad.

To be sure, we must remember that Germans in exile had a particularly hard time of it. They carried the burden of defeat without having fought. They often lived in the most difficult economic circumstances. And furthermore, the democratic foreign countries tended to respect or fear Hitler, instead of listening to the warnings or outright demands of German opponents of Hitler.

Despite their failings, it would be wrong not to recognize, or to belittle, the useful and—in my opinion—meritorious activities of German political refugees during the Nazi regime. Much of this became known in the years after 1945, and contributed to tearing down the walls of horror and suspicion all around Germany.

Among these activities was the not always welcome explanation and clarification of Nazism and of the "other" Germany. There were sensational campaigns, such as the one that resulted in the 1936 award of the Nobel Peace Prize to Carl von Ossietzky. And there were attempts to obtain the release of friends brought to trial in Germany. Sometimes these were successful, as when, with the aid of lawyers from Norway and other countries, we were able to exercise a felicitously moderating influence—for example when members of the national leadership of the SAP were convicted at the end of 1934. Or there was modest, unobtrusive help for those arrested and their families.

Among the German exiles, there were attempts to form a "Popular Front." Many of Hitler's opponents in the country thought that all differences of opinion must be subordinated to the common Opposition. "Abroad" there were numerous Social Democrats, mostly in France, but also "bourgeois" personalities who were ready to cooperate on a limited basis with the KPD. But the governing body of the SPD in exile, which was located in Prague until 1938, consistently refused such cooperation.

My own group endorsed, as before, the United Front of Social Democrats and Communists, and thought that later it would develop into a "revolutionary but independent" United Front. The question of the Popular Front was controversial. When, in 1936, a German Popular Front committee was formed, ugly differences soon appeared with representatives of the KPD who tried to run the proceedings. While I was in Berlin, my name appeared on the proclamation of the German Popular Front which was agreed upon and published in Paris. I did not sign it with Ulbricht, but my friends made use of my name, which they were authorized to do according to our regulations. But I want to add that I would have signed it myself, had the document been presented to me.

I never met Walter Ulbricht. I met other leading German Communists, among them men who later fell out of favor with their Party, but also such men as Hermann Matern, Herbert Warnke, Karl Mewis, who were to play a role in the other part of Germany after the war. The only central Popular Front congress which I attended took place in the fall of 1938 at the Hotel Lutetia, later headquarters of the Gestapo in Paris. It was a macabre meeting in more than one sense. It lacked clarity and strength; it also lacked inner honesty and truthfulness. I have never forgotten the tears in the eyes of Heinrich Mann, the chairman, when he said to me, his young compatriot from Lübeck: "I guess we'll never see the Seven Towers again."

THE DOMESTIC GERMAN RESISTANCE

During the war, of course, it became more and more difficult to keep in touch with the illegal groups inside Germany. From Sweden, we managed to maintain contact to a certain extent, partially through seamen who docked in German ports. Contact with central Resistance groups in Berlin was a whole other thing. It was important for me to feel reunited in this way with Julius Leber, who had meant so much to me during my youth in Lübeck. . .

Until the summer of 1944, it was not yet very clear to me what combination of forces were behind the 20th of July, or were drawn into those events. After the attempted assassination of Hitler, hopes for at least partial self-liberation were lost. . .

[8]   The Fascist ideology, according to Rosenberg, is based partly on the millenial struggle between fathers and sons. The tension between revolutionary and conservative ensures that "new life is constantly formed by perpetual movement." In practice, it worked like this: The Fascists took advantage of youthful rebellion against home, school and all authority in general. They guided youthful discontent toward the representatives of a weak, old order, wracked by crisis. A calcified and greatly degenerated labor movement—which bore a goodly share of the responsibility for its own predicament—could be made responsible for existing conditions—could embarrass "Marxism" and cause it to be rejected by the Fascist demagogues as belonging to the "old." *Fascism did not create the generation gap; it used it for its own ends.*

Though the generation gap played only a minor part in the past, remaining very much in the background, or even largely eliminated by social class differences, *the extraordinarily turbulent social climate of today* gives our young generation a more strongly unified character. This specific social situation *makes the generational conflict an eminently significant weapon in the social struggle.*

We have learned much too little to communicate with the great mass of the young. We have insufficiently understood their true problems. New generations growing up in the Reich know almost nothing about the labor movement before Hitler, or only learn of it through Fascist caricatures.

These youths will no longer understand us if we approach them in the old way. We have to develop new means of communication with them, and we must find a new language to make ourselves understood.

The problem of the new language has come up before. It is by no means one of the world's greatest mysteries. *How shall*

we talk? The same way as the young to whom we address
ourselves—just as simply; just as free from preconceptions.

THE REICH'S LOST VICTORY

[9] If Weimar had been accorded half of the concessions
made to Hitler's Germany, National Socialism probably
would never have come to power. Foreign policy victories
contributed most to Hitler's ascendancy. Preparations for war
were depicted as safeguards for peace. Large segments of the
German population who were otherwise totally dissatisfied,
commended Hitler for having rehabilitated Germany's
"national honor," having erased the "shame of Versailles."
National problems can, in fact, grow into external political
realities. . .

[10] The German victory at Munich had no more basis in
mystical factors than had former victories. National Socialism
repeatedly demonstrated its splendid talent for exploiting
the many-faceted weaknesses and antagonisms of capitalist
Europe.

The tempo of the offensive was further dictated by conditions inside Germany: the German stock market depression,
the actions taken against Jewish property, plans for new
taxes—all these gave testimony of growing economic difficulties. The military foundation for the invasion of
Czechoslovakia was laid by mobilization on a mighty scale,
beginning in August. By the time of the Nuremberg party
rally, one and one-half million soldiers had been concentrated
at various sites for military maneuvers. The general staff used
the opportunity to rectify any flaws that had shown up
during the invasion of Austria. If that had led to a military
engagement, Germany would have suffered a great fiasco.

The weakest points were troop transport and food supply. The totalitarian state conducted a totalitarian mobilization. Germany became an armed camp. Along with military preparations went propaganda preparation. But this was the Achilles heel of National Socialism. The uncertainty and unrest of the populace increased; the popular base of National Socialism became weaker than ever since the defeat of the labor organizations. It is extremely important to expose the true nature of the domestic situation in Germany, in order to debunk the legend that the victory of Munich was made possible by Germany's strength and inner unity. We must be armed against the propaganda of superiority disseminated by the dictatorships. During the summer months, growing discontent could be noted among the lower and middle classes, as well as among the peasants. They reacted against the economic difficulties and new tax pressures. The persecution of the Jews aroused little sympathy among the populace. And along with the mounting flow of propaganda and the growing extent of the mobilization, fear of war increased from day to day.

Reports by dependable foreign correspondents, and direct news from Germany, indicated that only a small minority of the German people was prepared for war. . .

The general impression was that Germany was so badly prepared in a military and ideological sense, that sober observers in Berlin said that for this reason alone, it was doubtful that those in power could "save" themselves through a catastrophic war. Few in Germany believe that peace was assured in Munich. The deeds of National Socialism during those last months only served to emphasize this view. The Jewish pogroms—assuming proportions unheard of till now, and employing medieval methods—were also designed (aside from the "safekeeping" of Jewish property for the State treasury) to improve morale in National Socialist circles. But though Hitler Youth and Storm Troopers were utilized in the persecutions, the plain people remained passive, and in many towns expressed scorn for a regime that used such methods.

The anti-Nazi agitation has often been oversimplified, but throughout all these years, and rightly so, it has pointed to the connection between National Socialism and war peril. The work which the German Socialists pursued after the defeat of 1933, in illegal groups and in exile, was a continual fight against the war policy.

The German Socialists agitated against Nazism. They did not agitate for war against Germany. They wrote and said that Nazi expansion had to be stopped. Their information from friends in Germany showed clearly that the complacent policy of the Western powers up to last spring, repeatedly weakened domestic opposition to the National Socialist regime. We reckoned that a firm position would assure peace and strengthen the forces in Germany that opposed a war policy. But broad policy took the opposite tack, and did not take into consideration—as can well be understood—what the German exiles were saying.

In more than one sense, the war created a new situation. First, it led to the the disappearance of one group of the German Opposition, namely, the Communists. Until the end of August, the German wing of the Comintern propagandized in favor of a war against Hitlerism if necessary—at the same time, ceaselessly promising that Germany would soon have a revolution. Then came the Russo-German Pact, and the German Comintern fell silent. The rest of the Communists in Germany felt deep disappointment; the exiles, confusion, while a few Party secretaries managed not only to defend the treaty that made it possible for Germany to invade Poland, but also the new Russian line which erased the expression "fascism" from the dictionary and put all the blame on the Western Powers, the neutrals and—the Socialist Workers' movement.

TEST CASE: FINLAND

[11] Only when Russian policy lashed out against Finland after subjugating the border countries, did there seem to be a more serious chance for a "peace offensive," although in a different way than Stalin and Molotov intended.

From the first moment on, heedless of consequences, we took our stand against the Russian attack on Finland, and sided with the Finnish workers' movement in its fight to repel the attack. But at the same time, we refused to give up our basic stand on this war. To us, Hitler and the Hitler regime were, are, and remain the chief enemy. We, the German, Austrian and Czechoslovakian Socialists, took that as a point of departure for our attitude on the war between Germany and the Western Powers. This also influenced our attitude toward Stalin's policy of making pacts with Hitler—not the other way around.

The pact with Germany led to the attack on Poland and to the declaration of war on Germany by the Western Powers. It extricated the Third Reich from a hopeless predicament. The entrance of Russia into the war sealed the fate of Poland. The war against Finland posed a series of new problems which can be of fateful significance in future developments.

There is nothing new in the picture of Soviet leaders embattled against the Socialist Workers' movement. They did it before, also, but today, the whole Socialist labor movement is forced to defend itself, and to draw clear lines between itself and the policy of the Soviet state. It is not the labor movement that has changed, but the Soviet Union.

Stalin's policy implies a strengthening of reactionary anti-Socialistic and anti-labor forces everywhere in the world. Behind the veil of a peace policy, the Soviet Union helped start the great war. Thus, the Soviet Union became a partner of Nazism and eliminated itself as a factor from the anti-Nazi front. On top of that, it used the same methods as Nazism by attacking a peaceful, democratic neighbor nation. The Soviet Union has become a reactionary factor in international politics.

SO THAT GERMANY MAY READ. . .

For me and my kind, Nazism was the enemy in our own country. Hitler had to be defeated so that Germany might live. But that did not mean we identified with other powers and their governments. My friends and I maintained our independence and skepticism toward the Western governments which had always evaded a debate as long as the risk of a great war was still relatively small. Regarding the policy of the Russians after the Russo-German Treaty and the attack on Finland, we established that they had compromised socialism and the peace policy of the Socialists. In my book, published in 1940, I said: "While the war machine on the European continent has not yet seriously been set in motion, it becomes apparent to everyone that there is a second front permeating the, at first, unclear and shifting front lines with the forces of the labor movement, freedom, democracy and historical progress on one side and the forces of capitalism, dictatorship, reaction and imperialism on the other side. It is the battle along this front which will ultimately decide whether this war will lead to a true peace, or whether it will be only another stage in the state of war that has lasted since 1914."

VANSITTART CONTROVERSY

During the war, the debate on Germany led to pro and con positions on "Vansittartism." This school of thought, named for Lord Vansittart, longtime secretary of state in the British Foreign Office, explained Nazism on the basis of the history and the national character of the Germans. Its conclusions were to lead to stern treatment of Germany after the war. Right from the start, this train of thought seemed to me unhistoric, unjust and above all unreasonable, though understandable viewed against the background of Nazi crimes.

There had been precursors of the Vansittart debate as early as 1939-40, in France. They were especially intensive during the period between the Munich pact in the fall of 1938 and the outbreak of the war, a short year later. The Right-wing publicist Henri de Kerillis represented the thesis of "realistic nationalism"—meaning that Hitlerism was a pre-destined expression of the German nation; that Germany had always been a robber nation and must be destroyed once and for all. Others reasoned in their own way that there should be no differentiation between government and people. They demanded that Germany be destroyed like Carthage.

The main speaker for the opposite point of view was the leader of the Socialists and former prime minister, Leon Blum, who—like so many others, was soon to suffer the hard lot of German captivity. He did not deny that Nazism had its roots in German history. But Hitler, he wrote, would hardly have risen to power if foreign nations had shown more comprehension of the Weimar Republic. Blum represented the view that after the war, a new type of international juridical organization would have to be created. A future democratic Germany must take its equal place within the united states of Europe.

In England, also, the discussion oscillated between these two poles, but significantly more toward advocacy of a just peace. It is touching to recall today what labor leader and later prime minister, Clement Attlee, announced as the first item on his agenda on September 8, 1939, after the outbreak of war: "The future peace shall not be a dictated peace. Germany shall neither be humiliated nor destroyed or divided. The victims of the attacks are entitled to compensation, but we must exclude ideas of vengeance or punishment."

RESPONSIBILITY AND GUILT

The Germans must bear responsibility. But responsibility is not the same as *guilt*. Those who do not feel guilty and are not guilty of Nazi crimes cannot—if they want to keep on working with and improving this nation—evade the consequences of a policy which a too-large proportion of the populace was ready to accept. They cannot disassociate themselves from mutual responsibility and interdependence. If they are in earnest about their reform and reeducation efforts, they would do well not to minimize the injustices other nations have suffered. They must beware of discussing the share of responsibility borne by foreign powers, as long as they have not told their own countrymen the full and complete truth. They must cease appealing for compassion when the bodies of the murdered have scarcely been buried.

But the fact of responsibility must be differentiated; must be brought up at the right time and place. And the question of guilt must focus on individual criminals and their criminal groups and organizations.

Once we have asserted, and made clear, that we do not intend to exonerate the Germans from something they participated in, we also have the right to point out that responsibility cannot be limited to Germany and the German people alone.

The foes of the Nazis—the true, democratic opponents of Nazism—not the desperados of anti-Nazism nor the last minute opportunists—are not guilty. But they cannot escape part of the responsibility for having allowed Hitler to rise to power. Neither can they escape the consequences of the Nazi murder policy. They must understand that their efforts will be viewed with a jaundiced eye for a long time to come. They cannot expect carte blanche. Trust cannot be forced. It must be earned, not by words but by deeds; by accord between word and action. Yet German democrats ought to be able to expect that all prospects will not be closed to them.

Between Nazis and anti-Nazis lies the broad mass of the more or less indifferent. Their responsibility is great. But there is no sense in loading them down with guilt. Guilt feelings imposed from without do not constitute the most felicitous beginning of reeducation. On the other hand, there is no reason not to let them know—until they have understood—that their indifference and servility made them responsible to a certain degree. I am not convinced that anything can be achieved through punitive measures which only elicit defensiveness and perhaps arouse new hatreds. But I am absolutely convinced that no one should be spared from seeing the films of Buchenwald and Bergen-Belsen. Not to make them admit they did something personally, but to reveal what it was they made possible. They cannot be allowed to consider everything that happened as a kind of natural catastrophe. The portrayal of historical responsibility must bring about a demand for a greater sense of responsibility. German experience has shown that wars are worthless. The people have seen where Nazism led them. They have seen race hatred at its worst. Now it is important that this newly acquired awareness will not be lost because the people are in despair, politically and socially.

Productive work is the best doctor and the best teacher.

AGAINST OVERSIMPLIFICATION

[5] Tremendous hatred against the Germans exists in all occupied countries. It is hard for people to believe in a "good" Germany if they are daily confronted with the "bad" Germany in its worst manifestations. This is the emotional foundation of Vansittartism. Millions and millions in tortured Europe are willing to endorse Lord Vansittart's thesis that "the great mass of the Germans developed, in the course of three or four generations, into a nation of wild, brutal, organized aggressors."

In *Black Record,* Vansittart goes back to Herman the Cherusker in the year 9 A.D.—"the first German national hero who earned fame through treason"—and then shows a clear progression through Charlemagne, Frederick Barbarossa, the Hanseatic League, Frederick the Great and Bismarck, to the new Hermann. Vansittart has asked to be relieved of all responsibility for everything connected with the phrase "Vansittartism." He also disassociates himself from ethnology, and goes so far as to calculate the number of "good" Germans at 25 percent. But at the same time, he uses German

"national character," "national soul" and "political mentality" as rather definite categories.

Vansittart's thesis becomes even more remarkable when it
deals with more recent history. He states that: Germany
started five wars since 1860, and that the people accepted
those wars as their own; that the ideology of the "master
race" and the defensive mentality were deep-rooted and still
alive; that democracy had never been on firm ground in
Germany; that the supposed democrats were just as bad as
the rest; that the Social Democrats played the role of the
Nazis in the First World War; that, during Weimar, everything
had been done to prepare for a new war; that representatives
of German culture had found their real vocation in preaching
nationalism and inciting aggression.

It is further stated that Hitler came to power through
democratic elections. That the majority of Germans supported Hitler's policies; that they wanted war and expressed
their endorsement of the aggression and occupation policy—
at least as long as everything went well.

Lord Vansittart wants a Germany according to the slogan:
"Full warehouses, empty arsenals," which conforms to the
Atlantic Charter and the proclamations of the Allied leaders
regarding disarmanent and economic parity of the Axis
powers. On top of that, Vansittart wants to have the
Germans declared incompetent, and wants to have their
country occupied for at least seventy-five years (as at first
suggested), or twenty to thirty years as later amended. That
the Germans should be educated as democrats and lovers of
peace, guarded by international police.

"Germany has to attend reform school; discipline will be
marsh and therapeutic, but there will also be rewards and
encouragement," says Vansittart. He also wants to teach the
Germans how to "be happy." He contemplates, first, inter-

national control of the educational system. The judicial and administrative systems should be changed to democratic types, and should be placed, to the extent necessary, in foreign hands for as long as the period of tutelage shall last. The Church, too, shall receive new spiritual meaning. Certain groups contemplate sending an expeditionary corps with foreign teachers to Germany. There are also proposals for the establishment of an Allied system of "gauleiters" or local area leaders.

THE "OTHER" GERMANY

The view antithetical to Vansittartism, holds that there really is a difference between the Nazis and large segments of the German people, and that this difference is one of the keys to the solution of the German problem. During discussions in France, before and after the beginning of the war, Leon Blum was one of the most distinguished personalities who opposed "realistic nationalism." He held to the working hypothesis of "another" Germany. Blum and his followers never stopped believing that there existed among the German people different and better elements than those represented by the Nazi regime. They hoped and wanted to help these elements attain power if possible. Blum accused the aggressive supporters of the political Right of employing a racist policy from a different point of view, but overall on the same basic premises as Nazism.

He did not deny that Hitlerism had deep roots in German evolution, but added that Nazism would hardly have succeeded if Europe had taken a clearer view of the German Republic. The peace of Versailles, said Blum, was founded on just principles, generally speaking, but had been irresponsibly administered. He cites the occupation of the Ruhr Valley as a drastic example. A logical conclusion from his attitude is that a future democratic Germany should occupy an equal place among the nations of Europe.

RELATIVITY OF GUILT

There are black pages in the history of all nations. Germany's history contains many, but they are not all dark. Douglas Smith's *Guilty Germans?* and Julius Braunthal's *Need Germany Survive?*, present numerous arguments against the Vansittart interpretation of history. As far as recent history goes, it is correct that Germany initiated five aggressive wars within seventy-five years. But an imperialistic policy was also being promulgated in other countries. France suffered through four wars in the eighteen years that Napoleon III reigned. In the seventy-five years of its existence, Italy fought eight wars. England set a record for participating in wars from 1850 until the turn of the century.

The existence of a "Prussian tradition" in modern German politics is undeniable. There is a direct line from Bismarck to Hitler. Prussia attained power primarily through military might, and assumed the role of a strong citadel of reaction and militarism. This was the Prussia that subjugated Germany.

Though Prussia might have written some of the darkest pages in German history, we still must be careful not to oversimplify. During the time of Napoleon and the 1848 Revolution, freedom-loving forces drew stronger support from Berlin than from some other parts of Germany. During

Weimar, the Prussian government's policy was considerably more progressive than that of the Bavarian government. Most of the leading Nazis are not of Prussian origin.

It is primarily through social conditions that the victory of Nazism can be explained. We tend to forget that Germany was a backward country when it suddenly plunged into imperialistic policies. It did not achieve national unification until very recently. As a result the middle classes had not been able to carry out a democratic revolution. The forces of feudalism were powerful, and blended with those of the upper middle classes. A great majority of the intelligentsia, just as in other countries, floundered in the wake of the governing class. Polarization was stronger in Germany than in many other places, because the labor movement quickly moved to the opposite extreme as a reaction. Despite Bismarck's anti-socialist laws, it had fought its way up to a powerful position, respected in the Second International, before the last world war.

The conflict between the "two Germanys" continued during Weimar. The Revolution of 1918 brought about no real decision. The old social forces kept their heads above water.

The major attitude in the labor movement was complacent, just as it had been soft toward nationalism at the outbreak of the war. Still, the Weimar Republic was not merely camouflaged "Prussian spirit" and revenge policy. Great masses of the people desired peace and were determined to attain it democratically. The reform policy was making significant progress. Pro-Fascist movements were quelled several times. Then came the Depression. It hit Germany especially hard. And in comparison with the seasoned democracies, it struck a country with little inner equilibrium.

THE GERMAN SACRIFICE

It is a fact that in 1933 only about half of the German population voted for Hitler and that only much later were many attracted to National Socialism. The elimination of unemployment was of great significance in this regard. The statement that all Germans became Nazis, however, is not valid. No labor leader of any consequence, and only very few liberals went over to Nazism. An underground anti-Nazi movement persisted, even if little was heard of it. Many more anti-Nazis were sentenced to death than is generally believed. At the outbreak of the war, there were about 300,000 persons in concentration camps or prisons for "political crimes." A million and a half Germans passed through the concentration camps.

GERMANY'S RUIN—EUROPE'S RUIN

The democratization of German society can be achieved only through cooperation with German democrats and in accordance with German democratic traditions. In Southern Germany, communal democracy has a relatively old tradition. Social legislation was already democratically codified before the First World War. Great reserves of democracy are to be found in the German labor movement. If democracy is to be reconstructed, the formation of political parties should not be impeded.

The Atlantic Charter and the official Allied declarations should prohibit the execution of extremist economic proposals. Carr points out that penalizing Germany economically would lead to the breakdown of Central Europe's economic unity. The European standard of living cannot be maintained without Germany's productive capacity. *Economist* stated the same thesis: "Germany's poverty means poverty for Europe. The ruin of Germany means that her neighbors lose their markets."

THE RESERVE OF YOUTH

[7]   Unlike Lord Vansittart, I do not believe that a nation can be forcibly educated and taught "to be happy." I believe —in spite of everything that has happened—in the moral, constructive force of a German minority which, little by little, could become a stable majority and leave its imprint on the whole nation. The occupation authorities can do a great deal in this regard. The new, and—I hope—peaceful and democratic existence of Germany nevertheless must be shaped by forces from within.

I don't want to depict German youth in an unduly favorable light and I would like it to become better. We must take into consideration that youth is fed up with propaganda. They are also suspicious of "party politics." It is hard for them to understand pre-1933 slogans. But they are receptive to a realistic approach. They can—they must—endure the ordeal of learning about actual conditions with no attempt at cheap idealization. That does not imply plunging our youth into black pessimism. They need a perspective, a goal that can rouse their enthusiasm; a "new faith" if you want to put it that way. Is not the work of reconstructing our country a great task that calls for true heroism? Especially if this reconstruction is given a European perspective, so that German youth can concentrate on an international goal. They must know that Germany will have its place in the new world—economically and culturally, rather than militarily.

It is my firm conviction that we should talk less about abstract democracy and more about basic human values, rights and duties—about decency, cleanliness, truth and honesty.

CONFLICTS WITH COMMUNISM

[12] The organizational techniques which the Cominterm developed over the years are in contradiction with the fundamental rules of the labor movement. Continuous meddling from above, even in the smallest organizational problems, and the heretical atmosphere created to fight "deviations" made it impossible for separate Communist parties to have a healthy development. But that did not bring about the disintegration of the Comintern. The various Parties' complete dependence on Moscow, its money and its agents, demoralized what was left of the Communist movement. After having "purged" the Communist parties of everyone who did not want a complete break with the Socialist movement, and also of any "Left" and "Right" opposition, practically all that remained were party hacks whose moral backbone had been broken. In this fashion, the Comintern became a politically coordinated bureaucratic machine with many venal and corrupt functionaries who blindly danced to Moscow's tune. And the purges and amalgamations still continue.

This battle of the Communist splinter parties takes on a special form. He who criticizes the dogma, orders or institutions of the one true "Church" is even worse than the enemy. There is always only one right opinion and that one is dictated from above. If the Party Line of the Comintern—meaning the Soviet hierarchy—continues to fail, it is the fault of the trusted leadership of each national party. These insiders then denounce each other as traitors or worse. Debates within a Communist party usually take place in order to manufacture an ideological justification for the purges that have taken place. Therefore such discussions become a mere farce.

As a result, Communist movement "insiders" are not to be trusted. Who knows if they will even be there tomorrow, or if they will be branded traitors and criminals next time around? A movement that has been conducted for years according to such principles, is doomed to decay. The Communists, of course, have the same rights as any other citizen in a democratic society—to voice their opinions, be they right or wrong. Facts and experience must demonstrate which is the correct policy. But the Communists proclaim as their first commandment, by which all must swear, that their policy is the only true one. All who refuse to obey this commandment are heretics and traitors.

Communist tactics are to shuffle the cards in such a way that their political opponents in the labor movement are branded criminals, thus justifying their brutal persecution.

Comintern policy must be vanquished. Their predictions have not been borne out. Their fight against the European labor movement has caused great damage. Their tactics were unsuccessful. Their methods have betrayed the labor movement, and their organizational principles turned out to be disastrous.

The old International collapsed in 1914 because the great labor parties did not manage to maintain their socialist independence from the warring bourgeois governments. The Comintern created a new dependent relationship.

The labor movement must be independent. Only then can it win over the whole nation and carry out a truly national policy which is not antagonistic to the internationalism of the labor movement, but constitutes its healthiest foundation.

[13] While the Russian Revolution of 1917 broke away from the old Great Power Policy, the Soviet Union returned to it in later years, and finally aligned itself methodologically with the aggressive Great Powers. Even if we cannot tell how far the Soviet Union intends to go, she has conveyed more strongly than ever that she is concerned only with herself. At least she does not intend to take the labor movement into consideration.

The British and French labor movements based their attitude toward the international crisis on the defense of democracy, the independence of each nation, and the fight for a Europe free of war policy and dictatorship. The underground Socialist movement in Central Europe is fighting for social change in the hope of gaining more ground for the labor movement, Socialism and democracy, and becoming the first member of a European New Order. In the neutral countries, the labor movement's main policy objective is the fight for peace and liberty, for the independence of small nations and against the dictatorship of the Great Powers. In all those countries, the labor movement felt betrayed by the Soviet Union's policies. In signing a pact with Nazi Germany, the Soviet Regime created a great schism between itself and the European labor movement. It set itself apart not only from the Socialist labor movement, but also from anti-Nazism. It made clear once again that it cares only for its own national interests, not for any development not directly linked to the intimate concerns of the home country. The Soviet Union has, therefore, eliminated itself from the international Socialist movement and from the fighting front for peace, liberty and independence of small nations.

Through its foregin policy, the Soviet Union lost all chance of exercising a positive influence in the task of creating a new Europe after the horrors and fears of the war. Only the Socialist workers' movement will be able to do that job. Looking ahead to these great historical tasks, the labor movement must prepare a Socialistic and democratic new order in Europe, independent of Great Power interests, thus eliminating the basis for further imperialistic Great Power conflicts and wars.

[12] Lenin, who was the leader of the victorious Russian Revolution, believed that the European working class was revolutionary in the Bolshevik sense, and that only a small minority—Party functionaries and "worker-aristocrats"— hindered the workers from proceeding to revolution actions. Experience proved that he had been observing Europe from a Russian point of view. In Russia, the rebellious but ignorant peasant masses became the foundation of a firm and resolute revolutionary leadership. What was possible in Russia should also be possible in Europe. So the most important task was to create in each country a party modeled after the Bolshevik Party, and then unite these parties into a great, centralized world party under the leadership of the Bolsheviks. The Russians and the Soviets, as political heirs of the Revolution, were to set the pattern for the labor movement in all countries.

But right from the start, there was less enthusiasm for Russian organizational plans and demands than there was sympathy for the Russian Revolution. Already in the fall of 1918, when she was still in jail, Rosa Luxemburg had written a polemic brochure opposing Bolshevism. She particularly warned against suppression of democratic liberties; that would lead to bureaucracy and Party dictatorship. In this connection, it is especially significant that she and other leaders of the German Spartakus-Bund (later KPD—German Communist Party), resolutely rejected the Russian plan to form a new International in the spring of 1919. Rosa Luxemburg's strongest argument was that it was not possible to organize an International with only one massive party, especially one which had developed along such special lines as had the Russian Party. An International dominated by the Russians would take the wrong path. One of the last decisions Rosa Luxemburg made with her directorate, a few days before her assassination, was to order the German emissary to the Russian conference, to vote *against* the founding of a new International.

[14] Since the First World War, there have been many meetings on a national and international scale, aimed at mending the split in the labor movement. Often only tactics were discussed. But there is no doubt of one fact: The Norwegian Workers' Party, during the conferences of 1945, honestly desired to reach an agreement. Rarely has a Socialist party shown such willingness to heal a schism. There ought to be neither victors nor losers. This stand of the Workers' Party was not based on insecurity and inner weakness. They felt that practical problems should not be an impediment if there was agreement on the policy to be pursued by the united workers' parties.

There is no doubt that the great majority of the members of the Communist Party desired unification. They were not the ones who wrecked the basis for negotiations.

The Communist leadership has no cause and no right to pose as mentor on matters of national policy. In truth, it took some time before the leaders of the Communist Party decided to join in the national resistance movement.

Neither do the Communist leaders have any right to act as if they alone saved Russia during the war. The war was won by the Allies, not by the Communist parties.

SPD—A NEW PARTY

[19] Certainly the representatives of social democracy are free to stress that their fight for the program of democracy and peace is based on a tradition going back eighty years. But they must also realize that although valuable traditional elements should be retained, we have to construct an essentially *new* party—a party that, in its organization, its structure, its resolute direction, does not cling to the past, but considers today's completely different social and international climate. Only such a party will be able to vanquish senility and become a party of the younger generation. That is all-important. It was unavoidable, in rebuilding the movement, that pre-1933 functionaries should dominate the proceedings. But this cannot and must not persist. During party conferences it should be repeatedly explained and stressed—taking local conditions into consideration, of course—how important it is to develop democracy *within the movement.* Leaders should be nominated on the strength of their brains, not their beards and bellies. We ought not to be narrow-minded, but we must declare war on internal diplomatic quibbling, splintering, and cliques within the parties.

AGAINST COMPULSORY FREEDOM

Clearly, it is insufficient to agree on common lists, programs, and job distribution. For it is a fact that the SP

(Socialist Party) has more followers and inspires more confidence than the KP (Communist Party). The same holds true for the Eastern Zone of Germany. It was also demonstrated in the South German elections. A unified policy cannot permit the SP to furnish the members and voters, and the KP to furnish most of the leaders.

[16] The way unified party policy was conducted in the East, discouraged the drive toward unity of a vast majority of Social Democratic workers. Today, throughout the West (and not only in the West), the KP is viewed with suspicion—a suspicion that has turned to open enmity in some quarters. Compulsory unity doubtless tends to tighten Zone borders. No amount of proclamations by the SEP can lessen that result. Vis-à-vis the Western powers, as well as the Western labor movement, the SEP policy calls itself spokesman for Russian foreign policy. It demands reciprocity. The result will be a wider gap instead of the stronger unification so badly needed.

TO BERLIN

[17] On the 28th of September, I was at the home of Halvard Lange. He said he heard that I had decided to return to Germany. In case this decision was not final, he wanted me to know that I could have a job with the Norwegian Foreign Service. H. L. had in mind the position of press attaché in Paris. It was a very difficult choice.

My German friends obviously expected me to participate in some way in the reconstruction of Germany. The party directorate in Hanover had asked me to take over as editor of one of the Zone news agencies. At first there was talk of DENA in Bad Nauheum, then DPD in Hamburg.

In May and September, in Lübeck, I had received several requests to return there. But I had a feeling that Lübeck would be too "tight" and that several leading Party figures were a little worried about their positions. That meant there would be conflict (of which we already had plenty). But I began to take a different view of this when I talked to M.P. Steltzer in Kiel, September 9. He pointed out a solution (referring to an earlier talk with Otto Passarge), by which I could become Mayor of Lübeck, while Passarge would take over the position of Provincial Chief of Police.

When I saw Halvard Lange again on October 19 (he had just arrived from Paris and was spending several days there before leaving for a United Nations meeting in New York), I was, basically, prepared to accept his Paris offer, hoping that from there I could make a reasonable contribution to European Democratic Socialism.

Halvard now presented me with a completely new situation. He said that while his Paris offer was still open, he would rather see me as a member of the press in Berlin, if only to observe the development of the East-West problem there. I agreed. Halvard telephoned Minister of State Gerhardsen, who was in accord with the proposal. Press chief Schive was consulted and ordered to discuss the practical problems with me.

I had made my decision.

IN THE SERVICE OF ENLIGHTENMENT

Oslo, November 1, 1946.
Dear Friends:
[18] It may seem strange to some of you that I am going to Berlin as a member of the Allied Forces, especially as I will

sometimes have to appear in Norwegian uniform. My status as an "ally" is nothing new, however. I became a Norwegian citizen in 1940, after having been exiled by Hitler several years before. I had no reason to resume German citizenship, which at the moment is sort of imaginary, and to ask Norway to release me from my allegiance.

The decisive factors cannot be formalities, nor disturbing attributes caused by conditions resulting from Hitler's war. What counts is where the individual can best serve in the European Renaissance and for German democracy. As you know, for years I worked simultaneously for "German" and "Scandinavian" interests. Those were not and are not contradictory. During the past year I tried, during my travels as a journalist, to help reestablish the connection between the Scandinavian and the new German labor movements, and to inspire understanding for the Socialist reconstruction of Germany. This program of mine will not be changed. I shall continue to work toward enlightening both sides and furthering understanding. I shall be useful to the German press, supplying it with Norwegian news and material about the Scandinavian workers' movement. Conversely, I shall inform the Norwegian government, the Scandinavian labor movement, and the press about German developments. Thus I can render practical services to the movement and to friends both here and there.

What counts more than anything is working to secure peace, for the development and stabilization of European and international cooperation. For years, the guiding principle of my political activities was to refrain from taking positions based on a narrow, nationalistic point of view. Each of you knows that the fate of Germany, which is struggling for new foundations, is being decided in large measure on an international level. But I take this opportunity to state to you explicitly that my inner attitude toward the German socialist movement is the same as before, and will remain so. Today I can best serve the movement by answering the call of my Norwegian friends. Later, we will have to test how and where I can serve best, considering common interests.

"YES" TO THE HOMELAND

[21] I would not have liked to miss out on the political opinions of my younger years, nor the experience I have gained since. I know today that my hopes for a "Third Force" which I expressed in the letter to Schumacher the day before Christmas of 1947, was doomed in view of the Cold War's onset. Today I am also better informed on German history and militarism. Today I can no longer get by with oversimplified class categories, not even to explain the victory of National Socialism in 1933. Today I would judge events like the Spanish Civil War from a more differentiated and more balanced perspective. Today I have long since shed my anti-clerical prejudices and have openly admitted "that the Church in a free society is not only entitled to tolerance, but that it must have a firm place in our society and that it can count on our help."

Since it appears that a long stretch of the journey that led to these realizations remains obscure to many, I wanted to document my early political development in a book. Anyone who wishes can now have a clearer picture of my experiences, thoughts, and writings "abroad."

Will there be understanding for what was written in 1933 by a nineteen-year-old, or in 1937 by a twenty-three-year-old? Will it be understood that this is not a justification, but an attempt to explain the thoughts of a man and to show whence he sprang and how he became what he is today?

I have always tried to find broadminded and honest answers to the pressing questions of our time. For example, I said in my speech to the Party Congress of the SPD at Dortmund on June 12, 1966:

Twenty years ago, only a few would have believed possible the great economic feats since accomplished by a diligent and capable people. Neither would most have thought it possible for Germany still to be divided twenty years later—both parts armed against each other and with no concrete prospects for a peace treaty. At that time, 20 years ago, everyone knew that Germany had lost the war. Today, many no longer want to know it. Then, there existed a strong desire to "reach new shores." In the course of the years, the propensity toward restoration of the past has become stronger. At that time, there was, in addition to considerable displacements, a reexamination of unity, of moral worth, of spiritual reserves. Later, economic success became the criterion for success *per se*.

Much of the original mission of Social Democracy still remains to be fulfilled. Large segments of the population still feel excluded from national events. The integration of the workers has not yet been achieved. The general theme is: equal opportunities, especially in education, and everything else pertaining to democracy, such as vanquishing traces of feudalism in the economy. For us, the democratic and social federal state is a permanent assignment. He who slanders systematic advance planning slanders progress. We can only satisfy our country's needs by a new kind of policy—a policy of honesty, of impartiality, of cooperation, of accommodation. We must do everything in our power to carry out what is recognized as true and right. That is our lesson from Weimar.

We need not fear *Communism as an ideology*. We do not need a Chinese Wall policy. Development does not stand still, even in the part of the world ruled by communism. We had contradictory answers to decisive political questions. Whether we like it or not, the Communists are a political power on German soil, but there is a fundamental, practical and political difference between us and the Communists. We became especially aware of this twenty years after the compulsory unification of the other part of Germany.

The relationship between the political and spiritual has been disturbed in the Federal Republic of Germany. There are many Pharisees in the German provinces. Mature citizens cannot be treated as if they were mentally retarded. It is essential for the building up of the Federal Republic that responsibility be shared by many. Spiritual forces have been crushed by materialistic profiteering. Complacency, selfishness, irresponsibility, have become widespread. But the nation as a whole is strong and basically healthy.

The people must be able to say *"Yes" to the fatherland* or they cannot go on living without losing their inner balance; without stumbling at times of temptation from within and without. We Germans cannot afford to forget history. But neither can we always run around confessing our guilt—the younger generation even less than the older. The most loyal subject is not the best patriot. We are patriots when we secure individual freedom in our land; when we help democracy economically and socially. We want to do everything in our power to save as much as possible of Germany for the Germans. Our patriotism should be regarded simultaneously as European and international responsibility in politics. Compared with peace, the nation is no longer the highest good. If our Federal Republic wants to stand for more than a rectified past, it must undergo changes in its social structure. Our nation can only maintain itself with a modern, mobile and humane social structure. The political leadership must have the courage to tell the truth, even if it is uncomfortable. Our people need clarity about the state of the nation. They must be on guard against empty phrases and illusions.

Meeting With Kennedy

THE WORLD MOURNS

The enthusiastic crowd was jammed tightly together; the rejoicing went on and on. Loud cheers arose repeatedly. Never before had Berlin beheld such a demonstration. Deeply moved, John Fitzgerald Kennedy, President of the United States, leader of the Free World, stood in the Rudolph Wilde Square—the square that was later to. bear his name. Already during the ride to City Hall, he had been amazed by the overwhelming evidence of trust and affection. And I, too, was stunned at the ecstatic joyousness of his reception. The American President's visit to Germany had reached a triumphal climax. In this unforgettable moment, no one could have foreseen that the year 1963, which had brought such personal triumphs to the American President, would end in sorrow and world-wide dismay.

Barely five months had passed since that 26th of June, 1963. On the afternoon of November 22, my wife and I had just returned from a trip to Africa. We were sitting in our home at the Schlachtensee with some of my closest associates. Gay, relaxed, happy to be home, we and our friends were catching up on the latest news. Suddenly—it was about 7:30 P.M. —I was called to the telephone. The voice of my journalist friend on the other end was shaky and deeply moved, as though he himself could not grasp what he had to tell me. An attempt had been made on the life of President Kennedy. Perhaps he was already dead.

Silently, we listened to the news from Dallas. Transported to the hospital. Hope? No, no more hope. Then the dreadful confirmation arrived via an official American telephone call. Was it possible? Could it be true? A heavy silence hung over the room. We looked at each other uncomprehendingly.

Each of us in his own way had to try to adjust to the tragedy. But we hardly had time. Again and again, the phone rang. City Hall, newspapers, friends from Bonn, American friends. Soon reporters and photographers crowded into the room where, just a short while ago, we had been so happy.

How much time had actually gone by on this black Friday night? Did not time stand still this night everywhere in the world where men's hearts beat?

I had to go to the television studio. From there, to City Hall. But first, I wanted to see General James Polk, Commandant of the American sector, to offer my condolences. He had ordered a funeral procession for the next morning.

Meantime, the students of Berlin had decided to organize a torchlight procession in Stein Square, and to march in silence to the City Hall. Small bouquets of flowers had already appeared on the steps of the hall. Around 1:00 A.M. the students marched up, carrying their torches. Tens of thousands of men and women had followed them. Again we beheld it—this moving spontaneity, characteristic of the people of Berlin; this simple, expressive presence; this glorious mixture of grief and defiance, of sorrow and vigor.

Deep silence hung over this already historic square. The best postwar tradition of Berlin was in evidence. Whenever Berlin was in extraordinary distress, whenever the citizens of this city wished to mingle their destiny with that of their fellows, they left their homes and gathered here. Those who assembled were not only the men and women who, in that first bitter postwar period, during the blockade and the subsequent war of nerves, had given proof of their courage and hardihood. Young Berlin was here too. In this midnight hour, Youth spoke for all of us.

There were larger demonstrations in Berlin, but few as moving. No order had been given, but the word went round. More than 60,000 persons gathered that night as living proof that it is not command which counts, but rather the heart and the spirit—that unconquerable spirit of a freedom-loving, fighting community. And part of that spirit was our feeling of gratitude toward our partner in combat.

Gratitude mingled with mourning in my speech to the Berliners, whose silence contrasted so sharply with the jubilation and enthusiasm that, only five months before, had filled the square in front of the City Hall in Schoeneberg. "The Americans have lost their President. Suffering humanity has lost the man so many thought would lead us on the path to a just peace and to a better life. Above all, we in Berlin mourn, for we have lost our best friend. I am deeply hurt and shaken this night, for I feel that I have lost someone with whom I could communicate in trust and friendship."

Kennedy assumed his post at a difficult time. But it is probably the best proof of his greatness that he did not falter under the load. The more the job demanded of him, the more he was able to give. This was particularly apparent in the reverses he encountered—for example, the unfortunate defeat of the Cuban invasion in the Bay of Pigs, which cast a shadow over the beginning of his career, and the Western Allies' undeniable loss of prestige in the Berlin crisis of August 1961. The man—the President—profited from these defeats. He rose above them. The man whose boyish, beaming smile graced all the world's illustrated news magazines was basically a very serious person.

The responsibility which the American people had entrusted to him developed to the highest degree qualities that must always have been latent in him. He had always been a passionate reader, driven by his thirst for knowledge. Now he became a tireless worker. More than almost any other statesman, he understood the complex interrelationships of world political and social problems. He studied them daily. His phenomenal memory served him well. I myself was amazed at how he had familiarized himself with even the smallest details concerning problems of Germany and Berlin.

Increasingly, this man who, as a naval officer, was seldom known to appear in proper uniform, and was almost always late, according to his biographer, William Manchester, developed an almost fanatical degree of organization. This was indicated by his growing propensity for clarity—for discipline in thought, and above all, in speech. He hated long-windedness, lack of concentration, idle chatter. Nothing was so foreign to this man of Irish descent as the tendency toward mysticism which is one of the basic characteristics of the Irish. He lacked that charming, but potentially dangerous love of the Irish for the theatrical—for sonorous tirades. He was a thinker of almost Roman consistency and self-discipline. William Manchester points out the President's spiritual debt to Tacitus. The Roman historian's motto: "Anxis et intentus agere"—always act, but never be impulsive—is indeed a saying which decisively influenced the work of President Kennedy. As a result, he was repeatedly accused of being cold and calculating; of being strictly a cerebral type. Was he really? He was cool, distant, but certainly not devoid of feeling. He seldom yielded to the dictates of the heart. He consciously controlled himself by disciplining his thoughts. But once he did yield, he could manage to touch the hearts of those he sought to influence. On the 26th of June, 1963, in Berlin, we saw this demonstrated in the most impressive fashion. When this man spoke of the fight for greater freedom—of self-determination for all nations; when he gave his word to do everything he could to prevent the self-destruction of humanity; when he pleaded for a Greater Europe as partner in the Atlantic Community; for a world without hunger and misery—then the people sensed that these were not just idle phrases. They realized that every word Kennedy uttered was thoroughly premeditated; that this sober, clear-thinking man, who understated rather than overstated, was an honest man.

THE YOUNG MAN FROM BOSTON

During my visit to the United States in March, 1961, I was received by John F. Kennedy in the White House. But that was not the first time we had seen each other. We had already met, three years before.

In February 1958, at the invitation of the Ford Foundation, I had flown to the United States with Senator Guenter Klein, Berlin's representative to the Bundesrepublik, the Federal Republic. This took place several months after I was elected Mayor of Berlin. The President, Dwight D. Eisenhower, invited me to visit him in Washington. There was a so-called "working lunch" at the Senate, in which John F. Kennedy, the young Senator from Massachusetts, participated. This type of lunch is supposed to provide an opportunity for an informal exchange of views and experiences—for an unconstrained discussion of important issues. Of course the conversation revolved mainly around Berlin. The luncheon developed into a regular question session, in which Senator Kennedy also took part. He had to leave a little earlier than the others, and excused himself. This luncheon impressed me with the fact that foreign policy discussions in the American Senate were much more open-minded and interesting than the press usually led us to believe. The men among whom I sat in Washington, including the future President, expressed their own, highly personal thoughts about the destiny and the future of our divided land.

I had been told that this Senator from Massachusetts, whom I sat with at lunch, was no friend of Germany. Maybe it was so. But he was certainly not "anti-German" as some later tried to label him. He was a man of his generation, his origins, his spiritual environment. It spoke well of him that he concealed nothing of this. He welcomed Germany into the Western community of nations. He understood the great importance of Berlin. He had a passionate interest in the thoughts and feelings of our youth. But at the same time, he asked questions: How could the events of 1933 and afterwards have been possible? In the new Germany, what was superficial and what lay deeper? Had the Germans found their inner equilibrium?

It must be understood that John F. Kennedy's impressions of Germany were formed, not by intellectual discussions, but through personal experience. Shortly before the war, when he was a student at Harvard, Kennedy came to Europe for a year's study at the London School of Economics where, incidentally, he studied personally with the British socialist Harold Laski. During this period, he visited the capitals of our feverish continent, and spent a few days in Germany. He spoke of this on the morning of June 26, as we stood on the wooden platform before the Brandenburg Gate, unable to see across to the Eastern Sector because the Communists had hung red cloth to hide the view. He asked what had happened to the Adlon Hotel, over on the other side, where he lived for a few days shortly before the outbreak of war.

His impressions at that time could hardly have been very favorable, during that late summer of 1939. Son of Irish Catholics, he was all too keenly aware of discrimination and mistreatment of minorities. Long before he became president, he was championing the right of all citizens to equal treatment. This young man demonstrated considerable political acumen. He wrote his father from Berlin: "There will be war before the week is out." He was right. In the summer of 1945, during the Potsdam Conference, Kennedy, who occasionally worked as reporter for the American news agency, International News Service, was in Berlin for the second time, and beheld the ruined wasteland that had been the capital of Germany.

VISITS TO THE WHITE HOUSE

On March 13, 1961, just two months after taking office, John F. Kennedy received me in the White House. My press chief Egon Bahr and I were kept waiting a moment in the room used for Cabinet sessions. The president's place is in the middle of the enormous table, with his back to the row of windows which overlooks the garden.

Kennedy entered the room, shook my hand, and greeted me cordially. His slim build made him appear particularly tall. In those March days of 1961, too, he looked younger than he really was. He took my arm and led me through a hall and a few antechambers into his study, and sat down, after having pulled up a chair for me so that I could sit across from him, at his desk. As he walked, his first comment was neither about world politics nor about Berlin. He inquired after my health and whether the coming election campaign would be a very strenuous one.

The moment we began our conversation, his facial expression changed. It became serious, intent, softened only occasionally by a fleeting smile. He had seen my televised press conference the previous night, and referred to it. He remarked that he was grateful to hear from a German that continual assurances of steadfastness, reliability and friendship were not necessary; that the United States guarantee of Berlin's freedom need not constantly be reiterated.

Our talk lasted about an hour. I reported on the spirit of my fellow citizens, on the growing economic strength of Berlin, and on our great confidence in the government and the people of the United States. I stressed that Soviet policy was not only directed against the people of West Berlin, but also at American prestige, credibility, and the position of the West in general. In his reply, Kennedy left no doubt of his determination to maintain the Allied position in the ancient German capital under any circumstances, in the interests of peace, and to defend that position if necessary. Who could ask for more?

The President had obviously prepared himself well for the

talk. He fired a series of questions at me that not only revealed his interest, but also his knowledge of our problems. He inquired about the situation in the Zone—East Berlin; about the practical and human relationships between West Berlin and the Zone. He asked about details that many a European had not brought up to me. All these questions were brief and precisely formulated—characteristic of a man who hasn't a moment to waste, but wants to be thoroughly informed. Kennedy had the habit of tilting his head back and gazing searchingly up at the ceiling before he answered a question or gave his opinion on a complicated point. Then he would look directly at his interlocutor again and reply, quickly, precisely, and in a low voice.

As in other conversations in these March days of 1961 in the United States, the coming German electoral campaign was always in the foreground. The President wanted to know my opinion on basic differences in the views of the two principal parties. Of course he was particularly interested to know whether foreign policy would be a major issue in the campaign. I explained that there presently existed no noteworthy differences of opinion between government and opposition on basic problems of foreign policy. In that respect, our election campaign would have no weighty consequences for the West. During the election campaign, the Federal Republic would not be undergoing gratuitous attacks from the Opposition regarding foreign policy.

Kennedy punctiliously avoided involving himself in German politics. But he was keenly interested in our domestic problems. When I mentioned our neglected community goals—furthering of science and education, community health standards, care for the aged, renoviation of roads and cities —he grinned and said it all sounded very familiar.

The President had in mind the task of abating, or at least

easing, tensions, especially in Central Europe. I was under the impression that he already had a definite plan in view. The Soviet Union demonstrated no readiness for an acceptable solution to the German problem. It would be unrealistic to disregard this fact. And yet the desired détente required that these problems be confronted.

(Immediately upon my return to Germany I reported to acting Chancellor Erhardt these views, together with Kennedy's desire to help improve German relations with Poland.)

During my visit to Washington, as is customary on such occasions, a draft of a joint statement was prepared for the President. We went over the text together. He asked whether I desired any changes or additions. These were taken into consideration. Then he found that the wording describing American responsibility for West Berlin was too legalistic. He crossed out that paragraph and replaced it with the simple words: "Bound by treaty and conviction, the United States stands by Berlin." The new administration thus convincingly reiterated the guarantee. The President wished me luck, in a way that denoted more than the cliché amenities.

I introduced several German correspondents who had accompanied me, and presented the President with a silver copy of our Liberty Bell. It occupied a place of honor on his desk.

THE WALL

A long hot summer was approaching for Germany. The world was racked by uncertainty. This summer might decide whether the Berlin crisis, which had been going on since 1958, would explode into catastrophe. President Kennedy made preparations for his first trip abroad. He planned to meet with General de Gaulle in Paris, Premier MacMillan in London, and with his adversary, Krushchev, in Vienna. Shortly before his departure, he explained in Washington why he sought a meeting with Krushchev. First, he would order resumption of atomic testing only after having done his utmost to reach an accord on this problem. Second, he intended to advise Krushchev to proceed with caution in Berlin. Kennedy and his experts on Eastern affairs were of the opinion that Berlin was the real hot spot in 1961. Certainly, the Laos crisis was ever-present, but in Southeast Asia, relationships were somewhat unclear; the American involvement was less explicit than in Berlin. Kennedy launched into the Berlin question at the outset of his talks with de Gaulle in Paris. He was not convinced that Krushchev realized how impossible it was for the U.S. to yield on Berlin. De Gaulle felt that Russia certainly did not want war. Kennedy expressed his intention of sending troop reinforcements from West Germany to Berlin, as a kind of trial balloon. The General remarked that it was a good idea to strengthen the military contingent in Berlin, and inquired about American capacity in case an airlift should be required. Kennedy replied that the United States was sufficiently prepared, in case an airlift was determined to be necessary. He must have been aware that the situation had changed drastically since 1948-49, and that it would no longer be possible to supply West Berlin by air for any considerable period.

From Paris, the President proceeded to Vienna. On June 3 and 4, 1961, the two most powerful men in the world met and talked for eleven or twelve hours. At first, the world heard little of the results of these talks. Pierre Salinger, steel-nerved presidential press secretary, limited his comments in the Hofburg, before the television cameras of half the world to the laconic statement: "The talks were open, courteous, serious—that's all I have to say."

Those who had the opportunity of seeing Kennedy and Krushchev descend the stairs of the Russian Embassy after the talks ended, both silent, wearing inscrutable expressions, could sense what a mighty clash of opinion and intention had taken place. The world was to know it soon enough.

Only toward the end of the talks had they touched upon the most delicate point of the agenda—Berlin. Until then, the conversation had remained within the bounds of cool politeness. Now Krushchev became loud and aggressive. He claimed that Roosevelt had planned in 1944 to withdraw American military forces from Germany after three or four years, at the most. His extraordinary memory now came to Kennedy's aid. He remembered the pertinent documents at once, and was able to reply that Roosevelt, at that time, had not counted on a divided Germany. Krushchev didn't know what to reply.

Toward the end of the meeting, over lunch in the Soviet Embassy, Krushchev rose to propose a toast. He said, shortly and succinctly, that he did not intend to yield. The President replied quietly and sensibly that he had come to Vienna to avoid, by all possible means, a war that would destroy Russia and the United States. Actually, the meeting was supposed to end with the luncheon, but Kennedy did not yet give up. He wanted to make one last effort to reach an agreement with his counterpart. In vain, because Krushchev announced harshly that his decision held firm—to sign a separate peace treaty with the "DDR"—the Deutsche Demokratische Republik—East Germany—by December. "If that is true, we shall have a cold winter," replied Kennedy. Those were the last words they exchanged.

Berlin, then, proved to be the point on which Kennedy was challenged—and he accepted the challenge.

Immediately after his return, on June 6, the President made a "Report to the Nation." He did not conceal his worry, and communicated his thoughts to the entire nation: The Vienna talks had been factual, thorough and objective. This meeting with the Soviet Premier, "as somber as it was," had been "immensely useful." They had gotten to know one another. The gap had not been closed, but they would remain in contact. Only the question of Laos had presented some immediate prospect of reaching an accord. Kennedy said that the same words—war, peace, democracy—had completely different meanings for each side. He and his opponent had very different concepts of where the world is and where it is going. The Vienna talks had given no cause for elation or relaxation, nor were they cause for undue pessimism or fear. "Our most somber talks were on the subject of Germany and Berlin. I made it clear to Mr. Krushchev that the security of Western Europe and therefore our own security are deeply involved in our presence and our access rights to West Berlin, that those rights are based on law and not on sufferance, and that we are determined to maintain those rights at any risk, and thus meet our obligation to the people of West Berlin, and their right to choose their own future. . . . We are not seeking to change the present situation. A binding German peace treaty is a matter for all who were at war with Germany, and we and our allies cannot abandon our obligations to the people of West Berlin."

On June 4, in Vienna, the Soviet Premier had presented a memorandum. It said that the Soviet Union proposed to call for a peace conference without delay. If the United States should oppose signing of a peace treaty, then the treaty would have to be signed by the nations willing to do so. This, then, was the threat—no longer a new one—to make a separate peace treaty. It also stated that in such case, the status of West Berlin as a free city, or, as we say in Berlin, "outlaw city," would be taken under particular scrutiny.

A crisis seemed unavoidable. When would it materialize? Certainly before December, the deadline established by Krushchev in the talks as well as in his memorandum. But most importantly, what form would it take? Then, in August, it became evident that Kennedy, his cabinet and his advisors had prepared themselves for a different type of crisis than the one which actually developed. At the meeting in Vienna, and from Krushchev's remarks on the German and Berlin problem, Kennedy had gleaned the impression that Russian attempts to sign a separate peace treaty, to block the access roads to Berlin, and cut off West Berlin from the Federal Republic, would precipitate acute danger of war. What really happened on August 13 was something different. Perhaps Krushchev, influenced by the Vienna encounter, had altered and abbreviated his plan. At any rate, the Americans were anticipating a different course of action.

The results of the Vienna meeting concerned us Germans directly. But it cannot be said that we—the Federal Republic, Free Germany—reacted to an appropriate degree. We were at the beginning of an election campaign. Berlin was supposed to be mentioned as little as possible, out of parochial considerations. I was involved in the election campaign, but at the same time was carrying out my duties in Berlin. In each speech I made in West Germany, I brought up the dangers that threatened not only Berlin:

First, there was the danger which I had emphatically indicated during my trip to America a few months earlier—

that the Berlin question would be increasingly narrowed down to West Berlin. I demanded that all of Berlin be taken into consideration in arriving at any agreement. Early in July I had the Senator for Federal Affairs, Dr. Guenter Klein, inquire of the appropriate department of the Federal Republic whether it would not be advisable to propose to the Soviets the reunification of Berlin, in order to lead international discussions away from the too-restricted level. The official point of view in Bonn was to maintain the status quo and to be very circumspect with new proposals. . . .

Secondly, it was important to me that the guarantees for West Berlin should not be too restricted. Already at the NATO conference in Oslo, in April of 1961, the "three essentials" had been mentioned. These three basic requirements for West Berlin, reiterated at the beginning of August by the foreign ministers of the three powers were: presence of the military; free acess; ability to survive. After this NATO proclamation in Oslo, one of my colleagues expressed anxiety: "This is almost an invitation for the Soviets to do as they like in the East Sector." On July 12, at a special session of the Berlin Senate, attended by Chancellor Adenauer, we had brought up the points that we thought must be taken into consideration. We believed that the presence of the Western powers in Berlin must be based on an unchanged legal position. The incorporation of the province of Berlin into the legal, financial and economic structure of the Federal Republic, which had taken place the year before, must be the keystone of the city's independent existence. Free access to Berlin must not be restricted. No agreement on Berlin should be made without considering the clearly evident desires of the Berlin populace. And Berlin must remain a place where Germans can meet freely. This communiqué was identical with a five-point declaration I had submitted on February 5, 1960, to the Berlin House of Representatives, in the presence of the Chancellor.

Third, I wondered whether it would not be advisable to accept the Soviet proposal for a peace conference, and so precipitate some action on the neglected German question. I did not count on instant success, since conditions for a pan-German peace treaty had obviously not been met. But I hoped that the Western powers would initiate some action that would win time for them and enable them to confront the unmistakable dangers.

In his speech of July 25, Kennedy took a very serious tone. The increase in the Soviet military budget was public knowledge. Krushchev and his deputies bristled with threats. Kennedy declared: "That we cannot permit. . . . The immediate threat to free men is in West Berlin. But that isolated outpost is not an isolated problem. The threat is world-wide. Our effort must be equally wide and strong, and not be obsessed by any single manufactured crisis. . . . West Berlin, lying exposed 110 miles inside East Germany, surrounded by Soviet troops and close to Soviet supply lines, has many roles. It is more than a showcase of liberty, a symbol, an island of freedom in a Communist sea. It is even more than a link with the Free World, a beacon of hope behind the Iron Curtain, an escape hatch for refugees.

"West Berlin is all of that. But above all, it has now become—as never before—the great testing place of Western courage and will, a focal point where our solemn commitments stretching back over the years since 1945 and Soviet ambitions now meet in basic confrontation.

"It would be a mistake for others to look upon Berlin, because of its location, as a tempting target. The United States is there; the United Kingdom and France are there; the pledge of NATO is there—and the people of Berlin are there. It is as secure, in that sense, as the rest of us—for we cannot separate its safety from our own."

During the first months of 1961, there were signs of a policy aimed at even stricter isolation of East Berlin. People who crossed the border were subjected to increasing pressures. In the early summer, the stream of refugees into West Berlin became a flood. In June, 20,000 refugees came over. In July, there were 30,000. The main reason for this development was the fear that access to Free Berlin would be cut off.

On August 11—it was a Friday, and I was en route to my party's convention in Nuremberg—I called on the Foreign Minister of the Federal Republic in Bonn. My deputy, Mayor Amrehn, and Senator Klein were also present. We urgently pointed out the danger of taking preventive measures to stop the flow of refugees. The menace was in the air, but there was as yet no German plan to avert it. Of course we did not know that attack was so imminent. Neither had we any idea of the form it would take.

In the afternoon of August 12, I spoke in the Nuremberg Market Square: "Tonight, Refugee No. 17,000 of the month will arrive in Berlin. For the first time, we shall have to take in 2500 refugees in the course of twenty-four hours. Why are these people coming? What anxiety swells this stream? The answer to this question is that the Soviet Union is preparing an attack against our people, the seriousness of which is apparent only to a few. The people in the Zone are afraid that the meshes of the Iron Curtain will be cemented shut. They are terrified that they will be locked into a gigantic prison. They are agonizingly worried that they might be forgotten—sacrificed on the alter of indifference and lost opportunities.

Throughout the difficult years in Berlin I have never

sounded a false alarm. I have never dramatized. But here and now I must proclaim myself the voice of a people that has come of age—that has the right to be addressed as frankly as President Kennedy spoke to his people and to the whole world."

Late in the evening of August 12, several colleagues and I boarded the special train which I was supposed to be using in those last weeks of the election campaign—along with a constant series of cars, airplanes and helicopters. We had slept only a few hours when the train arrived in Hanover about 4:00 A.M. There, a friend awakened us with the news of what had transpired in Berlin since midnight. We took the first available plane.

From Tempelhof airport I proceeded immediately to the Sector border on Potsdam Square and at the Brandenburg Gate. The incredible—and yet not totally surprising—was under way. East Berlin was being cut off from us by a huge military force. Giant posts were being rammed into the ground, and roll upon roll of barbed wire was stretched between them. The construction of the actual Wall began three days later.

That was one of the saddest days I have ever lived through. Berlin had again become a frontier city. Fear, desperation and rage were written on the faces of my fellow citizens. Was this only the first step? Would an attack on West Berlin follow? How were friends in the other part of the city reacting? Would there be outbreaks of mass fury, and attempts to break through to West Berlin? And what would the Allies do? Would they tolerate this violation of the Berlin treaty, or merely react with protests? If they did not, would there be any way out except war? The Allied commanders met at nine. The representatives of the Senate were called in two hours later.

I had already decided, on August 13, to cancel all my planned campaign appearances.

There was no lack of soothing, pan-German declarations. But the true burden fell upon living, suffering, anxious human beings. The city was very restless. There had not been such a critical period since the blockade. We called upon our fellow citizens to demonstrate in protest. Anyone attuned to the current of events could sense in the streets the possibility of incidents leading to unforeseeable consequences. The tension was not lessened by a newspaper report hinting that the Americans had known in advance what was going to happen. A word here or there could act as a spark. More than a quarter million men and women gathered before the Schoeneberg City Hall on the afternoon of August 16. After Mayor Amrehn's opening speech, I stepped to the microphone: "The people of Berlin have a right to know the true situation. The people of this city are strong enough for the truth. . . .

"Today we must be the voice of our fellow countrymen who can no longer speak out or come to us. In this hour, I address myself particularly to those of my countrymen who work in government offices and organizations in the Zone: Don't let them make bums of you! Conduct yourself with manly restraint whenever possible. Above all, do not shoot at your own fellow countrymen. . . !

"In this situation, I deem it necessary to lodge a protest with the world forum of the United Nations against the perpetrators of this act of inhumanity on the soil of Berlin and of Ulbricht's state. Our concern is not with the rights of the Western powers, but with human rights which must be restored. We Berliners have something to say to our protectors as well, on this day. This city wants peace, but it is not capitulating. There can be no other city in the world that desires peace and calm and security more than Berlin! But never yet has peace been won through weakness. There is a point where one can no longer retreat even a single step. This point has been reached."

Kennedy had told me to contact him directly whenever I thought it necessary and important. And now it was important.

My letter of August 16 was telegraphed to the President. I wrote: "The political-psychological danger, above all, is that inactivity and defensiveness might create a *crise de confiance* vis-à-vis the Western powers. We fear that the Ulbricht Government might interpret a wait-and-see attitude as a sign of weakness, a kind of license for further attacks, if not energetically countered. The Soviet Union has achieved half of its "free city" proposals. If a second act should follow, what remains of Berlin would become a ghetto. Then, instead of refugees moving into West Berlin, there would commence a massive flight from Berlin." I informed the President that I thought it appropriate in this situation for the Western powers to demand restoration of the Four-Power responsibility, at the same time proclaiming a Three-Power status of West Berlin. A strong statement should be issued to the effect that the Western powers considered the German question far from decided. On the contrary, the Western powers insist forcefully on a peace settlement based on the German people's right of self-determination. It would be desirable, at this point, to present the problem of Berlin to the United Nations, accusing the Soviet Union of having tampered in the crudest fashion with the Proclamation of Human Rights. "After suffering an illegal Soviet demarche, and considering the many tragedies that are taking place today in East Berlin and in the Soviet Zone of Germany, we must take the risk of assuming a firm stance. It would be desirable to reinforce the

American garrison as a show of force. I consider the situation grave enough to write to you, Mr. President, with the ultimate frankness that is possible only between friends who trust each other utterly."

THE DANGER LINGERS ON

Autumn came, the trees changed color, and the first leaves fell on the Wall. Here and there they covered blood that had seeped into the ground—blood of refugees mercilessly shot down. But again and again new attempts were made by men and women who risked everything to get through to us in West Berlin.

The political venture of Ulbricht and his henchmen forced people on both sides of the Wall to undertake ventures of their own. Tunnels were dug, identification papers were forged, and attempts were made to communicate through the sewer system. A young East Berlin man who had seen a magazine photo of General Clay's arrival, discovered that it would be easy to copy an American uniform. His girl friend in West Berlin smuggled the necessary insignia to him on the other side of the Wall. After exhaustive preparation, one day an American soldier left East Berlin at Checkpoint Charlie, the crossing point for foreigners. Nobody suspected him—not even the real Americans on our side. Here, as well as on the other side, daring plans were laid for crossing this frontier of cement and barbed wire.

How much courage and how much desperation was invested in those life-and-death efforts. Who will ever know the names of those helpers who, often after weeks of arduous labor, threw open the prison gates from below for a few hours, and guided father, mother, brothers and sisters, friends, and often complete strangers through to the West. Students from many lands deserve honorable mention. They tried to help where they could. Many made great sacrifices— some, the ultimate sacrifice.

Unforgettable pictures were seen round the world: people of every age who jumped out of four and five-story buildings, or from roofs, often to certain death. In those first days, it was still possible to use a rope, but when the houses were evacuated and the windows cemented up, many resolved on a leap of sheer desperation. The fire department stood by with safety nets; the nearest hospital was alerted; sometimes a plan was organized over a period of several days, triggered by a piece of paper fastened to a little stone, setting forth an individual's plan to jump. The waiting vehicles were not supposed to be seen from the Eastern Sector, and the photographers had to be deliberately misled so they wouldn't focus on the house in question too early and so give the Vopos—the "People's Police"—a chance to aim at the target.

And there were so many individual attempts. One man got himself a pickup truck, converted it into an armored car, and smashed through the sentry posts, barriers, barbed wire and machine-gun bursts. Another drove his automobile through the barrier, leaped out of the smashed vehicle, and jumped over the Wall. These are only a few highlights of a tortured people's situation. People kept coming up with new ideas and angles. Often, in this autumn of 1961, the escape route led through the cemetery, among the old graves.

This is a piece of German history, and I described it at a news conference I held in New York on October 6, 1961. It was the first time, after the Wall went up, and after the elections, that I expressed my opinion outside the borders of Germany. I was scheduled to receive a Freedom Award. I said that I had only done my duty, and many had assisted me. I would gladly receive the medal in the names of my fellow citizens of Berlin. For the first time, Germany received the Freedom Award: "... to a country in which freedom has been so unbelievably abused, and in part of which it is still cruelly suppressed. To a country where much blood and tears will have to be shed on the tortuous road to peace. I accept this award in the name of my fellow countrymen who suffered under the Hitler regime and who are still suffering today under Communist tyranny. And I proclaim solidarity with all who through mistakes and confusion, through misery and bitter grief, have endured. All of us, the overwhelming majority of my fellow countrymen, have taken our places in the camp of Freedom. For us, this is not a passing fancy—it is our unshakable position. The city from which I come endured the terrors of the Second World War to the bitter end. We know what another war would mean. Our place is with those who seek to do everything humanly possible to help keep the peace. I can honestly report to you that my fellow countrymen have taken admiring congnizance of the American plan to ensure peace, recently presented at the United Nations General Assembly. But we also agree with the government and people of the United States that it is an honorable peace we want, and not a graveyard peace of slavery and moral capitulation."

That night the American Research Institute gave a dinner at the Union League Club for numerous important leaders of industry. I made a report on Berlin, and solicited investment. During the evening I was called to the telephone. It was Kenneth O'Donnell, the President's appointments secretary. He said that his boss had tried several times to reach me at my hotel. Now the President had another appointment. Could he call me next morning?

The President said that his thoughts were ever with the

people of Berlin. He asked about the mood of the divided city. I made some suggestions, reported on our efforts, and added that the people expected a long-term arrangement which would convey a sense of stability. John F. Kennedy immediately agreed, and replied that he envisaged a settlement which would truly improve the situation in Berlin, so that new difficulties would not arise every few months. But, he added, the conditions for such a settlement were not yet ripe. In no case, however, did he intend to yield.

Kennedy also inquired after General Clay, whom he had sent to us in September as special emissary. He stressed that the General had his complete confidence. I assured Kennedy of our readiness to cooperate, and agreed that Lucius D. Clay would be of great help to us in Berlin. The talk ended with greetings from the President to the people of Berlin.

KENNEDYS AT THE WALL

The first member of the Kennedy family to visit Berlin after August 13, 1961 was Robert Francis Kennedy, the President's brother and Attorney General of the United States. American reporter Marguerite Higgins, who had become a "Berliner" during the city's most difficult years, informed us that Kennedy planned a world trip. I immediately invited him to visit us in Berlin. We received a cordial acceptance. This was a rare chance to give the personal center of power in Washington a spontaneous impression of the true situation in Berlin.

Robert Kennedy was full of energy. He was also a controversial man. The word "nepotism" didn't hold water long. The President's action in appointing his brother to the cabinet became understandable when the brother's real capabilities were recognized. It was obvious that he was equipped to serve his country effectively.

On February 22, 1962, we received Robert Kennedy and his wife Ethel. They had been in Asia, and now arrived from Italy. It was a cold, raw winter day. We really put our guest through an ordeal, driving through the city in an open car, to the Wall and then to the Schoeneberg City Hall. Together, we froze. It was Robert Kennedy's third visit to Berlin. The first time, he had been in our city as a reporter—two years after his brother John, who had also been in Berlin as a correspondent, in 1948, the year of the blockade, "when the people of Berlin and the Americans stood side by side, when Mayor Reuter and General Clay stood shoulder to shoulder as the Russians tried to force the proud city of Berlin to its knees." The second time was in 1955 after a trip through the Soviet Union. "I saw the pleasant streets, the attractive window displays, and the people here—and then I crossed into the Eastern Zone and it was as though I entered a nightmare world. . . ."

The people of Berlin stood freezing in the square before the City Hall. Robert Kennedy trembled with cold, but his words were clear and strong.

"In the past weeks, my wife and I have traveled thousands of miles, but nothing we saw in all those travels moved us as much as your welcome today. The warm friendliness of your greeting will remain in our hearts forever. And the message we take from here, we shall convey to the American people as a sign of your friendship for them. I want to assure you that these feelings are mutual, and that the American people feel friendship for you—deep friendship and admiration for your courage. I am proud to be in the city of Berlin."

During Robert Kennedy's speech, a number of Communist propaganda balloons came down over our heads. Our guest departed from his prepared remarks, saying quick-wittedly: "The Communists let the balloons come over, but not the people." He continued:

"I have seen the contrast between the Western part of this city and the Communist sector. I have drawn the comparison. Hundreds of thousands of people have made this comparison. That is why Mr. Ulbricht had to erect his Wall, for he could not tolerate having this contrast noted and observed. That is all he can do. He cannot stand the contrast between communism over there and freedom here. That is why he had no other recourse.

"We know how much heartache and how much grief this Wall has caused. But I ask you also to look at the other side of the question—to realize what kind of impression it has caused all over the world. This Wall is an admission of failure for the Communists. This is the first time in human history that such a Wall has been erected—not to keep bandits and thieves out, but to keep the populace in prison. The world will understand this. If the object of this Wall was the destruction of Berlin, then Mr. Ulbricht and his henchmen have made a fundamental error, for Berlin will continue to exist and to flourish. Communications between Berlin and West Germany will not be cut off. Firms from the United States and other countries will build up their business here and establish branches. The brightest and fairest pages in the book of West Berlin's history are yet to be written. Even though it lies on the fringes of the totalitarian system, West Berlin will not be attacked, for an armed attack on West Berlin is the same as an armed attack on Chicago or New York or London or Paris. You are our brothers and we stand by you."

After the rally, ignoring protocol, we climbed to the tower of the City Hall with the Attorney General and his wife.

They wanted to see the Liberty Bell. After signing our Golden Book, Robert Kennedy spoke again: "The U.S. would no more betray Berlin than it would one of our own states—Washington or Massachusetts." During the drive through the city, he had been deeply moved by the faces of the people and the awareness of their spirit. Now it was important to negotiate for improvement of Berlin's status. This would be done with our knowledge and consent. Difficult to comprehend as it might be for Berliners within sight of the Wall, he was filled with optimism for the future of the West.

On the night of February 23, Robert Kennedy spoke in the main auditorium of our Free University, at the invitation of the Ernst Reuter Society: "We are gathered here tonight on the 230th anniversary of the birth of a great and courageous man, George Washington, the father of my country, to honor the memory of another great man, Ernst Reuter, father of West Berlin's freedom. . . .

"George Washington led his countrymen in the defense of their independence against colonialism. Ernst Reuter led the citizens of Free Berlin when they asserted their independence against totalitarianism. Both were courageous, far-sighted, intelligent and steadfast. Both embodied principles mightier than themselves. Their fight for the independence of their fellow-citizens served the cause of freedom all over the world.

"George Washington's fight soon led to a happy ending. Ernst Reuter's battle goes on. This fight for independence concerns all free people. That is why Ernst Reuter is a twentieth century symbol of freedom. And the cause for which he fought is actively supported by nations like mine, thousands of miles from the Brandenburg Gate. . . ."

I have escorted visitors from many lands to the Wall. I have seen not only my countrymen weeping at the Wall. But I have rarely seen anyone stare at the stones and the barbed wire with such scorn and indignation as did Robert Kennedy. Surely he sensed the impact of the insult to human dignity being perpetrated here. Head bowed, he gazed as though hypnotized across Potsdam Square, as if he were trying to store away the memory of this scene of historical degeneracy for the rest of his life.

In the book *Just Friends and Brave Enemies* that Robert Kennedy published after his return to the United States, about the trip that had taken him through many countries of Asia and Europe, he devotes a special chapter to his Berlin visit. Of the enthusiasm and sympathy of Berlin's population, he writes: "Another thing struck me—the affection of the Berliners for the United States. The best illustration might be an event that occurred in a large market hall in the working-class district of Moabit. I was supposed to have visited the market hall during the morning, but the visit had been cancelled, unbeknownst to me, because we were running behind. When I learned that more than ten thousand people had awaited me there, I notified Willy Brandt that I would go to Moabit that afternoon, if he could meet me there.

"We arrived at 5:00 in the afternoon. An enormous crowd filled the street. The Mayor waited in front of the door. We tried to get into the hall to talk with some of the merchants, but it was almost impossible. The crowd was jammed tightly together. With police assistance, we squeezed about twelve feet into the hall. It became clear to us that someone might be suffocated in the crush. Since the door by which we had entered was blocked with people, we fought our way to a freight elevator, rode down to the basement, and left the building through a side exit. Incidentally, the next elevator, which we had almost taken, got stuck for almost twenty minutes, with the security officer and the press chief inside.

"In the meantime, the crowd in the street had grown. Now there were tens of thousands, filling all the streets leading to the market hall, jammed together. We managed to get to a police car equipped with a loudspeaker. Mayor Brandt and I each addressed the people, and the crowd responded by singing the Federal Republic's national anthem. It was a fantastic experience, sitting in the police car, listening to those thousands of voices."

In Berlin, too, he found the quality he particularly admired, being a Kennedy—courage. "Courage in Berlin today is an entirely commonplace quality. I found it in the faces of the crowds in the streets. I found it in the American troops I visited. And I experienced it first hand through two young students who had voluntarily taken unbelievable risks to get people out of East Berlin. . . . These students and their friends had organized something that might be called an underground railway. They used the sewer system to get deep into East Berlin and lead people to freedom. They said people all over the Soviet Zone asked them to help them find a way to freedom. They were handsome. They were young, strong, and determined to continue their work as long as possible. Only arrest or death could put an end to it. Because these young people are not alone, and because they are courageous, determined and unselfish, we shall win this fight."

A few months later, at the beginning of September, the President's mother came from Paris for a private visit. She enjoyed herself greatly as she sat among the spectators at the Police Sport Show in the Olympic Stadium. She was especially delighted by a transparent scroll unrolled by the top man on a motorcycle pyramid. It bore the inscription: "We are greeting Mrs. Rose Kennedy." It turned out that she spoke German quite well. She told us about her earlier visits to our city. As a young girl, she came here with her father, who had been Mayor of Boston, and was visiting the Berlin Zoo to gather information for a zoo in his home city.

Mrs. Rose Kennedy also told us of the deep impression his German trip had made on the President. He had shown the film of that day in Berlin more than once to family and friends. She herself was more deeply affected at the sight of the Wall than she had anticipated. She uttered the simple, but effective words: "When I think of my family living on the other side of the wall. . . ." The sentence remained unfinished.

RISKS UNDER DURESS

In September, 1962, we and the Allies received several confirmed reports of troop concentrations around Berlin. These reports were not easy to interpret. It was inconceivable that the Soviet leaders should be willing to precipitate a nuclear world war through their ventures in Berlin. On the other hand, we could not exclude the possibility that Soviet and Soviet-Zone groups were planning an isolated attack on West Berlin in hopes of bringing such an operation to a rapid conclusion. Counter measures would be slow in coming. Therein would lie the Soviet advantage in negotiating from a position of strength. We were prepared for anything, but had to be careful not to upset our people unnecessarily. About that time, McGeorge Bundy stated that atomic weapons might be used in Berlin. At that time, too, Defense Secretary MacNamara made a rapid inspection trip of American troops in Germany. That was the period when I, as Mayor of Berlin, speaking in America and in Germany, contributed to averting a miscalculation on the part of the East. My thinking was as follows: We in West Berlin have always been most circumspect about giving advice to our fellow countrymen in the Communist portion of Germany. We have always tried to prevent them from committing acts of desperation. If West Berlin were attacked, we would have to abandon our posture of reserve. Then we would no longer be able to exercise a moderating influence upon our fellow countrymen in the Zone.

Some West German politicians who were unable to grasp all the implications, inveighed against this carefully thought out advice. According to some, I was being too tough. I was playing with fire, they said. But they overlooked the importance of frightening others away from playing with fire. My advice was correctly interpreted in the United States. But above all, it appears that the warning had been taken seriously by the other side. What we knew about the condition of the Zone army did not vouch for its effectiveness in case of emergency.

This matter came under discussion when I visited President Kennedy in the White House on October 5, 1962. The President was strongly impressed by the realization that the East could provoke a crisis whenever it wanted, using the access routes to Berlin. He pointed out, and rightfully so, that the West still had no agreed-upon plan to deal with any one of a whole series of hypothetical cases. In this connection, the theoretical possibility was mentioned that the Zone might introduce by force the use of visas for land and sea access routes. We in the West could not simply wait until the East made a "peace treaty." I added that the example of the Wall had shown us we could anticipate regulations which we had thought would only be forthcoming in the context of signing a peace treaty. But I still thought it proper for the

West to work out a proposal setting forth its views on the bases for a true peace settlement.

The President thought the Germans should take the initiative in these matters. He had been turned down in Washington on his proposal for an international body to administer the access routes. He was sick of being pushed into these situations. The United States would now have to reserve the right to undertake nothing more in this area, awaiting the suggestions of those who were either wiser or ought to be at least as concerned about these problems as the United States. Then the United States would still have the option of voicing its opinion of such proposals.

I stressed the fact that Berlin still thought the idea of an international access administration a useful one. In any case, we had not shelved it. The President was pleased to hear this, as well as my suggestions for a new type of "Four-Power Umbrella" under which German experts could busy themselves.

Even today it is still inadvisable to quote certain passages of this conversation. They were indicative of Kennedy's strong sense of reality. In the face of all difficulties, he clung to his desire to get ahead politically and to pursue new perspectives. The President reiterated that what counted now was content rather than method. We would have to sit down together, for another *fait accompli* would make us look pretty silly. He favored any measure that would strengthen the position of the West—make that position more permanent. "I don't want to be under pressure of time after a period of idleness."

Kennedy also talked to me about the prospects of holding a popular election on the Berlin question. Two years ago, during his visit to the U.S., Adenauer had already hinted at

such a possibility, but at that time limited himself to the
question whether West Berlin was for or against the Allied
presence. I had visited the Chancellor at Cadenabbia on
September 21, and we had discussed the pro and con of a
popular election. My object was to get the Chancellor's
endorsement so I could bring up this topic in Washington.
The President and I agreed that first, the question should be
broadened and should be keyed to the interrelationship of
Berlin and the rest of the Federal Republic. Second, we
deemed it proper to propose an election take place in both
sections of Germany and Berlin. The expected Communist
refusal would still leave room for an expression of the
people's wishes in both parts of Free Germany—West Berlin
and West Germany. Such an operation—so I hoped, and
Kennedy agreed—would make it hard for the Soviets to
uphold their foreign policy. (The Soviets and the Soviet Zone
did react to the possibility of a popular vote with instantan-
eous, loud, phony arguments and threats. The proposal was
not followed up for a while, because the situation cooled off
considerably after the Cuban crisis.)

The official talk came to an end. Kennedy rose and took
my arm to convey that he wished to talk with me privately.
We left his study and went out into the White House garden.

The President was deeply preoccupied. He was not sure
whether a clash with the Soviet Union could be avoided in
the near future, but wholehearted efforts would have to
continue. The Cuban situation was causing him a great deal
of trouble. He would not allow any extreme right-wing newspapers and groups to tell him what to do. But he might have
to act on his own responsibility. It was certainly clear to me
that he had refrained from taking drastic steps up to now
because of the situation in general and not least of all because

of the threat to Berlin. Still, nothing in his words gave any indication of what, only a few weeks later would force him to a final decision.

CUBA

Monday, October 22, 1962. In the Berlin Congress Hall, an American movie premiere was taking place. In the middle of the show I was called to the telephone. The American Ambassador in Berlin, Allan Lightner, urgently needed to speak with the Mayor. He had an important message. Late that night, we met in my house on the Schlachtensee. Lightner was under orders to brief the mayor of Berlin on the speech Kennedy would be making to the American people on the Cuban crisis at midnight, European time. In the same fashion, Kennedy was informing other heads of friendly nations. He had made it a custom to keep Berlin posted as well as our colleagues in Bonn. While we were waiting for the speech, to be broadcast over the Armed Forces Radio Network, we reviewed the incidents in Cuba up to the present moment: the failure of the invasion by Cuban refugees at the Bay of Pigs in April, 1961, which had lost the President considerable prestige; then, towards the end of August, 1962, the Soviet announcement of a military assistance pact with Fidel Castro. Towards the middle of September, there followed Kennedy's warning that the U.S. would not tolerate the bringing of weapons into Cuba. At the end of September, there were alarming rumors of extensive Soviet arms deliveries to the sugar island.

Now the President cited clear evidence of secret preparations for establishment of offensive missile bases in Cuba, directed against the U.S. and the whole Western hemisphere.

Such a deliberately provocative and unreasonable change in the status quo could not be accepted. The thirties had taught a clear lesson: Allowing aggression free rein, unchecked, would ultimately lead to war. The path he had now chosen was strewn with dangers. But the greatest risk would be to do nothing. "The cost of freedom is always high—but Americans have always paid it. And one path we shall never choose, and that is the path of surrender or submission. Our goal is not the victory of might, but the vindication of right. . . ." It was clear that the world trembled on the brink of the abyss. The entire American military establishment was mobilized. Most of the Strategic Air Command took to the air. NATO declared a state of emergency. The next few hours could see catastrophe become a reality. Twice, in that speech, Kennedy had mentioned Berlin. Even if the immediate danger should abate, Berlin could become the scene of reprisals, in this time of utmost tension.

But we could not let that disconcert us. The law of mutual dependence and the affirmation of our linked destiny were more important now than ever before.

Allan Lightner and I discussed these matters. When I escorted him to the door, he asked if I had any message for Washington. That same night, he wired: "The Mayor thanks the President for emphasizing so opportunely the responsibilities toward Berlin and its people. He believes that the President must proceed on the course he has chosen—for the sake of freedom and peace. The risk could have been foreseen—we must be prepared to take the consequences."

Kennedy's reply came next day: ". . . It was reassuring to hear that you support the measures we deemed necessary in connection with the Cuban crisis. The complications of the situation in Cuba extend beyond our hemisphere, and subsequent developments will probably have important consequences for Berlin. These are the hard facts, and I am convinced that you are fully aware of them. For that very reason, your clear and unequivocal attitude is all the more gratifying.

"I hope we can remain in constant contact to ensure that everything necessary is done to strengthen the position of the Free World. . . ."

Berlin watched the Cuba week, observing developments intently. No further pressure was applied to our city. In the Caribbean area, the situation remained under control. The man in the Kremlin had understood and respected Kennedy's total determination.

In the night of October 26-27, Kennedy received that letter from Krushchev which was described by one of his few confidants as "one of the most surprising, emotion-laden documents of modern history." On Sunday morning, October 28, the third letter arrived from the Soviet head of government, announcing withdrawal of the missiles. On October 29 I wrote to the President: "Let me congratulate you. Your decision made it clear to the Soviet Union that the word of the United States must be taken seriously. I believe this will have a positive effect on the whole world. Certainly, the people of West Berlin have reacted very positively. It may even spare us more burdens and sacrifices. . . ."

The Cuban crisis was a turning point in international developments. John F. Kennedy had passed his most difficult test. Like his opponent, he had gazed into the abyss and had not shuddered. But with his awareness of conditions in the nuclear age, he had not gone to extremes. He had averted mortal danger from the United States and from the whole world. But he had not humiliated a powerful antagonist. That was not clearly understood by everyone, even in his own country. The experience of the Berlin crisis of August, 1961 lay behind him. Despite his intelligence, vitality and decisiveness, Kennedy, too, had needed time to reach a proper equilibrium.

THE PRESIDENT IN GERMANY

The year 1963 led off in Berlin with a short but lively election campaign which temporarily menaced even the city's political unity, even though the Wall was a daily exhortation to unity. On February 17, the polls opened and the noise abated. The Communists suffered a smarting defeat. Daily life was resumed within hours. After the results were published, disillusion set in. My party received 62 percent of the votes. The CDU (Christian Democrats) of Berlin suffered serious losses. The Free Democrats returned as a third party to the Berlin House of Representatives, and became coalition partners of the Social Democrats. Among the congratulations there was a greeting from the President of the United States of America, dated February 18:

"We are all very pleased with the results of yesterday's free elections in Berlin. The people of Berlin have clearly and unmistakably reinforced the cause of freedom by dealing the Communists a crushing defeat. Berlin is the focal point of freedom, and to defend this freedom is the primary task of the Atlantic alliance, so that what strengthens the Atlantic alliance, strengthens Berlin as well, and what strengthens Berlin, strengthens the Atlantic alliance. The United States will remain true to this twofold objective, and I know that Berlin will follow the same course under your leadership. . . ."

In my thanks to the President, I reminded him of the invitation I had extended back in 1961. I wrote that the morals of our people needed no encouraging demonstrations.

The fact that Nikita S. Krushchev had already visited East Berlin several times was no weighty argument to me. But in view of the general situation, a visit with us would be the signal for a great demonstration of Western unity which would attract world-wide attention.

Prior to this letter, European and American friends had already taken several other steps. Two things were of prime importance. First, we had to ensure that Kennedy included Berlin when he came to Germany. In retrospect that sounds so obvious, but at the time it seemed not at all so simple.

Secondly, it was important that the Presidential visit be more than just a conventional state visit. The Germans must have the opportunity to express their faith in the leader of the Free World, and their loyalty to the Western alliance. That meant Kennedy had to meet Germans outside of Bonn and Berlin. I was glad that, despite the restricted schedule, it was possible to include Cologne and Frankfurt at least.

June 23, 1963, the first day of John F. Kennedy's visit to Germany, already bore witness that he enjoyed the full sympathy of our people. Cologne and Bonn received the President with rejoicing, church bells, fanfares and fireworks. This reception surpassed anything Cologne had seen up to then. A great day for Kennedy—a great day for us Germans.

That night—a Sunday—after the triumphal journey through Cologne, Bonn, and Bad Godesberg, we were guests of the Chancellor at Palais Schaumburg. Two things particularly come to mind from the after-dinner speeches. Kennedy asked with humorous irony whether the many paper flags in the hands of the children got there on their own. And Adenauer's speech made not one reference to the partition of Germany.

On Tuesday, June 25, I joined John F. Kennedy for breakfast, shortly after 8 A.M. He was staying with the American ambassador. We were alone and could talk freely.

The President first brought up several questions on which he would have to express an opinion next day in Berlin. His close associate, Ted Sorensen had already mentioned them to me. I then suggested methods of proceeding, step by step, to change conditions in divided Berlin and partitioned Germany. It was quite clear to Kennedy that, if there should be a limited resumption of personal traffic between the two parts of Berlin, we must never allow ourselves to be placed in the position of sending back East Berliners, whether via the police or in other ways. The first important step—visits between relatives—which followed the issuance of passes at Christmas 1963, was not yet in view. I could report only one modest development—the Red Cross service which reunited families by enabling old and sick individuals to receive authorization to join their relatives in West Berlin or West Germany.

In another phase of our discussion, the President sought my opinion as to the probable outcome of the 1965 Parliamentary elections. Experienced politician that he was, he spoke of the special tasks that today face democratic parties seeking to attract the vote of heavily populated industrial areas and great cities.

The most important part of our June 25th talk was devoted to European and Atlantic cooperation. Kennedy thought that, despite the difficulties created by the French, there was a good possibility that in the next two or three years, constructive cooperation between Europe and the United States could be strengthened. Increasing social democratic influence would probably be felt. It seemed probable that Harold Wilson would become Prime Minister. In the Federal Republic, my friends and I could look forward to the prospect of exercising decisive influence. "In collaboration with the Scandinavians, we could accomplish much." He was worried about the unclear political situation in Italy, and about signs of an emerging Popular Front in the ranks of the French socialists.

I expounded my ideas on how to activate the European policy and again made it a people's cause. To do so, the "open-minded" Gaullist forces would be indispensable. Kennedy showed definite interest in strengthening contacts between European social democrats and friends in the U.S. "liberal" and labor union blocs.

Aside from that, the President urged me to have some more breakfast. He wished me good health before the helicopter took him off to Hessen for a parade. I wished fervently that this man might long be preserved for his people and for all of us.

A highlight of the Presidential visit to West Germany was his speech of June 25, 1963 in St. Paul's Cathedral, Frankfurt. Kennedy pointed out that today's problems were not just German or American or European. There were only world problems, and America was indissolubly linked with Europe on questions of war and peace.

The President warned that freedom would be threatened if we paused for the passing moment, if we rest on our achievements, if we resist the pace of progress. "For time and the world do not stand still. Change is the law of life. And those who look only to the past or the present are certain to miss the future. The future of the West lies in Atlantic partnership—a system of cooperation, interdependence, and harmony whose peoples can jointly meet their burdens and opportunities throughout the world. Some say this is only a dream, but I do not agree. A generation of achievement—the Marshall plan, NATO, the Schuman plan, and the Common Market—urges us up the path to greater unity. . . . Some say that the United States will neither hold to these purposes nor

abide by its pledges—that we will revert to a narrow nationalism. But such doubts fly in the face of history. For eighteen
years the United States has stood its watch for freedom all
around the globe. . . . We are proud of this record, which
more than answers doubts. But in addition, these proven
commitments to the common freedom and safety are
assured, in the future as in the past, by one great fundamental fact—that they are deeply rooted in America's own
self-interest. Our commitment to Europe is indispensable—in
our interest as well as yours . . . for war in Europe, as we
learned twice in forty years, destroys peace in America."

BERLIN'S GREAT DAY

It is not easy to describe those hours of June 26, 1963,
when millions showed their love for John F. Kennedy—when
a river flowed through the ancient capital—a river of enthusiasm and gratitude.

What the Germans hoped for, especially those in the East
Zone, became reality in Berlin. Kennedy's stay in the German
capital was the undisputed climax of his trip. Waves of
enthusiasm, of exceptional cordiality, joy and warmth enveloped the President and occasionally caused him to direct an
incredulous gaze on the crowds. The Berliners swept him
along. Deeply impressed by the first portion of his ride, John
F. Kennedy reached the Congress Hall, where he was to
address the delegates of the Trade Union Congress of German
Construction Workers. This was a special item on his agenda
which some had called superfluous. But they reckoned
without Kennedy. He said that he was not a stranger to
union meetings. We were all impressed by the way the leader
of the Free World—here in Berlin!—showed his respect for the

workers. He spoke of the achievements of American trade unions. He said the system of responsibilities within a free society was the best way that people can live. He called freedom the way to move ahead. He spoke of responsibility to other nations. "When I leave tonight, I leave and the United States stays."

A few minutes later the journey through jubilant Berlin continued. I pointed out places of interest on the route and the buildings, but most of the time we couldn't hear ourselves think. As we passed the Brandenburg Gate, we saw that it was concealed behind enormous red draperies, for the first time in the history of Berlin. That was Ulbricht's reply to the visit of the man after whose assassination he indulged in hypocritical posthumous tributes. Arriving at Checkpoint Charlie, scene of dangerous cold war confrontations, Kennedy gazed thoughtfully into the Eastern Sector where he could see the other Berliners—the imprisoned men and women, standing there by the hundreds, offering a silent greeting under the eyes of their guards and jailers. When the President descended from the platform, he yielded to an impulse to move forward to the cordoned-off public area and shake hands with the West Berliners. People surged around him in a frenzy of enthusiasm, and Kennedy's guards had a hard time getting him back into the car. In front of the City Hall in Schoeneberg, the storm of enthusiasm broke in earnest.

We paused briefly in my office to catch our breath. For the moment, the need to concentrate had passed. The crowd— the jubilant, elated crowd which we could still hear from below through the windows, allowed us time to take some refreshment and to think our own thoughts for a moment. The President went briskly up to the round table where visitors to the Mayor usually sit. He sat down on the chair which the host usually occupies, and waved McGeorge Bundy and another of his aides to his side. He glanced through the cards on which his speech had been written, and noted, by hand, a few additional, stronger points. After all he had experienced in this city within the last few hours, he wanted to express more clearly and with all sincerity how very close he felt to these people. The rest of us stood or sat around the room and exchanged a few words about this overwhelming experience, and what lay ahead for the rest of the day.

Federal Chancellor Adenauer sat at the Mayor's desk, reading, with amusement, a Communist newspaper. It expressed scorn and contempt for the President and for his visit. By now, our group had grown to fifteen or twenty persons—a motley crew of protocol officers, security men, translators, aides. My secretaries were in charge of the coffee, while my official advisor served orange juice.

After a few minutes the President pocketed his speech and went into the next room to change his shirt and freshen up. When he returned, he accepted a cup of coffee, but took only a sip and ate a couple of sugar cubes.

Then it was time to go back down to the square which today bears his name. The crowd's reception was something we had never before beheld. The Americans said that Kennedy himself had never experienced anything like it.

And as we emerged there were shouts, unending jubilation, handkerchiefs waving and flags flying from roofs, balconies, trees and lampposts. Somewhat disconcerted, the President confronted the surging crowd of hundreds of thousands of excited Berliners. Politics should not be confused with emotions, but emotions can corroborate politics.

Otto Bach, parliamentary president, led off this greatest demonstration ever to take place in Free Berlin, on Rudolph Wilde Square. Then Federal Chancellor Adenauer took the podium: "You have come here to hear President Kennedy, therefore I shall say only a few words. A popular vote has taken place here today which will echo throughout the world. We thank President Kennedy for his trip to Europe, for his trip to the Federal Republic, and especially for his visit to this part of the Federal Republic.

"The people of Berlin have distinguished themselves in these past years by steadfastness and patience. Fifteen years ago today, my friends, on June 26, the first planes arrived on the airlift that saved Berlin. I want to mention this particularly in the presence of General Clay. And now, my friends, if we compare that time, fifteen years ago with the world situation today, with the situation of the Federal Republic and of Berlin, which is part of it, we can say that we have made a great deal of progress and we shall progress further thanks to the help of our friends; thanks to our steadfastness and unity."

When John F. Kennedy appeared on the podium, the waves of enthusiasm of the Berliners again enveloped him. Not for many minutes could our guest say: "I am proud to come to this city as the guest of your distinguished Mayor, who has symbolized throughout the world the fighting spirit of West Berlin. And I am proud to visit the Federal Republic with your distinguished Chancellor who for so many years has committed Germany to democracy and freedom and progress, and to come here in the company of my fellow American, General Clay, who has been in this city during its great moments of crisis and will come again if ever needed.

"Two thousand years ago the proudest boast was *'civis Romanus sum.'* Today, in the world of freedom, the proudest boast is 'ich bin ein Berliner. . . .'

"There are many people in the world who really don't understand, or say they don't know what the great issue between the Free World and the Communist world is. Let them come to Berlin. There are some who say that communism is the wave of the future. Let them come to Berlin. And there are some who say in Europe and elsewhere we can work with the Communists. Let them come to Berlin. And there are even a few who say that it is true that communism is an evil system, but it permits us to make economic progress. *Lass' sie nach Berlin kommen.* Let them come to Berlin.

"Freedom has many difficulties and democracy is not perfect, but we have never had to put up a wall to keep our people in, to prevent them from leaving us. I want to say, on behalf of my countrymen, who live many miles away on the other side of the Atlantic, who are far distant from you, that they take the great pride in having been able to share with you, even from a distance, the story of the last eighteen years. I know of no town, no city that has been besieged for eighteen years, that still lives with the vitality and the force, and the hope and the determination of the city of West Berlin. While the Wall is the most obvious and vivid demonstration of the failures of the Communist system, for all the world to see, we take no satisfaction in it, for it is, as your Mayor has said, an offense not only against history but an offense against humanity, separating families, dividing husbands and wives and brothers and sisters, and dividing a people who wish to be joined together.

"What is true of this city is true of Germany—real, lasting peace in Europe can never be assured as long as one German out of four is denied the elementary right of free men, and that is to make a free choice. In eighteen years of peace and good faith, this generation of Germans has earned the right to be free, including the right to unite their families and their nation in lasting peace, with good will to all people. You live in a defended island of freedom, but your life is part of the main. So let me ask you, as I close, to lift your eyes beyond the dangers of today, to the hopes of tomorrow, beyond the freedom merely of this city of Berlin or your country of Germany, to the advance of freedom everywhere, beyond the Wall to the day of peace with justice, beyond yourselves and ourselves to all mankind.

"Freedom is indivisible, and when one man is enslaved, all are not free. When all are free, then we can look forward to that day when this city will be joined as one and this country and this great continent of Europe in a peaceful and hopeful globe. When that day finally comes, as it will, the people of West Berlin can take sober satisfaction in the fact that they were in the front lines for almost two decades.

"All free men, wherever they may live, are citizens of Berlin, and therefore, as a free man, I take pride in the words *Ich bin ein Berliner.*"

To the President I said: "This is a great day in the history of our city. We have lived through bad times, and for that very reason, we shall never forget, Mr. President, that you are here with us today and that you addressed us this day. I say this not only in my capacity as Mayor of this city, I say it in the name of all the people of Berlin, and most of all, for the one-and-a-quarter-million Berliners who have today participated in this tribute and demonstration of loyalty and friendship for John F. Kennedy. We could not have survived these years without the will to self-determination, but neither would we have come through without our good friends throughout the world. Together we can be proud that this is again a great and thriving city.

"We have heard the leader of the Free World. A fearless and progressive statesman has spoken. We know what a burden he carries on his shoulders. Our hopes are with him. They are directed toward peaceful change. We see the great possibilities of the peace strategy, as the President has been evolving it, before and during his trip to Germany. To it, and to construction of the new Europe, do we wish to make our contribution. This will be the path to self-determination. Thus will we achieve reunification of our people. And now, my friends, we partake of a truly historic moment in the history of this city. Let us share it in solemn silence. President Kennedy will sign his name in our Golden Book in the presence of the people of Berlin. And we shall listen to the Freedom Bell, on which is inscribed a quotation from Abraham Lincoln: 'May this world, with God's help, witness a rebirth of freedom.' "

It had become very still. The silence was the highest manifestation that Berlin could give of that accord and feeling of solidarity. No one who was present will ever forget that moment. The President signed the Golden Book of the German capital. The Freedom Bell rang out sonorously above the solemn crowd. The men bared their heads. Then the celebration resumed.

We went up to the Senate Hall which had been emptied of furniture. There, leading personalities were introduced. I no longer recall what was said there. Kennedy moved away from the group and again went to the window to look down into the square, still crowded with people, jammed tightly together.

He sat down briefly in an adjacent room. The Federal Chancellor joined him. Gifts for Mrs. Kennedy and the children had been prepared. An enormous table had been set in the Brandenburg Hall, and decked with the Hohenzollern silver, much to the delight of the Americans. Kennedy commented that he couldn't set such a table in the White House. He was greatly amused when he was shown an old book bearing the notation that a Johann F. Kennedy had moved from Cologne to Berlin in the middle of the eighteenth century, and had left owing eighteen Talers in taxes. Now it was proven that we had a real Berliner in our midst! Had the family moved to Ireland from Germany? The President laughed and asked for copies, which were, of course, presented to him.

From the City Hall the triumphal journey continued by way of Steiglitz to Zehlendorf. That was the first time I had seen a confetti shower in Berlin. It became almost a game to try to break through the cordon and throw the President a bouquet of flowers or shake his hand. There were some pointed remarks about the allegedly exaggerated security precautions. In Berlin they really were unnecessary.

The professors in their ornate ceremonial dress made a colorful picture. The President made a politically significant speech to the students. He applied his peace strategy to the example of Germany and developed it further. He said that it should not mark time behind the shield of American military commitments to the protection of Berlin, and maintain the status quo in anticipation of better times. It was the duty of every West Berlin student to formulate his own point of view, and to think on the goals to which this city aspired, and how best to attain them.

After eighteen years of oppression, even the countries of Eastern Europe are not unreceptive to the prospect of change. Truth does not die. Even after forty-five years of Party dictatorship, the people of the Soviet Union feel the might of historical evolution. Economic and political variations are appearing, for example, in Poland, Rumania and the Soviet Union itself. Dogmatic police states are an anachronism, just as the partition of Germany and Europe goes against the mainstream of history. The new Western Europe, a dynamic, varied and democratic Europe—must be exerting an evergrowing attraction on the nations of the East. Changes will not come about from one day to the next, but our efforts for a real settlement must continue undiminished. . . . "This process can only be helped by the growing unity of the West, and we must all work towards that unity. . . . This is not an easy course. There is no easy course to the reunification of Germany, the reconstitution of Europe. . . . There is work to be done and obligations to be met—obligations to truth, to justice and to liberty." By decree of its academic Senate, the Free University of Berlin bestowed honorary citizenship on the President.

Exhausted but elated by the events of the day, Kennedy arrived late at Tegel airfield. Once again he addressed the German people: "I said yesterday that I was going to leave a note for my successor which would say 'To be opened at a time of some discouragement,' and in it would be written three words: 'Go to Germany.' I may open that note myself some day.

"I know the American people naturally wonder on occasions whether all they have done since the end of 1945, all the responsibilities and burdens that they have accepted, whether any of this effort is recognized and appreciated. If they had any doubts, certainly it would seem to me that the warmth of the welcome of the last three days which was extended through me to the American people should have ended them. And for that reason, if for no other, I am happy I came, and I express my thanks to you, Chancellor, and to all the Germany people for the hand they held out to us."

Before the President boarded his plane, he said to General Clay that now he could understand him; up to now he had always thought him a little sentimental about Berlin. We also know from what Mrs. Shriver told my wife and what Princess Radziwill told my friend Nabokov, that he had not expected it to be as it was—neither the Wall nor the people.

FAREWELL IN WASHINGTON

The sun shone on the coffin as it passed through the mourning city of Washington. Hundreds of thousands kept silent vigil in the streets.

Ninety-two delegations from almost all the countries of the globe, sixteen presidents and heads of government, among them Federal President Luebke and the Federal Chancellor, accompanied Kennedy on his last journey—some satisfaction for the American people, but no consolation for a widow with two small children. Most of the world knelt at the grave in Arlington, but that is no answer to the question of why the assassination occurred.

The dead President left the text of a speech he would no longer be making. It is the speech of an optimist and a democrat who respects his opponent and who is certain of his cause. It is the speech of a man who pledged his life for his ideals. "Ignorance and misinformation can handicap the progress of a city or a company, but they can, if allowed to prevail in foreign policy, handicap this country's security. In a world of complex and continuing problems, in a world full of frustrations and irritations, America's leadership must be guided by the lights of learning and reason—or else those who confuse rhetoric with reality and the plausible with the possible will gain popular ascendancy with their seemingly swift and simple solutions to every world problem. . . .

"In today's world, freedom can be lost without a shot being fired, by ballots as well as bullets. The success of our leadership is dependent upon respect for our mission in the world as well as our missiles—on a clearer recognition of the virtues of freedom as well as the evils of tyranny. . . .

"Finally, it should be clear by now that a nation can be no stronger abroad than she is at home. Only an America which practices what it preaches about equal rights and social justice will be respected by those whose choice affects our future."

On November 25, 1963, I shared the grief of my American friends. I sat among the friends of the family in St. Matthew's Cathedral. I went to the veterans' cemetary at Arlington, and to the Swedish Embassy where Senator Hubert Humphrey, union leader Walter Reuther and other friends assembled. In the afternoon, Lyndon B. Johnson held a reception at the State Department for heads of state and chiefs of government who had come to Washington for the funeral. The special position of Berlin here became more apparent than I would have liked, for as mayor of a city I did not really belong in this company. Still, the President had sent me an invitation.

While I exchanged a few words with the King of Belgium, a message came from the White House. The widow of President Kennedy asked if I could pay the family a visit.

The wife of the Chief of Protocol took me to the White House. I rode up in the elevator. When the door opened, Mrs. Kennedy stood before me in a black dress, erect, controlled, as courageous as the whole world had seen her in those difficult hours. She took my arm and spared me the conventional phrases. We proceeded to one of the salons where I met the President's closest relatives again—Robert and Edward, the two brothers—Mrs. Shriver, Mrs. Smith and Mrs. Lawford, the sisters—Ethel, wife of the Attorney General— Princess Lee Radziwill, sister of the widow. After a brief greeting, Mrs. Kennedy invited her brother-in-law Robert and me to another room. There the three of us sat down and Mrs. Kennedy began to speak of her dead husband. In June, he had returned from his trip through Germany full of enthusiasm—above all from his stay in Berlin. How much he had talked about it, and how much he had enjoyed showing the movie of that day in Berlin.

"You just had to come here before returning to Berlin," said Mrs. Kennedy, and her brother-in-law nodded silently. Then this courageous woman expressed to me in brief, warm words how much she appreciated the sympathy of the people of Berlin in these hours. Berlin had been the first city to give her husband's name to a square that had meant so much to him: "How could you have done that—it was good that you did it."

I said that we also wanted to rename the German-American school in Berlin the John F. Kennedy School, and that the America Institute of our Free University which we are building with the aid of the Ford Foundation will be called the John F. Kennedy Institute. Then, in a few words, I described the tremendous outburst of mourning which had taken place in Berlin a few hours before, at the same time as Cardinal Cushing was celebrating the Requiem Mass in St. Matthew's Cathedral.

After I had described the Berlin demonstration, Mrs. Kennedy rose and said, "Please come . . . you must see it. . . ." We went to the big window and she drew the curtain back. Silently we gazed at the illuminated, snow-white Washington monument beyond the White House gardens, and the mighty Lincoln Monument, of the same stone, the same color.

Mrs. Kennedy said she wanted to experience this view once more, for soon she would be leaving the White House. Here, her husband had often stood; here he had drawn strength from the history of his country.

Robert Kennedy left the room.

It was difficult for me to find words. I told Mrs. Kennedy how courageous she was. I also wanted her to know that the President's ideas were immortal; that no one could shoot them down. And that we would try our best to see that his work was finished. Jacqueline Kennedy smiled. Then she replied that I was not the first to express those thoughts. But this was no consolation for her. This was her personal destiny.

Robert Kennedy, who had taken such an important place in the active life of his brother, escorted me to the car. We walked silently together. In farewell, he said, "He loved Berlin."

A Peace Policy for Europe

IN THE SPIRIT OF HISTORY

I indicated, when I took over the Foreign Office, something I was very aware of at the time: No one with a sense of history will find it easy to disregard the Great Coalition of Social Democrats and Christian Democrats, nor the fact that a man of my convictions has become the foreign minister of Germany.

I am presenting this book not as a man of my party, but because of my responsibility as German foreign minister. For me, this role involves three things:

1. The tradition and the creative determination of a freedom movement whose goal since its inception

From A Peace Policy For Europe *by Willy Brandt. Copyright © 1969 by Holt, Rinehart and Winston, Inc. Reprinted by permission of Holt, Rinehart and Winston, Inc.*

has been the validation of justice and morality in the coexistence of nations.

2. The knowledge that the history of one's own people cannot be evaded but must be borne as a legacy and as experience and that the objective must be to fructify the variegated energies of an indivisible history on behalf of the whole.

3. The duty of the day, which I take to mean that foreign policy must not be allowed to become the exclusive province of "experts" but must be explained in such a way that concerned citizens will understand what is at stake: peace and material existence, freedom and serenity.

The history of Germany is replete with blunders and missed opportunities involving all social and political factions. Down to the most recent decades this pernicious feature of an era has made even those who learned from the past the scapegoats for mistakes of others. This unhealthy trait of the past few decades can only be grasped in the context of an epoch of sharply contrasting blacks and whites.

I see no reason for not expressing myself straightforwardly about the historic personality of Bismarck. It was history that brought down the German Reich. The demands, however, for which Social Democracy was vilified as "the Reich's enemy," have become an integral part of German reality.

It is scarcely imaginable that a powerful diplomat like Bismarck—nuanced and many-faceted to the despair of friend and foe alike, condemned by his conservative class colleagues because of his lack of ideology—would have erred in the direction of recklessness or immobility. Such blunders were reserved for others. The word "dogma" was alien to his policy; his vocabulary lacked all "doctrine." Anyone who

remembers that, need not fear being reproached as an oppor-
tunist. But today we are dealing with the question of the
future of a people who live between West and East.

"Consistency in politics often becomes erroneous, high-
handed and arbitrary. One must recast oneself in accordance
with the facts, with the state of affairs, with the possibilities;
one must take the circumstances into account and serve one's
fatherland in accordance with conditions, not in accordance
with one's own opinions, which are often mere prejudices."

These words were spoken by Bismarck in January 1871,
shortly after his Reich was founded. It was a statement quite
free of arrogance and bombast; it was sober and modest—
though there really were grounds for pride. It is a statement
that should be pondered, especially in our schools, for it
confirms the recognition that a policy of interests does not
require unscrupulousness.

In our day, national unity can no longer be forged through
"blood and iron," even if some fool were to dream of that.
Smaller than Prussia of that time and in an utterly transformed European landscape, the Federal Republic of
Germany must demonstrate its political maturity by showing
if and to what degree it can overcome the attitude stigma-
tized by Bismarck as one of high-handedness—of "all or
nothing."

The great Chancellor succeeded in bringing about external,
but not internal unity. The premise of having a state en-
throned above its citizens was an agreement among princes,
was contrived in such a way, that it could have evolved into a
democratic constitutional monarchy and become an industrial mass society without any major upheavals if its rulers
had really wanted that evolution—but they were unable, and
for the most part did not really wish, to bring it about.
German liberals showed scant understanding of the working

class movement; they preferred coming to an arrangement with the rulers. Socialists invariably met with conciliatory reactions, but socialism was never understood as a spiritual movement. The universal and free ballot guaranteed in the national constitution was bound to remain an oratorical piece of patchwork as long as the insistence on thoroughgoing democratization was anathematized as seditious.

An autocratic and authoritarian state, its forms delineated in Prussia even more clearly than in the Reich as a whole, wanted to suppress a natural development toward democracy by police methods. This autocratic position had a long-drawn-out life, and has not yet entirely died out. In Germany, the image of the State as a strict and generally fair-minded paterfamilias has far too long been regarded as immutable. The persecution of "Reds," the harassment of "Blacks" and the contempt for "intellectuals," were bound to leave behind a trauma pregnant with consequences. Only now is that trauma gradually beginning to disappear, even though on occasion political shortsightedness would like to revive it.

Externally, we can only be as strong as we are internally. In his unpretentious way, the German Social Democrat, August Bebel once said that the upward striving strata of the people were part of the nation and did not want to belong to it passively, through mere obedience. He spoke of the "fatherland of love and justice" that was worth fighting for and realizing. The distance that separates us from Bismarck's era, and the democratic and social rights that have since become a matter of course, make it plain that the German Reich can be understood only by taking Bismarck and Bebel together.

The poorest son of the people has often been its most faithful. This statement must often have been understood only superficially, as in the allusion to the fact that the Social Democrats did, after all, vote the war credits in the Reichstag on August 4, 1914. In fact, they were more patriotic than a few years later when refusing such credits, because they were being requested not for defense, but for conquest. In World War I, those with responsibility thought they could talk on and challenge the world until the eleventh hour. Instead of putting an end to the murderous confrontations by means of an acceptable negotiated peace, they dreamed of annexations with such blindness that the inevitable happened.

Not only the monarchial form of the State fell; the Reich itself floundered. Germany was left an impotent, mutilated, vestige of a state, condemned by the verdict of the victors, and shaken by crises. With immense effort it devised a new constitution and attempted to bring it to life. That effort succeeded for only a short time. Then the forces of moderation, of reconciliation at home and of understanding abroad failed, and their failure was due not only to enemies within the nation.

No one will reproach me for being among those who would like to make people forget what our own guilt and our own weakness or arrogance have meant in our recent history. But, I must point out however, that while Germany acted, its neighbors merely looked on. Everywhere, or very nearly everywhere, the terrifying indications of chauvinism, short-sightedness, and irrationality manifested themselves. The democrats in Germany were not given an easy time of it by countries abroad after World War I. Too little was given and too late, when reasonable men—Friedrich Ebert, Walther Rathenau, Gustav Stresemann—pleaded and insisted. It was not recognized that their moderate and reasonable demands for Germany were also in the interest of Europe and peace. Outside our borders, also, it must not be forgotten, that the dictatorship was condoned or simply allowed to keep what it had seized.

It would be irresponsible to use foreign indifference as an explanation for the whole of the subsequent disaster. Its roots were embedded in the internal mechanism of the State; in the spiritual attitude of a society that was not ready to support that State. Republicans remained a minority in the German Weimar Republic. The fidelity to the State demonstrated by the democrats—in the postwar turmoil, in the fratricidal struggles of the revolution, and in their patriotic coalitions for the salvation of the republic—did not prevent them, these same democrats who had created and borne aloft the youthful State, from becoming scapegoats. Everything was blamed on them—all responsibility for external and internal difficulties, for misery, want, and unemployment. Social renovation was shattered at its very inception. The old forces, in key economic and social positions, had scarcely faltered; in the struggle against Weimar, they swiftly found each other again, supported and strengthened by a civil and military bureaucracy that was in reality sympathetic to the restoration.

On such terrain, no self-analysis could grow. On such terrain, domestic political hatred grew, the glorification of futile deeds of arms prospered, arrogance luxuriated. The gravediggers of democracy did not find it too difficult to seize control of a state that was being defended against them merely by an embattled minority. With the Enabling Act in March 1933, when the death certificate of the Weimar Republic was being signed, the Social Democrats became simultaneously the rearguard and the vanguard of the German movement of resistance and liberation.

Yet it is a bitter realization that by some of their own failures, the Social Democrats contributed to their exclusion from government in the Weimar period. And it remains a tragedy that the majority of the people could not be rallied for the defense of the republic against the forces of destruction. Then we Germans proceeded with open eyes through the rule of the Brown Terror, the horrors of World War II, and the desperation of total defeat.

Whether we like it or not, we must realize that even twenty-five years after the end of the war, we still have to bear the consequences of Hitlerism. No one who fails to realize this can forge a wise policy for Germany, and anyone who believes himself capable of managing without an emphatic break with the past, will flounder. Neo-Nazism is treason to fatherland and nation.

The world has changed since the days of Weimar, but the foreign policy of the Federal Republic is in large part characterized by the principles of Ebert, Rathenau and Stresemann. Peace, justice and freedom were the basic principles they wanted to have upheld through the vital forces of the German people. Through them, Germany was to assume a fitting place in the world and to carry out a reasonable mission in Europe.

With all due concession to the extent of the defeat and the division of Germany, Germany's foreign policy cannot and must not disregard the moral heritage of the German Resistance either—not to please former enemies, but for reasons of self-respect; not to preserve contradictions within the German people, but to conduct the reconciliation to a clearcut conclusion.

The statesmanlike figure of Friedrich Ebert stands out against the hate laden phrase, "the November criminals." Such men as Julius Leber and Wilhelm Leuschner represent the German resistance to Hitler. And for the self-affirmation since 1945, I nominate Ernst Reuter and Kurt Schumacher.

At all times and in all camps, there have been Germans to be proud of. As foreign minister, I am gratified to recall that members of the German Foreign Service took part in the resistance movement against Hitler. As chairman of the Social Democratic Party, I can state that, even in the time of persecution, my political friends never wavered in their well known national solidarity.

The achievements of Konrad Adenauer are esteemed even by those who opposed him. Yet the position of the Federal Republic on foreign affairs cannot be defined by the first federal Chancellor and his colleagues. Others, and Social Democrats not least of all, played an important role when the issue was to regain confidence in Germany.

In 1952, shortly before his death, Schumacher wrote: "What is at issue is giving the German people a new national consciousness, equally removed from the outrageous arrogance of the past and from the inclination, so widespread today, to see in every wish of the Allies a revelation of European thinking. Only a people that asserts itself can become a valued member of a large community." Today, sixteen years later, there is a great deal of talk in our country about the people's need for a new national consciousness. At that time, during the first postwar years, the bearing of Schumacher and Reuter was often mistakenly thought to be nationalistic. Yet it was, rather, an expression of the feeling of integrity, of personal freedom, and of a sense of the destiny of their compatriots. For these men, the end of the war was a genuine liberation, out of which they won the strength to make requests in the name of a people; the majority of whom felt only defeat. It is now clear how important it was for national self-confidence that those who spoke for the people had intact self-respect.

Those to whom I feel politically close, in the narrower

sense, were standing up for legitimate German interests at a time when others who wanted to jump on the nationalist bandwagon were still busy with insincere confessions of guilt or improbable affirmations of innocence. We knew that the guilt of twelve years of disaster could not be wiped out by the evasion of a common responsibility or by a sort of withdrawal from the nation. In the bitterest hours, we tried to appeal to the good qualities of our people and to liberate the substantial reserves of common sense that had fortunately survived.

National self-awareness is different from arrogance and from the overestimation of one's own value with respect to other nations. It rests on a sure judgment of one's own strength, capacity and virtue—and limitations. To recognize by ourselves the way things are, to know where we stand and where we want to go—that is part of the self-awareness of a mature people. And it can be a source of healing for the inferiority complex that keeps telling us that we are a misunderstood nation.

Just as Konrad Adenauer's name is bound up with France, with the Western European Alliance, and with the Atlantic Pact, so the names of Kurt Schumacher and Ernest Reuter stand for political self-assertion—and not only in Berlin—for the assent of the working class to the Federal Republic, for democratic solidarity, and for the campaign to equate democracy and the nation. One is almost tempted to perceive in this a remarkable dialectic that in domestic politics has led to a situation of intertwined fronts. Nevertheless, in spite of world political developments, independent of German politics and occasionally embittered altercations over foreign policy, the great parties (the Social Democrats and the Christian Democrats) have not wholly drifted away from each other. Our part of Germany had the strength and insight to cross the necessary bridges when, at the end of 1966, there was a question of preserving the essence of the Federal Republic and ensuring it stability and hope for the future in the second phase of the postwar era.

There have been rectifications of the course of foreign policy that can be scrutinized. If nothing had changed, a good deal of the polemics would not only have been superfluous, but incomprehensible to boot. No polemics, however, can change the fact that German foreign policy is geared to one common denominator: the ensuring of peace. This principle means, primarily, a European policy aimed at détente, collaboration, and accord. As long as I am foreign minister and the SPD is the party in power, that will not change.

In a world of exploding technology, of a balance of terror, of convulsive political and sociological changes, it is up to us, as a relatively small federal republic, partly to shield the nation and partly to collaborate on behalf of Europe. Anyone looking backwards will find that arrogance and a blindness that today seems downright incomprehensible to us, have made Germany ever smaller. The Reich had better premises than the Federal Republic for the attainment of the goals of reason. However, the importance of Germany would in any case have decreased even if there had been no Hitler. The war that was begun and lost by the National Socialist destroyers, and their betrayal of European and German unity have caused us to lose, in addition, something that can only partially be compensated for by economic strength.

Firmness in the representation of our interests and principles can help us to conserve both what has been maintained and the results of the reconstruction. But to help rebuild Europe and to determine its own destiny within the framework of a European peace order, what our nations require above all is a sure eye for proportion.

FRANCE-GERMANY: THE PRIMACY OF PROXIMITY

The reconciliation of the French and German peoples is one of the most important realities of the postwar world. It cannot be shaken, nor can anyone in the world maintain that the phenomenon runs counter to his interests. The reconciliation of these two peoples, who have been hostile toward each other for centuries, is anchored in the hearts of the younger generation of both countries and therefore is only conditionally dependent on the relationship between the governments. My conviction of this has been strengthened in many ways during the past few years, whenever I have had occasion to express myself on this theme. People have a feeling that an intimate collaboration between the French and Germans in the Europe of the future will be an abiding element in the consolidation of peace. They realize that friendship with our French neighbors must be one of the primary goals—one of the initial tasks—of German foreign policy in the wholesome spirit of German democracy. After everything we have been through, we must, on both sides, take as our starting point the union of our resources. Both here and there everyone knows that such a union is in our own self-interest, as it is in the interest of the preservation of peace and the welfare of other nations.

. . . We have explained that in our opinion a secure alliance with the United States is necessary for the achievement of European security and its guarantee. We said that Europe, in the midst of organizing itself, could not go on existing back to back with America, but only with a readiness for open cooperation across the Atlantic Ocean. General de Gaulle, like others, foresees a time in which the United States neither would nor could remain militarily present in Europe as it has been during the first two postwar decades. But whereas French policy is bound to appear as though it were consciously striving for a decisive diminution of the American presence in Europe, we interpret our own interests differently; to mean that Europe cannot renounce a close security policy association with the United States. This position would persist—as far as we can see at present—even if a satisfactory European security system were to be developed. Meanwhile, it may become important to strengthen the European component within the Atlantic alliance. Here our hope is that French cooperation within the alliance will be maintained as far as it is possible, for a total withdrawal of France would raise very serious problems. Furthermore a scrutiny of the data of changing world politics would be in the common interest. The joint studies of the world situation and European security in the 1970's, as agreed upon and initiated between Bonn and Paris, may be helpful in that respect.

Only when both countries, in spite of some differences of opinion, stand together—only if they constantly try to find a common approach to the most important problems—will this Europe, which General de Gaulle likes to call the cradle of civilization, be anything more than a geographical concept.

I had met the French President many times, beginning when I was mayor of Berlin. I paid no attention to the black and white impressions that many people had formed of him. To the annoyance of some, I said as much publicly in New York on May 15, 1964:

If we recall President Kennedy's vision, which brought so much hope not to my own city alone, it will become clear to us how remote we still are from the great goals. We still do not have a constructive Atlantic partnership. Instead, we are experiencing signs of crisis in NATO. And instead of a free Europe speaking with a single voice, we hear over and over the cacophonies of a strength-dissipating rivalry.

In my opinion, it is neither sensible nor fair to hold General de Gaulle responsible for all the difficulties we confront in the West. Some of the decisions made by the President of France are not easy to understand, but I have not come to the United States to complain about him. Rather there is cause for us to become aware of the fact that de Gaulle, in his own way, is thinking about the unthinkable with boldness and independence, and has begun to draw conclusions therefrom.

The equilibrium of terror held in balance by the two superpowers creates enough free ground to set the congealed fronts in motion. The President of France is making use of this in his own way. And sometimes I ask myself, as a German: "Why, really, should it be he alone? If we build bridges from the past to the future, it is not obligatory for us to forget the present."

The question of why he alone should do this is to be understood exactly as it was asked. The Americans and the British make use of the relative freedom of movement in their own way. Other states react similarly. And what do we do? The Federal Republic cannot, of course, play possum. Put less colloquially, it cannot give the appearance of having no interest and no will of its own. Hence the question of utilization of the possibility of movement arises for the Federal Republic too.

It was no surprise to me that after the formation of the new federal government there was no difficulty in finding a thoroughly close accord with Paris on questions relative to Eastern policy. Here there was no question of who had to adapt to whom, but rather the fact that German as well as French policy desired a détente, and consequently was bound to be interested in improved relations with the nations and states of Eastern Europe. Both of us, Paris and Bonn, envisage a joint European future; in this respect, German and French interests run parallel. Thus, a trustful and productive exchange of opinion in precisely this area was natural.

But the question has also been raised, understandably, as to why the Franco-German treaty of January 1963 was unable to lead to far more extensive joint political action. Here I must say, first of all, that I was one of those who was not convinced then, that the timing and form of the treaty had been well enough studied. Since then, I have come to the additional insight that the effectiveness of the subsequent consultations has been uneven. It will be necessary to make a point of not allowing a grandiose task to turn into mere routine.

At the beginning of 1965, the German side regarded as necessary, a statement of the federal parliament to make clear that the Franco-German treaty must not diminish or even bring into question the other obligations and political aims of the Federal Republic. This measure of the federal parliament secured the assent of the then Social Democratic opposition to the projected treaty. In fact, such clarification was also in the interest of France—even though official Paris took a different view of it—especially because France has always recognized the special situation of the Federal Republic with respect to its need for security and to the division of the country. It was this clarification that excluded any mistaken interpretation of the treaty as being a special alliance at the expense of other vital interests.

The German Social Democrats have committed themselves as formerly, and especially in the Weimar Republic, to friendship with France. After the last war, the German Social Democratic Party did everything in its power, when in the parliamentary opposition as well as a government party, to promote the reconciliation of the two peoples and to strengthen their collaboration. In the great questions of reconciliation and peace, it is precisely in this area that there is no party monopoly grounded in the accident of government responsibility. Governmental authority has given my political friends and myself abundant opportunity to prove that we are not merely proffering lip service to the unification of Europe and to cooperation with France.

In January 1968, when the Franco-German treaty was five years old, its purpose was certain to be questioned. We realized quite clearly that the treaty had three different designations. The official title is "Treaty Concerning Franco-German Cooperation." In political usage, the designations "friendship treaty" and "consultation pact" have also become common. These wordings undoubtedly, merely reflect different aspects of the same political subject. The practical cooperation that is specifically regulated by the treaty is a visible sign of the reconciliation of the two peoples. In accordance with the will of the signers, the treaty sets the seal on their solidarity. To be sure, there would have been no need for this treaty to bring about the historic fact of Franco-German reconciliation and solidarity. For, as I have already tried to indicate, the population and especially the youth of both nations had already directed its gaze to the future. Basically, the governments were merely realizing what the people were feeling and thinking.

Both governments are committed by the treaty to joint periodical cabinet consultations at relatively brief intervals. The meetings of the heads of government, of the foreign ministers and departmental ministers, together with subsequent plenary sessions—as a whole, all have been fruitful and useful. Of course, if it had been thought that as a result of such meetings alone, a joint policy might come into being, experienced has proved this hope to be unwarranted.

The useful instrument of a treaty cannot be made responsible for the blunders and unfortunate developments that have come about during past years. That does not lessen the value of consultation. In any case, it is important between two neighbors that are so dependent on each other. But that does not mean that governments must make themselves captives of procedures in the sense that their mere practice becomes the criterion of their relations.

At the first meetings that the Chancellor and I had with President de Gaulle, Prime Minister Pompidou, and Foreign Minister Couve de Meurville, a readiness was shown on both sides to fill the treaty of January 1963 with new life. We resolved to intensify our collaboration. Indeed, the economic cooperation between our two countries, including the voting on monetary matters, has made heartening progress. We are striving for further progress in the domains of technology, science and research, and such initial results can be seen as the joint projects of the Grenoble reactor and the television satellite. Others will follow. There has also been progress in joint plans and in political consultation in the area of developmental aid. In all this, it is only natural for us to be concerned also with securing an appropriate economic share for our achievements.

We stand behind the goals of the Franco-German treaty and remain resolved to use this instrument of cooperation and consultation for the good of both countries and for the good of Europe in order to serve peace in the world. As far as we are concerned, the bitter remark that General de Gaulle made a few years ago—to the effect that treaties, like young girls and roses, quickly fade—will not come true. We know that a decisive role for the future of Europe is going to devolve on the development of relations between Germany and France.

THE COURAGE TO SAY YES—
THE WEAKNESS OF SAYING NO

Our policy on Europe must not stand against something; it must stand for something. And it must link itself vigorously to the requirements of the scientific and technical revolutions.

The beginnings of the policy of European unification after 1945 were in point of time and in their political logic partially—yet surely not only—parallel to the growing threat from the East. The initial unification in the West was conceived by many as a consequence of the Cold War. Some people thought that integration was the political rounding off of what had been the military assignment of NATO, with the sole aim of building a dam against communism. In this way, the policy on Europe carried a defensive restrictive or almost negative feeling.

The Cold War of the postwar years lies behind us, but difficult confrontations continue that cannot be overcome by illusions or by becoming prisoners of outmoded formulations of questions. I consider the policy on Europe to be stronger if it is not defined as mere anti-communism. Rather, Europe should be unified for the good of the European people and for their constructive role in the world, and the policy of European statesmen must be harmonized with the long range goal of a European peace order.

Not only the West, but also the East is becoming aware of the importance of pan-European cooperation. Slowly, and hopefully not too late, it will become clear that the cooperation and unification of Europe is not directed against anyone.

Rather, in a dangerous epoch and strife-divided world, it could be an example of how nations and states, regardless of different kinds of governmental and social systems, can achieve prosperity and security by peacefully working together.

Reconciliation and cooperation, which we are striving for between West and East, have already become a fact in Western Europe and will succeed in spite of the above described difficulties. The economic and political unification of Europe is a substantive element of a worldwide peace.

It is true that Europe can no longer consider itself the center of spiritual and economic progress in the world. In disunion, our continent would only sink still further, but in cooperation, it will have a great deal to offer mankind. If that is what we want, we must not only overcome political obstacles, but we must also be prepared to participate in the explosive scientific and technical developments that, in the future, will determine the face of the world.

Europe must not slide into a peripheral position in relationship to the world powers. At one time, steam engines could be built by an individual; airplanes were much more difficult to tackle; and now, space travel has attained such magnitude that it transcends the power of individual European states. Thus, in our modern world, politics can no longer be thought of as independent of the effects of technological progress. These effects to a great extent will determine the future international significance of states and their coexistence. The scientific, technical, economic, and political potential of the individual states is governed today by direct interdependence. The viability of states in the future will depend more and more strongly on their participation in and their contribution to technological progress. The necessity of living up to the effects of technological development touches all the key areas of foreign policy. This factor is as relevant to our efforts on behalf of a peaceful and satisfactory future for Europe as it is to the relationships between industrial countries and underdeveloped countries.

Although the population of the earth is now growing by 70 million people a year, 25 million starve to death every year. The developed countries in the West and the East, despite their well-known conflict, are confronted by the question of whether or not they are capable of making a joint effort against hunger and poverty. Only if such a joint effort is successful, presumably, will they be able to avoid explosive developments in the relationships between North and South.

The population explosion and the scientific revolution are the two great moving forces of our time. The major developments in the future will no longer be derived only from power-political or ideological constellations, but also to a large measure from economic and technological capabilities. If a nuclear war of destruction can be avoided, which every reasonable person must yearn for with every fiber of his being, and if it is true that peaceful nuclear science, space travel cybernetics, and modern biology transcend all ideologies and lead to an objective community of thought, then the political difficulties of our backward present will appear as transitional and capable of solution.

We must look further into the future, for only thus can we gain the confidence that we need to accomplish the tasks of today. These tasks are numerous and hard for us Germans and Europeans. Only in a peaceful, cooperative Europe will the Germans find their place assured. Today we see only the beginnings of such a Europe. But in the Europe of the Six, there are already countries among whom there existed and still exist conflicts of interest—countries which have become so close within a period of a decade and a half that military conflict among them has become inconceivable. One need only think back thirty years to realize that this is a fantastic achievement and not something to be taken for granted, as it may seem to some today. And yet this can be viewed only as a beginning. I have explained why the community must develop far beyond what could have been envisaged in the Treaty of Rome. We are in the midst of a probationary period which this complicated process presents for all the participants. And none should think that we have a lot of time left for it.

An economic community during the coming decade is conceivable only if it is, at the same time, a closely knit community of scientific and technological progress—a community for the coordinated, peaceful exertion of strength. When we learn to think in categories like these, it will be easier to link together enduringly the West of our continent with its East. This progress, which is the only thing that can ensure our common future, must now be thought about and initiated. For this, preconditions must be created within the individual countries, without which the scientific-technical achievements which the future demands cannot be brought forth.

It is precisely ourselves, in the Federal Republic of Germany, who must not succumb to any soothing dreams of the future. It is precisely we who must be clear in our minds that a phase of the history of mankind has begun in which the importance, the weight, and the influence of a country will depend on whether or not it is capable of mobilizing the capital of its talents. We shall have to realize that we still have a research deficit and also an underdeveloped interaction between scientific and political practice. In former years, our means and capabilities were linked up far too much, to the detriment of our research, with short-range defensive thinking. I consider that we must now demonstrate an ambition for scientific and technical expansion; that our society must be put in the position of radically modernizing itself. For the decisive factor in the existence of a people is its I.Q.

It is old-fashioned to think that we are giving ourselves the luxury of too much expensive educational training. It is more accurate to say that we cannot afford to let even one person fail to take advantage of a vocational or college education if he is capable of it. It is a question here of the potential inherent in many families in broad sectors of our populace. The percentage of workers' children among students, in comparison with Western industrial states, is still frighteningly low. We have an untapped reservoir that can be explained by the peculiarities of a slowly changing and excessively heterogeneous school system in different parts of our Federal Republic. Finally, there is also a female reservoir that must be tapped if a mockery is not to be made of all the talk about modernity and equality of rights.

It is also the point of European unification that our continent must be able to link itself swiftly and purposefully to the dimensions of the twenty-first century. If the European communities extend and develop themselves, Europe's role in the world, economically and politically, will be greater. European unification is meant, after all, to serve that consistent policy of peace by means of which the political tensions between East and West can be overcome. We are convinced that the cooperation that the Western European countries have already found themselves ready for, will also be of decisive importance for the relations between Eastern and Western Europe. Western European unification not only is no obstacle for the accommodation of interests, but will prove itself to be a factor that promotes and stabilizes that accommodation.

A CHANGING ALLIANCE

We wish for the consolidation and the further development of the Atlantic alliance in tune with the times. What this calls for is the adaptation of the alliance to the changes in world politics.

We are in the decisive years between two eras in which the course is being laid down for a long time to come. Such a thing happens only rarely at spectacular conferences or in momentous political decisions of principle. It is not always wars, crises and revolutionary movements that determine the course of history. One is reminded of the saying about ideas that come "on the feet of doves" and nevertheless lead the world. This saying may apply to the development of Europe during the last few years, for it came about almost unnoticed.

We cannot speak of cooperation in Western Europe or of securing peace for all Europe without including the North Atlantic alliance in our considerations. Because of the necessary and desired participation of the United States and of Canada, the alliance reaches out beyond Europe, yet its center of gravity and its principal mission lie in Europe. This defense alliance is and remains necessary even though a changing world constantly obliges us to reconsider its goals and its methods and to adapt it to developments. Essentially there is nothing new in this. It applies to all alliances.

It is well known that a number of members of the alliances would like to improve the mechanisms for political consultation and coordination within NATO. This is to be welcomed. We have often made the point ourselves that the East-West policy has as precondition a certain measure of opinion research and communication between the Western partners.

On the other hand, the idea of a "joint policy" within NATO has been turned down, primarily by the French government. It is true that this idea does not involve a joint policy in the literal sense, but there is a divergence of opinion even about the necessity and appropriateness of up-to-date forms of consultation and cooperation. In such circumstances, any insistence on far-reaching claims can scarcely be successful. At the same time, however, all the Allies seem to be in agreement that the goal of our policy must be an enduring and just peace order throughout Europe. By this I mean an order that will eliminate the causes of tension and overcome the division of Europe.

Moving from an alliance that was concluded in a period of intense international tensions and for the purposes of defense against a very specific danger, to a policy of détente, very naturally raises a number of new questions that must be answered. A reduction of the tensions between East and West is useful and desirable, yet our policy aims at something further. It regards as its task the elimination of the causes of tension during a phase of the détente, and the creation of a situation that, as far as human foresight can reach, will offer no grounds for new and dangerous tensions. The period of détente, which we hope will be enduring, is to be used to give European security a solid foundation.

The revolutionary objectives of Soviet policy in Europe have receded. Nevertheless, the influence of ideology on the Communist leaderships in the future must not be underestimated, for it will often distort their analysis of the policies of non-Communist states and societies. More than one conference and publication have, even very recently, sketched a completely warped image of the West and of its political intentions. Such ideological prejudices restrict the readiness for a détente and for cooperation. They are deeply embedded, and it will not be easy to overcome them.

We have built up our state successfully in the hope that a new, free and united Europe would be created; in the hope of a European community in which our nation, with equal rights, and eventually also reunited, would be able to live side by side with the other nations of our hemisphere. It is toward such a Europe that the Germans of the Federal Republic have directed their policy; it is what they are working for. Our participation in Atlantic cooperation has always been related to our European objectives.

The very Constitution of the Federal Republic of Germany permits the transfer of sovereign rights to supranational organizations. The Federal Republic has subordinated all its combat forces to the supreme command of NATO. With respect to its allies, it has renounced the production of atomic, biological, and chemical weapons, subjected itself to restrictions on the production of other weapons, and accepted controls. In order to avoid any misunderstanding, it was unambiguously laid down in the federal government statement of December 13, 1966, that we do not aspire to national control over, nor national ownership of nuclear weapons. Furthermore, the Federal Republic has most earnestly cooperated in the building of the European community, and hopes it will be extended, politically and economically.

In short, we have sought a firm anchoring of the Federal Republic of Germany in the Western alliance. We have closely linked our destinies to the alliance and to the Western European union that is being formed under its protection. This affiliation was all the easier for us because our allies accepted our legitimate national objective: the right of self-determination for our nation, and a peace treaty that would enable the Germans to live under the umbrella of a single state.

The North Atlantic Treaty Organization is first and foremost an effective defense alliance. It prevents potential opponents from being tempted to exert political pressure on any one of the allies through military force. But constant effort is required to maintain this defensive strength in the face of constantly advancing technical developments. We realize that the commitment in Europe is a great burden on the United States and that some of its citizens feel it is too heavy. It is understandable to ask why a reduction of the burden should not be possible. It will become possible only when the East-West situation permits it. But I am afraid that the time for any significant lightening of the United States' burdens has not yet come.

The Atlantic alliance, for the reasons already pointed out, is not summed up by a military assignment. NATO was supposed to be simultaneously an instrument of political cooperation and of an understanding between governments that shared the same fundamental convictions. This goal does not prevent different governments from having different views of different problems, for tensions are characteristic of an alliance of free states during changing international constellations. What is at issue is a constant and at times painful process of adaptation. It is important to carry out the necessary adjustments, and simultaneously to maintain and further develop the alliance.

To me, the Atlantic alliance, European unity, and German-French amity have a logical and equally important relationship. The existence of difficulties and delays only indicates how large and how important our problems are. We do not live in a world of pat solutions.

The Federal Republic, I said as early as December 1966, before the council of NATO in Paris, will not evade discussions based on mutual confidence, aimed at a reform of NATO during the coming years. It wishes to contribute toward a policy of détente between the states of the Warsaw pact and those of the North Atlantic pact, while opposing any danger to the security of any country. The Federal Republic of Germany is no obstacle to the peaceful, secure future that is to the interest of us all. Nor shall we, in this respect, allow ourselves to be led astray by the aggressive speeches made against us by Communist leaders in their own countries, in neutral states, and in the countries of our allies.

NATO and a policy of détente are not mutually exclusive alternatives. On the contrary, the existence of NATO—that is, its political weight and its readiness to defend our territory against all attacks—has shown that a policy of tensions and crises is of no avail. The weakening of NATO would reduce the possibility of a détente and lessen its effectiveness. The military deterrent has ensured peace in Europe. It would be frivolous to encroach upon it and to risk losing what has been achieved.

Our policy of détente is not to be understood in the sense of underestimating and neglecting the vital importance of the Western alliance. On the contrary, we have warned against allowing the bilateral attitude in East-West relations to grow out of hand. In place of that, we have worked toward having the alliance as a whole take a stand with respect to new tasks.

GERMANY AND THE SOVIET UNION—
BEGINNING OF A DIALOGUE

In addition to economic and cultural relations between Germany and the Soviet Union, we hope for an improvement of the political relationship between us. Because it would not be realistic to expect an abrupt and fundamental change, we are exerting ourselves to attain an understanding step by step.

Obviously the special importance of the Soviet Union is rooted in its position as a world power, and for us, to be sure, also in its position as one of the four powers that still bear responsibility for the problem of Germany. It was no accident that in December 1966, the Soviet Union was mentioned first in the foreign affairs section of the government statement. It is no contradiction to acknowledge the Soviet Union as the leading Communist and East European power, and at the same time to take cognizance of the differentiations within the Communist world. But we are going out of our way to be fair to the role of the Soviet Union, and not to give it the impression that we are speculating on differences of opinion within the Communist camp.

Thus we have renounced taking the initiative concerning relations with the People's Republic of China. Nor have we pursued the possibility of formalizing our far from insignificant trade relations with China.

In any case, it is easy to figure out that we would not be so foolish as to implicate both world powers simultaneously concerning our relations with China.

This does not necessarily mean it might not be in the interest of a peace policy if China collaborated with the family of nations. A possible later settlement of our relations with the People's Republic of China will, however, have to avoid disturbing our relationships with friendly Asian governments, primarily Japan, and with the United States, as well as avoid arousing Moscow's suspicions that we might wish to exploit the Soviet Union's difficulties with China.

The Union of Soviet Socialist Republics has grown to be a world power, but the Soviet world power remains at the same time a European power. In the international situation of rivalry with the United States; of potential conflict with China; of incipient unification of Europe; and of insecurity in other parts of the world that constitutes a challenge the political intervention, the Soviet leadership has shown little or no inclination to give up power positions, even if in so doing it could secure new, better, and safer relationships. This, in essence, is what has characterized Soviet policy in Europe since the earliest postwar years. European developments have seemed acceptable to the Soviet leadership only insofar as they consolidate its power position. But détente without the reexamination of power positions is a dubious undertaking.

For us Germans, the rigid clinging to the status quo is particularly difficult because it does not open up any prospect of overcoming the division of Germany. For Europe as a whole, the present state of division cannot be final either. It is difficult to harmonize the rigid Soviet positions with the properly understood interests of Europe, which has a right to its own, peacefully secured existence, as Europeans are becoming increasingly aware. An accommodation of interests will not be easy, but it must be sought most tenaciously.

There will be no swift transformation of the European situation. Every sensible foreign policy in this connection must take into account a time factor. But it would be a grave mistake for anyone to regard Europe as the petrified excrescence of two spheres of power. It is a living community of peoples and states. And the transformation that some wish for and others would like to stop, is already making itself manifest.

It is making itself manifest in the West. It is also manifesting itself in the East, where the Warsaw pact has long since ceased to be the conspiratorial community of ideologists that wrongly advised propagandists still insist on seeing. This reference is not to be construed as a way of setting up artificial contradictions between the Soviet Union and the Eastern European states allied with it. It would be foolish and shortsighted, and for that matter, futile, for our policy to speculate on such contradictions. We are not going to try to play one off against the other. We must accept the fact that there is a far-reaching community of interests between the Soviet Union and its allies in Eastern Europe. But the uniformity of the Stalin era belongs to the past. Ideology has failed to extinguish national identities. On the contrary, ideology is increasingly influenced by changed national data and the requirements of the people.

In this age of transition—and against the background of the partition of Germany—it is a difficult enterprise to bring about good relations with the Soviet Union. A great deal of patience is required. We do not wish either our patience or our good will to fail. We owe that to Europe and to our own country. Our democratic Europe must and will oppose the Soviet Union if and for as long as it tries, by pressure or by other methods, to make its own ideas of state and social order an article of export and thus involve itself in other people's internal affairs. But our democratic Germany can be, and the German people would like to be a sincere friend of the Soviet Union. To this it might be added that greatness is also capable of showing greatheartedness. It is not that we are begging for this, but a Soviet Union that would respect the vital rights of the German people would not have to be afraid—and not only because it is powerful—of the German people. And we, those Germans of good will—that is, the great majority—want to see to it with equal concern that no danger of war can ever again arise on German territory.

The face of the Soviet Union has been transformed during

these past fifty years; the fact of Germany, too. What has remained unchanged is the geography that has made the people of the Soviet Union and of Germany indirect but close neighbors, and keeps them neighbors (always taking into consideration the vital rights of the Polish people). We have clearly explained that according to our understanding of history, the Polish people should have their borders assured.

The German foreign minister is not in a position to threaten, nor would this be appropriate to his character. I am merely making a statement based on experience when I say that it is not good—it is not wise—to allow a great people in the center of Europe to continue under the tension of its unnatural fragmentation. I am realistic enough to know that the national unity of the German people—the isolated realization of its right to self-determination—is not, today, on the agenda of practical politics. Only through the unfolding of a historic process will both portions of Germany be brought closer to each other and linked together; and that process revolves around Europe. But one must desire this process, envisage it, and begin it. That process is in the German interest, but it is also just as much—I am deeply convinced of this—in the interest of the Soviet Union and in the interest of all our neighbors, to envisage a peace that is secure beyond all need for precautions; beyond any desire for disturbing changes.

Today there are many contacts between the countries of Western and Eastern Europe. Although for a variety of reasons Germany's starting point was more difficult than that of others, the German government is vigorously striving to promote such relations. Meanwhile, we have emphasized again and again that we do not wish to isolate any state—including the other part of Germany.

Our assertion that relations with the Soviet Union occupy

a special priority in our considerations corresponds to the realities and to history. We have said to the Soviet Union that we are prepared at any time to initiate a discussion of all the substantive questions in our relations. We are well aware that such a phase of serious dialogue requires time.

The government of the Soviet Union knows that we are ready for an exchange of statements renouncing the use of force. Of course we do not wish to evade any question whose discussion is of concern to the Soviet Union.

I know that the Soviet Government does not want to talk about Germany unity for the time being, but I believe it does want to discuss peace in Europe. So do we. In details, our opinions may still differ considerably, but no one who takes the trouble to have a discussion with us will be able to hurl the cheap reproach that we are militaristic and revenge-minded. In reality, everyone knows that we include the DDR (East Germany) and the problematic question of the partition of Germany in our offer to renounce force.

As soon as the possibility arises out of any discussions with the Soviet Union, however difficult, problems will also manifest themselves in the West. The secrecy-charged atmosphere that made the word "Rapallo" a symbol and a nightmare to Western statesmen was, and obviously is still to this day, hard to eradicate. In that treaty we ended the state of war with Russia. It included economic cooperation and a most-favored-nation clause, and formulated a mutual renunciation of war indemnities. Many who talk about Rapallo do not know this. The contents of the treaty show, in contrast to today's situation, that these cannot be repeated, notwithstanding any fundamental changes in the world. Its essence— the restoration of normal and, if possible, friendly relations between Germany and the Soviet Union, remains a task that cannot be performed by any single feat of sudden dramatic nature. It demands tenacity and intense, quiet work, but also the readiness of the Soviet Union to join with us in examining such a course.

I am well aware of the encumbrances of the past. But I cannot accept attempts made to force the Federal Republic into a corner where it does not belong. The German people and the federal government want peace. I believe the governmental responsibility of the German Social Democrats offers an additional guarantee.

I have never for a moment believed in any rapid improvement of our relations with Moscow. Of course I also did not expect the government or the Soviet Union to identify itself to the extent it did with the hostile attitude of East Berlin toward the government of the Great Coalition. In December 1966, for instance, there was still no indication that Moscow would set up as many obstacles to the establishment of diplomatic relations with the Eastern European states as proved to be the case. There is some reason to think that the exaggerated polemic was supposed to serve as an instrument for holding the Warsaw pact together—incidentally, not with complete success. Its connection with events in other parts of the world, primarily in Vietnam, is also bound to come to mind.

We have not let ourselves be deflected, either by cross-fire from abroad or by a lack of understanding in our own country, from seeking an objective dialogue with the Soviet Union. I will not be made to deviate from this goal, nor shall I let myself be deflected from energetically continuing a dialogue which was initiated with so much difficulty, as purposefully and as intensively as possible. It is well known that big advances cannot be achieved swiftly. The terrain must be prepared, and for that, there must be favorable circumstances and necessary intervals of time.

THE POLICY OF DÉTENTE—MENDING THE BRIDGE
BETWEEN EASTERN AND WESTERN EUROPE

The primary goal of our policy on Eastern Europe is to arouse confidence and eliminate distrust. As we once had to do in the West, we must now, under more difficult preconditions, pay off the mortgages of the past in the East. Our Eastern policy, starting from the given circumstances of today, is intended to help overcome the division of Europe. Consequently, we are particularly concerned with demonstrating the peaceable nature of our means and ends. Statements renouncing the use of force can contribute to this.

In January 1967, we established diplomatic relations with Rumania on the occasion of Foreign Minister Manescu's visit. About the same time, East Berlin and Warsaw, supported by Moscow, succeeded in hampering our conversations concerning the establishment of diplomatic relations with other Eastern European states. The conclusion of the friendship treaties of East Berlin with Poland, Czechoslovakia, Hungary and Bulgaria does not, to be sure, bar the initiation of diplomatic relations with us, but it means a postponement of the course of normalization.

German policy with respect to Eastern Europe nevertheless showed a positive balance at the beginning of 1968. After the exchange of trade representations with Czechoslovakia, we now figure in all Eastern European states except Albania. We are the most important Western trading partner there, and all possibilities of economic cooperation have not been exhausted. Cultural exchange with most of our neighboring Eastern states is growing. In this connection I should not like to omit mention of the fact that the Federal Republic publishes by far more Eastern European literature than any other Western country.

In a number of capitals there is, as we know, a fundamental wish for political talks and the readiness not only to normalize relations but to improve their nature.

It can be stated that an important result of our endeavors and of the support of our friends is that no one who maintains that the Federal Republic of Germany is a mischief-maker or an obstacle to détente will be believed. Here we are in the midst of a genuine change of climate. The accusations that the federal government is preparing an act of aggression; that it is imperialistic; that it is jeopardizing the peace, and similar remarks—all such charges pass into a void. Anyone who advances them loses his credibility.

Furthermore, we have never thought we could carry on an active Eastern policy and a successful policy of détente at the expense of alienating the West. Anyone who interprets foreign policy in terms of swinging pendulums misunderstands both its own laws and—in our case—the position of Germany. It was always wrong to interpret the decision of the Federal Republic in favor of Western democracy as a decision against Central and Eastern Europe. I said, in this connection, that in foreign policy there were for me no spoiled darlings, no favorite children, and no stepchildren, but only the vital interests of the state and the nation—above all, the interest of securing the peace. Our Western allies have been urging us—rightly—over and over again during the past years, to contribute to this détente.

After ambassadors were exchanged with Rumania in the summer of 1967, a German-Rumanian accord was signed at the beginning of August for cooperation in technical and scientific domains. This accord was followed by negotiations for deepending economic relations. The conversations I conducted in August 1967 in Bucharest and at the Black Sea—the latter with the Party head, Nicolae Ceaucescu, who has since become president—initiated an untrammeled political dialogue that can be of service to other countries as well. This is an example of a realistic kind of cooperation that pushes solid bridges far beyond the differences of political conceptions.

The agreement on goods and payments exchange and on the exchange of trade delegations between Czechoslovakia and the Federal Republic of Germany in the summer of 1967 was also an interim result of more than ephemeral importance. The initiation of these official relations was particularly important because Czechoslovakia and the Federal Republic of Germany are direct neighbors.

Diplomatic relations between the Federal Republic of Germany and Yugoslavia were broken off at the end of 1957 because Belgrade recognized the German Democratic Republic. The present Federal administration declared that it was concerned with the restoration of diplomatic relations. We were quite clear in our minds about the special, uncommitted attitude of Communist-ruled Yugoslavia. We thought we were aware of the conditions under which its relationship to the Soviet Union, which for years had been so tense, had again been normalized. But above all, we were concerned with being able to work together with this important member of the European community of nations in a policy of détente and in the perspective of a European peace order.

The exchange of ambassadors was no reason for each side to feel triumphant, but it was more than an encouraging sign. The domestic reaction in Germany showed that our people do not hold much with dogmas and formulas that were the motivation for a policy of limited duration; mere accessories unable to withstand the course of evolution.

We had the impression that the governments of Hungary and Bulgaria, as well as that of Czechoslovakia, were concerned with normalization—that is, with the resumption of diplomatic relations. However, these governments thought it correct or timely to take into account the demands of East Berlin and of others. We respected their position and made it clear that in the interim we would work together to improve de facto relations within the framework of the possible.

Official Poland assumed toward our policy of détente an attitude that seemed to be irreconcilable. Although the federal government strongly emphasized its desire for reconciliation, the Warsaw regime seemed uninterested in talks. I will not conceal the fact that the nuances by no means escaped me.

I should like to reaffirm here my clear conviction that the reconciliation of Poles and Germans will someday have the same historical importance as the friendship between Germany and France.

We shall reach the stage when it will be even more obvious than it is today that whether the détente in Europe can be promoted by practical progress, agreements, or accords, will depend on the good will of the leaders of the Eastern European powers—not on the attitude of the Federal Republic. What is a reality is that the federal government is ready for this détente—that it is ready to be taken at its word.

I will not allow myself to be deflected from a path I regard as the right one, either by setbacks or by disappointments. We must cling to the goal of a reconciliation with our neighbors in the East, for otherwise there can be no enduring peace. But in the process, we must not view internal German connections—the relationship to East Berlin—in isolation. There is really a three-fold aim in our Eastern policy: improved relations with the Soviet Union; normal relations with the Eastern European states; and a *modus vivendi* between the two parts of Germany.

The policy of the German government rests on the expectation and the hope that we can create a basis for common interests in Europe while mutually respecting differing social orders. The geographical situation of the German people gives us a special responsibility for this. For centuries, Germany was a bridge between East and West. We are striving to build anew the shattered bridge, better, sturdier, and more reliable.

SAFETY FIRST

In our policy of détente and of the consolidation of the peace, we have been able to count on a large measure of agreement with our allies. That agreement has become clearly apparent in our regular consultations with our French neighbors as well as with the governments of Great Britain, Italy and other European countries. It must be made equally clear, to be sure, that the concrete political agreement between the Western allies and within the Atlantic alliance still leaves something to be desired. I myself have come out rather vigorously for stronger coordination and consultation, and was therefore somewhat startled when at the beginning of 1968 it was rumored—with a reference to "Washington circles"—that we were in favor of unilateral action.

The continued existence of the alliance, its effectiveness, and its further development are necessary from the point of view of a European peace order. There is a good deal of evidence, I am convinced, that an effective European security system could, on a short-range basis, be sensibly based only on agreements involving the two alliances, which would continue to exist.

So that nothing remains unclear: It is of great importance for our foreign policy that our contribution to defense (in the form of the Federal army, the Bundeswehr) correspond to the obligations that have been assumed.

I think it appropriate to say a word here concerning the Bundeswehr. I know things are not easy for it. I am familiar with the objective difficulties of defining a clear defense mission in a constantly changing world situation. The overcoming of this difficulty and of others is not made any easier by the continuing burden of the past on the position of soldiers in our present-day society. It may be said that after the horrors of our recent history, this is no cause for wonder. Nevertheless, I believe that it is time, twenty-three years after the end of the war, to strive for the right sense of proportion here too.

In the bitter years that followed 1945, there was not only the Allied order to demilitarize Germany; even without that there were some who had vowed never again to bear arms. The attitude summed up as "leave me out" never convinced me; yet if it was an error, it was an honorable one. Events have proceeded further, faster, and in a different way than most people could have foreseen. It is simply not accurate now to continue speaking of the dangers of German militarism.

We are faced with many still unsolved tasks. One of these consists of reducing foreign mistrust. Another is to resist energetically the tendency of every army to become a state within the state. A third is to provide the social equivalent, by means of a healthy historical continuity and a just assessment of values, for those demands that developed defense technology imposes on the soldiers. Here, much remains to be done. I assign a high priority to this task. We must not fail in this, for we require an army whose inner strength corresponds to its outer effectiveness.

The federal armed forces are not an end in themselves. They are an indispensable instrument of our defense within the Alliance. Discussing a reform of the Alliance necessarily raises the question of what mission the federal army is to perform.

It would be almost intolerable if our allies substantially reduced their military presence on the continent and then one day took the view that the Bundeswehr was too big. This means that in all future considerations, the overall balance of the Western alliance must be a criterion. In any case, we shall strive for this with vigor.

As for worldwide measures for limitations on nuclear and conventional armaments, the nonproliferation treaty was the center of international interest in 1967.

Although we ourselves are not members of the Geneva Disarmament Conference, we played a not insubstantial role in influencing the draft of a nonproliferation treaty, especially in clarifying the connection between further disarmament measures and the securing of peace. In my capacity as federal foreign minister, I must emphasize here the four-fold self-limitation of the Federal Republic in the nuclear domain:

Renunciation of the production of nuclear weapons.

Renunciation of control of atomic explosive devices.

Recognition of Euratom to control civilian uses of atomic energy.

Support of the principle of non-proliferation of nuclear weapons.

A European peace order must be conceived with the awareness that it is not enough to reduce the massing of military power. What is at issue beyond that, is the reduction of political tensions, the accommodation of interests, the harmony of nations, and the cooperation of states so that solid foundations may be laid for a healthy European future.

But to attain all this, one must make a beginning by blunting military confrontation, and while preserving the security of European peoples and nations, one must mutually reduce armaments and come to agreements on control measures.

It would not, as we know, be realistic to expect a complete solution of European problems either today or in the immediate future. It is, therefore, not very useful now to pursue the idea of a European security conference. One day there will surely also be a conference on questions of European security and the peace order. But it must be well prepared. The time must be ripe for it.

In East Berlin it is considered offensive when we say that a just and enduring solution of the German question must also be found within the framework of a European peace order. This position is said to be a proof that we would like to change existing conditions—a reprehensible goal, it is said, that conflicts with the consolidation of peace. Once again I ask what it means to want to change? Is it not true that all who have serious intentions toward peace and toward Europe must be ready to try to change a few things for the better? All who strive toward this goal wish to replace a dubious security system by a solid one. They want to replace mistrust by cooperation. They want to end the partition of Europe. Renunciation of force, including respect for the borders now laid down in Europe, does not, after all, mean that everything can remain exactly as it is today. Not only is the exaggerated military confrontation in the heart of this continent and on German territory unreasonable, but the Berlin Wall and the Death Strip across Germany are unreasonable, unnatural, and contrary to history.

It must be manifest to our partners that we clearly agree with the policy we have helped to formulate within the Atlantic alliance, and we stand by this policy.

It must be clear to the government of the Soviet Union and to our neighbors in the East that our defense policy does not contradict our striving toward a détente, but is subordinated to it.

A man who, since Kennedy's time, has been responsible for organizing the defense of the United States (and whose immense abilities, now that he is president of the World Bank, can also serve the underdeveloped countries), remarked that in the year twenty-two of the Atomic Age, the world needs no new arms race. What the world needs in this year twenty-two of the Atomic Age is—as he said, and I agree with him—a new race of reason. I can think of no better formula for our policy.

The Hour of Truth

SPEECH ON THE STATE OF THE NATION,
JANUARY 14, 1970
(condensed)

This is the first statement issued by the federal government in the first year of the seventies. It concerns the state of the nation—the situation in our divided fatherland. In truth, we are forced to admit that there is little hope for an early, fundamental change in this divided status.

Nevertheless—or for that very reason—the federal government is obligated to render a yearly report on the state of the nation. This report must necessarily deal with the problem of partition. Thus, it will become clear that we shall never cease to work on the problem, which has been a subject of international political preoccupation since the end of the war, under the label "German question."

I shall not deny that there exist many other problems and difficulties in the two parts of Germany, and of course also within the Federal Republic itself, which demand our attention. Some are of shorter duration, some longer. Some of them are with us constantly and must be dealt with continually.

The federal government has declared, and reemphasizes, that it seeks to be a government of internal reforms. Domestic political problems will continue to be of primary importance, but there will always be periods in which foreign policy considerations dominate or seem to dominate. The agenda of this distinguished House for the next few weeks shows to what a great extent we must and will dedicate ourselves to the domestic problems of our nation and our people.

With regard to our topic for today, it must be noted that twenty-five years after the unconditional surrender of the Hitler regime, the concept of the nation is the bond which unites divided Germany. In the concept of the nation, historical truths and political force are joined. "Nation" embraces more—signifies more—than common language and culture—state and social structure. The nation is based on a people's enduring feeling of solidarity.

No one can deny that in this sense there exists a German nation and that it will continue to exist as long as we can foresee. In its constitution, the DDR also recognizes that it is a part of this German nation.

DIVIDED THROUGH OUR OWN FAULT

We must have a historical and political perspective when we talk about the state of the nation; when we support the

German people's demand for self-determination. History, which caused Germany to be divided through its own fault, will decide when and how this demand can be fulfilled. But as long as the Germans have the political determination not to relinquish this demand, there remains hope that future generations will live in a Germany where political organization will be the result of the collaborative effort of all Germans.

National components will also play their part in the organization of a European peace. But there is a long and difficult road ahead until the Germans achieve self-determination within the framework of such a peace. The length and difficulty of this road should not deter us, if at all possible at this point in history, from achieving organized coexistence between the two states of Germany. The important thing here is the German contribution to an international climate in which, to repeat the words of President Nixon, a transition from confrontation to cooperation will take place.

The federal government has submitted to this distinguished House data concerning evolution of the German question, and concerning domestic German relationships. In preparation is a report which will contain a thorough-going comparison of conditions in the most diverse walks of life, in the Federal Republic and in the DDR. The preparation of this long report has already brought up or verified the realization that the concept known as Convergence Theory is simultaneously true and false. It is true because the exigencies of modern industry in West and East exert pressure for reforms, independent of existing political and social conditions. It is false because the two states of Germany do not automatically develop consecutively. This explains why several technical and scientific projects, as well as management of some structural problems in different areas of both parts of

Germany, point in the same direction. These facts are encouraging.

NO EASY COMPROMISES

Nevertheless, the two national and social orders which have now existed for more than two decades on German soil have completely different and irreconcilable ideas on German unity—on what should be the nature of a common future and how it could be achieved. Let us not delude ourselves that we can escape these arguments, for Germany is not only politically divided, but on its soil there is the confrontation of completely different social systems. On this point we agree with Ulbricht that between our system and the one now in force on the other side, there can be no affinity—no easy compromise.

WE INSIST THAT THE DDR IS NOT A FOREIGN COUNTRY

In my official statement of October 28, 1969, I said, and I reiterate today:

1. No one can convince us that the Germans do not have the right to self-determination like every other nation.
2. The questions raised by the Second World War and the Hitler regime's national betrayal can only be solved through a European peace arrangement.
3. The aim of practical policy for future years is to preserve the unity of the nation by easing the

currently tense rapport between the parts of Germany.

4. It is not only in the German interest to achieve active collaboration via an organized plan of coexistence. It is also meaningful for peace in Europe and for East-West relations.

5. Therefore the federal government offers the Cabinet Counsel of the DDR nondiscriminatory negotiations on a governmental level, with the object of reaching agreements on collaboration.

6. Our readiness to enter into binding agreements concerning mutual renunciation of the use or threat of force applies also to the DDR.

We insist that the Federal Republic and the DDR are not foreign countries to each other.

We further insist that we will not consider valid any international diplomatic recognition of the DDR.

It is absurd for East Berlin polemicists to claim, in this connection, that we wish to make the DDR an "inland Bonn," or force it into the status of a colony.

Furthermore, asking the so-called "cooperative," "peace-loving" forces in the Federal Republic to increase their influence leads nowhere. Neither would it lead anywhere if we asked the cooperative forces existing in East Berlin and in the DDR to lean harder on the dogmaticians and reactionaries of the Left who think their powerful positions more important than peace in Europe.

The federal government will not do these people the favor of getting trapped into counter-polemics. It will actively promote objectively feasible historical developments directed at improving relationships between the two parts of Europe and the two parts of Germany. Both in the East and in the

West, there are those who profit from the split. But the people at large suffer.

In the effort to demonstrate to their own side that they are competent, the DDR requests, among other things, that there be a vote on the draft treaty sent to Federal President Heinemann by the chairman of the council of state, Ulbricht. The most accurate part of this document is the term "draft." But I, personally, would not want to exploit this document for propaganda purposes. We are dealing with a serious matter.

Let me make one thing perfectly clear: A treaty between the DDR and ourselves must not become a smokescreen concealing unchanged circumstances oppressive to humanity. On the other hand, if one toys with the idea of a popular election, as East Berlin propaganda has already tried, then I could envisage different problems than those set forth in Ulbricht's plan.

We are dealing with a remarkable development. The countries signatory to the Warsaw Pact—except the DDR—have, with some reservations, understood that the Federal Republic acted in good faith. They have pointed out that deeds must follow words. We are convinced that this principle should be observed everywhere.

In the DDR there are dominating forces which constantly make new demands. It must be recognized that these forces are exceptionally obstinate. I would like to cite three examples: a) The DDR demands from us diplomatic recognition. The other states of the Warsaw Pact expect us to make treaties with the DDR which naturally would be as *binding* as the ones who have with them. b) The DDR demands that the Federal Republic review the Paris Treaties and reduce, or even discontinue, its obligations under the Atlantic Pact. The Soviet Union and other countries of the Warsaw Pact emphasize that a European Security Conference will be blocked by any party desiring to place on the agenda the reduction or the abrogation of existing pacts. Thus, the question of reciprocal troop reduction does not, for the present, seem topical or expedient.

THE NATO PACT IS NOT UNDER DISCUSSION

I hardly need to stress that neither the Paris Treaties nor our obligations under the Atlantic Pact are under discussion as far as the Federal Republic is concerned.

c) The DDR government explains that twenty years ago, they definitively recognized the Oder-Neisse line as the final border; literally "in the name of all Germans, therefore also in the name of the people of West Germany." I don't know whether this interpretation was very pleasing to the Polish government. Logically, this would lead to the conclusion that Poland's Western frontier is of no interest to us. As far as I know, the People's Republic of Poland does not share this opinion.

I really wonder how much arrogance the Federal Republic and other European states—not only in the West—are going to have to tolerate from the leadership of the DDR. Their know-it-all attitude will not heal Europe. Anyone with a minimum of self-respect and a sense of reality must reject any attempts made in East Berlin to force on everyone else conditions which would not lead to improved relationships in Europe.

At the same time, let me add that political efforts must be made under certain conditions, even if chances for success are slight. The completely negative attitude which our side some-times manifests would be, in truth, an acknowledgement that the German people renounce the regulation of their own affairs. Patriotism demands that we face facts and that we find out again what is *possible*. It demands the courage to face reality. This does not mean that a given reality is considered desirable, or that there is no hope of changing it in the course of time. But honesty, without which no policy can be implemented permanently, constrains us not to make demands whose fulfilment belongs in the realm of illusory wishful thinking. And it obliges us to protect our people from being led to their doom by pied pipers.

I am in favor of the "Hour of Truth" recently mentioned again. This implies saying the same things within this House as are said throughout our land. It means not raising in our countrymen hopes that cannot be realized. It's eyewash to convey the impression that policy should always produce immediately visible results. Respect for the mature citizen requires that difficulties not be kept from him.

UNRENOUNCEABLE POINTS OF ORIENTATION

There must, there can, and eventually there will be negotiations between Bonn and East Berlin. Violent, argumentative exchanges accomplish nothing. We have, however, several unrenounceable orientation points:

1. The right to self-determination.
2. The struggle for national unity and liberty within the framework of a European peace system.
3. The solidarity of West Berlin, without affecting the responsibility of the Four Powers for all of Berlin.
4. The federal government respects and will continue to respect the rights and responsibilities of

the Three Powers concerning Berlin and Germany as a whole. It is not our desire to undermine these rights or allow them to be undermined. They specify obligations for the federal government as well as for the governments of the Three Powers. I have worked long enough in Berlin to know that there are problems too weighty for us which the federal government cannot take on just in order to attain unlimited sovereignty.

Everything we plan vis-à-vis the DDR will not interfere with the above-mentioned rights of the Three Powers. Of course we have begun consultations with the three governments, as is the custom among allies and friends.

Documents known to all of us demonstrate how firmly and by how many ties the Federal Republic is linked to the West and the DDR to the East. I don't intend to do anyone the favor of starting a fruitless discussion about why it happened and who is responsible. Most of us have reached our own conclusions. Historical research will have to deal with some of the other points. The governments must proceed from what *is*—must keep their eyes on what can be done today for the sake of a better tomorrow.

SIXTY PLUS SEVENTEEN MILLION GERMANS

Let us all realize, please, that there are not many people in this world, aside from our nation, who are delighted at the prospect that these 60 and 17 million—these two economic potentials, not to mention the armies—will reunite. But a discussion on this point hardly seems worthwhile at this time.

I just want to explain what I hold to be the truth. National unity still exists. German unity depends on many factors: not primarily on the constitution, but on what we do; not primarily on what is written in agreements, but on the extent to which we win other nations as friends; not on Potsdam, 1945, but on healing the European split in the 70s, 80s, and—if necessary—the 90s. Already in 1955, Professor Hermann Heimpel, with a historian's detachment, made a telling point when he called the attention of the German public to the fact that there existed no ultimate, inherent right to reunification, and that we were confronted with a *process* whose future prospects could be gambled away.

UNIFICATION—ONLY A PROSPECT

German unification is a prospect, neither more nor less. That we do not gamble it away depends on all of us who are politically responsible in the Federal Republic, taking into consideration the limited power of the Republic, the rights of the Four Powers, the interests of all our European neighbors. Our aim must be, as stated by Herbert Wehner, to help the true sovereign—the German people—come into its own.

There exists not just *a* single German question. In discussing Germany, one confronts *several* German questions, which must be differentiated and can no longer be dealt with uniformly as was attempted in the fifties. Today they must be examined one by one, but not out of context, and above all, not in isolation:

The fate of the Eastern provinces and their people—the refugees, those who remained, those who are employed there, and those born there in the interim; the Soviet-occupied Zone which became the DDR; the three Western zones which became the Federal Republic—both no longer provisional arrangements, both of economic importance, both closely associated with one of the two super powers; and last but not least, the reality of West Berlin, part of a Four Power city under the unlimited supremacy of the Three Powers, including, by order of these Three Powers, ties to the economic, financial, and legal system of the Federal Republic and its foreign diplomatic representation.

WHAT ARE THE OBJECTIVES?

Such is the situation, rather tersely outlined. Much more can be said on these problems confronting Germany. In view of this situation, the question arises: What are the objectives of that Germany policy?

The first answer is that we must keep free the liberated parts of Germany, or, as has been remarked, the Federal Republic must acknowledge itself. The second answer is that we make our contribution so that more human rights may be granted and exercised.

DEMOLISH BORDERS THAT SEPARATE

There arises the logical question: How can German policy attain these objectives? No longer by the traditional means of nationalism, but only through agreements with others. In future, there will no longer be political solutions of important problems, other than treaties, security measures or common interests. Important German problems cannot be dealt with nationalistically and traditionally, but only in a step-by-step effort to build a European peace.

What counts is to recognize and to respect realities—truths—but not to accept existing wrongs resignedly; to alter the separatist character of European boundaries.

WESTWARD—MORE ACTIVITY

The federal government declared on October 28, 1969: "It is not in our national interest to stand between the West and the East. Our country needs cooperation and harmony with the West, and understanding with the East." There is only one unified German foreign policy, and no contradiction between our policies toward East and West. An impartial glance at the two-and-a-half months which have passed since the government's statement will verify that this government—in accordance with our natural inclinations—has been much more active vis-à-vis the West than towards the East. I remind you of the NATO meeting; of the defense minister's negotiations in Washington; of the summit conference in The Hague, where Europe regained its perspective. I remind you of the time-consuming and exhausting negotiations which culminated in the Common Market. Also, that the Euratom agreement is safe as of the last meeting of the Union of Western Europe.

It has become clear that we can count on the trust and accord of our friends and Allies during our attempts to achieve a détente with the East. It should surprise no one that developments are watched attentively in another quarter, as the federal government utilizes to the fullest its limited scope for action.

Of course I respect everyone in the Federal Republic who voices his doubts based on honest concern. But I would like it understood that in practical politics there are always areas where methods which were correct yesterday or the day before, can be wrong today. I have no sympathy for zealots who don't care whether their attacks on the government harm the Federal Republic itself. This government will not be misled or turned aside from its straight course by them.

The Federal Republic of Germany is no "wanderer between two worlds." Without the background and the security of reliable friendship and tried-and-true agreements, there could not even exist an active German contribution towards a policy of detente.

At the heart of our policy is the renunciation of force—the basis for improved relations with all of the East European countries. Since the German people as a whole cannot hope for a peace treaty in the near future, the renunciation of force could be the basis for solving specific political problems with various countries of Eastern Europe. We see in the renunciation of force something enduring, for the German people can exercise only a peace policy, as evidenced by our security contribution to the Atlantic Pact. The chairman of the CDU/CSU Party stressed in his statement of January 12: "We have supported the policy of the Great Coalition in the matters of renunciation of force, Poland and the DDR, and we again endorse these German policy objectives." After having heard very differently worded statements in the past, I particularly welcome this statement by the leader of the opposition, in the hope that we have at least the same aims and that differences of opinion on ways and means can be reconciled.

At this moment I can only say that we are having a broad-minded exchange of views with the Soviet Union, aimed at achieving a renunciation of force, and we will pursue it confidentially, as the nature of the matter requires.

The federal government intends, in the near future, to participate in an appropriate exchange of views with the government of the People's Republic of Poland.

CONVERSATIONS WITH POMPIDOU AND WILSON

The federal government's consultations with its Allies also touch on themes other than those of the moment. At the end of the month I shall visit President Pompidou in Paris, meeting with the British premier in London at the beginning of March, and probably pay a State visit to the American President at the beginning of April. We shall talk, among other things, of the proposed conference on European security which the federal government approves in its basic outlines. It must be prepared thoroughly enough to promise certain success for Europe. It can only be successful if all participants take on equal responsibilities within the framework of security.

It should be known that we are actively and constructively participating in the formulation of views on problems of European security, via the Atlantic Pact, including proposals for mutual disarmament, both of conventional and nuclear weapons. Questions of economic and technical-scientific cooperation should be dealt with on levels beyond mere statements of good will. The federal government will initiate or continue an exchange of views with any interested State(s). It would be particularly gratifying if a bilateral renunciation of force would encourage such a European conference and its results, as well as man-faceted bilateral cooperation.

But it should, in any case, be made clear that our participation in such a conference would make no sense if by then there had been no positive indications on the question of the two Germanys. I want to say this in all candor, not as a condition, but as an explanation.

BERLIN TALK WITH MOSCOW

The federal government supports the intention of the Three Powers to hold talks with the Soviet Union on Berlin, the confirmation of its status, and amelioration of its situation. I hope that these negotiations will have good results. These talks might have a good point of departure, since—despite noisy propaganda—none of the powers mentioned wants to change the city's status.

Among the realities are the growing ties between West Berlin and the Federal Republic, and the city's position in our common economic and monetary system. I regard it as an affront to the above mentioned talks when the DDR arrogantly demands for example, that the federal government cease holding work sessions of parliamentary groups or committees of the German Parliament in Berlin.

We have just as much right to be in Berlin as the *Volkskammer*—the "people's chamber," which holds sessions there regularly. Our right to meet in Berlin as members of Parliament or in any other capacity has always been recognized by the Three Powers who, as even the Soviets acknowledge, have the highest authority there.

When I talk about Berlin negotiations, I mean that they should not result in deterioration, but that a détente on Berlin should lead to an improvement in the condition of the inhabitants.

We learned with interest that the governments of Czechoslovakia and the People's Republic of Hungary are interested in improved relations with the Federal Republic. I hope that at the appropriate time, substantive points of contact will result therefrom.

MUTUAL RESPONSIBILITY

The Hungarian foreign minister, Janos Peter, in his interview on German television, expressed an idea with which the federal government is in total agreement. To the question whether historical unity or the current ideological division prevails in Europe, the foreign minister not only affirmed the presence of these two factors, but added a third: Mutual responsibility. He reminded us that the oldest "capitalist" and the oldest "socialist" states are European. "We must show the world that we are ready, in order to avoid the danger of war, to share mutual responsibility in spite of our differences." We heartily concur. We do not deny the contrasts; we do not "prettify" the antagonistic social systems; we see common causes and historical ties. This holds true for our own divided nation as well, with its dual system, which still must show responsibility for ensuring a more secure peace, and take a practical approach to a détente. This responsibility is equally great on both sides—not only in Bonn, but also in East Berlin. There must be action on both sides.

THESE ARE THE FACTS

The Federal Republic remains, through ties and conviction, a Western nation. The DDR remains, through ties and the will of its leadership, a nation of the East. These are the facts. They must not prevent us from organizing coexistence and together attempting to proceed from confrontation to cooperation. In this international objective, there is an important role for the Germans, here as well as on the other side. The federal government is determined to assume its share of the responsibility, with all the ensuing consequences. It will not be deterred from this intent by disturbances of threats or suspicions, wherever they originate. It submits to this test, and puts other governments to this same test of sincerity, reality and the good sense to do what is possible. To accomplish this, with security in mind, is my mission as Federal Chancellor today, as it was long my mission as mayor. It is my conviction that, despite fundamental differences, we must try everything to find ways of living together—coexisting—which, at Harvard in the autumn of 1962, I called a "forced risk."

CONGENIAL RELATIONS

In East Berlin, they took offense when we said that the two German states could not treat each other as foreign countries. That statement has no meaning under international law, they tell us. I don't want to go into that at the moment; rather I say that it has an eminently practical meaning. It represents realities which the other side likes to talk about so much, but which only too often it views one-sidedly. It is a fact that there exist more cordial relations between the people of Leipzig and of Hamburg, than between the people of Leipzig and Milan, or Warsaw. And the relationship of the people of the Steiglitz quarter of Berlin to those of the

Liechtenberg quarter is different from that of the Steiglitz people to those of the sixth *Arrondissement* in Paris.

Is there a Wall down the middle of Paris, London, Prague or Warsaw? Is there a single one of our neighbors who has a bleeding interior boundary such as has been forced upon us, with thousands of shootings and a still unfinished list of fatalities?

SPECIAL RELATIONSHIPS

Why did we speak of special relationships? Not to uphold the concept of guardianship, but neither to sustain the absurdity of our peculiar status. It is easier to travel from the Federal Republic to Czechoslovakia, Hungary and Rumania than to the DDR. Even from the DDR it is easier to travel to those countries than to the other part of Germany. And of course let us not even go into the problems of traveling between West Berlin and East Berlin.

If the leadership of the SED rejected these peculiarities, we would be in complete agreement. In the future, these peculiarities should no longer exist. There are peculiarities inherent in nonrelationships and in negative relationships.

Both German states are not only neighbors, but are parts of a nation with many other common characteristics. What is more natural than to take care of their practical problems as sensibly as possible? We are ready to do that. We are ready to participate in the creation of any agreements that might lead to mutually acceptable regulations in the fields of economics, science, transportation, postal service, culture, sports, information exchange, etc. In this way we would fulfill the need to have the interrelationship of the German states catch up to their relations with outside countries. This must be taken care of before we can establish close rapports as is appropriate for two state systems within one nation.

RELIEF FOR THE PEOPLE

Understandably, the East Berlin regime is concerned about political equality; also about certain abstract formalities. But it must also be understood that the federal government will only agree to discussion on many matters if this also results in concessions for the people of divided Germany. The welfare of the State is worth little if it is not also the welfare of its citizens.

READY FOR NEGOTIATIONS

The government of the DDR says it is ready for negotiations too. We have taken cognizance of this. We are ready, just as with other members of the Warsaw Pact. The federal government suggests to the government of the DDR negotiations on a basis of equality and nondiscrimination aimed at renunciation of the use of force. Now that an exchange of views on the subject is already in progress with the Soviets—not that anything can yet be said regarding a positive outcome—we think it feasible to enter into corresponding negotiations with the government of the DDR as well. These negotiations would offer a good framework within which, in a broad-minded exchange of opinions, we could discuss all the problems important to a harmonious relationship between the parties. Of course one side cannot say "This is my proposal—only it is acceptable." If that should be the attitude of the DDR, we would reject it. We think a settlement would be advanced by a direct exchange of views on related problems of interest to both sides, before proceeding to examination of details. This is the procedure which is now being observed between the Federal Republic and the Soviet Union.

BONN PRINCIPLES

This exchange of views, or these negotiations, whatever you want to call them, can begin soon. Each side must be free to present all the points it wants to discuss. In the near future, I shall present the chairman of the Council of Ministers of the DDR with a proposal in this regard.

The federal government will be guided by the following principles:

a) Both states have the obligation to preserve the unity of the German nation. They are not foreign countries to each other.

b) The generally recognized principles of international law must be followed, particularly nondiscrimination, respect for territorial integrity, the obligation to seek a peaceful solution of all arguments, and respect for the boundaries on both sides.

c) This also includes the obligation not to seek to change by force the social system of the other party to the treaty.

d) The two governments and their delegates should aim for neighborly cooperation, especially the regulation of technical cooperation. This will make it easier for government treaties to be signed.

e) The existing rights and responsibilities of the Four

Powers in regard to Germany as a whole and to Berlin, are to be respected.

f) The attempts of the Four Powers to reach an agreement on a bettering of the situation in and around Berlin, are to be supported.

There could be agreement on other points too. It must be clear that a settlement of the relations between the two parties should not be subject to time limitations. It must include the possibilities of improvement during the era in which these two states exist.

NO FALSE HOPES

Finally, in the name of the federal government, I state that our behavior is guided by a cool and realistic appraisal of the situation. That means that the federal government earnestly desires serious negotiations, and desires positive progress in the negotiations with the Soviet Union, with Poland and the DDR, and with others; that it has no false hopes about the difficulties of these negotiations; that concerning the firm position it holds and will continue to hold, it cannot exclude the possible failure of these attempts, though this is certainly not desired. But the federal government puts itself and other governments to the test of sincerity in its striving for a détente and for peace.

I would like to say a word about the "advances" sometimes used only in quotes. There was a time in the Federal Republic when noteworthy German overtures to the West were considered a proof of special diplomacy and capability. It is indeed noticeable that the Federal Republic achieved good results; confidence in us, equality of rights, and non-discrimination.

WHAT'S IN IT FOR US?

If we have begun after the terrors of the war, to solicit confidence also from the East, this is indeed a huge and difficult task. We would be tempted to label as cowardly and unpatriotic anyone who would ask, regarding this task: "What do you get for it in return?" To make peace more secure for our whole nation—is that nothing? To add to our friendship with the nations of the West, North and South, also the trust, reconciliation, and eventually the friendship of the Eastern nations—is that nothing? And Germany itself—will it not gain more security and a better peace? Will not each and every one of our people profit by it?

In a word: Because there will be less fear—because burdens will be lighter—because people who had not been able to meet for years will be able to see each other again—because, perhaps, two individuals from the two parts of Germany who today are separated by inhuman force, can marry.

These are the standards this government has set for itself—in all sobriety, conscious of the difficulties, the length of the road ahead, the well-calculated risk. This is a task we can face, because we are confident and because we have good friends.

Numbers appearing in the text refer to the following works by Willy Brandt:

[1] From "War Aims of the Great Powers and the New Europe," Oslo, 1940.

[2] From a letter to history professor Dr. Arne Ording, Stockholm, December 27, 1941.

[3] From a letter to Dr. Arne Ording, Stockholm, February 11, 1942.

[4] From the leaflet *War and Peace Objectives*, Stockholm, 1943.

[5] From "After Victory," a discussion on war and peace objectives, Bonniers, Stockholm, 1944.

[6] From an article in the *Lubeck Free Press*, September 7, 1946.

[7] From *Criminals and* Other *Germans*, H. Aschehoug & Co., Oslo, 1946.

[8] From the essay "Toward Our Solution: Socialist Front of the Younger Generation," 1936.

[9] From the article "Five Years of Hitler Rule," Oslo, January 29, 1938.

[10] From the essay "Germany Before and After Munich," December 1938.

[11] From the essay "Toward the End of the First Phase of the War," January 22, 1940.

[12] From the pamphlet *Division or Unity—the Cominterm and the Communist Parties*, DNAs Forlag, Oslo, 1939.

[13] From the pamphlet *Soviet Foreign Policy 1917-1939*, DNAs Forlag, Oslo, 1939.

[14] From the pamphlet *Facts About the Policies of the Communists*, Oslo, 1945.

[15] From a letter to Irmgard and August Enderle, Nuremberg, February 9, 1946.

[16] From a letter to Jacob Walcher, New York–Oslo, April 30, 1946.

[17] From remarks on his appointment as press attache in Berlin, October, 1946.

[18] From a circular to personal and political friends, Oslo, November 1, 1946.

[19] From *Abroad*, p. 13 ff.

[20] Ibid, p. 63 ff.

[21] Ibid, p. 366 ff.

FIRE
KEEPER'S
DAUGHTER

ANGELINE BOULLEY

ROCK THE BOAT

For my parents, Donna and Henry Boulley Sr.,
and their love of stories

A Rock the Boat Book

First published in Great Britain, Ireland & Australia by Rock the Boat,
an imprint of Oneworld Publications, 2021

ISBN 978-1-78607-904-6 (hardback)
ISBN 978-0-86154-090-7 (export paperback)
ISBN 978-1-78607-905-3 (ebook)

Printed and bound in Great Britain by Clays Ltd, Elcograf S.p.A.

Oneworld Publications
10 Bloomsbury Street
London WC1B 3SR
England

Stay up to date with the latest books,
special offers, and exclusive content from
Rock the Boat with our newsletter

Sign up on our website
oneworld-publications.com/rtb

MIX
Paper from
responsible sources
FSC® C018072
FSC
www.fsc.org

*I am a frozen statue of a girl in the woods. Only my eyes move,
darting from the gun to their startled expression.*

Gun. Shock. Gun. Disbelief. Gun. Fear.

THA-THUM-THA-THUM-THA-THUM.

*The snub-nosed revolver shakes with tiny tremors from the
jittery hand aiming at my face.*

I'm gonna die.

*My nose twitches at a greasy sweetness. Familiar. Vanilla
and mineral oil. WD-40. Someone used it to clean the gun. More
scents: pine, damp moss, skunky sweat, and cat pee.*

THA-THUM-THA-THUM-THA-THUM.

*The jittery hand makes a hacking motion with the gun, as if
wielding a machete instead. Each diagonal slice toward the ground
gives me hope. Better a random target than me.*

But then terror grips my heart again. The gun. Back at my face.

Mom. She won't survive my death. One bullet will kill us both.

*A brave hand reaches for the gun. Fingers outstretched.
Demanding.* Give it. Now.

THA-THUM-THA—

I am thinking of my mother when the blast changes everything.

PART I

· · · · · · · · ·

WAABANONG

(EAST)

IN OJIBWE TEACHINGS, ALL JOURNEYS BEGIN
IN THE EASTERN DIRECTION.

CHAPTER 1

I start my day before sunrise, throwing on running clothes and laying a pinch of semaa at the eastern base of a tree, where sunlight will touch the tobacco first. Prayers begin with offering semaa and sharing my Spirit name, clan, and where I am from. I always add an extra name to make sure Creator knows who I am. A name that connects me to my father—because I began as a secret, and then a scandal.

I give thanks to Creator and ask for zoongidewin, because I'll need courage for what I have to do after my five-mile run. I've put it off for a week.

The sky lightens as I stretch in the driveway. My brother complains about my lengthy warm-up routine whenever he runs with me. I keep telling Levi that my longer, bigger, and therefore vastly superior muscles require more intensive preparation for peak performance. The real reason, which he would think is dorky, is that I recite the correct anatomical name for each muscle as I stretch. Not just the superficial muscles, but the deep ones too. I want an edge over the other college freshmen in my Human Anatomy class this fall.

By the time I finish my warm-up and anatomy review, the sun

peeks through the trees. One ray of light shines on my semaa offering. Niishin! *It is good.*

My first mile is always hardest. Part of me still wants to be in bed with my cat, Herri, whose purrs are the opposite of an alarm clock. But if I power through, my breathing will find its rhythm, accompanied by the swish of my heavy ponytail. My legs and arms will operate on autopilot. That's when my mind will wander into the zone, where I'm part of this world but also somewhere else, and the miles pass in a semi-alert haze.

My route takes me through campus. The prettiest view in Sault Ste. Marie, Michigan, is on the other side. I blow a kiss as I run past Lake State's newest dorm, Fontaine Hall, named after my grandfather on my mother's side. My grandmother Mary—I call her GrandMary— insisted I wear a dress to the dedication ceremony last summer. I was tempted to scowl in the photos but knew my defiance would hurt Mom more than it would tick off GrandMary.

I cut through the parking lot behind the student union toward the north end of campus. The bluff showcases a gorgeous panoramic view of the St. Marys River, the International Bridge into Canada, and the city of Sault Sainte Marie, Ontario. Nestled in the bend of the river east of town is my favorite place in the universe: Sugar Island.

The rising sun hides behind a low, dark cloud at the horizon beyond the island. I halt in place, awestruck. Shafts of light fan out from the cloud, as if Sugar Island is the source of the sun's rays. A cool breeze ruffles my T-shirt, giving me goose bumps in mid-August.

"Ziisabaaka Minising." I whisper in Anishinaabemowin the name for the island, which my father taught me when I was little. It sounds like a prayer. My father's family, the Firekeeper side, is as much a part of Sugar Island as its spring-fed streams and sugar maple trees.

When the cloud moves on and the sun reclaims her rays, a gust of wind propels me forward. Back to my run and to the task ahead.

Forty-five minutes later, I end my run at EverCare, a long-term care facility a few blocks from home. Today's run felt backward, peaking in the first mile and becoming progressively more difficult. I tried chasing the zone, but it was a mirage just beyond my reach.

"Mornin', Daunis," Mrs. Bonasera, the head nurse says from behind the front desk. "Mary had a good night. Your mom's already here."

Still catching my breath, I give my usual good-morning wave.

The hallway seems to lengthen with each step. I steel myself for possible responses to my announcement. In my imagined scenarios, a single furrowed brow conveys disappointment, annoyance, and the retracting of previous accolades.

Maybe I should wait until tomorrow to announce my decision.

Mrs. B. didn't need to say anything; the heavy scent of roses in the hallway announces Mom's presence. When I enter the private room, she's gently massaging rose-scented lotion on my grandmother's thin arms. A fresh bouquet of yellow roses adds to the floral saturation level.

GrandMary's been at EverCare for six weeks now and, the month before that, in the hospital. She had a stroke at my high school graduation party. Visiting every morning is part of the New Normal, which is what I call what happens when your universe is shaken so badly you can never regain the same axis as before. But you try anyway.

My grandmother's eyes connect with mine. Her left brow raises in recognition. Her right side is unable to convey anything.

"Bon matin, GrandMary." I kiss both cheeks before stepping back for her inspection.

In the Before, her scrutiny of my fashion choices bugged the crap out of me. But now? Her one-sided scowl at my oversized T-shirt feels like a perfect slap shot to the top shelf.

"See?" I playfully lift my hem to reveal yellow spandex shorts. "Not half-naked."

Halfway through her barely perceptible eye roll, GrandMary's gaze turns vacant. It's like a light bulb behind her eyes that someone switches on and off arbitrarily.

"Give her a moment," Mom says, continuing to smooth lotion onto GrandMary's arms.

I nod and take in GrandMary's room. The large picture window with a view of a nearby playground. The dry-erase board with the heading HELLO! MY NAME IS MARY FONTAINE, and a line for someone to fill in after MY NURSE. The line after MY GOALS is blank. The vase of roses surrounded by framed photographs. GrandMary and Grandpa Lorenzo on their wedding day. A duo frame with Mom and Uncle David as praying angels in white First Communion outfits. My senior picture fills a silver frame engraved with CLASS OF 2004.

The last picture taken of the four of us Fontaines—me, Mom, Uncle David, and GrandMary—at my final hockey game brings a walnut-sized lump to my throat. I went to sleep many nights listening to Mom and her brother laughing, playing cards, and talking in the language they had invented as children—a hybrid of French, Italian, abbreviated English, and made-up, nonsensical words. But that was before Uncle David died in April and GrandMary, grief-stricken, had an intracerebral hemorrhagic stroke two months later.

My mother doesn't laugh in the New Normal.

She looks up. Her jade green eyes are tired and bloodshot. Instead of sleeping last night, Mom cleaned the house in a frenzy while talking to Uncle as if he were sitting on the sofa watching her dust and mop. She does this often. I wake up during those darkest hours, when my mother confesses her loneliness and regrets to him, unaware that I am fluent in their secret language.

While I wait for my grandmother to return to herself, I retrieve a lipstick from the basket on the bedside table. GrandMary believes in greeting the day with a perfect red smile. Gliding the matte ruby over her thin lips, I remember my earlier plea for courage. To know zoongidewin is to face your fears with a strong heart. My hand twitches; the golden tube of lipstick a jiggling needle on a seismograph.

Mom finishes with the lotion and kisses GrandMary's forehead. I've been on the receiving end of those kisses so often that an echo of one warms my own forehead. I hope GrandMary can feel that good medicine even when the light bulb is off.

When my grandmother was in the hospital, I kept track of how many times she blinked during the same fifteen-minute window each day. Mom didn't mind my record keeping until she noticed the separate tally marks for LIGHT BULB ON and LIGHT BULB OFF. The overall number of blinks hadn't changed, but the percentage of alert ones (LIGHT BULB ON divided by total blinks) had begun to decrease. My mother got so upset when she saw my tally that I keep the blink notebook hidden in GrandMary's private room now, bringing it out only when Mom isn't here.

It happens. GrandMary blinks and her eyes brighten. LIGHT BULB ON. Just like that, her focus sharpens, and she is once again a mighty force of nature, the Fontaine matriarch.

"GrandMary," I say quickly. "I'm deferring my admission to U of M and registering for classes at Lake State. Just for freshman year." I hold my breath, anticipating her disappointment in my deviation from the Plan: Daunis Lorenza Fontaine, MD.

At first, I went along with it, hoping to make her proud. I grew up overhearing people whisper with a sort of vicious glee about the Big Scandal of Mary and Lorenzo Fontaine's Perfect Life. I pretended so well, and for so long, that her plan became my plan. Our plan. I loved that plan. But that was in the Before.

GrandMary fixes me with a gaze as tender as my mother's kisses. Something passes between my grandmother and me. She understands why I had to alter our plan.

My nose tingles with pre-cry pinpricks from relief, sadness, or both. Maybe there's a word in Anishinaabemowin for when you find solid footing in the rubble after a tragedy.

Mom rushes around the bed, pulling me into an embrace that whooshes the air from my lungs. Her joyful sobs vibrate through me. I made my mother happy. I knew I would, but I didn't expect to feel such relief myself. She's been pushing for me not to go away to college, even encouraging Levi to pester me about it. Mom pleaded with me to fill out the Lake State admissions form back in January as a birthday gift to her. I agreed, thinking there was no way anything would come to pass. Turns out, there was a way.

A bird thuds against the window. My mother startles, releasing me from her grip. I only get three steps toward the window when the bird rises, fluttering to regain equilibrium before resuming its journey.

Gramma Pearl—my Anishinaabe nokomis on my Firekeeper side—considered a bird flying into a window a bad sign. She would rush outside, one leathered brown hand at her mouth, muttering "uh-uh-oh" at its crooked neck before calling her sisters to figure out which tragedy was just around the corner.

But GrandMary would say it was random and unfortunate. Nothing more than an unintended consequence of a clean window. *Indian superstitions are not facts, Daunis.*

My Zhaaganaash and Anishinaabe grandmothers could not have been more different. One viewed the world as its surface, while the other saw connections and teachings that run deeper than our known world. Their push and pull on me has been a tug-of-war my entire life.

When I was seven, I spent a weekend at Gramma Pearl's tar-paper house on Sugar Island. I woke up crying with an earache, but the ferry to the mainland had shut down for the night. She had me pee in a cup, and poured it into my ear as I rested my head in her lap. Back home for Sunday dinner at GrandMary and Grandpa Lorenzo's, I excitedly shared how smart my other grandmother was. *Gramma Pearl fixed my earache with my pee!* GrandMary recoiled and, a heartbeat later, glared at my mother as if this was her fault. Something split inside me when I saw my mother's embarrassment. I learned there were times when I was expected to be a Fontaine and other times when it was safe to be a Firekeeper.

Mom returns to GrandMary, moving the cashmere blanket aside to massage lotion on a spindly, alabaster leg. She's exhausting herself looking after my grandmother. Mom is convinced she will recover. My mother has never been good at accepting unpleasant truths.

A week ago, I woke up during one of Mom's cleaning frenzies.

I've lost so much, David. And now her. When Daunis leaves, j'disparaîtrai.

She used the French word for "disappear." To fade or pass away.

Eighteen years ago, my arrival changed my mother's world. Ruined the life her parents had preordained for her. I am all she has left in this world.

Gramma Pearl always told me, *Bad things happen in threes.*

Uncle David died in April.

GrandMary had a stroke in June.

If I stay home, I can stop the third bad thing from happening. Even if it means waiting a little longer to follow the Plan.

"I should go." I kiss Mom and then GrandMary goodbye. As soon as I leave the facility, I break into a run. I usually walk the few blocks home as a cooldown, but today I sprint until I reach my driveway. Gasping, I collapse beneath my prayer tree. Waiting for my breath to return.

Waiting for the normal part of the New Normal to begin.

CHAPTER 2

Lily's Jeep screeches into the driveway. Wearing all black as usual, my best friend hops out so I can climb into the back seat. Granny June sits in the passenger seat, headscarf tied under her chin, dark brown eyes barely peeking over the dashboard. Between tiny Lily and her great-grandmother, it's a wonder either can see the road.

Lily's been my best friend since sixth grade, when she came to live with Granny June. We look like opposites, and not just because of our height difference. I am so pale, the other Nish kids called me Ghost, and I once overheard someone refer to me as "that washed-out sister of Levi's." When Lily lived with her Zhaaganaash dad and his wife, they kept her out of the sun so her reddish-brown skin wouldn't get any darker. We both learned early on that there is an Acceptable Anishinaabe Skin Tone Continuum, and those who land on its outer edges have to put up with different versions of the same bullshit.

Lily's smile is outlined in glossy black lipstick. It grows wider as she takes in my outfit—jeans paired with one of my dad's hockey jerseys extending to mid-thigh.

"Lady Daunis in her finest gown. It's my pleasure to drive thee." She bows.

I grin, and it feels like when I slip off a backpack loaded with all my schoolbooks.

"I should sit back there. Too much work for you," Granny June says, watching as I flip the driver's seat forward and wedge my nearly six-foot-tall frame into the back. "Like seeing a baby crawl back into the womb." She says this every time we both hitch a ride with Lily.

"No way, Granny June, you're the best copilot."

You do not make an Elder accommodate you. You just don't.

We often drop Granny June at the Sault Senior Center on our way to work, depending on what's for lunch. She compares the monthly menus for the two senior-citizen lunch programs, monitoring them as closely as bingo cards during the cover-all. If Granny June thinks the Zhaaganaash are getting a better meal, she makes Lily drop her off at the Sault Senior Center downtown. Otherwise, a tribal van picks her up for the ferry ride to the Nokomis-Mishomis Elder Center on Sugar Island for lunch and social activities.

"Did ya do it?" Lily gives a knowing glance in the rearview mirror.

"Yup."

"Did ya use protection?" Granny June says. We all laugh, and as Lily turns a corner too quickly, even her tires add a squeal.

"No, Granny," Lily says. "Daunis told her ma and grandma about not going to U of M. It's official . . . Lake Superior State University, baby!" She does a high-pitched trill out the window, which startles a few tourists on the sidewalk. Lily's tried and failed to teach me how to lee-lee, which some Nish women do to call out an accomplishment.

Granny June turns to look at me and scowls. I wait for her to tell me to sit up straight. It's what GrandMary would say.

"My girl, some boats are for the river and some are for the ocean."

I think Granny June is right. I just don't know which one I am.

Lily gives me a sympathetic look in the rearview mirror. In science, a mixture has two or more components that don't join chemically. Like oil and vinegar. Lily knows it's how I feel: sad about not being in Ann Arbor, yet glad to share freshman year with her. Both feelings existing separately but swirling around together inside me.

We drive past gift shops along one side of the street. The other side follows the river, where a crowd of tourists watches a thousand-foot-long freighter pass through the Soo Locks.

I remember when we went to downtown Ann Arbor and took the campus tour last fall. GrandMary's enthusiasm contrasted with Mom's annoying questions about crime rates. Uncle David—who rarely sided against my mother—insisted that I needed to earn my degree far from home. But to me the University of Michigan meant more than just an education. It was freedom from the gossip that has surrounded me my whole life.

Daunis Fontaine? Wasn't her dad that hockey player, Levi Fire-keeper? He was one of the few Indians from Sugar Island with potential.

I remember when he knocked up Grace Fontaine. Richest, whitest girl in town.

Didn't he booze it up at a party on Sugar Island and crash his car with her in it?

What a shame when he broke his legs in the crash! Just when the scouts were coming around. Ended his hockey career.

Mary and Lorenzo sent their daughter to stay with relatives in Mon-treal, but when she came back with a three-month-old baby girl, Levi was married to someone else and had Levi Jr.

I heard mousy Grace stood up to her parents when they tried keeping that baby girl from Levi and all those Indian relatives.

Oh, and then there was that terrible tragedy . . .

We pass a billboard that usually advertises the Superior Shores Casino and Resort, but for the past month, the Sugar Island Ojibwe

Tribe has encouraged enrolled members to vote in today's Tribal Council election. Last night, someone graffitied it, changing one letter to make it read: VOTE! IT'S YOUR TRIBAL ERECTION.

"I'd vote for that," Granny June says. Lily and I crack up again.

Then Granny rants about how it doesn't matter who gets elected because they end up serving themselves better than any of the members.

"Now, when I die, yous gotta promise to get Tribal Council to be pallbearers at my funeral"—she pauses for dramatic effect—"so they can let me down one last time."

I laugh along with Granny June. As usual, my best friend just shakes her head.

"Teddie should've run," Lily says. "She would've cleaned up, hey?"

My aunt Teddie is the smartest person we know. She's so badass. Some rabble-rouser tribal members want Sugar Island to declare its independence from the United States. If they ever got Auntie onboard with their half-baked plan, Operation Secede might actually happen.

"Eh, Auntie says she can make a bigger impact as Tribal Health director," I say.

Granny June chimes in. "She'd never win, same as me. Teddie tells it like it is. Voters want pretty lies over ugly truths, hey?"

Lily nods, even though neither of us is eligible to vote in a tribal election because we're not enrolled.

"Listen to me, my girls," Granny June says. "Strong Ojibwe women are like the tide, reminding us of forces too powerful to control. Weak people fear that strength. They won't vote for a Nish kwe they fear."

Now I'm the one nodding along to my Elder's truth.

When we arrive at the Sault Senior Center, Lily does her unique method of parallel parking, pulling in nose first until she taps the rear bumper of the car ahead. We both climb out to help Granny June. She pauses before entering the center.

"Me and Teddie got skeletons in the closet. Slept with too many of their men." Her chin juts defiantly. "Well, that and our felonies." Lily and I give each other wide-eyed looks as Granny June waves us off.

Back in the Jeep, we burst into peals of laughter.

"Holy shit," Lily says. "I know Granny June's got a past, but do you think it's true about Teddie having felonies?" She reverses into the bumper of the car parked behind us and then merges into downtown traffic.

"Auntie says all those stories about her 'youthful shenanigans' are bull."

"Speaking of shenanigans, we set for tomorrow?" Lily asks as we head toward the Tribe's satellite reservation on the mainland.

"Yes. We need to celebrate," I say, focusing on the positive part of my decision.

"You were so worked up about telling GrandMary. How'd she react?"

"She, um . . . she let me know it's okay." I am touched again by that moment between my grandmother and me, when I realized she saw the situation clearly and that she understood.

"See? You always worry for no reason," Lily says.

We reach Chi Mukwa Arena. There are two polling locations for today's Tribal Council election: one here at the community recreation facility and one at the Elder Center on Sugar Island. Cars already line both sides of Ice Circle Drive. Lily bumps over the curb to park on the grass.

She catches me scanning the lot for any tribal cop cars. Lily's creative parking skills always attract police attention.

"Have you seen TJ yet? Do we really gotta call him Officer Kewadin?" She shudders. "You didn't invite him to the party, did you?"

"No. I did not invite a tribal cop to our party," I say, all peeved. "I'm not the one who gets back with my ex every other week."

Lily eyeballs me coolly. Her mouth twitches, but she stays silent. Just as we reach the front row of cars, she slaps my back. Hard.

"Ow! What the hell!" I turn to see my best friend looking all innocent.

"What? You had a black fly on you the size of a hummingbird." This time, she grins.

We crack up. Our laughter is as bubbly as I feel, knowing that everything will be okay.

A gauntlet of tribal members wave campaign yard signs for their favorite candidates as voters enter Chi Mukwa to cast their ballots. One lady perks up when we approach and offers us a plate of home-made cookies.

"They're not enrolled," her sidekick announces coldly.

The cookie lady sets the treats back down and impassively calls out, "Have a nice day."

We are descendants—rather than enrolled members—of the Sugar Island Ojibwe Tribe. My father isn't listed on my birth certificate, and Lily doesn't meet the minimum blood-quantum requirement for enrollment. We still regard the Tribe as ours, even though our faces are pressed against the glass, looking in from outside.

"As if we wanted their moowin cookies," Lily mutters, sounding exactly like Granny June.

I don't mention how we both licked our lips at that plate.

The lobby is packed. Voters line the hallway to the volleyball-court-turned-polling-location. Parents drop off their children for the Niibing Program. The summer recreational program provides full-time childcare for kids who need supervised activities intended to tire them out, but is way more effective at exhausting us group leaders.

Just before we part ways to join our different groups, Lily nudges me.

"Later, gator."

"After while, *Crocodylus niloticus*."

We do our special handshake: high five for the tall girl, low five for the shorty, elbow touch, Hacky Sack foot bump, and palm forward to lock thumbs for the butterfly-flutter finale.

"Love ya, geek!" Lily always gets the last word.

CHAPTER 3

When it's time for our last activity of the day, I bring my group of nine- and ten-year-olds to the locker room to put on sweatshirts, hats, and gloves for open skate. I turn it into an Ojibwe language lesson, naming each item in Anishinaabemowin as I put it on.

"Naabikawaagan," I say, wrapping my scarf around my neck as we step onto the ice.

"Hey, Bubble!" Levi shouts my least favorite nickname across the rink.

On Friday afternoons, the Sault Ste. Marie Superiors skate with the kids. The Supes are an elite Junior A league team, a stepping-stone for guys hoping to play at the college or professional level. GrandMary refers to the Supes as a "finishing school" for hockey players.

My younger brother, who will be a high school senior, was made team captain in only his second year on the team. In Michigan's Upper Peninsula, the Supes are regarded as hockey gods—which makes Levi like Zeus, possessing something special that transcends even natural talent and hard work.

We look nothing alike. I'm the spitting image of our father. But where Dad's facial features were proportional to his large frame, mine are like caricatures. Levi resembles his mom, right down to the dimples, bronze skin, and long eyelashes. Dad was a hockey god, so Levi lucked out there, too. Plus, my brother can be charming, especially when he wants something.

Levi and one of the new Supes are skating with the five- and six-year-olds, which include my six-year-old cousins Perry and Pauline.

"Auntie Daunis!"

I love when my twin cousins call me "Auntie." I ditch my group and skate over to them.

"Auntie, did you know today is Friday the thirteenth?" Pauline sounds like a teacher.

"Uncle Levi says bad luck is just made-up horseshit," Perry chimes in.

I imitate Pauline's schoolmarm tone. "Levi, did you know that responsible aunts and uncles don't swear around young, impressionable minds?" The Supe next to Levi snickers. "See, New Guy knows what I'm saying."

"It's Jamie," New Guy says. "Jamie Johnson."

"Eh. Let's see what you bring to the team before I learn your name," I say.

OutKast's "Hey Ya!" blasts over the rink sound system as I take off my extra-long scarf. Perry and Pauline latch on to the ends, and I pull the twins around the rink.

Dad used to do this with Levi and me—a kid on each end, with the middle of the scarf around his waist like a harness. My dad's scarf was jade green, the same color as Mom's eyes. Perry pleads to go faster. That girl is happiest on warp speed, with her long blue-black hair fanning behind her like jet vapor condensation trails. Impulsively, I double back to Levi, digging in my hockey skates for four quick lateral pushes. Enough to make Perry squeal but not get Pauline rushed out.

Just before I reach my brother, I halt with a quarter turn. My hockey blades shear the ice. The shavings hit Levi and New Guy. I flash a grin as they jump back a second too late. Levi is amused, but New Guy's jaw drops with something like shock and awe.

I check the twins' trajectory. Perry tries mimicking my stop. She falls over but pops right back up. Pauline keeps going until she bounces off the dasher board and lands on her back. I'm certain she's okay, but I skate over anyway. New Guy follows me.

When I reach her, Pauline looks up at me, breaking into a jack-o'-lantern grin. Her beautiful face is the darkest amber—a perfect and precious deep golden brown. She flaps her mittens at me.

"Pick me up!" she pleads.

I remember how, as a kid, I once fell hard, my helmet smacking the ice. Dad was at my side in an instant, deep voice booming, *N'Daunis, bazigonjisen!* I scrambled to stand while my eyes saw stars. *That's my girl!*

Whenever I fall, my dad's voice is the thunder following the crack of lightning, telling me to get back up.

"Eh, you're fine," I say.

She squeals with delight when New Guy helps her up.

"You should've let her lie there like a slug till she freezes," I tell him. I try not to smile when he spins Pauline on the ice and laughs along with her. People are watching and I'm not giving the gossips anything to comment on.

I look around for Lily. She's surrounded by preschoolers inching forward with their colorful plastic skate helpers. She makes eye contact, as well as a lewd gesture with her hand and tongue. Clearly, Lily agrees with everyone who's been yammering nonstop about the new Supe since the team for the 2004–2005 season was announced a week ago.

Jamie Johnson is crazy hot.

Jamie Johnson's scar makes him look mysterious.

Isn't it too bad that Jamie Johnson has a girlfriend back home? Yeah, that won't last.

And, worst of all . . .

Hey, Daunis, can you ask Levi to assign me as Jamie Johnson's Supe ambassador?

I sneak a glance at him. Empirically speaking, I suppose Jamie is good-looking. He's got huge dark eyes and dark brown hair long enough for curls to go in different directions. I'm more interested in the scar that runs from the outer edge of his right eyebrow to his jaw-bone. I study it. It doesn't have the plump overgrowth of a keloid, so that makes it a hypertrophic scar.

"Levi told me about you. You're headed to the University of Michigan," Jamie says, watching the twins skate back to their group leader.

"Oh, I . . . um . . . change of plans." I meet Levi's eyes as he joins us. "I'm gonna go to Lake State. My mom needs me." I clear my throat. "You know . . . with everything going on."

I don't mention Gramma Pearl's warning about bad things happening in threes.

"You're staying?" Levi shouts. "Woo-hooooo!" My brother picks me up and spins me until I'm nauseous. I whack at his back, laughing. His happiness is kind of contagious.

Levi sets me down. "Now we've got something to celebrate this weekend. Party at the big house tomorrow at eight, right? Beer will be ice cold."

"Lily and I will be there."

Still cheering, Levi skates away like the Pied Piper, leading a line of kids who imitate his footwork.

"So, you're sticking around." Jamie's smile extends to his eyes, and the last traces of nausea somersault in my stomach.

Nonempirically speaking, Jamie Johnson is hot when his eyes sparkle like that.

He keeps talking. "I wish you were gonna be a senior too. But, hey, at least you get to miss out on my uncle Ron as your science teacher."

I nod even as my nose stings with familiar tingles, which I force away with a clenched jaw.

"Is that a bad thing?" Jamie's voice deepens slightly with concern.

"No. It's just . . . Your uncle is filling my uncle's job at Sault High." The image of Uncle David adjusting the gas flame of a Bunsen burner triggers a tidal wave of sadness. And fury.

Jamie waits for me to say more.

"He died a few months ago. It was awful." I correct myself. "It's still awful."

When someone dies, everything about them becomes past tense. Except for the grief. Grief stays in the present.

It's even worse when you're angry at the person. Not just for dying. But for how.

My mother fainted when she heard the news about Uncle David. Later, when the police provided details, she insisted he had been sober for over thirteen years. Not a drop of alcohol since the day Mom returned from the library on campus and found five-year-old me on the sofa reading books to my passed-out uncle. She was adamant that her brother had never used other substances. Ever.

"I'm very sorry, Daunis."

My name sounds different in his almost-husky voice of concern. He stretches my name, so it sounds like *Dawww-ness*, rather than the way my Firekeeper relatives say it: *Dah-niss*.

Lily calls my name and points with her lips toward the dashers, where Teddie is waiting. My aunt motions for me. I skate over, a bit surprised when Jamie follows.

"Hey, I came here to vote and pick up the girls, but now there's a thing at work." Auntie notices Jamie. "Hi, I'm Teddie Firekeeper. You must be the new Supe everyone is talking about. It's a big deal whenever another Native player makes the team. Where are you from?"

"Jamie Johnson, ma'am." He offers his hand. "From all over. We moved a lot."

Auntie looks respectable, in a pantsuit with a gorgeous, beaded floral medallion. But, there's still the echo of the girl who would've throat-punched you for calling her Theodora.

"I meant which tribe," she clarifies.

"Cherokee, ma'am. But I didn't grow up around any family."

I glance at Jamie. I cannot fathom growing up without relatives. I have so many family members, not all blood-related, who have surrounded me my entire life. Plus a lot of matriarchs and mini-matriarchs-in-training.

"You need me to keep the girls awhile, Auntie?"

"Can you?" She sounds relieved. "Gotta go back to work. T-shirts came in for next week's immunization fair, and they have an owl saying, 'Be wise. Immunize!'" Auntie shakes her head. "No one caught it before ordering three hundred shirts, hey?"

"Holy." Lily skates over in time to add her succinct opinion.

"What's the problem?" Jamie directs the question to me, confused. Either Cherokees have different teachings about owls or else Jamie doesn't know his culture.

"In Ojibwe culture, the owl is a companion for crossing over when you die," I explain. "Not exactly the ambassador you want telling Nish parents to immunize their babies."

Auntie adds, "Not everyone knows their teachings. So I'm meeting the community health worker and her supervisor back at the office so we can rush-order new shirts."

"On a Friday night?" Lily's both appalled and impressed.

"Well, it's a problem they helped create, so they need to be part of the solution." Auntie calls to the twins in Anishinaabemowin. "Aambe, jiimshin." They hurry over for kisses and hugs.

After their mother leaves, Pauline asks Jamie to lift her up. He does, and she poses like it's their Olympic performance. I admire how he holds her with perfect technique, which I recognize from the years of figure-skating lessons I endured in exchange for GrandMary letting me play hockey as well. I wonder how long Jamie trained as a pairs figure skater before he switched to hockey?

Lily catches me watching him.

"I'd say it's too bad the new Supe has a girlfriend, but I know you don't date hockey players because of your moowin Hockey World rules." She sounds almost mad about it.

"Yup. Gotta keep Hockey World separate from Regular World." On the ice, I know the rules. But off the ice, the rules are always changing. My life goes more smoothly when Hockey World and Regular World don't overlap. Same with my Fontaine and Firekeeper worlds.

"But the good stuff happens when worlds collide . . . osmosis combustion," Lily says.

I grin. "You're thinking of collision theory. When two things collide and exchange energy if the reacting particles have enough kinetic energy."

"Oh yeah. How could I have gotten them confused?" She laughs. "But seriously, though, your rules are so black-and-white. Why can't you just—"

"Lily?" A voice calls out. We both turn, and I freeze when I see Lily's ex-boyfriend standing near the dasher door a few feet away. I tense at his familiar, hopeful smile, then look to Lily for my cue on how to react.

Back in the sixth grade, we were in the cafeteria when Lily first heard sweet, dorky Travis Flint burp the alphabet. She laughed so hard that she snotted milk from her nose. It was the best reaction he'd ever gotten; Travis instantly fell for Lily. When he grew up, in high school, revealing chiseled cheekbones and a square jaw, girls suddenly noticed the class clown was beyond handsome. Travis was radiant, especially when making Lily laugh.

That all changed back in December, halfway through our senior year.

I watch Lily closely. If she talks to Travis, I'll have to brace myself for another episode in *The Lily and Travis Saga*. It's a show that keeps getting renewed even though they repeat the same storyline.

Fortunately, she skates away, clearly uninterested in speaking with him. Travis isn't wearing skates, but I block the half door opening to the ice anyway, channeling every inch and pound of my body into becoming an impenetrable wall. Every hockey team needs a goon, someone to start shit or avenge wrongdoing. I am Lily's goon.

"Aw, Dauny, don't be like that." The hollows under his cheekbones are concave to the point of sickly. Any softness is gone. He seems like a shell of the funny boy who once made me laugh so hard that I peed my pants a little. "I swear I'm clean. Just wanna talk to her."

"Not gonna happen, Trav." I put my hands on my hips to become even wider.

"I'm clean," he repeats. "I'm staying clean for her."

"I know," I say. I believe he truly means it, but that doesn't mean it's a good idea for him to be near Lily. I usually call guys on their crap, but the sincerity in his voice almost makes me want to hug him. It's different from the typical Guy Lies.

Guy Lies are the things guys declare in the heat of the moment, which fade with time and distance. I've heard quite a few Guy Lies thanks to TJ Kewadin, the Sugar Island Ojibwe Tribe's newest cop. *I can't stop thinking about you*. Or *U of M is only two hours from Central, we can make that work*. And my personal favorite? *I love you*.

Travis is not lying when his anguished voice cracks. "I just miss her so much. I'll do anything to get her back."

"I know you'll do anything. That's why I'm going all goon on you." Lily told me what he did: *C'mon, Lily-bit. It's a love medicine. It'll make our relationship stronger. Try it for me.*

"Trav, maybe you should stay clean for yourself. Go to ceremonies. Get healthy."

Travis's eyes brighten, and for an instant I remember how funny and beautiful he used to be. He was my favorite of Levi's friends. We took nearly every Advanced Placement science class together. Travis Flint was my friend, too.

"That'll do it, won't it, Dauny?" he says excitedly, turning as if to run for the nearest sweat lodge. "I'll promise to go to Traditional Medicine. See the healer."

"Get healthy for you. Not for her!" I shout at his back.

As I watch Travis run off, I feel unsettled. I quickly skate around the perimeter, looking for Lily. She can always use a hug after a Travis encounter. I'll listen to what she says, and doesn't say, and support whatever she decides.

I really don't like *The Lily and Travis Saga*. I only watch because my best friend stars in it and she needs my protection. And my support. After all, goons get called upon to do what other players can't or won't.

I've seen Travis in bad shape before, but this felt different. He looked desperate, like he wants to do the right thing but for the wrong reasons. I resolve to keep an eye on Travis to make sure he stays far away from Lily until he's doing better. I'm worried that Lily may be in danger of more than a broken heart.

CHAPTER 4

After dinner, I borrow Mom's car to drive the twins home. I'm planning to stay the night at Auntie's, like I do every few weeks. Even with Pauline and Perry acting up in the back seat, the ferry ride to Sugar Island is like a five-minute meditation. I wonder if it was the same when my ancestors crossed the choppy water in birchbark canoes. If their hearts lightened because they were coming home.

I glance over to the car next to me and spot Seeney Nimkee. I quickly look away and hunch down in my seat. Seeney recently turned sixty, officially making her an Elder. She's a mentor to Auntie and works for the Tribe's Traditional Medicine Program. She once yelled at our Tribal Youth Council for sitting down at a community event while there were Elders standing. Even when I scrambled to my feet, she eyeballed me the entire time. I cried in the bathroom afterward and have been treading carefully around her ever since.

Two dogs, Elvis and Patsy, bark at Mom's car as I pull up Auntie and Art's winding driveway, which opens to a chalet-style log home overlooking Canada to the north. The front yard is bookended with a pole-barn garage and an elaborate tree house. As soon as I park, the twins tumble out of the car and pull me toward the tree house.

Their favorite game is Castle, where we fight imaginary dragons and trolls down the entire length of the tree fort. My battle cry is always, "We don't need no stinky prince!" Perry's a believer, but Pauline takes some convincing.

When Auntie comes home, I help with the girls' bath time and story time. After we put the girls to bed, I help my aunt fold laundry at the granite island in the kitchen.

"So you excited about Lake State?" Auntie asks.

"Yeah, Lily and I registered for classes, but my schedule's totally screwed up," I whine. "Eleven credit hours isn't full time. What if I can't get into that one biology seminar?"

"You worry too easily about shit. Lake State's not gonna screw you over. Your last name is on a dorm, for crying out loud."

I fall silent and focus on carefully folding one of Perry's T-shirts. After a minute, Auntie gets up and fixes a cup of lavender tea for me. She sets down the mug and smooths my hair.

Sometimes when I'm around my Firekeeper relatives, my older cousin Monk will call me Waabishkimaanishtaanish when Auntie is out of earshot. If she ever heard him call me White Sheep, even when he's giiwashkwebii, he'd be leaving the party with two black eyes.

But, every once in a while, Auntie herself makes a comment with an edge in her tone that sinks into the pit of my Fontaine stomach.

Art comes in from his garage workshop and greets me with a bear hug, breaking the awkward silence in the room. Even if I hadn't known where he'd been, the smell of orange hand cleanser, burning sage, and WD-40 would have been a dead giveaway.

When Art kisses Auntie, she relaxes into a softer version of Teddie

Firekeeper. With me and the twins, her love has layers—a tender core wrapped in an exoskeleton of tough love. But when she's wrapped in her husband's dark amber brown arms, Auntie can drop her guard.

My phone buzzes in my back pocket. I expect to see Levi's number, because ever since he got a Nokia with a full keyboard, my brother is more likely to text than call. But the text is from an unfamiliar number.

> ###-###-####: Its Jamie Johnson. Levi invited me 2 ur party. I asked 4 ur # 2 make sure u wont throw out the new guy. All cool?

My first thought is *Jamie texted me?* My second is *What the hell is Levi up to?* And my last is *Who else has he invited?*

The party Levi apparently told Jamie all about isn't exactly supposed to be a party. Lily and I sometimes sleep over at my grandparents' house and help ourselves to the liquor cabinet and wine cellar. We're supposed to make sure everything is fine at the big house since no one is living there. Mom won't consider selling it because she thinks GrandMary will want to move back home once she's recovered. I can't bring myself to say anything to her about that yet.

Lily had the idea that we should invite a few friends and celebrate my decision to go to Lake State. Asking Levi to help us get beer was probably not my smartest decision.

Art chuckles. "That's one conflicted reaction to a text."

They're both watching me. I stuff my phone into my pocket, feeling my face heat up.

"Probably the new Supe I met today," Auntie says with a smirk. "Cherokee. His name's Jamie. I'm nosy about his scar." Auntie describes it to Art, ending with "That cut's too straight to be accidental."

"His uncle is taking Uncle David's job at Sault High." My voice catches.

"Life moves forward, Daunis," Auntie says gently.

"But it's so unfair," I say. I frown to keep from crying as Art gives me another bear hug.

"I don't remember fairness being one of the Seven Grandfathers," Auntie says.

The Seven Grandfathers are teachings about living the Anishinaabe minobimaadiziwin—our good way of life—through love, humility, respect, honesty, bravery, wisdom, and truth. I include one in my prayers each morning to help me become a strong Nish kwe like my aunt.

I get her point. Auntie's right, as usual. Maybe my mother isn't the only one having difficulty moving forward from unfair events.

We hang out until Auntie and Art say good night and head upstairs holding hands. I begin to get ready for bed, but before I plug my phone into the charger, I reread Jamie's text.

I think back to today on the ice, when I first met him. Before he even opened his mouth, I'd already heard his name plenty of times from Levi, always with an awed tone. According to Levi, Jamie showed up at the open camp right before the team was announced. The Superiors had already hosted their pre-draft camp, goalie camp, and invitation-only camp. For a nobody to make the team as a walk-on from open camp, he had to be fantastic.

I review what little I know about Jamie, gathered from rumors and our brief conversation. First, I remind myself firmly, he has a girl-friend. He also has an interesting scar on his face. He used to be a fig-ure skater. He's Cherokee but isn't connected to his tribal community.

I wonder if it was hard to move around all the time. I wouldn't know. I've lived in the Sault since I was three months old and have always been surrounded by family. The Firekeepers are one of the oldest families on Sugar Island. In addition to the dorm on the hill with my grandfather's name, there are streets in town named after GrandMary's people. They were some of the first French fur traders who showed up centuries ago along with the Catholic missionaries.

I'm definitely local.

Yet even with such deep roots, I don't always feel like I belong. Each time my Fontaine grandparents or their friends have seen my Ojibwe side as a flaw or a burden to overcome. And the less frequent but more heartbreaking instances when my Firekeeper family sees me as a Fontaine first and one of them second. When they say things about the Zhaaganaash and then, a beat later, remember that I'm in the room too. It's hard to explain what it's like being so connected to everyone and everything here . . . yet feeling that no one ever sees the whole me.

Is that how Jamie feels whenever he moves to a new place? Unseen? I sigh and reply to his text.

ME: all cool. see you tmrw.

I get cozy on the oversized sofa in the great room, with stars filling two stories of windows. Normally I drift off quickly when I'm on Sugar Island. Tonight, however, curious thoughts about Jamie Johnson seesaw with concern for Travis and how his decline is affecting my best friend. Plus, Levi's actions, inviting Jamie and sharing my cell phone number, seems suspicious. My brother always has an agenda.

Auntie's footsteps on the stairs wake me. It's still dark, with even more stars than before.

I'm instantly alert at the sound of her voice: low and harsh, whispering through gritted teeth.

"Where? Tell her not to go anywhere . . . Yes, I'm on my way . . . No, you keep her away . . . Because it's a blanket party, not a murder scene . . . Damn it . . . I'm on my way."

I bolt upright, but Auntie just shoots me a warning look and keeps walking past the sofa. I quickly get up and follow her into the mudroom, my heart beginning to pound. A blanket party is when a guy does something bad to a woman and her female cousins take him into the woods, rolled in a blanket, and beat the moowin out of him. I asked Auntie when I first heard about it; she called it Nish kwe justice. Lily and I made a pact that if either of us finally got to attend one, we'd tell the other about it.

"Take me with you," I plead as she rummages for her keys.

Lily is usually the one who tells me about rez happenings. This would be a chance for me to have something exciting to share with her for once. Auntie's my only entry to Ojibwe ceremonies, and sometimes she brings me to full-moon ceremonies, but going with her to a blanket party would mean something different. It would be another way for the other Nish kwewag in my community to see me as part of the Firekeeper family. Not just a Fontaine.

Plus, what if this blanket party got out of hand and Auntie needed my help?

"No way." She tucks her cell phone into her bra.

"But I want to go." I'm surprised at myself. I have never talked back to Auntie; her word is law.

She whirls around and steps toward me, but I stand firm. Auntie glowers. Something shifts in her, energy imploding to simultaneously magnify and focus her anger. The hair on my arms and neck stands on end.

"This shit is ugly and messed up and I don't want you anywhere near it." She practically spits in my face, "Go to college. Snag Jamie. Live your nice life."

She turns and is gone. I stand there in the dark, hands trembling. Her dismissal stings like a slap across my face.

My cousins always tell stories about my aunt's fighting days. Tales of Fierce Teddie and her legendary shenanigans that grow more hilarious with each retelling. Like the time when she was at a bar with friends and a Zhaaganaash guy kept asking each girl if she was an Indian and how much Indian was she? He leered at Auntie and asked if she'd show him which body parts were Indian. She throat-punched him. While he was gulping for air, my aunt told him he just experienced a real Indian fist and she had another if he wanted to see that one too.

Tonight is the first time I glimpse the scary version of Auntie.

There is nothing funny about it.

CHAPTER 5

The next morning, I wake up with Perry wedged between me and the back of the sofa. Half my butt hangs off the edge. I shift onto my side to snuggle her. She sleeps with her mouth open; her breath smells like sweet corn. Just as I start to doze off again, a finger pokes my shoulder. I wince.

"You know that's my sore one," I grumble, rolling over.

"Will you make pancakes?" Pauline whispers loudly. Her breath smells like corn chips.

"I want pancakes," Perry says, eyes closed, still on the bridge between asleep and awake.

Sometimes you know you're up against forces too powerful to ignore. I reach around Pauline's sturdy body and roll her over to smush Perry in a hug.

"Ninde gidayan." *You have my heart*. I kiss each girl.

I sit up and spot Auntie's car in the driveway, letting out a sigh of relief. Auntie's dismissal last night rushes back to me, but I push away the hurt, telling myself that at least she's home safe. By the time I finish getting ready in the bathroom, Perry and Pauline are waiting for me at the kitchen island. They love my pancakes. I place the electric griddle in front of them and plug it in to heat up while I brew a pot of coffee.

"Tell me where you went last night," I say once the drip-drip of the coffee maker begins. They also love telling me their dreams. I listen while adding the pancake ingredients in the blender.

Perry found herself inside a bank vault filled with fancy jewelry. She brags, "I was the bad guy, Auntie Daunis. I was really good at it."

"Pearl Mary Firekeeper-Birch, jewel thief!" I laugh. "And what about you, Sis?"

Pauline says a mysterious boy visited her dreams and told her she was a princess.

"You know, Pauline, you can be a princess even without a boy saying so," I say while sipping a cup of coffee with hot cocoa mix added. Pauline rolls her eyes.

"Aho." Perry chirps the Ojibwe equivalent of *amen*. I spit out my coffee at her response.

Today the girls want bear-cub pancakes. As I pour batter onto the hot griddle, Auntie's words come back like a boomerang. *Live your nice life.* Distracted, I mess up the bear-cub ears. I curse under my breath and fix them by glopping on more batter and declaring them alien pancakes. Pauline pouts, but Perry happily crams hers in her mouth.

When Auntie and Art come downstairs, the twins are stuffed full of pancakes and maple syrup made at last year's Sugar Bush, watching *SpongeBob SquarePants* on TV.

"Miigwech, Little Sister," Art says warmly. He always thanks me for giving them their private morning time.

I glance at Auntie, who avoids eye contact. I'm not sure what time she came home, but I can tell something happened last night. Bigger than the blanket party. I don't know if I should say something first or wait for her to mention it. Either way, I doubt she'll say much in front of the twins.

Sure enough, Auntie just makes small talk until it's time for me to leave. The twins sit on each foot like usual, begging me to stay as I drag them toward the door. Once I shake them off, Art gives me another hug. Ordinarily, Auntie would nod and tell me to stay out of trouble, own my power, or aim true when kicking Harry Pajog. Standard Nish kwe anthems.

Today, she makes a point of embracing me. She holds on long after I let go.

"Ninde gidayan," she says into my ear.

I feel like crying but I'm not sure why. Auntie is full of remorse today. I just wish she didn't have the need for her regrets. Or maybe the blanket party didn't solve a problem but created a new mess instead.

The blanket party stays on my mind all day. Lily meets me at the big house in the afternoon to move artwork and other valuables to my grandfather's library as a safety precaution. I want to enjoy the party instead of worrying about something getting damaged.

As we work, I tell Lily about the blanket party.

"I wonder who they got?" she muses. "Can you imagine a Council member or the mayor or, like, a teacher walking around with a black eye? Pretending they walked into a door or some such foolishness?"

"I just hope whoever the blanket party posse was helping, that she feels safer now," I say.

Levi shows up at my grandparents' house with the beer around eight p.m. Ice cold, as promised. I can tell Lily's pissed.

We set up the keg in the kitchen. Then Levi leaves to pick up his friends, calling over his shoulder, "Don't drink all the booze before I get back!"

"I don't know why you're mad," I say as we head to the library off the dining room, where the liquor cabinet is located. "Levi just did us a big favor."

She gives a frustrated growl. "You're so clueless sometimes."

"Hey. I'm not legal in Canada till October, and Auntie told me never to ask her to buy alcohol. So, unless Granny June was gonna buy us this pony keg, we were shit outta luck." I lower my voice, teasing. "C'mon, Lily, do you know how humiliating it was to ask my younger-by-three-months brother to get us beer?"

"It's just . . ." Lily holds back, as if choosing her words carefully. "You bitch about Hockey World, and then you invite the king of Hockey World to our party. What happened to just having a few friends over?"

"Calm your tits, Lil. We're celebrating. Lake State. Woo-hoo!" I say with minimal enthusiasm. "It's just Levi and his minions crashing the party. And Jamie Johnson. What can I do to make it up to you?"

"You invited *Jamie*?" She eyeballs me. "Oh, I get it now. Calm your own tits and stick your tongue down New Guy's throat, hey."

"No tits to calm, Sis," I say, looking down at my flat chest. "And I'm not kissing Jamie. Levi's the one who wanted him here. And he's got a girlfriend." Anticipating a comment from Lily about my defensive tone, I decide it's grappa time.

I walk over to the liquor cabinet. My grandparents' foolproof security system was to hide the key on the hook on the back of the fancy cabinet. The alcohol equivalent of writing your password on a Post-it and sticking it on your computer screen. I select a bottle of imported grappa. I take a big sip, and the Italian brandy burns all the way down to my gut.

"If the girlfriend's dating a hockey god who's playing for a team thousands of miles away—where the hell is he from, anyway? Whatever. She knew the sitch," Lily says.

"Is that what you would've said to my mom?" I take another swig of grappa. "You know she's never gotten over walking in on my dad and Levi's ma."

"I know, I know. I only said to kiss him 'cause you haven't dated anyone since TJ, and that was two years ago. Stupid hookups don't count." She lets out a sigh that feels too big for her body. "I'm pissed 'cause your brother takes over shit and makes it about him. This was supposed to be for us."

She's right. I take another drink. It's only the first swig that burns. This one spreads a relaxing warmth throughout my body.

"We're gonna have a great night. It's still about us. Three weeks from now, we start college. You gotta tell Granny June how much your books are gonna cost so you can redeem one of her coupons." Lily's graduation present from her great-grandmother was a sheet of eight handwritten coupons: *This coupon is good for one semester of books and supplies for Lily June Chippeway with love from Granny June. Nontransferable.*

"You're right, and once we're at Lake State, no more Levi and his boys." Lily scopes the liquor cabinet and pulls out a bottle of Frangelico. She clinks the odd bottle, shaped like a priest, against my bottle of clear liquor, which has a grapevine twig floating inside.

Before we drink, Lily holds out her left hand to begin our special handshake.

"Lake State, baby," I say at our butterfly-flutter finale.

Lily trills a lee-lee that nearly shatters my eardrum.

Two hours later, my little goon is loudly scolding Levi for playing music too loudly.

"Do you *want* the cops to stop by?" Lily sounds exactly like Granny June giving someone hell. Levi ignores her until Lily adds, "All them tribal cops are cross-deputized to handle calls off the rez, so maybe TJ will be the one who responds to the loud noise complaint."

My brother immediately turns down the volume on Hoobastank.

"And I told you to play Amy Winehouse," she reminds him.

"And I told *you*," Levi counters, "none of your weird music that nobody else knows."

As Lily launches into a profanity-laced speech about the genius of Amy Winehouse, I count twenty-four people in the big house. I take a swig of grappa for every half-dozen people. The pony keg won't last much longer. Levi and his friends will leave. Lily will calm her tits. Everything will be fine. I already feel fine. So fine, in fact, that when Jamie Johnson stands next to me, I hold out the bottle of grappa so he can feel fine too. He takes a small sip and coughs.

"What is this, moonshine?" he sputters.

"Grappa. Italian brandy," I say. "Made from the stuff left behind after the grapes are pressed for wine." I take another swig and offer to give Jamie a tour of the big house.

Daunis the friendly host—that's all. I'm definitely not trying to be alone with him. Some creeper girl Levi must have invited tags along when we go upstairs. Damn wannabe anglerfish auditioning for the part of Jamie Johnson's next girlfriend.

Anglerfish. That's what I call the hockey girlfriends. A bottom-dweller fish that bites its mate and fuses with it. A parasitic appendage unable to exist separately.

"There's a master bedroom suite, three more bedrooms, two other bathrooms, and a secret door to the scary attic." I fling my arm awkwardly toward all the doors.

Jamie smiles at my wild gesturing.

"Wait, so you grew up here?" the girl asks.

"Till I was six. Then my mom finished college, started teaching kindergarten, and bought a house four blocks away." I narrow my eyes at the anglerfish circling Jamie like a shark. "But, yeah. Sunday dinners and major holidays here."

I lead them down a paneled hallway, pointing to the hidden attic door and pressing a finger to my lips to emphasize its secret existence.

Jamie pauses to stare at my senior portrait on the wall. GrandMary made me curl my hair. I have a dreamy expression on my face. My mother's and uncle's portraits are next to mine. They barely look like who they became.

Mom graduated high school a year after her classmates, the only one with a toddler. Her dark brown hair was shellacked into a tall wave of bangs and angel wings curving around each ear before cascading past her shoulders. There is something heartbreaking about her stylish efforts, and the way she smiles into the camera, her beautiful green eyes filled with hope. I want to hug that version of my mother. She has no idea of the losses to come.

In his portrait, Uncle David looks as if seeing the Sault in the rearview mirror cannot happen quickly enough for him. Eager to flee and go someplace where people are more interested in being colorful than coloring within the lines. He wears a boring suit and a fresh haircut to please his mother, but the purple tie and pocket square are my uncle's tribute to Prince.

"Pay no attention to the curious photos on the wall," I say. "These people will be unrecognizable soon. Even to themselves."

"You're weird," the girl says.

I shrug and take another swig of grappa before leading my tour back to the staircase.

"I can hold that for you," Jamie says, reaching for the bottle.

"Yes. A hockey god with manners. Good for you, Jamie Johnson. And welcome to Sault Sainte Marie." I gesture like a game-show hostess. "Now, don't be like tourists and pronounce it like *Salt*. It's *Soo*."

"Noted," he says. "You're full of fascinating facts."

I catch his gently mocking tone. "Miigwech, hockey prince." I look around. "Hey . . . where did that girl go?"

"I think you lost her," Jamie says.

"C'est la vie." *Such is life.*

"Qui n'avance pas, recule," he says. *Who does not move forward, recedes.*

I stare at him. Jamie speaks French? Before I can ask him about it, I get distracted by his eyes. He's standing close enough for me to notice that his irises are lighter toward the pupil and have a darker brown perimeter that sort of bleeds into the tawny part. Grappa must sharpen my eyesight, because I'm noticing every detail.

"You're staring," Jamie says.

"Um . . . girls are after you," I tattle. It sounds stupid as soon as I hear myself.

"Thank you for the warning." His wide smile tugs at the end of his scar.

"Hey, Bubb!" We both turn to see Levi taking the stairs two at a time to join us. My brother puts an arm around me. "Got a favor to ask."

I brace myself. Previous favors have included me being his best friend Stormy's date to Shagala last year and providing Anishinaabe-mowin nicknames for his friends and teammates. One guy kept pestering me for an "Indian name better than everyone else's," so I told him that Gichimeme meant the biggest and most powerful bird. He went around for weeks, loudly crowing his new name before a Nish-naab friend finally pulled him aside and explained it meant, "big pile-ated woodpecker." In other words, Big Pecker.

"Would you be Jamie's Supe ambassador?"

"Me? But . . . I'm not part of the club," I say in surprise. "Them girls call dibs on the new Supes."

"Right." Levi gives Jamie a knowing look before adding, "That's why you'd be perfect. Jamie's got a girlfriend. So you'd be keeping all the puck sluts away."

I growl. "You know I hate that term."

"Sorry, Bubb," Levi says quickly. "What I meant is, he could go running with you, so you could tell him all about the town." He turns to Jamie. "Did you know that Daunis made the boys' varsity hockey team all four years at Sault High? Plus, she was the class valedictorian."

"I did notice she knows a lot of fun facts," Jamie says with a wink.

"Hey, this feels like a setup," I say as the realization hits me.

"It's a help-up, Bubb. Any other girl as Jamie's ambassador would result in catfights."

"Don't flatter yourself." I roll my eyes. "But if you think that's true . . . won't they be mad at me?" Did Levi just invent a word: *help-up*?

"No one will mess with you," he says. "You're a total badass. Just like Aunt Teddie."

And with those magic words, along with the pleased look on New Guy's face and the warmth of the grappa, I agree to be Jamie's ambassador.

CHAPTER 6

Two mornings later, Jamie Johnson is in my driveway, stretching his arms overhead in the dawn twilight. He must live nearby, since I don't see a car. I nod hello before putting semaa down and whispering at my prayer tree. Joining him in the driveway, I take in an eyeful of my new Supe buddy.

The guy is all lean muscles and ligaments stretched over bones. He has no body fat whatsoever. We are the same height, but I outweigh him by a good thirty pounds. Even more on puffy days.

As I size Jamie up, I imagine him doing the same to me: *Tall, sturdy chick, ginormous ass, ghostly white skin, wide mouth, big nose, and—what cruel irony—small tits.* I fight an urge to shout back that I'm powerful on defense, I'm smart, and I don't ever give up.

He interrupts my internal dialogue. "You ever run with your brother?"

"Sometimes," I say, beginning my side stretches. "He and his friends go a lot faster than my normal pace." I leave out the part about Levi's impatience with my warm-up routine.

"You're really close to your brother." Jamie squats and stretches one leg to the side.

"Um . . . I suppose. Sometimes he's a pain." I stare at the taut gracilis muscle of his inner thigh, how it forms a direct line into his loose shorts . . . I force myself to reestablish eye contact. "Do you have any siblings?"

"No siblings. Just my uncle. My parents divorced when I was little. They aren't into hockey. Uncle Ron's always helped pay for my gear and travel teams. When he got a teaching job here, I took him up on his offer to do my senior year in the Sault." He looks pleased getting the town nickname right.

I catch myself mirroring his proud smile as I go through a quick version of my warm-up. Jamie matches his stretches to mine.

"Ready, buddy?" I jut my chin and lips toward the road.

"Yes, Ambassador." The smile hasn't left his face.

I take my normal route through campus.

"Hey, look," Jamie says when we pass the new dorm. "It's got your last name on it."

"Yup."

He laughs. "That's all you got to say?"

"Yup." I flash my cheesiest smile.

When we reach the overlook behind the student union, I stop.

"Hold up," I say. Jamie walks back a few steps to stand next to me. "Over there, a few miles away, is Lake Superior." I point to the west before following the river. "It feeds the St. Marys River, which is the international border with Canada. The city on the other side is also called Sault Sainte Marie, but it's a lot bigger than our town." I end with another game-show-hostess flourish. Something about Jamie makes me want to show off. "The river curves around the east end of town, and those pretty hills are part of Sugar Island. That's where my dad's family is from. Mine and Levi's, I mean."

"Wow. It's beautiful."

The awe in his voice makes me feel the same as when I ace a quiz.

"Ready?" I ask, easing back into our pace. We follow the road from the bluff to the river a half mile away.

Jamie watches a freighter moving slowly and quietly into the nearest lock. As he observes the long ship, I sneak a look at his profile, the side of the face that isn't scarred. The freighter blasts its horn fifty feet from us. Startled, Jamie swears loudly. I laugh.

"I'm gonna need my ambassador to explain all this," he says.

"Remember when I pointed to Lake Superior?"

"Five minutes ago?" he says dryly.

"Yes, smart-ass. So, ships pass by on their way to or from the other Great Lakes to reach Lake Superior, which is twenty-something feet higher than everything downriver. There used to be rapids here. It was a major gathering spot for Anishinaabeg, with fishing villages on both sides of the river and on Sugar Island. The government took over the area and cut through the rapids to build the Soo Locks, which work like a water elevator to raise or lower the ships."

Jamie's eyes are on me instead of the freighter across the street. "What happened to all the Anishinaabeg people and their villages?"

I raise an eyebrow. I'm not sure if Jamie knows what a big question he's asked. Tourists like Jamie never think about the ones who got pushed aside for progress. I don't know if he really wants to know my tribe's history, or how I'd even begin to tell him.

"That's a story for another time," I say. "Now it's your turn to talk. Tell me about you."

"That's a story for another time," he says, grinning. "I have more questions."

I smile back. "How did I get stuck with the most curious one of yous?"

"What's the deal with 'yous'?" Jamie asks.

I laugh. "Ah, that's the most important question. Yous is the Yooper version of y'all."

"And . . . Yooper means a person from the U.P., or Upper Peninsula?"

"Wow. I got the smart buddy." I point for us to take the next turn.

We fall easily into a comfortable silence that lasts for a few miles. When we turn by the Dairy Queen, he gestures toward a small house.

"That's where my uncle and I live," he says, continuing to run beside me. "Oh, one more question. When people say Anishinaabe, do they mean Native or Ojibwe?"

"Anishinaabe means the Original People. Indigenous. Nish. Nishnaab. Shinaab. Mostly we're referring to Ojibwe, Odawa, and Potawatomi tribes from the Great Lakes area. Ojibwe language is called Anishinaabemowin or Ojibwemowin. Levi calls it Ojiberish." I roll my eyes. "If you hang with him long enough, he'll give you a Nish nickname."

Jamie quickly looks my way. "Levi said to ask you how to say Scarface in the language."

We burst into laughter at the same time. I inhale some spit and have to stop for a coughing fit. Once we catch our breath, I motion toward EverCare, surprised at how quickly the miles flew by with Jamie.

"I end my run at that nursing home. My grandmother's there. She had a stroke."

"I'm sorry," he says. "That's a lot to deal with after losing your uncle, too. How are *you* coping, Daunis?" The directness startles me. Something about the way he asks makes me wonder if he might be familiar with loss, too.

Other than Lily, no one really asks how I'm doing. People ask about Mom, or what will happen with the big house. It's odd to have the person who has known me the least amount of time ask how I'm doing, and in such a genuine way.

"It's okay," Jamie says as I fumble for words. "Tell me when you're ready."

By the time we reach the parking lot, I still have no answer. I look over at Jamie. His skin glistens like a shiny penny, smooth and new. His hair is damp with sweat, the curls going in every direction. My thoughts about Jamie go in every direction as well.

Regular World needs some Hockey World rules, I decide.

"Miigwech for the run, buddy," I say. "Tomorrow, it's your turn. You can tell me about your last hockey team, your last school, your uncle, and your girlfriend, hey?"

Jamie smiles, gives a thumbs-up, and jogs away.

I call Lily while walking home from EverCare. After I fill her in on my run with Jamie, she and I try guessing what he might reveal about his girlfriend.

"Car accident," Lily declares. "They bonded over their scars."

"Nah. Auntie says his scar is too straight to be accidental."

"Her ex-boyfriend cut Jamie in a jealous rage," she says.

"Holy. Not every relationship is a drama shit show," I say.

"Well, all the ones I seen are."

We are silent for half a block. I hear Granny's dog barking on the other end. Lily doesn't say much about her mom or her life before coming to live with Granny June, but sometimes she'll take Mom's side when I gripe about the overprotective stuff.

Lily finally says, "Okay, Fancy Nancy Drew, what's your hypotenuse?" The smile in her voice is contagious.

"My hypothesis is that they lost their virginity together," I say, breaking into a wide grin. "By the way, a hypotenuse is the long side of a right triangle."

"Whatever," she says as she heads off. "Later, gator."

"After a while, Crocodylus niloticus."

"Geek!"

It rains hard the next morning, so I text an alternate plan to Jamie before dawn. He swings by in a black pickup truck and we go to the fitness center at Chi Mukwa. I don't like running indoors, but it's better than going through the day feeling like something's off.

We hop on our treadmills and, a minute in, I notice that Jamie's settings are the same as mine.

"You know, you don't have to keep pace with me," I say. "That's the upside of running on a treadmill. Go as fast as you want."

"Nah. It's good. I still have practice and conditioning with the team later," Jamie says.

I shrug and keep running, but secretly, I'm pleased. It takes two miles for me to find my rhythm. That's the downside of a treadmill, right up there with feeling like a hamster on a wheel.

"You're quiet today," Jamie says. "Everything okay?"

"I was waiting for you to talk, remember? It's your turn."

"Ah. That's right," he says. "Well . . . what do you want to know?"

I want to know everything. My prayer this morning, though,

was for manaadendamowin. Respect. Respect for relationships—my ambassador thing with Jamie and his relationship with his girlfriend. I won't be a wannabe anglerfish, trying to latch on to a guy who is already taken.

"Whatever you want to tell me, buddy."

"Well, Ambassador, I was born on a dark and stormy night . . ."

I look over to see his full smile tugging the bottom of his scar.

"I don't like talking about myself, I guess," Jamie says. "My dad's Cherokee. Him and my mom got divorced when I was little. She and I moved around a lot. He got a new family. Uncle Ron checked on me more than my dad. I played hockey all over. That's it."

Jamie's background is kind of like mine. Native dad. Parents not together. And an uncle who stepped in because his own dad wasn't around anymore. Maybe that explains why it feels easy to be around him.

"And you figure skate," I say. "You left that part out."

"How do you know that?" I feel Jamie eyeballing me.

"I dunno. The way you lifted Pauline the other day?" I shrug again and feel a painful twinge in my shoulder. "My grandmother, the one I call GrandMary, she made me do figure skating for a few years. I hated it. But it was the only way she let me play hockey."

"What about your mom? Didn't she have a say?"

"Ha! You never knew GrandMary. She was like Eta Carinae, and my mom and I were kinda like wobbly planets sucked into her gravitational pull."

"Eta Carinae?" Jamie asks.

"The largest star in the galaxy," I say quietly. Something sinks inside me as I realize I used the past tense about someone who is still alive. I increase my pace setting. Jamie seems to sense the shift and cranks up his setting too, quietly keeping pace. We go silent for the rest of the run.

On the drive home, I ask Jamie to drop me off at EverCare.

"But it's still coming down." He gestures at the frantic wiper blades.

"Eh, I won't melt." I open the truck door and steel myself for the sprint to the building. I glance over to him. "Thanks for the run and the ride, buddy."

"You're welcome, Ambassador."

I kiss GrandMary before applying her red lipstick. Mom hasn't arrived yet, so I retrieve the blink notebook from the top shelf in the small closet. Settling into the chair beside her bed, I talk to my grandmother, pausing to make tally marks in the two columns: LIGHT BULB ON and LIGHT BULB OFF. She seems tired today; I stay only for the fifteen-minute data-collection session.

When I leave, Jamie's pickup truck is still in the parking lot.

"You didn't need to wait," I say, climbing in. Surprised yet grateful.

"Eh," he says, mimicking me. "I wanted to."

As Jamie pulls into my driveway, I remember the girlfriend. She needs to be real to me.

"You didn't say anything about your last town or team . . . or your girlfriend."

"My girlfriend's name is Jennifer. Jen," he says. I try to imagine her, but all I see is a cool girl with long, shiny hair and a long side bang over her left eye like the late singer Aaliyah. "We've been together for three years. Her dad's military, so she moves all the time too." I should feel happy for Jamie, having a girlfriend who understands being the new kid in school. "It's just nice to have something solid no matter how much everything else changes. Know what I mean?"

I nod, though I don't know what Jamie means. Ever since Uncle David died, nothing's felt solid. Even before he went missing, my uncle began acting strange. Distant. We found out about his relapse afterward. The last time my life felt solid was . . . Christmas?

"Well, I'll see you tomorrow morning . . . and, Jamie? Chi miig-wech." *Big thank you.* I say it to cover everything—the ride and telling me stuff about himself, even though he has difficulty sharing details about his life.

"You're welcome, Daunis."

I don't understand why I'm jealous of a girl who can relate to the closed-off parts of Jamie.

By Friday, the line between Hockey World and Regular World has blurred as if drawn in charcoal pencil that Jamie smudges a little more with each morning we run together. I wake up, brush my teeth, pull my hair into a thick ponytail, throw on running clothes, and grab a pinch of semaa from Gramma Pearl's birchbark basket on the entry table. Jamie is always in my driveway when I whisper my morning prayer. Then we do our warm-up and hit the road.

When we pass the row of gift shops across from the Soo Locks, I smile at a memory.

"Levi sold sweetgrass to tourists here when he was little," I say.

"What's sweetgrass?"

"It's one of our traditional medicines that smells really good, like a mellow, sweet spice. In Ojibwe it's called wiingashk, and in science it's *Hierochloe odorata*. There'll be some for sale at the Tribe's powwow this weekend."

"I've never been to a powwow. Are you going tomorrow? Can you show me around?"

"Sure," I say, surprised at his eagerness. I remind myself that he hasn't grown up around his tribe like I have. "How about an ambassador-guided powwow experience?"

"That'd be fantastic," he says with a grin. I have to force myself not to grin back. "So, Levi sold sweetgrass to tourists?"

"Yup. He and our friend Travis picked and braided it. Levi told people he was descended from a powerful chief and a medicine woman. He claimed that his sweetgrass was magical. You know, that hokey stuff tourists like to believe." I roll my eyes.

"That sounds like Levi," Jamie laughs. "Natural businessman. I'm sure Stormy was in on it, too. Those two are trouble." Stormy Nodin is Levi's best friend, since their tribal Head Start preschool days. He made the team, along with Jamie, after bombing at Supes tryouts last year. True, Stormy's mom was in jail at the time for fighting some Zhaaganaash guy at a bar downtown, but hockey doesn't give a rat's ass about your personal problems.

"Nah, Stormy's dad didn't want him collecting medicines with people outside the family. His dad is kinda scary, like it's not just Zhaaganaash that he doesn't want to be around. Even some tribal members don't make the cut with Mr. Nodin. They only did it for a couple of summers, though. Then the casino opened, and per capita started."

"I heard some guys on the team talking about it. Tribal members get money from the casino? That's kind of crazy." Jamie shakes his head in disbelief.

I stiffen. "It's no different than Walmart or Ford paying dividends to shareholders." I keep my voice smooth while awaiting Jamie's reaction. Hoping he won't reveal himself to be a jerk.

"Wow, I never thought of it that way," he says. I feel my shoulders relax. "Can I ask how much? Or is that rude?"

"It's okay," I say. "I've heard Levi blab that adult members get thirty-six thousand dollars a year. Not sure how much it is after taxes. Kids who are tribal members get a third of that amount."

"Don't you get it?" Jamie sounds confused.

"I'm not enrolled. My dad's not listed on my birth certificate. One of many decisions that my Fontaine grandparents made because my mom was only sixteen when she had me."

Jamie must have heard the shift in my tone because he pauses and asks, "Are you okay talking about this, Daunis?"

"Yes," I say, realizing my ease at sharing about myself. Maybe not everything, though. I'm not ready to admit how angry I feel over their decision that affected my tribal enrollment.

"It's hard when being Native means different things depending on who's asking and why," he says.

"And to some people, you'll never be Native enough," I add.

"Yeah. It's *your* identity, but it gets defined or controlled by other people."

His words mirror my exact thoughts. What GrandMary and Grandpa Lorenzo took from me when they meant to exclude my dad.

Jamie meets my eyes and I know that we see each other.

We're both silent for the rest of the run. There's a steady breeze off the river and not a cloud in the sky. The cool air feels wonderful and tingly on my arms and legs. My breathing is deep and steady. I feel so good. As if the rays of sunshine aren't landing on me but coming from inside me. Jamie looks over and I smile back.

Then, it happens. The zone. My body feels strong, as if I could run like this forever. I'm both in my body and somewhere else. I'm whole. Running is where all the different parts of me fit together perfectly, like a jigsaw puzzle. The zone is where I'm a step removed from the puzzle, so the lines fade, and I can see myself clearly.

By the time we reach EverCare, we're both panting. Jamie usually gives a thumbs-up and jogs the rest of the way home. Today he doesn't make any move. Just stands next to me, running his hands through his wet hair, leaving waves from his temples to the back of his neck.

"Would you like to meet my grandmother?" I ask impulsively.

"Yes," he says, looking surprised but pleased. "I'd like that very much."

We pass the front desk, both easing into regular breaths. I feel nervous as we walk into my grandmother's room. I'm not sure why I've decided to invite Jamie along. Not even Lily has been here to see GrandMary.

"GrandMary, this is my friend Jamie," I say after kissing her cheek. LIGHT BULB OFF.

"Bonjour, madame. C'est un plaisir de vous rencontrer." Jamie kisses her hand, where raised blue veins thread beneath wrinkled skin. He looks across GrandMary's bed to me.

I do a double take. For as much time as I have spent this week with Jamie, I still know so little about him. He spoke French at the party last Saturday and now again to my grandmother. The line between Hockey World and Regular World isn't blurred; it's been rendered nonexistent by the new guy on my brother's hockey team. Dangerously nonexistent.

"Who are you, Jamie Johnson?" I ask, perplexed.

He looks down as if embarrassed or uncomfortable. When he meets my eyes, there's something determined in his expression. He speaks French again, this time to me.

"Je suis celui qui attend avec impatience demain." *I am the one looking forward to tomorrow.*

CHAPTER 7

Saturday morning arrives with the same excitement as my former game days. Because of today's powwow, the Supes have an early-morning practice. I run by myself at a quicker pace than usual. During GrandMary's alert moments, I tell her about Jamie's visit and my plans to take Jamie to the Tribe's powwow. She doesn't show much of a reaction until I mention my other activity for the day. The news that I'll be pricing textbooks with Lily merits as big a smile as my grandmother can manage. I wrap GrandMary in a hug and kiss her cheek. It makes both of us feel so happy that I hop around to kiss her other cheek before leaving.

Later that morning, Lily drives us to the campus bookstore.

"All that pep in your step wouldn't have anything to do with a certain hockey player, would it?" she comments as we walk through the parking lot.

"Just excited to check out our textbooks and highlighters," I say.

"Yeah, right," Lily says. "The old magic-pencil theory." She doesn't share my belief that the perfect pen or pencil can improve my academic performance.

We laugh, sharing a good mood that evaporates the second we're staring at the prices of the books required for American Literature.

"Holaaay." Lily's voice carries over to the next aisle.

"You ain't kidding," a stranger shouts back.

After Lily drops me off, I eat an early lunch. Mom calls from EverCare while I wait for Jamie.

"You and Lily headed to the powwow?" she asks.

I give a distracted *mmm-hmm* as I pet Herri.

"You girls be safe. Call or text me if you make plans for later."

"Love you," I say, brushing away the smallest pang of guilt.

Protecting Mom from full disclosure isn't the same thing as lying. She won't care that Jamie is just a friend. Once she learns he's new in town, Mom will launch the inquisition: *Who is this boy? Where is he from? Who are his parents? How do we know he's a good person?*

It's a kindness to us both, really, to spare her from anxieties kicking into high gear. My mother's superpower is turning my ordinary worries into monsters so huge and pervasive that her distress and heartache become almost debilitating. I can protect her from that hurt.

Jamie's truck pulls into the driveway. I slide my cell phone into the pocket of my cutoff jeans while jogging over to the passenger side.

"Hey, buddy," I say, climbing into the truck. "Thanks for the ride."

After I told Lily everything that happened during yesterday's run with Jamie and at GrandMary's room, I decided I needed to pull back and emphasize the *buddy* part of the new friendship.

"No problem. Thanks for letting me go with you and showing me around, Daunis."

"It's my duty as ambassador. Everything you ever wanted to know about powwows but were too afraid to ask?" I say. My back pocket buzzes. It's a text from Lily. She rarely texts, because her cell phone plan charges for each one sent or received.

> LILY: Can I PLEASE text sex stuf aboot jj and u not b mad
> ME: This seems v imprtnt 2u
> LILY: VVV IMP
> ME: u have free pass 4 filth let it fly my fren

Jamie takes the scenic route to the powwow grounds. The Superior Shores Casino and Resort spans across a massive amount of riverfront. It looks like it should be on the Las Vegas strip rather than in our small town.

"Okay, I got a question. Why's the Tribe called the Sugar Island Ojibwe Tribe, but the casino's on the mainland?"

"The Tribe had claim to land along both sides of the river," I say. "They settled a land-claims case with the federal government twenty years ago and used the money to buy an old factory and dock. Ten years later, they opened the casino and just kept expanding. Per cap started about five years ago."

"It sounds like you have some feelings about the per capita payments."

I pause to read the incoming text.

> LILY: tell jj ambassadors reward their supe 4 evry goal
> ME: u lil perv

"Sorry. Lily needed something," I say, shoving my phone into my back pocket. "Auntie says per cap isn't good or bad. It just kinda amplifies whatever's going on with a person or family." I point for Jamie to turn toward the satellite rez. "People judge how a few members spend their money and say petty stuff. But there's lots of good things happening too. Families travel. Buy a nice car or put a down payment on a house. Go to college."

My words instantly echo with the biting tone from Auntie last Friday as she left for the blanket party. *Go to college. Snag Jamie. Live your nice life.* My giddy buzz about bringing Jamie to the powwow deflates a bit.

This weekend, she and Art are parking their RV on the edge of the powwow grounds by the woods. They'll visit with friends from other tribal communities who travel to powwows across the country and into Canada. The twins will play with cousins and powwow friends. It would be a good time to sit with Auntie and tell her what's still on my mind from the night of the blanket party.

Jamie opens his mouth to ask another question.

"So, buddy," I cut him off. "Do you speak other languages besides French?"

"Spanish. What about you?" He follows the small directional signs that are on nearly every corner the closer we get to the powwow grounds.

"Eh. French, a little bit of Anishinaabemowin, and a bit of Italian . . . but that's mostly for the swear words." He turned my question back on me, I notice. "Oh, and another good thing about per cap: More Nish kids play hockey. Figure skating too. When my dad played, the Firekeepers took up a collection for new skates and gear. He always said there were other guys on Sugar Island who should've been on the best teams with him." Another text buzzes.

"Sorry." I apologize again, with the explanation, "Lily."

LILY: Tell him u lost ur v in a ice shanty. Thats so yoop
ME: More yoop than losing it in a deer blind?
LILY: i was 12 dint kno bettr

This time I turn off my phone and set it in the drink holder between our seats.

"Can I ask what happened?" Jamie asks. "To your dad, I mean."

I blink in surprise that Levi hasn't filled him in yet. "Um . . . bit of a scandal back then. My mom was sixteen when she got pregnant, and my dad was a poor Nish from the rez on Sugar Island."

I'm not sure why I am telling him this. Maybe because I get to be the one to tell him, rather than someone filling him in with juicy gossip.

"The night my mom told him she was pregnant, they got into an accident on the island and my dad broke both legs. He didn't get the right medical treatment, so his legs didn't heal properly. It was before the casino opened, and he couldn't get work anywhere in the U.P."

"It must have been really high unemployment back then, huh?"

I stare at my buddy. Has Levi really told him nothing? "My dad couldn't get a job because my Zhaaganaash grandpa was the mayor of Sault Ste. Marie and owned one of the biggest construction companies in the U.P. And he and GrandMary didn't care much for Indians. Especially ones who'd knocked up their only daughter."

"But . . ." Jamie lingers at the intersection even after the other cars turn. "You're Indian."

"Yup." I stare out the window when he resumes driving. "Anyways, he needed a job so he followed a cousin to northern Ontario. I didn't have much time with him before he died in a logging accident when Levi and I were both seven."

"Daunis, that's awful. I'm so sorry." Jamie's compassion is his best trait, I think.

"Miigwech," I say.

"You and Levi were both seven? How does that happen?"

I shrug. "I heard it was the whiskey."

Jamie waits for me to say more, but I'd rather stay quiet until the complicated feelings—which arise whenever my Fontaine and Fire-keeper worlds collide—make sense. And there's no telling how long that might take.

☀

The lot at Chi Mukwa is filled to capacity with powwow overflow. Jamie manages to find a narrow spot along Ice Circle Drive and demonstrates expert parallel-parking skills.

"That's Lily's Jeep." Cell phone in hand, I point to the lone vehicle in a clearing beyond the ice arena.

"Why does she park all the way out there? Is she worried about getting blocked?"

"No. She's just really bad at parallel parking."

"I could teach her," Jamie offers.

"Eh. She thinks her method is fine." I smile mischievously. "I'll bet if you spoke French when you offered, she'd agree to anything."

Jamie blushes, and I feel my giddy buzz return.

We follow one of the many clusters of people spilling from the sidewalk into the road. Drumbeats grow louder with each step toward the powwow grounds. A steady breeze and intermittent shade from puffy cumulus humilis clouds save us from frying in the August sun like ants under a magnifying glass. Perfect powwow weather.

A tingle runs the length of my spine as I observe a hulking figure squeezed behind the steering wheel of an approaching tribal cop car. TJ Kewadin.

I love you, Lorenza. The only person to call me by my middle name. We dated for two months before we started snagging. But once we did, he thought it was pervy to use my first name, which translates to "daughter."

He dumped me without explanation one month later. Stopped calling. Wouldn't look at me in the AP classes we had together.

I flip the bird in a smooth pan motion as Officer Kewadin passes by. So much for staying under the radar.

Jamie gives a low chuckle. "Not a fan of law enforcement, huh?"

"Nope." I change the subject. "Have you been across the river to Sault, Ontario?"

"Yeah, my uncle and I went to the mall. I had to get a new suit for game days."

"I'm guessing yous get searched at the border on your way back to the U.S.?"

"Yeah," Jamie says slowly. "Why?"

"I just assumed your uncle is also . . . um . . . visibly Nish."

Jamie nods, confused, and I continue. "Border guards in Canada ask if you're bringing any firearms into their country. On this side, they just wanna know about cigarettes. Unless you're visibly Nish. Then you get the full questioning. And if you're Nish and Black, like my uncle Art? You get a gun pulled on you at the border with your Nish wife and baby daughters in their car seats."

Jamie studies me. "Man, Daunis, I had no idea that racist bullshit happens here. It makes me angry that your aunt and uncle had to go through such a horrible experience."

"And *that's* why I'm not a fan of law enforcement. Among other reasons." I look down. "My aunt Teddie rarely crosses the border now, and when she does, she never has Art or the girls with her. As soon as I could drive, she had me shop for them across the river. Not only am I the palest Nish, but I have a Canadian birth certificate because I was born in Montreal, so it makes my border crossing less complicated."

Jamie's been incredibly sympathetic throughout our conversation, so I expect him to respond the same way now. Instead, he remains quiet and focuses on the birch trees nearby.

"Do you ever wish you could do something to truly make a difference?" he says finally. "Solve a problem and improve things for people? Not just for those you know, but something big enough to impact even people you'll never meet?"

"Of course," I say. "I want to become a doctor and help people heal. And do research that can benefit tribal communities. But for now, I do small things to help. Like go across the river to get my aunt the Limpa rye bread she likes from the Swedish bakery. My mom has me bring back over-the-counter medicine that's way cheaper over there. Plus, Tim Hortons coffee for Art." I glance down and pull at a thread on my cutoff jeans. "It probably seems insignificant, but I know it makes a difference to my aunt and uncle."

"Kindness is something that seems small, Daunis, but it's like tossing a pebble into a pond and the ripples reach further than you thought." Jamie smiles and—as if confirming his words—the warmth of his kindness ripples through my body.

I hope I am not blushing.

"You must think it's strange," I begin, eager to change the subject. "A foreign country is right next door and I go for coffee and Sudafed. And Canadians cross the river for gas and milk. But when you live somewhere forever, I suppose everything seems normal."

Jamie gives me an odd look, curious and melancholy at the same time. "I never live anywhere long enough to find out what normal feels like."

He hesitates, like he just admitted something he shouldn't have. Before I can ask him more, we're interrupted by a group of skateboarders rolling past us. Like a flock of birds, they curve their route in unison to avoid a cluster of people in the road ahead.

There is a startling *POP! POP! POP!* sound.

In the next instant, I am facedown on the road.

CHAPTER 8

Something is crushing me. Jamie. He's thrown himself on me, pressing me into the ground. A moment later, he pushes himself off and the absence of his weight instantly expands my lungs, and I gulp deep breaths. My vision comes into focus just as I realize it's gone dark. Jamie's hand is on my back, forcing me to stay down.

"What the hell?" I push myself up anyway, shaking him off. Firecrackers. Tossed onto the road by local boys stirring up mischief. A few years ago it might have been Levi and his friends.

The boys laugh as they skateboard away. Most people are turned in their direction. An older man shouts at their backs. A few people gawk at Jamie and me.

I get up and bend over to dust off my legs, observing my bloody knee an instant before it begins stinging.

"Shit," I say, as the pain grows and blood trickles down my leg to my running shoe.

"Daunis, I'm so sorry. I thought . . . I panicked." Jamie kneels to inspect my injury. He quickly removes his T-shirt, and even in my confusion I am struck by how lean he is. Sleek. His tanned chest is a human anatomy lesson; each muscle is clearly defined. His hand on the back of my knee feels so hot that I wonder if it will leave a mark. With his other hand, he pours water on it from a bottle that someone hands him and dabs at the wound with his shirt.

I focus on his bent head. His curls look soft. A few strands shine copper under the sunlight.

"You thought it was gunshots?"

His hands freeze for just a second before he resumes cleaning my knee, as if I haven't said anything.

I continue. "You lived in some dangerous neighborhoods?"

He doesn't quite meet my eyes. I fight an urge to trace the length of his scar. I read about scars once. Hypertrophic scars are reddest in the first year; they fade with time. Jamie's scar is fresh. *That cut's too straight to be accidental*. If what Auntie said was right, then someone cut him on purpose. Recently.

"Danger can turn up anywhere," he says.

As soon as Jamie and I reach the powwow grounds, the twins shout my name. They're dressed in Jingle Dress regalia. Skirts with waved rows of small, silver-colored cones clink melodically as Perry and Pauline run toward me, Auntie close behind. Their eyes go to my knee.

"Holy. What happened to you? Something bloody?" Perry asks hopefully.

"Someone set off a bunch of firecrackers. Caught us off guard, and we dove for cover. But Jamie patched me up." I make it sound like an exciting adventure. Jamie shoots me a grateful smile.

When Auntie approaches, I hear her before I see her. Sewn onto her yellow Jingle Dress are bands of orange and white ribbons, and attached to those are 365 jangling golden cones. She bends over to inspect my injury.

"Looks like you cleaned it pretty well," she tells Jamie. "There's antiseptic spray in the first aid kit in the RV," she reminds me. "Get some on your knee right away."

Lily approaches in her Fancy Shawl regalia, which includes a simple black floral fabric dress with black ribbon around the skirt hem. She holds a black shawl fringed in long black and silver strands. She eyes Jamie's shirt, which still has traces of my blood, and wrinkles her nose at my threadbare yellow GIRLS ON THE RUN T-shirt, cutoff jeans, and old running shoes.

"Holy wah. Yous look like you fought a pack of rez dogs and lost."

"But we put up a good fight," Jamie says. I snort and Lily raises an eyebrow at me, eyes glinting. Just as I'm bracing myself for one of Lily's pervy comments, we hear the emcee make the final call for dancers to line up for Grand Entry.

Lily heads off while Jamie and I jog over to Teddie and Art's RV at the edge of the powwow grounds. I douse my knee in antiseptic spray, swearing at the fresh sting.

I rummage for a shirt and hand it to Jamie. "Hurry up, we're going to be late," I say. It's one of mine from the last time I went camping with them, and is too big on him, but at least it's clean.

Jamie turns away when changing, but I can't resist taking a peek at his back muscles. For science.

We make our way to the covered bleachers forming a perimeter around the dance arena. At the very center is a large, cedar-covered arbor with more than a dozen drum groups warming up for Grand Entry. Each drum is the size of a round coffee table. Men are seated around it, each one beating it with a drumstick that has a leather-wrapped bulb on the end, while the women stand behind them.

We all rise for Grand Entry. Carrying a staff of eagle feathers, the head veteran leads the procession. Each veteran in the color guard brings in a different flag: U.S., Canada, Michigan, Tribe, and several clans. The head dancers come next, a man and woman in regalia, dancing side by side. They're followed by the two teens who are the junior head dancers. Then a seemingly endless line of dancers enters the arena by category, announced by the emcee.

Jamie is on the edge of his seat, taking everything in. He has questions about everything. When a woman near us makes a high-pitched trilling sound, a few other women join in.

"What's that?" he asks, wide-eyed.

"Those are called lee-lees. Nish women trill them, mostly to honor someone. Other times there's more to it. Something else. But I'm not sure what." I make a mental note to ask Auntie.

I point out Granny June at the front of the Women's Traditional dancers.

"That's Lily's great-grandma. She named her dog Tribal Council just so she could yell at him." I imitate Granny. "Fetch my slippers, Council. No, Council. Bad Tribal Council."

Jamie throws his head back and laughs. I scold myself: *Don't be That Girl.* I think of Levi's mom, Dana. The one who got to take the Firekeeper name. *Sometimes That Girl wins.*

Auntie and her girls pass our section with the rest of the Jingle Dress dancers. My aunt is like a golden flame flickering around the arena. When the twins raise their tiny feather fans at the honor beats, I feel so proud that the breath catches in my throat.

The Fancy Shawl dancers are the last to enter the arena. Lily's shawl drapes over outstretched arms. The fringe blurs as she spins. A lone black butterfly surrounded by color.

I lean into Jamie, speaking into his ear as he scans the panoramic kaleidoscope.

"All these dancers. Imagine that each one is an atom, forming molecules of dancers for each category: Traditional, Fancy, Grass, Jingle. You see the whole entity."

I point with my lips at the sea of dancers. They entered the arena single file, but their line has spiraled around the drum arbor. Not a speck of grass is visible in the space.

"Now focus on just one dancer—say, a Jingle Dress dancer." Jamie dutifully fixes his gaze. "Every atom has subatomic parts. Her regalia includes a dress, belt, moccasins, and a lot of other items. Dancers don't start out with their full regalia; they get it bit by bit. Each piece is a connection to her family, her teachers, and even to ancestors generations back. If you know the story of her regalia—who and where and why each item came to be—then you know her."

We all remain standing as the singing is led by drumbeats so powerful they reverberate through the bleachers to my feet, as if pulsing my own heart. I can feel Jamie's gaze.

I breathe deeply, inhaling the songs, then meet his eyes. "You know the saying 'The whole is greater than the sum of its parts'?"

Jamie nods.

"Grand Entry is the whole," I continue. "It's the synergy of all the teachings."

My macro theory of Nish connectivity may not make sense to anyone except me, but seeing Jamie's excitement, I want to share it with him.

After a long moment, Jamie says, "I like how you see the world, Daunis."

We watch in silence until the flags are posted and the veterans' honor song has finished. As we take our seats, Jamie turns to me suddenly. "Hey, why aren't you dancing? You didn't skip it to show me around, did you?"

I look down at my hands. "I'm taking a break for a year, as part of grieving my uncle." Even though I'm angry at Uncle David, I thought it would help me get past what he did.

"I'm sorry." Jamie seems embarrassed. "I didn't mean to pry."

"You can ask me anything, Jamie. We're friends."

His smile reaches his eyes. "You have no idea how much that means to me."

I will not be That Girl, no matter how much Jamie's eyes sparkle with delight that ripples warmly to every cell in my body.

After, we roam the vendor booths that form an outer ring surrounding the bleachers. I keep an eye out for Lily. We run into her and Granny June near the first aid booth.

"Hey, we wanna sit with yous when it's time for the twins to dance," Lily says.

I tell Jamie it's the first time the girls are dancing in a competition category. "Last year they were still in Tiny Tots. They're so good . . . better dancers at six than I'll ever be."

"I bet you can dance," Jamie says, grinning. "Levi's always talking about what a star athlete you are."

"Eh. I have the endurance. Just not light on my feet. Or graceful."

Granny June nods. "Your brother is the dancer in your family."

"Yeah, but Levi never wanted to dance Fancy or Grass. Just hip-hop," I say.

Lily nudges Jamie. "You'll get to see Levi in action at Shagala. All you Supes hafta go. You should take Daunis."

"I'm sure Jamie's *girlfriend*, Jennifer, will visit for that." I glare daggers at Lily.

"Shagala," Jamie says slowly, like it's a foreign language. "Is that Nish—"

"No," I say. "*SHA* for Sault Hockey Association. And *gala* because it's a fancy dance."

"Shag-ala, *snag*-ala," Lily says. We all crack up, except for Jamie, who may not know that *snagging* is what we call . . . Eh, I'll let Levi explain that one.

"You a hockey player?" Granny June narrows an eye as she scans Jamie head to toe.

"Yes, ma'am." He straightens himself up a bit taller.

"Hockey players are all hype, hey," she grumbles. "Best lover I ever had was an accountant." Granny June lowers her voice in a conspiratorial whisper. "Zhaaganaash."

"Granny June, he's not a boyfriend. He's a boy who's a friend," I clarify.

"And I thought you were a smart college girl," Granny June says. She takes a second look at Jamie before pointing her lips in my direction. "You gonna do right by her?"

Jamie stares at Granny before answering. "Yes. I will."

"Good. Because things end how they start," she says before wandering off to haggle with vendors for senior discounts.

"Granny June's got opinions." I roll my eyes and hope I'm not blushing.

"I like her," Jamie declares.

"You like her now," Lily begins. "Just wait till you realize everything she says is either raunchy or a quote from a fortune cookie."

"Don't forget her rants against Tribal Council," I add.

Jamie grins. "Her dog? Or the actual Tribal Council?"

"Both!" Lily and I say in unison, followed by, "Jinx!" Before she can say "double jinx," I shout, "Jinx infinity!" I give her a bratty smirk. "Infinity wins."

Lily tells Jamie, "Never argue with a geek. They use science and math like weapons."

His laughter reverberates through my body, and for just one second, I let myself imagine what it'd be like if there wasn't a Jennifer. But, isn't this how Dana started?

As a shiver runs the length of my spine, Travis suddenly appears at Lily's side. Without a thought, I put myself between them. A buffer for Lily. A pause for Travis.

"Hold up, Dauny. I just want to talk." Travis attempts to peer behind me. "Lily, can we talk?" He has the audacity to glare at me. "Without your goon?"

"That's a bad idea," I announce while raising my fists. If he wants to call me a goon, I'll act like one.

Travis shifts from foot to foot as he attempts to soften his stance. He flashes a familiar smile that reveals the beginnings of tooth decay at the gumline. *Oh, Travis.* A pang of sadness seeps through a crack in my goon armor. Then he transforms his face into his *Please, Lily, just one more chance* expression. His hands shake as he grips a two-liter bottle of Mountain Dew; a coffee filter floats inside like in a snow globe. I see Jamie notice it too, and we lock eyes.

"Not here. Not now." Lily looks nervously in the direction Granny went.

"Aww, c'mon, Lily-bit." I've heard Travis call her that nickname a million times, but this time, there's an edge to it. The hairs stand up on the back of my neck.

"Just go, Travis," I say, tensing.

"Hey man, let me help you." Jamie offers a hand to shake.

"Who are you?" Travis snarls, the pleading look on his face evaporating immediately.

"Stop, Travis. Jamie is Daunis's friend. He's a new Supe." Lily tugs Travis's arm. "Just go. Okay?"

Travis snorts, his expression twisting. "Dauny finally got herself a puck fuck?" The ugliness of his mean-spirited glee reveals a Travis I don't recognize at all. Where is the boy who convinced me to place my textbook beneath my pillow the night before a test in case its contents might permeate our brains through osmosis?

"Shut up, Travis." Lily shoves him. "Please, just go."

"I'll go if you promise you'll come find me later, Lily. I just want to talk."

"Fine, but only if you go now."

"Okay, you promised." Travis flashes a grin, all smiles again, before darting away.

"Holy shit, Lily," I say. "Don't talk to him. He looks really rough. And you know what that coffee filter stuffed into his pop was laced with. He can't even get through a day without it. He's in deep."

"I know," she sighs. "But what am I supposed to do? It's Travis. I'll talk to you later. I need to find him now—Granny can't see him, or she'll raise hell."

"Lily, don't." I reach for her arm, but she moves away.

"No! I can take care of myself." Lily rushes off.

"C'mon, Lily . . . ," I call to her before realizing I sound exactly like Travis trying to cajole her into doing what he wanted. Lily can take care of herself, and Travis won't try anything with so many people around.

"So that's Travis," Jamie says as we watch the small black figure disappear.

"Yup." I'm still disturbed by the change in Travis, and my trying to get Lily to do what I wanted. And my embarrassment that Jamie saw what just happened. I clear my throat. "Travis used to be sweet and so funny. In school when it was time for announcements, he'd do this drumroll thing on his belly." I shake my head. "He looks so bad."

"Has he always been like this?" Jamie asks. I'm relieved he doesn't seem rattled by Travis's behavior.

"Well, he's another Lost Boy." I shrug, but it's a hollow gesture that causes a familiar jolt of pain in my left shoulder. I don't know why I tried making light of it; Jamie's demonstrated unexpected compassion again and again. "People call them Lost Boys, like from Neverland, never taking anything seriously and seeming stuck in place. But I think there's more to it."

"What do you think is going on?" Jamie asks. His voice is low and calm.

"My aunt once described a rough patch in her life as self-medicating the pain. Maybe that's what's really going on when guys like Travis quit school and fixate on video games and weed—well, more than that now . . . and drinking garbage. Literal garbage."

Jamie's expression reminds me of Uncle David during class, waiting for the final answer.

And I've known the answer for several months.

"Travis is a meth head," I admit. Lily made me promise not to tell anyone, but Jamie doesn't know anyone in town. Besides, if Travis is showing up at powwows drinking meth tea, then everybody will know soon. The moccasin telegraph is powerful.

I reach for my phone to check on Lily.

ME: Sorry 4 grabbing u. R u ok?

CHAPTER 9

The powwow emcee breaks into my thoughts:

"Intertribal dance. Everybody welcome. Swish and sway the Oh-jib-way!"

I nudge Jamie. "Let's walk around before we go back to our seats. I'm too worked up about Travis." The latest episode of *The Lily and Travis Saga* has set me on edge. Damn meth ruining people's lives. Travis's and . . .

Nope. I don't want to think about him.

"Hey, would you mind if I went for a quick run or something?" I ask. Suddenly, I'm feeling anxious, like maybe I've shared something that I shouldn't have. "You can browse the vendor booths, or I'm sure Levi is around somewhere. I just . . . I don't like feeling like this."

"Daunis." The intensity of the way he says my name grabs my attention. "I'll come with," Jamie says. "You wanna talk, I'll listen. If you don't, that's okay. We can just run together."

Jamie is doing it again, being kind and sympathetic. Making it so easy to open up to him. I realize that running with Jamie has become the best part of my day—the only normal part in this New Normal.

I nod gratefully. We make our way past people leaving the pow-wow grounds.

"You know what would help?" I say as we reach Ice Circle Drive. "Set the pace. Push me so I burn off this anger. Okay?"

"You got it." He grins, and something flips in my stomach. As if I've swallowed magnets and Jamie is made of steel. *Don't be That Girl.* I force myself not to smile back.

"Let's see what you've got," he says, launching into a sprint.

It works. We do a fast two-mile loop that requires all of my physical and mental energy. I give a thumbs-up as we catch our breath. Running is good medicine.

"Do you want to talk about it now?" Jamie asks.

"Travis drank at parties," I say as we walk back to the powwow grounds. "He didn't make any teams, so he wasn't under any player code of conduct. Two years ago, he started dabbling in other stuff."

There's a relief in telling a secret. A burden lifted, just by sharing it with someone. And Jamie listens patiently. When I tried telling Levi last fall and winter, he didn't seem to take my concerns about Travis seriously. I saw my brother giving Travis hell after that, so I guess Levi did listen; he just wasn't sympathetic in the moment, the way that Jamie is.

"Meth's cheaper than booze and lasts longer. His mom got into meth. People call her the Meth Queen. Travis started skipping school a lot and took fewer AP classes. Lily caught him making meth over Christmas break. Like, actually cooking it, Jamie. Since then, it seems like more people in town and on the rez are using." I take a deep breath before adding, "Sometimes it's people you never in a million years thought would get mixed up in it."

Even though Jamie is listening without a trace of judgment, I cut myself off. It feels disloyal to say anything more. I'd be revealing the worst parts about someone I love. I never thought about secrets being like a bull's-eye. The smaller the circle, the bigger the secret.

We reach the vendor booths. "Thanks for listening, Jamie, but I think that's all I want to say for now. Let's just browse a bit. Okay?"

"Whatever you want, Daunis," Jamie says gently. "Any recommendations?" he asks, pausing at a table of books for sale.

I scan the titles quickly and point to *Custer Died for Your Sins* by Vine Deloria Jr.

"Auntie got me that book when I was fourteen. That was the year we made my Jingle Dress skirt. Each day, she had me sew one jingle cone on my skirt. Three hundred sixty-five days, three hundred sixty-five teachings."

"You're so lucky to have her in your life," Jamie says, paying for the book.

I lead Jamie over to my cousin Eva's stand with her gorgeous beadwork: strawberry earrings, floral medallion necklaces, and even an ornate checkbook cover. She's also set out braids of sweetgrass for sale. Since Eva is in deep conversation with customers, I tuck a twenty-dollar bill beneath her bottle of pop and take two green braids of grass the length of my arm. I hand one to Jamie and we hold the sweetgrass up to our noses. Jamie closes his eyes as he inhales the fresh, delicate sweetness.

I catch a whiff of fry bread and my stomach gurgles. "Oh man, you've got to try this." I pull Jamie toward a small trailer with a big window and order one piece of fry bread for us to share, hot out of the fryer. I add butter and maple syrup, and Jamie and I sit down at a nearby picnic table. I tear one half for Jamie, and he holds it in a paper towel until it's cooled off enough to eat. It's perfect—crispy outside and fluffy inside.

I sit up straight when Jamie moans. "Oh, Daunis. This is so good," he says, mouth still full of his first bite. "We gotta run extra miles tomorrow." He swallows and takes an even bigger bite. "So worth it."

"So worth it," I mumble in agreement, cramming more into my mouth.

As we split up to go to the bathroom and wash the sticky syrup from our fingers, I text Lily, who still hasn't responded to my previous text. She'll see it when she checks her phone after the intertribals finish. She's more likely to reply to a raunchy one anyway.

ME: jj moaned while eating frybrd. his gf vvvlucky

During the dinner break, I bring Jamie back to Auntie and Art's RV. The twins are in shorts and T-shirts now; they've decided to skip the evening dances to play with their cousins and conk out early. Auntie finishes unbraiding Pauline's hair, pulling it into a high ponytail and wrapping it into a bun. Art calls Jamie over to the grill to fix a plate for supper. When Art cracks a joke, I feel Jamie's hearty laugh all the way to my toes.

When Pauline runs off, it's my turn. I walk over to the picnic table where Auntie is still perched. I plunk myself on the bench, my back facing her. She picks up the hairbrush and starts working through my thick mop, pulling it into a high ponytail like Pauline's. Jamie sets his plate down at one end of the picnic table.

"Will you fix me a plate, too?" I ask sweetly. Jamie grins and heads back to the table where the food is spread out.

"Auntie, why did you snap at me about the blanket party?" I ask.

"Daunis, I love you like my own daughter. The Nish kwewag who show up at those blanket parties . . . they know that violence firsthand." Auntie's hands move quickly, dividing my ponytail into thirds, which she will braid separately before weaving the three braids together into an elaborate braid that she'll wrap into a bun. It's her favorite hairstyle for me, one she's done many times since I was a child. "It's just . . . in that moment I was pissed you were so eager to go. I hate going, but I thank Creator each time that you're not with me. I keep hoping your privileges will keep you safe. Your last name. Your light skin. Your money. Your size, even."

Auntie spots Jamie heading back from the grill area and finishes with "I'm thankful for you having those advantages. But I get mad and scared because my Black and Ojibwe daughters don't."

She's right. All the things I've been uncomfortable with, advantages I've done nothing to earn, they are privileges. The twins will face struggles that I never will. I think back to how I begged to tag along to the blanket party and feel ashamed.

She kisses the side of my head as Jamie hands me a plate with fried whitefish, potatoes, and green beans. I accept it gratefully, her words still ringing in my head, and we both dig in.

"So, Jamie, I see Daunis has been showing you around our town. Is she also taking you to the minor forty-niner?" Auntie asks.

"A minor what?" Jamie looks up from his plate.

"Powwow parties are called forty-niners," I explain. "When it's not for adults, it's a minor forty-niner."

"So it's a party just for teens?" Jamie asks as if to clarify for himself.

"Yeah." I motion taking a sip of an imaginary bottle. "Beer and shenanigans." Jamie glances at Auntie to gauge her reaction.

"It's okay to have fun and not be stupid about it," Auntie says, then gives me a pointed look. "I mean, throwing a party at your grandparents' big, fancy house in town would not be smart at all. But, I suppose, having a beer or two in the woods with friends while one person stays sober"—she eyeballs Jamie—"and sleeping over at a relative's house on the island is a more intelligent and safe option. Right, Daunis?"

"Yes, Auntie," I say meekly. Of course Auntie knows about my party last weekend. I can never hide anything from her. Even when I try, my aunt has informants everywhere, it seems.

"Don't worry about Elvis and Patsy," she tells me. "The dogs are staying at Seeney's this weekend."

"Make sure they don't come back all mean like her," I grumble.

Auntie gives a wry smile. "You think you're the only one Seeney ever made cry?"

When we leave, Art shakes Jamie's hand the way Nish guys do, reaching around to grasp Jamie's thumb rather than the fingers.

Auntie hugs me, whispering, "I'm sorry I took out my fear on you. I'll do better. I love you, Daunis."

"I know," I whisper back, squeezing her tight. "I'm sorry, too, Auntie."

As we walk away, Auntie calls after us.

"Let your mom know you're going to the island, so she won't worry about you."

On the ferry ride to Sugar Island, I text Mom. Auntie knows that I have to strike a delicate balance by giving my mother enough info so she won't fret, but not too many details and trigger new worries.

> ME: Hanging with lily and friends on island. Will stay at aunties.
> DONT WORRY ILL BE SAFE.

Technically, I'm not lying. Jamie and I are friends. Lily will be at the party after she deals with Travis. I shoot a text to Lily. Still no response to either of my previous texts.

> ME: Headed to 49er with jj. What happened with Trav?

"Hey, if you need to let your uncle know where you're at, text him now. You can't get a signal except on the north side where it's close enough to some Canadian cell towers. Rest of the island is a dead zone. Plus, the east side is all cliffs and caves, so signals just bounce around."

"Cliffs and caves?" Jamie asks.

"Yeah, it's really remote. Some caves are only accessible from the water." Jamie raises an eyebrow, so I go into tour guide mode again, lowering my voice to a whisper. "Did you know that Al Capone smuggled liquor across the border during Prohibition? He'd go to Waishkey Bay over in Brimley. Supposedly he also had a stockpile on Sugar Island."

"Did you know that Al Capone's nickname was Scarface and he had syphilis and gonorrhea when he went to prison for tax evasion?" Jamie says. "But we just have the nickname in common."

I laugh and then feel compelled to mention the girlfriend. "Jennifer is a lucky girl. Will I get to meet her at Shagala? It's the first Saturday in October. You should tell her now because there are only two flights a day into the nearest airport." I force myself to stop babbling. As we approach the next intersection, I motion for him to turn. Roads narrow until it's just a two-track—two ruts on an unpaved trail. Cars fit into spaces between trees. He backs into a spot.

"Thanks for the guidance," Jamie says. "About the directions here . . . and about the dance. I'll let Jen know." Hearing him say her nickname makes her more real to me. "Jennifer" is too formal, while "Jenny" is too cutesy. But I could imagine sitting next to a "Jen" at the round dining tables in the Superior Shores ballroom and helping her to feel welcome. I'll need to line up a date for Shagala before Levi asks me to be Stormy's escort again.

Lily. I'll ask her to go with me. We can kick off our shoes and dance to every song.

We follow the sounds of people singing forty-niner songs, funny songs about rez life set to drumming. The singing and laughing grow louder as we approach an old barn. A group of guys stand in a circle, each with a small, handheld drum. One guy sings and drums while everyone else listens.

Have you seen my powwow snag
Prettiest girl, ain't no brag
Dancing barefoot on the grass
Red tube top and flattest ass
Can filet a fish and gut a deer
Works at Indian Health, got a career
Showed her off around my rez
That's your cousin, my kokum says

The beer is ice cold and goes down like water, so I get another. I feel a prickle of worry when I look around but don't see Lily anywhere. I don't bother checking my phone because there's no signal out here.

My brother shouts my god-awful nickname, repeated like a chorus by his friends and fans. My former teammate Macy Manitou chants it the loudest.

"Bubble. Bubble. Bubble."

It feels like swimming upstream to reach them across the barn. Macy's shiny, long brown hair covers one eye, but her other eye takes in my GIRLS ON THE RUN T-shirt, cutoff jeans, jacked-up knee, and old running shoes. She wrinkles her nose as if I stepped in moowin. In contrast, Macy wears a black bandanna top, low-cut jeans with an unfinished waistband, and black Chuck Taylor All Star low-top sneakers.

Levi throws an arm around me. He pulls Macy next to him with his other hand.

"Jamie, you never talk about your girl! Is she like these two?" Levi asks Jamie. "Mad hockey skills, but perfect princesses off the ice?" He tilts his head each way. "This brat is Macy."

"So, what's the deal with your scar?" Macy dives right in. Rude as usual.

"Car accident," Jamie says. He turns to me. "So, Bubble, huh? What's with the nickname?"

I chug my beer and pretend I don't hear him, but Macy gleefully pipes up.

"Bubble is short for Bubble Butt. Chi Diiyash Kwe. Big Butt Woman." Her laughter is a wind chime of glass shards, quick and pretty but with dangerous edges.

Everyone cracks up, but Jamie doesn't join in, just gives me a small smile. Macy spins out of Levi's grasp and over to the drummers.

"Guilty," I say with a shrug, but my face is burning. *I'm going to kill Macy. Then Levi.* I scan the crowd for Lily again; she'd help me kill them. Be my alibi. Or be Thelma to my Louise.

"In middle school, I wore oversized glasses and had a growth spurt so all my pants were too short and everyone called me 'Urkel.' Even my teammates," Jamie tells me before stepping away to refill my cup. I flash him a grateful smile. I try picturing him as the dorky television character, but it doesn't align with the athletic, confident guy I watch. Maybe his compassion stems from that early teasing.

When Jamie returns with my beer, we join the crowd watching Macy twirling around the drummers. As annoyed as I am with her, I have to admit she's mesmerizing to watch. She does Fancy Shawl steps to a forty-niner version of the theme song to *SpongeBob SquarePants*. She's another one with smooth dance moves. Macy holds her arms out, as if to display an imaginary shawl. Her black Chucks barely touch the concrete as she dances.

I finish my third drink as quickly as my first and start heading back to the keg. I offer to get Jamie a drink, but he shakes his head. I notice he's been sipping the same can of pop since we arrived. Lots of hockey players won't drink for the whole season. Maybe Jamie's a rule follower too.

As I refill my cup at the keg, Levi appears. He swipes it and downs the entire thing.

"You being a good ambassador to the new 'skin?"

I bristle. Levi knows I hate it when he calls Nishnaabs 'skins. As if using the redskin slur ourselves makes it okay.

"Yup," I say, grabbing the cup back.

"You gonna make your move tonight?" he asks with a sly smile.

"Hells no. Levi, he's got a girlfriend."

"Eh," he says dismissively, watching me refill it once more.

"I don't poach boyfriends," I say evenly. Levi and I have both grown up with the rumors of what his mom did. "Besides, you know I don't date hockey players. I'm not some clingy-ass anglerfish girl- friend." I exaggerate a shudder.

"Don't tell me this is because you're still not over Toivo Jon," Levi groans.

My brother gives everyone a nickname, except TJ. Levi always uses his real one—the Finlander name TJ shares with his dad and grandpa even though they go by different versions.

"Hey," I snap. "We don't do this. Stick our noses in each other's relationships. Because if we do, I'd be saying shit about all the girls you use and toss away like Kleenex."

He raises an eyebrow. "What am I supposed to do when they make it so easy?"

"Um . . . maybe treat them with respect?"

"I always say *miigwech* afterward," he says.

I've never wanted to smack the smug from my brother more than at this moment.

"Levi, I hope someday a girl you really truly love walks away from you. And that you know that it's totally your fault."

"Why? Oh right, what do you call it . . . Guy Lies?" Levi clicks his tongue and shakes his head in mock pity. "Toivo Jon really messed you up."

"Screw you, Levi." Something churns in my stomach like magma. The music, laughter, and conversations fill the pole barn, suddenly overwhelming my senses. I push my way to the barn's side opening.

Weaving around the maze of parked cars, I swat away the image of TJ. His face illuminated by the glow of a tiny woodstove inside the ice shanty. Intertwined in a large sleeping bag on a camp mattress. Whispering how much he loved me between gasps.

Toivo Jon Kewadin. The rotten lying liar. My introduction to Guy Lies.

That's not true. He wasn't the first one to lie to you.

I am dizzy and queasy. My feet find every stone and exposed tree root as I stumble on the way to Jamie's truck. Something flaps large wings over my head. I veer a few steps into the woods, and the sick erupts from inside me.

I collapse on my knees, one still sore from earlier today. As I wipe my mouth, I hear strange sounds. I pause, listening. Arguing. Crying.

I jump up as I see Lily and Travis walking down the two-track, ten feet away from me. Lily looks upset and she begins to speed up. *That jerk.*

I open my mouth to call out to Lily and ask if she needs help when suddenly Travis halts. He grabs Lily's arm to stop her from walking away. When she yanks free, he pulls a gun from the back of his jeans.

My scream is trapped in my throat; only a gurgle escapes. Lily snaps her head in my direction, and I see the fear in her eyes, knowing it's reflected in mine.

I freeze as Travis spins around to aim the snub-nosed revolver at me. Only my eyes move, darting from the gun to Lily's horrified expression. Gun. Shock. Gun. Disbelief. Gun. Fear.

My ears are pressure-filled by the pounding of my heart. There is no other sound.

THA-THUM-THA-THUM-THA-THUM.

Travis's hands shake with tiny tremors. We sat next to each other in every AP class. I rooted for him to get his act together.

I'm gonna die. Lily will watch me die.

The oily sweetness is familiar. Art's garage. Someone used WD-40 to clean this gun. More scents: pine, damp moss, skunky sweat, and something sharp. Cat pee?

THA-THUM-THA-THUM-THA-THUM.

Suddenly, Travis acts as if the gun transformed into a machete. He makes odd diagonal slicing motions toward the ground at invisible targets surrounding him.

Maybe he'll forget about me. Lily and I can run away or jump into Jamie's truck.

Terror grips my heart. The gun. Travis aims at my face again.

Mom. She won't survive this. One bullet will kill us both.

A brave hand reaches for the gun. Lily's fingers outstretched. Demanding. *Give it. Now.*

THA-THUM-THA—

I am thinking of my mother when the blast changes everything.

CHAPTER 10

L ily lands on her back, arms outstretched, like she's floating in a pool. But not moving.

This moment lasts an eternity. Or an instant. It is both but I don't know how.

Travis looks at her before turning back to me. His mouth moves, but I can't hear him. All I hear is an echo of the blast. He raises the gun to his temple. I squeeze my eyes shut, then open them to see his head snap sideways. His body crumples at Lily's feet, as if groveling for one more chance.

This isn't real. It didn't happen. I must have passed out on the way to Jamie's truck. I'll wake up and go back to the barn. Find Lily and hug her. Tell Levi that I'm over TJ. I'll reveal every secret to Jamie that I've been keeping. The truth about Uncle David's death. Why I don't play hockey anymore. What my mother did after she found Dad in bed with Dana at a party on Sugar Island the night she planned to tell him about me. How Guy Lies started.

It's just a bad dream. Any minute now, I'll wake up.

A figure moves behind a car. Jamie. Here in my dream. Crouched low. His head jerks around, scanning for people, but the rest of his body glides as if on skates. He kneels at Lily's side. Gently sweeps the hair from her forehead.

Why isn't he panicking? Why is he so calm? Even in my numbness, I notice the way he's kneeling. Attentive and focused, just like when he cleaned my bloody knee. Messy curls glimmering copper. The only person who reacted to the firecrackers as if they were gunshots.

Jamie feels for a pulse at her neck. His index and middle finger go to her lower neck where the common carotid artery is located. Exactly like when Teddie taught me CPR.

His head drops forward as if his neck can no longer bear its weight. Then it slumps backward while he releases a long sigh to the trees above.

Something bleats in agony. He spins to look at me. Huge, surprised eyes.

"Daunis!" He rushes toward me. "Are you hurt?"

I mean to shake my head but my entire body trembles instead. When I take a step toward him, my legs wobble. He pulls me up and half carries me the few steps to his truck. Quickly places me in the passenger seat. Gently. So I won't break.

"S-s-secrets." It doesn't sound like me, too high-pitched, but I felt the word start in my gut. I look out the window for any path I could take to get away. Another word escapes as I reach for the door. "S-s-stranger." The secrets I want to run from aren't mine.

"Shhhhh," he says, breath in my ear. "We gotta get out of here, Daunis. Now."

Lily is dead.

Jamie Johnson is not who he says he is.

And this is not a dream.

Jamie retraces our earlier route. The two-track and dirt roads are like capillaries threading through Sugar Island, leading to veins that will take us back to the ferry. Veins flow to the heart; arteries flow from the heart. Everything starts at the heart.

"I'm gonna be sick." I put a hand to my mouth as the other grips the door handle. Jamie takes the first side road. I'm out of the truck before he can shift into park. I have nothing left to puke, but my body still goes through the motions.

"Daunis, I'm so sorry. But we really need to go. I've got to get you home."

"Is she dead?"

This can't be happening. He needs to say he made it all up. His reaction was fake. She's still breathing back there. We need to save her. How could we leave her behind?

"I'm not making it up," he says. "There wasn't anything we could do for her."

I realize I must have said everything aloud. To be sure it doesn't happen again, I clamp my hand over my mouth. Dirt and minute bits of gravel stick to my lips. My knee hurts, so I sit back instead. Jamie stands in the road as if he's guarding me. But from what?

He looks at me. I look up at him, my mind racing. I hear Uncle David's voice in my head, telling me to piece together what I know. I take a deep breath and focus.

Things That Don't Make Sense:

1. Lily is dead.
2. Jamie told Macy his scar was from a car accident. Auntie said it was too straight to be accidental.
3. Jamie is full of questions but doesn't like answering them.

4. Jamie made the Supes as a walk-on from nowhere. He's a complete unknown.

5. Jamie checked for Lily's pulse like a first responder, not a high school student. He cleaned my knee well enough to earn Auntie's respect, and she's a nurse.

6. Jamie reacted to the firecrackers like gunshots. Soldiers and cops train repeatedly so they have muscle memory and their reactions are automatic.

It hits me.

Jamie Johnson is a cop.

My eyes widen. He blinks. LIGHT BULB ON. He knows that I know his secret. I uncover my mouth and stand in front of him, shaking. I repeat the question I asked yesterday, when we stood across from each other by GrandMary's bed.

"Who are you, Jamie Johnson?"

He pinches the bridge of his nose and looks away.

I continue, "Let me guess. You're gonna give no response, or an evasive one, or a half-truth, or—and this is my favorite—you'll turn it around and ask me a question instead. Like this one: 'Daunis, how did you figure out I was a cop?'"

He looks at me, this time not blinking. Not flinching. Instead, I'm the one who looks away, down the dirt road leading to the north end of the island.

Auntie. She will make sense of everything.

I jump to my feet and I run. Not with him. From him. Fleeing in a panicked frenzy. I run as fast as I can, each breath ripping from my lungs. I won't stop until I reach the driveway marked with stone light posts like sentries standing guard, where I know a wood sign reads:

Firekeeper-Birch

Bigiiwen Enji Zaagigooyin

(Come Home Where You Are Loved)

His footsteps get closer. Looking back would only slow me down. I will my legs to stretch, lengthening my stride beyond what I ever thought possible. How can he be gaining on me? He's going to catch me. There are no houses nearby. No one to hear me scream. As my thighs spasm from quadriceps pushed to exhaustion, he races ahead. His controlled breaths remain steady even when he turns to run backward—nimble and lightning fast. Jamie hasn't just hidden his true identity and purpose . . . he's refrained from showing his full speed, agility, and stamina.

"Daunis, listen to me. I know you're scared, but we can't go to your aunt's house. Trust me, you don't want her involved in this." Fear flashes through me as I realize he knows where Auntie lives. I've never told him. "She's at the powwow all weekend, right?"

I halt, my feet taking root in the middle of the road. He's right; she's not on the island.

My words are jagged gasps. "What do you mean by 'this'? Why can't Auntie be involved in it?" I get in his face, goon-style. "You talk or I'll ditch you right now for the woods that I know and you don't."

Even as I say that, I realize that maybe he is familiar with these woods. He's already proven that he knows things he shouldn't know. I'm not sure I can trust anything he's told me.

"I need to take you home. You'll be safe with your mom," Jamie says gently.

I look at the sugar maples, taking a deep breath as I prepare to run from that kind voice.

"Okay. Daunis, get in the truck and I promise, I'll answer your question." He sounds too weary to fight. But he isn't tired. His breathing has returned to normal while mine is still beyond my control. I need to regain control. Turning to walk back to the truck, I want my anger to build with each step. Fury is better than fear.

I get in the truck and slam the door shut. I stare expectantly at him. "Answers or I run and make you regret ever coming here."

"You're right. I am an undercover law-enforcement officer." He starts the truck and turns around to get back to the main road.

"That wasn't a net gain of information," I point out.

"I'm sorry, but I can't say anything more until I clear it with my supervisor," Jamie says.

"Your supervisor?" Another puzzle piece clicks into place. "Your uncle isn't your uncle, is he?"

We approach a line of cars waiting for the ferry to arrive from the mainland. Kids walk from vehicle to vehicle, hugging each other. Some cry. Others look dazed. Someone must have found Lily and Travis. Heard the gunshots and realized they weren't fireworks.

I feel numb. Outside my body. Not in a good way, like in the zone. I should be there with Lily, but I'm running away with a stranger who has lied to me since the moment we met.

The ferry arrives, full of law-enforcement vehicles. Every variety: tribal, state, county, city. Even Border Patrol. They practically fly off the ramp, one caravan of flashing lights.

Jamie follows the deckhand pointing to a lane on the ferry. We are just one vehicle of many. It's a full load of traumatized kids from the minor forty-niner. The captain blasts the horn and we leave Sugar Island.

I'm sorry, Lily. I look behind as the distance grows between my best friend and me.

Across the river, several cop cars have their lights flashing in the parking lot. There is a roadblock set up just beyond where cars will exit the ferry.

I've never seen or heard of anything like this before.

Jamie calls someone. Probably "Uncle" Ron.

"I've got her. Taking her home now," he says.

I pull my phone from my pocket and flip it open. I've missed nineteen calls and eight texts. My heart skips a beat at the first one.

LILY: Headed 2 party. Telling T its over. Needs 2C my face & hear
my voice 2 kno its final. BTW jj watches u when ur not looking. Got
it bad 4 u.
LEVI: Where r u
LEVI: R u wit Jamie
LEVI: ????????
LEVI: ANSWER UR GD PHONE
AUNTIE: Is it true about Lily?
LEVI: At Teddies wit guys call when u get this
MOM: Call now

I reread Lily's text. Over and over. Then I scroll through the missed-call numbers: Levi, Teddie, Mom. None from Granny.

"I need to tell Granny June. She doesn't know yet." My voice breaks.

"Daunis, listen carefully to me. It's very important that you not talk to anyone right now," Jamie says as he inches the truck forward. "It was instant for Lily. She didn't suffer. You were with her and she wasn't alone when she died. Please hold on to that."

Although meant to be soothing, Jamie's words infuriate me. I consider kicking open the car door and just making a run for it, but we're next in line. An enormous tribal cop talks to the driver ahead.

TJ Kewadin.

"Do you have your driver's license with you?" Jamie pulls his wallet from his back pocket. "Let me do the talking. If the officer asks, we left the party early and were driving around, just talking about the powwow. Then the texts and missed calls came through. You were too distraught to return any, and now I'm taking you home."

I hand over my license to the stranger next to me. The secret cop who is a very smooth liar. I thought TJ was bad, but Jamie Johnson takes Guy Lies to a whole new level.

"ID," Officer Kewadin orders, even though Jamie already has our cards held out.The instant TJ sees my driver's license, he quickly bends down to look me in the eyes.

"Are you okay?" His deep voice is alert, urgent. I could blurt out everything to TJ right now. About Lily. Travis. Jamie.

I'm almost there, Lorenza. Oh God. Yes. Oh, I love you.

I nod but remain silent. My stomach contracts. There's nothing left to spew.

A week after TJ began ignoring me, Lily hunted him down in the school parking lot. She hid in the bed of his truck until he opened his door. Then she leaped on his back like a tenacious baby wolf spider. When he finally pulled her off, his massive wingspan kept her fists from reaching him, so she tried kicking him. My little goon swore a blue streak and told TJ that his Harry Pajog had better hope she never learned any bad medicine.

TJ says our names into a walkie-talkie.

"Where were you tonight?" he asks.

Jamie responds, "We were at a party and left early to—"

"Wasn't asking you," TJ barks at Jamie. His voice softens a fraction, sounding uncomfortable. "Lorenza, have you talked to your mom or Teddie?"

I shake my head.

"Take her straight home," he orders Jamie. "Her mom's waiting."

Jamie sets his jaw, but nods. TJ must say something into the walkie-talkie, because a city police car escorts us all the way until we pull into my driveway. The officer rolls down his window and watches as Jamie leads me up the front steps.

"Remember, Daunis," he whispers before knocking. "Please don't say a word about what you saw or heard. I'm sorry I can't say more right now, but I'll explain more as soon as I can. Let your mom take care of you."

I refuse to look at him or acknowledge a single word he's saying. The door flings open and Mom pulls me to her, squeezing me more tightly than ever before. Every muscle in her body shakes. Her words come out as terrified sobs.

"Levi said he couldn't find you. I thought Travis shot you, too."

"I'm sorry, Mom," I murmur into her hair. "I didn't mean to make you worry."

Jamie stands in the doorway. He mumbles to my mother. Introduces himself. Teammate of Levi's. A senior at Sault High. Friend of mine. Gave me a ride home.

Mom releases me and rushes toward him. She hugs Jamie.

"Thank you for bringing her home. Thank you. Thank you." She chokes out the words.

Our eyes meet and something passes between Jamie and me. We will be smooth liars together. With one look, he knows I will say nothing to anyone about what happened.

Until we talk again.

I need answers as to why a cop is in Sault Ste. Marie, Michigan, posing as a high school senior. On my brother's hockey team. Because my best friend is dead, and Jamie Johnson has something to do with it.

CHAPTER 11

M y mother hands me a pill and a glass of water. Watches as I
drink. Helps me into bed as I begin to shiver and my teeth
chatter. She is the steady one now.

I have a faint memory of shaking like this during my coming-of-age
fast at fourteen on Sugar Island. For two nights and two days during a
cold and rainy October, I shivered beneath a wool blanket and a tarp
on a boulder in the woods. Prayed and waited for my vision to come.
I had to wait a month, until the next moon had passed, before I could
tell Auntie about my experience. How no vision had come to me, but
that every muscle in my body spasmed the entire time.

*Cold and shivering is fine, Daunis. It's when you stop shivering that
you're in trouble.*

I blink and . . . it's morning. Sunlight whispers against my eyelids. At
some point, I fell asleep. Mom stirs at my side. Why is she . . .

Lily.

Something jolts through my body. Lily is dead. I see it all again:

my best friend falling onto her back. The memory is painful; every part of my body hurts.

I get out of bed, still dressed in a ratty T-shirt and cutoffs, and head to my mom's bathroom. I know the pills are in the medicine cabinet. I need to go back to sleep. To forget this. Forget last night. Lily. Travis. Jamie. TJ. Lily. Lily. Lily.

My hand stops short of the orange prescription vial.

Lily is . . . somewhere. By now, Auntie and Seeney Nimkee will have washed her body with cedar water. Even if Seeney didn't work for the Traditional Medicine Program, Granny June would have asked her to prepare Lily for the four-day journey to the next world. It isn't part of Auntie's job as Tribal Health director, but I know she will assist Seeney.

Each day has a purpose. Today, Lily's first day, she will mourn her family. Loved ones.

Me. She will mourn me. I can't sleep through it.

I close the medicine cabinet and go to the table next to the front door. Gramma Pearl's birchbark basket in the shape of a blueberry. A pine cone hangs from each point of its flared crown. I reach inside for a pinch of loose-leaf tobacco.

My bare feet touch cold concrete steps and then grass slick with dew. The bumps and dents of the lawn remind me of dancing in my moccasins. Drumbeats reverberating from uneven ground, up my legs and into my heart. I felt that same medicine yesterday, sitting in the bleachers.

I hold the semaa in the palm of my left hand, the one closest to my heart. Release it to the poplar where I always begin my day. After my introduction, I inventory the Seven Grandfathers—love, respect, honesty, humility, bravery, wisdom, and truth.

Which one will help with this unfathomable anguish? I don't have the answer.

When I go back inside, my mother is pouring hot water into a dainty teacup.

"Want me to run a bath?" she asks gently.

If I say yes, Mom will set the kettle down and take care of me. She will skip visiting GrandMary to stay by my side. She has always put my needs first. Even before her own. Whenever I'd complain about Mom smothering me with her unending questions and hovering, Lily would say, *Cut her some slack.* One time, she snapped at me. *Some of us would love to have a mom who puts their kid first.*

Lily adores my mother. Adored my mother.

"Thanks, but I need a quick shower before I go sit with Granny June at the funeral home. Can you drop me off on your way to EverCare?"

She opens her mouth. I know she will gently suggest I stay home.

"Mom, I need to be with Lily and Granny June. I need to help."

That my mother understands perfectly.

When Granny June hugs me, I rest my chin atop her head. My nose stings. I visualize frost spreading inside my nasal cavity like feathery ice crystals on a window, overtaking the inferior turbinate, closest to the tip of my nose, traveling up the medium turbinate, and, finally, covering the superior turbinate. I'm grateful—the cold keeps the pins and needles at bay.

Granny June takes my hand. We walk to the simple pine casket. Its wood-burned etchings are in a traditional Ojibwe floral design that includes butterflies. I inhale deeply, numbing frost spreading to coat my lungs, and look down at Lily.

My best friend looks like she's napping. She's wearing her black regalia. Black is her spirit color. One time, Macy Manitou sneered about how Goth was so nineties. Lily joked, *Black makes me look slimmer, hey*. She weighed maybe ninety-six pounds.

The longer I stare at Lily, the less real she seems. A mannequin with bubble-gum-pink cheeks and lips. No black lipstick or heavily winged eyeliner. Nothing about this feels real.

I look around for Auntie. If she isn't here at the funeral home, then she must be at the ceremonial fire Art will be tending in the woods behind their pole barn. My father's family was named for its role in the tribal community for generations: Firekeeper. Auntie happened to marry a man from another Ojibwe community who was also taught firekeeper duties.

Firekeepers strike the fire for ceremonies, funerals, sweat lodges, and other cultural events where our prayers are carried by the smoke to Creator. A ceremonial fire is special; you don't roast marshmallows or sing forty-niner songs at it. Firekeepers ensure that protocols are followed the entire time it burns: no politics, no drinking, and no gossip. Only good thoughts to feed the fire and carry our prayers.

Art must have struck the fire last night upon hearing the news. He will take care of the fire for the four nights and four days of Lily's journey. At the end of the fourth day, as the fire goes out in this world, it is struck in the next world, where it will burn without end for Lily.

I am proud to come from people who served their community in this way. Auntie married a good man who continues this responsibility. The part I cannot fathom is Art tending a ceremonial fire for Lily, for her wake and funeral. She is only eighteen. Was only eighteen.

Granny June leads me to the food table at one end of the room. There will be another at Art's workshop. Slow cookers filled with different versions of hominy soup, pork and beans, and macaroni soup. A cast-iron pot of wild rice mixed with tender chunks of venison roast. Foil-lined pans of fry bread. Trays of smoked whitefish, fried baloney, and venison sausage. A brick of commodity cheese sliced into cracker-sized bites. Deviled eggs dusted with paprika. Veggie trays. Bags of chips. Pans of blueberry galette. Homemade cakes and pies next to store-bought varieties. Bowls of strawberries and tiny wild blueberries.

We sit down with full plates and we eat. With each bite, I observe a different person at the funeral home. *Do you know what is going on? Are you involved?* Jamie's strange warnings have me looking at everyone with new eyes.

Lily's mother Maggie arrives on the second day. She repeats herself to everyone who hugs her: "I had to get the kids packed. Shop for church clothes."

If it were me in that coffin, my mother would be fused to it like an anglerfish.

I remember once when Lily told me she was her mom's practice baby. Same with the next kid—a half sister in Lansing. Auntie overheard us talking and sat us down. She talked about the boarding school that Granny June's daughters had been scooped up and taken to. Years spent marching like soldiers and training to be household domestics. They had the Anishinaabemowin and cultural teachings beaten out of them. When they came back to Sugar Island, one of the girls had scarred palms that looked like melted plastic, and she ran into the woods at the sound of a kettle whistle. Her sister was afraid of men and had to sleep with her back against the wall. Auntie had told us, *When you criticize Maggie, just remember she was raised by one of those sisters, the one who didn't kill herself.*

I spot Auntie now, holding Maggie's hand while they both cry. I was quick to judge Lily's mom, even today. My aunt's words were remembered as an afterthought.

Maggie's two little ones sit with relatives near the food tables. The toddler girl, in a pretty yellow dress, has a contagious laugh that's bigger than she is. The boy, in a matching bow tie, is a year younger than the twins. He flashes a shy smile that is the same as Granny June's, where one side claims more of the happy than the other. I continue watching as Maggie walks over to where they're sitting. The little girl reaches for her mom, who kisses her toddler's forehead slowly. There is healing medicine in those kisses.

When Auntie spills coffee on herself, I offer to drive her car to the house for a clean blouse. On the ferry ride to the island, I think about the second day of Lily's spiritual journey. It is for atonement. She will face every living creature she ever harmed during her lifetime.

I glance at the car next to me and recognize one of Travis's cousins. The car to my right is filled with his relatives. The Flint family would have a fire lit for him at the lodge behind the Elder Center. Tribal members can use its community room for wakes and funerals. Anger flashes through me as I think about how it's Travis's second day as well. He will be unable to move on until he accounts for the harm that he is responsible for. Including taking Lily from us.

Time is a concept of our earthly minds. In the spirit world, his second day might last an eternity for him. As it should. My nails dig into my palms. I want Travis to suffer. To feel our pain. For his atonement to be a mirage just beyond his grasp.

I can't be around the fire like this. Filled with such fury.

Only good thoughts for Lily.

I look down at my hands, expecting to see blood. The curved indentations resemble tiny scars.

CHAPTER 12

The third day is for Lily to learn about the next world. When I sit next to her casket, I keep going over everything I know about Jamie's identity and the reason he's here.

What I know for sure about Jamie: He used to be a figure skater.

What I know for sure about why he's here: Two undercover cops are in the Sault working on a case. One is posing as a high school science teacher; the other is pretending to be a high school senior and a hockey player on a Junior A team.

What else I know for sure: Lily shouldn't be here.

Jamie and his "uncle" show up at the funeral home. When Jamie asks to speak with me outside, I'm both curious and irritated. I follow them to a nearby bridge over the power canal.

Ron Johnson, or whatever his real name is, looks a few years older than my mom. He has a barely there mustache I recognize in Native guys whose facial hairs present as lone wolves determined not to get too close to one another. He is smack-dab in the middle of the Acceptable Anishinaabe Skin Tone Continuum. I'd bet my trust fund no one has ever told him, *Oh, you're Indian? You sure don't look like one.*

"Ron Johnson," he says, shaking my hand. "Senior agent with the Federal Bureau of Investigation."

"For real? Ron Johnson?" I scoff.

"It's better not to provide actual names at this point."

I eye Jamie. "Let me guess, Jamie Johnson?"

"For your protection, Daunis," Jamie says. "But I really am a law-enforcement officer on loan from the Bureau of Indian Affairs."

The FBI and BIA . . . two federal agencies that tend to make things worse instead of better for tribes.

Ron asks, "Would it be possible for you to come with us so we could talk with you about the investigation?"

I wanted this. Answers. Truth. But how can I leave Lily now?

The purpose of the third day is suddenly clear: to gain new ways. Just as Lily is finding her way now, there's a new world for me to learn. Lily would want me to do this.

"I'll let my aunt know I'm leaving with you," I say.

We pass the movie theater downtown on our drive from the funeral home to . . . wherever Ron is taking me. Denzel Washington in *The Manchurian Candidate* and Hilary Duff in *A Cinderella Story*.

"Oh look," I point out. "Two movies about people faking identities." Since Ron and Jamie have yet to say anything, I decide not to be the naive girl who accepts half-assed stories.

The corner of Ron's mouth twitches. In the back seat, Jamie pinches the bridge of his nose.

"Fake identities are necessary for protection," Ron says. "An operative's cover is a shield with two sides. To protect the people he comes in contact with as well as the agent."

He turns left at the corner with the Dairy Queen, toward the middle school and high school. I remember standing in a snowstorm with

Lily last April when DQ opened for the season. I ordered my usual Buster Bar and she got a Blizzard with goofy combinations of stuff in it.

A few minutes ago, I was sitting next to Lily, racking my brain about how little I know about Jamie's true identity and whatever this investigation is. Now I'm in a car with Jamie and Ron, but all I can think about is Lily. It's as if Jamie and his investigation are lodged in my brain's left hemisphere with facts, logic, and analysis. Lily is in my right brain, part of my imagination, intuition, and feelings. Between the two hemispheres is a divide as deep and wide as the Grand Canyon.

I force myself to pay attention to Ron, who's mentioning other cases he's worked on. "My last investigation involved the BIA, local tribal police, and the Royal Canadian Mounted Police. High-profile case. It was over twenty-five years old, but last year we identified the people who murdered a Native woman. Her family got answers." He pulls into the high school parking lot and turns to face me. "Answers can't bring a person back, but a successful investigation can help loved ones grieve and carry on."

I feel his words sink in as we get out of the car. Is that something I can do? Help Lily's family now, because I couldn't help her Saturday evening on Sugar Island?

It feels strange to walk back into the high school. Surreal. As if I was here only yesterday. And in the next step, as if I've been gone for years instead of months. When we pass the front office, the school secretary comes out with her arms widening for a hug.

"Daunis, I'm so sorry to hear about Lily Chippeway," Mrs. Hammond says, embracing me. "And after what you've already gone through. First that terrible business with your uncle and then your grandmother's stroke."

Mrs. H. releases me. I remain in place. Gramma Pearl's warning rings through my head. Lily's murder was the third bad thing. I was supposed to be on guard. Watch for signs. But I didn't stop it. I failed Lily. She's gone and I was supposed to protect her.

"Hi, Mrs. Hammond, I'm Ron Johnson," Ron says as he steps forward to shake her hand. "We spoke on the phone earlier."

"Oh yes." Mrs. H. looks at Ron. "You must be the new Indian science teacher."

"I am the new science teacher, and, yes, I am Native American," Ron says amiably. "Ron Johnson. This is my nephew, Jamie. He and Daunis are friends. Jamie's on the Superiors team with her brother, Levi."

"Okay, then." Her voice brightens. "Any friend of theirs should do well here."

Jamie asks, "Ma'am, is there a vending machine nearby? We need something to drink."

Mrs. H. gives directions before chatting with Ron about the upcoming district-wide pre-service conference for all faculty. My mother won't be there this year; she is taking an indefinite leave of absence to take care of GrandMary. The surreal part is that Ron sounds like any other new teacher having an ordinary conversation with someone. It's like an iceberg—a minuscule amount of blah-blah chitchat above the surface, while deep below is a giant mass of secret info.

Jamie returns a minute later with a bottle of water, which he opens and hands to me.

"Thank you." I take a sip before holding the cool plastic to my sweaty forehead. Jamie stays at my side, an echo of all the mornings we ran together. I remind myself that easy comfort wasn't real. It was manufactured as part of an undercover assignment.

I move away from Jamie and walk over to Ron. I remain next to him when he heads down the dimly lit hallway, the linoleum amplifying the squeak of Ron's shoe each time his right heel lands. It's the opposite of stealth. I suppress a giggle that comes from nowhere and tickles like Pop Rocks fizzing against the roof of my mouth.

Is it normal for my emotions to go all over the place? Debilitating grief one instant, and giddy hilarity in the next? And sometimes abandon me completely?

When we reach Uncle David's old classroom, the funny moment leaves as quickly as it arrived. Turning on the lights, Ron motions for me to sit at my uncle's vintage steel desk at the front of the room. He sits next to me on the stool at the lab workstation. Jamie remains in the doorway: neither in nor out. He watches me.

I used to sit at this desk every day after school. Uncle David kept snacks in the bottom drawer. I open it, hoping to see protein bars and bags of trail mix covering the false bottom he once showed me, but Ron has already filled the deep drawer with file folders and textbooks.

"Why are we here?" I ask, as my legs begin to shake. I haven't been back here since I collected Uncle David's personal items after his death and right now, the persisting sadness compounded with my fresh grief over Lily is almost too much to bear.

"Jamie and I are part of an investigation involving multiple agencies, federal and Canadian. There's been a significant increase in drug trafficking throughout the region—Michigan, Wisconsin, Minnesota, and Ontario." Ron is calm and matter-of-fact, but he missed the point of my question.

I'd meant *here*. In Uncle David's classroom.

"Okay, then why is *he* here?" My lips point in Jamie's direction. "On the hockey team," I clarify, so Ron won't explain that Jamie is standing guard and listening for any sounds in the empty school.

"The substance we're most interested in is methamphetamine," Ron says.

Meth. A prickly chill travels up my spine.

Lily on her back, arms outstretched. Her fall reverses, as if I'm rewinding her final moments in my head. She is upright, eyes open. Startled. The bullet leaves her chest and is back in Travis's gun. The reverse action speeds up, Travis showing up at the powwow. Back at the ice rink. Years unhappen. When it halts, Travis is a chubby boy who burps the alphabet and makes Lily laugh until milk sprays from her nose.

"There's a pattern of distribution," Ron says. "Similar batches of meth show up in hockey towns and on reservations in the Great Lakes area. We're trying to identify the manufacturers, the ones cooking it."

Travis. In eighth grade, Travis and I walked together every day from the middle school to Sault High for chemistry. When we became official high school students, we took every Advanced Placement science class together: biology, physics, earth science, and physical science. Uncle David advocated for kids like us who tested out of the standard classes at the school.

My legs bounce dramatically. The prickly chill is itchy now too.

"You think the person making the meth is from the Sault?" I look from Ron to Jamie, who is still observing me from the doorway. "How do you narrow it down? My aunt goes to Indian Health meetings in Minnesota. Meth isn't just here, it's everywhere."

"We identified hallucinogenic additives in samples of the meth-amphetamine," Ron explains. "Mushrooms. *Psilocybe caerulipes* from near Tahquamenon Falls."

I do a double take at Ron, at his ease in speaking the language of scientific classification.

He shrugs. "Undergraduate degree in chemistry."

The other part of what he said registers with me. Tahquamenon Falls is only seventy-five miles away. Auntie and Art got married there, alongside the larger, upper waterfall.

As I struggle to keep up with what Ron's telling me, I feel Jamie's eyes on me, continuing his silent assessment.

Ron keeps talking. "Another batch included a variety of *Pluteus* from Pictured Rocks National Lakeshore."

Our Tribal Youth Council went to a youth powwow there. Every tribe in Michigan had their tribal youth groups represented. Lily made me dance the two-step special with a guy from downstate. *Go on! It's a chance to kiss a Nishnaab you're not related to.*

"There was another sample that had a mushroom from the southern end of Sugar Island."

Travis came from a large family that has always had family members on Tribal Council and were hired into the few good-paying tribal government jobs during the lean years. Practically the entire eastern half of the island is owned either by the Tribe or by the Flint family.

Ron and Jamie clearly suspect that Travis was the person cooking the meth that the FBI is interested in. But he did his deep dive into meth over last winter break, and meth has been a problem since long before Christmas. So who else could have been involved?

I inhale deeply. This classroom smells different from other ones. I don't know if it's the actual scent or just the memory of countless experiments. Bunsen burner gas flames. Sulfur.

"Okay, but you haven't explained why we're *here*? In my uncle's classroom?" I ask.

But even as the words leave my mouth, my leg stops bouncing. Every part of me goes numb. Why did they bring me to this room I know so well to talk about the investigation?

Uncle David didn't show up for dinner on Easter Sunday. No one could reach him. GrandMary immediately suspected he'd relapsed and was on a bender. Mom didn't believe it. I would have sided with my mother if not for the fact that Uncle David had been acting strange for weeks—no, months—before he went missing.

Someone found his car two weeks later, on a seasonal private road near the county line. A fifth of bourbon next to him. The toxicology report came back a month later, and the gossips had a field day. David Fontaine, the chemistry teacher, had died from a meth overdose.

I know why we are here.

"You think my uncle David was manufacturing meth?" I try sounding indignant, but there's no heat in my words.

Ron's jaw drops. He takes a minute to recover. "No, Daunis, your uncle was helping us. He was a CI—a confidential informant."

I gape at Ron in absolute shock.

"His death was suspicious," he says. "David thought someone he knew was manufacturing meth. A student. He refused to provide names or evidence until he knew for certain. After his body was found and the toxicology reports came back, the FBI green-lighted a UC—undercover—operation."

"Oh my God." Hiding my face in my hands, I cry tears of shame. Mom was right. She had faith in her brother and never wavered. I believed the worst. My uncle didn't fail me. I failed him.

I sob until my palms are slick with snot, not caring if Ron or Jamie is uncomfortable. When I lower my hands, Ron has placed a box of tissues in front of me. I blow my nose and wipe my eyes and hands.

"Tell me more about the investigation." I need to know everything now.

"Last February, a group of kids got really sick," Ron says. "On a reservation in northern Minnesota, a few days after a Superiors hockey tournament in Minneapolis. The kids couldn't eat or sleep; they just wanted more meth. And it wasn't that they hallucinated . . . those kids had group hallucinations. Something about that batch was different. We call it meth-X."

Uncle David was trying to help the Nish kids. *I'm so sorry, Uncle.*

Ron continues. "We're focusing on distribution. From there we can backtrack to the manufacturers. We think Travis Flint was one of the students David Fontaine was concerned about." His expression softens. "Daunis, you were a person of interest as well."

"Seriously?" Me? Wait . . . are they going to arrest me? I sit back in my chair.

"Hear me out." Ron puts his hands up, like, *Be calm.* "The person cooking the meth has been experimenting with batches. Adding different things—hallucinogenic mushrooms, mostly. We think there's a cultural connection. It's highly likely the person is Ojibwe and familiar with plants in the area."

"You thought that *I* made the meth that killed my uncle?"

Jamie clears his throat. "Daunis, we read about your science-fair project. Junior year. Honorable mention in the state competition. You should have won, by the way."

Wait, what? How long has this investigation been going on? I feel prickles on the back of my neck.

He continues, "You showed that traditionally prepared choke-cherry pudding had cancer-fighting properties. The seeds—grinding up the seeds in the traditional way instead of filtering them out—that's what had the medicinal value. You know science and you know your culture."

How dare Jamie of all people suspect me of being a secret meth creator? A secret anything?

"I'm not the person pretending to be someone else." My voice drips with acid. "You did win, by the way. Top honors in Guy Lies. No contest, you fake son-of-a—"

Ron cuts in. "Daunis, we know you're not involved." He rises and takes a half step closer. "You have the means and opportunity, but no motive. With your trust fund, there's no financial incentive for you to risk so much. And while you're extremely competitive, you don't seek the limelight, so you're not motivated by ego."

Ron meets my stunned expression with a shrug. "Master's degree in psychology."

"Then why bring me here and tell me all this?" They've brought me to Uncle David's classroom. Told me about the investigation. Made a connection between Travis and the meth showing up in hockey towns and on reservations. The meth that turned Travis into a shaking addict who murdered Lily. The meth that was cooked with something that might be connected to Ojibwe culture. The meth that my uncle was investigating as a confidential informant.

You know science and you know your culture, Jamie's voice echoes.

"You want me to take my uncle's place in the investigation."

"Yes," Ron says.

CHAPTER 13

I jump to my feet. Jamie has been playing me. Every stride we ran together was one step closer to roping me into their plan. And I had actually thought . . . *felt* something for the person who was so kind, funny, and sympathetic. I am such a fool.

"Oh, hells no," I say, voice rising. "I don't want anything to do with yous." Three quick paces and I reach the doorway and Jamie. "Take me back to the funeral home. Now. And stay the hell away from me. If you contact me again, I'll blow my entire trust fund on lawyers to get you for harassment. I'll blab . . ."

I expect Jamie to block my path. Instead he steps aside after giving me a look somewhere between pity and disappointment. How dare he? I stomp down the hallway, Jamie and Ron following close behind.

We drive in silence and they drop me off at the funeral home. As I undo my seat belt, Ron finally speaks.

"The investigation will give closure to your community. Healing to people who are grieving. Knowledge to people who need to know the truth about your uncle's death and your best friend's murder. Justice to the ones responsible for it all. Daunis, you have the ability to help your family, your loved ones, and your community. Please think about it and let us know if you're on board."

I slam the car door and don't look back.

The next day, I'm still shaking with anger as I sit next to Granny June at Lily's funeral. Granny has aged twenty years in the past four days. She rests her head against me, as if I am a sturdy oak. I can be that for her.

Today, the final day, Lily will come back to say goodbye and then cross over. Art will let the ceremonial fire go out tonight after the supper. Once the last ember fades, the fire is lit in the next world, where it will burn without end for her.

I haven't run since the powwow. My body protests this Newer New Normal. I am exhausted and cannot think clearly. All I do is eat. I'm constantly grazing. Pants won't zip over my distended stomach, so I wear the only thing that fits. A shapeless orange dress.

Mom and Auntie are in the second row, directly behind us. They pat our shoulders at random intervals. Maggie is on Granny June's other side, along with Lily's two youngest siblings. Does Lily's other sibling even know what's happened?

Throughout the past four days, whenever my mother has been at the funeral home, or here at the tiny Catholic church, she hovers. Every trip I take to the food table or even to pee, she's two steps behind me. Asking if she can get me anything. Asking how I feel.

I caught myself drafting a text to Lily.

ME: swear2god moms bugging the shit outta me

She won't ever reply.

One of the Tribal Council members walks down the aisle and makes the sign of the cross beside Lily's open casket. I look around for any other council members. Two out of ten leaders. Both women. One is a distant cousin of Granny June's. The other is someone who travels frequently to Washington, DC, to represent the Tribe.

I'm not surprised by the lack of council presence. Lily is—was—a descendant, not an enrolled tribal citizen like Travis. Their funerals are both today, the fourth day, per the traditional Ojibwe teachings. Travis is a murderer, but he's also from one of Sugar Island's largest families. Council members are paying their respects at the Elder Center with the Flint family of voters.

My aunt squeezes my shoulder before approaching the lectern near the open casket. Granny asked me to give semaa to Teddie before asking her to speak at the funeral mass.

Auntie clears her throat. She introduces herself and says a prayer in Anishinaabemowin. Then, she translates what she just said into English.

"Hello. My name is Teddie Firekeeper. Bear Clan. From the Place of the Rapids. We pray for Lily June Chippeway. Creator knows her by her Spirit name: Thunderbird Woman. We are thankful for the time we shared with her. We honor her gifts. We wish her a good journey. We keep her love in our hearts. Thank you most greatly, Creator. That is all."

After the prayer, she adds, "The burial at the cemetery on Sugar Island will take place immediately after the mass. The ferry tickets are covered. On behalf of Granny June and Maggie, I invite everyone to my home for supper after the burial." Her voice cracks. "Everyone who loves Liliban is welcome."

I choke up at the sound of Lily's new name, indicating she is now in a different time and place. We traditionally add "-iban" after some-one has changed worlds.

The funeral mass begins with "Amazing Grace" sung in Anish-inaabemowin. It is beautiful. Layers of sorrow and salvation.

Many tribal members, including Maggie, are Catholic. Others, like Auntie and Granny June, keep the Church at a distance because the churches operated some of the Indian boarding schools, along with the federal government. Granny June told Lily and me, *They came for our ceremonies and then for our children.* She didn't say, *They came for my children.* Why didn't she tell us about her daughters? Did she want to protect us?

When we recite the Lord's Prayer in Anishinaabemowin, the words stick in my throat.

"Miinshinaang noongom gizhigak inbakwezhiganinaan minik waayaang endaso gizhigag, boonigidetawishinaang gaawiin ezhi-nishkiigoosii'aan, ezhi-bonigedetawangidwaa gaa ezhi-nishkinawiyangidwaa. Gego gaye ezhi-wijishikangen gagwedibeningwewining, miidash miidaawenimiyaang dash maji-inakamigag. Ahow."

Ron's words about closure and justice come to mind. Does closure come from forgiving others and being forgiven for our failings? Do we resist temptation from evil by believing in a righteous justice? My thoughts and the words to the prayer swirl around me and continue outside.

As if following their path, I look behind me and see Levi standing next to Jamie. My brother catches my eye and gives a gentle smile. Emotion washes over me. He chose to be here, to pay his respects to Lily, instead of being at the Elder Center on Sugar Island. Travis was his longtime friend. Levi chose me.

A hundred tiny needles stab the inside of my nose.

It isn't until the funeral director is closing the casket lid that it hits me. This is it. The last time I'll ever see Lily. I want more. It isn't fair. I want to shout for him to stop. Just one more look.

I failed her. That bird flying into the window was a warning. My chance to stop the third bad thing. Instead I spent time showing the new guy around town. Each time Jamie's eyes sparkled and laughter tugged at his scar, I felt desire and guilt.

I'm so sorry, Lily. I wipe away hot, angry tears with the sleeve of my pumpkin dress.

Toward the end, the priest walks around Lily's casket dangling a shiny gold vessel on a chain. Smoke rises from the incense. *Church smudge,* Granny has always called it.

We stand as six men in dark suits approach the casket. My brother is one. So is TJ. His black suit jacket is enormous. TJ was always a big guy, but he's bulked up even more. Two years of college football will do that. He surprised everyone when he left Central Michigan University for the police academy. And again when he came home this summer for a job with Tribal Police.

How dare TJ come to Lily's funeral? Pretend to be a good guy. A helpful pallbearer. Why do all the liars find their way to me? Because all men are liars.

Except Uncle David. He was good and tried to help the FBI. He didn't lie; he just didn't disclose the truth. He was trying to protect me and Mom.

I failed him, too.

They escort the polished wood casket past us. Granny June holds my hand so tightly I nearly cry out in pain. Lily's family leads the recessional, but Granny and I remain behind. Her body shakes. I embrace her, absorbing her sorrow.

I am her oak tree.

A few people approach us to offer comfort to Lily's great-grandmother, but she is still inside my sanctuary. Auntie accepts their hugs as proxy.

I help Granny June into my mother's car. Mom sobs quietly at the steering wheel. I shut the car door and glance across the lot.

Then I see *her* and my blood boils.

Angie Flint, Travis's mother, has the audacity to be here. She stands beside Travis's rusted pickup truck at the far edge of the funeral home parking lot, looking lost.

I tell Mom I'll ride with Levi, before stomping across the blacktop. I'm nearly to Travis's truck when my brother intercepts me.

"Daunis," Levi says cautiously. "Don't do anything."

Angie's eyes widen when she sees me approach, but she quickly looks away, her eyes darting anywhere but at me.

"What are you doing here?" I snarl. Travis's funeral must be later today or this evening. The cigarette in her fingers tumbles to the ground.

"I came to pay my respects." The Meth Queen cries some *Crocodylus niloticus* tears.

Most of the cars have followed the hearse, behind my mother and Auntie, but a few stay behind, because a good fight—whether at a party or a funeral—is something not to be missed.

"Pay them in your own way, but don't you dare show your face here."

"She was like a daughter to me," Angie says, steeling herself to meet my glare.

"Then it's too bad your son killed her." I start toward her, but someone grasps my upper arm, firmly but not painfully.

"This isn't helping the situation," Jamie says into my ear as he pulls me away.

I want to charge at Travis's mother and watch her cower. I know she wasn't the one who pulled the trigger. But she's the one in front of me. And this rage feels so much better than grief.

Levi puts his arm around Angie, comforting her, and she looks at him gratefully. TJ stands next to his enormous red pickup truck. Watching the entire spectacle.

"Gawk much?" I shout at him. "You never should've come home. Protect and serve? What a crock of shit. We don't need you."

"Daunis, this is bigger than TJ," Jamie urges in a low voice. "Bigger than Travis and his mom. Can't you see this is gonna keep happening? Over and over. More funerals. More pain."

Even as my heart pounds in my chest, I know he's right. I don't want anyone else to feel such heartache.

The most horrible thought comes to me. *What if this ever touches the twins?*

I couldn't live with myself.

I take a deep breath and pick up the scent of the cedar bush a few feet away. Giizhik. One of our traditional medicines. The one we use for protection.

"Daunis," Jamie says softly. "Let's go to the cemetery. To Lily. You ready?"

"Just give me a second. There's something I have to do first." I kick off my black patent-leather stilettos. Shiny like polished onyx. Jamie frowns in confusion.

Lily made me buy them at the mall across the river. She called them fuck-me shoes. At first, I balked at adding four inches to my height. Her eyes danced as she handed me the shoebox.

Trust me. You need this.

What, the heels or a good snag?

Both!

I wore them today because anything connecting me to Lily felt like the right thing to wear to her funeral.

Auntie's friends made tobacco ties for Lily's wake and funeral, to use with our prayers. I take mine from my pumpkin dress pocket, untie the yarn, and release the pinch of semaa with my prayer. I give thanks for the giizhik before I break off two flat sprigs. I place one in each shoe before slipping my feet back inside.

Auntie does this before meeting with Council. Giizhik protects us from bad intentions.

I, too, need any help I can get, because I've made my decision.

I am going to be their confidential informant.

I'll find out what led to Travis killing Lily.

What Uncle David found out, and who killed him.

I pull myself up to my full height. My spine is a steel rod. I tower over Jamie. I give one more glare at TJ across the parking lot. I will protect my community. Me.

The stilettos aren't fuck-me shoes.

They are fuck-you shoes.

"Yes," I tell Jamie. "I'm ready."

PART II

· · · · · · · ·

ZHAAWANONG

(SOUTH)

THE JOURNEY CONTINUES INTO THE SOUTHERN
DIRECTION—A TIME FOR WANDERING AND WONDERING.

CHAPTER 14

The next morning, I step outside dressed in running gear. Heavy fog conceals the rising sun. I say my morning prayer and ask for gwekowaadiziwin. Honesty. Walking through life with integrity means not deceiving yourself or others. The prayer sticks in my throat. In this Newer New Normal I am living a lie as a confidential informant for the meth investigation connected to the deaths of my uncle and my best friend.

I can't find my rhythm. Something feels off. It's the same route. Same pace. It isn't until I run past the Dairy Queen that I realize what's missing.

Jamie. I shouldn't have gotten used to him running with me. Or liked it so much.

Mrs. B. greets me at the front desk. I wave. The invisible cloud of roses itches my nose. I twist my back until I hear and feel the satisfying crack on each side. All my normal routines.

Mom sits at GrandMary's bedside, reading *Pride and Prejudice* aloud. Jane Austen has mediated their tumultuous relationship my entire lifetime. GrandMary has always found passive-aggressive ways to convey disappointment in my mother—snide comments about Mom's inability to lose the baby weight, and refusing to carry plus sizes in the dress boutique. Spirited discussions about Englishwomen of the early nineteenth century were the only time they could spar on equal footing.

I turned down their repeated requests to join them, offering Lily in my place. My best friend loved Jane Austen. Loved reading and taking deep dives into the classics. Lily basked in my mother's attention, while I was all too eager to escape it. I wonder if Mom has told GrandMary about Lily, or if she ever will.

"Too sweaty," I declare when Mom rises to hug me. She holds me anyway.

"Are they doing anything special at the Niibing Program for Lily?" Her voice is gentle against my cheek.

I nod. "They have counselors doing activities with the kids all week. When I called Mr. Vasques for time off, he offered to have last Friday count as my final day. He asked if I could drop by between now and Labor Day Weekend so the kids can say goodbye." I swallow the lump in my throat. "TJ's cousin Garth is interning at Behavioral Health and can sub for me. Mr. Vasques said one of the counselors took Lily's spot to help her kids with their grieving."

"I'm glad the tribal programs work together like that to support the kids," Mom says. "And that Mr. Vasques understands what you need during all this." She rubs my back before releasing me.

"I'm gonna run errands today. Check on Granny. Buy my books for my classes. Try to add that biology seminar," I say. Surprise deepens the creases in my mother's forehead. I soften my voice. "Lily will be mad if I don't follow through on our classes."

I leave out the day's biggest errand—a long day trip with Ron and Jamie to Marquette, where the United States Attorney's Office for the Western District of Michigan is located.

Ron's car pulls up while I'm still combing my wet hair. I grab a bottle of water for the road and slide the comb and a hair tie into the pocket of my sleeveless short romper. Uncle David brought the fabric—red cotton with white hibiscus flowers—back from a trip to Hawaii, and GrandMary had it made into a romper customized for my flat chest, thick waist, and long legs. I couldn't fathom any occasion I'd wear it to, but meeting federal officials seems to call for a dressier outfit than a T-shirt and jean shorts. And sandals rather than running shoes.

I open the car door, and the air-conditioning is a relief from the late August humidity. The romper is already sticking to my back. I fix my hair into a side braid that falls over one shoulder.

Jamie sits directly behind me. His audible sigh ticks me off. I'm the only person in this car who has a right to be irked. In fact, I want Jamie as far from me as possible.

There's a scene in *The Godfather*, my brother's favorite movie, where a character named Clemenza positions himself behind the guy he intends to strangle while they're in the car.

"Hey, Clemenza, sit behind Ron," I tell Jamie.

"Leave the gun. Take the cannoli," Ron says without missing a beat.

I laugh. My own shield to protect myself from Jamie, the smooth liar.

Jamie pinches the bridge of his nose, as if it pains him to shift three feet over.

"Secret Squirrel training starts now," I say, diving right in. "What do I need to know?"

"Secret Squirrel?" Jamie asks.

Ron answers. "Secret Squirrel . . . a cartoon squirrel. Wears a fedora and trench coat."

"He was a secret agent in the International Sneaky Service," I add. "I know my classics."

"The car was searched for listening devices and is clean," Ron says. "You should assume everywhere else is bugged and only speak about the investigation when we tell you it's safe."

I make a mental note.

Secret Squirrel lesson #1: I'm not paranoid, but the men listening to me are.

"I'm showing you a drop-off site," Ron says, turning off the highway toward Dafter.

"Drop-off?" I imagine suitcases filled with meth, cash, maybe dismembered body parts.

"I'll explain but first, let me say, we need CIs to obtain useful and credible information that will aid our investigation into criminal activities. Information you share with us might be included in future warrant applications, but your identity won't be. That's the confidential part of being a confidential informant. It doesn't mean that we provide you with confidential information about the investigation. Only what is deemed necessary and appropriate for you to know." He makes another turn down an unpaved road. "It's important for you to understand these limitations, Daunis. If an LEO, meaning law-enforcement officer, directs you, as a CI, to do something—say, search the hockey team's gear bags for disposable cell phones—you become an agent of the law. If you, as an agent of the law, obtain evidence illegally, then the information is inadmissible in court under the Fourth Amendment. It's called fruit of the poisonous tree. It's better for you to volunteer information and let us ask for clarification."

Secret Squirrel lesson #2: Beware the fruit of the poisonous tree.

Ron turns down a gravel driveway next to a dilapidated trailer. The path snakes through pine trees to a three-car garage. He pushes one of two door openers, revealing a modern workshop.

"This is where you can drop off bags of trash from the hockey players' homes. Including your brother's," he says.

The mouthful of water I just took sprays the front windshield.

"Trash hits are legal," Jamie says. "Once it's in the can, we don't need a warrant."

"Oh, hells no," I sputter. "I'm not hauling my brother's trash. You can't be serious."

"It would be helpful." Ron pushes the gadget again to close the door. He hands me the second device. "But it's not mandatory. Daunis, you have access that we don't. Just tell us about things you see and hear. We'll figure out the trash hits on our own."

Secret Squirrel lesson #3: I am not my brother's keeper . . . of trash.

I'm helping to investigate Travis and the other meth heads in the Sault. I won't be snooping on Levi or any of my friends. *The FBI won't change who I am,* I vow silently.

Halfway to Marquette, Ron mentions I'll need to learn how to make meth.

"For real?" I squeak before realizing that, logically, it makes perfect sense.

Ron smiles. "Yes. You need to learn different methods of production, so you can identify any evidence you might come across. We're asking you to figure out what Travis Flint did to create meth-X. You have to know the recipes before you start adapting them."

"You want me to make meth and experiment with it," I say, for my own confirmation.

"Well, the more you know, the better a CI you can be," he tells me. "Before the season opener, you and Jamie will take a weekend trip together to a federal lab outside of Marquette."

"Wait . . . what?" I glance back at Jamie, his head resting on a sweatshirt against the window. His eyes are closed. Probably taking a nap. I lower my voice to a whisper. "That's not normal for new friends to take a trip like that. Besides, he has a girl . . ." I stare at Ron. "There's no girlfriend, is there?"

"Easier to keep girls away if he's being loyal to someone back home," Ron explains.

"But . . . everyone will think I poached him from his girlfriend." I don't know which disturbs me more: being That Girl Who Steals Boyfriends or spending a weekend with Jamie.

But I do know that spending a weekend with Jamie is a more disturbing thought than learning to make meth.

Secret Squirrel lesson #4: All's fair in love, hockey, and meth.

"It's your choice, Daunis. Posing as friends or as something more."

I see where this is going. The logical choice is to pose as the girlfriend. But after a lifetime of following the rules, I'm sick of logical. It felt good to shout at Angie Flint and watch her cower. And to tell TJ off. I want to be more like Lily: jump a curb and park in the grass.

"Isn't there a better cover story?" I grumble, as logic refuses to take a back seat so I can jump the curb. "I mean, the whole romantic charade seems . . ." I grasp for the right word. *Stupid. Torturous.* "Basic?"

"Occam's razor," Ron says. "The simplest solution is easiest to believe."

"That's not what Occam's razor means. It's a problem-solving principle about competing hypotheses and starting at the one with the fewest assumptions."

Ron stares at me with his jaw dropped. Then he chuckles. "Okay. I just mean it's the most believable scenario."

"But why can't you come along on the meth weekend, like today?" I need Ron to be a buffer between Jamie and me. Even the sight of that smooth liar is irritating.

"Because we can get away with it once or twice for a fake college visit, but if the three of us keep going away together, it gets hinky.

People accept normal patterns, Daunis. When there's a disruption in the pattern, people notice. Their Spidey senses go on alert, even if they aren't consciously aware. You and Jamie need to establish relationship patterns for people to observe. He has to be your main point of contact."

"Yeah, well, what about Murphy's Law?" I mutter, shifting in my seat.

Secret Squirrel lesson #5: Whatever can happen will happen.

"Daunis, I have a feeling you're gonna keep all of us on our toes." Ron glances in the rearview mirror. "Especially him."

We arrive in Marquette at an office building. I follow Ron and Jamie inside. Next to the elevators is a sign that reads: UNITED STATES ATTORNEY'S OFFICE, WESTERN DISTRICT OF MICHIGAN. Ron leads us into an office where some big cheese's name is engraved on a brass nameplate.

Big Cheese introduces himself and another attorney. Explains that ordinarily the field agents would review the confidential informant documentation with me. Due to my age, Big Cheese will read verbatim the official CI instructions. Little Cheese will serve as the witness.

It expands on what Ron covered on the drive this morning: My job is to provide truthful information. My help is voluntary. The government strives to protect my identity but cannot guarantee it if there are legal or compelling reasons. Any promises or considerations in exchange for my cooperation are at the discretion of federal officials other than the agent. Agreeing to serve as a confidential informant does not give me immunity from following the law, and I risk arrest and prosecution for any illegal activity I might choose to do.

But, hasn't Ron already said I'm going to learn how to make meth?

Ron registers my confusion. "If you have any questions about legality, ask for clarification before you act."

What if he isn't around? What if there isn't time to get an answer? I don't know enough about what I will be doing to know if these are questions to bring up now or later.

Big Cheese finishes reading the document. I only catch every other word: Not employee. Can't obligate government. Payments taxed.

"People get paid?" I scowl. "I don't want anything." It would feel weird to get paid for this. I'm just trying to make sense of what happened to Lily and protect my community.

Ron chimes in that they want me to provide information about the team, the Tribe, and the town. Any information that might reveal who was working with Travis Flint, and what traditional medicines he used to create at least one batch of something more powerfully addictive than even the purest meth.

When it's time to sign the agreement, the pen is fancy, like the one I received as a graduation gift from one of Grandpa Lorenzo's business partners. It weighs more than an ordinary pen. Maybe the U.S. Attorney's Office does this on purpose: The heavy burdens begin with your signature.

This feels wrong. I've researched our medicines before, but for science projects like the chokecherry pudding. I wanted to show people that our traditional healers are—and always have been—scientists who use plants as medicine. But . . . this? Looking for traditional medicines to experiment with meth at the request of the FBI? It's not right. In my heart, I know this.

What would Lily do? My brave friend's last act was reaching for the gun to protect me.

What would Auntie do? My badass aunt would punch first and ask questions later.

Gramma Pearl also comes to mind. Her parents hid her and her sisters whenever the dogs barked. When she was growing up, dogs barking meant men might be coming to take the kids to boarding school. I was with her once when she heard barking. Even though the last church-operated boarding school in Michigan closed two years before I was born, my nokomis grabbed Grandpa Ted's rifle and put me into the hidey-hole beneath a trapdoor under the bed. Told me to stay quiet or the Zhaag-anaash would get me. Gramma Pearl would have killed to keep me safe.

Maybe it isn't about helping the FBI, but about protecting my community. Can I do one without the other? If I don't sign on, they will find someone else to be their confidential informant.

Jamie is right—I know science and Ojibwe culture. I also know that I am strong enough to do this. There is one more thing I know . . . My definition of being a good Secret Squirrel is not the same as theirs.

Maybe there isn't one investigation taking place, but two.

Theirs. And mine.

I sign the agreement.

The car ride back is silent. I blink until the trees fade away. I haven't played my daydream game in a while. Blinking to change the scene in front of me.

At hockey games growing up, I'd imagine my dad watching me in the stands with the other parents, getting high fives from everyone around him. When Levi was named team captain earlier this summer, the youngest one in the North American Hockey League, I blinked until Dad stood next to me. Hugging me and saying how proud he was of my brother and me.

My name is Daunis Lorenza Fontaine and my best friend is Lily June Chippeway. We are shopping at the campus bookstore. Lily needs to price her books so she can redeem one of Granny June's coupons. I'm excited to shop for mechanical pencils and highlighters. Lily says every pen and pencil writes exactly the same, but that's not true. I feel smarter with certain ones. Calculations come more easily; words flow more smoothly on the

page. She teases me about my magic-pencil theory. I am her favorite geek in the whole world.

I shop with Lily, even for groceries, because her dark brown skin means security personnel will follow her around most stores. She doesn't need me to be her goon—Lily's perfectly capable of calling them out for their bullshit shoplifter profiling—but having a witness is always helpful. The college bookstore should be different. More enlightened. We are two ordinary freshmen in a sea of people.

Ron and Jamie appear at the end of the aisle, next to the protractors. Why are they . . . ?

Danger can turn up anywhere, Jamie says.

I turn to warn Lily, but she's disappeared. They showed up. Now she's gone.

As I wipe tears from my cheeks, I catch Jamie watching me. He looks away quickly.

We have an hour more to go. The turn for Tahquamenon Falls State Park is just ahead.

"Follow those signs," I tell Ron. "Yous need to see this."

There are two entrances a few miles apart. We go to the Upper Falls, instead of the one for the smaller series of Lower Falls. Outside the car, the temperature has cooled off. That's the thing about living near Lake Superior; the winds can change without notice.

Jamie offers his sweatshirt, which I begrudgingly take. I'm surprised it fits me; it must be two sizes too big for him.

I lead them from the parking lot to the trail through the woods. The roar of the waterfall intensifies as we get closer. We glimpse the Tahquamenon River through the trees before coming upon a set of one hundred steps down to an observation deck.

It's a gorgeous day. Leaves are beginning to transform from lush green to faint shades of red, orange, and yellow. Not peak autumn colors yet, but the promise of a momentous change.

The frothy brown water of the wide river resembles root beer as it cascades over a fifty-foot drop that will continue to the Lower Falls downriver. Ron and Jamie look awestruck.

We have the deck to ourselves after a large group departs.

"There's more to the U.P. than meth and hockey!" I shout over the deafening torrent.

"Why is the water that color?" Ron yells back.

"Tannins are leached from the cedar swamps upriver."

I take pride in the spectacular beauty of this place. Jamie and Ron are here to investigate something horrible. To shine a light on the bad things. That's not the entirety of our story.

"Giizhik is one of our traditional medicines. Cedar. One of the big four," I say, deciding to volunteer information. "It's a cleanser, a purifying medicine."

"You put it in your shoes," Jamie says. He doesn't need to add *at Lily's funeral.*

"You offer semaa, tobacco, to give thanks before you take any. Giizhik is protection. When you walk on cedar, you're asking for help and goodness to surround you."

We remain there for a few minutes. Or maybe it's hours. Time seems to stand still here.

I need to tell them what I should've disclosed on the drive to Marquette.

"Ron, I don't know if Jamie mentioned it, but I'm honoring my traditions—grieving my uncle and Lily. I can't collect medicines for a year, because my grief affects them. It means I won't be part of the gathering sessions, which is when a lot of teachings are passed along." I take a deep breath. "I'll need to find other ways to get information, but I swear, I'll figure it out."

Ron nods. "I understand. But that brings up another subject I wanted to discuss."

I tense my body and feel the familiar throbbing in my left shoulder.

"I know you're not enrolled," he continues. "But your tribe allows for you to apply for membership until your nineteenth birthday. That's October first, right? Would you consider trying to apply for special consideration? It might help the investigation if you strengthen your connection to the Tribe."

"No way." The investigation and my enrollment status are two areas of my life I want to stay separate. Jamie the Blabbermouth must have repeated what I told him about my birth certificate. Or else Ron memorized dates when he researched me.

"It's just a suggestion, Daunis. I didn't intend any disrespect," Ron says.

"What was in the case file about my uncle's help?" I'm eager to change the subject.

As Ron recites it from memory, I keep my face an unreadable mask. I pinch my upper thigh when he gets to the part about mushrooms and Sugar Island.

"David Fontaine wouldn't give the exact location, but we knew he was on the southern end of Sugar Island, near Duck Lake. He collected samples of mushrooms and fungi."

Why wouldn't Uncle David have told them his exact location? And if he didn't, then how did the FBI know where he was on the island? Were they following him? Why would they?

Wait . . . will they be following me?

Assume everywhere is bugged. Did Ron mean the FBI will be checking on me? Is Jamie's job to keep tabs on me?

Ron motions toward the stairs. "Let's head back."

"Secret Squirrel time," I say with an empty smile.

I start climbing the mountain of stairs at a normal pace. Jamie quickens his steps, as if it's a competition. That asshole! I take two steps at a time to surge ahead. He catches up. We reach the top at the same time, both huffing.

"What's with all the cartoon stuff?" Jamie says between breaths. "This is serious shit."

"You think I don't know that?" The stitch in my side feels like a knife. I yank the sweatshirt over my head and throw it at him. "Here. I'm fine now."

He catches it with lightning-fast reflexes and a scowl that pisses me off.

"Did you tell Ron what I told you about my dad not being on my birth certificate? And the stuff about my grandparents keeping him from getting a job? Because I didn't share that with you to put it in one of your reports."

"Keep your voice down," Jamie says, looking around the empty parking lot.

"Here's something for your next report," I hiss, flipping both middle fingers at him. "We are not friends. Not even buddy and ambassador. Unless it has to do with the investigation, you don't exist to me."

Jamie's tawny brown eyes blaze with something intense—anger, exasperation, defiance.

I serve it right back. It feels like a staring contest. No . . . a glaring contest.

"Don't know why you're both in such a hurry," Ron says when he finally appears. He walks between us like a knife cutting the tension. "I'm the one with the car keys."

CHAPTER 15

The next day, Granny June calls me to ask if I can bring her to lunch at the Elder Center on Sugar Island.

"Sure," I say without hesitation. "I'll let my mom know I need the car."

"Don't worry about that. I'll see you at eleven, hey?"

My heart skips a beat when the Jeep pulls into the driveway. Granny June is the tiny figure behind the wheel. She hops out and gives me a wave before walking around to her usual spot as copilot.

If Granny can drive, then why does she need me?

It feels weird sitting in Lily's seat. My head grazes the roof; my knees wedge uncomfortably beneath the steering wheel. I lower the height of the seat and move it as far back as it will go.

When I turn too quickly into the ferry parking lot, the tires call out for Lily. Granny smiles through tears. In that instant, I want to tell her about the investigation. Justice for Lily.

I stay quiet.

On the ferry ride, she takes a pouch of semaa from her purse and offers me a pinch.

"This constant flow means it's a new river each time we cross, and we should honor the journey," Granny tells me. "These are old teachings. I haven't always kept them up, hey?"

I join her as she tosses the semaa out the window, where it and our whispered prayers are carried on the breeze to float downriver.

Granny June crushes my hand in hers when we walk into the Elders' dining room. This is why she needed me. It wasn't about the ride at all.

She takes a seat next to Minnie Mustang. Minnie's actual last name is Manitou, but when she bought a Ford Mustang the color of a ripe tomato, Minnie got a new nickname. She purchased it when she turned seventy-five, telling everyone it was her midlife-crisis car.

Granny pats my hand when I bring her a cup of coffee.

"Miigwech, my girl. Mmmm . . . dark and bitter, just like my first husband."

"Gets you riled up, too. Hot stuff," Minnie adds. They both laugh.

I get in line behind Jonsy Kewadin, TJ's grandpa. He used to be nearly as tall as TJ, but now he's closer to my height.

"You call this a pasty?" Jonsy grumbles when the lunch lady hands him a plate with a baked meat pie, folded in half with crimped edges, filled inside with diced beef and root vegetables.

"What do you got to say about dis here pasty?" she asks in mock indignation.

"I don't have enough years left to tell you what all's wrong with it," he yells.

She gives me a wink as Jonsy walks away. I fix a tray for Granny. Elders are always served first. I'll come back for my own food after the line goes down.

I bring Granny June a salad, a pasty, and a bottle of ketchup. Minnie makes the sign of the cross at the sin of frosting a pasty with anything but gravy.

Minnie asks about my classes. I rattle them off.

"American Literature? That college better include Michener." Granny says it like a threat.

Lily and I used to drive Granny and Minnie to garage sales in their quest for James Michener hardcover editions with pristine book covers. I once tried reading *Hawaii*, but never made it past the initial chapter describing the islands' origins millions of years ago: lava eruption breaking the ocean surface and birds pooping out seeds from faraway lands.

I get myself yogurt and salad, thankful that my eating habits have returned to normal.

Auntie walks into the dining room and I'm wrapped in her arms a heartbeat later. Everything goes quiet as I inhale her wonderful Teddie smell: designer perfume, contraband cigarettes, and a scent that reminds me of the woods just after it rains.

My throat closes up the instant I think about telling her what's going on. Granny June mentioned Auntie having felonies. Why neither woman can run for Council. If it's true, would I be putting her at risk if I said anything about the investigation?

Auntie has a peaceful life with Art and the girls. She used to date hell-raisers. *Bad dudes,* she called them. Art taught her that love wasn't supposed to be a roller coaster; it could be a walk in the woods. She told me there's a phrase in our beautiful language for when you no longer walk alone on your path but are together for the journey on this earth: wiijiindiwin.

I stay silent.

From across the room, Jonsy shouts his usual greeting at her. The one he uses on every Tribal Council member and program director who drops by for lunch.

"Hey, Big Cheese, how much are we paying you?"

Auntie responds, "Not what I'm worth, Jonsy, but just enough so I'll stick around."

Granny June and I stay after lunch for the social activities. Some Elders speak Anishinaabemowin while they work on puzzles together. Others speak English, with Ojibwe words added liberally like salt on bland food. There's a book club and a tai chi group. Granny usually argues about tribal politics with a cabal of fellow dissidents who don't care for most of the Tribal Council's decisions but spar loudly over the alternatives.

Since today is Friday—euchre day—Granny and Minnie sit opposite each other at a card table, blinking secret codes to let the other know what suit they're holding and if they've got any bowers. It would be an unfair advantage if their opponents weren't doing the same damn thing.

Jonsy comes over and asks if anyone wants to go bottle collecting with him. I remember his obsession with finding collectibles down at the old landfill site south of town.

At a nearby table, Seeney asks Auntie about harvesting giizhik aniibiishan, cedar leaves, on the island. A group of Nish kwewag will be going this weekend.

"Gaawiin." Auntie shakes her head. *No.* She speaks quickly in the language. I manage to catch two words: inigaazi and kwezan. *Grief* and *little girl*.

I fight the urge to run back into her arms and cry like a baby. Auntie is joining Granny June and me as we honor our mourning period for Lily. Not harvesting medicines for a year, among other protocols. The traditions I told Ron and Jamie about yesterday at Tahquamenon Falls.

I reassured Ron I'd find other ways to obtain information about traditional medicines, especially those that might induce hallucinations.

I should have prayed this morning for manaadendamowin, since to act without harm is to know respect. There is power in what I am going through; it's my responsibility to observe the protocols and protect others during this traditional grieving period.

Jonsy walks behind each euchre player, checking out their cards. He grimaces at Minnie's hand.

During the three months that I was TJ's girlfriend, I spent a lot of time with the Kewadins. I always liked TJ's family. Especially his grandpa. Jonsy was always telling stories. Sometimes I'd need to hang in there to find the teaching in his meandering, animated anecdotes.

Wait a minute . . . Jonsy is a talker. Full of teachings.

TJ didn't like his grandpa going by himself to the landfill in search of antique treasures.

"Hey, Grandpa Jonsy," I call out. "You still looking for someone to go collecting with you?"

CHAPTER 16

Jonsy struts over as if I called his ticket number on a fifty-fifty raffle.

"I always knew I liked you," he says. "Let's go, Sis. We're burnin' daylight."

"Can you follow me to Granny June's? Then I'll ride with you," I say.

We arrive at Granny June's house on the satellite reservation on the south end of town. Half the homes on the rez are cookie-cutter houses, part of a federal housing project funded by Housing and Urban Development in the 1970s. The other half are what everyone calls "per-cap mansions." Ordinary but nice homes that, contrasted with the nondescript HUD homes, make the street look like a suburb where the moms take turns hosting Tupperware, Mary Kay, and Longaberger parties. The two neighborhoods are a Before and After of tribal economic prosperity. Granny June lives in the Before neighborhood.

Braking in the driveway sharply enough for the tires to shout for Lily again, I share a bittersweet smile with Granny June. I hold out the Jeep keys for her. Still clasping the tobacco pouch, she wraps both hands around mine. The key ring becomes a pearl in an oyster.

"I went to settle up for Binesikwe's funeral and he said it was taken care of already."

Hearing Lily's Spirit name, I look down at my jeans.

She continues in a voice as soft as I've ever heard from her.

"You didn't need to use your zhooniyaa for that. Miigwech. And for being her friend, chi miigwech." She squeezes her hands like a hug. "I want to see this Jeep tooling around town. On campus. At the mall across the river. On the ferry. Can you do that for me, my girl?"

I nod. The lump in my throat bobbles as well.

Jonsy's voice startles me. "C'mon, Sis. I've got women to woo and bets to place." He taps his watch dramatically at my open window.

I laugh. He's been married to the same woman for fifty-plus years and plays poker for dimes.

Granny waves me off when I get out to walk her to the front door.

"You be careful at that bad place," she calls out.

I follow Jonsy's powder-blue Lincoln Town Car with the FRYBREAD POWER! bumper sticker. The old landfill site, several miles south of town, is bordered by a small parking lot, a creek, and a forest of birch and black ash trees.

He opens his trunk to reveal a mini workshop of plastic storage bins arranged like a Jenga masterpiece. Each blue lid is labeled in TJ's distinctive block lettering.

Jonsy retrieves the bin for his collecting adventures:

TREASURE HUNTING
BANDOLIER BAG · MAGNIFYING GLASS · STORAGE BAGS
BACKPACK · DISINFECTANT WIPES · DISH TOWELS
GLOVES & MASKS · ANTISEPTIC SPRAY · BOTTLED WATER

He slips the wide strap of a well-worn brown leather bandolier bag over his shoulder before putting everything else into the oversized backpack. I need to adjust the backpack straps from their maximum allowance to fit me. TJ must be his grandpa's usual collecting buddy.

Jonsy rolls his eyes while handing me a pair of latex gloves and a breathing mask. TJ must have ingrained safety precautions into his reluctant grandfather.

"Stay here, good pony." He pats the hood of his car as we begin our adventure.

The landfill is haphazardly arranged in reverse chronological order, with the newer junk toward the road. Mattress stains are still identifiable. Black garbage bags are shiny. Console televisions molt their veneer. A dollhouse with furniture inside. Why would anyone throw away . . . Nope. Not gonna follow that thought.

Jonsy has no interest in the easily accessible stuff. He must know every acre, because he quickly leads me through a trail visible only to him. Maybe time warps here, because he crosses the uneven terrain on nimble feet that align with the stories of his boxing days. Meanwhile I stumble like a toddler past the different decades of junk.

The silence should feel tranquil, since we are away from town and the highway. Instead it's unsettling. Accompanying Jonsy was such an impromptu decision that I didn't think to put any giizhik in my sneakers. I need to be a smarter Secret Squirrel going forward.

Maybe Jonsy doesn't care for the stillness either, because he starts humming. Once we reach his intended destination, he gives instructions.

"Now, we're looking for old glass bottles that have raised writing or designs. No broken ones. Colored bottles are good too. If they still have a hat, that's even better."

"A hat?"

"A cap," he says in a tone that, if Perry had said it, would've been followed by *Duh*.

Jonsy resumes humming and pokes around piles of junk. Soon his sounds grow lyrics. Finnish folk music from his mother's side of the family. He grunts while lifting a huge piece of corrugated metal and heaving it aside.

"Grandpa Jonsy, I could've helped with that. And shouldn't you check for spiders first?"

His look matches the *Duh* of his bottle-cap answer.

"Sis, do you think anything living stays around here?"

That is why it's so eerily quiet. No birds in the trees. No insects. I haven't swatted a no-see-um once. Not a single mosquito.

These birch trees, with their scars of fungus resembling burnt charcoal, will never be harvested for the medicine within the Chaga. The black ash trees will never be pounded with a mallet to loosen the layers that hold a story for every year. No one will split their bark into thin strips, soaking some in berry- or flower-dyed water, before weaving the black ash into exquisite baskets.

Instead, these trees absorb contaminated groundwater and breathe virulent fumes.

"The Sault is an old town, hey." He resumes poking around for glass treasures. "Factories and farmers hauled their moowin here before the EPA and OSHA and whatever alphabet soup of laws said they couldn't. People who weren't thinking seven generations ahead ruined the ground. No bugs. Birds won't stick around if there's nothing to eat. Spiders, neither. The four-leggeds got the sense to avoid it too."

"Um . . . if they don't hang around here, maybe we shouldn't either?" I say.

He swats the air in my direction. "Eh. Now you sound like TJ." He stands, stretching his still-formidable wingspan. "You two were quite the pair. Didn't last long, though."

There's no way I'm blabbing about his pride and joy dumping me. I've moved on.

"Silent about it." He shakes his head. "Just like him, too."

The bottom of a brown bottle angles from the ground like an iceberg. I use an old license plate to carefully excavate it. As I rub the glass with the wipes, bumps become raised lettering.

"Hey, Grandpa Jonsy, this one says 'Warner's Safe Kidney and Liver Cure.'" As I walk over to show him my find, I glimpse a stretch of grayish cloud in the southwest direction. The sky beneath the shelf cloud is dark teal.

"We need to get back to our cars," I warn. "Squall coming in."

He stands and sniffs the air. Nods his head. "Let's get away from the trees. Walk back along the creek," he says, placing the bottle inside his bandolier bag.

I feel like an owl, turning my neck to check our pace against the shelf cloud. Jonsy's agile steps remind me of TJ on the football field. He sidesteps a single black garbage bag at the edge of the creek. I zero in on it.

Wasn't the newer junk supposed to be closer to the road? This bag, still shiny, is fresh.

The hair at the nape of my neck stands on end an instant before my brain registers the whiff of . . .

Travis's hand shakes, making the revolver jiggle. I follow the tip of the barrel pointed at my face. He stinks. Meth rotting his system from the inside out. Burning my nose.

"Hey, what are you doing?" Jonsy's voice is like a phone call with a bad connection. His giant hand jostles my bad shoulder; the sharp pain jerks me from the memory.

"What's going on?" He looks down at the bag, squatting to inspect it closer.

"Don't touch that." I push him away so quickly that he stumbles backward. "Sorry. Sorry. I'm so sorry." My words rush as I steady him. "It's just that . . . there's bad stuff inside that bag."

"It doesn't stink like dead body," he says, dusting off the back of his jeans. "Should we call TJ?"

"No," I bark. I don't know if the FBI is working with Tribal Police. Ron hasn't shared that information with me. I didn't think to ask. My mind scrambles for a plan. "Let's just leave it and get in our cars before the storm hits. We need to get home."

Once I'm inside the Jeep, I wave to Jonsy and go through the motions of following the Lincoln Town Car. When it's my turn to pull into the road, I wait for him to speed away. After he rounds the curve, I reverse and turn back to the landfill.

I want that bag.

CHAPTER 17

L ily keeps two blankets in the Jeep. *Snag rags*. One is a quilted moving pad, which I spread on the ground. I set the shiny garbage bag in the middle and use the moving pad to swaddle it. Squatting, I lift the meth garbage baby and gingerly place it in the back of the vehicle.

I race home for the garage-door opener Ron gave me yesterday. I'm back on the road when hail starts pelting the Jeep like shrapnel. I pull into a store parking lot along the business spur. Straight-line winds rock the vehicle from side to side. It's darker than I thought possible in an afternoon.

Supes' afternoon practice must be ending, so I call Jamie, who answers with "Hey."

"Hey," I mimic, as lightning flashes an instant before a boom of thunder shakes the Jeep.

"Where are you?" he asks. It must sound as though I'm at a battlefront.

"Kmart parking lot," I shout over the cacophony. "On my way to haul some trash."

He's silent a moment. Did Jamie catch the significance of my trash reference?

"Are you in your mom's car?"

"No. Lily's Jeep."

"I'll meet you there. Don't drive in this storm," Jamie says.

"Wasn't gonna . . . partner," I say in fluent sarcasm. Does he think I'm an idiot?

"Don't call me that." He ends the call before I can swear at him.

Twenty minutes later, the rain eases enough for me to watch Jamie turn in to the lot and drive past the Jeep. I am about to tap the horn when I realize he's parked close to the store so anyone who recognizes his car will assume he's merely shopping. Okay . . . that's smart.

I drive over to him, giggling as I imagine a spy-worthy intercept with Jamie making a slow-motion running leap. I reach for my phone to tell Lily, then slam the brakes.

She isn't around to answer my calls or texts.

Jamie sprints the rest of the way to the Jeep. He's drenched when he opens the door.

"What the—" he begins in a raised voice before shifting tone. "What is it?"

I open my mouth, but nothing comes out. He looks genuinely concerned. I focus on his tawny brown eyes.

"Switch seats," Jamie says softly. "I'll drive."

I climb over to the passenger side as Jamie takes my seat. We sit, surrounded by lightning, rumbling thunder, and heavy rain. Gramma Pearl loved a powerful nichiiwad like this.

I blink until my head rests on Gramma's lap and she smooths my hair, as she did whenever I wasn't feeling well. It's how she comforted me after pouring my pee into my ear to cure the earache. I researched it years later, discovering what she had known: Urine is sterile and a substitute for hydrogen peroxide.

What would my Firekeeper nokomis think about the surreal situation I'm now in? Could I even explain that I'm helping law-enforcement officers from the same government that tried taking her to boarding school? If I told her about Lily, and Uncle David, and the sick kids on a rez in Minnesota . . . would she know that I am trying to protect our community, and others, too?

Once the storm lessens, Jamie drives to the garage in Dafter. He places the meth garbage baby on the countertop along one side of the garage. I grab the other snag rag, a threadbare quilt, and stand at the open bay.

The air is a good thirty degrees cooler than it was an hour ago. Jamie stands next to me and runs a hand through his wet hair. He's completely soaked. I sit down, positioning one half of the blanket under and around my right side. I motion for Jamie to sit next to me and wrap the left half around him. The soft blanket still has the wonderful smell of campfire smoke. We watch the last of the storm blow over. When I finally speak, my voice is scratchy.

"My gramma Pearl loved storms. She'd sit in the garage like this and talk about the thunderbirds that brought our loved ones, our ancestors, from the other world to check on us. She'd say, 'Tell them how you're doing, my girl.' The thunderbirds blinked lightning, so every time it flashed, I'd wave and shout, 'We're doing good!' The gigantic birds I pictured had rows of Elders, like in an airplane, waving back."

I wipe away my tears and meet Jamie's luminous eyes.

"Do you think Lily was with them today?" I ask.

He inches over until his shoulder touches mine. I focus on his damp T-shirt, warm skin, and calming breaths.

Jamie doesn't need to be kind to me; I'm on board with the investigation now. We established that yesterday in the parking lot at the falls. We are partners and nothing more.

But . . . I relax my shoulders and don't move away. I stay next to him. Just until the rain stops.

⚹

Ron arrives as the sun reclaims the late-afternoon sky. While searching through the workshop cabinets, he commends my quick thinking about the bag of trash.

"I wasn't sure if you were working with any tribal cops. Or if that information is confidential," I say. Ron is silent as he finds industrial gas masks and latex gloves in one of the workshop cabinets. It isn't until he hands each of us the protective gear that Ron responds.

"You should assume no one knows about the investigation," he says. "No LEOs. Not tribal, state, city, or even border patrol. Talk only to Jamie or me." Ron opens another cabinet and reaches for a packing-tape dispenser with a thick roll of clear tape. My eyebrows raised quizzically prompt Ron's explanation. "For lifting fingerprints."

Jamie puts a small plastic tarp over a picnic table behind the garage, as if we are having a cookout. He sets the meth garbage baby on the tarp and pulls out one item at a time like Santa at a Christmas party.

The table fills with dented containers of brake fluid; individual pop bottles with gray, opaque residue; lithium batteries cut in half so their guts could be scooped out; drain cleaner; thin, white tubing bunched like spaghetti; and a dozen boxes of cold-and-flu tablets, the plastic sheets all having hatched their pills.

"How could anyone buy that much medicine without being noticed?" I ask.

"Michigan restricts pseudoephedrine sales. Canada doesn't," Ron explains.

I remember how Jamie laughed when I told him about buying stuff across the river. He had pretended to be surprised, but he'd been fishing for information. I don't buy cases of cold medicine . . .

[150]

but I could. It isn't illegal, and you don't have the hassle of showing identification and filling out a form for the pharmacist.

"I thought you and Jamie could go to Marquette in a few weeks to spend time at the forensics lab, but now I'm thinking we shouldn't wait." Ron makes up a plan as he speaks. "If I can arrange for the lab tech to work next weekend, can you think of an excuse to get away? Labor Day weekend might be the best time to be in the lab."

What would Gramma Pearl do?

I take a deep breath and hold it, remembering when the dogs barked and she had me hide. I watched her sit in a chair angled toward the door. Her hands were steady so her aim would be true.

She was smart, resourceful, and incredibly brave.

When I exhale, it's a long, controlled release.

"My new boyfriend and I can have a romantic weekend in Marquette."

CHAPTER 18

A last-minute spot opened up for a Labor Day weekend geology seminar at Michigan Tech that will transfer to Lake State. At least that's what I tell my mother on Monday. She accepts the lie without question.

The lie is cover for Jamie and me having a romantic weekend in Marquette, which is a lie to cover my Secret Squirrel meth tutorial, so I can be a confidential informant and help the FBI.

Each lie is a fish, with a bigger fish swallowing the one preceding.

I call my aunt and tell her about the romantic weekend. Mom won't check on me, but Auntie would. She isn't happy about the lying part, but it's not the first time we've deceived my mother.

"You sure you're ready? Grief can make us do things we normally wouldn't," she says.

"Normal left town a while ago." I brace myself for the half-truth I'm about to tell. "Spending time with Jamie is the only thing that makes sense right now. Can you understand?"

Please understand, Auntie. The investigation will help everyone.

"I do." Auntie sighs as if she was the one holding her breath. "Can you promise you'll be careful? Your Norplant doesn't protect against STDs."

"You think Jamie is a skanky puck fuck?" I giggle.

"Girl, you don't know everything about his history."

Girl, you said a mouthful there.

She ends the call with "Be a smart kwe. Lust doesn't last, but herpes is forever."

On Tuesday, I make it as far as the parking lot next to the campus bookstore. I sit in the Jeep. "I'll go in after the next song," I say aloud. An hour later I give up. "Tomorrow," I announce.

I drive to Chi Mukwa arena to spend time with my Niibing Program kids like Mr. Vasques had suggested. When we shoot baskets, I notice how TJ's cousin Garth interacts with the kids. He chats easily and offers encouragement.

I miss shot after shot, even more than usual. My kids find it hilarious for a tall person to be so bad at basketball. I don't mind; besting me brings them inordinate delight.

When I leave Chi Mukwa, I catch my smile in the rearview mirror. I coast on my good mood all the way back to the campus bookstore. This time, I decide to pretend I'm on a game show where I race against other shoppers to complete my mission the quickest. Sometimes pretending is good.

I keep busy all day to avoid thinking about the weekend trip with Jamie to Marquette. Pesky questions still manage to creep into my thoughts. *What do I wear to a federal meth lab? Will Jamie and I spend every minute together? What if I'm bad at making meth and they fire me from the investigation?*

Ron calls on Wednesday with details, asking if I would be okay with staying in the same hotel room with Jamie.

"Separate beds, of course," Ron assured me. "Jamie will mention the trip to your brother. Sharing a hotel room is a precaution in case Levi and his friends make an impromptu visit."

Levi will know about the trip? Everyone will think Jamie and I are dating?

※

On Saturday I park the Jeep in the Secret Squirrel garage and get into Jamie's truck for the drive to Marquette. We're halfway there when I ask how his conversation went with my brother.

"I told him I broke up with my girlfriend back home and was interested in you." Jamie shrugs. "He was happy about it and said I'd better treat you good."

I'm surprised to hear Levi's reaction. He must *really* like Jamie. Levi's overprotective and always gets kind of weird whenever I start seeing someone. Like, he can be a player, but I'm supposed to be chaste. Unless I'm with a hockey god, I guess.

"You told him we were spending the weekend in Marquette?"

"Yeah . . . he recommended an Italian restaurant. Said to make sure we're back on Monday for some cookout at the lake?"

"Coach Bobby hosts a Labor Day bonfire. He's the varsity hockey coach at Sault High."

I shake my head. I still can't believe Levi's green-lighting this weekend. Is he really this eager for me to be fully immersed in Hockey World?

We arrive at the hotel, an elegant historic building on a hill overlooking downtown Marquette and Lower Harbor along Lake Superior. As Jamie checks in, I sneak a peek at his driver's license and credit card, both with his fake name: James Brian Johnson. His address is the one he and his fake uncle are renting in the Sault. I'm not quick enough to eyeball his date of birth, but I figure it must be a fake one that says he's eighteen.

"How old are you really?" I ask as he unlocks our hotel room door.

"That info is off-limits to you," he says, stepping aside to let me enter first.

"You don't think my knowing truthful things about you will help me live the lie better?" I toss my overnight bag to claim the queen bed closest to the window.

"Nope."

He drives me to the federal crime lab outside town. I hope he will drop me off, but he stays at my side. Jamie is the herpes of my Secret Squirrel life.

We start with a documentary about the history of meth. I wait for Jamie to sit before taking a seat across the room. The video is an arms-crossed, detached chronicle narrated by what sounds like a combination robot-scientist-reporter.

"The ephedra plant was used in Chinese medicines for over five thousand years, as a tea to help open the lungs and ease breathing. In 1919, a Japanese chemist figured out how to reduce the essence of the ephedra plant, known as ephedrine, into a crystallized form, thereby creating the first crystal meth."

History and facts aren't what matters. This is hurting my community, I tell the robot.

"Meth was once a legal, medicinal product. In the 1930s, you could buy amphetamine inhalers to treat asthma. People liked the side effects—bursts of energy and euphoria—so pharmaceutical companies developed a pill version."

Angie Flint was always a beautiful woman. But last week in the funeral parking lot, she looked as rough as her son did. At the powwow, Travis was nearly unrecognizable. Visible physical effects of meth. But what about the damage on the inside? The toll on them and their loved ones?

"During World War Two, troops were given meth pills to make them better soldiers: able to stay awake for long periods, with hyper-alert senses and an increased willingness to take risks."

Is that how it starts, Mr. Robot? Lost Boys trying meth to play video games longer? Partiers wanting an all-night buzz? Dieters thinking it's the answer to a prayer?

"The negative side effects also became known: paranoia, hallucinations, delusions, and heart irregularities, including heart failure."

There are places in town everyone knows to avoid—the alley behind the seediest bar, and a bunch of small houses down a dirt road people call Dogtown. Even an area behind the fitness center at Chi Mukwa and the last stall in the second-floor bathroom by the sophomore lockers at school.

"Meth has become the most abused hard drug in the world. Over the past three years, from 2000 to 2003, the meth industry has grown from eight billion to seventeen billion dollars. It is on track to top that in 2004."

Why can't I stop thinking about those Nish kids in Minnesota?

When the video ends, the guy in the lab hops up from his seat.

"So, who's ready to make meth?" Lab Guy is eager—like, meth-boner giddy.

"This isn't fun and games," I snap, recalling Travis's jittery hands.

Lab Guy dials it back, acknowledging the seriousness of the situation. Blah, blah, blah.

The meth tutorial begins with us putting on protective jumpsuits with hoods closed around our faces, breathing masks, and goggles. I stay peeved during Lab Guy's review of beakers, digital scales, flasks, and condensers. We're starting with the most complicated process for making meth because it takes longer and needs overnight drying time.

As soon as I pick up a Kjeldahl flask, I'm transported to a familiar place. Science World has laws, standards, order, and methods. I'm fluent in its language. I immerse myself, grateful for the single-minded focus required of Science World inhabitants.

On the drive back to the hotel, Jamie glances at my legs bouncing anxiously.

"Where do you want to get dinner?" he asks.

I shrug and look out the window. My jittery legs continue.

When we finished at the lab for the day, we removed our masks. The off-gases, which smelled like nail-polish remover, a fish-cleaning shack, and cat pee, are embedded in my nose. I can't un-smell them, and I forgot to pack anything to smudge myself with except semaa.

"Jamie, what can you tell me about the kids from the reservation in Minnesota?" When he doesn't answer right away, I ask a more precise question. "What do you know about the group hallucination they had?"

"The kids were out of it when they were brought to the emergency room. They were aggressive and seemed paranoid. They wanted more of whatever substance they had been using. Their drug screens came back positive for meth. The kids were hanging out in the woods and they snorted crystal meth together. The medical providers noted the kids alternated between pleading for more stuff and being scared and not making any sense. Each one had the same hallucination of men coming after them."

"Men chasing them in the woods?" I say. "Everyone saw the same thing?"

"Yes. Whatever was added to that batch of meth brought on a group hallucination. Once their parents arrived at the hospital, the kids wouldn't say anything else to the medical staff." Jamie pulls into the hotel parking lot. He remains seated in the truck, so I stay put as well.

"The FBI had been investigating meth activity. The incident in Minnesota was unusual enough for the FBI to look into the different substances being added during production."

"Do you know how the kids are doing now?" I hope their community has good resources to help them.

When Jamie admits he doesn't know, it reinforces how different we are. The FBI is interested in learning what caused the group hallucination. I want to know if the kids are okay.

Back at the hotel room, I take a long, hot shower. My skin is bright pink and tingly when I dry myself. Mom always sneaks a travel-sized bottle of lotion into my toiletries bag. Lilacs are to Mom as roses are to GrandMary. Tonight I'm thankful for the sweet, cloying scent.

Smelling like a lilac bush after a gentle June rainfall, I emerge from the bathroom wearing stretchy knit shorts and one of my dad's old T-shirts. My stomach comes to life a second before I register the pizza loaded with everything, waiting on the table.

Jamie ordered dinner and had it delivered to the room.

"I wasn't sure how you like your pizza, but I figured it was better to have to pick stuff off than leave out something you like," he says while flipping TV channels.

When the screen shows an early scene in *The Godfather*, I give a thumbs-up. He turns up the volume. We watch Levi's favorite movie while I demolish half a pizza and a side salad.

While Jamie is in the bathroom, I call Mom and then text Auntie.

ME: In mqt. All good.
AUNTIE: YOUR PLEASURE IS EQUAL TO OR GREATER THAN
HIS. MAKE SURE HE KNOWS THAT.

Shaking my head at Auntie's shouty text, I shut off my phone.

After Jamie exits the bathroom, I go back in to brush my teeth. The scent of his soap lingers in the steam. When I agreed to be a Secret Squirrel, I had a hazy notion of what it might involve. I never imagined repeatedly inhaling the soap that makes Jamie smell like a surfer on a tropical beach.

I don't know what to do with Jamie's thoughtfulness. It's easier for me when everything is black-and-white. He is my point of contact for this investigation. He's not my friend.

I climb into my queen bed and stare out the window.

"You want to talk about today?" Jamie asks softly in the dark from the other bed.

"Nope."

I am a frozen statue of a girl, standing in the woods. Unable to move. Carved from stone with my eyes wide open. The woods smell of earth, bark, and simultaneous life and decay.

Lily walks away from Travis, but he grabs her arm. She jerks away from him.

I can smell the chemical odor seeping from his skin.

He pulls a gun from the back of his jeans. Spins around to point it at me.

WD-40. Someone used WD-40 to clean the gun.

Lily is stunned to see me at the edge of the woods. Her mouth moves as Travis makes slashing motions with the gun at random points.

He aims at my face once again.

Lily reaches out for the gun. Brave hand demanding it.

He shoots and she falls backward.

Acrid gunpowder.

His mouth moves, but there is no sound here. Only scents that don't belong in the woods.

Copper. Acetone. Urine.

He raises the gun to his temple.

I wake up like a chased rabbit, shallow bursts of breath and heart skipping in its haste. Chemical odors are absorbed into the pores of my skin. They're even on my tongue. I swallow, and taste the odors that burn like cheap whiskey.

It's the first time I've dreamed the smells from that night.

Jamie snores softly. I count each loop of his respiratory cycle. The low rumbling happens when he exhales, followed by a gentle inhale. I make my breathing mimic his pace. It sounds like calm waves stroking the shore.

I become the sand and let his snores caress me back to sleep.

When I wake the next morning, I have an annoying headache, menstrual cramps, and dampness between my legs. The selling point of the birth-control implant is not worrying about missing a pill. The downside is the unpredictable periods.

Jamie is up by the time I finish washing the stain out of the sheet. We have an unspoken pact: I will not mention his morning boner and he will say nothing about bloody sheets.

"Can I run with you?" Jamie asks when he sees me dressed in running clothes.

Hells no. I can't get used to running with Jamie again. Secret Squirrel World needs to be black-and-white.

"Jamie, I need time to myself. We're gonna be at the lab all day."

I look away from his dejected expression.

Since I'm on my Moon, I don't set down any semaa with my morning prayer. Women are at their most powerful during menstruation, connected to life-giving forces. Auntie gave me teachings: The reason we don't use traditional medicines and we're not around ceremonial fires during this time is that we carry our own medicine and fire within. Others may act as if it's something annoying or unclean, but even the way we refer to menstruation is respectful. Auntie said, *None of this "being on the rag" or "the red curse." Your Moon is a mighty time, Kwe.*

I feel better after a five-mile run on a path along Lake Superior. Even more so after a shower and a quick breakfast with Jamie. We take a cab to the federal building, leaving his pickup truck in the hotel parking lot in case Levi and his friends decide on an impromptu trip to Marquette. If they see the truck, they'll assume we're having a marathon snag-fest.

We begin by donning our protective gear and checking on yesterday's meth. Lab Guy sets up dehumidifiers to accelerate the drying process. Then I learn four simpler methods for making meth. Quicker and less complicated, these are the versions I am likely to come across.

Throughout the day, Lab Guy teaches us meth lingo, so I can pick it up in overheard conversations. I mentally catalog the slang into three categories: familiar, unfamiliar, and camouflage. The familiar ones are the obvious words like speed, crank, and ice. The unfamiliar words are weird ones like pookie, gak, and yaba, that would catch my attention. The most difficult slang words are camouflaged as common terms such as chalk, cookies, and quick.

"How do you know when 'cotton candy' means meth or, you know, actual cotton candy?" I ask Lab Guy.

"Context." The succinct response makes me feel like there's an exception to the saying: *There are no stupid questions.*

Jamie asks about gangs.

"The only gangs I know of ride snowmobiles and live for hunting and fishing," I say.

Jamie laughs. The sound reminds me of that brief time when I thought maybe everything would be okay. When we were buddy and ambassador. Before Lily reached for Travis's gun.

I can't revisit that Before. It's too complicated.

Lab Guy shows us meth paraphernalia to look for. I focus on holding it, smelling it, getting familiar with it. We look through photographs of meth lairs: closets, sheds, trunks of cars, motel rooms, remote cabins, a bathtub and toilet, a three-foot-tall plastic drum, and campers.

At the end of the day, Lab Guy inspects the results from our various batches and tells us what a teener of our meth would sell for. *Teener* is short for *teenager*, as in Sweet Sixteen, a sixteenth of an ounce. There isn't much difference between our batches from today, but when Lab Guy checks our results from yesterday, mine looks like clear glass and would fetch a higher price than Jamie's product, which is decent but slightly cloudy. It feels petty of me to take satisfaction in the comparison, but I ride that petty horse all the way back to the hotel.

At the hotel room, I take another marathon shower and slather myself with lilac body lotion. Jamie eyeballs my dad's T-shirt, which serves as my nightgown, when I emerge.

"We really should go out to dinner. To that restaurant Levi recommended."

I sigh. My brother's behavior is confounding. I suspect there's an ulterior motive for why he's so pro-Jamie.

Jamie explains, "It's called backstopping when you make sure your story checks out. In case anyone asks questions, you have something solid as proof."

"Like your fake ID?" There is a hint of an edge to my voice.

Now it's his turn to sigh. He also adds his signature pinch to the bridge of his nose. He never used to do that before. That must be the real Jamie, the one he hid from me.

I leave an exasperated Jamie in the room while I change in the bathroom.

Years of traveling to hockey games made me an expert in packing a weekend bag. We always had to dress nicely for post-game activities. For this weekend, I included a pair of black slacks, black clogs, and one of the many elegant blouses GrandMary gave me from the boutique. Tonight's top is red draped stretch jersey.

Jamie is dressed for dinner when I exit the bathroom. He is wearing a button-down shirt, black pants, and smooth black leather dress boots. The cream-colored shirt contrasts nicely with his tanned skin. His hair is slicked back, which makes him look a little older. More sophisticated.

Is this Jamie's normal image when he's not posing as a high school senior? Should I tell him that he looks too polished? That messy hair suits him?

I say nothing.

The Italian restaurant has classic rustic decor: checkered tablecloths and tall candles melting over vintage Chianti bottles in wicker-wrapped holders. An elderly couple at the next table hold hands. Jamie's left arm rests on the table just like the older gentleman's arm.

I am unsure how far we take the backstopping precautions. Do I hold his hand? Or keep gripping my thighs beneath the table?

Jamie watches the couple next to us before meeting my eyes.

"I'm twenty-two," he says.

It would be easier if I immersed myself in the fake-girlfriend role. I was able to be a good Secret Squirrel at the lab, learning about and cooking meth.

Why can't I simply play along now?

Because I felt something for Jamie when I was getting to know him. It was real for me, but not for him. He played along too well.

"I think you had it right the first time," I say, breaking away from his intense stare. "Probably best if I don't know real things about you."

Shields have two sides for a reason.

"Okay," Jamie says quietly. A waiter brings crusty bread, still warm from the oven, and a plate of olive oil with grated Parmesan and a dash of balsamic vinegar. I rip off a chunk, dip it into the oil, and shove it in my mouth.

We eat dinner in silence. Anyone looking at us would surmise we are on a very bad first date. We appear to have zero connection. Ron said we needed to establish relationship patterns so people would buy into our cover story.

We have failed miserably.

CHAPTER 19

When you go on a trip, the drive there usually feels twice as long as the ride home. For Jamie and me, it's the opposite. The drive from Marquette is agonizingly protracted.

Lily's voice pops into my head, as clear as if she were leaning forward from the back seat and whispering to me. *Your black-and-white shield keeps osmosis combustion from happening.*

"So, tell me about Coach Bobby," he says as we pass through Au Train.

"Coach Bobby? He's been the hockey coach at Sault High forever. Teaches business classes. Always stood up for me when other coaches acted like I shouldn't be on a guys' team."

"Did you get a lot of shit?"

I shrug. "Eh. Levi taught me some filthy smack if anyone messed with me." He raises his eyebrows again, this time curious. "I'm not telling you," I say with a small laugh that lowers my Secret Squirrel shield a smidge.

Somewhere along the Seney Stretch, a curveless twenty-five-mile portion of M-28 that cuts through the swampy wetlands of a wildlife refuge, I decide to take charge of the situation.

"Okay. We gotta come up with . . . relationship patterns, like Ron said."

Jamie nods his agreement.

"We can hold hands," I say. "And kiss on the cheek only. Not on the lips."

"No tongue?" He flashes a grin that makes his eyes sparkle.

"Hells no." I look away. Focusing on the jack pines that we pass, I take deep breaths until my voice can be casual. "I want to touch your hair. Smooth it down or ruffle the curls."

"Okay. Then I get to touch yours."

"No," I blurt, as the ghost of TJ's meaty paw strokes my hair. I don't want any reminders of that liar.

"That hardly seems fair," Jamie says lightly.

"Fairness isn't one of our Seven Grandfathers . . . didn't you know?"

"And the Seven Grandfathers are . . . ?"

"Teachings about living a good life. Nishnaab way. Humility. Respect. Honesty. Bravery. Wisdom. Love. Truth." I let out a half chuckle. "Levi calls them the Seven Godfathers."

Jamie gives a half smile but doesn't say anything until we reach the gas station at the edge of the blink-and-you'll-miss-it town of Seney.

"Would it be okay to put my arm around you when we're next to each other?" he asks.

"Yeah. That makes sense." I add, "Now, all these rules are for when we're around other people. When we're alone like this, it's coworkers only."

He turns his head to give me a look, eyebrows raised like, *Duh.*

"Well, I just wanted to put it out there. So there's no misunderstandings," I say.

When we reach the four-way stop at the intersection with M-123, I point to turn north.

As we drive through the tiny village of Paradise, Jamie makes the requisite crack about driving through Paradise. I roll my eyes. He smiles, twitching the tail of his red scar.

"How did you get your scar? For real. And don't say car accident."

He's quiet as the road takes us along Lake Superior, past rustic cabins and the odd new, fancy vacation home.

"I got held down and sliced with a knife." He shakes off a shiver. "In case you were wondering, yes, knife wounds hurt like hell."

It's somber in the truck for the last mile to Coach Bobby's cabin. My thoughts spiral. Did Jamie get knifed on the job? How often do investigations result in injuries?

I don't want us to show up at the party like this. Both of us glum. I motion for him to turn in to the next gravel driveway.

"Yeah, well . . . at least my dick is bigger than yours," I say—to Jamie's utter astonishment. I quickly add, "I swear that's what Levi told me to say on the ice."

He throws his head back and laughs. The sound is deep and reverberates all the way to my toes.

But the good stuff happens when worlds collide.

I roll my eyes at the echo of Lily's voice before I give in and join Jamie.

Still laughing, we follow the music down weathered driftwood steps to the beach party. Nickelback singing about "Someday."

When we arrive, three dozen people stop what they're doing and stare at us.

"Lovebirds!" Levi shouts above the music.

Macy Manitou finishes a back walkover. Her mouth gapes like a flounder out of water.

Jamie reaches for my hand and squeezes it in tacit understanding. It's showtime.

☀

It's a perfect Labor Day: one last glorious, cloudless day. As if the summer days when rain chilled your bones were in exchange for this.

Lake Superior is calm, with only minuscule waves teasing the shore. Some of my former teammates are roasting hot dogs around a large bonfire. Others play touch football on the sugar-sand beach. Levi is surrounded by girls enthralled by some story he's telling.

I lead Jamie to a gazebo where Coach Bobby flips burgers on a large gas grill. When he sees me, my old coach sets down the metal spatula and holds out his fist so we can bump knuckles. I suspect we will greet each other this way forever.

"Hi, Coach, this is Jamie Johnson. He's one of the new Supes."

Jamie lets go of my hand to shake Coach Bobby's.

"Robert LaFleur. Everyone calls me Coach Bobby." He resumes his grill-master duties, adding cheese slices to half the burgers. Coach tilts his head my way. "Best left defenseman I've ever coached. You got yourself one hell of a girl there, son."

"Yes, sir . . . Coach Bobby," Jamie says.

"She should be headed to Michigan to play D-one," Coach says with exaggerated gruffness.

I know him well enough to hear the kernel of true disappointment deep within the bluster.

"Time to try new things," I say, reaching for Jamie's hand.

It almost sounds true. Maybe Coach can hear beneath my bluster as well.

We sit at an old picnic table to eat cheeseburgers. I get two cups of lemonade from the large drink cooler. Jamie's plate is loaded with tiny kosher dill pickles. I wonder if he actually loves pickles . . . or if he's just playing the part of someone who loves pickles.

Levi sits with us, along with Stormy Nodin, who has fit three cheeseburgers on his plate. For all his voracious appetite, he's scrawny—not slender-yet-lean muscled like Jamie. Stormy's taken off his shirt, not at all self-conscious about his practically concave chest. Smooth cinnamon skin glistens under the bright sunlight. His hair is pulled back into a thick braid.

"So, how was Marquette?" Levi wants to know.

Answering for us, Stormy belts out a pervy-sounding "Bow-chicka-wow-wow."

"Thanks for the restaurant suggestion, Levi," Jamie says. "It was great."

Mike Edwards swaggers over with military precision. His blond hair is freshly buzzed and gelled, which makes his big head look like a square porcupine. He's kept his T-shirt on to keep from getting a sunburn, but his muscular Zhaaganaàsh forearms are already pink.

"So, the rumors are true. Dauny Defense plays offense, too," Mike says.

"Where's your girlfriend?" I ask, knowing full well of his hockey-season chastity vow.

"Gotta keep the hockey temple clean," he says.

"Um . . . girls aren't unclean and you're not Samson. You don't have to worry about some Delilah chick snipping off your power."

"Delores who?" Mike eats his burger perimeter first, until there's one perfect center bite left.

"Holy. Read something other than hockey magazines and computer manuals," I say.

"Hey, Bubble," Levi says in a gentle, unfamiliar tone. "I heard Granny June gave you Lily's Jeep." When I nod, he adds, "That was really nice of her." He smiles kindly.

My shoulders relax. I hadn't realized I'd been so tense.

He grins. "Starting tomorrow me and Stormy are seniors, Mike's a junior, and you're a lowly freshman."

"College," I say, pointing at myself first and then the guys. "High school."

"I wanna run with you." Levi looks at Stormy and Mike, his two best friends, and revises himself. "Us lowlies want to run with you tomorrow morning. Sound good? Jamie, too." His voice is playful, but there is a seriousness behind his eyes.

Sometimes my brother drives me crazy. And other times, like now, he does something sweet and thoughtful. Our dad would be proud of Levi. Being supportive when I need it most.

I smile. "I'd like that." I explain the sequence of events to Jamie. "You come by my place before seven. We'll warm up, and swing by Levi's before we pick up Mike along the way."

"Welcome to Hockey World," Levi tells me.

So that's why he's been so accepting of Jamie. Because I've blurred the lines between Regular World and Hockey World.

Guilt nibbles away at me. My brother doesn't know I'm just acting the part of a hockey girlfriend. I hadn't given any thought to what I might need to reconcile after Jamie and Ron leave. The whole aftermath. It's their investigation, but it's my life.

The rest of the afternoon flies by. We play touch football with the guys. When I throw a perfect spiral to Levi, Stormy makes a wisecrack about all the things I learned from TJ Kewadin. My stomach cramps from either the burger, which was pinkish red in the middle, or from my Moon. I ask Macy to sub in so I can go to the bathroom in Coach Bobby's cabin.

It's been a year since Coach's last party. He's renovated his kitchen. I'm impressed with the high-end finishes; he has the same brand of appliances that GrandMary has in the big house.

Sunset means a rapid temperature drop. Jamie and I go to the truck; it's easier to change behind it rather than in the tiny cabin bathroom. When it's his turn behind the truck, I glance at the side mirror as Jamie pulls up his jeans. I look away, but not before his trio of well-defined hamstring muscles—semitendinosus, biceps femoris, and semimembranosus—are etched in my brain.

Wait . . . was he able to see me when our positions were reversed?

We chat with the guys until I see two seats open up at the bonfire. I move quickly to claim the spots for Jamie and me.

I watch Coach Bobby supervise the fireworks setup. My brother always brings the good kind you can only buy on the rez. A blur moves next to me as Macy sits in the empty seat.

"That's for Jamie," I tell her.

"Aw . . . saving for Jamie." Her syrupy voice mocks me. She leans closer. "Didn't know you had it in ya to be a shark off the ice. His girl back home never stood a chance."

Macy's superpower is the ability to give a backhanded compliment.

"All's fair in love and hockey," I say, silently adding, *And meth*.

Heather Nodin, one of Stormy's many dozens of cousins, leans across me. Her weed fumes overpower the bonfire smoke.

"You're just mad Daunis got to him before you could. Now be gone before somebody drops a house on you," she tells my nemesis.

"Fuck you, Heather," Macy says without any heat. She leaves to chat with some other girls. They look over at Heather and say snarky things between giggles.

Heather is dressed oddly for a bonfire. Her red Roots hoodie is normal, but the skintight capri jeans are open at the side seams, an inch wide from hip to mid-calf, and held together by oversized safety pins. Her black flip-flops are the impractical platform kind that I'd bust an ankle in.

"Thanks," I tell Heather. "Or as they say in my village, miigwech."

She laughs a little too hard at the way I echo stuff the Elders always say.

Heather's eyes are half-shut. Her laughter is hollowed out. Paper thin, empty inside.

When guys do nothing but smoke weed and play video games, we call them Lost Boys. As in Peter Pan's gang in Neverland. Never growing up. Never leaving home. Never holding on to a job. I suppose there can be Lost Girls, too.

"Hey . . . ," Heather says, pulling a clear plastic bag from the pouch of her hoodie. The pills look like speckled candy. "I got some Molly V. You and your new boyfriend can go all night long. Got other stuff too." She holds out another sandwich bag, this one with a half-dozen rolled joints.

I stare at her.

"Heather, we just buried Lily. You remember my best friend who got shot through the heart by her meth-head ex-boyfriend? So, no . . . I don't want any ecstasy boner pills."

She stares back with eyes that are suddenly laser-focused.

"Fine, but you sure do have a strange way of grieving, Daunis. Showing off your new boyfriend at a party?"

Heather Nodin leaves me at the bonfire, where I seethe over truths I cannot tell.

After the fireworks, the crowd thins out. We all fit around the bonfire now.

"Tell us a story, Firekeeper's Daughter," Levi says to me from across the fire.

I shake my head. "There's no snow on the ground."

Auntie says we honor our traditions when we save stories for the wintertime.

Macy scoffs. "That's just so snakes don't overhear the teachings." She glances around. "All clear," she says with a grin before launching into a story.

"Creator gathered all the animals and birds, along with First Man and First Woman." She lowers her voice to sound like her dad, Chief Manitou. "'I'm Creator and I've got a gift for each one of you.'"

People laugh.

"So Creator named a gift and waited for someone to claim it as theirs. 'Who wants to fly higher than any other bird and bring prayers directly to me?'"

Macy waves a hand toward the sky.

"Migizi says, 'Me. Me. Pick me.'

"'You got it!'"

Everyone laughs more. She waits a beat before continuing.

"'How about big teeth to cut down trees for a house that can purify a river?' Amik nudges First Man, whispering, 'You better not wait till the end and get stuck with a bad gift.' Then Amik jumps up and shouts, 'Creator, that gift sounds perfect. Please choose me.'

"'You got it!'"

Macy looks around the fire, pausing for dramatic effect just like her dad when he's making a big speech.

"Now, First Man grew anxious as he watched the four-leggeds and the winged claim their gifts. He tried raising his hand a few times, but others were quicker. Finally, it was just First Man and First Woman left. Creator announced the next-to-the-last gift.

"'How about the ability to pee standing up?'"

The laughter is even louder.

"First Man pushes past First Woman. 'Me. Creator. Me. Pick me.'

"'You got it!'"

Macy's eyes glitter like the crackling embers at the base of the bonfire.

"First Man asks Creator, 'Oh . . . by the way . . . what was the last gift?'

"'Multiple orgasms!'"

CHAPTER 20

The next morning, Jamie is in my driveway stretching his legs in the dawn twilight. I nod hello before whispering my prayer at the tree. I omit putting down any semaa because of my Moontime. When I begin my warm-up routine, Jamie aligns his stretches with mine. It is as if no time has passed since our last run. Before Lily flew away and I became a Secret Squirrel.

"Last night, Levi called you Firekeeper's Daughter. What was that about?" he asks.

I put one foot forward to stretch my quadriceps and hamstrings in a lunge position.

"Well, there's a teaching about the daughter of the original firekeeper," I say. "She starts each day by lifting the sun into the sky and singing."

We do lunges on the other leg. He looks expectantly at me, waiting for more info.

"My brother calls me that sometimes . . . our dad's last name and all. He thinks it's ironic because I'm a really bad singer." I roll my eyes and continue stretching as the sky lightens. "I don't like her story, because she doesn't even get her own name in it. Her identity is in relation to her dad, Firekeeper, and then her husband, First Man, called Anishinaabe, and then her sons, named after each of the four directions. She gets stuck with the responsibility of lifting the sun every morning." I do a few jumping jacks. "What if she was tired one day and said, 'Screw it . . . I'm going back to sleep'?" I motion toward the street and begin jogging. "Just seems like a raw deal—all that responsibility and you don't even get your own name."

Jamie follows my gentle pace for the few blocks to my brother's place. The houses get bigger the closer we get.

I think about the extra name I add to my morning prayer so Creator will know who I am. What if Creator knows exactly who I am? I've been the one tying my identity to my father. Telling Jamie her story brings out the contradiction in my prayers each time I introduce myself.

Ishkode-genawendan Odaanisan. *Firekeeper's Daughter.*

I decide that from now on I'll leave out that extra name. My Spirit name is enough.

I should ask Auntie the word in Anishinaabemowin for the beams of light you can see when the sun hides behind clouds. In science, they're called crepuscular rays. I think the word is *zaagaaso.* If I'm right, that's what I'll call Firekeeper's Daughter from now on. Her own identity: Zaagaasikwe.

I make out the shapes of two guys stretching in a driveway.

"Levi lives in a studio apartment over the garage at his mom's," I say. "Stormy, too, most of the time."

Jamie raises an eyebrow.

"Well, Stormy's family is kinda messed up."

Stormy used to hitch a ride from Sugar Island whenever his parents fought. He'd toss pebbles at Levi's window until my brother woke up and let him in. It happened so often that Dana put a key under the garden-gnome statue by the back door for him.

Anything she did for Levi, she did for Stormy. Going shopping for school clothes or hockey gear, she'd buy Stormy his own stuff. Not hand-me-downs, either.

It's what I like most about Dana Firekeeper.

She grew up poor and made sure Stormy didn't feel the way she did. Levi told me that when his mom was a little girl, she shared a bed with her sisters, and they'd wake up to snow dusting their blanket from a hole in the roof.

Levi and Stormy fall in beside us.

"Hey, Bubble, wanna take a detour past the mansion?" Stormy attempts to rattle me.

I glare at him, but he keeps talking.

"Weren't you at the party at the big house, Jamie? What did you think of it? Us per-cap Nishnaabs are new money. Bubble is *old* money. *Trust-fund* money." He does a half laugh, half snort. "You could've bought a car anytime you wanted."

"Geez, Stormy. Did someone piss in your oatmeal today?" I say.

Levi sticks up for me. "It's all cool, Storm. She wants to earn it and not coast by." He smiles my way. "I respect that."

I have complicated thoughts about my trust fund. GrandMary explained it was for my education, a car, and a "good start in life." She said it was a safety net so I would never be trapped in an "unfortunate situation." I am conflicted about using it because I was my mother's "unfortunate situation." What choices would she have made if she'd had access to a trust fund?

Like me, Stormy's weird about zhooniyaa. I can see why. Before Levi turned eighteen, Dana deposited his minor money—a monthly check one third the amount of an adult member's per-cap check—into a joint account for him to access. Stormy's mom doesn't do that.

Shawna Nodin is Ojibwe, but from a band in Wisconsin. One time, she rented the Ogimaa Suite at the Superior Shores and threw a huge party that lasted the weekend. The Monday after, she filled out an application at Tribal Social Services for the Emergency Needs Program to pay her shutoff notices. Ever since, they call her Shawna Shutoff.

As we approach the Edwards's house of steel and glass, Mike appears from nowhere, like a ninja. He immediately matches his stride with the group's.

The guys blather, but I cannot manage any words. Their pace is halfway between my normal speed and a full sprint.

Mike farts loudly and everyone cracks up.

"Damn, Boogid, that one sounded wet," Stormy says.

Levi tells Jamie, "Boogid is Mike's honorary Indian name. It means 'fart,' but we should've named him Moowin, because I think he just crapped hisself."

"How you know it wasn't Bubble?" Stormy asks.

"'Cause GrandMary would disinherit her if she ever cut one like that." More laughter.

The downside of hanging out with the guys is that they're super gross. If I had a dollar for every fart that I've endured around them, I wouldn't need a trust fund.

I tune them out, focusing instead on the sound of my breathing.

Their route takes us along the river to where it curves past the ferry launch and the country club. I catch a fragment of the story Levi is telling Jamie. About me.

"So, I'm walking on top of the climbing thing like a little badass. A few drops of rain make it slippery, and the next thing I know, I'm flat on my back looking up at it. That's when Daunis comes running over, yelling not to move me."

We cut through the southern edge of the golf course to reach a trail that will lead us to the powwow grounds. Levi keeps blabbing.

"My sister gets on all fours to keep the rain off my head. She orders the playground monitor to call for an ambulance." Levi looks my way. "And we were, what, eleven?"

"Nine. It was right after that *Superman* actor fell off his horse and became paralyzed," I say, able to manage words only because we've slowed down on the trail.

I don't mention how scared I was that day. I nearly peed my pants at the thought of my brother being seriously injured. Up to that day, Dana had treated me politely, though not warmly. I even thought she deliberately held Levi back a year so we wouldn't be in the same grade together. But when Auntie and I arrived at the hospital to check on Levi, Dana hugged me for the first time. Between sobs, she repeated *miigwech* into my ear for what seemed like an hour. Our relationship changed, bonded by our love for Levi.

I look at my brother's back as we run single file. For all the times he annoys me, there are many more times when I am profoundly thankful for him.

"Ball out," Levi shouts over his shoulder to the rest of us.

The guys break into a sprint for the final quarter mile across the powwow grounds and along Ice Circle Drive to Chi Mukwa. I should've known that this was just a warm-up for them, and now their real workout will come from lifting weights at the fitness center.

By the time I catch up, they're well into their post-run stretches. I collapse onto soft, cool grass, facedown and arms splayed. I want to lick the moisture from each blade.

Once the guys finish their cooldown, they shout their goodbyes. Jamie follows behind Levi, but at the last minute he says something to my brother and runs over to me. I roll over and flop onto my back. Jamie eases into push-up position, rising into a plank so his face is slightly above my raised head.

Jamie plants a quick kiss on my cheek.

"Is Levi watching?" he whispers.

I glance over to where my brother stands, grinning at us from an entrance.

"Yup."

⚛

I walk slowly and stiffly to EverCare. The scent of roses fills the hallway outside GrandMary's room. Pausing in the doorway, I watch Mom massaging lotion on her mother's toothpick legs. She exhausts herself looking after GrandMary, who wasn't always kind to her.

What if it's a strength to love and care for someone you don't always like?

Mom was adamant that Uncle David hadn't relapsed. I know now that he didn't, but even if he had, she would have continued to love and support him.

What if my mother is actually a strong person disguised as someone fragile?

I walk over to Mom instead of plopping down on GrandMary's bed like I usually do. Bending down, I kiss my mother's cheek. I inhale a whiff of lilac perfume at her neck, gentle as a whisper in a room where the roses shout over one another. I kiss her again. Just because.

"It's my first day at Lake State," I tell GrandMary after a blink brings her back to us. She breaks into a huge smile. "I have class at nine, so I can't stay long. I love you."

After a quick shower and yogurt for breakfast, I race in the Jeep to the parking lot behind the student union. I run across the quad, past Fontaine Hall, to arrive at class, breathless and anxious. The only seats left are in the front row. I sit and glance at the empty one next to me.

You should be here, Lily.

The professor reviews the syllabus for Principles of Macroeconomics. Every other sentence is an admonition.

"This is not high school."

"I don't take attendance."

"I don't check on missed assignments or reschedule exams."

"I don't speak with parents."

"You, and only you, are responsible for your academic performance."

"If this is not what you signed up for, leave now or forever hold your peace."

I don't want to be here without my best friend.

I get up and leave.

Now what, Lily?

Pinpricks stab my nose and a fist-sized lump swells in my throat. I struggle to take deep, gulping breaths. Water. Maybe water will help. I dig in my backpack but come up empty.

As I reach for the door of the student union, TJ Kewadin exits. Surprise flickers across his face before it's replaced with a smooth, impersonal mask. He walks past, dressed in a plain white T-shirt, jeans, and rugged work boots. He smells clean and woodsy.

That asshole is still wearing the cologne I bought for him.

I grab the first item in my backpack. *Macroeconomics: Understanding the Wealth of Nations* lands with a thud two feet from TJ. He spins around, something angry flashing across his face before the mask returns. I don't know which is more infuriating—that he's pissed off or that he covers it up like a big faker.

Just then, Robin Bailey walks past TJ. She picks up my textbook. One hand passes me the book and the other hand firmly pulls me inside the student union.

"Girl, you gotta get over TJ," she says while handing me a bottle of water from her backpack. "No guy should have that kind of power over you. No matter who he is or how much everyone adores him. Or how much you might still want him."

"I do not want TJ," I say, bristling.

She gives me a look verging on pity.

Robin graduated two years ago, with TJ. Class of 2002. Her sophomore year, she was the first girl in the Sault ever to make the boys' varsity hockey team. I joined her the following year as a freshman. We were teammates for the two years we overlapped at Sault High. She played one year at Cornell before transferring to Lake State last year.

"It's just . . . he just happened to catch me in a low moment," I say.

"Yeah, I know how that goes," she says in sympathy. "You don't have to be a superhero. Dauny, it's okay to not be okay. I'm kinda surprised you're even here."

"I thought it was what Lily would want me to do." I wipe away a tear.

Robin is content to sit with me in the café and let me be sad.

"How about if you pick two classes and drop the others? What class was Lily looking forward to the most?" She hands me napkins for my runny nose.

I smile. "American Literature of the Twentieth Century."

"And what class were you most excited about?"

"Plant Morphology."

"Of course." She shakes her head in amusement. "When's your next class?"

"Ten. American Lit."

"Give it a try. No pressure. See how it goes. You like it, you stay. Same with plant class." She takes my phone and calls herself before handing it back to me. "Call if you want me to go with you on Friday to the registrar's office to drop anything you aren't excited about."

"Miigwech," I say.

She stands to my left and raises her right arm in front of me. I grin and do the same with my left arm to make an *X* with hers. We used to do this with our hockey sticks when we skated onto the ice before every game. It was her idea. For all the little girls like us, who chose hockey skates over figure skates.

I walk to my next class, American Literature, and sit in the back row, closest to the door. Scanning the reading assignments on the syllabus, I look for one in particular.

Uh-oh . . . no Michener.

Granny June's harangue on the literary underestimation of James A. Michener lasts from the time I pick her up for lunch until I bring her home that afternoon.

❋

The following day, as I help her into the Jeep, Granny picks up where she left off.

"You better tell that Zhaaganaash smarty-pants that James A. Michener is the greatest American novelist of my lifetime," she yells.

"The professor is Black," I say. "And, yes, I will for sure tell her about your opinion."

"Not opinion. Fact."

❋

After I've brought Granny June her tray of Indian taco with whole-wheat fry bread, I stand in line for myself. Jonsy Kewadin knocks over the coffee mug he's just filled. I grab napkins to clean up the mess. When I hand him a fresh mug, he motions toward the sugar.

"But what about your diabetes?" I say.

"I'm not a diabetic," he shouts. "I'm a Presbyterian."

I laugh. Jonsy's a twice-a-week Catholic.

"Hey." His tone changes to a conspiratorial whisper. "I took TJ back to the landfill after the storm, and that bag was gone . . . You didn't take it, did you?"

"Hauling toxic garbage doesn't sound like something a rational person would do, Grandpa Jonsy," I say, leading him back to his table of friends.

Jonsy's brother Jimmer gets my attention. "Hey, Firekeeper. My grandson got me a iTunes card. What the hell am I supposed to do with that?"

"You can buy any song online for ninety-nine cents and burn a CD," I explain. "Like making a tiny album of your favorite songs."

"Jimmie Rodgers and Ernest Tubb?"

"As long as their stuff is in the iTunes catalog," I say. "I'll grab my laptop after lunch. We can use your gift card today and I'll bring your CD tomorrow."

I tell Granny that after lunch I'm helping Jimmer Kewadin buy songs online.

"That old gangster?" she says.

The Elder Center director makes announcements before they do the fifty-fifty raffle. Tribal Youth Council will be there Thursday afternoon to help anyone set up their cell phones.

"You can get emergency alerts. Or send a group text to your friends with ferry updates."

"Holy wah," Jonsy says loudly. "Modern-day moccasin telegraph."

"Oh, and a young woman's missing. Tribal citizen. Heather Nodin was last seen walking through Paradise on Monday night. Anyone with info should contact Tribal Police."

Heather is missing? I don't remember seeing her around the bonfire when Macy told the story about Creator's gifts. Maybe she left right after offering me drugs and telling off Macy. I make a note to let Jamie know that I might have been one of the last people to interact with Heather Nodin.

By Friday, I've dropped down to two courses and have become an iTunes mix master. Granny and I spend most of the afternoon on the island. She and Minnie rehash old arguments. I cannot imagine sparring for decades like that with Macy.

What I have decided, as a Secret Squirrel, is that while I'm helping an Elder buy songs from iTunes, I can ask about medicines and stuff. Good trade, as Jonsy would say with a wave of his hand, mimicking a scene out of *Dances With Wolves*.

Jimmer Kewadin tells me that Al Capone did, indeed, hide whiskey in a cave along Lake George. The east side of Sugar Island.

"Do people explore the caves looking for anything he left behind?"

"Every now and then a dead body washes up. That scares away most with good sense."

Leonard Manitou—Minnie's son, Chief Manitou's dad, and Macy's grandpa—reveals that when he was five years old, he went missing for two days, and nobody except his mom and grandma believed the Little People had kept him safe.

Bucky Nodin—who everyone calls Buck Naked—catches my attention. He is Heather's great-uncle, I think, and might want to know when I last saw Heather. Instead, he seems scattered and asks how much it would cost to get every song Patsy Cline ever recorded. Before I can answer, Buck mentions the time he accidentally snared his own cat instead of a rabbit. Then he tells me he used to go picking mushrooms with his great-grandma on Duck Island.

"Mushrooms? On Duck Island?" I say before he can jump to another random topic. My heart beats so fast, I'm sure Buck can see it through my Red Wings T-shirt.

When Ron brought me to Uncle David's classroom, he named three locations where hallucinogenic mushrooms had been found: Tahquamenon Falls, Pictured Rocks, and Sugar Island. On the drive back from Marquette, Ron provided an important detail about the location where Uncle David had been—Duck Lake on Sugar Island. Duck Island is bordered on one side by Duck Lake.

"Yeah," Buck says. "That little island within an island is full of them. Something about the soil and moisture. All them old trees ain't never been chopped down."

I look around, flush with excitement over picking up Uncle David's mushroom research. Seeney Nimkee scowls across the dining room, as if she knows what I am thinking.

This Secret Squirrel is in search of a nut. A hallucinogenic mushroom of a nut.

CHAPTER 21

On Saturday, I stare at the Tribe's billboard on my way through downtown. Despair drops anchor in the pit of my stomach. The left side has NEVER FORGET in white letters on a dark background. Heather's senior picture, along with her description and the phone number for Tribal Police, fills the other half.

It isn't until I pass by that I notice the outline of the Twin Towers behind the bold lettering. They had meant to never forget about 9/11. Two separate posters.

Heather's mom looked rough last night on TV. Hard living and more than one stint in county jail. She claimed the police weren't doing enough to look for her daughter. I make a mental note to ask Jamie or Ron if anything can be done to increase the search efforts.

On Sugar Island, I head south and east until the asphalt ends. The Jeep rocks side to side on the uneven dirt road beyond. "Whoa, good pony," I say, patting the dashboard when I park.

Taking my cue from Jonsy's masterpiece of organization, I have a backpack with clear storage bags, a roll of tan masking tape for making labels, and a black Sharpie. I've also packed a map of the island—folded so the panel shows only Duck Island—along with bottled water, latex gloves, bug dope, red cotton yarn, tiny scissors, a digital camera, and a notebook with a pen tethered by a yarn leash to its spiral binding.

On my walk to the narrow section of land that makes Duck Island a peninsula instead of an actual island, I come upon the caretaker's cabin on the preserve.

I halt. A memory washes over me like a gentle rain.

My dad carrying me on his shoulders as he hiked past the cabin to his best secret fishing spot on Duck Lake.

I want to stand here and blink until he's next to me. I hear Jonsy's voice instead.

Get to work, Sis. You're burning daylight.

Somewhere on Duck Island, Uncle David found a unique variety of mushroom.

To explore the area methodically, I decide to view it as the torso of a body getting a CAT scan. I stand at the southeastern side of the peninsula at the edge of Lake George and tie a snip of red yarn around a birch tree to mark my starting point. I take ten paces north along the shoreline and mark another tree with yarn.

The average person's stride is about thirty inches, but since I have such long legs, my strides are probably closer to a full yard. So my cross sections will be thirty feet deep for the width of the island east to west.

Cutting through the middle of Duck Island, I reach Duck Lake to the west. I head south until I'm at the narrow starting point of the peninsula and mark the first tree. Marking ten paces north along the shore of Duck Lake, I establish my northwestern boundary.

I canvass the section, looking for the damp places—soil or soft wood—where mushrooms grow. When I find something, I take pictures, log it in my notebook, and collect a sample in a sandwich bag. Later, I'll look up each sample in the three mushroom encyclopedias that were among Uncle David's books. Mom had me add all of his books to the library at the big house after we emptied his apartment. In addition to my uncle's reference books, I found a mushroom-foraging website that is searchable by location or species.

My goal is to find something that hasn't been cataloged. I'm not looking for a match—rather, for the absence of a match.

Daunis, we don't prove a hypothesis is true; we search for evidence to disprove a null hypothesis. Uncle David's voice is as clear as if he is walking behind me.

He taught me so much. I can follow in his footsteps—do what he would have done.

Is it wrong to be excited about a research project that has so much at stake?

The woods are medicinal. Engaging all my senses and connecting me to something timeless. Like being in the zone, except I'm not running. Leaves flutter to the ground. Critters scurry nearby. The scents of pine, cedar, and moss mixing together.

When I complete the first section, I begin again with ten paces north along Lake George. I explore Duck Island in cross sections for the rest of the morning.

I take an early afternoon break to eat some cheese and crackers and a juicy Honeycrisp apple. I check my watch. My mother thinks I am studying all day at the university library. My plan is to do a few more sections before I go home and look up today's samples. Tomorrow I'll come back as soon as Mom leaves for Sunday mass and put in more hours.

I take ten paces north and mark a tree. There's a patch of pansies just beyond my boundary. Yellow with purple markings or with their coloring reversed.

Gramma Pearl gathered these vivid flowers. She mixed them with melted bear grease as an ointment for my dad's eczema. I drank tea made from dried petals she kept in a coffee tin. She boiled purple petals to use as a dye for the strips of black ash that would be twisted into the weaving for a colorful accent in her baskets.

I've always liked pansies. When I did my coming-of-age fast, it rained the entire time. It stopped only once. Enough for me to take in the woods surrounding the large boulder where I huddled, which was like the hull of an overturned boat. There was a patch of colorful pansies, and their markings looked like little faces. When the rain returned and I went back under my tarp, I imagined them as spirit helpers keeping me company.

Something black darts past. A raven, pausing to rest on a small boulder at the water's edge beyond the pansies.

I recall Macy's story at the bonfire. The way I heard the story from Gramma Pearl, Gaagaagi was away making mischief when Creator handed out gifts.

What will I do? Oh, why was I so naughty? How can I ever find my purpose?

Gaagaagi visited Makwa to see if he could learn her ways, but he grew bored. All she did was lumber through the woods finding medicines.

He flew away and observed each of his friends using their gifts. Again he scolded himself for being naughty and missing out on receiving his own gift.

One day as he was flying around, he heard Ajidamoo crying in a hole in an oak tree surrounded by the acorns he had collected.

What is the matter, Ajidamoo?

I am sad and I have no joy for anything I once loved doing.

Maybe you should go see Makwa. She knows about medicines. Maybe there is a tea she can make for you. Come with me. I will take you there.

Gaagaagi led Ajidamoo to Makwa. Sure enough, Makwa had the right medicine for him.

A pleased feeling came over Gaagaagi as he flew away.

He kept going until he came upon Waabooz crying.

What is the matter, Waabooz?

I cannot relax as long as that sly Waagosh is trying to eat me.

But, Waabooz, Creator gifted you long ears and quick feet. You can hear things that others cannot. No one moves more quickly than you. You will have a head start on Waagosh if you honor your gifts.

That is true, said Waabooz. Miigwech, niijii.

As he flew away, Gaagaagi had that good feeling again. He had spent so much time flying around, watching his friends using their gifts, that he had come to know their strengths and how they might help one another in their time of need.

And that is how Gaagaagi discovered that his gift was in solving problems.

I am smiling when I approach the black bird on the small black boulder.

"And how will you help me, Gaagaagi?" I ask quietly.

The smell hits me when I realize something is just beyond the boulder along the shore.

A body.

Pulling my sweatshirt to cover my nose, I take hesitant steps aligned with my shallow, halting breaths. I reach the boulder and peer around.

Eyelids still half open. Eyes gone. Pecked or nibbled.

I stumble backward.

It doesn't smell like dead body.

How would Jonsy know what a dead body smelled like?

Because rotting flesh is unlike anything else.

I know that I, too, will never forget the smell of Heather Nodin's body.

CHAPTER 22

I t isn't until I'm close to Auntie's that my phone connects with a
cell tower across the river. I burst into the house, talking to the
911 operator.

"No, she doesn't have a pulse. I told you she's dead."

My aunt comes running from the laundry room, wide-eyed with
concern.

"Heather Nodin . . . washed up . . . Lake George down by Duck
Island." I gesture to the phone, telling Auntie, "I've told her twice
now." I shout into the phone, "I DIDN'T NEED TO TAKE HER PULSE
BECAUSE SHE WAS ALREADY DEAD."

Auntie grabs my cell phone. With her other hand, she yanks me
into half of a bear hug.

"We'll meet the police at the caretaker's cabin," she says into the
phone before flipping it shut and tossing it on the kitchen island.
Auntie's other arm wraps me tightly.

They do this to calm cows at slaughter. My first year playing
hockey for Coach Bobby, he brought me home from an away game.
We listened to an NPR interview with Temple Grandin, a scientist

who has autism. She invented a "squeeze machine" for cattle process-
ing that also relieved her own sensory overstimulation. Mom came
outside to check on me when Coach's car remained parked in the
driveway and I still hadn't exited. I had wanted to finish listening
to the interview. Coach Bobby rolled down his window when Mom
approached.

No worries, Grace. She's safe with me.

Four cop cars are followed by an ambulance. Auntie grips my hand
as we lead a half-dozen cops and two EMTs along the shoreline. TJ is
among the law enforcement officers.

When I recognize the boulder the raven showed me, I stop and
point.

"There." I don't want to smell her again.

Auntie and I walk back to the small clearing by the caretaker's
cabin where the cars are parked. We sit against the front bumper of
her SUV. I focus on the late afternoon sunlight still above the tree line
and make a point of ignoring TJ when he approaches us.

"What were you doing out here?" Officer Kewadin asks me.

I lean forward and throw up on his police boots.

Auntie pours water on a paper towel and wipes my clammy forehead. She hands me a second towel. I wipe my mouth. I take deep
breaths, as she hands damp paper towels to TJ.

"School assignment," I say finally. "Plant morphology."

"Can you radio someone to call her mother?" Auntie asks him.

Shit. Mom will freak out.

Double shit. I forgot to notify Jamie or Ron about this. But . . .
maybe Heather isn't connected to the investigation.

*I got some Molly V. You and your new boyfriend can go all night long.
Got other stuff too . . . if you want.*

"I need to call my . . . boyfriend." I cough on the word.

"Your brother's teammate?" TJ's jaw clenches.

I nod and dry-heave.

Officer Kewadin doesn't take any chances. He backs up and walks away.

For once, I don't resist when my mother insists on taking care of me. I know she's serious as a heart attack when she skips Sunday mass and her daily visit with GrandMary to watch movies with me all morning. It's kind of annoying, though, when she keeps hopping up from the recliner to top off my dainty teacup of never-ending chamomile. Each time she does it, my flash of irritation at her hovering is replaced with guilt for being selfish and ungrateful.

I am not the only brat in our house. Herri naps on my flat chest. Her tuxedo coloring—mostly white with a few black spots—makes her look cute. It's an effective disguise because she is a demanding little pest. If I pause too long from stroking her silky fur, she bites at my fingers.

My cell phone buzzes once. Herri gets pissed when I stop petting her to flip it open.

> JAMIE: Call?
> ME: No. Come over.

Last night I called Jamie. Long enough to provide a recap of finding Heather, before my mother interrupted with an offer to run a bath for me. She hasn't let me out of her sight since.

When the movie ends, Mom asks what I want to watch next.

"*Hocus Pocus*," I say.

"Is that a good choice? Doesn't it have"—her voice drops to a whisper—"dead people?"

"It's fine, Mom." I roll my eyes and instantly regret it when she blinks, hurt.

I push Herri off me and rise quickly. My arms go around Mom the way Auntie held me tight yesterday. Something breaks my heart when her tense shoulders shake.

This is how we've always been.

GrandMary was like Herri. She pushed me, and I could push back, confident in knowing exactly where the limits were. As with Herri, my formidable grandmother and I nipped at each other, not enough to break the skin but just enough to get a point across.

But my mother is always moving the line so that I never know what will make her crack. All I know is that her fragile emotions are like pond ice during spring thaw.

When she stops crying, I kiss her cheek.

"A friend is coming over. Is that okay? You met him . . . Jamie. We are . . . more than friends now," I babble.

Mom's conflicted emotions are so easy to read: surprise, happiness, concern.

I answer her unspoken questions. "Jamie is a good person, Mom. Very respectful of me and all I've been through."

I let go of her and take my teacup to the kitchen sink. I rinse it out, and set it upside down in the dish drainer. I need to talk with Jamie, which won't be possible if Mom is filling teacups and baking a batch of cookies for my friend.

"Would it be okay to have some privacy?" I ask gently.

Again, her anxious face reads like a script: *no, yes, no, okay.*

"I'll fold some laundry and ride the exercise bike," she offers reluctantly.

When Jamie arrives, my mother greets him with a hug. She asks if he's nervous about next weekend's season opener and he admits that, yes, he is very anxious.

Mom makes her polite retreat to the basement. As soon as I hear the television in the family room, I look at Jamie and put a finger to my lips.

He watches with a bemused expression as I go to the bookcase to retrieve the baby-monitor sensor that will convey all upstairs sounds when my mother is in the basement. I move it to the antique armoire that has been retrofitted to hold the television and DVD player. Mom will either listen to *Hocus Pocus* or shut off the baby-monitor receiver downstairs.

Daunis, Secret Squirrel extraordinaire, is a sneaky ajidamoo.

I motion for Jamie to follow me as I tiptoe down the hallway. When I reach my bedroom, he's not directly behind me. He got sidetracked by the multiple oversized framed photo collages along the way. The life story of Daunis Lorenza Fontaine. I bat at his arm the way Herri does when she wants me to pay attention to her. Jamie hones in on a picture of seven-year-old me looking miserable in a sequined pink figure-skating outfit tight as sausage casing.

Finally I have to drag him into my bedroom.

Jamie eyeballs my room. He pauses in front of the dresser. A framed photo shows Lily and me dressed up for Halloween as two of the sister witches from *Hocus Pocus*. She thought it would be funny if I was the glamorous sister, so I wore the blond wig. Herri jumps onto the dresser and nudges Jamie's hand to pet her.

"Who's this?" he asks while rubbing behind Herri's ears.

"Herri . . . Herrington, actually. She's named after NASA astronaut John Herrington, who is a member of the Chickasaw Nation and was the first Native American to walk in space." I keep babbling, "Did you know that John Herrington brought an eagle feather to the International Space Station?"

"I didn't. That's really cool," he says. Herri purrs loudly, approving of Jamie's nimble-fingered technique. I nearly forget why I invited him over.

"So I didn't mention it before," I whisper. "Heather offered me ecstasy mixed with Viagra at the bonfire. Weed, too."

"You're supposed to tell me things right away," Jamie quietly admonishes the Daunis in the mirror above the dresser. "Not a week later."

"I didn't think it was anything, but now I do."

"Her death wasn't suspicious, according to Ron."

"Drowning in September? Washing up on Duck Island? How is that not suspicious?"

The gold-framed mirror makes us look like a photograph. I turn my back to the dresser.

"She used to be Heather Swanson," I say. "Everyone knew her dad was Joey Nodin, but he denied it. Supposedly he threatened Heather's mom when she asked for child support. But once the casino opened and the Tribe started paying per cap, Joey claimed paternity and enrolled Heather in the Tribe. People say Joey paid her mom's shady boyfriend to set her up for a drug bust so she would lose custody. The custodial parent gets the kid's minor money."

Jamie raises the eyebrow on the perfect side of his face. I keep whispering.

"I told you before that per cap can be good or bad, depending on how it is used. There's a lot of good things about per cap. Auntie buys back land on Sugar Island that got sold to the Zhaaganaash during hard times."

He says nothing.

"But when it comes to the worst aspects of per capita payments, everyone mentions Heather. Auntie said her case led to Tribal Council amending the tribal enrollment code. There's a process now for non-tribal members claiming their babies are tribal. DNA tests to establish paternity right from the start."

Jamie interrupts me. "DNA tests can tell you what tribe you're from?"

"Shhh." Finger to lips again.

He turns to me. Awfully close. I move a step away and keep talking in a low voice.

"You're thinking of those bullshit ancestry tests where you mail your spit in a test tube and they say you're eighteen percent Native American. Those tests are imperfect. They generalize results to geographic regions, not specific countries or tribes or bands. People take those tests and think they can enroll in a tribe. It doesn't work like that."

He frowns. Jamie works undercover, going into tribal communities and playing a role. *I never live anywhere long enough to find out what normal feels like.* Is it possible that, whoever he really is, he has no community?

I could tell him what I know. Share information that isn't about the investigation, but might be of interest to whoever he is behind his shield.

"Paternity tests use any type of body fluid to extract DNA to compare the child to the father or his siblings. The Tribe requires a blood test. They were going to require hair instead, until some of the traditional pipe carriers reminded everyone about the violent history of our hair being taken from us . . . scalps that were cashed in like animal pelts, and boarding schools cutting children's hair as soon as they were taken from their families. When Council debated using blood for the testing, that got heated too. Some said too much blood had been spilled already. But there were others who talked about blood memories. It wasn't just generational trauma that got stored in our blood and passed along, but our resilience and language, too. So the Tribe voted for blood as the way to help children reestablish their blood connection. And for adults who got adopted out to find their way back to their family."

Jamie isn't looking at me anymore. He's at my desk now, staring out the window as he absentmindedly pets Herri. His mind is elsewhere; I've bored him with my impromptu speech: Everything You Always Wanted to Know About DNA But Were Too Afraid to Ask. Maybe he wasn't curious after all.

"Anyway, Council tried fixing it so no one else would go through what Heather did."

"You knew her, so I don't want to say anything bad," Jamie says. He turns from the window. "But, evidently, running off without telling anyone and having a bag of weed and one full of pills and crystal meth in her hoodie pouch wasn't out of character."

"I don't care about that. She deserves to have someone give a damn."

Now he is the one to raise his finger to his lips.

Something pulls me away from the red-hot flare of anger.

What he just said about the contents of her hoodie pouch. Could it be a clue?

"Jamie, there wasn't any meth in the bag she showed me. Just speckled pills."

I want to join Jamie in talking with Ron about the drugs found on Heather.

"You had a traumatic experience yesterday, Daunis. Take it easy today," Jamie whispers in my ear as I pick up the baby monitor to return it to the bookcase.

I cover the microphone part just in case Mom is listening.

"Don't tell me what to do."

He pinches the bridge of his nose and heads to the front door.

I fight the urge to throw the damn baby monitor at him. Following behind, I catch up as he reaches his truck. Just as I do, Macy's royal blue Corvette turns onto my street.

You two need to establish relationship patterns for people to observe, Ron said.

Did I think to pray for zoongidewin today? No, because why would I need bravery to stay home all day with Mom and Herri? I offered semaa this morning and prayed for zaagidiwin for Heather Nodin. To know love is to know peace. I wish that for her in the next world, because I think it eluded her in this one.

I embrace Jamie from behind. His body goes rigid. My arms circle his waist and I hold him in an impromptu squeeze machine.

"Macy's car is coming. We gotta make this look good," I say quickly.

He smells like the beach and sunshine.

Jamie gives a casual wave to the passing car.

I kiss the side of his neck. The pulse of his carotid artery beats against my lips.

And that, Macy Manitou, is called acting.

Jamie leaves. Mom stands at the door, weeping. Sighing, I go inside to decipher her tears and figure out how to comfort her.

Reading people was something Lily and I had in common.

My best friend said that when she lived with her mom, Lily could tell within three seconds whether Maggie's latest relationship was good or bad. Assessing the situation to determine if she needed to be Funny Lily or Invisible Lily. I thought I could relate. Mom carried herself differently on Sad Days, still mourning her relationship with my dad. I'd need to comfort my mother—make tea, give hugs, and watch a lighthearted movie together.

It's kinda the same thing, I told Lily.

No. It's not, she said. *Your mom never took it out on you when a relationship ended.*

It takes all of five seconds from the driveway to the front door to discern Mom's mood.

Observation: Tears, but without her Sad Days slouched posture, and a wistful half smile.

Diagnosis: I'm growing up, and Mom wishes my uncle were here to see it.

Prescription: Hugs. Sympathy. Suggest a nap afterward. And tea.

"David won't be there to walk you down the aisle," Mom says.

I resist the urge to tell her, *Holy wah, I'm eighteen going on nineteen.* Instead I hold her until she's done crying.

"Mom, why don't you lie down and I'll bring a cup of tea. Chamomile."

While my mother naps, I try finishing the movie. It's no use. I'm too fidgety. Herri nips my fingers because I'm ruining her plans to nap on my chest.

My mind won't stop racing.

Jamie and Ron are communicating with the FBI to find out everything that was on Heather, a complete inventory. Meanwhile, I have to stay home. Be a useless Secret Squirrel.

Work the problem, Daunis.

Uncle David taught me to think like a scientist. It wasn't enough to make haphazard lists; you needed to sequence the order of tasks.

I miss him. Not just because Mom was as carefree as she could ever be around her little brother, but because he was good and kind. He loved me and my boundless curiosity.

Once, GrandMary grew weary of my endless questions over Sunday dinner.

Curiosity killed the cat, Daunis, GrandMary said.

Yes, but satisfaction revived her. Uncle David scored the equivalent of a hockey snap shot. Quick. More about surprise than power.

I can't talk about the investigation with Auntie or Granny June. Uncle David would understand. He'd help me work the problem.

He taught me the seven steps of the scientific method: observe, question, research, hypothesize, experiment, analyze, conclude. Order from chaos.

Organize and document everything, Daunis.

That's it. I stand so quickly that Herri flees from my eureka moment.

My uncle logged every experiment, each step of his beloved scientific method. He filled notebooks with his messy handwriting—the only part of him that was not meticulous.

Uncle David went missing before he could provide any evidence. He discovered something he wasn't supposed to know. That's why he isn't here.

I'll trace his footsteps, but carefully. Curiosity killed the cat. But satisfaction revived her.

CHAPTER 23

GrandMary, Mom, and I packed all his belongings after he died. My mother couldn't bear to get rid of anything, so it all went to GrandMary's basement.

I write a note for Mom and put it next to the teakettle for her to see after her nap.

Going for run—didn't want to disturb you.
Don't worry about me for dinner.
Might go visit GrandMary or Auntie. Love you.

I pass Dana's house on my way to my grandparents'. People still shake their heads when they talk about her unforgivable sin of painting her dark brick home ivory and adding bold indigo shutters. Levi told me his mom saw a house like that in Ann Arbor when she was in law school and wanted a house like that someday. Dana Firekeeper, chief tribal judge, is nothing if not tenacious.

My grandparents' house, meanwhile, looks as if it was reconstructed stone by stone from the French countryside. An imposing chateau in a cul-de-sac overlooking Sault Sainte Marie and Sugar Island off to the east.

I jog to the side entrance off the kitchen and use my key to enter. It smells like lemon furniture polish; the cleaning lady must've been here yesterday or Friday. She still comes twice a week to keep everything pristine while my mother clings to the hope that GrandMary will recover and demand to return home.

I turn on every light as I make my way through the dark basement, passing the laundry room and the wine cellar before reaching a heavy wood door leading to a large storage area. The cleaning lady doesn't enter here, so it has a musty smell. My grandfather had sturdy wood shelving units installed around the perimeter. Dusty cardboard boxes, plastic storage bins, and wooden crates line the shelves. Most, but not all, are labeled.

Uncle David's belongings fill a section of wall, and his furniture takes up most of the floor space. Mom cried when she told me that he would want me to have his dining room set in my own house someday. She cries whenever she talks about him, like today, when she got choked up at the sight of me embracing Jamie and says something about how David would have loved meeting him.

I look for the bins marked OFFICE and lift lids to peer inside until I find the ones with his notebooks. GrandMary and I did that room, while Mom insisted on boxing things from his bedroom. My grandmother, who thought his being gay was something he would outgrow, was content to let Mom box up the parts of his life she herself couldn't understand.

If it had been me who died, would GrandMary have felt the same way about my black ash baskets from Gramma Pearl and my Jingle Dress regalia?

I'm ashamed of myself for the thought.

When you love someone, but don't like parts of them, it complicates your memories of them when they're gone.

The notebooks were tossed haphazardly into the bins. I dump out the contents of the first bin to check the beginning and ending dates of each college-rule spiral notebook. Anything prior to 2004 or 2003 will go back into the bin. One by one they return. Bin by bin, I make my way through the experiments and scientific musings of my uncle. Everything I read reaches my brain in his voice.

There are notebooks from before I was born. I'm tempted to get lost in the pages. What was he working on when I was a secret zygote? When the genetic material from my mom and dad had already combined to decree that I'd have my dad's frame and my mom's backside? His nose and her superpower of overthinking everything. That I would be like Mom and GrandMary and Grandpa Lorenzo, able to drink wine and grappa and feel just fine the next day, instead of like Uncle David, who had decided that sobriety was the path that worked for him.

When he died, Mom insisted he hadn't relapsed. She was right, but at the time, I noted his odd behavior and drew the wrong conclusion.

I stare at the bins now back on the shelves. Something heavy weighs me down, as if I'm no longer on this planet but on Jupiter, with its gravitational pull 2.4 times stronger than Earth's.

David doesn't have any notebooks from this year because he was preoccupied with his confidential-informant activities for the FBI. He was holding himself back.

I was clueless. In not seeing what was going on right in front of me, I allowed a seed of doubt to plant itself in my heart. I had been so convinced that yet another person I loved had disappointed me with their failings.

The week flies by. Uncle David stays on my mind all day, every day, as if he is perched on my shoulder like a parrot dispensing mini science lectures. He's with me in the Newer New Normal, during my morning run with Jamie and the guys. In Plant Morphology class, he confirms my answers before I say them aloud. He cheers me on at the library on campus, where I do my assignments for the next day. Even when I pick up Granny June for lunch. And when I attend Heather Nodin's funeral.

On Friday, I help an Elder make a CD of music from iTunes. Nothing but Dolly Parton. When I finish, I wander over to the euchre table to say goodbye to Granny June.

"Go to classes, my girl," she says.

Granny thinks I have afternoon classes, so she takes the Elder van when she's ready to come home.

"I still don't know why you don't catch a ride with Minnie," I say, shaking my head.

"Have you seen her drive?" Granny points her lips toward her euchre partner. "She never lets that damn Mustang gallop."

Minnie holds her cards with one hand as she flips her middle finger at Granny.

I leave the Elder Center but head south to Duck Island. I park at the end of the dirt road, grab my backpack, and hike past the caretaker's cabin. I make my way north along the peninsula to where I left off yesterday.

Every afternoon, I forage for wild mushrooms and document every variety I come across. I pause only to drink water, enjoy a Honeycrisp, or pee next to a tree. My progress every day this week has been steady and orderly.

Today, however, I'm distracted by the stunning autumn leaves. Shades I've never noticed: saffron, claret, mustard, coral, rust, canary, and vermilion. The pictures I snap all afternoon are of leaves instead of mushrooms.

The Supes' season opener is tonight. I should be eager for Levi's first game as team captain, but it is also my first game as a dreaded anglerfish. So I snap more pictures of leaves.

All week I have avoided the spot where the raven showed me Heather Nodin's body. Today I find myself standing in the patch of yellow and purple pansies along Lake George. Dropping my backpack, I sit with my knees pulled up to my chest.

Each blink reveals different memories of Heather.

Her face aglow from the bonfire. Eyelids half open. Speckled pills. Jeans that showed a lot of skin beneath the large safety pins holding together the cutout side seams. Ridiculous platform flip-flops in which, even as stoned as Heather seemed, she walked more steadily than I would've.

A quiz in English class our freshman year. Everyone else scribbling furtively, but Heather sat at her desk and stared out the window. She was living with her dad by then. Her mom was in county jail.

Dodgeball in seventh-grade gym class. At the start of each match, she'd walk to the line, get picked off immediately, and go sit down on the sidelines. That was the year the Tribe began distributing per capita payments to members.

A little girl in a purple dress at the school Daddy Daughter Dance. Heather was the only other girl besides me who showed up without a dad. The only girl I wasn't envious of. Heather went with her mom's latest boyfriend, a man she called Uncle. I showed up with Uncle David, the first year he took me there after my dad died.

Auntie told me once that a girl needs at least one grown man in her life who sees her worth as inherent. Values her just as she is, not dependent upon her appearance or accomplishments.

Are Lost Girls the ones who received other messages about their value?

※

I arrive at the season opener against the Shreveport Mudbugs during the first intermission. Just in time to watch the anglerfishes skate onto the ice. They wear identical Supes team jerseys, navy blue with an ominous cresting white wave outlined in silver. Each anglerfish has her boyfriend's last name on the back. They toss Supes-logo hockey pucks and rolled-up T-shirts to fans.

People stare as I walk to the anglerfish section of the arena. Daunis Fontaine as a Hockey World girlfriend. I should have expected this sort of attention, but I'm still not prepared. I haven't been part of their anglerfish clique. I don't watch the Supes practice. They will probably shun me. I'm not one of them; I'm just a faker.

To my surprise, their faces light up when they return to their section and see me hovering. They squeeze more closely together to make room for me. They rattle off their names too quickly for me to process. The one next to me gives me a side hug; her name might be Megan, but I'm too embarrassed to admit I don't know it.

Their excitement swirls around me like fairy dust. By the time the players return to the ice for the second period, I join in their laughter. Just a little.

I follow Jamie's every move, analyzing his technique as only another player can.

He is a talented but quiet player. He must have played Junior A or college level. There's something enthralling about the way he skates, a smoothness that's almost ballet-like. He never needs to confirm that in his real life he began as a figure skater; I just know.

The girlfriends congratulate me, as if I have anything to do with Jamie's prowess. They also give me credit for Levi.

My brother is a completely different type of skater than Jamie. Levi is commanding on ice. Full-throttle, never-back-down, born to play center. He doesn't look a thing like our dad or play the same position, but Dad's talent is in Levi's DNA.

He and I grew up on the ice. At first it was us three: Dad, Levi, and me. Then just my brother and me. Stormy and Travis joined us, and, later, Mike.

Although Levi is three months younger, I was his protégé. During my own games on the girls' leagues I played in before high school, I tuned out all sound except my brother's voice. When Levi gave praise, I truly believed it.

My heart bursts with pride as Levi skates past. His captain's letter patch, *C*, is stitched on the upper left breast of his light blue jersey. Over his heart.

I have many reasons for becoming a Secret Squirrel: Lily, Uncle David, the Tribe, my town, and those Nish kids in northern Minnesota. Watching the Supes on the ice, I add to my list of reasons Levi and his team.

"I wanna show you my latest tattoo," Maybe-Megan says in the bathroom after the game. "By the way, you and Jamie make such a cute couple."

I used to mock anglerfish girlfriends for the inability to pee solo. Now I hold up my end of the conversation from the next stall.

"Aw, thanks. So do you and Tanner." It's probably unwise to mention how Tanner eyeballs Levi's latest conquests when he thinks no one is watching.

Being a Secret Squirrel has opened my eyes to deception. It doesn't filter the insignificant from the significant. It's like when Cousin Josette got a cochlear implant and heard every sound as an amalgam flooding her mind. She needed to learn how to tune out the noise.

When I exit the stall, Maybe-Megan has her pants unzipped to proudly display a dream-catcher tattoo below her belly button. An imperfect spiderweb design, complete with feathers dipping to where her pubic hair was waxed away for a smooth canvas.

"Cool, right?" she says.

"Your kiden needed protection from bad dreams?" I raise an eyebrow.

She laughs while zipping her jeans. "Dream catchers are sexy."

When Lily and I were on Tribal Youth Council, we all played a game called Bigotry Bingo. When we heard a comment that fed into stereotypes, we'd call it out. Dream catchers were the free space. Too easy. There were so many others, though.

You don't look Native.

Must be nice to get free college.

Can you give me an Indian name for my dog?

Maybe-Megan's tattoo would have been good for another square: Native Americans as a sexual fetish. The more she talks, the more squares I mark on my imaginary bingo card with an imaginary dauber.

"I'm honoring Indians," she says in response to my lingering scowl.

"Plus, I'm part Indian, so it's okay."

"My great-grandma was an Indian princess."

Lily, we have a winner!

"Bingo," I whisper as we leave the bathroom.

I wait in the congested lobby to cheer for our victorious Supes. Ron finds me. When Mike's parents wave us over, I provide background information along the way.

"Mike Edwards is a high school junior and made the team this year, which was his first year of eligibility. His dad is a defense attorney, one of the best in the U.P. Mr. Edwards sponsors the Booster Bus for superfans to attend the away games." I recall some juicy gossip. "Supposedly, everyone signs an agreement to keep quiet about the Booster Bus shenanigans."

"So . . . we want to get on the bus," Ron says.

"Well, good luck with that. There's a huge waiting list and annual fees."

Ron shakes his head in disbelief at that level of fandom.

We reach them, finally. Mr. Edwards is deep in conversation with Coach Bobby.

"How's your grandmother?" Mrs. Edwards asks. She always smells like Chanel No. 5.

"The same," I say. "This is Jamie Johnson's uncle. Ron Johnson." I turn to Ron. "Mrs. Edwards bought my grandmother's clothing store a few years ago."

They shake hands.

"Helene Edwards. I don't believe we met when the team was announced. My son Michael plays goalie. Nice to meet you."

Coach Bobby winks at me as Mr. Edwards finishes raving about Mike's performance. Coach holds out his fist for our usual fist-bump greeting.

I make the introduction. "Ron, this is Coach Bobby."

"Bobby LaFleur. I coached this one for four years," he says, smiling at me. "Best hybrid defenseman. Hockey sense like you wouldn't believe. Even better than her brother's."

Embarrassed, I focus on Macy talking with some guy next to the vending machines. He reaches out to grab her hand and she acts like it burns her. Her dark eyes flash. He watches her go before staring at his shoes for a long time.

Whatever he had going on with Macy is over now.

I'm pulled back into the conversation when Mr. Edwards interrupts

Coach Bobby to introduce himself to Ron and engage in a handshake that appears almost combative. He must have come right from the office, because he's still in a suit and tie. Mike has his dad's pale blue-gray eyes. I wonder if he will shave his head like his dad if he goes bald before his time too.

"Your son made a great shot," Mr. Edwards tells Ron.

"Nephew," Ron clarifies. "Yes, he's been sweating bullets over this first game."

I crack a smile.

"Mr. Edwards—" I begin.

"Call me Grant. You're all grown up now." His light eyes twinkle.

"Grant," I say, as if I'm just learning English and this is my first word. "Ron and I wanted to ask you about the Booster Bus. Is there any chance we can be added to the waiting list? I'm interested in all the away games. Ron would like to join when he can get a sub on Fridays. He's teaching at Sault High."

Call-me-Grant grins. "Let me see what I can do. You want to try it next weekend? See what you both think?" He looks from me to Ron.

"Really? That would be fantastic," I gush.

Players emerge from the locker room in their dress clothes, shower-damp like wet puppies. Eagerly seeking their people.

While Jamie and Mike make their way through the crowd, I watch Levi, with Stormy at his side, as they are absorbed into the mass of excited fans. It's like watching a human depiction of phagocytosis, with my brother and his best friend playing the part of bacteria getting swallowed by the crowd as one giant feasting amoeba.

"You did great," Ron tells Jamie, patting him on the back.

Jamie holds my hand as we listen to Call-me-Grant's recap of the night's best plays.

Levi breaks away from his fans to hug me. Stormy trails behind.

He and I were teammates last year at Sault High. Stormy's parents attend his games unless one or the other is on a bender. Neither is here tonight for his first game as a Supe; that's rough.

"Great game, Stormy," I say. His face lights up.

Next I turn my attention to Mike. He is my target. I will be a take-charge Secret Squirrel, instead of waiting around for a clue to rub its head against my leg and purr to be petted.

During varsity hockey season, Mr. and Mrs. Edwards hosted Sunday dinners for post-game rehashing. I always attended. We'd watch videos of the game and analyze our mistakes.

Call-me-Grant's home office might hold a clue. He does represent a lot of shady clients. Maybe he keeps files at home? My Secret Squirrel goal is to engineer an invitation because Levi mentioned that Mike's parents planned to host similar post-game dinners for the Supes.

I give Mike a shove with my free hand. "You were fantastic."

It's true. He appears bulky and methodical, but in truth, Mike is deceptively quick. He has an innate sense of what will happen next and can react instantly. It makes him a phenomenal goalie.

"Ah, but he let one slip by," says Call-me-Grant in a casual tone that rings hollow.

Mike looks away. Mrs. Edwards rummages for something in her Dooney & Bourke handbag.

Countless times I've witnessed Mike's dad pull him into the corner of an arena lobby and berate him in a low hiss while fake smiling at people passing by.

"Isn't it strategic to let one messenger live?" I point out.

Call-me-Grant does a double take.

"It's hockey, not *The Art of War*," Mike says with the tiniest of smiles.

"Son, hockey is *The Art of War*," Call-me-Grant says while

assessing me. His left eyebrow and the corner of his mouth lift simultaneously. "You read Sun Tzu?"

I smile demurely. No one needs to know I learned military strategy by watching the Disney movie *Mulan* a hundred times with the twins. The villain let one scout live to warn the emperor that the Huns were on their way.

"Mike, will you help me set up my new BlackBerry?" I ask, attempting to ingratiate myself with my brother's tech-savvy friend.

"Why didn't you get a Razr?" Levi breaks in. "They look sweet."

"Sweet," Stormy echoes.

"Sure thing, Dauny Defense. Tomorrow?" Mike says.

"Tomorrow's game day," Call-me-Grant reminds his son. "Why don't you come over Sunday for dinner buffet and game videos?" He glances at my hand in Jamie's before looking up. His intensive stare is a truth-seeking laser; I always feel guilty of something whenever he's around.

"Daunis, please bring Jamie and his uncle, too," Mrs. Edwards says.

I nod before wandering over to the vending machines. It's the only excuse I can think of to get away from Call-me-Grant's ice-blue laser stare. What was that word Ron used to describe when your Spidey senses are tripped?

Hinky.

CHAPTER 24

On Sunday, we ride together in Ron's car to Mike's house. Carefully holding a crystal bowl of homemade tiramisu, I answer Ron's questions about who will be at the dinner.

"Levi, which means Stormy, too. One or two of the better players. The Supes' head coach and both of the assistant coaches. And Coach Bobby will probably be there. He and Mr. Edwards have been good friends ever since Coach helped Levi, Mike, Stormy, and Travis over a shooting incident about three years ago."

"Shooting incident? Daunis, this is the type of stuff you're supposed to tell us about." Jamie pinches the bridge of his nose.

"Travis was goofing off with a BB gun after hockey practice," I say. "Levi, Stormy, and Mike were with him. A BB hit a minivan passing by, broke a window. Glass shattered all over the driver, a teammate's mom who ended up losing sight in one eye. The guys wouldn't say who had done it. Coach convinced them to tell the truth so the one who did it could accept responsibility. Travis came forward. He was shunned by everyone in town and didn't play on any team after all that."

"That's really important background information you should've mentioned sooner," Jamie says. "Anything else you've conveniently forgotten to relay? What do you know about Grant Edwards?"

I bristle at Jamie's tone. "You should've gotten Granny June or Minnie Mustang to be your informers. They know all the dirt."

"You're helping to paint a picture about the town for us," Ron says.

"You guys want a snitch?" I bounce my legs so hard that the dessert on my lap wobbles. "Dana Firekeeper's parents were killed by a drunk driver when she was little. She graduated from law school and was the first tribal member to be appointed as a judge at Tribal Court. Before her, all the judges were non-Native or from other tribes."

I turn to stare down Jamie, who sits in the back seat behind Ron.

"Mike's mom was Miss Michigan and her talent was rhythmic gymnastics. Supposedly she's from a big crime family downstate. Mike's dad was a superjock at Sault High. He was offered full-ride athletic scholarships in two sports. He picked hockey over wrestling."

Ron is on the receiving end of my next Angry Snitch glare.

"Stormy's mom got held for ransom when she owed too much to the big-city drug dealers who came around when per cap started. His dad and uncles cashed their checks and bailed her out."

Gossip pours from me like a spigot on full blast.

"Granny June's been married five times. Twice to the same guy and once to his brother."

Jamie is subjected to my Really Angry Snitch glare.

"That Labor Day bonfire Coach Bobby hosts each year? Did you notice any beer? No. Because he wants to provide a safe and fun celebration for the players before school starts. He doesn't put up with any drinking or drug use. He used to drive me home after games so my mom wouldn't have to wait at the school parking lot in the cold. He defended me and before me, Robin Bailey, when the other high school coaches didn't want us on the team."

I stare forward, too worked up to look at either of them now.

"I know what you're here to do. But these are good people. Mrs. Edwards started a donation program at my grandmother's boutique so girls who can't afford a dress for Shagala or prom can get one. During the last huge snowstorm, tribal police organized teams of snowmobilers to check on every Elder and deliver meals. When the ferry gets iced in, the Tribe offers rooms at the hotel for Sugar Island residents who are trapped on the mainland. I don't like the way you come into town, turn on a light, and expect to see cockroaches scurrying everywhere."

It gnaws at me, the way they want bad stuff without knowing the good stuff too.

"It's like . . . you haven't earned our stories," I say.

"Fair point," Ron says. Jamie is silent—just stares at me for a beat before turning toward the window.

If the community were an ill or injured person, the FBI would cut out the infection or reset the bones. Amputate if necessary. Problem solved.

I'm the only person looking at the whole person, not just the wound.

Ron's navy sedan is out of place among the luxury cars parked in front of the glass-and-steel house. Jamie's eyebrows rise higher with each make and model we walk past.

Sighing dramatically, I point to each vehicle. "Dana's Mercedes. Levi's Hummer. Mike's Jaguar. And Coach Bobby's BMW." I catch Ron's expression mirroring Jamie's. "There's nothing sketchy about having nice cars," I say. "They all have money except Coach Bobby. And he won his car in a poker tournament a few years ago."

Mrs. Edwards greets us at the door. I hold out the dessert like a bomb, which she takes graciously. Jamie carries the bag with my new BlackBerry. When Ron contributes a bag of potato chips, I can't help but smile despite still being ticked off. He reminds me of a cousin who shows up to potlucks with a box of Jell-O.

Dana gives me a quick hug on her way out. She always drops off a pan of lasagna for Sunday buffet.

It's only been six months since I was last here at one of the Edwards's Sunday dinner buffets, watching our Sault Blue Devils game videos on the giant wall-mounted plasma screen, analyzing each play, and looking for ways to improve. Coach Bobby and Mr. Edwards reenacting moves like performance artists. The Before was a lifetime ago.

In the Now of this Newer New Normal, I hold hands with Jamie on the sectional. The hockey game on the big screen isn't mine. I'm not here as a player, but as an anglerfish to my Supe boyfriend. Looking around, I realize Jamie probably sees everyone as suspects. My brother and his friends—correction: *my* friends. Mike's parents. Coach Bobby. And, sitting next to Levi, Coach Alberts, the Supes' coach for the past two years.

Some people were against hiring Coach Alberts, because he's Black. *Maintaining our proud hockey heritage,* which is just code for *hockey is for rich Zhaaganaash boys.* My dad went through similar bullshit. Hockey might not give a rat's ass about skin color, but some of its fans certainly do.

Mrs. Edwards tells everyone to fix a plate and sit at the dining table. She reminds me of GrandMary. No one was surprised when Mike's mom bought the boutique. She had been the manager and, before that, its best client. Mrs. Edwards even resembles GrandMary: slender, French bob hairstyle, impeccably dressed, and never without the requisite strand of pearls.

I'd get mad when GrandMary praised Mrs. Edwards in front of

Mom. My grandmother valued timeless style and "taking care of one-self." I remember visiting the boutique to try on dresses a few years ago, and overhearing GrandMary mention that I was at risk of out-growing the sizes carried. Mom forbade her from ever speaking to me about my body, my weight, or anything about my appearance. *Daunis and I will leave town without a backward glance if you ever cross that line.* I'd never heard my mother use that tone. But GrandMary must have heard it at least once before when Auntie first showed up at the big house to see three-month-old me and Mom insisted to GrandMary and Grandpa Lorenzo that I not be kept from my Firekeeper family.

I only wished for my mother to stand up for herself like that.

When I see Mike head to the kitchen island where the buffet is set up, I make sure Jamie and I are right behind him. I plant myself next to Mike at the mahogany dining table, gleaming beneath a rectangular chandelier of a thousand crystal icicles. We sit on uncomfortable, clear acrylic dining chairs. Floor-to-ceiling windows provide a spectacular view of the red, white, and blue lights of the International Bridge and the cityscape across the river. It feels like we're in a diorama or on a stage. Tonight, I'm expanding my usual role as Jamie's Girlfriend to also play Girl Who Is Interested in Everything Mike Edwards Says.

"Shagala won't be the same without your grandmother," Call-me-Grant says, his somber expression held for a respectful moment. "It's the town's finest night," he tells Jamie and Ron. "Dinner, dancing, and our women lovelier than ever." His eyes hold my own for an extra beat.

I narrow my eyes. This must be how he gets juries to acquit his clients: just the right attention to each one. Before the whole Call-me-Grant nonsense, I never thought of him as anything other than Mike's dad. Now he's kind of a gross pervert.

"Don't you think it's silly?" I keep my voice breezy. "All that time and money spent on a fundraiser? Wouldn't it be easier if we donated what we spend on tickets and dresses and everybody just stayed home for the night?" I smile sweetly.

Call-me-Grant laughs at my absurdity. "Well, what's the fun in that?"

"It's our best month at the store," Mrs. Edwards points out.

"It helps the team," Levi says. "People are more loyal to something they're part of."

"Speaking of dresses," Mrs. Edwards tells me, "I went ahead and ordered something for you since Shagala is coming up in two weeks. I hope you'll trust me." She turns to Mike. "Macy's dress came in, and she's already done her fitting. I'll order her corsage for you."

I sit up straight. "You're going with Macy?" I ask Mike, trying to hide my irritation. Macy Manitou is like a UTI, flaring up at the worst times.

Levi answers for him. "She's in between guys and Mike needed a date. Me and Stormy are going with some twins from St. Ignace . . . Carla and Casey or Colleen or something."

"I'm sure they're honored by your enthusiasm," I say.

Levi grins. I might be the only person in the world who gets away with teasing him.

The conversation moves on as Coach Bobby boasts about a girl from across the river who made Canada's national women's team. I'm not surprised; she's the best center forward I've ever played against.

"It's not too late," Coach Bobby tells me in a wistful, singsong voice. He explains to Jamie, "Daunis could establish dual citizenship and be eligible to play for either country's national team."

I tense under the sudden spotlight. It still hurts. Becoming a doctor wasn't my only big dream. Medicine and hockey. Playing for a national women's team was a longtime goal. Coach doesn't know that that dream crashed and burned a year ago. Auntie is the only one left who knows what I did. Two summers in a row now, I've made a huge decision that changed me.

"She should be playing D-one and getting ready for Torino," Coach Bobby says in a scolding manner, referring to the next Winter Olympics.

"No, I get it," Levi cuts in. "Family's here. Leaving's hard. I'm glad you stuck around, Daunis." He nods at Jamie. "Bet you are too."

"Yes." Jamie gazes into my eyes as if I'm the only person in this suddenly too-hot room.

My stomach somersaults at the sincerity in his voice. I pinch my thigh under the table to snap out of the dreamy moment. For an instant, I forgot that Jamie is acting a part.

I change the subject. "So . . . what do we think will happen with the lockout?"

Any mention of the NHL lockout is like tossing chum to sharks. Coach Alberts and Call-me-Grant predict the lockout will shut down the entire season. Levi and the guys take Coach Bobby's side that it won't come to that. Ron is Switzerland, declaring his neutrality. At one point, as Jamie and I are gleefully joining in, I realize that Ron is quietly observing us.

As the debate dies down, I tell a few stories about Mike's best saves.

"Remember the time he spiked the puck? It was coming in high and he just . . ." I imitate a perfect volleyball smash. "And when he fell on his back, but still blocked the puck with his leg?"

Mike's parents beam at their son, who has turned beet red.

"All right, that's enough. C'mon, Dauny Defense. Let's set up your new phone," Mike says to shut me up.

Secret Squirrel time. I follow Mike as he grabs the bag with my phone.

"We're gonna keep telling stories about ya," Levi shouts as we go downstairs.

My plan is to leave something in his bedroom, so I have an excuse to return a few minutes later. Call-me-Grant's home office is next to Mike's basement lair. My heart races at the thought of seeing the office furniture that used to be Grandpa Lorenzo's. When GrandMary sold the business and the building downtown to Mrs. Edwards, she included the furniture from my grandfather's office on the second floor. I imagine my feet are as heavy as uranium to avoid breaking into a Smoke Dance—tiny staccato steps as quick as a hummingbird's wings.

I've been in Mike's bedroom before, on Sunday evenings when there was a line for the main bathroom. There is a Jack-and-Jill bathroom between his bedroom and his dad's office. It was easy to forget about because you couldn't access it from the family room.

Mike's bedroom cracks me up, especially the shrine to Gordie Howe. A number-9 jersey is mounted in a huge shadow box on the wall, hanging above a fancy table with a lit candle burning in front of a framed autographed photo of the Red Wings legend. I spy the latest iMac computer on Mike's desk. A king-sized bed with a poster above the headboard: the 2002 Red Wings team posing with the Stanley Cup. Bookcases lining an entire wall, filled with hockey trophies, many books, and assorted Red Wings memorabilia.

We sit on the edge of his bed, and I pull out the BlackBerry. Mike coaches me through each step. Although I like the way the BlackBerry feels in my hand, I make a show of grumbling so he'll feel needed.

"Why's it called a BlackBerry if it's blue? And rolling the side ball thingy feels weird," I whine, thumbing the small tracking knob on the device.

Mike looks at me and we both giggle childishly. When he finishes his BlackBerry tutorial, I let my old phone slip through my fingers at the far side of the bed. The thick carpet muffles its fall. We return upstairs.

Coach Bobby and Call-me-Grant reenact plays from last night's game. They're the same height and build, and with their jeans and Red Wings T-shirts, they look like twins.

While everyone watches their performance, I seize the opportunity to go downstairs and "search" for my old phone. I rush through Mike's room to the bathroom. My actions sync with the plan I make up as I go: lock Mike's bathroom door, turn on the light and the noisy exhaust fan, try the doorknob to Call-me-Grant's home office, exhale a sigh of relief when it opens.

I'm in.

Operation Secret Squirrel:

1. Eyeball the room layout using only the light from the bathroom.
2. Grab the Red Wings throw blanket on the love seat and fold it against the bottom of the door to the family room.
3. Turn on the overhead light.

My breath catches at the sight of the office furniture: desk, credenza, and matching bookcases. The deep, purplish-brown rosewood has simple lines, unlike the ornate, hand-carved mahogany furniture of Grandpa Lorenzo's library at the big house. I run my fingertips along the desktop.

The pre-cry sting inside my nose is like someone holding a bottle of ammonium-carbonate smelling salts to jostle me back to alertness. *C'mon, Sis, you're burning daylight.*

4. Remove a small digital camera from my sports bra to snap pictures of each bookcase shelf to document the contents: books that might include an interesting title, perhaps chemistry-related, and framed photographs of Mike's dad at hockey events that might place him at locations that align with drug activity in the Great Lakes area or show his contact with someone the FBI considers to be a suspect.

Whenever Auntie tucks her cell phone and lipstick in her bra, she calls it her Nish purse or "the high pocket." My high pocket is a shallow space barely able to fit the camera without creating a plateau-like uniboob.

5. Check the file drawers in the credenza to photograph the label on each file folder.

Locked. Minor obstacle. No worries. I have a backup plan.

6. Pull the top right drawer of the desk all the way out, to reach the key that should be on the tiny hook in the back.

It's not there. Major obstacle. Mouthing silent curses, I look around for any ideas for a backup plan for my backup plan. What I see makes my heart thud instead.

My footsteps. Recorded in the plush ivory carpet like a trail through snow.

Uncle David's voice urges me. *Think through the problem, Daunis. Identify your need. Assess your resources. Develop a plan. Sequence your steps.*

Steps—footsteps—are my problem. But I have no resources, only trophies, framed awards, and books. Loads of books.

Books.

I rush to the bookcase and pull out an art book that looks to be the same length as the width of the vacuum. Gripping the spine, I drag the edge of the art book to retrace the vacuum marks. The result is not exact but it's close enough. I turn off the light and return the throw to the love seat. Working my way backward to the bathroom, I feel sweat trickle from my forehead along my face and down my neck.

Back in the bathroom, I hide the art book in the vanity cabinet. The girl in the mirror takes deep breaths. I stare at her, this girl who feels separate from me. I blink until I am back to myself again. I flush the toilet, wash my hands, and splash cold water on my face. The last step in my sequence is to spray air freshener as if I've just taken the biggest dump of my life.

I open the bathroom and jump back in alarm.

Mike. Standing in front of me. Half smirking. Blue-gray eyes twinkling.

"It's no use, Daunis. I know what you're up to," Mike says.

CHAPTER 25

The food in my stomach instantly sours. Mike knows. He blocks my path to the bedroom door. His hands are in the front pockets of his jeans. He's . . . amused.

"You came back." He states the obvious.

Mike Edwards knows.

"Bathroom," I say, getting my own obvious statement out there. "Plus, I forgot my phone." Retreating to the far side of his bed, I scoop up my old flip phone. I wave it at Mike before shoving it in my pocket.

"Nah . . . I know what this is really about." He closes the space between us. Sauntering, actually. Full of himself.

Shit. Okay, how do I get out of this? Shout? Knee his pajog? Or do both?

Mike stops in front of me. I close my eyes, bracing for him to tell me that I'm a rotten spy looking for dirt on his dad . . .

Wet lips mash against mine.

"What the hell?" I push him away.

"What?" Mike sounds as surprised as me. "You been hanging all over me tonight."

"I—I . . . um . . ." I quickly replay my words and actions. Shit. I did hang on his every word, just not for the reason he thinks.

"I saw your face. You're jealous I'm taking Macy to Shagala," Mike says. He appears genuinely confused. "And . . . we aren't teammates anymore."

"But we're friends," I say. Ever since he made the best travel teams with Levi.

"You were friends with TJ before you guys started snagging."

"TJ wasn't part of Hockey World," I point out.

"Is it because I'm younger?"

"What? No. Yes. No." I'm still trying to make sense of the conversation. "I've known you forever. You're like a brother to me."

"I am not your brother," he says evenly.

"But, Levi—"

"Believe me when I tell you I'm not afraid of Levi. This could be our own little secret." That smirk. I instantly know what Call-me-Grant looked like at seventeen.

Jamie. I remember only now that I already have a boyfriend.

"I'm dating Jamie," I say primly.

"Eh, I don't see that going the distance. Seems like someone who's here for a season or two and moves on."

"Maybe I don't wanna stick around either."

"Really?" He laughs as if I've said something ridiculous. "I figured you bailed on leaving because you're like royalty around here. Connected to everybody. Out there"—he gestures to somewhere beyond—"you're nobody."

Is Mike right? Is that how it appears to other people? I've always felt a step outside the inside, both in town and on the rez.

"I—I—I'm not interested in you. Not like that." I grasp for a lifeline. "But there's lots of girls who do . . . think of you that way."

"Is it because you think you're too good for me?" His voice lowers menacingly. "Because you're not . . . you know. Better than me."

This Mike—instantly aggressive—scares me. I scramble for the right words to defuse his escalating anger. Nothing comes to mind. I want Jamie to come looking for me. Right now.

"My dad's right," he hisses. "Girls are just distractions. I thought you were different. But you're not." With a look of disgust, he turns and leaves.

This wasn't how I envisioned tonight going.

I thought I knew Mike Edwards. My brother's goofy friend and teammate. *My* former teammate. The tech-savvy guy who set up my new phone tonight. I know that guy.

But the one who kissed me and refused to listen to any of my refusals?

I don't know who that person is.

Is this what will happen over the course of the meth investigation? I'll learn things about everybody I thought I knew?

Back upstairs, I stand next to the kitchen island, on the edge of the living room. The video is still going; everyone cheers when Mike blocks a Hail Mary last-second shot by the Mudbugs.

Jamie approaches. His eyebrows are raised like antennae detecting concern. "Everything okay?" he says into my ear. I nod and he continues. "Then can I put my arm around you?"

I nod again, this time meaning it. His arm slides around to rest casually on my hip.

I lean into him, suddenly exhausted.

When it's time to go, Mrs. Edwards returns my mother's crystal bowl, now washed. I thank her for a nice evening. I avoid looking at Mike when the guys do a round of fist-bumps.

"See ya bright and early," Levi says.

I don't want to be around Mike, especially during my morning run.

"Hey," I say. "I wanna increase my mileage, so I gotta slow my pace. But don't let me hold yous back. I'll go on my own."

"Can I join you?" Jamie asks me.

"Ditching us for a girl? C'mon, man," Levi says with a huge smile.

"I'd really like that," I say.

I sit in the back with Jamie for the ride home. He reaches for my hand. I don't pull back.

"Mike's parents do this every Sunday night?" Jamie asks me.

"Yup. Every Sunday during hockey season. Last year it was for our varsity hockey games. I'd have Sunday dinner at the big house in the afternoon and have second dinner at the Edwards's in the evening."

"Do Mike's dad and Coach Bobby always do their routine?"

"Yup. Dinner and a show," I say.

Jamie laces his fingers through mine. My body does the opposite of tensing up; I melt from a solid state to liquid.

"The dessert your mom made was my favorite. Please let her know."

"Your real favorite?" I tease.

"My real favorite." He squeezes my hand. "Man, how cool to analyze the games we just played. And their house? I've never been in a place like that. It was like something from a magazine. Do you think we'll get invited back?"

I can't help but smile. Jamie has the same level of enthusiasm as a kid experiencing Disney World for the first time. He's played on plenty of hockey teams, I'm sure, and been to plenty of team dinners. What is it about the Sault Superiors that's so fascinating to him?

When Ron pulls into my driveway, I ask if he's tried the new car wash on the business spur. That's our code for asking if it's safe to talk about the investigation in his car.

He nods.

"I took pictures of every bookshelf in Mr. Edwards's home office in the basement." I reach into my bra and feel Jamie shift awkwardly next to me. I roll my eyes as I pull out my camera. "Unfortunately, I wasn't able to dig around for any client files that he might be keeping at home instead of in his office. His desk used to be my grandfather's, and I thought the key to the file drawers would be where I remembered, but it wasn't."

Ron gives me a long look before saying, "This is helpful. Thank you."

I say good night and grab the dessert bowl. Jamie gets out, too, and we walk together to the front steps.

"Should I kiss you in case your mom is watching?" he whispers.

The front entry light turns on. We laugh.

Jamie leans in. His kiss lands on my jaw instead of my cheek.

"Holeeey." I drag out the word. "I thought Supes had way better aim than that."

His back is to Ron's car. I'm the only one who sees Jamie's full smile reach his eyes and tug at his scar. I want to kiss it. Instead of analyzing the impulse, I give in. *Osmosis combustion.*

My lips brush his cheek, feeling for the ripple in the smoothness. Jamie's breath catches, sending a delicious tingle through my body. I kiss him. One perfect, soft kiss that moves as his scar is pulled taut from a smile I feel but cannot see.

I leave Jamie on my sidewalk as I scale the three front steps in a single leap.

Jamie isn't in my driveway the next morning. It's not like him to be late. I've been looking forward to running only with him, especially since kissing him last night.

What if he didn't like it? I recall feeling his smile mid-kiss. He liked it.

I focus on my prayer. This morning I ask for gwekowaadiziwin. The irony is not lost on me. Praying for honesty as I deceive people today. Flakes of semaa land on yellow leaves at the base of the poplar tree.

Leaves. Falling.

The first day of autumn is this week. The fall colors peak early in the U.P.; the first snowfall generally happens anytime between early October and late December. My birthday is October first. Less than two weeks away.

Shit. The weather could disrupt my mushroom hunting at any time.

I finish stretching in the driveway as Jamie jogs toward my house.

"You're late," I say, meeting him in the road.

He mumbles an apology but provides no details.

We head in the opposite direction from our usual route. The less I see of Mike Edwards, the better. My pace is close to what we've been maintaining with the guys since fall semester began.

"Thought you were going for distance," Jamie says. He keeps up with me easily, barely winded.

"Change of plans . . . Need to . . . get to Duck Island . . . look for mushrooms . . . before everything . . . covered in leaves."

"You're skipping class?"

"Think . . . of it . . . as . . . independent . . . study . . . on fungi."

We run upriver toward Sherman Park. It feels good to push myself this hard. The faster we finish, the sooner I can get to the island.

"I don't think you should skip classes," he says as we loop around the parking lot next to a playground along the waterfront.

"Why . . . are you . . . still . . . thinking . . . about . . . it?"

"Because, Daunis, when the investigation is finished, you should go back to your life. Put this—and everybody involved—out of your mind. Play hockey at Michigan. Or go somewhere new. Don't let this investigation change everything for you."

I halt. The nerve of Jamie giving *me* advice about change when he's the one who changed. From last night to today. My anger has an afterburn of embarrassment as I recall impulsively kissing his scar last night.

"What," he says, jogging back to me. His clueless expression infuriates me.

"Everything *is* changed." I take pleasure in Jamie flinching at my words. "It changed the instant Travis shot Lily," I manage to say between heaving breaths. "No. Before that—when he pulled the gun from his jeans. No. When my uncle died . . . or when he began acting strangely because he was helping yous."

I stare coldly at him. "And there is no college hockey for me." Jamie thinks I should play hockey at U of M. As if my life could ever go back to the Before.

"Why is that?"

"That info is off-limits to you," I repeat his words from the meth weekend in Marquette. He doesn't get to know about the foolish decision that changed my future. After all, Jamie is only here temporarily. Once the investigation is finished, he will go back to his life too.

I sprint the rest of the way home. Unlike the night he chased me down a dark road on Sugar Island, Jamie doesn't catch up.

This time, he lets me go.

My mother is walking to her car when I finish my run. She blows a kiss to me so as not to get drenched by my sweat. When Mom reverses out of the driveway, she rolls down her window to wave at Jamie, who waves back.

"My girl bested you today," she declares proudly.

"She sure did." His smile is pleasant but doesn't tug at his scar.

Jamie doesn't join my cooldown, but he also doesn't leave. He stands there, watching me.

"Daunis, I think I should run with the guys from now on."

"Oh." More change. *Don't let the pretender know he got under your skin,* I tell myself.

"They're starting to treat me like more than just a teammate," he says quickly. "It would be good for me to hear their stories. Get more info that could help the investigation."

"Sure," I say, keeping my voice breezy. "No problem." I motion awkwardly toward my house. "Well. I gotta shower and catch the ferry. Hallucinogenic mushrooms await."

I don't look back as I limp up the front steps.

"Hallucinogenic mushrooms await"? You're such a geek.

Lily, I think my fake relationship is over for reals.

I make good progress by Friday late morning. Not that I've found an unknown mushroom, but I'm near the north end. I could finish today if not for three things.

First, the leaves are slowing me down. Every day this week, there have been more leaves on the ground. A magnificent carpet of color that makes it take longer to get through each cross section.

Second, I stop each day at eleven, race to the ferry, pick up Granny June on the mainland, and bring her to lunch as usual. My break costs me nearly three hours of prime daylight.

It's worth every minute.

I made a bargain with myself. I can be deceitful about my whereabouts, let people assume I'm at class or in the library, as long as I take care of Granny and help the Elders.

I avoid Auntie, because I'm not a good enough actor to maintain my deception in front of her. She texts and calls every day, asking me to come over. Each time, I text back a false excuse. Studying. Spending time with Jamie. Doing something for Granny June or my mother. It's hard and I miss sleeping over with Pauline and Perry, but I know that she would immediately sniff out that something was off. Auntie doesn't miss a thing.

Today there's a third reason keeping me from completing my mushroom research. I need to catch the ferry as soon as lunch is served, to meet Ron at the loading spot for the Booster Bus. It's a five-hour trip to Green Bay, Wisconsin, where every team in the league participates in a showcase weekend of games.

Operation Secret Squirrel is going on the road.

Granny June and I enter the dining room, which seems more crowded than usual. They must be serving liver and onions today. I don't know why spongy cow organ always brings every nokomis and mishomis from all corners of Chippewa County. It just does.

I freeze upon seeing Auntie next to Minnie Mustang. The room falls silent. Everyone watches me. Even Seeney Nimkee eyeballs me from across the room. Auntie motions me over.

Shit. This looks like an intervention.

What the hell did I do?

CHAPTER 26

After a quick hug, Auntie motions for me to sit down.

"I need to get Granny's coffee and lunch," I say.

"No, my girl," Granny June says. "You need to sit down."

Granny's part of the intervention? Shit times infinity. Chi moo. What if this is about the investigation? How much do they know? What is the least amount of truth I can say before it feels like a lie?

Auntie places a large yellow envelope in front of me. Huh?

"What's this, Auntie?"

"Just open it," she says. "I didn't want to do this here, but you've been avoiding me."

Guilt makes my cheeks feel hot. I open the envelope and two pictures fall out. My heart skips when I glimpse two children skating with a large man.

A color photograph of Dad with Levi and me. I search for his jade-green scarf, but it's not there. The other is a black-and-white photo of my father holding me on his lap. I'm a baby, my dark hair sticking up. Big eyes. Pale skin contrasting with his. He's looking at me and smiling.

Speechless, I meet Auntie's eyes.

"Turn it over," she says.

It's my father's distinctive handwriting. He wrote one word on the back: N'Daunis. Putting the *n* in front of the word adds the possessive *my*. *My daughter.*

"Josette found them when she was cleaning her mom's attic. Great-Aunt Nancy had some round tins full of old photographs. Go on." Auntie nudges me.

I slide a stack of documents from the envelope. The one on top makes me gasp.

APPLICATION FOR TRIBAL ENROLLMENT—SPECIAL CIRCUMSTANCES.

Auntie nods, urging me to look at the papers.

A notarized letter from my mother explains that she was a minor when she gave birth and her parents refused to include my father's name on the birth certificate. Affidavits from Theodora Sarah Firekeeper-Birch, Josette Elaine Firekeeper, and Norman Marshall Firekeeper—who has written his nickname, Monk, in parentheses because no one has used his given name since the priest baptized him. There is a Firekeeper family tree with the three relatives' names highlighted. Auntie labeled each with the official relationship. I never knew Cousin Josette is my second cousin once removed. Or that Monk is actually my great-uncle even though he is a year younger than Auntie. All three have attested that Daunis Lorenza Fontaine is the biological daughter of Levi Joseph Firekeeper Sr.

"You have until your nineteenth birthday to file the application, along with a paternity test that you and I take to verify lineage," Auntie says.

My birthday is October first. Seven days away.

This.

I have wanted this ever since I understood that being Anishinaabe and being an enrolled citizen weren't necessarily the same thing.

My mind races, remembering Granny's unsuccessful efforts to get this for Lily.

I can become a member. Except . . . it changes nothing about me.

I am Anishinaabe. Since my first breath. Even before, when my new spirit traveled here. I will be Anishinaabe even when my heart stops beating and I journey to the next world.

My whole life, I've been seeking validation of my identity from others. Now that it's within my reach, I realize I don't *need* it.

"Miigwech." I take a deep breath. "But I don't need a card to define me."

"I know you don't, Daunis. But think about it," Auntie says. "This is a gift from your dad."

I sit with that. I have his facial features. His height. His skill on the ice. Mom says I have his laugh. My father has given me many gifts. All I ever wanted was more time with him.

Once, during the three months that I was TJ's girlfriend, I was at his house for the Packers-Lions game. TJ's little sister Teela snuggled next to their dad on the sofa, laying her head on his chest. Everyone was cheering loudly, but she fell asleep listening to her daddy's steady heartbeat. I had hungered for that moment for myself.

Granny says, "Your decision isn't just about you. It's for your children. Grandchildren."

People say to think seven generations ahead when making big decisions, because our future ancestors—those yet to arrive, who will one day become the Elders—live with the choices we make today.

The investigation. I think back to Ron's suggestion that enrollment could help my efforts. Could he be right? I feel ashamed for allowing the thought to flicker even for a second.

Another thought vies for brain space: As he reminded me this morning, Jamie is here temporarily. The FBI is concerned only with what's happening right now. They cannot fathom that their actions might have far-reaching effects.

Maybe it's even more important for me to be part of the investigation because I'm the only one thinking seven generations ahead.

"Okay." I nod. "I want to enroll."

Auntie breaks into a smile. I've missed seeing it.

"There's one more requirement," my aunt says. "You need three affidavits from tribal Elders who are not related or who are more distantly related than third degree."

My mind scrambles through people who might come through for me. Granny June for sure. Minnie, too. Maybe I can ask Jonsy Kewadin?

Seeney Nimkee approaches the table. She places a paper in front of me. It is an affidavit attesting my parentage, with her signature. Certified by Judge Dana Firekeeper.

I try to speak, but the words get stuck in my throat. I stand and hug her. She pats my back gruffly.

When Seeney releases me, Granny hands me a second affidavit. I blink repeatedly. Not to conjure my dad, but because through my tears, I can barely see the line of people forming behind Granny June and Minnie.

My application for tribal enrollment will include twenty-six Elder affidavits.

I alternate between grinning and sobbing all the way to Chi Mukwa Arena. The cargo-hold doors are already closed, so I leap onto the Booster Bus with my overnight bag in hand. The Booster's treasurer takes my check for transportation, community refreshments, and two nights' lodging. I pause, wondering if the rumors are true and she's about to hand me a nondisclosure agreement to sign.

"You're all set. Go find a seat." She cracks open a beer and offers it to me.

Her nephew graduated with me; she knows I'm not twenty-one. I accept it.

Someone shouts my name from the back of the bus. Call-me-Grant motions toward an empty seat near him. I scan for any other option and am delighted to see that Ron saved a seat for me.

The team left yesterday. The players still in high school have special schedules where attendance rules take a back seat to hockey schedules. Ron's request for a half-day substitute teacher was approved without any fuss because special allowances always get made when it comes to hockey.

Most of the Boosters are Zhaaganaash; I see only two tribal members. I tell Ron there's a caravan of RVs following the bus, and a good number of those are filled with Nishnaabs who prefer their own campers and trailers.

"Why is that?" Ron asks, surveying the fifty or so people drinking and chatting amiably.

When the bus speakers blast out the opening piano chords of Journey's "Don't Stop Believin'," four rows of women lose their shit, squealing and jumping up and down.

"That's why." I point with my lips toward them. More than a few are already giishkwebii and we haven't even left the city limits. I've heard enough stories to know.

Ron snickers and gives a discreet eye roll.

I whisper, "Some of them are the same ones who say Indians can't hold their liquor or that per cap doesn't buy class."

One of the ladies is so overcome by the magic of Steve Perry's vocals that she flashes a truck driver next to the bus as we head south on I-75. Everyone cheers when the trucker blasts his horn in appreciation. I laugh at Ron's astonished expression.

I am still giddy, riding a wave of happiness as I replay the memory of each Elder handing me an affidavit and hugging me. It is a feeling so profound, there must be a word in Anishinaabemowin for it. Nouns in the language are either animate—living—or inanimate. I'll ask Auntie if feelings are animate too, because this one has good energy to it.

As the ride continues, I grab a book from my bag. According to the American Literature syllabus, there will be an essay due next week on *The Sound and the Fury*.

I spend the next two hours attempting to read. From the corner of my eye, I catch Ron observing me.

"What?" I say, closing the book.

"You haven't turned a page in twenty minutes," he remarks.

"Well, this is crazy hard to get through! It's someone's stream of consciousness, his thoughts go everywhere, and time jumps around. It's so hard to follow."

Lily was supposed to help me dive beneath the surface to find the deeper meanings.

"Benjy." Ron names the narrator of the book's first section.

My jaw drops. "You know Faulkner?"

"Time is a theme, Daunis. Benjy's thoughts aren't bound by time, but his brother Quentin is tethered to it."

Whoa. There it is: the deeper meaning beyond my grasp. Does everyone understand except me?

"Stories should go from A to B to C," I say.

"Maybe it's the scientist in you. Wanting everything to follow a precise sequence."

"Uh-huh. You're a scientist too, Ron." Plus, why is order a bad thing? Like taxonomy—categorizing living and extinct organisms by an eight-level classification system: domain, kingdom, phylum, class, order, family, genus, species. Same with the periodic table of elements. Rules are a good thing. How can you trust the unknown?

Ron smiles. "Non-linear thinking can be disjointed, like Benjy's thoughts, but if you step back or follow it to the end, sometimes it comes full circle."

"Hmmm," I say, unconvinced.

"Maybe the point is patience. Trust that the answers will be revealed when you're ready."

Surprised, I turn away and pretend to bury myself back in my book, blinking back tears as the bus crosses into Wisconsin.

We just had a conversation that had nothing to do with the investigation.

Ron reminds me of Uncle David, who always took time to explain things I didn't understand. I don't recall thinking about my uncle today. Does that mean my grief is shrinking?

Will there come a day when Lily isn't part of my everyday thinking? Grief is a cruel and sneaky bastard. You love a person and then they're gone. Past tense. You forget them for an hour, a day, a week. How is that even possible? It happens because memories are fickle; they can fade. I wanted to help the investigation for Lily. Now my motives seem less clear. I am terrified at the thought of the world—and me—going on without Lily.

The rest of the bus ride is a like a fog. It doesn't lift until I'm sitting in the bleachers at the game, when Call-me-Grant plants himself next to me. Mrs. Edwards doesn't travel to away games leading up to Shagala, which is quickly approaching; it's her busiest and favorite time of year. I know he won't try anything with Ron sitting next to me, but I still do my best to ignore him.

Instead, I focus on the conversations around me. When I overhear someone behind me mention per cap, my ears perk up. It happens all the time; I overhear some Zhaaganaash talking about the Tribe in general, or some particular Nish. And what they say about my tribal community when they think no one is listening? It is never good. Now's my window to walk away before actually hearing anything.

I prepare to leave, but realize I'd need to climb over Ron and a bunch of people to my left or Call-me-Grant on my right to escape. Shit.

"Tina Cheneaux's boy," says one of the guys. I recognize him as the attorney who once offered his services to ensure that I received my "fair share" of Grandpa Lorenzo's estate. I told him to go to hell.

He must mean Ryan Cheneaux, a guy I graduated with.

Ryan is a smarmy jerk, always saying shit about Nishnaabs. Wanting you to explain why tribal members can hunt at different times than allowed by state law. Or pay a reduced price for gas that doesn't include the state taxes. I've watched Nish kids try to explain about treaty rights, which he would loudly declare outdated legal concepts, as antiquated as fiefdoms and feudalism. The more frustrated and angry they become, the more smug Ryan seems. As if his goal isn't to become enlightened but, rather, to make you waste your time and energy.

"No kidding?" someone chimes in. "When's his hearing?"

"October fourth. Their enrollment committee forwarded it to Tribal Council for action. He had to file his case before he turned nineteen."

Ryan Cheneaux is applying for membership in the Tribe? Now I'm hanging on to every word, even as they twist my insides.

"I didn't know Ryan's dad was Joey Nodin," says one of the guys.

"Yeah, Tina Cheneaux didn't want anyone knowing either. Joey'd have fought for custody of that per-cap check too."

"Can you blame her?" They all laugh.

"Kid just hit the lottery." More laughter.

"You get any of his winnings?" someone asks.

The lawyer answers, "Percentage of his per cap for ten years." They cheer. Someone claps him on the back.

I don't realize my hands are clenched until Ron pats my arm. He gives me a look of understanding; he heard too. Unclenching my fists, I try focusing on the game. But my mind goes to Lily.

Each tribe has the sovereign right to determine who is a member. My best friend couldn't get enrolled because of the way the Sugar Island Ojibwe Tribe's enrollment office calculated Indian blood quantum: fractions of Indian blood based on lineage. Granny June's first husband was from a First Nations band in Canada, so Lily's pedigree didn't meet the standard. Too many ancestors from across the river, not the right kind of Indian blood. Granny filed an appeal with Tribal Council, telling them, *No one told me I wasn't supposed to snag on that side of the river. We were here before that border existed. Every one of yous got cousins over there.* But Council rejected her appeal for Lily's membership application.

If I submit my documentation before October first, Tribal Council will vote on my and Ryan's applications at their next official meeting.

His identity is not my concern, I remind myself.

Instead I remember the joy that grew inside me with each hug from my Elders. I wish Lily had known a moment like that.

When Ron and I walk back to the bus for the ride to the hotel, he deliberately slows his steps to separate us from the Boosters.

"I hope you can understand, Daunis, why I told Jamie it might be better to cool it with the boyfriend-girlfriend act," Ron says quietly.

Huh? Is that why Jamie acted strange on Monday and has been so standoffish this week?

I consider my response to Ron. I'm thinking like a Secret Squirrel: I want information without giving anything in return.

"You're gonna need to explain it to me," I say in my best Ryan Cheneaux imitation.

"Undercover operatives, especially young field agents, sometimes get too enthusiastic about their assignments. They develop emotional connections with suspects or informants. It happens often enough that senior field agents, like me, know what to look for."

Ron waits for me to say something. When I don't, he stops walking.

"What I saw Sunday night? At least one of you was not acting."

CHAPTER 27

The hotel lobby is regarded as "international waters" because it's the only place where Supes and fans can hang out together after the game. Supes can't be on the Boosters' party floor; girlfriends can't be on the players' floor. International waters are patrolled by sharks—coaching staff and vigilant do-gooder chaperones.

Coach Alberts announces that his players have exactly one hour in international waters. Tomorrow they will be allowed a later curfew. But they have ice time early tomorrow for drills.

When I sit next to Jamie, he looks around.

"Ron is upstairs partying with the die-hard Boosters," I say, reaching for his hand. Now that I know Jamie backed off at Ron's direction—what will he do when his supervisor isn't here? My stomach flips with a delicious thrill when he doesn't move his hand from mine. I want things to change back to the night I kissed him and felt his smile. A good change for once.

Jamie remains motionless while everyone laughs over Levi's imitation of Mike blocking goals. My brother looks like he's playing a solo game of Twister.

Moving on to Stormy, Levi puts up his fists.

"Let's go, then! Let's go, then!" He repeats it until the words blur into "Skoden." My brother high-fives his best friend and dubs him "Skoden Nodin, the baddest goon Sugar Island's ever seen."

That's not true. Dad was the ultimate goon.

Sometimes I worry that Levi forgets things about Dad. Whenever I mention the scarf that we'd hold on to as Dad pulled us around the ice—jade green, soft, and extra long—my brother swears it was sky blue. He also swears that it's in their house somewhere, but he hasn't been able to find it.

Levi moves in front of me and Jamie. My brother flashes his perfect smile before gliding from side to side, mimicking Jamie's finesse. He adds his best version of Patrick Swayze from *Dirty Dancing*.

Jamie gives an embarrassed smile that doesn't reach his eyes or pull at his scar.

"Loverboy got some smooth moves," Levi says.

Leaning over, I kiss Jamie's cheek. His jaw clenches. I break away at the realization that, even when done for show, my kiss wasn't welcomed. The sting of rejection intensifies as I comprehend the mannequin-like stiffness of his hand in mine.

Stop it, Daunis. I begin my internal pep talk. *Don't let Jamie cloud your focus. The investigation is about protecting your community. Getting answers.*

When my brother continues his imitation game on the other players, I motion for Jamie to follow me. I lead him to the farthest corner of international waters.

"Listen," I start. "I don't care what Ron says about emotional connections or whatever. I won't kiss you if you're not comfortable, but we should still hold hands in front of other people. For the investigation. Us posing as a couple is the best way for you to be accepted in town."

More irony. The same people who might not accept me will embrace the new guy in town because he's a Supe who fake dates me.

Jamie doesn't say anything. He looks down at our shoes. His black dress boots are so different from the rugged ones I'm used to. These are polished leather. Stylish. Urbane.

"You need to trust me. I can handle this." I nudge him. "I'm here to help."

"I know you are," he says, meeting my eyes. His Adam's apple bobs as he gulps. "What happens when someone finds out which tribe they're from?"

What does this have to do with the investigation?

"There are over five hundred federally recognized tribes, Jamie. Each one is different." I take in his pleading expression. Is it possible there are other reasons why he's working undercover in a tribal community? "I can only talk about Sugar Island. First off, is the person an adult or child?"

"Adult. Does that matter?"

"It's less complicated to enroll a child who's eligible. If their parent is enrolled and listed on the birth certificate it's an easy process as long as the kid meets the blood quantum minimum. It's different for adults. Once the Tribe built the casino, there was a push to close enrollment for adults. So people have until their nineteenth birthday to enroll. But with per cap, it's rare for someone to wait that long." I search his face for a clue as to why he's brought this up. I thought his pensiveness was due to Ron's warning, but maybe there's something else on his mind.

"So if you don't enroll before you're an adult, you miss out?" Jamie asks.

I think about Ryan and me, both trying to make the deadline. "Not necessarily. Sugar Island makes exceptions for people who got adopted out and . . ."

His eyes widen at the word. *Adopted.*

"That's what happened to you, isn't it?" I've been speaking quietly this whole time, but now my voice is a whisper.

Jamie doesn't answer. He looks away again.

"Families search for babies who were adopted out before ICWA." I pronounce the Indian Child Welfare Act by how its acronym sounds: ick-wah. "You know? The federal law to prevent the removal of Native children from their homes and tribal communities. Some people set an extra place for them at feasts."

I've seen those plates, but I never really thought about how it might feel to be the person it was intended for.

"Hey." I reach for the sleeve of his maroon dress shirt, before pulling my hand back in case he isn't comfortable with my touching him anymore. "We have ceremonies when someone comes home, after Tribal Council votes on their enrollment." I step as close as I can without actual physical contact. "Those ceremonies are powerful. Healing. Other tribes might do that too. Your tribe might do that. We don't forget our lost ones."

He blinks quickly and clears his throat. When he opens his mouth, I can't hear his voice. But I feel it like a warm blanket on a cold night.

Miigwech.

Coach Alberts gives a five-minute warning for curfew.

We walk past couples kissing as if about to be separated by catastrophe. We squeeze into the crowded elevator. Jamie's hand grasps mine. It isn't for show because nobody can see.

Just before it stops at my floor, Jamie's thumb caresses my hand, gliding smoothly back and forth across my fingers. Casual yet tender stroking that makes me catch my breath. I distract myself by reciting the muscles he's touching. *First dorsal interosseous, second dorsal interosseous . . .*

At the ding of the elevator, my eyes meet Jamie's. While anglerfishes detach from their boyfriends, Jamie leans in, pausing when his lips are an inch from mine.

"Okay?" he whispers.

"Yes," I reply. His lips are soft, like a down feather. Perfect and gentle.

No one comments about it. After all, why would they? One kiss out of many happening in the elevator. They don't know it was our first kiss on the lips.

The post-game party is going strong as I step out of the elevator. People ricochet from room to room. Every door is propped open. Music blasts down the hallway: Big & Rich instructing us to "save a horse, ride a cowboy."

I bump into Ron. His goofy smile tells me it's not his first can of beer.

"Jamie doing okay?" he asks.

"Yup," I say, passing him. "I'm turning in for the night. Keep it down out here."

"Yes, boss," he calls from behind.

I glance back and chuckle as Ron heads into another room for more reconnaissance.

At the end of the hallway, the door next to mine opens and the bus flasher exits. She's married to an old guy whose family bought land on Sugar Island from Nishnaabs who fell on hard times. Their house is at the southern tip of the island. Right now, her hair looks like a family of squirrels has claimed it for their winter nest.

Call-me-Grant, towel wrapped low around his hips, stands in the doorway, watching her leave for just an instant before turning his gaze to me.

His expression is so unabashedly proud, I wonder if he will strut down the hallway to receive high fives from everyone. No one bats an eye. In Booster World there are different rules, or rather a suspension of rules. Or maybe guys like him know the rules don't apply to them.

I brush past him, trying not to look at his naked torso. There's a scientific name for his six-pack, but it escapes me.

"Hello, Daunis Fontaine." His voice reverberates low, like a high-performance engine toying with first gear.

I enter the key card the wrong way and a light flashes red. I turn it around and get another red light. He chuckles and pulls the latch on his own door, so it won't lock him out. His bare feet bring him to my door in three quick steps.

"You're jiggling it." He takes the card without asking and smoothly pushes it into the slot. The light blinks green.

"The right moves make all the difference, Daunis Fontaine."

"Thank you," I say, sounding like GrandMary in her prim and formal tone.

He laughs. "Happy to help anytime."

I close the door before he offers any suggestions. It's week two of a six-month season. Twenty-two or so more weeks of avoiding Call-me-Grant.

The next day, Coach Bobby gets huffy when I reach for one of the boxes of hockey pucks he has stacked to carry into the arena.

"You shouldn't be lifting with that shoulder of yours," Coach says.

"I'm all healed up, Coach." I can tell he wants to protest, but his hands are full, so he can't stop me from taking the top box and following him.

When I reach the visitors section of bleachers, I set the box of pucks next to the other one. I decide to be even more helpful and use my keys to open the clear packing tape across the top. The girlfriends will walk up and down the steps in our section handing out these souvenir pucks to the fans. I decide to join them tonight, since it won't involve going onto the ice.

The box I open has plain hockey pucks.

"Coach Bobby, are these the right pucks? They don't have the Supes logo."

"Ah, that's because those are donated." He rushes over to show that some have a dream-catcher design printed on them. Coach looks around, tilts his head toward where Call-me-Grant sits next to the bus flasher.

"Grant Edwards is donating these to a tribal youth program," Coach says. "Don't mention anything, though, because he likes to keep that stuff quiet."

"Wait, so the local Nish kids get defective pucks?" I am instantly pissed, because half the dream catchers look smeared.

"Fontaine, we're all just trying to do our best out here," he says.

※

When it's time to take a seat, I glance at the empty spot between Ron and Call-me-Grant before squeezing next to Maybe-Megan.

"Hey, everyone, it's Daunis!" One quick side-hug later, Maybe-Megan hands me a large gift bag. "This is from all of us. We meant to give it to you yesterday, but someone misplaced it." She glares down the row at a fellow anglerfish.

Reaching into the bag, I feel the stiff fabric of a new hockey jersey. I hold up an extra-long, navy Supes jersey with the white and silver wave logo on the front.

"We were gonna put Jamie's last name on it, but some wondered if you'd want Levi's on it too," one of the girlfriends says. "And Megan said you were former teammates with Mike and Stormy. And you're kinda like the team's ambassador. But all those last names would be . . . a lot."

"So we figured your own name was just fine," Megan declares.

I turn the jersey to reveal DAUNIS on the back in silver-edged white letters.

"It's perfect," I manage to say before my throat constricts from rising emotions. Shock and awe at their generosity. Humility and gratitude for the thoughtful consideration they gave me when I hadn't done the same for them. Most of all, I am overcome with joy.

During the first intermission, I proudly wear my new team jersey to hand out a stack of pucks with the Supes logo through the visitors section. I recognize most of our fans. The lady who took over the War Memorial Hospital Auxiliary after GrandMary's stroke rubs my arm.

"I'm praying for your grandmother," she says.

My BlackBerry vibrates in my back pocket. I ignore it to continue tossing pucks. When I hold one out to a girl who graduated a year before me, she reads something on her cell phone that causes her to burst into tears. Another vibration.

My heart races. Someone else looks at their phone. People share shocked expressions, and I see one girl cover her mouth with her hand. Dropping the pucks, I reach for my phone to read whatever bad news is rippling through the bleachers.

AUNTIE: Robin dead. TJ said meth OD.

CHAPTER 28

Word spreads quickly. Our entire section buzzes. I have to get out of here. I catch snippets of conversations as I run up the steps to the upper-level exit. A lot of people are upset and confused, but my ears pick out certain voices above the murmur of the crowd.

"Robin Bailey? No way."

"I thought she was one of the good Indians."

"That's what you get for taking easy per-cap money. I told you they don't know how to handle their money or their alcohol."

"My God, even the smart ones are dumb."

The vultures are already tearing into Robin's dead body.

Hot, itchy anger races through my veins. I rub my nose as I sprint to the bathroom. The mixture of odors won't go away: acrid smoke, rotting flesh, WD-40, chemicals, and sweat. I can smell and taste the coppery tang of blood at the back of my throat. Laboratory chemicals and off-gases. Urine. Lily's bladder releasing as she fell backward. The body does that when you die. All your muscles fail.

I can't take this. I'm smelling everything again.

When I reach the last stall, my legs give way as I latch the door. I scurry to the corner and pull my new Supes jersey over my head. Like a turtle. I breathe in until the only thing I can smell is my own sweat and deodorant as I continue rocking back and forth. In shock over another girl gone too soon.

The girlfriends gather outside the stall. I hear them whispering, then Megan tries to crawl underneath the door. I kick a long leg at her. I have no room for their thoughtfulness inside my grief bubble.

"Daunis, the game is over. We gotta go back to the hotel," they take turns saying.

One of them must think to get Ron. I hear him tell the girlfriends to go; their van is waiting. It's okay. He'll wait for me and we'll take a cab back to the hotel instead of the Booster Bus.

After they leave, he just sits there outside the stall. Quiet except for occasionally telling someone to mind their business when they say something about a man in the women's restroom.

"Go on," he says. "No one's bothering you."

All I see is his bottom half, with his knees pulled up to his chest like mine are. His shoes are the same ones he wore the day he brought me to David's classroom. The ones with the squeaky shoe.

Someone must have told security, because heavy footsteps approach.

"Sir, we've received a complaint of a man in the women's rest-room."

"That would be me," Ron says. "I'm looking after my nephew's girlfriend. He plays for the Superiors. She got some bad news tonight. I just want to make sure she's okay."

Ron's voice is firm. He isn't leaving until I do.

I don't want security to escalate things.

"I'll be out in a minute," I say. My voice is raspy even though I haven't been crying.

Ron's right shoe squeaks as we head outside to wait for the cab he called. Strange as it seems, focusing on his noisy shoe helps me put one foot in front of the other.

Ron brings me back to the hotel and when he sees Jamie waiting for me in international waters, he leaves us there alone. He must have decided to cut Jamie some slack.

We sit on a love seat near the fireplace. Jamie puts his arm around me without asking. I lean against him and exhale.

Tonight's mood is different. Everyone is subdued. The players must have found out about Robin during the game, because they had a really bad third period.

Levi sits by himself, staring out the window. I can't imagine what he is thinking. My brother escorted Robin to Shagala her junior year when he was in the eighth grade. I debate going over to him but cannot summon the energy to move.

Levi rises and faces the room. "We played for shit tonight because we aren't reading each other yet," he says.

Wait . . . Robin is nowhere on his mind?

Levi continues, "We gotta be brothers. We gotta know what the other is thinking before he even says it. We gotta play smarter."

The players nod their heads, even the local guys who knew Robin. No one says a word about her or the fact that this is yet another drug-related death in our community.

No one cares.

Jamie holds me closer. He observes my right leg shaking as if every ounce of anger has settled in that one limb. Makes eye contact with me: *What can I do to help you?*

We are reading each other.

I stand and stretch my legs, trying to reverse everything suddenly tightening up.

"What? You got an idea for how we can gel as a team?" Levi asks. "Give us your wisdom, Dauny Defense!"

I'm bouncing on the balls of my feet as if about to start a race, but when I see all eyes on me, I freeze in place. Jamie's expression is now a silent warning: *Think very carefully about what you say next.* I am scared that I'm growing fluent in Jamie. What if Ron was wrong and Jamie is just a better actor than me? A smoother liar? Smooth moves through and through.

Every morning now I pray for gwekowaadiziwin. To be honest, if only with myself.

"Robin Bailey just died! Is this how players from the Sault mourn a former teammate?" Glancing around the room, I see that half the people are looking at their feet while the others stare at me like I'm having a meltdown. I glare at Levi. "But you go ahead and focus on hockey, because your loss tonight is the real tragedy."

I storm off to the farthest corner of international waters. Levi intercepts me. His arms wrap me in a tight hug.

He whispers into my ear, "It's okay. It's okay."

"No. It's not okay. How many more people are gonna die before our community does something about it?" I choke out. "Robin was your friend, too. And you're just acting like nothing's happened!"

We stand there for a few minutes while the room slowly resumes normalcy. Robin's name is peppered into some of the conversation fragments I hear.

Levi sighs, then breaks away from our hug.

"Hey everyone," he calls out. "Daunis is right. We need to do something." Everyone's looking at Levi. "Robin was one of us."

"What are you thinking? Like, a fundraiser?" Mike says, joining us.

I forgot that Mike escorted Robin to Shagala her senior year. She laughed when people teased about her taking eighth-grade boys her last two years at Sault High.

"Yeah," Levi says. "That's it!"

"Hey, everyone," Mike announces. "Levi had a great idea. A charity game." He beams at Levi. "Like, us playing a non-league game?"

"We can collect donations and do something in Robin's name." Levi gives me a side hug. "We can donate and raise awareness for drug-prevention programs."

"Hey, Levi. What about Sault High?" Mike asks. He looks at me; it's the first time since what happened in his bedroom. He smiles just like normal. "C'mon, Dauny Defense. We always said we could kick Supe ass if we had a chance. Now I'm a Supe and I say, 'Let's do this.' Supes versus Sault High Blue Devils, current and former players. Fundraiser and ass-kicking."

The room starts buzzing. Heads nodding. Excited conversations. It's decided that they'll hold the fundraiser game next weekend, the night before Shagala.

As I watch my former teammates rally, the tears that felt locked inside me in the bathroom stall release now. A flood of tears. The guys *do* care. Proud tears. For my brother making something good happen. Maybe even tears of relief that things with Mike can go back to how they used to be. Me as one of the guys. Dauny Defense. Bubble.

Suddenly, it's all I want. For things to go back to normal. To the Before, when Bubble lived in a bubble. Before the investigation—the chaos of not knowing what's real and what isn't.

Firekeeper's Daughter is over the lifting-the-sun gig. Being in the dark is fine by me.

Jamie approaches. He hugs me and doesn't let go.

"What are you doing?" he says into my ear, low and deep. "This isn't part of the plan."

The hotel lobby feels different. People are excited. Hopeful. The guys huddle with a cluster of players and girlfriends who have formed an impromptu planning committee.

"But . . . this is good . . . isn't it? My community. Doing something positive?" I use the sleeve of my Supes jersey to wipe the last of my tears from my cheeks. Jamie tugs me over to the side, out of earshot of everyone else, and lowers his voice.

"We need to stick with the plan," he insists. Jamie folds his arms across his chest. He shifts uncomfortably before putting his hands on his hips.

I step back to eyeball him. His stance changes, becomes unyielding. A cop doing his job.

I understand at last.

"Hold on. When you say 'we,' you don't mean you and me. You mean the FBI," I say, mouthing the initials while pretending to rub my nose so no one can read my lips. "Jamie, don't you remember what my aunt told us about making some workers stay late to fix the owl T-shirts? They learned about the problem and had ownership in the solution? *We* have to fix it. The community, not the"—my hand hides my mouth from the room again—"FBI."

His jaw clenches as if I've said something unpleasant.

"Well, you guys haven't fixed it yet," Jamie points out.

"Don't you see how warped it is to think we can't get it done without the . . . ?" I don't bother with the initials this time.

"Honestly, no," he says, even more quietly than anything he's said to this point.

I don't know this person, and he sure as hell doesn't know me, either. Or my community.

Jamie Johnson doesn't see us.

"You swoop in, want to save us, and then leave," I say. "You won't be here for the fallout. You aren't thinking about the community at all. Don't you get that?"

Jamie's face is devoid of any emotion. It's a mask to protect himself . . . from me.

The sting in my nose infuriates me. Robin comes to mind.

No guy should have that kind of power over you. No matter who he is . . .

Maybe I need a shield to protect myself from Jamie. Glancing around to see that no one is paying attention to us, I advance. This asshole will see how Dauny Defense plays offense.

"Maybe you'd understand if you actually had a community?"

He takes a step back. Blinks his tawny eyes.

I've drawn blood. It was a deeper cut than I intended.

James Brian Johnson, or whoever he truly is, walks away.

Instead of feeling victorious, I'm hollow inside.

I am on my knees, hunched over, wiping my mouth, when I hear arguing and crying. Lily and Travis walking down the two-track.

"Travis, I told you. You gotta get help. This is bigger than you. You need real help."

He grabs her arm when they're ten feet away from me.

"Tell me how, Lil. Just tell me what to do and I'll do it."

She yanks free. "First off, you gotta leave me alone. No more coming around to snag when Granny's away. I gotta focus on school. You focus on yourself. We gotta stand on our own feet separately. Don't you see? I can't stand on my own if I'm always holding you up."

"No. I can't do it on my own. I need you. I love you." His voice trembles.

"Need and love aren't the same. Your need is ruining the love part. Travis, I'm done. I'm really done."

Travis pulls an old revolver from the back of his jeans.

I wake up, choking on the smell of Travis's body odor. Chemicals and sweat that seemed more pungent than ordinary guy stink.

Why haven't I remembered what they said to each other before now?

Was Ron right when he said that I had to trust that the answers will be revealed when I'm ready? Will the rest of my memory come back? Or am I creating something out of nothing?

My BlackBerry vibrates on the nightstand.

JAMIE: I am sorry.

I don't know what he's sorry about. For thinking so little about my community? For shutting down when I took issue with the FBI? For revealing a clue about himself having been adopted out from some tribe somewhere? For kissing me in the elevator?

Maybe he's sorry for accepting this assignment in the first place.

ME: Me too.

Maybe I'm sorry for everything too. For agreeing to help the investigation. That sometimes my community disappoints me in ways too complicated to process, but that doesn't mean the FBI is the solution. That it didn't take much for me to lean into Jamie. Or maybe I'm sorry for lashing out at him because I like him more than I should. Seeing his cop mask slide into place was a reminder that he will leave after his job is done.

Getting left behind doesn't get any easier the more it happens.

JAMIE: Whats ur room number?
ME: 740

I listen in the darkness for the stairwell door next to my room to open and close with the cautious movements of someone sneaking where he shouldn't be.

My heart races when I open my hotel-room door and he enters. Jamie, in sweatpants and a T-shirt, with his hair going in every direction. I close the door behind him. We face each other. Time slows the way it does on the ice, everything pausing for one long, clarifying breath.

I kiss Jamie tenderly, like we had in the elevator. Only I don't stop. The thoughts that went through my mind as we texted moments ago are still swirling around us. But, in this moment, I don't want to spend time with my concerns. Just for tonight, I want to be part of something that feels good. In the Now of this Newer New Normal, that means being with Jamie.

I inhale his scent, the soap that reminds me of a far-off sunny place. He tastes faintly of mint. My fingers weave through his soft curls, which feel better than I imagined.

He kisses me back. Slowly. As if he wants to savor every moment of this. His arms are wrapped around me. Lean, strong muscles.

Our lips part and my tongue finds his. We remain in this embrace, as soothing as gentle waves upon the shore, for hours, it seems.

When Jamie steps back, I reach for him, not wanting this to end. I feel his low chuckle from his body pressed against mine.

"We shouldn't, Daunis," he whispers. "Not until we're on the other side of this. We have no idea what's coming. Let's wait for *Someday*."

"It's already Sunday," I say, pretending to mishear. We laugh together, louder than we should.

Jamie carefully opens the door and steps into the hallway, gives me a long look that nearly has me chasing after him. I watch him enter the stairwell and close the door behind him. As I stand there alone in the hallway, the final click of the door breaks through my happy bubble.

What have I done? I kissed the guy who is investigating my community. The guy I have very real feelings for. This entire situation got more complicated tonight, and I'm still not sure how I feel about how Jamie is approaching the investigation.

The door next to mine opens; Call-me-Grant pokes his head into the hallway like a turtle. He has a sleepy twinkle in his eye as he raises an eyebrow at me. He holds up a finger to his lips.

"Shhhh. Your secret is safe with me, Daunis Fontaine."

Shit times infinity. This just reached chi complication level.

CHAPTER 29

The next morning, I'm the first to board the Booster Bus. I slide over to leave the aisle seat for Ron. I stare out the window, replaying every moment with Jamie. If I pretend last night was a dream, maybe Ron won't find out.

Someone sits next to me. I turn to greet Ron, ready to play innocent. My stomach twists when I see it's Call-me-Grant instead.

"I thought you were a good girl," he says conspiratorially. "But you're a bad girl who doesn't follow rules."

"I didn't realize it was an either-or situation."

"There are always choices one must make. I admire people who make interesting choices." He glances sideways, appraising me as if I were one of my grandmother's necklaces.

"Doesn't your income as a defense attorney depend on those who make poor choices?"

"Indeed, Daunis Fontaine. Indeed." He rises when Ron enters the bus and begins walking toward us. "Sometimes poor and interesting go hand in hand."

The closer we get to the Sault, the heavier my heart sinks. I wish everything that happened to Robin Bailey were a bad dream that she could wake from and have a fresh start.

How could Robin get mixed up with meth? She has her act together. Had.

What secrets did she have?

She was a rez girl. Her mom is a Nodin. Stormy and Robin were distant cousins. Her dad is from another tribe. They live in the After neighborhood on the satellite rez. Everyone liked her.

I can't let anyone else die. I need to become a better Secret Squirrel. More active and less passive. Maybe I should pull on threads from Robin's life . . . see what unravels?

My take-the-initiative efforts with Mike turned into a disaster. Should I try again, but with Stormy? He's related to Robin. Heather, too. Maybe I can ask him about them? Offer to be a sympathetic listener, but not hang all over him like with Mike and have him misinterpret my attention. I won't make the same mistake twice.

But first I need to finish my mushroom research on Duck Island. Uncle David found a unique species of a hallucinogenic mushroom he suspected Travis added to a batch of meth.

Ron clears his throat gently and slides a folded paper into the book on my lap. I wait a few minutes before looking.

The inventory of everything found with Heather Nodin: her safety-pin jeans, a crop top, and hoodie. No mention of a bra, panties, or black platform flip-flops. She had a small, zippered fabric wallet with her driver's license, laminated tribal enrollment identification card, single ribbed XL condom packet, and $174.00. Her red Roots hoodie sweatshirt pocket held two resealable plastic sandwich bags—one had two joints and the other bag contained shards of crystal meth alongside pills that were a reconstituted mix of methylenedioxymethamphetamine and sildenafil citrate.

When the bus flasher begins a striptease to Beyoncé's "Naughty Girl," I take advantage of the diversion. I point to the unfolded paper, the line listing two joints.

"There were six in the bag when she showed me," I murmur.

The cheering grows louder. I point to the next item, the second bag in her hoodie pocket.

"She offered me the ecstasy boner pills. They were light with dark flecks."

I share my percolating thoughts with Ron, whispering as quietly as I can.

"She wasn't shy about selling stuff at the bonfire. If she'd had meth on her, I'd have seen it in the bag. So she must have gotten it from someone after she talked to me. People supposedly saw her walking through Paradise." My voice rises along with my excitement. "Can you find out where that info came from? They might remember something—a car, or who else may have left at the same time. Whoever she had contact with may have done something to her."

He raises a finger. *Shhh.*

I lower my voice again and grin. "We need a secret language like my mom and Uncle David."

Holy shit. I quickly turn to look out the window so Ron won't see my expression.

What if Uncle David did keep a journal? But he wanted to make sure no one else could read it?

I know my uncle. My doubts when he disappeared came from observing behaviors and drawing a faulty conclusion. What I know for certain is that he collected evidence and documented everything.

There has to be a last journal somewhere. And I'd bet it was written in code, in a language that only my mother and I can speak.

If I can find it and prove what Uncle David tried to do, everyone will know the truth about him and why he died. They'll also know my mother's faith in her brother wasn't naive or misguided.

My thoughts are racing. I haven't forgotten Jamie's views about the FBI's role and the community's role. Am I helping the FBI or am I helping my community? I had doubts from the start that it was the same thing. The more enmeshed I become, the farther apart my investigation is from theirs. It's no longer on two parallel tracks. For the rest of the bus ride, I sequence the steps I will take when I return.

1. Finish searching Duck Island.
2. Ask Mom about Uncle David's last journal, where he might have kept it separate from his other notebooks.
3. Ask Mom if Grandpa Lorenzo kept a second set of keys to his desk.
4. Watch for opportunities to reach out to Stormy about Heather and Robin.
5. Talk to people who knew Robin and try to dig for any details about what she did besides take classes at Lake State.

For now, I won't mention the notebook to Ron. Or Jamie. Once I find what I'm looking for, I'll figure out what, if anything, I should share with them.

It's early afternoon when we return to the Sault. I race across town to catch the ferry to Sugar Island. By the time I hike to where I left off last Friday, I've got about five hours of light.

I collect three samples. Two are familiar. One is unlike anything I've seen before. Could it be that Duck Island saved its secrets until the end? I'm excited to get home and check my mushroom and fungi books and internet databases.

It's sunny and brisk, but cools considerably once the sun nears the treetops across Duck Lake. Autumn is a fickle season. Sometimes lingering, sometimes making only a brief appearance.

On the causeway, my phone vibrates repeatedly with texts and missed calls. I wait to check it until I park in line for the next ferry.

JAMIE: Hey back in town. U free
JAMIE: What u up 2
JAMIE: Is this a bad time
JAMIE: Why u not respond
JAMIE: Will u call so I know ur ok

Holy. He's as bad as my mother.

I call. Jamie picks up before I hear a ring.

"I'm fine," I say as a greeting. "Just finished research on the island. I told you I can't get a signal unless I'm on the north end or close to the ferry."

"Well, I didn't know where you were."

"Um . . . Jamie . . . are you ticked off? I'm not someone who checks in with a guy."

"This isn't an ordinary situation, Daunis. You're exploring remote parts of Sugar Island. Alone. Where you found a dead body." His voice softens. "You promise to text me when you go off somewhere?" When I don't answer immediately, he adds, "For safety reasons. Okay?"

"Okay. But you need to promise too. For safety. And fairness."

He laughs. "Okay. Promise."

"I gotta go. They're waving me onto the ferry," I say.

Once I park in the row, I shut off the Jeep and glance around. Robin's mom is in the passenger seat of the car next to me.

We make eye contact. She gives me a teary smile. My body reacts before my brain can sequence what I should do. I exit the Jeep. Instead of rolling down her window, she gets out of the car.

We hug.

"I am so sorry, Mrs. Bailey."

Robin's mom cries as the ferry rocks from side to side on the choppy water. I don't know what I might say to comfort her, but I try.

"Robin helped me a few weeks ago. On campus. It was so good to see her. I hoped we'd end up in classes together. Is there anything I can do to contact her professors?"

Mrs. Bailey looks confused. "Robin wasn't taking any classes," she says.

My face must mirror hers from a moment ago. "What do you mean? I just saw her taking classes at Lake State."

"That's not possible. Robin's been addicted to painkillers ever since she re-broke her collarbone last year." Mrs. Bailey breaks into raw, choking sobs. "Then she admitted she was doing meth."

Mr. Bailey gets out of the car and comes around to hold his wife as the ferry docks.

"We were trying to get her into rehab, not college," he tells me in a broken voice.

CHAPTER 30

I drive home in a stupor. The day Robin helped me, she had a backpack and we went into the student union together. We were just two college students hanging out in the café.

Except . . . Robin Bailey wasn't on campus to go to classes. I realize I didn't actually see her walk into any classroom. So why was she there?

As I close the front door behind me, a bad thought pops into my head. Why a girl who was addicted to pills and meth might be carrying a backpack around campus . . .

Shame washes over me. I'm no better than those assholes talking trash about Robin at the hockey game the minute they found out she overdosed.

Two girls possibly dealing meth. Both dead.

Should I tell Jamie and Ron what I learned about Robin? And about my suspicion that she was dealing meth or pills on campus? Or do I wait until I'm certain?

C'mon, Daunis. Focus. Something has to make sense.

I hear the crinkle of plastic in my backpack. The mushrooms.

I sit at my desk and research the three samples I collected today. Cross-reference them with photographs in the three different field-guide books and the mushroom-identification websites I've come to know as well as their creators and web administrators.

The first two are confirmed to be well-documented varieties.

The final one is black with bumpy white warts on its irregularly shaped cap. It stinks too much to take it from the bag. Once I get a closer look, I realize the white spots aren't warts. They're minuscule white fungi growing from the dark mushroom. Like the mushroom equivalent of an anglerfish, completely dependent on its host for nutrients.

This could be it. A new variety. Anticipation builds.

In the next instant, I crash and burn.

It's in the database. *Asterophora parasitica.* A rare variety, but not an undiscovered one.

I throw the sandwich bag of anglerfish mushrooms across my bedroom. All that time wasted on this wild goose chase.

Not a waste, Daunis. Ruling things out is part of the process, Uncle David reminds me.

Frustration churns inside me like magma. I must have missed something. Somewhere.

Shit. Triple. Quadruple. Infinity. Shit.

The scent of freshly baked cookies wafts under my bedroom door, along with Herri's paw reaching through the gap for the bag. I jump up to grab it before she can hook the plastic with her claws.

I need to be more careful. The mushrooms could've been toxic to Herri. My rash actions could be dangerous to others.

I join Mom in the kitchen, take a warm macadamia nut cookie from the parchment paper on the counter. It melts in my mouth. The sweetness jolts my molars. Okay, the mushrooms didn't reveal any answers, so it's on to the next step of my plan.

"Mom, did Uncle David keep journals anywhere else besides his home office?"

She gives me a quizzical look, before her eyes shift upward to tap into her mental data files.

"He started with a diary, you know, when we were kids. Always writing down what he did that day." She smiles at the memory. "He kept them in our tree house. Nothing like what the twins have, but it was perfect for us. We'd read and play cards. He'd write in his diary and leave it in an opening where a squirrel once made a home." She pulls a cookie apart and eats one half, sighing contentedly. "They tore it down when we were teens to make room for the gazebo. The tree, too." She shakes her head. "Why do you ask?"

"I've just been missing him and thinking about him. Especially those last weeks," I say carefully. "Just wondered what he was pre-occupied with."

My mother tenses. GrandMary and I didn't believe her. I put my arm around Mom and wish I could give her more than a silent apology. But I don't know what I can say without revealing too much. My reticence is a lie by omission. One that's hurting my mother.

When the investigation is over, I can tell Mom the truth. She was right all along.

"He was spending all of his time at school, as far as I knew," she says. "You would've seen him more than me those last weeks."

"I remember him organizing his chem storage room," I tell her. "He didn't bother with anything so easy as alphabetical order." I smile and hug her more closely. "He had to put them in reverse order of their group number and then in descending order of their atomic mass."

Everyone who looked at his storage room would see random labeled jars. Only people who knew the periodic table frontward and backward would see the order. Sometimes he'd tell an AP Chem student, *go get a metalloid with an atomic number that's second small-est in their group.* We'd wait for them to return with the jar labeled SILICON.

It seemed like just a nerdy Uncle David quirk. Only now do I realize that maybe he did it to tell if anyone had moved things around.

Ron must have inspected the chem storage room and dusted for fingerprints. There would be students' prints. Nothing to narrow down anyone stealing chemicals. Plus, Uncle David didn't have anything toxic or unstable. Just an inventory of the chemicals he might want to use for lessons or his own research.

Okay. Mom didn't provide an instant answer. I'll regroup and try again later. For now, I move on to the next task in my sequenced list.

"Hey, Mom. Did you think it was okay for GrandMary to include Grandpa Lorenzo's office furniture when she sold the building to Mrs. Edwards?"

"Where did that come from?" she asks, taken aback.

I shrug. "Just wondered if she asked you first."

"No," Mom says curtly. "She did not."

Change is so hard for my mother. Was she always like this? Even in the Before, a part of her was stuck in 1985. The accident on Sugar Island, when she told my dad about me.

"I wonder if GrandMary remembered to tell Mrs. Edwards about the desk drawer that stuck when it rained and about the key hook at the back of the top drawer?" I say.

"I'm sure she went over every detail when she turned it over to Helene and Grant. David would hate to admit it, but he got that quality from our mother."

"Even down to the spare key for the desk?" I keep my voice as casual as possible.

"Oh, I'm certain. Your grandmother was very thorough."

My heart sinks again. No instant answer.

And an even more distressing thought . . .

Mom just used the past tense when speaking about GrandMary. A tiny, subconscious slip. Change comes even when we consciously try to avoid it.

On Monday, Auntie and I have an appointment at the hospital lab. She made the appointment there instead of at Tribal Health, where she is the director, so no one can claim she used her position to influence the outcome.

"Would someone really do that?" I ask.

"I don't put it past anyone," she says wearily.

The results of the blood tests, showing a familial relationship between my paternal aunt and me, will be sent directly to the tribal enrollment clerk to be added to my membership application file.

I drive from the hospital to the tribal enrollment office to drop off my application and supporting affidavits. Stormy is there, asking the receptionist if his tribal ID will be enough to get him across the International Bridge. He can't find his passport.

"You know how CBP is with tribal members," she tells him. "It's hit or miss if them officers ever heard about the Jay Treaty."

The Jay Treaty is supposed to let Nishnaabs cross the border freely, but people always complain that CBP asks for different documentation every time. Sometimes they'll wave you through; other times they require an ID, a birth certificate, and a statement on official letterhead listing your blood quantum and your parents', too.

When he turns around, he looks so dejected. Sometimes Stormy is such an asshole, and other times you just feel bad for the hand he got dealt.

"What's across the bridge?" I ask.

"Eh," he says, trying for nonchalance. "Greyhounds hockey tonight.

Coach Alberts got us tickets to go. The whole team. Going to the mall first and dinner."

"Where do you think your passport could be?"

He shrugs. "Probably at my ma's."

I look around. "Is Levi waiting for you?"

"No. I walked here after fifth period."

It's really windy and there's a storm gaining power over Lake Superior.

"C'mon," I say. "I'll take you to the island and you can look for it."

"Really?" There's just enough hope in his voice that I almost forget about the times he's a jerk.

On the ferry, Stormy takes semaa from the pouch I keep in a cup holder and makes a silent offering to the river. I'm initially surprised by his knowing the old ways, but on second thought, his parents attend ceremonies when they're doing well. *Clear eyes and open hearts,* as Auntie says when she means drug- and alcohol-free.

The closer we get to his mom's house on the original rez, the less confident he is.

"Yeah. Probably won't find it. Doesn't really matter," he says.

"I believe in you, Stormy," I say, keeping my voice light so he knows I'm just teasing.

He laughs and goes inside. I wait in the Jeep, until his mom opens her front door and waves for me to come in. Shawna Nodin must have clear eyes and an open heart these days.

She offers me coffee, and even though I don't drink it often, I accept her hospitality. Her small house is spotlessly clean.

There are school pictures of Stormy taped on the wall. They're the only decoration except for one poster advertising last year's Anishinaabemowin conference. The print image is of an institutional-looking boarding school in the background; in the foreground, there are teepees set up just beyond the fence surrounding the school. I've never seen that old photograph before, but there is something defiant and reassuring about it. The proof that even when their children were taken away, there were some parents who followed them. Maybe they drummed and sang and prayed, while their children were forbidden from speaking the language on the other side of the fence. Maybe, just maybe, a kid heard the familiar songs in the distance. Maybe even smelled the smudge carrying their parents' prayers to Creator.

There's a pot of soup or something simmering on the stove. It smells good.

I'm glad for Shawna.

I'm even more glad for Stormy.

My shoulders tense when Stormy's dad comes down the hallway. A lot of the Nodins think of me as more Zhaaganaash than Nish. My childhood nickname of Ghost was started by a Nodin boy a year older than me.

Stormy's dad sits across from me and lights a cigarette. Blows a puff of smoke my way. Gives a cold, silent appraisal of me while Shawna pours him a cup of coffee.

Stormy is making a ruckus in his bedroom. Slamming dresser drawers and swearing.

When the cigarette is nothing but a stub in an ashtray, Stormy's dad speaks. "Your grandma hosted those 'Cards 'n' Crafts' things. Do-gooder shit for the hospital."

I give a half nod. GrandMary and the hospital volunteers' auxiliary. Stormy's dad continues like he's just been stewing for years, waiting for me to show up in his living room so he can tell me exactly how he feels about my family.

"Old, rich Zhaaganaash ladies played cards in the center of the room. Then they took a break, walked around the tables where we had our stuff set out for sale. Beadwork, leather, wood carvings." Smoke from the next cigarette puffs my way. "Them ladies could've paid ten times over for everything on our tables. But they still haggled, looking for a deal."

His simmering hostility makes me uncomfortable.

Down the hallway, it sounds like Stormy is demolishing his bedroom down to the studs.

Shawna joins us at the table. She puts a hand on her husband's sleeve and rubs it gently while he continues talking.

"I went with my grandpa. Your grandma wrinkled her nose at his baskets. At his prices."

I don't know what to say in response. All Stormy's dad sees in me is my Zhaaganaash family. GrandMary loves me, but she did not care much for Indians. Even before my dad came along. It's hard to reconcile not liking, even despising, parts of someone you love.

Is it possible the heart can expand to hold love as well as all the complicated emotions?

"Your grandpa's baskets are beautiful," I say. "Worth more than he ever asked for."

He makes a dismissive sound, "Pshhhhhh," as he grinds the cigarette butt into an ashtray.

Stormy enters with a navy-blue passport booklet and a victorious smile.

"Hey, Ma," he says. "You got any money so I can get something to eat with the team?"

Shawna shakes her head. "Just paid October rent."

His dad stands up and pulls out a wallet. Counts the dollar bills. Stormy and his dad get per-cap checks each month, but his dad's is garnished by the county court for some legal trouble and attorney fees. I think Stormy's check is their only income.

"Nine bucks," he says, handing his son everything he's got.

Even with the favorable exchange rate, that won't cover more than a hot dog and a pop.

Stormy, Macy, and I did our coming-of-age fast the same time, although I was more than a year older. I heard Stormy's dad drumming and singing every so often, from a tree stand in the distance. Just so Stormy would know he was nearby.

"Miigwech for the coffee," I tell Shawna.

"Makade-mashkikiwaboo. Niishin," she says. "Black medicine drink. It is good."

"Aho," I acknowledge. *That is all.*

Stormy and I are silent in the Jeep. He stares out the window as I drive to the ferry. The dark storm clouds are visible in the distance. Leaves whip around us.

My sequenced list calls out to me and . . . I just can't. It doesn't feel appropriate to use this ride to pump Stormy for information about two dead girls who happen to be his cousins. The perfect Secret Squirrel would stay on task, but I'm no longer going by the book.

Once we're on the ferry, I finally speak because the silence grows more awkward with each passing minute. "Your mom and dad looked good, hey."

"Pshhhhhh," Stormy says, sounding exactly like his dad. "This week."

He makes another offering to the river. After all, it is a new river each time.

My phone buzzes with an incoming text.

LEVI: Hey do u got ur debit card 4 canada
ME: yes
LEVI: I cant find mine. Can I borrow
ME: yes. Do a favor no questions. Sit w stormy mike jamie at dinner. Say ur treat BEFORE they order.

Exiting the ferry ramp, we pass the line of cars waiting to board the ferry to the island. In the middle of the convoy is a tribal cop car. Stormy motions at the large figure behind the wheel.

"Ghost of Christmas Past," he says of Officer Kewadin.

"Pshhhhhh. I ain't 'fraid of no ghost," I say, mimicking both his dad and the *Ghostbusters* movie.

Stormy laughs. I drop him off at Chi Mukwa for the bus to the Greyhounds game. Levi catches me before I drive away. He comes over to get the debit card just as Jamie pulls into the parking lot. My brother greets Jamie with a fist bump.

"Have fun at the game," I say. "And, Jamie, don't forget to text if you go anywhere besides the mall and the arena. For fairness."

Jamie gives a brief smile before leaning his head through the open window for a kiss. His peck on the cheek is . . . underwhelming. I hide my disappointment beneath an extra-cheesy grin.

"C'mon, Loverboy," my brother tells Jamie. "We're late for the Naughty Nickel."

"Levi Firekeeper, you'd better not take him there!" I play up my outrage.

The guys laugh.

"Do I want to know?" Jamie says.

I roll my eyes. "Strip club. Your coach isn't taking you there, no matter how much Levi pesters him."

The sky becomes a dark gray ceiling with a curtain of cold rain whipping sideways across the parking lot. The guys dash to the team bus. I wait until they're safely inside before I drive away through the sideways downpour.

Gusts of wind rock the Jeep all the way home. I try concentrating on the road as fragmented thoughts lurch back and forth: *Duck Island's a bust. Uncomfortable around Stormy's dad. No journal yet. Why uncomfortable? No spare key for that desk. Unflattering story about*

GrandMary. When to ask Stormy about his two girl cousins? Entirely plausible for GrandMary to behave that way. Make sure there's enough money for Levi to pay for dinner. Jamie's peck on the cheek felt blah. Who else has info on Robin?

I glance at the time once I'm back home. I need to check the balance in the account. Make sure there's enough to pay for dinner. Levi can be careless with his spending, and who knows what they'll get up to tonight?

I look through the Longaberger basket where Mom puts all the bills and bank statements. My trust account statement is there, along with the one from my savings account in town.

Nothing from Canada . . . that's odd.

It isn't until I go through last year's financial documents in the metal filing cabinet in the basement that I find an old statement from the joint account. I run back upstairs and call from the house phone, giving my name, account number, date of birth, and address.

"I show a different mailing address on the account," the customer service lady says, giving Levi's address. "Is there a problem? Do we need to freeze the account?"

"No," I say quickly. "That's my brother's address. He's on the account too. He uses it more than I do."

I should text Levi to let him know how much is in the account. In case he wants to shop at the mall before or after dinner.

"What's the current balance?" I ask.

We usually keep the equivalent of about four hundred U.S. dollars in the account. With the exchange rate, it should be around five hundred dollars Canadian.

"Four thousand eight-hundred fifty-six dollars and seventy-seven cents."

Holy.

"Did you say four *thousand*?"

"Yes." A few heartbeats later she says, "I'm sorry, I made a mistake."

I breathe an enormous sigh of relief.

The bank lady continues. "I gave you the amount from your August statement. The current balance is ten thousand eight-hundred fifty-six dollars and seventy-seven cents."

CHAPTER 31

That is more money than we've ever kept in our shared account.

A sick feeling washes over me.

Is Levi involved?

It's ludicrous. There must be a plausible reason why Levi would keep so much money in our account. I'm certain of it.

The bank lady asks if I'm still there.

"Uh-huh," I manage.

"The statement for September's activity will mail out on Monday. Would you like to change the address back?"

"No. Keep everything the same." I'll get the statements from Levi, along with answers about the unusual activity. I ask, "Is it possible to put two addresses on the account?"

"No. Our policy is to mail one hard copy." A beat later she adds, "But you could give your email address and authorize monthly statements to be sent electronically also."

After I follow her suggestion, I end the call but remain standing in the kitchen. Herri rubs her head against my leg.

I do the math on Levi's per capita payments. He turned eighteen in January, which means he's been getting the adult amount for almost nine months now. Thirty-six thousand dollars a year means three thousand each month, minus taxes. Last year, as a minor, he got twelve thousand dollars, which probably worked out to around nine hundred dollars a month after taxes. Plus, he's reimbursing his mom for payments on the Hummer she financed for him.

When the bank lady said the current balance, my first thought had been to question whether Levi was involved somehow. I feel ashamed. I had believed the worst about Uncle David. Haven't I learned anything about jumping to the wrong conclusions about a loved one? But I'm supposed to follow clues wherever they lead. Aren't I?

It feels like a battle raging between my brain, gut, and heart. In the Before, I usually relied on science and math. Linear thinking. But does that mean I should ignore my gut instincts? Is it like a pie chart where making one slice larger takes away from the other slices?

Herri bites my chin, annoyed by my leg jiggling under the covers. I push her away.

"Go bug Mom, you pest."

I put her in the hall and close my bedroom door, only to toss and turn. I try pushing away every troubling thought from today by thinking about Jamie. His kiss in the elevator and, later, in my hotel room. I imagine what Someday might be like with him, and slide my hand under the blanket.

But . . . why did Jamie's kiss feel different this afternoon? Right before the storm hit. Storm. Stormy. I've got to figure out how to question Stormy. Stormy's dad . . . I know the sour look GrandMary gave Mr. Nodin's grandfather. She had given me the same look when I told her about Gramma Pearl fixing my earache with my pee.

Pshhhhhh. The moment is ruined.

I'm left with no choice but to recite the periodic table of elements: Hydrogen, helium, lithium, beryllium, boron, carbon, nitrogen, oxygen, fluorine, neon . . .

"Do you even know what I did to prove my love for you?"

Travis pulls an old revolver from the back of his jeans.

He follows the sound of my gasp ten feet away. Aims the shaking gun at my nose. Cheek. Mouth. Forehead.

"Don't shoot. It's Daunis." Lily gapes at me. "What are you doing here?"

Each scent finds me: WD-40, pine, Travis's stink, damp moss, decaying bark, ammonia.

I'm gonna die. Lily will watch me die.

"She's for real?" Travis asks. "'Cause the Little People won't leave me alone. They're out here. All around me."

He slashes diagonally at invisible enemies as if his gun has become a machete. He isn't paying attention to me. I can grab Lily's hand. We can run from him. Or get into Jamie's truck.

Travis aims at my face again. I'm terrified. I don't want to die. I want my mom. This will kill her too.

"Travis, the Little People aren't tryna get you. Just gimme the gun," Lily says.

She reaches for it. Insistent. A steady palm with fingers outstretched. Give it. Now.

He holds it out for her to take. His hands are twitchy to the point of spasming.

"Travis, give me the gun before you hurt Dau—"

"I can't do this without you." His hand steadies. "I love you."

POP!

Lily falls backward, landing on her back, arms outstretched.

Travis stares at her before turning to me.

"They're so mad at me," he whispers. "The Little People. I just wanted her to love me again. She's the only person who ever loved me. Believed me when everyone else ditched me. If only she just tried it, Dauny. But she wouldn't. So I added it to my cookies. She didn't want those either. This was the only way."

He raises the gun to his temple.

I snap upright. Grateful for the noise beyond my bedroom door, pulling me away from that dream. No, not just a dream—a memory. The horrible moment when Travis steadied his aim and shot Lily.

I've known Travis practically my whole life. How could he do that to Lily? Travis killed her, all while saying how much he loved her.

Wait. I dreamed the words. Lily's last words were to protect me.

Travis said something about . . . the Little People.

Am I unlocking memories? Or just inventing them?

One of the Elders had mentioned the Little People. It takes me a minute to remember: Leonard Manitou. Macy's grandpa. He doesn't eat lunch at the Elder Center every day. I want to ask him about the Little People. Asking the right way means bringing semaa to him. I'll need to pick up more pipe tobacco today before I get Granny June. Just in case he's there.

I hear the noises outside my bedroom start up again, the squeak of the mop wringer. Water splashing back into the bucket. Familiar pine scent drifts beneath my door. Mom's midnight cleaning frenzy.

"He loved me. I know it, David. Even after what I did."

My brain automatically translates the spoken mishmash of Grand-Mary's French, Grandpa Lorenzo's Italian, and the language Mom and her brother invented together.

"I should've told the truth. No matter how angry I was at him. Everything could've been different. My baby would have her dad."

Mom must be dipping the mop in the bucket, sloshing water with frantic motions.

"David, he promised we'd have everything after he made a team. He thought Mom and Dad would accept him then. 'Be patient, Grace; we're on Indian time is all.'"

My mother's laugh is a delicate giggle as she compresses the mop wringer again.

"I said, 'Doesn't that mean always late?' But Levi said, 'Indian time really means that things happen when they're supposed to.'"

She begins to cry.

I usually pull the covers over my head at this part. Tonight I slip from my bed, open the door, and tiptoe down the hallway.

"Why can't Indian time let you go back in time? Change the things that weren't supposed to happen? We never should've gone to the island. I shouldn't have looked for him. Never should've opened that bedroom door. He said she got him drunk. Well, I was at the party too, and no one was twisting his arm to do all those shots."

As I move through the living room, her words are unintelligible between raw, choking sobs. My brain fills in the gaps. This is not my first time hearing her heartache.

"Why did he jump in the truck at the last minute? He should have just let me go. Why did I drive so fast? Why didn't I just hit that god-damn deer instead of swerve? Why did I lie and say Levi was driving? Why?"

I answer from the kitchen threshold. It's the first time I've interrupted her confessional.

"Because that night you wanted to tell Dad about me, and instead you found him in bed with Dana," I say as gently as possible.

She rushes into my arms, still weeping.

I continue, "Because you were shocked and angry that he cheated and broke his promises to you. Because you were a sixteen-year-old girl who was scared about what your parents would do when they found out you were three months pregnant."

I lean down to kiss her forehead, the way she did to me every night after a bedtime story. The way she still does whenever I have a fever. There's healing medicine in these kisses.

"Because you panicked when the police showed up and when you tried to tell the truth later at the hospital, no one believed you. Then your parents sent you to live with family in Montreal. By the time you came back with me, Dad was married to Dana. And Levi was born."

Her voice is a resigned whisper. "It's so unfair. Dana got everything he promised to me."

My heart breaks for her, for her life altered by secrets and scandals. By wounds so deep the scar tissue keeps building up. Layers of bulging, dark red keloids encasing her until she cannot move. Leaving her stuck somewhere in the past.

Scars made by the broken promises of Levi Joseph Firekeeper Sr.

The king of Guy Lies.

Maybe my first wound was so deep that it never healed.

My mother wasn't the only person he made promises to.

My dad was the first guy who ever lied to me.

I was seven years old.

It still hurts.

CHAPTER 32

Three days after her heart seized from too much meth, Robin Bailey's family and friends fill the church at St. Mary's. Her parents are Catholics who don't follow Ojibwe traditions about the four-day journey.

Some Nishnaabs blend their religious faith and traditional Ojibwe spirituality, like adding semaa to the incense during mass. Others, like the Baileys, maintain a clear division.

I sit in the pew closest to the stained-glass window that has the engraved plaque honoring GrandMary's parents and Grandpa Lorenzo's as well. My grandparents unofficially claimed the pew as theirs. Mom sits alone here on Sundays now.

I stopped going to mass when I was a sophomore. One Sunday, GrandMary likened Catholic Indians to converted Catholics, claiming that organized religion was something brought to Indians by French missionaries, so people who converted to the faith were somehow less than "original" Catholics.

"Where do I fit into that hierarchy?" I asked her.

"Don't be obstinate, Daunis Lorenza. You're a Fontaine, not one of *them*."

Every Sunday from then on, I joined Uncle David in a booth we unofficially claimed at our favorite restaurant. He'd realized long ago that, as GrandMary's gay son, he wouldn't be admitted to the VIP section of her heaven.

The God I pray to is here with us, Daunis. With you, me, and our pancakes.

I'm surprised when the familiar Catholic prayers and responses come so easily from me. I'm even more surprised to find them comforting.

My mind goes back to sitting with Robin in the student union after I threw my textbook at TJ Kewadin. She was so helpful that day.

You don't have to be a superhero. Dauny, it's okay to not be okay.

I only wished she had taken her own advice. I knew about her broken clavicle; it happened the same time as my first shoulder injury. The last home game of my sophomore year, Robin's senior year, an opponent slammed into the two of us like we were bowling pins and he was going for a strike. He got ejected from the game, but not before receiving high fives from his teammates. Robin and I ended up at War Memorial Hospital.

Auntie was with me because Mom couldn't handle seeing me in pain. When my aunt looked at the prescription the new doctor had written for me, she handed it back. *I'm not giving oxycodone to my sixteen-year-old niece.* The doctor puffed up in indignation. *I assure you it's safe for short-term use.* Auntie wasn't having it, telling me, *Girl, you're sticking with Tylenol and ginigiinige tea.*

Is that how it started for Robin? A ten-day prescription for oxy and no hypervigilant auntie? Maybe her parents believed the doctor about it being safe.

Maybe she didn't think she could ask for help.

It's hard to let people down, and harder still when your expectations for yourself are even higher. Especially knowing that some people enjoy pecking at your mistakes and flaws.

No guy should have that kind of power over you. No matter who he is or how much everyone adores him. Or how much you might still want him.

Who had Robin given her power to? There was something bone-weary in her sigh that day on campus. Which guy had made her feel the opposite of powerful? Had she felt there was no one on her side? Not even the guy she still wanted?

Would Jamie and Ron see Robin only as an addict or—if my suspicions are correct—as a meth dealer? They don't know her story. I don't know her story either, but I know she has one. *Had* one. I can try to find out and share the stories that might help the investigation.

I need to be part of the investigation.

The community needs to be part of the solution.

The funeral home director closes the lid of the casket. Robin's mother makes a sound that is an amplified version of the one I made when I saw Lily's body. The horrible bleating that I hadn't realized came from inside me.

How many more loved ones will know this anguish before the investigation ends?

After the funeral mass, Robin's uncle invites everyone to the grave site for the burial and Rite of Committal, followed by lunch at Chi Mukwa. He also announces the benefit hockey game on Friday, three days from now, for the Robin Joy Bailey Memorial Foundation.

Mrs. Bailey looks my way and smiles through tears.

I've agreed to play on the Sault High team. Coach Bobby first asked those of us who had been Robin's teammates on the boys' varsity team to participate before filling out the rest of the roster with current varsity players.

The entire town is pitching in. Call-me-Grant donated his services to set up the nonprofit foundation. Dana pledged a huge donation on behalf of the Firekeeper family. The Sugar Island Ojibwe Tribe donated the full billboard in town, advertising the fundraising event with Robin's senior picture in her Blue Devils hockey jersey and leaning against her stick.

It had to come together quickly, because this coming weekend is the only one without a Supes game until the league pauses for Thanksgiving break. The Superiors always take the first weekend in October off for Shagala Saturday. It's the biggest weekend all year for the town.

Not just the town—it's special for me, too. My birthday is on Friday.

I skip the funeral lunch so I can take Granny June to the Elder Center. Passing the little convenience store on the way to the ferry, I remember the semaa for Leonard Manitou. I am relieved when they have a decent variety of tobacco. Auntie says the kind for rolling cigarettes is harsh on the lungs and it's better to get the good pipe tobacco for gifts. I purchase a few pouches.

When we arrive for lunch, I eagerly scan the room. A few weeks ago, Leonard mentioned the Little People. Just like Travis did on that terrible night. Leonard's story had something to do with being lost in the woods. Maybe he was hallucinating from the freezing cold.

After a minute, my heart sinks. Leonard isn't here today.

Minnie makes the sign of the cross at Granny slathering ketchup on a pasty. I eat my lunch while scrambling for a backup plan. Minnie might know what her son is doing today. But . . . how to ask her? My mind goes blank.

Granny June and Minnie talk about how to determine if someone is fluent in Anishinaabemowin.

"When you can say, 'There's a man sitting on a horse, eating a slice of apple pie.' If you can get through that, you're fluent," Granny says.

"Eh," Minnie counters. "It's when you know which words are animate or inanimate because you just know which ones are alive."

Jonsy and Jimmer pause while passing by to chime in.

"You're fluent when you can tell the difference in dialects," Jimmer says.

"It's when the language teacher says you passed the test," Jonsy says in fluent smart-ass.

Seeney speaks up from the next table over. "You're fluent when you dream in the language."

The room falls silent with a consensus of nodding heads and pursed lips.

Right then, Leonard Manitou walks in. I sit up, blinking in case I'm daydreaming. He comes over to our table and drops off Minnie's prescription medicine refills. After he kisses her cheek, Leonard gets a cup of coffee but nothing to eat. He joins a table of friends. If Leonard ate somewhere else, he might not stay long.

As soon as Granny June and Minnie finish, I rush to take their trays to the dishwasher area.

"What's your hurry?" Granny asks. "Minnie didn't get any better at pinochle overnight."

"What you don't know about cards could fill a book," Minnie retorts.

After dropping off the trays, I cross the dining room. I'm nearly to Leonard's table, when Auntie comes in. Jonsy shouts across the room, "Hey, Big Cheese, how much are we paying you?"

Ignoring him, she grabs my arm and drags me outside.

Holy shit. Auntie is pissed.

"Is it true you're playing hockey on Friday?"

"Yes. It's for Robin." I glance around the parking lot.

"Bullshit. She wouldn't want you to risk—"

"But she's not here," I snap. "That's why there's a game."

Auntie narrows her eyes at me. "I don't know what's going on with you, but I'm gonna find out. You can count on that." She pokes a finger at my chest.

I expect her to walk away, but my aunt is just getting started.

"You're making stupid decisions. You're running around with a different crowd. You don't come around and play with the girls."

She's right. I'm such a bad auntie. But she doesn't understand that I'm doing this for our community. So the twins never have to lose a friend . . . or each other. I shudder at the thought.

I can't tell you, Auntie. I know I'm hurting you, but it's for your protection.

"You return maybe one in four texts. Your ma says you're never home."

"Classes are—"

"Daunis Firekeeper, don't you dare lie to me!" Auntie shouts. "Is it that Supe you're snagging? You're really gonna be one of those girls who forgets herself as soon as she's in some guy's bed?"

Does my aunt think so little of me? That I am capable of losing myself over a guy?

"I'm not—"

"TJ said he doesn't trust Jamie."

What? I'm too stunned to respond immediately; we just stare at each other.

"You talk with him? After what he did to me?" I hate the shrillness in my voice.

Auntie takes a deep breath, but before she can say anything else, I cut her off.

"TJ Kewadin has no right to speak to me or about me, ever again."

"There's more going on—" she tries to interject.

"No. There isn't." I take a few steps backward. Before I turn away, I leave her with "Auntie, I thought I could trust you to always be on my side."

I wait for Auntie's SUV to leave before returning to the dining room. The Elders make a point of not looking at me. All they know is that Auntie yelled at me and that, knowing her, I probably deserved it.

But I had yelled back. Something is shifting between my aunt and me. I don't know if it's good or bad. Maybe it's both. Hadn't Lily told me I had black and white thinking?

They go about their normal activities. Granny June and Minnie play pinochle with Jonsy and Jimmer. Seeney works on a puzzle but glances up periodically.

When Leonard Manitou returns from refilling his makade-mashkikiwaboo, I am sitting next to his seat. I slide the pouch of semaa onto the dining table next to his coffee mug.

"Mishomis, would you please tell me about the Little People? If now isn't the best time, we could meet up whenever works for you." Auntie taught me that when you gift semaa and ask for something, it's good to give the person an option in case they need to think about your request.

Please be ready now, I silently plead. My leg bounces beneath the table.

Leonard puts a hand on the pouch of pipe tobacco and gives a single nod. My relief turns to eagerness.

"You said you were lost in the woods?" As soon as I offer a starting point, I feel ashamed for taking it from him. My impatience got the best of me. I can hear Auntie scolding me: *You know better than that, Daunis!*

His eyes look up and to the side. Accessing his memory files.

"I was five. Chasing a rabbit with my slingshot. That was good eating then. Still good eating. What I wouldn't give for some waabooz-naboob."

As he swallows the memory of rabbit soup, I say a quick prayer that it's savory and warms him through and through.

"The snow came down heavy. Snowflakes big as my thumb. Got turned around, but I kept walking. Figured I'd reach home or the next house. I was a quick little guy. I'm sure my mom called for me, but I was too far away."

He looks out the window. Lost in thought.

"Didn't get scared till dark. I tucked my arms into my shirt beneath my coat, like this, hey." He crosses his arms and tucks his hands into his armpits. "Looked for a pine tree to crawl under and lean next to her trunk. But it got so cold. You ever know cold like that?"

I think of shivering on the fasting boulder, with my thick wool blanket and plastic tarp. Stormy's dad drumming in the distance. If I had needed to, I could've shouted to him. Someone would have come for me. My experience was not like Leonard Manitou's. I shake my head.

"Pretty soon the Little People were there. Smaller than me, but not young like me. The stories I heard about them weren't nothing to be afraid of, hey. Little mischief makers, enjoying some shenanigans. Tying my mother's laundry on the clothesline into knots. I always like a good shenanigan, so I followed them. Came to a boulder. One of them old grandfather rocks that have always been here. I was at the rock and then I was passing through it. Traveling on a stream beneath the island. Like a highway. Crisscrossing I don't know where."

His face lights up.

"We took Macy to a water park when she was a kwezan. She rode down the tunnels. Fearless. Laughing each time she shot into the pool where her dad waited for her. Made me think back to them underground springs. My granddaughter's like me. I wasn't afraid."

I wait for him to say more, but not with a sense of urgency. It is enough to sit with Leonard Manitou and hear whatever he wants to share, whenever he's ready. We are on Indian time.

"They led me back through the rock. I heard my dad shouting for me. I called out and he found me. Gone two nights and two days, hey. I told my parents where I was. My dad said that couldn't be. But my mom and my nokomis always left gifts for the Little People. A copper thimble. Tiny knitted toques. Semaa. Bear-grease medicine."

Gramma Pearl left items like that outside. When Art takes care of a ceremonial fire, Auntie always fixes a small plate of food and sets it at the edge of the woods. I've always heard about the Little People, but I've never paid much attention to the stories.

Left your boots outside and now they're by the outhouse? That's the Little People.

Shoelaces tied in knots? Them Little People are playing a trick on ya.

Firewood scattered on the ground instead of stacked? Must've been the Little People.

I never heard anyone say anything bad about the Little People . . . until Travis.

"Do you think they have it in them to be malicious or get mad?" I attempt to be casually curious rather than heart-poundingly, did-Travis-provide-a-clue, Secret Squirrel inquisitive.

He thinks awhile. Long enough that I wonder if he forgot my question.

"I had a cousin who used to sniff gasoline. We'd find him passed out next to the car. One time, he said the Little People yelled at him. But he kept on sniffing. I asked if they still came around to yell at him.

He wasn't always there, know what I mean." Leonard Manitou taps the side of his head. "He told me, the last time they came 'round, they cried for him. He never saw them again."

"This was your cousin?" I say.

He nods. "Skinny Manitou. Only his gramma called him Elmer. He could draw an idea and you'd swear it was a photograph. Damn shame. He caught himself on fire—gasoline on him and he lit a cigarette." He shakes his head.

"Chi miigwech," I say.

"Someone you know sniffin' gas?"

I nod. "Something like that."

CHAPTER 33

L ike everything about the investigation, Leonard Manitou's story leaves me with more questions than answers. I wake up the next morning no closer to resolving any of yesterday's questions. What was Travis messing with, and why did he think the Little People were so mad at him? Did he really see something, or was he hallucinating? Do any other Elders have stories about Little People or mushrooms that I could try to learn?

Is it possible to solve one riddle without tumbling down more rabbit holes?

I head to the ferry with my scattered thoughts. Leonard Manitou was nearly the same age as the twins. The Little People took him through a stone? Fearless Macy launching off the end of a waterslide. Knowing her, she'd strike an action pose—fist raised in the air, Buttercup from *The Powerpuff Girls* cartoon I watch with the twins.

Auntie's words still sting. How can she think I'm acting foolish over a guy? Ditching her and the twins for the new guy in town. Telling me that TJ Kewadin claims he's no good. It's none of her business, and it's definitely not his.

If TJ wants to look for bad guys, I've got a mirror he can eyeball.

Crossing the river, I make an offering from a new pouch of semaa. I give thanks for Leonard Manitou's story before asking for help.

"I really need a win today," I say aloud.

I check the time. Last period at Sault High. The guys will be headed to Chi Mukwa for Supes practice. Now's the perfect time to ask Levi about the joint bank account and hopefully clear everything up.

The quiet lobby at Chi Mukwa feels unnatural. It's the calm before the convergence of hockey practice, city volleyball league, drop-in basketball, dance classes, after-school programs, moms pushing strollers around the indoor walking track, and satellite courses for the Tribal College.

There is a SUPES FUNDRAISING bulletin board next to the concession window. Today's newspaper takes up most of the space, with small photos of Robin tacked around the front page. The headline announces: SAULT SUPERIORS VS. BLUE DEVILS ALL STARS ON FRIDAY! There is no mention of Robin. Team captain Levi is in the main photo, along with both coaches, Call-me-Grant, Dana, and other big cheeses who've donated. I scan the article and finally spot Robin's name in the fourth paragraph.

She is already an afterthought.

I distance myself from the bulletin board, walking backward until I am in the hallway leading to the volleyball courts.

The lobby doors open. Guys laugh. Mostly familiar voices. Boasts about girls they're snagging or hope to snag soon. Sighing, I decide to remain hidden. I don't feel like joining Hockey World just yet.

"Who's that pretty Indian girl with nice tits?" asks a voice I don't recognize.

"Macy Man-Eater?" Mike says. They laugh.

"Wait up," Levi calls out. Footsteps approach as he catches up with them.

The unfamiliar voice asks, "Well, who's the Incredible Bulk that Johnson's boning? She's got a nice ass." My hands ball into fists.

"Are you fucking kidding me?" Levi shouts a second before there is the crunch of a fist connecting with bone. "Don't you ever talk about her like that. She's worth ten of you."

"Dude, that's his sister," Mike tells the clueless guy.

I peek around the corner, torn between being grateful to Levi and being upset that he resorted to violence. Stormy and Mike pull my brother away from a guy catching blood in a hand cupped under his nose.

"You so much as look at her and I will end hockey for you," Levi seethes, while flexing his fingers to assess any damage.

I react as if jolted by an electric shock. I've never seen my brother so enraged. His voice and coiled stance are unrecognizable.

Mike notices me and quickly nudges Levi.

"Hey, Daunis," Mike says with exaggerated friendliness.

"Go on ahead," Levi tells them. "Not you." He gets in the bleeding guy's face. "You apologize to her."

His teammate makes the briefest eye contact with me. Enough for me to see his shame and fear. "I'm sorry," he says, voice muffled by his hand.

Levi watches the guy hurry away while I observe my brother. I don't like the glint in his eyes. Because it isn't from anger but, rather, satisfaction. It's gone from his face by the time he wraps me in a massive hug.

"Did you see me go all goon on him?" Levi lightens his tone, jostling me before he lets go. "Dad would be proud of me, defending your honor, hey?"

"Levi, you were beyond goon. It was . . . disturbing, to be honest," I admit.

"Hey, nobody disrespects my sister."

"But guys say stuff about girls all the time. *You* talk about girls like that." My shock finally crystallizes into thoughts. "If you're that provoked when the comments are about me . . . maybe you should think about the comments you and your friends make about any girl."

Dumbfounded, Levi stares at me. It takes a half a minute before my brother has a LIGHT BULB ON moment.

"I never thought about it like that," he says. When Levi hugs me again, I'm filled with hope. He's not a violent goon; he's my brother. Not perfect, but capable of growth. I hug him back, even more tightly.

Then, for some reason, we both laugh like little kids sharing a private joke and Levi playfully shoves me away.

"What brings you here anyway?" he asks. "Waiting for Loverboy?"

As if on cue, Jamie enters the lobby. His smile reaches his eyes. In one fluid motion, he grabs my waist, twirls me once, and continues on his way.

Holy wah. That was hot.

"Smooth moves," my brother calls out as Jamie heads to the locker room. Then Levi looks at me expectantly, waiting for me to answer his question.

What did he ask me? For a second, I can't think of anything except imagining Jamie and me on the Shagala dance floor. And today's appointment at Mrs. Edwards's store, which I've been dreading. I haven't been there since it was GrandMary's boutique. It might not be so bad. A fitting for a dress when I have no idea what it looks like. Or how much it will cost.

Money. Bank. Eureka. I laugh.

"I called the bank across the river to make sure there was enough money to cover dinner. Why are you keeping so much in the joint account?"

Levi looks momentarily confused before he has his own eureka moment.

"Oh, that." He laughs too. "I'm buying land near Searchmont. Sweet investment, ya know? Figured it'd be easier using our Canadian account."

"Holy Tycoon," I say, giddy with relief. I got my answer, and that's that. "Why Ontario? Coach Bobby's always looking for property here."

"None of Coach Bobby's businesses ever take off in a big way," Levi says. He tilts his head. "Can I ask you something and you promise not to get pissed?"

"Okay," I say hesitantly.

"GrandMary's not, like, getting better . . . right?"

I stare at my shoes.

"If she passes away, will you transfer to U of M? Or stick around now that you got something going with Jamie?"

It feels good to show genuine surprise. "I don't know. I had a plan for my life, but everything is different now."

"Maybe you need new plans," Levi says. "Remember, Coach Bobby always says, 'Failure to plan means planning to fail.'"

I smile. "How come you've spent half the time I did with Coach, but you quote Bobby LaFleur's wise words more than anybody?"

He shrugs and flashes his perfect smile. "What would you think about investing with me?" Levi asks, suddenly boyish in his earnestness. "A business opportunity where we could work together? Your genius brain plus mine? We'd be unstoppable."

"Um . . . GrandMary always said not to mix business with family or friends," I say.

He raises an eyebrow. "Why not?"

"Because they'll think it's a democracy, but a successful business needs one leader who can make tough decisions and be an asshole."

"GrandMary said *asshole*?"

"I translated it for you," I say.

We laugh.

"Seriously, though," he says. "It might be good advice for everybody else, but we're special, hey? We look out for each other and keep it real."

Levi's right. When the shit goes down, we've got each other's back.

"Speaking of failing to plan, what you gonna do for your b-day?" he asks.

I mimic his exaggerated shrug from earlier. "Play hockey for Robin. Go to Shagala the day after with Jamie."

"Mike's parents are doing their usual Shagala after-party in the Ogimaa Suite. We could throw our own all-nighter at his house. Is there anything special you want?"

It comes to me immediately, something I want. No, something I need.

"Dad's scarf. You always say it has to be somewhere in your house. Can you look for it?"

My eighth birthday was the first one without Dad. Levi tried cheering me up, but nothing helped. Until one day my brother gave me a photo of us with Dad. Levi and I were wrestling him tag-team-style. I had just leaped off Grandpa Ted's recliner onto Dad's back. Levi was supposed to tag out, but he kept attacking from the front. The camera captured Dad mid-laugh. I'd been so afraid of forgetting things about him, until I looked at the photo. That's what Levi's gift was on my eighth birthday: Dad's deep, rumbling laughter.

He'd laugh like that pulling us around the rink with his extra-long scarf. Although I know now that it must have been so painful for him to skate on mangled legs, Dad was happy to be with us on the ice.

Levi hugs me. "For you, absolutely."

I show up early for my dress fitting.

"My, my," Mrs. Edwards says. "I half expected you to be a no-show and thought I'd need to send a search party for you."

I follow her to what used to be Grandpa Lorenzo's office overlooking Ashmun Street. The windows are now draped in sheer curtains that puddle on the floor. Her desk is a fancy glass dining table in front of a huge, ornately framed bulletin board covered in fabric swatches. On the opposite exposed-brick wall, she's mounted a trio of matching oversized mirrors. The outer two are hinged to create a dressing-room area complete with a small raised platform.

"Oh, Mrs. Edwards, it's beautiful," I say in genuine awe.

"That's right, you and Grace haven't seen it since we renovated. I'm expanding into bridal gowns. Even trying my own designs." She pauses before asking, "Will your mother be okay with the new look?"

"Mom doesn't do well with change," I say, in the understatement of the year. "But it doesn't matter, because this is amazing. GrandMary would have loved it."

Mrs. Edwards gets a little misty-eyed before collecting herself and waving in the tailor she inherited from GrandMary. The tailor displays a red gown with a flourish. I force a smile, because they're watching me. Dresses have never been my thing.

My first surprise is that I have to step into—rather than dive into—the garment because it's pants. Silky wide-legged pants with a fluttery transparent overlay. When I step onto the platform, the elegant pants flow like a skirt. There is a deep pocket along each side seam.

"Bra off," the tailor says.

"Really?" I glance around. "But what about my top?"

"You're wearing it."

I stand topless on the platform and twist around to stare at multiple angles of myself in the red pants, before noticing a weird train attached to the back of my waist.

With a grin, the tailor bends to lift one panel of the train and drapes it over my shoulder. She does the same with the other before pinning the ends of the red silk into my waist.

The sleeveless top exposes skin to just above my belly button.

"Holy," I say.

Mrs. Edwards laughs. "Is that good or bad?"

"I don't know. Um . . . it's all out there."

"Listen, you're the only person who can carry this off," she says, appraising me in the mirrors. "Anyone with cleavage would be too exposed. Oh, don't look at me like that. We'll fix you up with some double-sided fabric tape so there are no wardrobe malfunctions."

No one can forget seeing Janet Jackson's boob during the halftime show at this year's Super Bowl.

"Now, do you have hot rollers?"

"Um . . . no?"

Mrs. Edwards tsk-tsks. "Stop by tonight and you can borrow mine. You'll want to blow-dry your hair, spritz it with setting spray, and roll small sections until your head is a helmet of rollers. When you take the rollers out, you pull up the front half into a high ponytail and wrap your mother's strand of pearls around it and pin into place. Not the real pearls but the good fake ones. And ask Grace for your grandmother's ruby-and-pearl drop earrings."

I only have pierced ears because Lily made me do it. She said I could either get it done at the mall across the river or she'd make me drink grappa until I passed out and do it herself.

Mrs. Edwards scrunches her nose. "I'm not going to get makeup on you, am I?"

I shake my head, already overwhelmed by her hair tutorial.

"Indulge me with some red lipstick. For your grandmother."

I sigh and nod.

As I pay for the dress and the golden tube of red lipstick that Mrs. Edwards insisted was perfect for me, my BlackBerry vibrates.

AUNTIE: Come over tomorrow night. 8 pm. Important.

I mull a response, still hurt that she would listen to TJ over me. But it doesn't feel right when Auntie and I aren't on the same page.

When my mother returned to the Sault with baby me, it was Auntie who told her about my dad and Dana and Levi Jr. It was Auntie who brought me to Sugar Island to spend time with my dad and Firekeeper grandparents. She was the one who told us the horrible news when my dad died.

I've always been a Firekeeper. Auntie made it more than a name. She made me family.

ME: Ok. 8

Mrs. Edwards tries opening the top drawer of the antique dresser that serves as a checkout counter. It's where the smallest paper shopping bags are kept.

"Daunis, this piece is gorgeous, but each drawer has a mind of its own. Either they stick when it's damp out, or the drawer guide won't stay in place."

GrandMary had me behind that counter for so many hours; I know every inch of it. I laugh. "I know, I always searched for a hidden treasure. I was convinced I'd find a secret drawer in the dresser, but I never did."

"So many lovely childhood memories here," Mrs. Edwards says with a smile. "The alterations will get done tonight or tomorrow morning. Stop by anytime tomorrow after lunch," she says. "You know we'll be open late tomorrow and Friday, but it's only going to get more chaotic."

I practically float all the way to the Jeep. I've never been this excited about going to Shagala. The way Jamie led me in that one spin at Chi Mukwa . . .

Oh, Lily. I wish you were here. How can I be so happy and still so sad?

GrandMary . . . I should stop by EverCare with Jamie on the way to Shagala. Maybe she will have a LIGHT BULB ON moment. She won't approve of the low-cut top, though.

I wish Dad could see me.

Uncle David, too. My uncle would have helped Mom get over how much skin I'll be showing on Saturday. He always helped her through all the secrets and scandals.

Secrets.

My heart skips a beat.

It was Uncle David's desk at school that had the secret drawer.

CHAPTER 34

I am relieved when Ron's car isn't in the staff parking lot at Sault High School. If there's nothing to be found, I don't want him witnessing my disappointment and embarrassment. And if my hunch is correct? It means Uncle David wanted me to find it.

After I read his research, I'll know whether he intended for me to share it with the FBI.

Part of me wishes I could ask Jamie to come along. I want him to be with me whether there is a hidden notebook or not. But . . . if it's there, Uncle David meant for me, and me alone, to read it.

The secretary makes me sign in even though it's the end of the school day. As I do, she asks about GrandMary and Mom.

"My grandmother is the same. Thank you for asking, Mrs. Hammond." A plausible lie comes to me in a flash. "But my mom has been having a hard time lately. She's still grieving. I wondered if I could go to Uncle David's classroom. We left some of his things there. Framed posters and stuff. It might help her to have them now."

The day I boxed up his belongings, I had an odd mix of feelings. Devastating grief. Surreal disbelief. A sliver of doubt as I replayed his inexplicably distracted behavior over the weeks and months prior to his disappearance. It was just enough to spark fury and, then, deep shame that I was angry at Uncle for abandoning me to hold Mom together without his help.

"Of course, dear. You go right ahead. I'll be here until five."

I sprint to the science classroom.

Breathless, I sit at the desk that looked like a gray military tank. Mom was supposed to arrange for movers to haul it to the big house, but it was still in his classroom. Three drawers on the left side; two on the other. The bottom right drawer was where he kept snacks for me so I could power through hockey practice. Sometimes Levi would stop by after school to mooch snacks for himself and the guys. Uncle David never minded. He would say, "Plenty for all. That's why I keep the biggest drawer full." I remember the third day of Lily crossing over: the day for learning about new worlds. When Ron and his squeaky shoe brought me here. I'd pulled out the snack drawer, disappointed by the sight of file folders hiding the false metal bottom.

Uncle David showed it to me only once. I was ten. He was so excited for his new job.

The dissecting kits are across the classroom in the storage case next to the microscopes. He kept his more elaborate dissecting kit on the top shelf. I remove two identical tools from the zippered case. A mall probe and seeker is a six-inch chrome rod with an angled tip on one end. It's like a dental pick but less delicate.

I extend the bottom drawer fully and kneel next to it to begin my task. The folders are filed alphabetically, so I make neat stacks on the floor, in order. My fingers touch the barely visible holes in each corner of the metal bottom. Focusing on two corners diagonally across from each other, I slide the bent tips into the minuscule openings before straightening the tools. Heart pounding, I lift the probes' angled ends to hoist what resembles a metal lid covering a hidden bottom two inches deep and just a hair smaller than the width and length of the drawer.

This could be it. The most important clue so far.

I can't look. I have to. But what if . . .

I look down to see an ordinary blue spiral notebook. There. It's right there.

I knew it. Uncle David documented everything. I do know my uncle.

I set the metal lid against the wall. It promptly slides and clangs loudly.

"Daunis? Are you still here, dear?" Mrs. Hammond calls down the hallway.

"Yup." I slide the notebook into the back of my jeans.

Her footsteps approach as I quickly put the false bottom back into place and return the file folders. I nearly drop one stack.

I close the drawer three seconds before she reaches the doorway. It's enough time for me to spot the probes on the floor. I sit back against the wall and cover the tools with my leg.

"It's harder to be back here than I thought," I tell her.

Channeling any bit of stealth, I scoop up the probes as I rise. Mrs. H. takes a step closer and I fear she might try to comfort me. I hold up my left hand to keep her at bay.

"I'm fine," I say, sitting on the edge of the desk. I pretend to compose myself, which requires a stellar performance because I'm shaking for real. It's possible the secret that Uncle David took to his grave is in the notebook pressed against my sweaty back. My body provides cover to slide the probes into the dissecting kit and zip it shut.

I glance around the room for anything that belonged to my uncle. I spy the shadow box with his collection of Lake Superior rocks and minerals.

"That was Uncle David's." I point to it before going over and carefully lifting it from its multiple picture hooks. "This case and his dissecting kit on the desk are all that's left. Well, besides his desk. Thank you so much, Mrs. Hammond, I know my mother would want to have these. I'll make sure she arranges to move the desk during Christmas break. And I'll tell my mother you said hello."

She offers to carry the kit for me, and I let her. I am riding a wave of Secret Squirrel satisfaction, fueled by jittery nerves and the secret tucked against my back.

We walk to the Jeep. I thank her again while loading the two items. She reaches to hug me. I pretend to misunderstand her movement, quickly clasping her hands in mine. I squeeze gently in a gesture of appreciation as if words fail me.

"Once your mother is feeling better, I hope you'll rethink staying home. I know Indian kids struggle in college because they're not prepared academically or socially, but Daunis, you're not like them."

Words truly do fail me. All I can do is gape at her in disbelief.

"Well, I don't mean anything bad about Indians." Mrs. Hammond looks around anxiously. "You know I'm not prejudiced."

As I attempt to put Mrs. Hammond's Bigotry Bingo out of mind, I run through possible locations where I can read Uncle's notebook undisturbed. Definitely not home, because Mom will be there fixing dinner. Nothing on campus, because I know too many people. Same goes for coffee shops. Maybe the big house? Or what about EverCare?

That's it. I'll sit with GrandMary and tell the nurses I'm studying. I send identical texts to Mom and Jamie.

ME: Studying for exam. Shutting off phone. Will be home late. Talk tomorrow.

Walking down the hallway, I crack my back out of habit. The muscles in my neck and shoulders feel like guitar strings tightened one turn too many.

I enter my grandmother's room to find Mom crying in the recliner. Next to an empty bed.

"What happened?" My mouth is the only part of me that can move. The rest is numb with icy fear.

Mom looks up, surprised. "GrandMary's okay," she says, rising quickly. "There's an issue with the plumbing. They needed to move some patients around."

I study her, and she doesn't avoid my eyes. Hers are puffy and bloodshot from crying. Her face is open, unguarded . . . drained.

"Did you have a rough day?" I ask gently.

"No, sweetheart, I had a good day. GrandMary too. It just caught up with me." Next to the recliner, the blink notebook is on the bedside table. The closet is empty. She found it while moving things to the new room.

"I didn't mean to upset you with that," I say, collecting the notebook. When I shove it into the back of my jeans, I feel Uncle David's spiral notebook. Uncle David's secret.

"I know," she says. "I really did have a good day. I ran into one of my students at the store. Such a happy little girl." Mom glows. "It felt like a roller coaster when I looked through the notebook." She considers her words before asking, "Do you ever have days where every different emotion seems to cling to you and it's just . . . too much?"

As if to prove that I do, indeed, have those days, I smile and feel the pre-cry pinpricks in my nose.

"I'll leave the Jeep here and hop in your car. Let's rent a video and get takeout," I say, pleased when Mom nods happily.

The two notebooks at my back will need to wait. Because it's been one of those days.

⁕

On Thursday, I finish my run, check on GrandMary in her new room, and drive the Jeep home. My day includes the usual: shower, class, Granny June, ferry, Sugar Island, lunch, and listen to Granny's tirade du jour. Today she's mad at the Elders' book club members. They shot down her James A. Michener book suggestion. But what got Granny even more riled up was Seeney Nimkee saying, "If we read a story about Hawaii, I'd rather support Native Hawaiian authors."

As usual, Seeney is spot-on.

I thought I'd be excited for my afternoon plans to pick up my outfit for Shagala and then go to the big house and read Uncle David's notebook. It's what I've been hoping for—information that might help the investigation. My uncle's last communication.

Instead, I take the scenic route back to Granny June's house. I offer to run errands with her. When she declines, I make my way to the dress boutique. Mrs. Edwards tries to rush me in and out, but I insist on letting others check out before me. All the while, a growing sense of dread builds until I find myself sitting in the Jeep, with the engine shut off, parked in the garage at the big house.

What if Uncle David's final thoughts reveal what happened to him? What if he was scared or hurt? What if his notebook raises more questions than it answers?

What if? What if? What if?

I shake my head. What if it helps someone? What if it could bring comfort to Mom?

I repeat those two what-ifs as I make my way to the library and sit at Grandpa Lorenzo's desk in his leather chair. My entire body trembles. I stare at the blue notebook.

Should I start at the last page? I run my hand across the back cover, tempted to jump into the deep end.

No. I turn the notebook over to start where he started. In the Before.

I need to earn Uncle David's story.

His first entry was on September 2, 2003, the first day of my senior year. My uncle wrote in English, mostly. Nearly every school day had an entry. He enjoyed jotting down the more intriguing questions asked by students, leaving room for follow-up notes, which were often in a different color of ink.

Instead of students' names, he mostly used initials and a class period. A few students were assigned a symbol instead. I pick out mine right away—a heart. When Uncle David spoke in code with Mom about me, I was *N'Coeur*. The French word for heart, with the Anishinaabemowin *N'* in front to make it possessive. *My Heart.*

My uncle loved me and trusted that I would find the clues he left for me. When my nose stings and my throat tightens, I decide not to fight what my body wants to do. I reach for tissues and let myself feel however I feel.

He included ideas we'd discussed for my senior-year science-fair project. I forgot about my plan to compare resting heart rates before and after smudging with sage and sweetgrass. The goal was to identify whether there was a significant difference in Nishnaabs who used traditional medicines compared with a control group of those who did not use the medicines. His side notes included *Reduce variables?* and *Likert scale for cultural identity?*

We'd had a heated debate about trying to quantify cultural identity. I wasn't comfortable asking participants to assign a number value to something like *How Nish are you?* Uncle David challenged me to come up with a research question that might work with a Likert rating scale.

> I believe smudging (a cultural practice of burning and breathing in smoke) with traditional medicines, such as mashkodewashk (sage) and wiingashk (sweetgrass), will improve my overall physical and mental well-being.
> - ☐ Strongly Agree
> - ☐ Agree
> - ☐ Neither Agree nor Disagree
> - ☐ Disagree
> - ☐ Strongly Disagree

In the end, I didn't do any project my senior year. I was eating, breathing, and dreaming hockey at that point. When Uncle David didn't question my decision to opt out, I thought something about his behavior was odd.

In October, Uncle David began writing more about one student in particular. Their symbol was a light bulb with a face, including a full smile like a watermelon slice. The student—Light Bulb—asked many clever questions.

Ryan Cheneaux was known to the entire school as someone who always asked questions. But his "questions" didn't always end with an actual question mark. They were more like stream-of-consciousness exercises or monologues with a lengthy buildup that ended with, "Isn't that so?" Which isn't an inquiry; but rather, fishing for validation.

Question: Could Ryan Cheneaux be Light Bulb?

Answer: No. Ryan Cheneaux fails to meet the threshold for "clever."

When it came to "clever," Macy Manitou was all that. Probably even more so than Levi. I remember how once, Uncle David asked me what the difference was between cleverness and intelligence. I'd figured out that a person could be intelligent without being clever, but not clever without also being intelligent. Cleverness also required a measure of shrewdness and creativity, neither of which were necessary to be intelligent. No doubt that Macy could ask a clever question, a bold question, a snarky question . . . if she wanted. But I'd been in a few classes with her and she never raised her hand. If called upon, she would give the correct answer. Macy plays offense everywhere except the classroom.

Question: Could Macy Manitou be Light Bulb?

Answer: No questions = No Light Bulb.

I think back to Travis asking endless questions, even in middle school. He would jabber nonstop the entire time we walked over to the high school for chemistry. Sometimes he and Levi would get into deep discussions just with one or the other starting off with, "Riddle me this . . ." Travis was in every AP class with me until he started skipping and then dropped out our last semester before graduation. Travis made classes fun. Even when Mike or Levi or any of my brother's friends were in an AP class with me, Travis was always the one I sat next to. He was intelligent as well as clever, and he asked smart questions.

I can't imagine the brilliant and smiling Light Bulb as anyone but Travis Flint.

A month later, around Thanksgiving break, Uncle David wrote down, verbatim, a question from Light Bulb:

If a poisonous plant got tossed into compost, would it poison the whole batch of compost? Would it kill crops grown with the compost, or could the crops survive the poison? If they did survive, would poison remain in their roots or leaves?

I stretch my legs while mulling over what I've read so far. Was Light Bulb's question actually about the origin of meth-X? I do a set of deep lunges from the library to the kitchen and return with a bottled water from the refrigerator. Was that when it all started . . . with a precocious student's inquiry?

When I resume reading the notebook, I sit on the edge of the seat. My legs bounce with jittery tension as the entry dates approach the holiday break.

In early December, Uncle David tried helping Light Bulb develop a research methodology for testing plant toxicity and its spread into surrounding organic material. Light Bulb became impatient. Instead of a carefully thought-out plan with sequenced steps, Light Bulb wanted to jump ahead. Soon after, the daily entries mentioning Light Bulb were crossed out and a comment added in the margin each time: *No-show.*

I recall multiple instances of Travis skipping class, only to show up the following day and ace an unannounced quiz.

On December 8, 2003, Uncle David wrote one word. *Champignons.* The French word for "mushrooms."

Uncle David's entries from then on are in the code he and my mother invented. It takes longer to get through his notes because I need to translate. I'm used to hearing—rather than seeing—the hybrid of French, Italian, and quirky made-up words.

One of the next entries references *canard isola*. *Canard* is the French word for "duck"; *isola* is the Italian word for "island." *Canard isola* means Duck Island. He doesn't abbreviate it as DI; instead he uses CI, which is confusing at first because I keep thinking it means "confidential informant."

It was in December that he must have picked up on Travis's increased drug use. He wrote in code about his growing concern that Light Bulb was messing around in things he shouldn't.

That was around the time that I noticed Travis skipping school more and looking really out of it when he was in class. Lily and Travis began arguing—and not their normal cute spats, like whether Zamboni was a cooler name for a boy or a girl.

Lily found out over winter break that Travis was cooking meth. She tried talking to Angie Flint about getting help for him. Lily fumed to me about moms who made excuses for their sons. *It's so fucked up, when a mom enables her boy instead of raising a man.*

I resume reading. In January, an entry mentions *Cheelegge*. I don't recognize it as any of Mom's and David's nonsense words. I try enunciating different parts of the word, like when Lily would say *SHAG-ala* instead of *Sha-GAH-la*.

"Cheel-egge. Cheel-eggy. Chee-leggy. Chee-leg. Chee-leh-jeh."

That's it.

C-h-e-e is a phonetic way of spelling the Anishinaabemowin word *chi*. Big. *Legge* is Italian for "law." *Big law.*

Cheelegge was David's word for the FBI.

CHAPTER 35

U ncle David started working with the FBI in January. They told him about the hallucinogenic mushrooms in the meth that was showing up in different hockey towns and Indian reservations. Maybe that's when David realized that Light Bulb's research question about poisonous plants was actually about fungi.

Spring had come early, and Uncle David could forage for mushrooms. He wrote an entry reminding himself to research growing seasons and made a plan to return each month. There might be new growths once it became warmer and the days were longer. Rain was another variable; a heavy rainfall might produce something that had not been around a month earlier.

He began with land owned by Travis's family on Sugar Island. His entries become a log of his exploration of Duck Island. He foraged for mushrooms in cross sections just like I did, except he started at the north end and worked his way south. He used orange biodegradable seedling pots to mark his boundaries instead of yarn.

I smile. His lessons are part of me. I really am the best person to pick up the investigation where Uncle David left off.

He documented each specimen of mushroom or fungi he came across in the unusually early spring. He left room in the margin to list its scientific name once he had identified it using his guidebooks. There were no blank margins—every specimen had a name in the margin.

With one exception.

On April 4, 2004, Uncle David found a variety of parasitic mushroom that wasn't listed in any guidebook or online directory. He drew a picture of the culprit. It looks similar to *Asterophora parasitica*. His notes indicated it grew on a documented variety of mushroom that was hallucinogenic. The parasitic mushroom was nourished by a decaying, or composting, hallucinogenic host and was likely hallucinogenic as well. An anglerfish of a mushroom. He added a row of alternating question marks and exclamation points, which was his signature indication of being excited about this unknown specimen.

My own heart quickens at the possibility of discovering Uncle David's discovery. This could be a previously unknown hallucinogenic mushroom that might have been added to a batch of crystal meth—which found its way into the hands of a group of thirteen kids on a reservation in northern Minnesota.

I turn the page.

My heart sinks as I read the results of Uncle David's analysis of the anglerfish mushroom. It did not share the same hallucinogenic qualities as its hallucinogenic host.

He wrote: *There is no connection between champignons and cattiva medicina*. He had given an Italian translation for meth, calling it "bad medicine."

I think about what he has just told me. The mushrooms are a dead end. Uncle David knew and withheld the information from the FBI. And he wanted me, and only me, to know both of these details.

Uncle's last entry was April 9, 2004. On Good Friday. He wanted to talk to Light Bulb's mother.

He hid the notebook in the false bottom of his desk.

My mother reported him missing two days later when he didn't show up for Easter Sunday dinner. I cry again. This time it feels as if my sorrow has settled in my lungs—heavy, raspy, shallow breaths. I am so sorry for pushing my grief away to make space for the anger. I wish I could remember my last conversation with Uncle David beyond saying hello and helping myself to snacks from the desk drawer.

If you knew it was the last time you were going to see someone, would you say something profound? Would you share how much they meant to you? Would you ask any burning questions? Would you ask for forgiveness? Would you thank them?

The library is dark when I push away from the desk and go to the formal dining room. I sit in my usual seat and remember that last Easter Sunday dinner. GrandMary at the head of the table. My mother next to me. Uncle David's seat empty. I blink away my tears until I hear him come into the house, apologizing to GrandMary before he even sits down. Traffic was backed up on the International Bridge all the way into Canada. It's never taken over two hours to cross back into the U.S. He winks at me.

"Uncle David," I say across the table. "Thank you for leaving the clues for me to find. And for giving me the skills to decipher them. I am so grateful for you."

I drive to Jamie and Ron's rental house. Jamie answers the door. Ron grades papers at the kitchen table. *JAG* is on TV.

"Do yous wanna go for a walk?" I say.

They do.

We walk a few blocks away to Project Playground, by the ballfields.

It's one of those gigantic wooden structures like the one Art built for the twins. This one was built by community volunteers, with the Tribe providing most of the materials.

I need more information before deciding what to do with the notebook.

"Well, I finished my mushroom research project on Duck Island." My words in the cold night are visible puffs that dissipate after a few seconds, as if truly cloaked in secrecy.

Their faces light up.

"I didn't find anything," I say quickly. "But I was wondering when the FBI started working with Uncle David, like what month?" I already know, but I need them to do most of the talking.

"January," Ron says. "The kids in Minnesota got sick the last week in February. Is the timing important?"

"It could be. There are so many different varieties and growing seasons. It was a mild winter; maybe it grew only then, during a fluke early spring. Unless we can replicate the conditions from February, we aren't collecting from the same sample Travis had."

Ron's frustrated sigh lingers in the air.

Okay. What other information can I mine from them?

"It might help if I knew more about what was in the file about the kids. Which community? And how are the kids doing now?"

Ron won't name the reservation and doesn't know how they're doing. I keep my face a smooth mask to hide my anger at being stonewalled.

"Jamie told me they hallucinated men coming after them in the woods. Did they mention any other details about the hallucination? Was it visual only or did it involve other senses too . . . and maybe cross the senses? Doesn't that happen sometimes? I forget what it's called but it's where people see music or taste colors?"

Talk less and listen more, I scold myself.

Ron shrugs. "It didn't make any sense. The kids were scared one minute and pleading for more meth a minute later. They told the ER staff that men came after them. Most of the kids wouldn't say anything else, especially after their parents arrived. Maybe that stuff happened, what you said about jumbled senses, because their vision was distorted. One boy mentioned that the men chasing them were small men."

Little People.

The Little People found the kids in the woods and scolded them.

The FBI assumed whatever had been added to the meth-X was a hallucinogenic mushroom, because the Anishinaabe kids who tried that particular batch of meth saw something that didn't make sense. The team working the investigation was alarmed by the group aspect of the hallucination and thought it was an unusual side effect of an unknown variety of mushroom. Whatever was added to the batch of meth-X, it didn't cause hallucinations.

Because the Little People are real.

Travis said the Little People were mad at him. But what if they were warning Travis, like they had with Leonard Manitou's cousin Skinny?

What was so bad that the Little People went after the kids in the woods to warn them?

If the meth-X additive wasn't a hallucinogenic mushroom, then what was it?

I've got to go somewhere to think about what I still need to figure out. There are connections that I'm on the verge of making, but I need to go through the information again, uninterrupted and undistracted.

Step 1: Don't show any reaction that might tip them off that you're on the verge of a eureka moment.

Step 2: Think of an excuse to make an exit.

Step 3: Go home and think.

I sigh the way Ron did earlier.

"Well, what should I work on next? Because I'm all out of ideas."

Ron starts to say something, but I keep talking.

"I know, I know. Fruit of the poisonous tree. You're not supposed to direct me." I smile at Jamie leaning against the tube slide. He's letting Ron do all the talking so far. "But couldn't you be sneaky and drop a clue, like 'Whatever you do, Daunis, don't buy drugs from the Boosters'?"

I turn sharply to Ron.

"Wait . . . you did. Ron, in the car on the way to Marquette you said, 'We can't tell you to search the hockey team's gear bags for disposable cell phones.'" I shake my head and give Ron a begrudging smile. "I see what you did there. You're a clever one."

We head back to their house. Ron says good night and goes inside. Jamie leads me behind the Jeep. I put my arms around him, already hungry for his kisses.

Instead, Jamie places one gentle kiss on my forehead like my mother does.

I pull back, puzzled. He leans in to kiss my cheek.

Except he doesn't.

"I see what you did there. You're the clever one," Jamie whispers in my ear.

I drive away, mind racing. What did he mean? What does Jamie suspect I've done?

Turning onto my street, I notice Auntie's vehicle in the driveway.

Shit. I forgot I promised to come over tonight. It's ten o'clock and I said I'd come over at eight.

I park next to her. Before my hand touches the key in the ignition, she's already slamming her door and stomping around the front of the Jeep.

"Auntie—" I begin, intending to explain my exhaustion. My sentence halts in my throat.

My aunt has the same *Do not fuck with me* look from the blanket-party night.

"The only choice you got is whether your ass rides shotgun with me or in your own ride to the island," she says. "But, make no mistake, Daunis Firekeeper, you are coming with me."

CHAPTER 36

I decided to take my own car. Our vehicles are next to each other on the ferry. I look straight ahead, not turning a single degree. I feel for the pouch in the drink holder and toss a palmful of semaa to the river.

"Help me with what's coming next," I say.

Auntie's timing is the worst. I need this time to put together all the clues, not spend it getting yelled at by my aunt. Plus, Jamie's parting words still linger on my mind. What does he think he knows?

She follows me all the way to her house. There is the glow of a fire in the woods behind the pole barn. It's not a full moon tonight, so it can't be a ceremonial fire for that. Perhaps someone passed away and I haven't heard about it yet.

When I pull up to the house, Josette's car is there. She must be babysitting the twins if Art is tending a fire. I park next to her car.

My aunt walks beside me to the clearing, which overlooks the First Nations reserve across the river's north channel. Our breaths appear and disappear together.

Art stands next to the fire, stoking it with a shovel. There are several large rocks in the pit. We call them grandfathers because they have been here forever, seeing and hearing all.

I glance over to the madoodiswan. The curved dome of the sweat lodge is covered in old blankets and tarps. The entrance blanket is flipped above the eastern opening.

"What's going on, Auntie?"

"Intervention sweat," she announces.

"Can you even do that?" I've never heard of it before.

"I'm a modern Nish kwe and I just invented it, hey?"

She holds out a floral gathered cotton skirt for me. Her unwavering hand is like Lily's, demanding Travis's gun.

I reach for the skirt. After stepping into the skirt, I pull it over my jeans before taking off everything underneath. I remove my toque, coat, Red Wings sweatshirt, socks, and shoes. Although I'm barefoot and wearing only a T-shirt and skirt, I am not cold. The fire is strong.

It should be. It had an extra two hours to strengthen.

Auntie holds a small round bundle of mashkwadewashk. There are different varieties of sage, as well as male and female versions. Mashkwadewashk is for clearing negative energy. She lights one end from a glowing ember that Art holds out on an old shovel. We smudge ourselves with the smoke from the female sage to prepare for the sweat.

Auntie crawls into the madoodiswan.

Art waits for me to enter so he can use the shovel to place one of the glowing grandfather rocks in the center of the lodge before lowering the blankets over the entrance.

There is ceremony inside the madoodiswan. Healing. Returning to balance. *Madoodiswan* means "Mother Earth's womb." You enter your mother and leave reborn.

I lower to all fours, like a baby, and follow my aunt's lead. Crawling forward, I pray. Not asking for help with one of the Seven Grandfathers, but acknowledging the Grandfather instead. Dabaadendiziwin.

Humility: the knowledge that I am part of something larger than my existence.

I give myself up.

Afterward, Auntie and I sit at the fire, fully dressed once again. When I couldn't find my toque, she handed me a spare knit cap to pull over my damp hair.

We gulp cold spring water before tasting the hominy soup and blueberry galette that Art brought us before retiring for the night. We enjoy our small feast while watching the glowing embers. Salty broth and mushy kernels of hominy nourish something deep inside me. When I bite into the galette, the tang of the wild blueberries mixes with the faint sweetness of the biscuit-like cake, taking me back to my berry feast.

I got my first Moon when I was thirteen. Mom alerted my aunt. If I chose to do a berry fast, Auntie explained, I wouldn't be able to eat any berries for one whole year. No fresh strawberries in early summer. No tart raspberries or fat blackberries to fill my mouth. And, hardest of all, no blueberries—my absolute favorite.

Auntie even took me wild-blueberry picking, testing my resolve. In the woods north of Paradise, which felt like a secret from the intense August sun. She wandered off, leaving me with a bucket for collecting the tiny, ripe blueberries. I had to constantly remind myself of what I couldn't have, for fear of forgetting and popping a blueberry into my mouth without thinking. At the end of the day, Auntie eye-balled me as if with X-ray vision. I met her strong gaze with my own. I resisted temptation, knowing I'd never be able to hide any dishonesty from her radar.

Sadly, I now know that I can.

My year-long berry fast ended with a feast. Auntie, Mom, Gramma

Pearl, and my Nish kwe cousins and aunties gathered to honor my passage into womanhood. My mother held a plump strawberry for me. I had to refuse it three times, but on the fourth offer, I leaned forward and took it into my mouth. Its sweetness reached the tips of my fingers and toes. When I took a handful of my beloved blueberries, I marveled at each one, appreciating the nuanced range of tart to sweet. It was like experiencing them for the first time. My entry to womanhood was filled with joy, pride, belonging, and seeing ordinary things with new eyes.

I am overcome with deep gratitude as I sit here next to Auntie before the fire. Auntie has shown me how to be a strong Nish kwe—full of love, anger, humor, sorrow, and joy. Not as something perfect: She is a woman who is complex and sometimes exhausted, but mostly brave. She loves imperfect people fiercely.

Her eyes open; she smiles tiredly at me.

This is when I should tell her what's going on. But I know it's not safe to involve Auntie. The stakes for her are different. It's not just her. She is not alone on her journey. Wiijiindiwin.

Instead, I focus on a plate of food Art placed on a stump at the edge of the woods. Next to the plate is the bundle of female sage, a copper spoon, and my toque.

"Offerings for the Little People," Auntie explains. I quickly shove more galette in my mouth to hide my surprise.

"Art heard them in the woods while we were in the madoodiswan," Auntie says. "They check on us, like Animikiig during thunderstorms. Hoping to see us living Anishinaabe minobimaadiziwin."

"And maybe getting angry if they see us messing with stuff we shouldn't be around?" I hold my breath and watch Auntie's face, all shadows and light from the glowing embers of the dying fire.

"I suppose so. But most who know about bad medicine aren't going to leave it lying around unprotected. In the wrong hands, people can do harm by not knowing what they're messing with." She holds my gaze. "Those who know the old teachings, the medicines on the opposite side of healing, they respect its power."

We sit in silence for a long time. Uncle David and Auntie used the term *bad medicine*. So had Lily . . . the day she went all goon on TJ after he dumped me. My uncle stated clearly in the notebook that there was no connection between the mushrooms and the bad medicine—his code for the meth-X. Auntie said bad medicines were the opposite of the healing kind.

"You need to be careful, Daunis, when you're asking about the old ways." She looks at me the way Seeney Nimkee does sometimes at the Elder Center. "There's a saying about bad medicine: 'Know and understand your brother but do not seek him.'"

Auntie reaches over to a birchbark basket filled with semaa. Taking some in her left hand, she says a quiet prayer.

I rise, repeating her actions. Releasing the semaa into the last embers of the fire.

Auntie's voice wraps me like a blanket. "Please be careful. Not every Elder is a cultural teacher, and not all cultural teachers are Elders. It's okay to listen to what people say and only hold on to the parts that resonate with you. It's okay to leave the rest behind. Trust yourself to know the difference."

My aunt hasn't been around lately, because I've engineered it that way. But she seems to acknowledge my forging ahead without her. Something changes between us as we watch the fire simmer into ash. As if I've crossed over from a place where I was a child and am now a grown woman.

"I trust you to know who to share yourself with, and when not to," she says. "I love that you are figuring it out so much sooner than I did. I've made so many foolish choices. Messed up so badly and so often in my life. I gave too much of myself to men who didn't deserve me."

As I listen to Auntie, it begins to snow: big, beautiful flakes. Softly floating all around us like tiny feathers.

"I met Art a long time ago. Met him at ceremonies. Didn't think of him in any romantic way. Art was too mellow. Not my type." She smiles to herself before sighing.

"I used to be with this one guy. I thought the sun rose just to shine light on him. He was handsome and smart and the life of the party. But oh, when we fought . . . it was so bad." She shivers and pulls the coat around her more tightly. "He consumed all the oxygen in the room and left nothing for me to breathe. If the sun dared to shine on me instead of him, it was my fault. The only way to keep him happy, to see the version of him he was when other people were around, was to make myself small."

Her voice cracks. "It's hard when someone says they love you, but they need to contain and control the things that make you *you*."

She pauses to put semaa onto the ashes. "So I left him. I came back to the sweat lodge. Stayed sober for ceremonies. It felt like Creator breathing air back into me. I ran into Art again. Saw him clearly this time."

Auntie closes her eyes as the snowflakes land on her cheeks.

"Oh, I still managed to screw up plenty. I used to start fights with Art to see what he would be like when he was angry. I'd say hurtful things . . . and then turn away quickly. He asked me why I did that." Tears roll down her cheeks. "I told him I was bracing for his punch. 'That's not love,' he told me. 'Love honors your spirit. Not just the other person's but your own spirit too.'"

When she looks at me, my aunt seems at peace.

"I found my way back to minobimaadiziwin, our good way of life. I love and am loved. I am true to Creator and to wiijiindiwin." She points her lips to her home, where her husband and babies sleep. "Honor your spirit. Love yourself."

I gotta focus on school. You focus on yourself. We gotta stand on our own feet separately. Don't you see? I can't stand on my own if I'm always holding you up.

When Lily told Travis that she was done for good, he pulled out a gun. Love is not control. If he had truly loved Lily, he would have wanted her to have a good life. Even if it wasn't with him. Instead, he did the opposite of love. Travis steadied the gun in his hand and thought only of himself.

As we head back from the fire, Auntie invites me to sleep on the sofa, but I decide to catch the last ferry back to the mainland. As I drive, the snow lets up.

At the launch, I park under the light pole. Mine is the only vehicle waiting. I wrap myself in Lily's quilt and page through the notebook.

The ferry horn signals its departure from the mainland. It will be here in five minutes.

I open the notebook to my uncle's entry on the fourth of April from his mushroom search on Duck Island. That page and the four pages that follow are his notes from when he found the previously undocumented parasitic mushroom and analyzed it for hallucinogenic qualities, as well as his questioning whether there even was a connection between hallucinogenic mushrooms and meth-X.

I tear the five pages so there is no trace of anything regarding the dead end. Anyone reading the notebook will assume Uncle David's efforts were incomplete, rather than unsuccessful.

The Nish kids in Minnesota didn't have a shared group hallucination. They had a shared encounter with the Little People warning the kids to leave the bad medicine alone.

As long as the FBI continues their wild goose chase in search of a hallucinogenic mushroom, they will leave our other medicines alone.

I gather any torn-page remnants left inside the spiral binding, along with the matches Lily kept in the glove compartment. All the evidence of Uncle David's additional research goes up in flames on a flat rock off the shoulder of the road. It burns quickly, and I am back inside the Jeep when the deckhand motions me to drive forward.

The ferry is all mine for the last trip of the night. Stepping from the Jeep midway through the crossing, I release a pinch of semaa over the railing. It carries my prayer of thanks. *Miigwech for trusting me with the information about the mushroom. And chi miigwech for the responsibility of protecting my community by not sharing the information with the FBI.*

Because I think I know what Travis did to create meth-X.

CHAPTER 37

After Lily broke up with Travis over Christmas break, he kept trying to win her back with romantic gestures. Travis had a heart-shaped pizza delivered to her during AP English class. He spray-painted her name in the snow outside her homeroom. He stood in the parking lot at the end of the school day holding a boom box above his head, blasting their official love song as if he were John Cusack in the movie *Say Anything*.

Sometimes his efforts worked and *The Lily and Travis Saga* would get picked up for another episode, but it always ended like the previous seasons.

Travis was no longer the class clown. His handsome looks disappeared along with a shocking amount of his body weight. Yet even as he was wasting away, there were still girls who told Lily how romantic it was when he did one of his *Give us another chance* routines.

She and I wondered what grand gesture Travis would do for Valentine's Day. He'd been building up to something that had all indications of being epic. There were the deliveries of floral bouquets. Her locker filled with her favorite candy. When it snowed all day long, Lily's Jeep would be the only one in the parking lot that had been brushed off and shoveled out. I could feel Lily softening more toward Travis with each grand gesture.

Valentine's Day fell on a Saturday. We thought Travis might make his romantic declaration on Friday, because he wasn't welcome at Granny June's, and his grand gestures always took place in or around school.

On Friday the thirteenth, Travis followed Lily onto the ferry after she dropped me off at Auntie's for the weekend. He darted from his truck to her unlocked passenger door before she realized what he was doing. He made his grand romantic gesture: offering her love medicine. No details of where or how he had come into possession of it. They could make plans to take it together, on Valentine's Day.

Lily exited her Jeep, leaving him inside, and went upstairs on the ferry to the small waiting room. She called and asked me to come get her. When I met the ferry on its return trip to the island, my heartbroken best friend told me what he had done.

Then one day a few weeks later, I was running errands with my mother's car and saw Travis at the gas station on the rez. My heart sank. Travis looked horrible. He was deep in the throes of meth addiction.

By then, Travis Flint had created meth-X and been its first customer.

The night he killed Lily, Travis told me that the Little People were mad at him. *I just wanted her to love me again.*

Somehow, Travis had come across a love medicine. The kind of bad medicine that Auntie warned me against asking too much about.

When Lily refused to try the love medicine, Travis must have added it to a batch of meth, also known as his cookies. What he thought was a love medicine was actually the opposite of love. Real love honors your spirit. If you need a medicine to create or keep it, that's possession and control. Not love.

A couple of weeks later, on a rez in Minnesota, a group of kids tried it while they were hanging out in the woods. Every single one got sick. Not lovesick for some girl they'd never met, but infected with an insatiable desire for more meth.

I can do my part to protect our medicines, while trusting that there are those in the community who are doing their part to preserve and protect many different medicine teachings.

On my drive home, I stop at Jamie and Ron's again. This time, I slide the spiral notebook through the mail slot in their front door.

When I walk back to my Jeep, my steps grow lighter. It feels as if a huge weight has been lifted off my shoulders. I shared only what Ron and Jamie had a need to know.

The following morning, I rush through my bathroom routine, throw on running clothes, and practically burst out the front door. Each sunrise is a minute or two later than the prior day. Even in the darkness, I see the familiar figure stretching beside my Jeep.

"Happy birthday, Daunis," Jamie calls out.

It may not be visible to him, but I flash my widest smile anyway, unable to contain my excitement. I'm glad his first words are not about the investigation. Today is too special.

My whispered prayer is for zaagidiwin. Love is the first Grandfather teaching we receive as babies—even before birth, as new spirits traveling while our bodies are forming to the cadence of our mother's heartbeat. Love from our parents, family, and Creator is with us as we draw our first breath in this world.

I wonder what Dad felt and thought the first time he held me. Mom said Auntie reached out two weeks after we returned from Montreal. Asked if she could give Mom and baby me a ride to Sugar Island. My Firekeeper family wanted to meet me. My father wanted to hold me.

After our warm-up stretches, Jamie and I run toward Sherman Park. Our invigorating pace makes it a silent run. When we reach the park, Jamie halts instead of turning around like we usually do.

"Gotta take a leak," he says, walking to a nearby tree.

I stretch my legs while staring across the river. Marveling at the way the sunrise behind me lights up the Canadian horizon.

"Ron won't be at the benefit game tonight," Jamie says, coming up beside me. "He's going to Marquette, to enter the notebook into evidence and analyze its contents with another agent."

I nod but say nothing. The investigation continues. The FBI has their work and I have mine. The truth about meth-X was one part of the investigation. I still need to find out who is distributing the meth and who has taken over production with Travis gone.

"What are you doing today for your birthday?" he asks, changing the subject.

"Run, EverCare, class, lunch with Granny June, and spend the rest of the afternoon with my mom before heading over to the game."

"Could I take you to dinner after the game? To celebrate your birthday?"

"I'd like that," I say.

"You didn't tell me what color your dress is. I wanted to get one of those corsages like Mike's mom did for Macy."

"It's red, but I don't like corsages. I think they're kinda weird. It's not a big deal." I decide to dive into what is the bigger deal. "What did you think was I being clever about last night?"

"You were interrogating the interrogator," Jamie says. "Getting information but not giving anything significant in return. And then there was the whole thing with your body language."

Apparently, my attempt at a poker face last night failed.

"What did you learn?" I say, both eager and hesitant for his analysis.

"You are a passionate person. You love deeply. You have flashes of anger and sadness. You can be silly. Even dorky at times." I hear the smile in his voice.

After a few paces, he continues. "Last night, Ron was telling you details about the investigation that killed your uncle. And you were too calm, Daunis. You asked about what happened to the Nish kids in Minnesota and when Ron didn't have an answer, you didn't get irritated like when you asked me about them in Marquette. You care deeply about them and what's happened since their group hallucination. The only time you reacted was when you remembered what he said about burner phones."

Could I be any less stealthy? I must be the squeaky shoe of spies.

"You're going rogue. Hiding things," Jamie says.

"I'm not—"

"It was a hundred-fifty-page notebook with one hundred forty-five pages."

Shit. There it is.

"Does Ron know?"

"I counted the pages while he was taking a shower." Jamie looks at me. "I think they'll figure it out soon. Probably today."

I don't respond until we are doing cooldown stretches in my driveway.

"Can you trust me, Jamie, that what I removed wasn't meant for the FBI?"

He answers with a question of his own.

"Can you trust me?"

Jamie leaves me to ponder whether both questions share the same answer: *I don't know, and the stakes are too high for uncertainty.*

CHAPTER 38

It's late afternoon when I walk into Chi Mukwa with my large duffel bag of hockey gear slung over my good shoulder. Once I enter the women's locker room, the oddly intoxicating aroma brings back the thrill of every great play I've ever made. The whiff of industrial cleaning products mixed with the skunky stink of sweat smells powerful.

"Happy birthday to me," I whisper before practically skipping to my old locker. One glance at Robin's locker next to mine wipes the smile off my face. I figured today would be a mixture of highs and lows. Playing hockey one more time . . . but for the worst possible reason.

My phone buzzes while I'm changing into my gear.

AUNTIE: Not sure I can watch you play. I get why but it is still foolish.

I swallow the lump in my throat. Auntie has never missed a home game of mine.

"You still remember how to play? Been a while." Macy laces up her black hockey skates, which are adorned with acrylic-painted flowers.

"Yup. Starters have good memories," I shoot back. Just a little reminder about which one of us started the game on the ice and which one watched it from the bench.

Once we are ready, Macy and I leave the locker room together. The bleachers are already filling up with people who want to watch our warm-up. We step onto the ice side by side and automatically cross our sticks for all the kwezanswag who feel alive the moment their hockey skates touch the ice.

When it's game time, my body feels the delicious tingle of battle. My stomach clenches, my legs are jittery, and I feel like puking. Classic adrenaline rush. On the ice, it is music to my ears, feast to my hunger. Coach Bobby puts me in as left defenseman, and it's like my second skin. I breathe it, I transform, and everything that is not a tenacious beast falls away.

I join center ice, waiting for the referee to drop the puck for Levi and my teammate to fight over. Levi will aim the puck to Stormy on my right side. Sometimes they operate as a single-cell entity, as if Levi's brain controls two sets of arms and legs. Levi as host and Stormy doing his bidding without independent thought.

Just when I think my body will explode from adrenaline overload, the ref releases the puck and something magical, yet familiar, happens. Time slows for an instant, enough for a quiet calm to wash over me. I watch the puck drop, as if in slow motion, not even touching the ice before Levi's superhuman reflexes have responded and his stick smacks it to Stormy. I intercept and pass it to Quinton, my high school teammate, who rushes to the Supes' net.

Time now races and I am the Terminator. With laser focus, I

instantly compute actions into strategic countermoves and proactive aggressions to force opponents into changing course.

My team quickly finds its rhythm, defending the puck and setting up plays. We know Quinton will be halfway to the net, ready for the pass. We won the state championship my junior year and made it to the quarterfinals last spring. We are fluent in playing as a cohesive unit.

The Supes, individually, are better players. But they haven't gelled as a team yet. Or as my brother would say, they aren't reading each other. Levi loses his temper, swearing at a teammate for not sharing the same hive mind as Stormy and Mike. Although both are rookie Supes, they've been on the ice with Levi for ten years.

In the final period, I take a hip check from Stormy and keep going. That goon ain't getting in my way. I back-check and steal the puck. Macy, who subbed in a few minutes ago, is waiting on the periphery. We've danced this number before. Stormy bounds back for another go at me, but I pass behind my back to Macy, who chips it to Quinton. She races to the net, where, three seconds later, she gets it back and fires the puck. Mike's arms seem elastic, stretching to reach the upper corner of the net to block Macy's shot.

Damn. She nearly had it in.

Stormy crashes into me. I'm thrown into the plexiglass and boards, bouncing off and landing in a heap on my shoulder. I gasp at the pain.

N'Daunis, bazigonjisen!

I quickly get up and roll my left shoulder to assess the pain.

It stabs. No. No. No. Maybe I just need to shake out a kinked nerve.

Coach Bobby pulls me out. My sub and I fist-bump with our right hands as we cross paths. I sit on the bench, moving my left shoulder in circles. It hurts like hell.

A minute later, Macy subs out and sits next to me.

"Stormy got you good," she says.

"Eh," I reply, as pain radiates from my bad shoulder. Keeping my eyes on the puck, I fight the temptation to look anywhere else. If Auntie is here watching, I am absolutely certain she is glaring at me from wherever she is seated. I bounce my legs, dreading the inevitable confrontation.

"Your guy is pretty smooth," Macy says. It takes a few blinks to realize she means Jamie.

"Eh." Truthfully, I haven't paid him any notice.

She laughs. "Holy, you're a supportive boo."

"Screw him. He ain't on my team," I say.

"All's fair in love and hockey?"

"Off ice, he's mine. On ice, he's theirs." I point my lips toward Levi.

The part about Jamie not being on my team—I don't think it's true anymore.

Can you trust me? His voice echoes.

I watch as the guy who replaced me does a crappy job on defense. Crappy Sub was a year ahead of Robin, so he has never played with Levi. My brother sees every opportunity and weakness. The only way to beat Levi is to stay at his side and strategize your best countermove if he ever lets down his guard.

If I've figured out Crappy Sub in two minutes, then Levi has as well.

"Put me in," I shout to Coach Bobby, standing so I can jump over the boards.

"Sit down and shut up, Fontaine," he yells back.

I grumble and stew in the burning pain.

Macy laughs. "You only got one good arm. What're you gonna do?" She imitates a penguin, keeping her arms pressed to her sides and flapping her hand next to me.

Crappy Sub leaves an opening for Levi to skate through, receive a

pass from Jamie, and take a shot. The blast of the Supes' goal horn—
from an actual freighter—confirms my brother's aim.

"I would've skated into Levi. Drawn a penalty and made a sacrifice
for the greater good," I shout over the deafening noise to Macy.

We lose, but just barely. Although my team played better, we
couldn't get anything past Mike. One look at my brother during the
post-game handshake line and it's clear: He is pissed. Levi knows we
handed the Supes their sloppy asses.

Jamie's face lights up when we meet in the handshake line. My
stomach somersaults at his touch.

Do you trust me?

In the locker room, I check to make sure Auntie isn't waiting to
give me hell. Once I know the coast is clear, I text my doctor. Then I
peel off my jersey sideways and wince in pain.

"You want me to get Coach?" Macy offers while helping me out of
my gear.

"Nah, I just texted Dr. B. to meet me at War Mem after I shower."

"Yeah, good thinking on that shower. You're really ripe." She
scrunches her nose as if we are trapped in a Sugar Island outhouse
in July.

"Bitch," I say, without any heat behind it. I walk toward the
showers.

"Bigger bitch," she replies, following me.

"The bigger the better." I turn on the water and wash with one
hand, keeping my left arm glued to my side.

"If you say so," Macy laughs.

Petty bitch always trying to get the last word in.

"I know so," I throw back at her, letting our smack talk distract
me from the pain. I towel off gingerly and get dressed. As I attempt to
zip my jeans, she huffs a tortured sigh and helps me.

When we reach the lobby, the packed crowd cheers. The roar feels familiar, like a real high school game. I'd forgotten how great this moment is: all the community love.

Hockey brings my community together. Native and non-Native. All ages. All neighborhoods. Here in Chi Mukwa, a community recreation building funded by the Sugar Island Ojibwe Tribe, everyone stands united for our teams. I just hope they remember today was for Robin Bailey.

With my duffel bag slung over my unhurt shoulder, and my jacket over the bag like a saddle blanket, I push through the crowd. Jamie stands a few feet behind the other guys. When I touch his arm, he stares at me in astonishment.

"What?" I check to see if I put my sweatshirt on backward.

"I figured you were a decent player." Jamie's hushed voice reaches me through the surrounding chaos. "But, Daunis, you're incredible."

I don't know what to do with his admiration. I shrug my shoulders, wincing in pain.

He takes my duffel bag before I can protest.

"You okay?"

"Eh, took a hit," I say, faking nonchalance.

"There she is," Mike interrupts. "Dauny Defense."

"We kicked your asses," Stormy declares.

"That's not what I saw." I ignore Stormy's glare.

"It's all good," Levi says, bumping into Jamie robustly enough to dislodge my gear bag. "The point was to start playing better as a team."

The point was to do something for Robin. I scowl at my brother, who helps Jamie with my bag. How could this be just another game? Levi took Robin to Shagala her junior year.

No guy should have that kind of power over you. No matter who he is or how much everyone adores him. Or how much you might still want him.

Robin's words ring in my ears. Did she mean Levi? He does have a reputation for loving and leaving. Or, as the guys say, *Snag and brag.*

"What's with the stink eye?" Levi asks me. "Ya mess up your shoulder when Stormy bodychecked ya?" He tells Jamie, "She's got a bum shoulder. Always popping its socket."

"Really? How long has it been an issue?" Jamie asks Levi while looking at me.

Mike's parents join us. I avoid eye contact with Call-me-Grant; I haven't been near him since the bus ride back from Green Bay.

"Happy birthday, Daunis," Mrs. Edwards says. "How did it feel to play for the Blue Devils one more time?"

"Great," I say. It feels good to let my true feelings show. Tonight, Secret Squirrel is taking a break.

"One helluva birthday," Call-me-Grant says. "Hockey and becoming a tribal member."

I gape as he puts his finger to his lips like he did from the doorway of his hotel room.

Shhhh. Your secret is safe with me, Daunis Fontaine.

He continues, "You didn't know? Tribal Council met today instead of next Monday because Chief Manitou and a few other council members are traveling to Washington, DC, that day."

"Woo-hoo!" Levi shouts, reaching to hug me and spin me around. I keep both arms glued to my sides, mimicking Macy's penguin impersonation from earlier.

It feels like I'm in a centrifuge. When he stops, I am nauseous, only partly from the spin. The other reason is Call-me-Grant being so interested in Tribal Council business.

My heart lifts when the twins shout for me from across the lobby. They sit on Auntie's and Art's shoulders. Pauline chews on a section of her ponytail. Mom is with them as well. I check Auntie's face for any indication that she is upset with me, but all I see is a big smile.

I wave back with my good arm and head over. Jamie remains at my side.

"Please don't say anything about my shoulder," I tell him before we reach my family.

I hold hands with Jamie, keeping him close to my left side so I won't need to move it. The twins, now hopping around, get side hugs from me with my right arm. Mom kisses me and whispers how proud she is of me.

"Happy birthday to our newest tribal member!" Auntie's voice cracks as she leans in to hug me. I hide my wince and pretend that Call-me-Grant didn't hijack this special moment.

"Oh, Auntie, this means so much. Miigwech for helping me."

Mom wipes away her happy tears. I know she always wanted this for me.

"Jamie wants to take me out to dinner to celebrate," I announce.

"Have to spoil the birthday girl a little," he says.

Mom gives Jamie a huge hug, and I can tell she means it. Jamie laughs at Art's jokes and nods when my aunt tells him something I can't hear. The twins want to do a simultaneous high-five clap with him. Jamie encourages them with each attempt to sync their leaps in the air to reach his raised palms. He laughs when the girls intentionally smack each other and, again, when they finally perfect it.

Our eyes meet. His are sparkling with pure joy as an incandescent smile tugs at his scar. It feels like we are in the zone together. Where we are here with everyone, but also somewhere else that is entirely ours.

In that place, James Brian Johnson is eighteen years old and hoping to get scouted by U of M or Michigan Tech. Any school with an excellent premed program for me. We make plans to stay in the dorms for our first year and move off campus after that. His hockey schedule works well because I need to come home often to check on Mom. Waking up tangled in each other's arms is the best start to our day. He joins me in offering semaa each morning, giving thanks because every day feels like a gift.

It is a beautiful dream.

You are fluent in a language when you dream in it. I assumed Seeney meant nighttime dreams. I didn't think about the ones that sneak up on you during the day.

A tear falls down my cheek without warning.

He isn't eighteen; he's twenty-two.

He has a different name. A past. A life beyond this assignment.

I try to imagine a place for us to be together in the After of the investigation. But that dream, the one based in reality, is too murky and too far away to see.

We walk to my Jeep. He loads my duffel bag into the back.

"Where would you like to go to dinner?" he asks.

With my good arm, I reach to touch his damp curls. My fingertips trace his scar and settle on his carotid artery. Each pulse is an affirmation that he is a real person. Here with me in the Now of the Newer New Normal.

I kiss the pulse on his neck. Each heartbeat throbs against my lips. I inhale deeply, holding it in as if it might stay with me. His familiar soap and natural scent fill my lungs.

Can you trust me?

"Jamie, would you drive me to the emergency room?"

The nurse tells me to change into a gown and that Dr. Bonasera will be right in. She instructs Jamie to tie my gown in the back and to leave my hurt shoulder free.

As soon as the door closes, I turn my back to him and try wriggling out of my oversized sweatshirt, retracting my unhurt arm through the sleeve. Jamie lifts the sweatshirt over my head. He moves my hair over my right shoulder, exposing my bare back.

I didn't bother with a bra after the shower. I would have had to ask Macy for help, and it was easier to freestyle.

He kisses my hurt shoulder with lips soft as a whisper.

From behind, he holds the gown in front of me, arms over my shoulders, and I put my uninjured arm through the armhole. He drapes it carefully over my hurt shoulder and ties it loosely in the back.

"You smell like strawberries," he says simply, sniffing next to my head.

There is a knock on the door a second before Dr. B. enters.

At the sight of Jamie, my doctor greets him. They shake hands. Jamie introduces himself as my boyfriend. I tell Jamie that Dr. Bonasera's wife is the head nurse at EverCare.

"Okay, Daunis, let's see what's going on here," Dr. B. says in a soothing tone.

I steel myself as he touches my shoulder. It's painful, but I've known worse.

"It's not dislocated," he says to my relief. "But you did bang it good."

"So, no sling. Just be gentle with it?" I prescribe my own treatment plan.

"Hold on. Not so fast, Daunis," Dr. B. says. He takes a pen from the pocket of his white coat and presses one end into the back of my upper arm.

"Do we need to do this now?" I ask Dr. B., focusing on my hands resting on my lap.

"He doesn't know?"

"Doesn't know what?" Jamie asks, instantly alarmed. I remain fascinated by the ulnar artery threading along the back of my hand, a faint blue river barely visible beneath the skin.

"You didn't tell your boyfriend?" Dr. B.'s voice is gentle, though disappointed.

I want to remind Dr. B. about doctor-patient confidentialit, but when I look up, his eyes are kind and filled with concern. I give a half shrug with my one good shoulder and make a decision.

"It's okay, he can see," I say. I keep my eyes on Jamie now, as Dr. B. slowly drags the pen down my arm. I only know what my doctor is doing because I'm familiar with the sensory test. It isn't until the pen reaches just above my elbow that I say, "There."

I spell it out for Jamie.

"That's where I feel the pen on my skin. Everything above it is numb."

CHAPTER 39

D r. Bonasera pulls a small retractable tape measure from his pants pocket. He measures up from the bony knob of my elbow and makes a notation in my chart.

"You were extremely lucky today, young lady. You risk further nerve damage every time you reinjure that shoulder." Dr. B. looks at Jamie. "A complication from the surgery she had last summer to treat her chronic shoulder instability."

The summer before my senior year, when everyone thought I was at Marie Curie camp at Michigan Tech, I was in Ann Arbor with my aunt. The surgery was supposed to fix my shoulder. I didn't want to risk any injuries in my last year of varsity hockey. We had a shot to be repeat state champions. The University of Michigan wanted me to play on their women's hockey team. Auntie paid for the surgery so it wouldn't show up on my mother's health insurance and used the medical power of attorney Mom had signed years before just in case anything ever happened to me while I went somewhere with my aunt.

The surgeon explained the risks, but I was so certain that my surgery would take care of the problem. I was Levi Firekeeper's daughter. Hockey was in my blood.

"Seriously?" Jamie looks at me. "Why did you even play tonight?" He sounds mad.

I feel like an ant under the glare of a magnifying glass.

"My team lost because Levi got past my crappy sub," I say.

Dr. B. looks over his glasses at me before telling Jamie, "She's a pistol, isn't she?"

"She's something," Jamie says, pinching the bridge of his nose.

Back in the Jeep, Jamie asks where I'd like to go for my birthday dinner.

"How about cheeseburgers at the drive-in?" I say.

He laughs. "I was expecting something more . . . celebratory?"

"You ever have one of their bacon cheeseburgers?"

When we get our food and my celebration strawberry shake, I give directions for Jamie to drive past the golf course and follow the river.

"Turn here," I say, a few miles downriver.

"It's a trail in the woods," he comments.

"I know. Just follow it." A branch scrapes the top of the Jeep. "My aunt and Art almost bought this lot instead of the property on the island. It's still for sale."

"Whoa," Jamie says when the trail ends at a clearing with Sugar Island across the river.

"Right? It's even prettier in the daylight." I hand Jamie our bag of burgers, his iced tea, and my shake. I grab Lily's blankets from the back, thankful I washed the smell out of the one I'd wrapped around the meth garbage baby. "C'mon. Dinner and a show."

We walk past a stone fireplace and crumbling chimney, all that's left of the house that used to be here. At the end of the lot, I spread the moving pad on the grass at the edge of a steel breakwall with a small swatch of beach beyond. Still favoring my injured wing, I ease onto the pad. I take off my clogs and sit cross-legged. Just as I did the day of the squall when we sat together in the garage bay, I wrap half the soft quilt around me and hold out the other half for Jamie. The blanket still smells like campfire. He sits next to me and we tear open the bag with my birthday dinner.

"The first sip of strawberry shake is the best," I declare, offering the white Styrofoam cup to Jamie. He drinks from the straw.

"You are correct," Jamie says, and leans over to kiss me. It's so sudden my smile is captured in his mouth.

My birthday dinner continues as we alternate kisses with bites of bacon cheeseburgers and a shared strawberry shake, listening to the gentle waves lap the shore.

Several hundred feet away, a freighter silently passes by.

"Here comes the after-dinner entertainment," I tell Jamie. "You know how ducks leave a V-shaped pattern that fans out when they move across a pond? Boats do that too. It's called a Kelvin wake. In a few minutes, the waves from that freighter out there will hit the shore."

"Well, then, let's make good use of the time," he says.

This kiss feels urgent, our tongues meeting and retreating. When Jamie moves his lips to my neck, I look up at the stars. My good arm rises so I can rake his curls with my fingers.

"Daunis, can I do that to you? To your hair?" he asks at my neck.

Jamie remembers the rules we made up on the drive to Coach Bobby's bonfire.

Smoothing my hair had been TJ's move, and I didn't think I could bear to have anyone be close to me like that. Especially someone faking it.

Jamie is asking for real.

"Yes," I say to the stars.

Rising to my knees, I sit on my heels and face Jamie. He follows my lead. The blanket slips from us as the waves grow louder.

Jamie kisses my lips softly as his hands brush against my temples. His kisses grow more urgent as his fingers tangle in my hair.

I move my left hand to test my injured shoulder. It is sore, rather than painful. I rest my left palm against Jamie's chest, my good arm slides around him. I reach beneath his jacket and shirt to feel the lean muscles of Jamie's back.

The waves increase in intensity, strong enough to reach the break-wall. A succession of crashes that align with Jamie's deepening kisses as he follows the length of my hair from the top of my head to the middle of my back.

As the waves recede, I push against Jamie's chest.

"Lie back, please," I say.

He does, stretching out and reaching for me. I lie in the crook of his arm and pull the soft blanket up to our shoulders. We look at the stars.

"You missed the Kelvin wakes," I tell him.

"Worth it," Jamie says, hugging me closer.

We laugh.

"Can I ask you something, Daunis?" His voice is gentle but no longer playful.

It's an odd feeling for me, dreading his question while also wanting to open up. Maybe I've been so good at being guarded that it's my default reaction?

I nod.

"Why would you risk more nerve damage to play in the game today?"

I wait for my first response—telling Jamie it's none of his business—to recede. The pause allows me to dig deep and truly consider his question, as well as what I feel ready to share.

"Being on the ice is where I feel closest to my dad," I say, starting with the easiest truth. "I pretend he's at my games. Something about the smell of the rink and having a stick in my hand . . . it opens up a memory portal, I guess."

We are quiet as the blinking lights of an airplane cross the sky. I like that Jamie doesn't rush to fill the silence and I can think about what I want to say next.

"Surgery was supposed to fix the problem. Instead, the upper part of my arm went numb. It was a small portion, so I kept playing. I reinjured my shoulder once during regular season and again during playoffs. Each time, the numbness traveled further down my arm."

I sit up and face Jamie.

"Can you understand how hard it was to give up something I loved so much? Does it make sense now, my giving into temptation—just this once—to imagine my dad cheering for me?"

I trace the length of his scar. Jamie traces my face, as if I have a scar there too.

"I want to be with you," I say.

"I want you, too," he says. "But we need to think it through. We're in the middle of this situation and we don't know how it will end." Jamie's comment cuts at me. It's a painful reminder that as much as he seems to fit into my world, he can't stay in it.

I've been left behind before, but I was always caught by surprise. I thought it would hurt less if I saw it coming. But now I realize that knowing doesn't lessen the pain, it just gives it a head start.

Tonight, I would choose not knowing.

"For tonight, Jamie, can it not be about that? Can it be you and me, in the eye of the hurricane? Tomorrow, we'll be back in the storm. But tonight, it's just us."

The stars have nothing on this guy when his eyes sparkle.

I bring up the necessary details. "No STDs and I have a progestin implant for birth control. But you still need a condom."

"I don't have any STDs either," Jamie says. "We need to swing by a store, though."

I kiss his cheek. "Box of condoms in the glove compartment, courtesy of Lily."

"I really liked her, Daunis. She was a good friend to you." He kisses me back.

I nod. "The best."

He runs to the Jeep and a blink later is next to me. It takes athletic maneuvers to manage the logistics of removing items of clothing while remaining inside the blanket sandwich. We laugh each time the top layer shifts and cool air touches skin. I keep my lips on his, even swallowing our laughter.

His warm hands reach underneath my sweatshirt. I tingle from the feathery strokes of his thumbs working in unison.

He looks up at me. "You sure this is what you want, Daunis? We can stop anytime."

"I know," I say. "I want this."

I shift myself until I find the perfect angle. Nothing beyond us matters.

When Jamie groans, I silence him with my fingers flat against his mouth. He chuckles softly and kisses my fingers with such tenderness. He tries holding me in place, but I keep moving until I cry out, and, for once, the Newer New Normal makes perfect sense.

"I love you," he whispers.

No. No. No. Please. Not this.

I scramble out of the blanket cocoon, gulping crisp air while pulling on my jeans and fumbling with the zipper. My feet slide back into my clogs.

Jamie jumps up as well. He follows me, zipping up his black dress pants. His maroon shirt is open. Shadows dance along his chest and abdomen; his panting makes his muscles ripple.

"Daunis, is everything okay? What's wrong?"

I bend over as if punched in the gut. Drawing in a deep breath before shouting at my feet, "You had to ruin everything by saying that."

"Wait . . . you're upset because I said I love you?"

My nose tickles and my throat constricts.

"Telling you I love you is ruining it?" he repeats. He makes it sound like I'm messed up.

"I know all about Guy Lies," I say, rising to face him. "It's okay. We can pretend this never happened." I scoop up both blankets and hurry to the Jeep.

Behind me, Jamie inhales deeply like he has to steady himself, then rushes up behind me.

"Guy Lies . . . that's what you call it . . ." His voice rises. "Did that tribal cop lie to you?"

"Shut up. This isn't about him." I climb into the passenger seat and turn up the heater.

"Who else lied to you?" he says, walking around to the driver's side.

"Everyone."

I'm fishing with Dad. His favorite spot on Duck Lake. My feet dangle in the water.

A leech on my pinkie toe. Dad sprinkles salt to make it release. Pretends to eat it.

We laugh. Dad and me. His face changes as he looks across the lake.

"Therefore I must be lying when I say I love you?" Jamie shakes his head, as if he's sorry for me. His pity pisses me off.

"You're the biggest liar of all," I say. A tiny voice from somewhere deep in my heart reminds me: *That's not true. You know who the biggest liar is.* "Your lies sound so believable because you don't know what's true. You don't even know which parts of you are real and which ones are bits and pieces you invented for this assignment."

It is quiet except for the engine and the heater.

"Daunis, I don't know what just happened." His voice is soft. "Why are you pushing me away?"

"Take it back," I whisper. "What you said about loving me."

"Please tell me why."

"He took me fishing on Duck Lake," I say. "I dangled my feet in the water and ended up with a leech on my pinkie toe. He kept a saltshaker in his box of fishing tackle. Sprinkled salt and told me he was seasoning it. He plucked the leech from my toe and pretended to eat it. We both laughed. Then he looked across the lake at the sunset and got sad."

When I repeat the words to Jamie, it's not my voice that I hear.

I have to go away, N'Daunis. Just for a little while. When I come back, everything will be different. We're gonna have such a good life together. Ninde gidayan, N'Daunis.

"'You have my heart, my daughter.' That was the last thing my dad ever said to me."

I'm sick of the quivering in my voice. I make up for it with volume.

"Don't you know, Jamie? Love is a promise. And promises you don't keep are the worst lies of all."

CHAPTER 40

We are silent on the drive back to Chi Mukwa, where we left his car. When I walk around to the driver's side, Jamie wraps me in his arms.

"Daunis, it's okay if you don't say it or feel it or are too scared to consider it. There's the investigation and then there's you and me. I love you and I'm not going anywhere except to that dance with you tomorrow."

I close my eyes. How can he even say that he's not going anywhere? It might be true for tomorrow, but he can't promise anything beyond that.

"Anytime you feel sad or worried, squeeze my hand. I'll squeeze back so you won't feel alone."

He breaks away and takes my hand. Squeezes it with each word.

"I. Love. You."

The next evening, I'm in the middle of the living room when Jamie knocks on the door and Mom lets him in. The instant he sees me, his jaw drops. He stands there—in a black suit and with his hair slicked back—and doesn't move. It feels as if we are in the zone together again, except with my mother dabbing away bittersweet tears. Jamie doesn't need to say anything; it's all in his eyes.

I give silent thanks to Mrs. Edwards and her tailor. My scandalous jumpsuit fits perfectly. The double-sided tape is doing its job. The lipstick is in a side pocket so I can reapply as needed. Grand-Mary's ruby-and-pearl drop earrings have replaced my starter studs. The only instruction I didn't follow was the hairdo. I left it natural so something will be the same when I look in the mirror tonight.

Mom laughs and hugs Jamie when he's still fumbling for words by the time we are heading out. It isn't until we are both in the truck that he manages to speak.

"You look incredible."

Jamie hands me a small present.

Inside is a bracelet of beaded strawberries against a black velvet band backed in black leather. I instantly know it's cousin Eva's bead-work. She varies the shades of red glass beads so that each strawberry looks as if it would actually taste sweet. It is exquisite.

"I know the investigation can change things in a heartbeat, Daunis. But there are things that are certain in the world. The way I feel about you. And what happened last night."

Jamie's fingers tickle against my inner wrist, where blue veins show through my ivory skin as he connects the jewelry clasp. I hold out my arm, marveling at his gift.

I hold on to the memory of last night. The certainty of his touch. And the way my heart opens a sliver to allow trust to enter and take root.

We stroll through the Superior Shores Resort as if it's a parade and each couple is a float. The crowd cheers along the entire length from the hotel entrance to the grand ballroom.

Levi and his date are ahead of Jamie and me. Stormy and his date follow us, with Mike and Macy behind them.

People ooh and aah over the kaleidoscope of dresses. Macy's strapless ball gown, an explosion of rhinestones, is a crowd favorite, a showstopper. People gawk at my jaw-dropper—their mouths gaping like trout on a dock. I just laugh and wave with the hand that isn't holding tight to Jamie's.

Auntie and the twins shout for us, so all four couples break away from the parade. As Jamie and I walk over, we come up to a slow-moving couple in our way. Jamie squeezes my hand twice and leads me around the obstacle.

"Well, I know three squeezes means 'I love you.' And I'm guessing two squeezes means to speed up?" I ask.

He squeezes once and halts. I laugh when he pulls me back to kiss me. Then he gives a double squeeze and continues on.

We pose for pictures on the grand staircase leading to the second-floor conference level. The vibrant floral carpeted steps and polished mahogany banister make for a beautiful backdrop. Teddie directs the photo shoot as if we are on *America's Next Top Model*. I just focus on Perry's and Pauline's excited faces.

Finally, Auntie says, "Last one, I promise. Daunis and all the guys."

The twins grab Jamie's hands, so he begs out of the picture to twirl them like ballerinas.

"C'mon, Bubble," Levi says.

My brother is on top of the world, standing a few steps up on the staircase and surveying the crowd below. His family, friends, team, town. He beams.

"Pose like a superhero, Auntie Daunis!" Perry shouts.

"Yeah!" Jamie says, lifting Pauline as if she is the prima ballerina in *Swan Lake*.

Putting my hands on my hips and trying not to laugh, I stare into the camera. Levi, Stormy, and Mike pretend to cower at my feet. Once again, Jamie looks at me with something that mixes awe and reverence.

When everyone is seated in the ballroom, the festivities begin. Call-me-Grant welcomes everyone to Shagala 2004. Chief Manitou gives a blessing in the language. Macy trills a lee-lee for her dad.

Coach Alberts introduces my brother and praises his leadership as team captain, then calls Levi to the stage to give the keynote address. He pauses to hug me on the way.

"I am so proud of you," I whisper. "Me and Dad. I know he's here too."

As Levi walks past them, people comment how handsome he looks in his tuxedo. Everyone smiles as the hockey god steps to the podium. He begins by apologizing to his ancestors if he says any of our Ojibwe words incorrectly. He introduces himself in Anishinaabemowin, then translates what he said. When Levi continues with his speech, I raise my eyebrow. The voice I hear is not his normal one.

My brother speaks with exaggerated inflections and dramatic pauses. The more Levi talks, the more I hear him doing that forced *I am but a humble Indian* routine. A nearby Zhaaganaash lady wipes tears from her eyes because she is so touched by my brother's words, his story about what hockey means in his life. When he mentions being a hope for his people, I actually wince. The only thing missing is mystical flute music in the background and an eagle landing on his shoulder.

Levi sounds like a few cultural leaders who make a big show about being capital *T* Traditional. They're quick to judge others, but bristle and turn mean when anyone points out their own shortcomings.

My brother finishes, and the audience roars their admiration. He shakes hands with people and high-fives the other Supes as he returns to his seat.

Levi grins at me. "So, how'd I do?"

"Um . . . It was kinda . . . fake. Like you were performing for the Zhaaganaash."

Levi laughs, as if my stunned reaction was his entertainment for the evening. "Just giving the people what they want." He begins eating his salad.

"Holy. Who are you to call out anyone?" Macy laughs across the table. "You got in by one vote."

I flush with anger and embarrassment. Even with the familial paternity test and twenty-six Elder affidavits and all the other paper-work, it still wasn't good enough for some council members. They still let me know that, to them, I will always be on the outside looking in.

Macy's superpowers are snarky insults and teasing comments with just enough truth to sting. Some Nish kwewag have the ability to convey that they aren't laughing with you; they are very much laughing at you. It bugs me to no end when Macy Manitou scores a direct punch.

My brother waves his white napkin cease-fire.

"C'mon now, Mace. That's what siblings do." He smiles warmly at me. "They tell the truth. Dauny's just keeping it real. Besides, it's time for her birthday present."

Levi sets a wrapped shoebox on the table.

My heart races. He must have found the scarf.

Opening the gift, I remove layers of white tissue paper to reveal . . . not a scarf. It's a man's choker, with beads carved from bone, solid and timeless.

I stare at Levi with an unspoken question. He smiles and nods.

"It's Dad's choker from his regalia. I found it when I was looking for the scarf." Levi looks down at the slice of cake placed before him. "I'm sorry I couldn't find it, but I wanted you to have this."

I can't speak or else I will cry. My dad wore this. He wore it when he danced.

When I hug my brother, he whispers in my ear.

"I left a surprise at your house."

My voice cracks when I tell him, "Chi miigwech."

After dinner, Call-me-Grant and Mrs. Edwards take turns introducing each player and his date. They start with team captain Levi and his date, who head to the dance floor. The players are then announced in chronological order of when they made the team. It takes a while for them to get to the rookie Supes.

"From Rockville, Maryland, Jamie Johnson, and our very own Daunis Fontaine."

There is applause, along with shouts of my name and various nicknames.

I grip Jamie's hand as he leads me to a spot near Levi and his date. He squeezes back three times. My breath quickens and my stomach tumbles in the most pleasurable way. I am not ready to squeeze back, but I am ready to enjoy tonight.

When the music begins, I put my arms around his waist, admiring my beautiful bracelet. We sway to a slow song. Jamie inhales my hair and sighs contentedly. I'm glad I didn't use any styling product that might have covered up the scent of strawberry-scented shampoo.

"Chi miigwech, Ojiishiingwe," I say for his ears only.

He raises an eyebrow.

"Ojiishiingwe. It means 'He has a scar on his face.'"

"Oh-JEE-sheeng-weh," Jamie says slowly. He repeats it until the name flows smoothly. Then he adds, "Miigwech . . . Do you have an Indian name?"

"A Spirit name, yes."

He waits for me to tell him what it is.

I gave away too much of myself to men who didn't deserve me, Auntie has said.

Jamie and I are in a good place right now. We have so much to learn about each other. I don't know his real name. Until I know it—and much, much more—I think that I am comfortable with what I shared today. But not anything else.

"Not yet, Ojiishiingwe," I say. "Once we're on the other side of this. Someday."

"Tomorrow's Sunday," he says.

We both smile.

The next song pulses with energy, bringing a swarm of people to the dance floor. Dancers form two lines, couples facing each other, spaced far enough apart for the couple at the start of the line to dance their way down the aisle. I look across at Jamie as we sidestep our way to the front of the line. I am curious if he will be as good a dancer as I suspect.

Levi is next to me. When it's his turn to dance, he tries to pull me to dance with him.

I yank my hand back and laugh. "Holy. Dance with your date, clueless guy."

He laughs too and joins the girl with the frozen smile who is waiting for him.

Levi shows off vintage moves like the Electric Slide and the Running Man. Granny June was right: My brother is the dancer in the family.

When it's our turn, I meet Jamie at the start of the dance line. "I apologize in advance for my dancing. Be gentle with my shoulder."

"I've got this," he says with a wink.

Jamie twirls me and everyone cheers. He stands behind me, holding my hurt arm close to my side, bent at the elbow and with his hand atop mine at my stomach. He extends the other arm out with a firm grip. He leads me down the dance line. Jamie dances the same way he skates, grace and skill blending effortlessly.

When Levi imitated him in international waters, it was a comic exaggeration of Patrick Swayze. Jamie's moves are as smooth as skate blades, hot off the sharpening machine, slicing through the ice. Every few steps he spins me by my good arm, always protecting my clipped wing. We finish to thunderous applause and hoots.

We looked fantastic. It was all Jamie.

Mike and Macy are up next, his robotic moves contrasted with her slinky belly-dancer gyrations. Her parents follow, and everyone goes wild when Chief Manitou and his wife do a variation of a powwow two-step.

Then TJ dances with Olivia Huang. She graduated the year between TJ and me. He is surprisingly light on his feet for a big guy. He smiles at her as they make their way down the dance line. His forehead is shiny, and sweat trickles from his temples.

I don't feel my insides churning. It's more like, *I used to know that person, and now I don't.*

Jamie and I smile at each other. He motions for us to go back to our table.

"All good?" he says.

"Yes." I plant a kiss on his cheek. "And I'll be even better after I hit the ladies' room."

The line is out the door at the restroom closest to the ballroom, so

I run up the floral staircase to access the restroom by the conference rooms. Halfway up, Ron calls my name.

I wait at the landing for him to catch up.

"We need to talk. Now," he says.

This is not good.

We find an empty meeting room next to a loud private party. I don't want to stand close to him, but we can't have anyone overhear what is going to be an unpleasant conversation.

"What happened yesterday?" He waits for my answer, not rushing to fill the awkward space with additional chatter.

"What do you mean?"

"Cut the crap. Don't answer my question with a question. What happened last night?"

I am not about to snag and brag. It's not any of his—

"And before you tell me it's not any of my business, let me remind you that everything he does is my business."

"You know about the benefit hockey game last night. Well, I hurt my shoulder and Jamie took me to the emergency room so my doctor could make sure I hadn't damaged anything. And now we're here."

"And now you're here. Doing what exactly? I saw you two on the dance floor. What was that?"

I say nothing.

"Did he tell you how he got his scar? His first UC assignment. A drug bust goes bad and someone decides to slice him. If backup hadn't come through, they were going to keep cutting."

Stunned, I try to reconcile what Ron is telling me with the smooth dancer waiting for me downstairs. What else has Jamie been keeping from me?

"Now this assignment," Ron continues. "He's getting emotionally entangled with a CI and it could jeopardize the entire investigation."

"I'm not just some emotional entanglement," I say. "Jamie and I can handle being part of the investigation and having something that's not so neatly defined."

Ron shakes his head. He's frustrated, I think, but what else can he say about it?

"Daunis, you do get that there is no actual Jamie Johnson, right? There is just a rookie officer who will do anything it takes to redeem himself after his first UC assignment went to hell. Including using you."

"What do you mean?"

"Jamie was the one who proposed that he get close to you."

I stare at my reflection in the ladies' room mirror, Ron's words echoing in my ears.

It was Jamie's idea to start something with me? How could that be true and last night be true also?

My BlackBerry chimes and I'm thankful to be pulled out of my trance.

###-###-####: Its TJ. Outside bathrm. Coming in.

I have just enough time to go into the nearest stall as the door opens.

"Daunis?" My name sounds strangely impersonal coming from TJ. I sigh. "What."

He checks the stalls to make sure we are alone. His big feet plant themselves outside my locked stall.

"The guy you're with is no good."

Wow. People do not like Jamie tonight.

"Go back to your date," I say tiredly.

"I will. This isn't jealousy. You moved on; I moved on. It's just that he's bad news."

"How do you know." My voice is a monotone.

TJ is silent for what feels like five minutes. He takes a deep breath and blows it out. "If he's new best buds with your brother, then he's bad news."

That does it. I slam open the door and glare at him.

"How dare you say that? You of all people criticizing anyone."

"I figured we'd get into that eventually," he says. "Look. I dumped you because Levi and his goons threatened me."

I shake my head. "That makes no sense. You were a senior. The biggest guy in school. They were, what, freshmen? Mike was an eighth grader."

"They said they'd find a way to get me."

"Oh, come on. Because we started dating?" I shake my head.

"Because we started having sex."

"That's crazy."

"I told Levi to piss off. He got mad I wasn't afraid of him. Scary mad. Said he'd find people to hold me down so he could slash my Achilles tendon and end football for me."

You so much as look at her and I will end hockey for you.

My head begins to swim. I push past TJ and walk unsteadily to the sink. The bathroom has a basket of cotton washcloths instead of paper towels. I dampen one with cold water and wipe my face.

TJ continues. "I went to Tribal Police. The officer said good luck getting anyone to believe me against Golden Boy."

He tries to lock eyes with my reflection in the mirror.

"I am many things," he says. "The worst was being a coward for breaking up with you without a word. But I'm not a liar."

I look in every corner of the mirror, never finding his face. "You're wrong, TJ."

"I'm not wrong about your brother. I feel a responsibility to make sure you know who you're with and what your brother is capable of. Just thought you deserved to know—that you'd want to know." TJ shakes his head. "Turns out the person I was wrong about is . . . you."

Returning to the ballroom, I catch my breath next to a speaker blasting dance music. Grateful for thumping bass beats pushing all bathroom revelations from my throbbing brain.

The song ends as someone sidles next to me. "Ahh. Daunis Fontaine."

Gramma Pearl always said that bad things happen in threes.

I brace myself.

"That was a nasty hit on the ice yesterday," Call-me-Grant says. "How's your shoulder doing today?"

"Much better," I say.

"Oh, that's great." He sounds overly relieved. "Let me know if you need anything for it."

"Thanks. I'm good." I keep my face a polite mask.

"Wonderful." His voice is now a purr. "I have an interesting video. Come up to my room. I'll tell you all about it."

I'm about to tell his old pervy ass to go snag himself when he continues, "A security video from my home office."

My blood turns to ice as Call-me-Grant's grin stretches wider. "What a curious cat you are, Daunis Fontaine."

CHAPTER 41

I glance over my shoulder on the walk to the hotel. Call-me-Grant is ten steps behind, greeting someone. My legs tremble. I'm an ant on a sidewalk; his laser focus is the magnifying glass.

Think of a plausible explanation, Daunis. You're a smooth liar in your own right. Calling out every guy who's ever lied to you, but never holding a mirror to yourself.

Call-me-Grant takes the lead as the conference center connects to the hotel. I follow when he detours down a smaller hallway. Another turn reveals a service elevator. I feel my insides twist as I realize we're bypassing the main elevators because Call-me-Grant doesn't want us to be seen together.

He presses the call button and the door slides open. As he motions for me to enter first, his smile is pleasant. Normal. The one he uses with the other parents.

I release my held breath and stride forward on steady legs.

You got this. He likes talking. Let him tell you what he knows. If there's any hint he knows about the undercover investigation, you need to alert Ron and Jamie.

Jamie. He never mentioned the fake relationship was his idea from the start.

Can you trust me?

The spot warms where his soft lips kissed my bare, injured shoulder in the hospital. A memory tattoo. Last night, being with him.

Ding.

The elevator opens on the top floor. When did it shut?

Forget about Jamie. Focus. Be like Gaagaagi, the problem-solving raven.

An idea sparks as I walk toward the Ogimaa Suite, where the Edwards family hosts their annual Shagala after-party. It gains strength with each step. Because it's rooted in truth.

You were in his home office to take pictures because it was a chance to be around Grandpa Lorenzo's furniture. Mom found refuge from Grand-Mary's boutique in her father's office upstairs. Where he hid treasures in the shelves—books for her, Uncle David, and you.

Maybe he will let you buy back the furniture for her. Because when someone you love dies, you find comfort in things connected to your memories of them.

Entering the room, I blink my surprise. It isn't a suite. Just an ordinary hotel room.

"Why—"

I land face-first on the bed. Question still in my throat.

Grant. He shoved me. I feel the weight of someone pressing down on me, but this time it's not Jamie. There are no firecrackers.

This can't be happening.

"Why so curious about me, Daunis Fontaine?" His breath is hot on my neck. "I'll tell you anything you want to know. Just ask real nice."

My arms and legs flail as I reach around, trying to grab or scratch him. Unable to kick behind me. I scream in frustration, but the sound is muffled by the bedspread.

"You hockey girls are my weakness."

Hockey girls. Did he mess with Robin? Is he the man she was talking about?

I channel my white-hot anger and fight harder. Try to dig in my elbows and knees so I can flip over, but I can't get any leverage beneath Grant's wrestler's pin. "All that vigor and skill. Grit and curves," he says.

His hand finds the zipper at my lower back. I freeze. His hands keep going.

It's not supposed to happen to me.

The bedding smells clean. Like a fresh sachet. Lavender.

An instant later, I watch from high above. What he does to her.

Alone in the elevator, I catch my reflection in its mirrored walls. The girl in the mirror takes shallow breaths. She combs her tangled hair with shaking fingers. She blinks repeatedly.

Blink.

Blink.

Blink.

Ding.

By the time the door slides open, her hair is no longer a tangled squirrel's nest.

See? Nothing happened.

I return to the ballroom, music growing louder. Jamie sits at the table, along with Stormy and his bored date. Shagala is in full swing.

"Holy," Stormy says. "Didn't think you were one of them girls who takes forever in a bathroom."

Ignoring Stormy, I shine my widest smile on my date. "Let's dance."

We are so unevenly paired. Jamie is all smooth moves. Baryshnikov and Denzel in a black suit and polished dress boots. Jamie Johnson, dancer and actor.

Don't think about it, Daunis. Nothing happened. Just dance.

So I dance.

There's an awkward pause when the song ends and the DJ cues the next one. The instant a drumbeat thunders from the speakers, the ballroom fills with cheers and lee-lees.

I giggle at Jamie's wide-eyed reaction to the pandemonium. Every Nish rushes to the dance floor for an honor song. Most Zhaaganaash flee; a few look scared. I laugh even harder.

Hands on hips, I stand in place and bounce on the balls of my feet to the drumbeats. It's the closest I can get to dancing while still honoring my grief.

Jamie stands off to the side, watching my favorite part of Shagala as if he has never seen anything so magnificent.

Stormy dances next to me. I always forget he's a wolf dancer like his dad. Their regalia includes a wolf's head and hide worn like a hooded cape. He hunches forward with arms bent at elbows as if holding a feather fan in one hand and his tomahawk in the other. Jerking his head from side to side, Stormy raises his tomahawk fist in the direction of the nearest round table. A Zhaaganaash man at the table does a double take before mimicking the movement to his friends and adding a war whoop.

The people at the table don't see that Stormy's dance honors Ma'iingan. Wolf is part of Bear Clan. We are protectors and healers.

I reach into my pocket for Levi's gift just before the four distinctive honor beats in the song. When they come, I raise my dad's choker to give thanks. I use my left hand, holding the gift as high as I can. The pain stabs my shoulder. When I lower my arm, the spasm reverberates through my entire body.

Levi makes his way over to me. His hip-hop dance moves synchronize to the drumbeats. When our eyes meet, I kiss the choker and raise it once more to Creator. My brother's smile radiates brighter than ever before.

I'm the luckiest kwe to have such a great brother.

After another fast song, the DJ gives us a breather. Acoustic guitar strumming slowly. Keith Urban singing about making memories.

Jamie kisses my shoulder. I jerk back.

"Is it still tender?" Beautiful tawny eyes full of concern.

"No, it's not that . . ." I look away. Retrieving the choker from my pocket, I hold it out to Jamie. "Would you help me put it on?"

He lifts my hair, letting it cascade over one shoulder. My hands press the straps of my top, so he won't attempt another kiss there. His fingers brush the nape of my neck as he joins the leather ties, and I force myself not to flinch away.

We sway wordlessly, my head on Jamie's shoulder. He won't see me blinking Call-me-Grant away.

It works.

I'm six. A happy little kwezan, wearing the dress GrandMary picked for me. My dad lifts me so my feet can be on top of his shoes and our steps will be the same. I look up in alarm, remembering that his legs hurt even more when it's rainy like tonight. He smiles. Full of love.

Gizaagi'in, N'Daunis.

I tell Jamie I'm ready to go home.

"You sure? Levi said something about an after-party."

"No," I snap, before catching myself. "Sorry, I'm just tired. Day caught up with me is all."

We leave hand in hand. He squeezes three times.

We pass Macy exiting the ladies' room, looking beautiful and flushed from dancing all night. Letting go of Jamie, I rush to Macy and push her back inside. She knocks my hands away.

"What the hell are you doing?" she yelps.

I growl into her ear. "Don't *ever* be alone with Grant Edwards."

Jamie and I continue walking in silence; our words are to others. I tip and thank the coat-check lady who hands over my mother's wool shawl. He does the same to the valet with his truck. It's only after we leave the Superior Shores Resort that Jamie speaks to me.

"What was that back there with Macy?"

"Nothing." My shawl hides how tightly I'm hugging myself.

"Well, it looked like you were gonna fight her or kiss her," he says lightly.

I shrug my one good shoulder. "Just needed to tell her something that couldn't wait."

"Is everything okay, Daunis? You seemed so happy on the dance floor." He looks over. "But it's like seeing Macy set you off."

"Jamie, I told you it's been a long day." My exhaustion is no act.

He follows the river back through town. I focus on a freighter entering the Soo Locks.

You hockey girls are my weakness.

An aftershock ripples the length of my spine.

Grant Edwards messed with Robin. Robin was addicted to painkillers but died from a meth overdose.

Mr. Bailey's broken voice. *We were trying to get her into rehab, not college.*

Grant Edwards's remark about my shoulder injury. *Let me know if you need something for it.*

Jamie's route home cuts through campus.

You're supposed to tell us stuff instead of waiting to be asked, Jamie scolded.

"Park behind the student union," I say before I can change my mind. "I want to talk."

Jamie gives me a look, but drives through the empty lot to its edge overlooking the International Bridge. If he floored it, his truck could baja the curb and go airborne.

Can you trust me?

Oh, how I wanted to, Ojiishiingwe.

I play out how it will go.

ME: Grant Edwards might be involved with the meth cell. For sure he had something to do with Robin's addiction to painkillers.

JAMIE: How do you know?

ME: He asked about my injured shoulder today. He said he could help if I needed anything for it.

JAMIE: That's not enough evidence.

ME: Well, how's this for evidence. Grant Edwards sexually assaulted me tonight in his hotel room. He held me down and, when he was done, squeezed my bad shoulder. Said he could make the pain go away. When I didn't respond, he laughed and said I'd be back for more . . . just like Robin. Is that enough for the FBI to go after him?

JAMIE: What possessed you go to a hotel room with Mike's dad? How could you make such a stupid mistake? You're supposed to be so intelligent, but all I see is a shit-ton of book smarts and not one ounce of common sense. Why didn't you scream for help? And how in the hell could you just go limp like that?

Odd how Jamie's scolding voice sounds exactly like mine.

We walk toward the ledge. I halt, shaking and dizzy, while my bravery tumbles down the hill. Away from me.

I can't tell Jamie.

Ron's FBI-agent confessional replays. *Daunis, you do get that there is no actual Jamie Johnson, right?*

I turn to him. "What's your real name?"

Startled, Jamie collects himself before answering. "I really want to tell you. But I won't."

He stares at the International Bridge for a long time. Probably buying time counting the lights of the double arches on the U.S. side.

"Daunis, if something goes wrong in this investigation, it's safer for you to know as little about me as possible. Once we find out who's running the drug ring, if they thought you had information of use to them . . . you'd be in danger. Telling you could get you hurt."

I'm the one who's dumbfounded now. Staring at him as cold fury courses through my veins. When I speak, my voice is ice.

"Because confidential informants risk getting injured. Or killed. Right?"

"Daunis, what's going on?"

"When you joined the investigation, you read all the materials. Got up to speed, hey?"

"Yeah . . . ," he says cautiously. Aware of a conversation land mine somewhere nearby.

"So you knew that a CI, my uncle, had died under suspicious circumstances." I take his grim expression as affirmation. "And you researched me. Learned about my science-fair project. Knew I had one parent who was Native and one who was white. Something we could bond over."

Jamie takes a step toward me, reaching out to embrace me.

I hold up my hand to keep him at bay. "Who had the idea for an undercover cop to get close to me? Whose idea was it to recruit the grieving local girl as the next CI?"

Surprise and guilt wash over Jamie. I wait for him to pinch the bridge of his nose, but he only stares at me. I make it a contest. He blinks first.

"What you need to understand . . . ," he begins, stepping closer.

My fist connects with his face. The crack of his nose and Stormy's goon advice from long ago register simultaneously. *Aim beyond his head. The power's all in the follow-through.*

"What the hell!" he shouts, hands rising to protect his nose after the fact.

That's my girl! My dad's deep voice is as clear and strong as if he were beside me. Pride eclipses my anger momentarily. Levi Joseph Firekeeper Sr. was more than a hockey god; he was the fiercest goon on either side of the International Bridge.

A car barrels through the parking lot. Headlights capture us in its high beams.

"That's for coming up with the idea in the first place!" I yell.

Rushing toward him, I raise my fist again. "And for going through with it, knowing I could get hurt. Even after you met me."

I swing and miss as he moves just beyond my reach.

With nothing to break my momentum, I stumble and land face-first on the ground. Instead of smelling grass, it's lavender that fills my nose. Terrified, I roll onto my back. My arms and legs swing at air. All the punches and kicks I couldn't deliver earlier.

Ron bolts from the car. In an instant, he's crouched by my side.

"Are you okay?" He helps me up.

My lungs hurt from huge gulps of crisp October air.

Ron looks over to Jamie. "What the hell's going on?"

Jamie freezes, aghast.

"Ron, something's hap—" Jamie begins in alarm.

"You're done," Ron interrupts. "I'll get you removed from this case. You'll be lucky if anyone lets you write parking tickets."

Jamie must not have heard his partner basically fire him, because he's still eyeballing me.

"What happened to you, Daunis?" His voice cracks.

I really want to tell you . . . but I won't.

Ron walks me to his car. Opens the passenger door.

I glance over my shoulder. Jamie stands ten feet away. Arms at his sides. Bloody nose dripping onto his white shirt. Still waiting for my answer.

I give it.

"What happened to me, Jamie? You did."

CHAPTER 42

Ron assumes I'm shaking from the temperature. He grabs a blanket from the trunk and wraps it around me like a burrito. He eases me into the car before clicking my seat belt.

We speed away.

"I'll drive wherever you want to go," he says. "Home? Sugar Island? June Chippeway's?"

"Home," I say without hesitation. For once, I don't want to be anywhere else.

"If you're able to tell me, I'd like to know what happened between you and Jamie tonight," Ron says, turning in to my driveway. Mom left the entry light on.

I remain seated. Sitting with him as the car idles. It feels familiar. Comforting, even. Like when Coach Bobby drove me home after away games. I half expect my mother to check on us.

Why am I upset with Jamie, but not with senior agent Ron, for putting me in danger? A hypothetical that became very real tonight?

Ron's focus has always been on the investigation. He's kind to me. I'm a helpful CI. But when this investigation is over, Ron Johnson will get up the following day and open the next case file. His professional compass always points north; at the first sign of an issue, he'll recalibrate to stay focused on the mission.

Jamie made me feel like I might be more important to him than the job.

There's a story about Original Man, who was given the name Anishinaabe. He was on a journey to find his parents and twin brother but became distracted by a beautiful song in the east.

Maybe that's what Ron observed. The reason why Jamie might not be cut out for undercover work. Jamie isn't good at recalibrating.

"I confronted Jamie about the fake relationship being his idea from the start and . . . may have broken his nose. My second punch missed completely, and that's when you showed up." I add for clarification, "It was a one-sided fight."

Ron takes a minute to gather his thoughts.

"He's had two undercover assignments. First one leaves him with a scar. Now a broken nose. His face is literally a road map of bad decisions." With a slow shaking of his head, he adds, "That guy better make a career change before he ends up looking like Quasimodo."

I surprise myself by laughing, then snort while attempting to rein it in. Ron joins in and I lose it completely. Our belly laughs fill the car as I wipe tears from my eyes.

Finally, I say good night. Ron waits until I unlock the front door and wave to him before he backs out of the driveway. I brace myself for Mom wanting a Shagala recap, but the house is quiet. She left a note next to the key dish.

I'm sleeping at the big house tonight.
Hope you and Jamie had a nice night.
See you tomorrow after mass. Love you—Mom

She hasn't stayed overnight at the big house since GrandMary's stroke. Why tonight? Unless . . . Mom was giving me privacy? Did she think I'd invite Jamie inside?

Maybe Mom—who had to sneak around with my dad—wants to be supportive in a way her parents never were.

I get ready for bed and lie under my comforter, exhausted but unable to settle myself. Instead of reciting the periodic table of elements, I reach for the choker still around my neck.

My fingers touch each bead as if it were GrandMary's rosary. Instead of a Hail Mary or Our Father, I say my Spirit name. The name that begins my prayers to Creator. The name I will only reveal to someone worthy of me.

The strange day leaves me before I reach the end of the choker.

Travis stares at Lily on the ground before turning to me.

"They're so mad at me," he whispers. "The Little People. I just wanted her to love me again. She's the only person who ever loved me. Believed me when everyone else ditched me. If only she just tried it, Dauny. But she wouldn't. I added it to my cookies. She didn't want those either. This was the only way."

He raises the gun to his temple.

My eyes squeeze shut, to make this all go away. The words he is saying now.

"The whole town wrote me off when I said I shot that BB gun. Glass nicked that lady's eye. Damaged her cornea. One more person sacrificed to the hockey god. Levi swore he'd be so grateful if I said it was me. He was the only freshman hockey player to make the varsity team. Everyone loved him. On the ice. Off the ice. On the rez. In town. Levi was supposed to be the best of us. I said okay. I told Coach Bobby it was me. Lily

believed me when I told her the truth. She just couldn't hurt you with it.
She's the best. Don't you see? I had to take her with me."

I open my eyes in time to see his head snap sideways.

One hand touches my choker while the other muffles my sobs. I stay like that until Zaagaasikwe dutifully lifts the sun to begin another day.

When sunlight fills my bedroom, my eyes are drawn to the red outfit draped over the desk chair. I never want to see it again. Instead, I focus on the gift-wrapped box on the desk. Green metallic gift wrap. Silver ribbon and bow atop the shoebox-sized present.

I left a surprise at your house.

Levi's whisper brings back the incandescent glow on his face as I kissed Dad's choker and raised it during the honor beats.

My fingers flutter at my neck. Each bead is a memory from last night. Jamie. Grant Edwards. TJ. Stormy. Macy. Ron. And . . . Travis.

Levi was supposed to be the best of us.

I bring the gift back to bed, where I unwrap the shiny package.

It's a framed picture of Levi, Dad, and me. As I pore over it, I feel the stretch of my wide smile. My brother and I each sit on a knee. Dad has an arm around each of us. Levi and I are four years old. My smile is a copy of Dad's. Levi's face is his mother's but the laughter in our eyes is the same.

Levi swore he'd be so grateful if I said it was me. Everyone loved him. On the ice. Off the ice.

I love my brother. But what if he is less than who I thought he was?

I dress in my running clothes—leggings and layers of shirts beneath a hoodie.

My morning prayer begins with my Spirit name, my clan, and where I am from. Which of the Seven Grandfathers should I include?

What if I ask for something I shouldn't? I could be a bird asking

Creator for love, only to be so enamored of my new mate that I fly into a clean window and break my neck.

Everything has strings attached. Unintended consequences. The shove from behind that you never saw coming.

Flakes of semaa flutter from my trembling hand.

My prayer ends with a confession: *I'm scared.*

I run as if chased by something menacing. Hot breath at the nape of my neck.

It isn't until I reach the wooded lot that I take in my surroundings. Sugar Island across the river. The grass still flattened from the Jeep tires.

Two days ago, I was happy. Kissing Jamie. Sharing myself with him.

It seems a lifetime ago.

Yesterday, my brother was on top of the world. Team captain. Hockey god. The prince of Shagala. The pride of Sault Ste. Marie and Sugar Island. TJ called him Golden Boy.

What if the terrible things about Levi are true?

Creator, I can't take any more. I just want to be a clueless girl living in her own bubble.

Retracing my steps, I jog back. My pace slows the closer I get to home. Exhausted and with dread growing inside me.

Mom hasn't returned from Sunday mass yet. A hot bath might ease the tension throughout my body. While waiting for the water to fill the deep soaking tub, I go to my bedroom and stare at my laptop.

It's October 3. The bank lady said monthly statements are sent after the first of the month. Of course, maybe they wait until the following business day, and September's bank statement won't show up till tomorrow.

All I have to do is check for an email from the bank in Canada. If it's not there, I can soak until my fingers are pruney before getting on with the rest of my day.

And if it is there? I want it to confirm Levi's explanation about investing in land near Searchmont. Because, just like with Uncle David, I've allowed a tiny seed of doubt to germinate.

I hold my breath while logging into my email account.

It arrived Friday afternoon. Right after Mrs. Bonasera's email titled *Read this to your mother*. Mrs. B. always sends medical-journal articles pertaining to GrandMary's condition. I'm supposed to translate them for Mom.

I click on the attached bank statement.

The starting and ending balances for September are what the bank lady told me on the phone: $10,856.77. But over the course of the month, my brother deposited $20,000 and then wired it to a bank in Panama.

My heart breaks with a thud.

Levi is the mule.

The water drains from the tub. I don't remember changing my mind about taking a bath.

Levi is the mule.

I stare into the vanity mirror. Questions multiply exponentially in my mind. Grabbing ahold of one question to steady myself, I ask my reflection:

"For how long?"

I halt at the painted brick house with its indigo shutters and the studio apartment over the two-car garage. The driveway is empty. I peek in the garage window. It's empty. Dana Firekeeper always stays at the Superior Shores Resort for the entire Shagala weekend. Levi and Stormy should be at Mike's parent-free house.

The back entrance to the garage is unlocked. I enter, and Waylon growls from behind a door leading to the house. When I call his name, his tone changes from protector to friend. A set of narrow stairs at the farthest garage stall leads to a second entrance to Levi's room. I try the door. Locked. Figured as much.

I stand in the backyard, looking up at the three dormer windows above the garage. My empty stomach somersaults. I shiver from hot skin gone clammy in the crisp October morning.

The spare key is still kept underneath a garden-gnome figurine in the flower bed next to the back entrance. I unlock the door and return the key to its hiding spot.

When I enter the house, Waylon drops a stuffed bear at my feet. I toss his toy, and the German shepherd dashes down the hallway.

Levi's school pictures run the length of the stairwell, beginning with his brand-new senior portrait. My brother becomes younger with each step. Middle school photos show a confident preteen with zero awkwardness. His charming smile never changes, but his face softens during his elementary school years. At the top of the stairs, he is a round, sweet, three-year-old preschooler.

Waylon nudges my hand with his toy. I fling the bear, which lands in front of senior-year Levi. French doors at the top of the stairs open to a small wrought-iron balcony overlooking the wooded backyard. The stair landing leads either to the main house or to the garage apartment. I try the door to Levi's space. Also locked.

I take a deep breath and blow it out in an exaggerated sigh.

A few years ago, I watched my brother break into his bedroom. He had lost his key and Dana hadn't hidden the spare yet. Stormy, Mike, Travis, and I were in the backyard, watching Levi scale the trellises framing the back entrance to reach the balcony. Mike led us in chants of "Spi-der-man" to cheer on Levi as my brother jumped to the garage roof and slid open a dormer window. As with everything, he made it look effortless.

Waylon races up the stairs to join me. I wrestle the slobber-damp bear and throw it back to senior-year Levi. It feels like a race between the dog and me . . . who can reach our goal first?

I turn the handle on one of the French doors and step onto the shallow balcony. I shut the door behind me. My fatigued quads twitch in anticipation and I hear the guys shouting, *Spi-der-man*. I only have time for two deep breaths before I jump the short distance to the garage roof.

I land on all fours, my shoulder screaming in protest. The peak of the roof didn't seem this steep from the ground, or in my memories. The instant I tell myself not to look down, I do and feel an urge to pee myself.

This was stupid. Does it really matter how long Levi's been distributing meth? What more proof do I want?

Waylon barks from the other side of the French doors as if agreeing. I force my breathing to slow down and lie there until my heartbeat matches.

Moving sideways in tiny increments, I reach the nearest window. When I looked up at the windows, each was open slightly to let in fresh air. Dana blasts the heat like a sweat lodge from October through April. She doesn't care how high their heat bills run; Levi will never wake up shivering.

My heart beats double time as I pry the screen from the window. The plan, which I am making up as I go along, is to put the screen back once I'm inside the room. The screen takes more effort, coming loose all at once. I teeter off balance. Dropping the screen, I grip the windowsill.

The screen hits the fieldstone patio below and I register the time it took to reach the ground. If I fall off the roof, it will take approximately two seconds until I splat.

I push the window up until I can fit through the opening. I land clumsily inside while Waylon barks from outside Levi's bedroom door. I stand.

Now what?

I start with the nightstand beside the queen-sized platform bed. Next to the lamp is a large bottle of ultra-moisturizing hand lotion and a box of tissues. Gross. I brace myself. Searching my brother's bedroom means I can't ever un-see stuff.

Moving to Levi's desk and dresser, I go through every drawer in the bedroom. I pull out each one to look underneath and behind for any secret documents.

Levi doesn't have a wall of bookcases like Mike, just a set of bunk beds along one wall. The bedding on the lower bunk is messy. Stormy sleeps there, further confirmed by a half-empty bag of Cheetos within reach on the floor. The top bunk is perfectly made, as if made by someone in boot camp. Mike stays over, though less frequently than Stormy.

I look under each mattress, careful to leave each in its pre-search state. Outside the door, Waylon paws at the door, reminding me he still wants to play.

An enormous plasma screen takes up the wall above a rectangular coffee table with precise stacks of video games next to Levi's PlayStation 2 and Mike's Xbox. Facing the screen are a trio of video-gaming chairs, low to the floor like a cross between bean-bag chairs and children's car seats. A fourth chair is banished to a corner. Travis's chair. But maybe Levi will let Jamie be their fourth.

I slide the closet door open to view half of the contents. Clothing, shoes, and plastic totes filled with hockey gear. I quickly go through each box. Most are filled with hockey tournament program booklets, hockey magazines, and hockey playbook drawings on graph paper: Xs and Os in formations with dotted lines.

This is stupid. What am I doing here?

I am sweating from the heat and understand Levi's need to keep windows open. A glance out the screenless window reveals a squirrel squawking from a nearby tree, also agreeing with my stupidity.

Returning to the closet, I move on to the other side, where my brother keeps his clothes. The shelf above has smaller boxes and a black ash basket. I go in order. There is a shoebox, the same brand as the one Levi wrapped Dad's choker in. Inside are bank statements from our joint account.

He hasn't received the statement from September yet, so I start with August. I check the beginning and ending balances before eyeballing the activity during the month. He wired $10,000 to the same bank in Panama. The month when Lily was killed.

I go through July's statement. Another wire transfer.

And again for June.

And May.

In April, the amount wired was $15,000.

It was $20,000 per month for March, February, and January. In 2003, he wired the same amount for December, November, and October.

Hockey season runs mid-September through mid-April. He wired more money in hockey months. But he was still running money through our account during non-hockey months.

How could he be a meth mule year-round? Is that why he's always using Dana's boat for trips to Mackinac Island in the summer?

There was no unusual activity in September 2003. It was a partial hockey month, but the statement shows nothing but normal purchases at stores at the mall across the river. Same for the summer months before that.

What was so special about October last year? Why did Levi start being a meth-mule then?

The common-sense realization comes far later than it should.

The wire transfers began when Levi became a Supe. But how could a minor authorize wire transfers from a Canadian bank to one in

[388]

Panama? Levi was a junior when he made the team. He wouldn't turn eighteen until January.

Meanwhile, I was a senior. Turned eighteen in October and . . .

My brother was a minor; I wasn't.

I am frozen on the floor next to the shoebox. More than a year of bank statements are laid out around me.

Could Levi have made the wire transfers in my name?

The floor rumbles as the garage door rises. Waylon rushes downstairs, barking.

Someone is home.

CHAPTER 43

I quickly refold the statements as a vehicle enters the garage. It sounds like Dana's Mercedes rather than the behemoth Hummer. I finish just as she enters the house from the garage.

Waylon barks persistently.

"What's going on, big guy?" Dana calls from the bottom of the stairs.

He's ratting me out is what's happening.

Waylon runs upstairs as I finish putting the statements in order in the shoebox.

Squawk.

I jump at the noise. A squirrel shouts at me from the windowsill. I reach for the nearby bag of Cheetos and toss one wrinkled orange stub toward the window. The squirrel is supposed to flee. Instead, it comes further into the room and protests more.

Squawk.

Waylon dashes upstairs. His barks set off the squirrel, which does a frantic lap around the room, too scared to retrace its steps back to the window.

"What the hell is going on?" Dana shouts, running up the stairs.

What if she can unlock the door?

My hands shake so badly that I knock the black ash basket while returning the shoebox to the shelf. It slips through my fingers.

Dana tries the door handle.

When I turn to scoop up the basket, its matching lid is a step away. I pick up the basket by the opening. Something soft brushes against my fingertips.

My heart skips a beat.

I tip the basket upside down. Staring at the floor where Dad's scarf lands.

Green, like my mother's eyes.

Levi kept it from me. He had it all along.

Heart racing, I shove the scarf into my hoodie pouch.

Waylon goes crazy on Dana's side and the squirrel dashes around on my side.

"This is Judge Dana Firekeeper." I think she's talking to me until she says, "I live at 124 Hilltop Court. Someone's in my house. My dog's going crazy and someone's in my son's room."

Dana called 911.

I put the lid on the basket and return it to the shelf. *Please, Waylon, bark louder so it masks the closet door.*

BAM.

Dana kicks at the door while I dash to the other one, leading to the garage.

BAM.

I turn the dead-bolt latch and grasp the doorknob with the push-button lock in its center. Opening the door, I push the button to relock it. I can't do anything about the deadbolt.

BAM.

I reach the top step and close the door behind me.

CRACK!

Dana bursts into Levi's bedroom as I practically ski down the stairs. While I race to the back door of the garage, Dana shrieks at the squirrel running around the room. Waylon loses his damn mind.

I stay close to the garage. Beneath the overhang of the roof, in case Dana looks out the window. Then I tiptoe along the side of the garage. Listening for footsteps chasing me. Eyeballing my target: the street beyond the trees at the end of the driveway.

The barks grow fainter, like Waylon is tearing down the hallway. There's the shattering of something delicate—a crystal vase, maybe—and Dana swearing.

I take my chances and run like hell.

Mom's car is gone, but I still lock myself in the bathroom. My heart thumps like Waabooz after a narrow escape. Something sour churns in my stomach an instant before I violently heave greenish-yellow bile. It leaves me exhausted and hunched over the toilet.

The emptiness inside me is replaced by something far worse.

Nibwaakaawin. Auntie told me the translation, breaking down each part of the word so it made perfect sense: *To be wise is to live with an abundance of sight.*

My whole life I've wanted to be like my aunt. The way a person dreams about being a ballerina, but not of broken toes and years of practice. I wanted to be a strong and wise Nish kwe, never considering how that abundance of sight would be earned.

I wanted to find out who was involved in the meth madness that took Lily and Uncle David. Robin and Heather, too. And the kids in Minnesota who got so sick from meth-X.

The person I was searching for this whole time was Levi.

Wisdom is not bestowed. In its raw state, it is the heartbreak of knowing things you wish you didn't.

Mom comes home while my stomach heaves. I turn on the fan to muffle my retching. Her feet make dark shadows at the bottom gap of the door, next to Herri's paw reaching underneath for invisible prey.

"Are you okay, honey?" Her soft voice is full of concern.

"Yeah. Just ate something bad."

I wait for her to move away from the door. She does, but returns a few moments later.

"I've got some Gatorade for you."

Once she mentions it, my dry throat wants nothing more.

"Can you leave it by the door?" I croak.

Mom can't help with this situation. I try to dry-heave more quietly, so she will leave.

I don't hear her anymore; she must have stepped away. I slide the pocket door. Herri bursts in as soon as there's clearance for her fat body.

"Are you pregnant?" Mom sits with her back against the wall opposite the bathroom door.

I shudder while reaching for the neon yellow drink. "No, um . . . I'm on birth control." Thank God for Norplant.

Mom looks away. I watch for clues to her reaction.

"I'm glad you have Teddie." Mom doesn't seem glad, more like disappointed. "But you have me, too. You . . . you can bring your problems to me instead of keeping secrets." She takes a deep, steadying breath. "If you ever get into a situation . . . I will always help you."

"If I robbed a bank, you'd drive the getaway car?" I say, smiling weakly.

She nods. "I'd make sure you wore a seat belt, too."

I crawl to her. She kisses my forehead. Leaning against her, I rest my head on her shoulder.

The weight of my secrets is exhausting. My whole life has been filled with them. Even as a zygote, I floated in an embryonic sac of secrecy.

If I tell Mom one secret, will I vomit the rest of my secrets all over her? And which one would I open with? Do I start with the earliest one and work forward? Or last in, first out? Uncle David would have me tackle the highest priority first, and list all the rest in descending order.

I decide to begin with the secret that provides the foundation for all the rest.

"It's hard to tell you things because I don't want you to worry or to let you down. I've already caused you so much pain."

"Pain?" Her surprise is genuine. "Daunis, you're the greatest joy of my life."

"But . . . I'm the reason your life is stuck in limbo now. If I hadn't been born, maybe everything could've been different for you and Dad."

Then I say the worst thing I've ever heard about myself. "I was the first of all the bad things for both of you."

She looks at me in astonishment, until an epiphany flickers in her eyes. It lights up her face.

"Children are never to blame for their parents' lives. Parents are the adults; we are the ones responsible for our choices and how we handle things." She sits taller at the revelation. "If I'm in limbo, it's because I chose to remain there. Even inaction is a powerful choice."

Mom rises with an abundance of sight. Holds out her hand for me. I take it. She lifts me into a tight embrace that flows through me. Continues through the Earth's crust and mantle, making its way to the solid inner core.

"My life. My choices," she says. "Not yours."

My second attempt at a bath goes better. Mom runs the bathwater for me and adds her favorite bubble bath. When my thoughts go to Levi and what I need to do next, I turn on the bath jets and disappear beneath a mountain of lilac-scented bubbles.

An hour later, I zip my black jeans with pruney fingers. The sports bra I grab is also black and has wide straps to cover the purple bruise branding my shoulder. To hide the evidence. As I pull on a black Henley, there's one moment when my raised arms are immobile. And I feel his words on the back of my neck.

The hallway cameras recorded you coming here willingly.

Will it be like this from now on? Flashbacks? A scent? Remembering things he said that I hoped to forget? A bite-shaped bruise I'll still see long after it fades?

I wish I'd never agreed to be a CI.

"Daunis, honey. I just remembered—Levi stopped by yesterday on his way to Shagala. So handsome in his tuxedo." Mom's voice travels down the hallway ahead of her footsteps. "You haven't said a word about last night. How was everything?" I quickly check my appearance in the full-length mirror next to my bedroom door.

"It was fine," I say. *Fine. Fine. Fine.*

Mom continues from the doorway. "Just fine? Did you and Jamie have a fight?" Her brow furrows.

"Something like that," I say.

"Do you want to talk about it?"

"I'm good, Mom." I smile so the crease at the top of her nose will smooth out. It does. She looks around my bedroom, zeroing in on the unwrapped gift.

"What did Levi give you?"

I reach for the framed photo already on my nightstand. Turn it toward her. Mom's first smile is for the overall image. Her second is for my father. After twenty years, she remains besotted with him. I'm torn between seeing her devotion as a triumph or as an anchor weighing her down. Can it be both? I don't see how.

Reluctantly, she tears her gaze away from him. "Didn't Levi give you another present?" she asks. I look around.

"I think this is it," I say.

"But he walked in with two boxes, one gift wrapped and one plain. He said he'd leave them in your room."

I shrug, feeling my sore left shoulder. I must be imagining it, but I can almost feel the clenching of his fingers.

Mom tells me it's time for her to head to EverCare. Do I need anything before she leaves?

I want answers.

No. I don't. Curiosity killed the cat. Doubt tore her into pieces.

Mom leaves. As soon as the front door closes, I look for Levi's second box. My brother gave me the choker at Shagala last night and the framed photo for me to find today. Where is the other gift?

It feels like déjà vu from searching Levi's bedroom earlier today. I check beneath my mattress, under my bed, each desk drawer and dresser drawer, every bookcase shelf. I pause to ask myself, aloud, if I am losing my mind. I get no response. I continue to the closet. Top shelf. Second shelf. Boxes of shoes. My Fuck-You pumps. I slide hangers of outfits GrandMary hoped I'd wear. The bottom of my closet has a laundry hamper and my hockey gear duffel bag. My stinky uniform will rot if I don't wash it. I pick up my bag to drag it into the sunlight.

There is a cardboard box beneath the gear bag. Is this what my mom saw?

Why would Levi hide a birthday gift for me?

I forget about my smelly undershirt, clingy shorts, team uniform, and socks.

When I open the box, it's filled with plain hockey pucks. I don't understand why this would be a gift for me. I claw my way to the middle of the box, grab a random puck, and raise it like buried treasure.

It's a smeared dream catcher hockey puck. The same kind from the weekend in Green Bay.

Things That Make Me Angry About the Damn Puck:

1. Dream catchers . . . seriously.
2. Substandard printing of said dream catchers on pucks going to Nish kids.
3. Donated by Grant Edwards, Coach Bobby said.
4. The pucks aren't even regulation weight.

I only realize the last item on the list when the puck is in my hand. It's slightly lighter; most people would never notice. But as someone who played for years—and slept with a puck under her pillow the night before every game—I can tell.

My thumb slides along the bottom of the puck, feeling a hairline crack. Yet another complaint for my list. Eyeballing the bottom of the puck, I see that the crack runs just inside the perimeter. Not a crack. The puck has a lid. I use the rubbery underside of my mouse pad to hold the bottom of the puck in place while I twist the lid.

A folded paper towel nests in the partly hollow middle. I peel back its corners to reveal the hidden treasure that has devastated my community and countless others.

The crystals resemble uncut, raw diamonds. Cloudy, lesser-quality specimens. Made haphazardly, without regard for precise protocols. My meth was so much better. Even Jamie's would score a higher price than this crap.

The hidden treasure is the answer to a question I hadn't thought to ask until now:

How does Levi, the mule, distribute meth to other communities? The question I don't want to ask myself: Why would my brother leave a box of these hockey pucks in my bedroom?

Mathematics, like science, has a language. Although I'm not passionate about math the way I am about science, I am functionally fluent in its numbers, letters, notations, symbols, and jargon.

Scientists and mathematicians approach problems differently. Scientists collect data in order to disprove a null hypothesis—the absence of a difference or relationship. In contrast, mathematicians seek to prove a theory, rather than disprove it. A proof is a set of conditional statements that build logically to a conclusion, thereby turning a theory into a theorem. A deep theorem is a proof that is particularly lengthy or complex, or includes unexpected connections.

Right now, I need both approaches to work through this. I sit on my bed with Dad's scarf draped over my shoulders, the paper towel of crystal meth in one hand and his choker in the other. A fierce battle is being waged in my head.

The Null Hypothesis that Levi Firekeeper Has
Nothing to Do with the Meth Devastation
versus
Daunis Fontaine's Deep Theorem of Her Brother's
Involvement in All the Bad Things

If the FBI is investigating meth activity aligning with the Supes team schedule, then people of interest include players, players' families, coaching staff, and fans.

If Uncle David hid his notebook where only I could find it and wrote in a code he knew I could decipher, then he clearly wanted me to know that the new mushroom he found was not connected to meth-X and did not cause the group hallucination.

If the Nish kids weren't having a mushroom-induced group hallucination, then what they saw was a shared encounter with Anishinaabeg spirit beings.

If my uncle chose not to reveal the dead-end information with the FBI, then he intended for them to continue on a wild goose chase.

If Uncle David went missing after sharing his concerns about Light Bulb—the bright student involved in meth—with Light Bulb's mom, then the parent—Angie Flint—needs to be questioned about my uncle's suspicious death.

If the fake pucks were how meth was being distributed, then the person donating the pucks—Grant Edwards—is involved.

If bank statements showing foreign wire transfers were found in the team captain's bedroom, then that player—Levi Firekeeper—is part of the meth operations and laundering his share of the profits.

If the wire transfers were made in *my name* to an offshore account and the pucks were planted in my closet, then that player—my brother—is setting me up.

If Levi has been setting me up, then he is part of the meth cell, and he is connected to the devastation meth has caused in our community and everywhere else it has been distributed.

If Levi has been weaving this web around me, tighter and tighter, then what will he do next?

My BlackBerry buzzes with an incoming text at the same time as I hear urgent knocking at the front door. I react like a guilty person, hiding the scarf inside the pumpkin dress at the back of my closet. The puck fits in the dress pocket.

I grab my phone while rushing to the front door.

Ron: Have you heard from Jamie since last night?

My first thought: *Hell no!*
My second: *That must be Ron at the door.*
My third: *Why would Ron be texting and knocking at the same time?*
At the door is the last person I expect to see.
Dana.
Fear grips me. Did she see me running away from her garage?
She's shaking and crying. Not angry. She's scared.
"Can you help me?" she pleads. "It's Levi. I think he's in trouble."

CHAPTER 44

A frantic Dana rushes inside before I can react. She's hyperventilating so badly that I automatically usher her to the nearest chair in the dining room.

Brown paper bags—Mom keeps some in the pantry for student treat bags.

I'm back in a flash with one. Guiding Dana to bend over and breathe into it.

"Um . . . when you hyperventilate, your body expels carbon dioxide too quickly," I say. "Recycling your breath restores the correct balance of oxygen and carbon dioxide."

She coughs a laugh into the bag.

Embarrassed, I look away from her. "Sorry. I'm rambling."

I bounce on the balls of my feet, anxious for Levi's mom to calm down enough to let me know what the hell's going on.

Dana rubs her throat. Must be dry.

Tea—Mom and both my grandmothers would fix a cup in this situation.

I dash back to the kitchen and fill half a kettle from the tap. After I turn the gas burner to its highest setting, I return with a teacup and basket of assorted tea packets.

"Please," Dana says, looking up from the bag. "You too. I have a lot to tell you."

Can I really turn in my brother to the FBI?

I grab a teacup for myself. When Dana selects chai, I do the same. By the time the teakettle whistles, Dana's breathing has returned to normal. I pour the steaming water into our dainty china teacups and return the kettle to the cooktop. On my way back to the dining table, I bring a carton of milk and the sugar bowl.

My hands shake, along with Dana's. Neither of us can wait for the tea to steep properly. We use milk to cool it down. I sip it and realize Mom must not have rinsed all the dish soap from my cup. I grimace and add sugar to make it drinkable.

Whatever it is that she wants to tell me must be truly awful, because I finish my tea waiting for her to begin.

"Levi is mixed up in something bad," Dana says finally.

"What is it? How bad?" I hope I'm doing a decent job of looking shocked.

"It has to do with that Travis mess. I'm so sorry about your friend Lily."

I blink at the mention of her name, surprised at how fresh the grief still feels.

Dana continues. "Travis was bad news, but my boy is a loyal friend. He'd go to Sugar Island to talk sense into Travis. Even Stormy knew when to cut his losses, but Levi kept trying."

My brother goes to the island often, but I've always thought it was to take Stormy to his house. Stormy doesn't like going alone because he never knows how his parents are doing until he steps inside.

"My boy used to think goodness was stronger than darkness."

Dana taps her teaspoon as if sending an urgent message in Morse code. "But my nokomis always said you can't be around that much darkness without some of it touching you."

Dana thought Levi was spending time with Travis for well-intentioned interventions. When in fact he was the mule for the meth that Travis was making. At what point did Dana catch on?

"The darknesh—I mean, darkness touched him?" I ask.

One corner of her mouth twitches before she nods.

"He used to confide in me. Most boys don't tell their mothers much, but Levi did. Once he made that team, became a Supe, I noticed him shutting me out. Just a little at first."

As Dana continues talking about Levi, her voice sounds far away. Like it's coming from the end of the hallway instead of across the table. I concentrate on her words.

"I tried talking him out of getting the Hummer. It was too much for a sixteen-year-old boy. He got so angry. I ended up buying it for him. I know I shouldn't have, but I wanted things to go back to the way they were between us."

Levi can be relentless when he wants something. He pestered me to be Stormy's date for Shagala last year when that was the last thing I wanted.

"I went to Shagala with Stormy . . ." I trail off. Unsure what point I was trying to make.

That's odd.

Dana's mouth is moving, but all I hear is Ron's last text. Inside my head. His voice repeating it. Growing more urgent each time.

Have you heard from Jamie since last night?

Have you heard from Jamie since last night?

Have you heard from Jamie since last night?

". . . one of Levi's teachers noticed it too. Came to see me."

Have you heard from Jamie since last night?

"Would you excuse me? I need to text someone," I say, but I'm not sure if the words actually make it out of my mouth.

I push away from the table. My hands touch the rug before I realize that I'm on the floor.

Get up! N'Daunis, bazigonjisen!

Herri boops my nose with her tiny, cold one. I laugh.

Dana coos as if I'm a baby. A wobbly baby deer. She helps me stand. So good to me.

I recognize her perfume. Same as Mom's. Did they smell the same to my dad?

She walks me to the front door. We slowly ease down the steps. Everything spins.

"Whish teascher?" It's important, I think.

Dana sighs wearily. Helps me into an old pickup truck.

"All you Fontaines ever do is mess things up."

Uncle David went to see Light Bulb's mom.

It wasn't Angie Flint.

PART III

· · · · · · · · ·

NINGAABII'AN

(WEST)

**IN THE WESTERN DIRECTION THE JOURNEY FOCUSES ON THE RIPENED
BERRIES AND THE HARVEST, A TIME OF CONSTANT CHANGE.**

CHAPTER 45

I love camping. The smoky scent fills the air and burrows into fabric, hair, and skin.

Hold on. It's camping but mixed with stale air. A closed-up, musty space.

My head throbs with my heartbeats. More smells: musky sweat and a nearby piss pot. I strain to open one eyelid, like breaking the crusty bond of a miniingwe eye.

Thin rectangles of orange light come from a woodstove across a small room. The light flickers, casting faint orange stripes against the walls and curved ribs.

I blink both eyes in slow motion, trying to focus on my surroundings.

It's an old aluminum trailer with a rounded ceiling and only one window. The kind people use as powwow food-vendor trucks. Art calls them canned hams.

I lift my head. Or try to. The trailer spins like a centrifuge.

"Daunis."

I jerk my head at the sound of Jamie's voice. He sounds like he caught a cold, but it's my head that feels foggy. He repeats my name. Each one pulses inside my skull.

"Daunis. Daunis. Daunis."

My groans form a word.

"Sssstop."

"Are you okay? What did they do to you?" Jamie's breath is sour. He tries wrapping me in his arms, but something about being held makes my heart race.

"D-don't." I push him away. "Your breath reeks."

"We're kidnapped. In a trailer somewhere. But my bad breath is what's bothering you?" Even Jamie's soft laughter has a stuffed-up, nasal tone.

Kidnapped. Trailer. I pop up.

"Oww," I say, vision blurring from the fireworks in my head.

Once it clears, I look around the trailer, which is gutted inside. Just a woodstove, a card table, some metal folding chairs, and the squeaky bed I'm in.

"How long have I been here? Why are you here too?"

"The guys came by last night as I parked in my driveway. I thought Levi found out you punched me, and he wanted to kick my ass for whatever I did to deserve it."

The memory of my fist smashing his nose catches up with me. Followed by why I did it.

There is just enough light from the woodstove to see the raccoon-like bruising around Jamie's eyes. Two black eyes from a broken nose.

"I did deserve it, Daunis. Ron shouldn't have been the only one getting you up to speed on that first drive to Marquette. You had a right to know—before you agreed to pose as my girlfriend—that I was the one who had the idea of us posing as a couple. But I swear, that was before I got to know you. When you were just a person in a case file, and I thought taking the initiative might help my career."

It takes more effort than my groggy synapses can handle to fully process his words. Jamie takes my silence as his cue to keep talking.

"Levi dropped by, but he seemed happy, not mad. He invited me to Mike's party and then asked about my nose. I was thinking of an explanation when Mike tasered me. They must've stuck a needle of something in me, because I woke up here this morning." He glances at his watch. "It's just after eight p.m. You've been here six hours."

Wisps of memories come back. Tea. Herri. Dana.

She drugged me with something . . . it must've been that date-rape drug. The name swims through the cloudiness. Rohypnol.

"Did Dana say anything when she brought me here?" My voice shakes as rage breaks through the roofie haze.

"Levi's mom is involved?" Jamie is taken aback. "Daunis, a guy in a snowmobile helmet that covered his face carried you over his shoulder. He dumped you inside the door before tasering me. I couldn't move. That's when he shackled your leg to the bed frame."

Shackled? I move each leg. There's a heavy clanking with my left one.

Dana didn't bring me here? Then . . . who else is part of this?

Jamie's still talking. It takes effort to focus on his story.

". . . removed the Taser barbs and threw a log in the woodstove. Five minutes tops."

Memories form . . . unless I'm creating mental images to fit his story.

What did you do to her? Answer me, you—Jamie's voice from a foggy dream.

"I was on the floor and you swore at someone?"

"Good! You remember," Jamie says. "It was right before he tasered me."

"Was it Grant Edwards?" My eyes dart around the trailer before

I scramble to look under the bed. Upside down, my head feels like someone is using it as a drum.

"I never saw his eyes, but he was the right size, I suppose."

I flinch at Jamie's hand on my arm as I return to a sitting position.

"Hey, you're okay. No one's here, Daunis." There is a seed of disquiet in his voice.

Avoiding Jamie's probing gaze, I focus on the distorted memories coming back to me.

"I was in a truck with Dana. The ferry horn sounded overhead. She laughed when I asked for semaa to make an offering." A shiver runs through me. I meet Jamie's eyes. "My mom will call my aunt; they'll look for me and contact the police. When they try reaching you, Ron will tell them you're missing too, and that he's been looking for you."

"He is? You talked to him? Why isn't he here with backup?" Jamie eyeballs the door, expecting Ron to bust in.

"He texted this afternoon and asked if I had any contact with you since last night."

"That can't be." Jamie looks confused. "Ron should be getting a tracking signal from my watch." He holds up his wrist.

"Really?" I say, impressed that his watch is a James Bond gadget.

"Yeah. Through satellites. My location coordinates are relayed to the FBI."

Satellites. I hold up my hand to silence him.

Assess the problem.

We're trapped inside a trailer on Sugar Island.

The rusty bed frame creaks when I rise. A wave of nausea and more centrifuge pile onto my headache. Jamie is at my side in an instant with steady arms.

He held me like this on the dance floor, leading while protecting my shoulder. It was just last night. How is that possible? A lifetime of bad things have happened since then.

"Thanks." I break away.

The heavy chain is a tether; I get as far as the card table in front of the window.

"Are you—"

"Shhh," I interrupt. "I'm listening."

We stand absolutely still, listening for any sounds beyond the window.

Gentle waves lap a nearby shore.

"What do you hear, Jamie?" Uncle David taught me to avoid leading questions. Otherwise, you steer the responses to what you hope to hear.

"Waves," he confirms. "I've heard them since I woke up."

"What can you tell me about the wave pattern?" It feels good to think like a scientist.

"They're just small waves, Daunis."

"If we're on the west shore, any freighters passing by will generate a . . ." My mind goes blank on what it's called when those ripples hit the shore. I hate this brain fog.

"A Kelvin wake?" Jamie offers. "Like Friday night at the break-wall?"

"Yes! Like that," I say. "The bigger the ship, the bigger the wake. Did you hear any change in the waves? Depending on freighter traffic, it could take hours for a ship to go past."

"Why does it matter which side . . ." His voice trails off.

I witness the awful moment when the answer gut-punches Jamie.

"Cliffs and caves." His voice is a sinking anchor in the deepest part of Lake Superior. "You said the east side of Sugar Island is all cliffs and caves. You can't get any cell phone signals except near the ferry or the north end. Satellites can't pick up GPS signals through stone, cement, or water."

The despondent look in his eyes leaves me completely rattled. He's a grown adult. Twenty-two years old. A cop.

Yet, somehow, I am the less-terrified person in this trailer. The one who will say out loud what we both need to hear.

"The FBI doesn't know where we are, Jamie. They think you're dead in the water like Heather. Ron's not coming."

CHAPTER 46

In the disheartened silence that follows, we hear voices approaching the trailer.

"... bet you a hundred bucks someone budges this week."

I recognize Mike's voice.

"Players or owners?" Levi asks.

They're talking about the NHL lockout. Goddamn hockey.

Quickly removing his watch, Jamie squats in front of me and grabs my untethered leg.

"It wasn't turned on when they tasered me, but it's been on since I woke up," he whispers, taking off my running shoe and sliding the stretch watchband up to my ankle. "There should be enough of a charge still." My laces are loose enough for him to slip my shoe back on my foot. "If there's a chance for you to leave with them, you take it." He rises and locks eyes with me. "No matter what, Daunis. Understood?"

I'm too scared to even nod.

A faint light is barely visible through the grimy window as they reach the trailer.

"Doesn't matter," Mike says. "Whoever makes the first offer has the weaker position."

"Nuh-uh." Levi sounds like he's ten years old.

Wood clunks against wood. Someone fumbles with a lock.

Levi comes in first. Never making eye contact, he sets a camp lantern on the table and retrieves the plastic bucket that serves as a piss pot. Levi heads to the door with it, stepping aside when Mike enters with one section of log.

"Hey, lovebirds," Mike says with a toothy smile. "We interrupt anything?"

I expect Stormy to waltz in, making his usual *bow-chicka-wow-wow* noises, but he doesn't. Must be on goon duty, standing guard outside. Figures.

Mike opens the door of the stove and pushes the thick cylinder of wood atop whatever pieces are still going strong.

Levi returns, setting the bucket next to an angled line of dark tape across the floor. A parallel line of tape is several feet away.

Boundary lines marking the reach of the chains. One line for our feet; the other for our grasp. The bucket, table, and window are within the caution zone. Beyond it, the woodstove, the trailer door—and freedom.

Mike takes off his puffer vest and hangs it on a hook by the door. He stands behind the table, leaning casually against the trailer wall with an amused expression.

I stare at Levi, but my brother still won't look at me. Instead, he removes his backpack and pulls out a roll of paper towels before dumping the rest of the contents on the table. Bottled water, sports drinks, and protein bars scatter. My thirst springs to life when a rogue bottle of water rolls off the table to join us by the bed.

Jamie drops the bottle when picking it up. He hands it to me after grabbing a second time. I chug half before offering him the rest. He motions for me to finish it. Cold water sloshes noisily in my empty stomach.

"Your reward for being so nice to Dauny Defense." Mike tosses a water to Jamie, who fumbles that bottle as well. "Good thing you're not playing football."

I grit my teeth. *Let's see how you guys like Dauny Offense.*

"What's going on, Levi?" I demand.

"We need your help," he says, finally meeting my eyes.

Jamie reaches for my hand.

Now is not the time for him to get mushy with a triple squeeze.

He stops at two. His code from Shagala. Two squeezes meant *Keep going.*

"We who?" I say. "You and the guys? Your mom who drugged me? Who all is 'we'?"

Levi shakes his head. "Forget about everyone else. *I* need your help."

"This is how you ask for help?" I shake my leg iron. "Did you buy these shackles at Home Depot or Ace Hardware?"

"We found them in a shack. Figured those Al Capone stories were true."

"So, you're a wannabe gangster?" I repeat my first question. "What's going on, Levi?"

"A business opportunity—"

"A *what?*" I bellow.

Jamie's hand pumps mine once, like a shock. Shagala squeeze code: *Stop.*

I serve it back with more force: *No, you stop.*

"Just hear me out." Levi's Adam's apple bobs with the gulp he takes before continuing. "I tried bringing it up that day at Chi Mukwa. When I punched the asshole who insulted you."

"You did?" My surprise is genuine.

"Yeah. I asked if you were gonna stay in the Sault because you were dating him." He half nods at Jamie. "If me and you could go into business together someday."

The day I asked Levi to look for Dad's scarf. The scarf he later lied about not having.

"What kind of business has you doing this bullshit?" I shake my leg again for the sound effect. "Because I thought you meant, like, buy a house to rent to college students."

The double squeeze from Jamie means I'm back on track.

"Here's the thing . . ." Levi starts his team-captain pep talks this way. "Sometimes I'd wait in the hallway outside your uncle's classroom. Before hockey practice."

"You were out there just lurking in the hall like a creeper?" Levi came by once in a while to mooch snacks for him and the guys, but I always assumed he strolled right in.

Levi shrugs and continues, "He'd ask you about chemicals. What would happen if you mixed this with that? You'd think out loud till you figured out if it was poisonous or what the reaction might be."

Coldness washes over me. He listened to Uncle David and me playing What Would Happen Next?

"I knew you were smart, Daunis," Levi says. "But, hearing how your mind worked, I realized what a genius you really are."

I'm surprised to see his expression filled with admiration. I hate that my first impulse is to bask in his proud smile.

"Watching you two dance around this shit is excruciating," Mike cuts in, moving closer.

Jamie's firm grip pulls me a half step backward. His adrenaline flows through our joined hands to flood my system too.

"Here's the thing." Mike mimics Levi's earlier lead-in. "Two years ago, I'm helping Levi and Stormy write a business plan for Coach

Bobby's class. We're tossing around bullshit ideas, like franchising the Naughty Nickel. And Levi goes, 'Why should big-city drug dealers end up with more per-cap dollars than any tribal member?' He was right: If people are gonna buy the stuff anyway, why not buy local?" He turns to Levi. "You and Stormy turned in a different plan—to put a Tim Hortons in Chi Mukwa, right?"

Something's off, but I can't pinpoint it. The stuff Dana put in my tea . . . it's as if I'm two seconds behind every play on the ice.

"How about you tell the next part, about Travis?" Mike says, grabbing a folding chair to sit just inside the caution zone. He doesn't offer the other one to my brother.

As Levi opens his mouth to speak, my own thoughts whisper from some other place. *This is it. How it happened. How we all ended up in this trailer.*

"Travis's ma dated some guy from Las Vegas who got hired in the VIP room at the casino. He made serious bank in tips and spent a lot of it on Angie. Even got her a new ride."

I try to identify what's different about Levi. He seems younger somehow.

"Turns out high-stakes poker wasn't the only thing Vegas dude was dealing," Levi says. "He got her to switch from vodka to meth. Angie could party all night with no hangover. Lost weight, too. She gave free samples of go-go juice to her rez friends."

It's his breezy use of meth lingo that pisses me off.

"How can—" I start to lay into him, but Jamie's hand pulses for me to stop. His thoughts are inside my head as well: *Don't get riled. Just let them talk.*

Levi continues. "Travis wasn't playing in a league anymore, so he'd hang out at the old city rink looking for a pickup game. He never said whether the Vegas dude gave him a free sample or he helped himself to it. Travis told us meth wasn't a big deal. It just made him skate faster. Gave him stamina to play for hours."

My brother leaves out his own role in why Travis wasn't on any league team.

Mike jumps in. Tag-team storytelling like the guys always do.

"Vegas dude starts knocking Angie around for not meeting her sales quotas. As long as he did it on the rez, Tribal Police couldn't touch his non-Native ass. But they could harass him, and the casino could fire him. My dad says the Tribe gets rid of troublemakers during the one-year new-employee probation period. They don't have to give a reason, and the fired person can't appeal it." Mike gleefully adds, "Someone gave Vegas dude a free sample of advice to get the hell out of town."

"Travis could help Angie with the business," Levi says. "He wanted to, Daunis. No one twisted his arm. He was smart and figured out how to make meth even better than Vegas dude. Their only problem was in scaling up production. All we did was invest in a growing business."

That's all they say they did. But—

Levi doesn't know that I know he did way more than invest. And he wasn't a mule forced to do it; Levi was a distributor, risking his hockey career . . .

What would you do, if you could get away with anything? If you grew up getting special treatment? If you had a friend like Travis to take the fall for a big mistake?

Mike tag-teams back into the story.

"Travis became his own best customer. He started adding psychedelic mushrooms to batches of meth. And last Christmas, when he was crying over Lily, he experimented with all kinds of wild stuff in the product."

My breath catches at hearing her name.

"Levi tried experimenting with the meth, but it's the one thing your brother actually sucks at." Mike shoots him a look of . . . annoyance.

The hair prickles at the back of my neck.

"Well, two things," he continues. "Levi couldn't pitch a simple business plan to his sister last winter when it would have prevented all the fuckups that happened since then."

My brother doesn't tell Mike to fuck off. He just stands there and takes it.

There is a lilt to Mike's voice now. "If you had been part of our team, Dauny, we could've gotten help for Travis. Lily would still be alive."

"Don't talk about her!" I snap, but my heart is in my throat. It's true. I could've saved her. If only . . .

Don't fall for it, Daunis. Jamie is inside my head again.

The scientist part of my brain steps in. I think back to all the times Levi had an idea and Mike provided a key suggestion and a sequenced plan. Sometimes a chemical is harmless in one form but becomes toxic under specific conditions. Mike is a catalyst.

When Mike kissed me, one of the excuses I gave was that my brother wouldn't like it.

Believe me when I tell you I'm not afraid of Levi.

Levi may be team captain on the ice, but in this trailer, Mike Edwards is in charge.

"You're the brains," I hiss at Mike. The goalie who can always anticipate where the puck is headed.

Jamie squeezes my hand. *Stop.*

"Oh, Dauny, it's hard being the smartest person in the room." Mike rises. "I thought you and I had that in common. Turns out, my dad was right." He imitates Grant, "'Winners outthink the losers. Winners see opportunities the losers notice in the rearview mirror.' I used to think my dad was full of shit, but Tenacious G outthinks everyone. He always plays the long game."

A look passes between Mike and Levi. My brother exits, casting a worried look behind his shoulder, and I brace myself for the finale he didn't want to witness.

"Now, I've got a story for you, Firekeeper's Daughter," Mike says. "Once upon a time there was a smart princess who fell in love with the new guy in town. The prince that her brother encouraged to date his sister. She was presented with an opportunity to help her brother. A choice to make: to help or not help. To save the prince or be responsible for a tragic ending." Mike yawns while casually stretching his arms above his head. "We'll be back tomorrow for your answer. For Jamie's sake, I hope you go with happily ever after."

Mike walks to the door and reaches for the doorknob. He turns to tell us one last thing.

A shudder runs through me. My sweaty hand is still intertwined with Jamie's.

"I never thought I'd want to be like my old man. Turns out, all of his lectures and lessons taught me how important it is to set a goal and do whatever it takes to see it through." Mike turns the doorknob. "My dad can be extremely persistent when he wants something." He smiles. "But you know all about that, don't you, Dauny Defense?"

My chest tightens. Mike knows what his dad did to me.

CHAPTER 47

I can't breathe. The trailer is too hot. I blink to find myself sitting on the bed. Jamie presses something damp and cool against my forehead. I need to know what it is, as if this one fact will provide comfort. The handkerchief from his suit-jacket pocket.

"You're okay, Daunis. They're gone. I'm here with you. You're safe." His voice is soothing, but I get stuck on his last word: *safe.*

My dad can be extremely persistent when he wants something. But you know all about that, don't you?

Jamie saw my frantic kicks and air punches last night. He tried alerting Ron that something was wrong. I wait for him to repeat his question from the overlook.

What happened to you?

He doesn't. I think Jamie is starting to figure it out.

I watch for a recriminating glance, a tsk-tsk, a lecture.

It doesn't come.

A trickle of sweat runs the length of my back. It's a sauna inside the trailer. Jamie gives me a sports drink and pats my forehead again. I take a few sips before offering it to him. He peels the wrapper of a protein bar like a banana before handing it to me. My stomach growls as I devour it. Chain smoker–style, he unpeels another bar while I chew my last bite of the first one.

"Let's have you turn off the tracker on the watch to save the battery. Okay?" He motions toward my ankle. "It's the knob on the side. You push it *in* to power down the tracker, so it's just an ordinary watch."

I reach down and push the knob in.

"We know the guys will return for you. They need you wherever their lab is set up. We have to hope that it's off the island or at least somewhere a signal could be detected. As soon as you're away from these rocks, pull the knob out and turn the tracker back on. Okay?"

I look at this person, backlit by a lantern and dancing orange lights, kneeling in front of me. What do I actually know about him?

He is twenty-two. He has strands of copper hidden in his curly brown hair. His deepest laughter tugs at the bottom of his scar. He was a pairs figure skater before he switched to hockey. He pinches the bridge of his nose when frustrated. He doesn't know his tribe or clan. His fingertips are as soft as a whisper against my skin. He takes the black olives off his pizza.

He kisses with confidence, no holding back. His eyes look ordinary from a distance but, up close, they are glorious. He was abandoned before. He always drives the speed limit. He speaks French and Spanish. He thought he was going to die when they cut his face. He prayed to Creator when he felt for Lily's pulse at her carotid artery, prayed to find it. He wants to belong to something bigger than himself. He is stronger than he appears. He loves me. And, finally: When he agreed to this undercover assignment, he never envisioned any of this happening.

Unable to keep my eyelids open, I lie down on the mattress with my back pressed against the wall. The cool metal against my shirt keeps me from dripping with sweat like Jamie. My hands shake with the tiniest of tremors. A side effect of the Rohypnol, their plan, or both.

I drift off to the sound of gentle waves stroking the shore somewhere on Sugar Island.

Orange lights move against the walls. Only it's not a trailer anymore; it's a rib cage illuminated with orange stripes. I'm not just inside the tiger; I am the tiger.

I crouch low, unseen, watching three boys. My eyes never leave them until a beautiful black jaguar, Panthera onca, *glides past. He's not supposed to be this far north. It's not his territory. He doesn't see the threat until they circle him. An owl hoots in the distance. Something slithers nearby. I remain hidden; no one ever needs to know I am here.*

They transform. Three boys become a creature with Levi's face, spiky blond hair, a concave chest, and six muscular arms, which extend like rubber.

Jamie, in a black suit, stands where the panther was. The creature's punches are like machine-gun fire. Jamie's white shirt rips to reveal abdominal muscles already forming purple bruises. The only sounds are the cracking of his ribs as he tries to catch his breath.

Ron shouts from a distance, "I can't find him, Daunis!"

I leap from my safe spot, already tasting the creature's warm blood in my throat. But I am jerked back and hit the ground with an "oof." My ankle is tethered to an old bed.

The creature transforms into three guys I no longer recognize. I roar at each one. The first won't meet my eyes. The second fades as if he was never there. The third smiles, revealing teeth that are much sharper than mine.

Jamie falls to the ground face-first, rolling over to frantically swing and kick at the air. I listen for breath sounds, but there aren't any. His movements slow until his arms and legs go still.

I cannot reach him. Jamie will die believing I abandoned him.

Hot breath on my neck turns me into a frozen statue of a tiger. Petrified, as a snake slithers up my leg.

I wake up, heart racing, with my forehead and palms pressed against the cool wall.

I'm scared. I want my mom. I gotta get out of here.

I turned over in the night, but Jamie didn't. His arm found my waist and his face is buried in my hair. Each time he exhales, his breath seeps through the tangled mess to tickle my neck. I know Jamie's breath is not Grant's, but rational fears are still terrifying.

As I climb over Jamie, my full bladder shifts uncomfortably. It's not my first time using a piss pot. Super-rustic cabins and hunting camps in the U.P. don't have running water. A bucket outside the front door means no trip to a spider-filled outhouse in the middle of the night.

After finishing, I sit on the floor at the center of the closest masking-tape line, staring at the woodstove. I wrap my arms around my knees pulled up to my chest. The only sounds are the gentle waves beyond the trailer and the sizzling pop of one sizable log in the stove.

Wood isn't solid; it's made of cellulose, which transforms during combustion into a gas. The gas builds up until it breaks through the cell wall at its most vulnerable spot. That's all the popping is—pressure finding a weakness.

I try to shake off the bad dream by organizing my thoughts.

What I Know:

1. The guys, Grant, and Angie Flint are responsible for the meth.
2. Dana drugged me and had me brought here.
3. They are using Jamie as incentive for me to cook meth for them.
4. There is no way they will let Jamie go.
5. Levi is the weakest link.

What I Don't Know:

1. What is Mom doing right now?
2. Did Levi have anything to do with Uncle David's death?
3. What is the extent of Dana's involvement?
4. How were Heather and Robin mixed up in this? Were their deaths accidental or intentional?
5. What does Mike have planned for Jamie?
6. How far would Stormy's inner goon go without any limits?
7. How do I stop loving the brother I don't recognize anymore?

I sit until the trailer lightens with Zaagaasikwe's song beginning a new day. Rising, I stretch my stiff limbs. My tailbone is sore. The tiredness behind my eyes feels permanent.

At the window, I use my sleeve to rub away soot to stare at a wall of darkness just beyond. Metamorphosed igneous peridotite. We are in a trailer hidden in black rock.

"East side," Jamie says from the bed. Not a question at all.

He gets up to pee in the bucket before returning to bed. Bone-weary already and the day is only minutes old. I heard waves and pops in my trance bubble . . . but no snoring. Jamie was awake the entire time as well.

Jamie's in the spot I had last night, his back against the wall. He pats the bed in front of him for me to join him.

"Let's sleep for a bit. They won't be back for a while and we're too exhausted to think straight. We can come up with a strategy when we're less fuzzy," he says. I lie on my back next to Jamie and stare at the curved aluminum ceiling.

It's comfortable in the trailer, not too hot or too cold. It will cool off steadily, though, as the fire dies down through the day. At some point, Jamie will try to cuddle for warmth.

"You need to face the wall," I say.

His eyebrow rises, but he rolls over. The trailer lightens with the only sun that's likely to reach us.

I say a silent prayer to Creator for zoongidewin. Today is a day for courage.

"Would it be okay for me to put my arm around you?" I ask.

"Of course," he says.

I turn toward Jamie and drape my arm over him. I like the feel of his body next to me this way. It calms me to know I'm not alone. I take a deep breath.

"You can't put your arm around me like this because . . ."

Jamie tenses. I pause, then continue slowly, ". . . because Grant Edwards held me down from behind when he attacked me last night in his hotel room. I went with him because he said he had a security video of me snooping around his home office from that Sunday night we were at their house."

Jamie doesn't say anything for what feels like an hour.

"You're gonna leave here today," he says finally. "The tracker will lead Ron to you. Tell him everything; he's a good agent. The FBI will take it from there. They'll get Grant Edwards and you can put this behind you, Daunis. You're gonna be okay."

I don't know whether I believe him or just want to so badly, but I finally relax. He rests his hand on top of mine in front of him. His thumb strokes the soft pad between my thumb and index finger with the same rhythm as the waves from Lake George.

We wake at the same time, as the voices approach the trailer. Both of us scramble to stand next to the bed. We each reach for the other's hand at the same time.

I'm light-headed from standing too rapidly and my heartbeat racing in fear.

"I'll agree to whatever they say," I whisper. "I'll tell Ron everything as soon as he finds me. We will come back for you."

Jamie gulps the air, as if he's about to dive into the deepest pool.

"I love you," he says quickly. "No matter what happens, Daunis, I love you. If everything goes bad, save yourself and get away from here."

My lips are at his ear now. "Trust me. Levi is the weakest link."

Someone fumbles with the lock.

I don't know why the truth matters now. Only that it does.

"I love you, Ojiishiingwe."

CHAPTER 48

They repeat their entrance from last night. Levi enters first and goes straight for the bucket. Mike goes to the woodstove. He's brought only one small log. My stomach drops at the implication that Jamie might not be alive long enough to warrant a larger one.

"Well, Princess, what's it gonna be?" Mike says when they finish their tasks.

Letting go of Jamie's hand, I step forward.

"What assurance do I have that Jamie will be safe if I agree to help you?" I ask Mike. "Because I don't trust Levi."

Mike blinks his surprise.

"What?" Levi says with high-pitched shock.

"Did I stutter?" My voice is ice. "You're a liar and a snake." I look to Mike and repeat my question. "What assurance do I have that Jamie will be safe if I agree to help you?"

Mike assesses me with a tilt of his head, furrowed brow, and lips pursed as if he's a Nish giving directions.

"What are you talking about, Daunis?" Levi asks.

"You lied about Dad's scarf," I seethe. "You knew how much it meant to me, and you said you couldn't find it. But you knew exactly where it was." I take another step forward, as far as the chain will allow. "I found it in your closet yesterday. If you'd lie about Dad, anything out of your mouth is sketchy." I give one last disgusted look at my brother before turning to Mike. "At least with Mike, we understand each other. Don't we?"

Mike does the smirk that reminds me of his father. I swallow the bile rising in my throat. My mask is one of cool detachment with Mike and unbridled fury toward Levi.

"What are you doing, Daunis?" Jamie says, clearly alarmed.

"You were the one who broke into my room?" Levi is bewildered, outraged, and embarrassed. A mixture of emotions swirled together yet still discernible.

"Yup."

"I'm impressed, Princess," Mike says as he steps into the caution zone. "Put your leg on the table."

"My leg?" I fight to keep my voice calm. How could he know about the watch around my right ankle?

"You want to lose that leg iron, don't you? But you, Prince Charming"—he nods toward Jamie—"lie down on the bed facing the wall so you don't try anything funny. Unless you prefer to get tasered."

We follow Mike's commands at the same time. Behind me, the rusty bed frame squeaks with Jamie's movements while I pull the card table closer so my left leg can rest on it.

Mike leans over the table to insert a key in the padlock at my ankle.

My newly unshackled leg feels as if it might float away. It's my right leg, now, that has the weight of the world around it.

"Thank you," I say.

Mike smiles benevolently.

"You can get back up, Prince Charming," he says. "Princess Dauny, he will be safe because I will tell Levi to keep him safe."

"So, you're taking me to your meth setup?" I ask Mike, adding a glimpse of relief for him to see.

"That's the plan," he replies. "Although, I must say, you're awfully concerned about the safety of a guy you cheated on."

"What?" Levi and Jamie say in unison.

"Dauny banged my dad at Shagala." At last, Mike's smile reaches his ice-blue eyes.

I recoil. Mike thinks it was a consensual hookup? I want to combust in a ball of fury.

I can't take back my clearly visible reaction, so I transform it into anger at being tattled on. To further sell it, I add uncomfortable fidgeting and a guilty look at Jamie. Jamie picks up the cue immediately. I know he is just playing his part, but his look of hurt and confusion cuts at me.

"You're a cheater?" Levi stares as if I am a stranger. He doesn't give me time to answer, instead turning to Mike. "You knew?"

"I always know when my dad chases tail." Mike shrugs. "He's so predictable. He won't let me have a girlfriend during hockey season. Meanwhile, he screws everything, and my mom pretends not to notice." Mike struts right up to me. "He gave Robin the heave-ho and started scoping you out. Out with the old. In with the new."

As I glare at Mike, a disturbing thought comes to me. He took Robin to Shagala three years ago and kissed me a few weeks ago. Maybe Mike's attentions had nothing to do with me and were about proving something to his dad instead.

I can't get distracted. I need to stick to the plan I made while staring at the woodstove this morning. My plan to get to the weakest link.

"Well, now that you've told Levi what a snake he is," Mike begins, "and he knows the truth about his cheating puck-slut sister . . . I think he should be the one to take you to your new work site. I'll stay here with Prince Jamie while you two siblings go on."

Mike is pleased with himself. He set up this hat trick—a hockey trifecta where a player scores three goals in one game. Revealing a secret to turn Levi against me. Ruining my relationship with my boyfriend. Showing me that he's in charge and capable of outsmarting me.

"Anything you want to say before you go?" Mike asks me.

I pivot toward Jamie and say in the most pathetic voice I can, "I am so sorry. It was a stupid mistake and didn't mean anything. I'll do anything to make it up to you."

My back is to Mike and Levi, who cannot see my wink. *Trust me. Levi is the weakest link.*

The plan was to find a way to separate Levi from Mike somehow. My only chance to talk sense into my brother is to get him alone. I was hoping that if they were going to take me away from the trailer, that it would be just one of them and not both. I had to make sure it was Levi, and the best way to do that was to make Mike believe I didn't want anything to do with my brother.

Mike showed me last night that he enjoys opportunities to shake me up. It's part of his need to prove he's the alpha in this operation.

I keep my mask on, playing the part of a girl who just got shown who the boss is.

"Oh, and Dauny, if anything keeps Levi from getting back here within two hours, it will not be a happy ending for Prince Charming."

Mike motions for me to go to the door with Levi. I shoot one last angry look at Mike while, inside, I try to keep from breaking into a gleeful, triple-speed Smoke Dance. My plan is going exactly as I'd hoped.

CHAPTER 49

I follow Levi north along the shore as if shackled to his leg. I scan the surroundings, looking for something familiar to indicate where we are. My nose twitches from all the wonderful, non-trailer scents: clean water in the air, fishy-smelling lichen on rocks, the sweet tobacco-like aroma of decaying leaves, and the familiar comfort of cedar and pine.

Levi turns at a cave in the black cliffs with a creek flowing toward the river. The cave turns out to be a tunnel passageway opening to a forest. We cross the creek by stepping on flat rocks that form a bridge of sorts.

My right foot hits the last rock just so and skids on the slick surface before my shoe drives off the edge. My toes dip in the cold water, jolting me as if electrocuted.

I could've ruined everything had my shoe completely submerged and soaked the watch.

Pausing to rub the side of my foot with shaking hands, I pull the tracker knob on the old-timey watch around my right ankle. Ten seconds later, I've caught up to Levi as we approach a grove of pine trees.

An old truck is parked between pines. It isn't so out of place; rusty trucks like this are scattered across the island and throughout the county. Both Nishnaabs and Zhaaganaash call them rez trucks, regardless of who actually owns them. Some die a slow, oxidized death in an overgrown field or behind a shed with other discarded relics. This rez truck is still perfect for going mudding or hauling an ice shanty onto a frozen lake.

Levi starts it up with a key left in the ignition. The gearshift extends from the steering column like a skinny arm raised in greeting. Something about the truck feels familiar when I sit on the passenger side of the front bench seat. My finger finds a tear in the olive-green vinyl that I knew would be there.

This is the truck Dana used to bring me to Sugar Island.

The pine trees quickly give way to maple trees. Levi's zigzagging route makes sense only because the fallen leaves are flattened ahead where the truck must have come from. The tire tracks are like a trail of bread crumbs.

It isn't until the winding path in the woods becomes a narrow road that Levi speaks.

"I can't believe you cheated on Jamie. I thought you were better than that."

This is the first thing he wants to say to me? "I didn't cheat. His dad raped me."

Levi jerks his head to gape at me. "That's not what Mike told me."

"Do I need proof for *you* to believe me?" My voice falters because his question is my answer.

I unzip my jacket and yank my shirt and bra strap from my shoulder. The bruise from his fingers is turning from dark red to purple.

"Well, how did he get you alone?" he chides me. "I thought you were smarter than that. Everyone knows he's a creep."

"Is that the part that matters, Levi?" I blink away tears and force myself to focus, making a mental note of the dome-shaped rock along the path that looks like a mini madoodiswan. "You were gonna kick your teammate's ass for disrespecting me at Chi Mukwa the day you asked if I wanted to go into business with you," I say.

He swerves around a fallen birch tree blocking the trail, eyes glued to the path while I keep talking.

"It's so wrong, Levi. All of this is wrong. You being involved with this meth business. You defending me every time but now. You letting Mike run the show. Your birthday present in my closet. Your mom drugging me. And Uncle David . . . did you have anything to do with his death?"

"No," Levi says quickly. "Mike thought that once your uncle tried meth, he'd be incentivized to produce good stuff. Your uncle injected too much at once. Mike thought he might've done it on purpose. I wasn't there when it happened."

"Incentivize." I say dully. "Is that why you put that box of pucks in my closet?" His Adam's apple bobs but he doesn't respond. "What happens when you guys go too far with Jamie and take him out of the equation? I know you won't let him go. Will you go along with them when they want to 'incentivize' me?"

"Mike would never hurt you. The box of pucks was just a backup. Insurance if you tried to take the high road. I never would've played that card, but Mike said to be stealth and direct your opponent's fate."

"I'm your opponent?" I ask quietly.

"No," Levi sputters. "It's just a safety net to keep you on board. We'll let Jamie go and he'll stay quiet. We can scare him into keeping his mouth shut," he insists.

"Like how you threatened to end TJ's football career?" I say. "You can't trust anything Mike says. He kissed me in his bedroom that Sunday night when he helped me set up my BlackBerry. I had to give him a half-dozen reasons why I wasn't interested. When I mentioned you, he said it could be our secret from you. Mike's not the loyal friend you think he is. Please listen to what I'm saying, Levi."

Levi falls silent as we leave the woods. We drive across a field that's morphing from a farm into something else. Returning to an untamed state. A patch of mashkodewashk grows. I wonder if it's the male or female version of sage. Then I wonder why I'm wondering about it.

We drive down a dirt road. I read a bent street sign and at least recognize where we are. He is headed west, toward the main road that runs north-south through the island.

My heart pounds in anticipation of Levi's next turn. If he takes a left, we're going somewhere on the island with no chance for a signal to be sent. If he goes right, we might be headed to the ferry, or a secondary location to the north where a signal might get through.

My only chance is a right turn.

When Levi reaches the main road, he pauses for so long I might vomit out my own heart. I look down at my lap, my hands resting on my black jeans.

He turns north, and I nearly cry out my joy.

We might have a chance.

If Jamie's watch around my right ankle is transmitting anything.

If I switched it on properly by the creek when Levi's back was turned.

If Ron can be waiting on the mainland, maybe set up a checkpoint for all the cars exiting the ferry, like the night Lily was killed. This time it would be to find Jamie and me.

If I can get back to the trailer to reach Jamie before two hours are up. How much time did it take us to come this far?

After arrests are made, will Sugar Island and my tribe be ripped to shreds by people in town who will be quick to distance themselves?

"Who else is mixed up in all this?" I name the other two tribal members on the team—one graduated with me and the other with TJ.

Levi shakes his head. "You got it all wrong. It's not Mike and some 'skins.'" I resist the urge to yell about his use of a racial slur. "It's me and Mike and some poor guys who could use the money. Rob, Max, and Scotty."

My relief at hearing the names of three Zhaaganaash guys is chased by guilt and anger. Now they can't say it's an Indian thing. Because they would.

"Levi, why are *you* involved in this? It can't just be for the money. I mean, you already get per cap."

"Sure, to *you* money's no big deal." It's the first time he sounds angry. "My mom says that when the casino implodes like all of our boneheaded tribal business ventures eventually do, we won't be dependent on the Tribe for anything. We'll never go back to being poor pitiful Nishnaabs fighting over scraps. If you want something, say it out loud and decide in your heart to do whatever it takes to make it happen. She said that's how she got everything she wanted."

"Like with Dad?" I blurt out, before I think about how it might not help the situation.

"It wasn't just her," he says hotly. "She wasn't the cheater. He cheated on your mom."

Levi sounds like a little boy. A scared one.

"Levi, why did you lie about Dad's scarf?" I ask quietly as he drives north on the main artery through Sugar Island.

"I don't know!" His voice cracks. "I found it when I was little, and when my mom saw it, she got real mad. Said it was a present from your mom to him. Fancy cashmere scarf that matched her green eyes. Whenever Dad wore it, he was letting my mom know that he should've been with your mom instead." He floors the truck so hard it shakes, like an old man forced to sprint. "Maybe I thought if you had the scarf, you'd wear it, and it would be like rubbing my mom's nose in what she did that night on the island. She had Macy's dad do shots with Dad till he could hardly walk, so she could take her shot with him."

I want to freeze time so I can digest each part of what my brother is telling me, but I need to focus on my plan. Our lives depend on it.

Levi turns west toward the causeway to the ferry launch. We hear the ferry horn, and I'm racked with fear that we've missed it and will have to wait a half hour for the next one.

"My mom wanted Dad so bad, she wished for me and made it happen. I couldn't let you wear that scarf. I just couldn't. Daunis, please don't ever wear it around her."

I breathe a sigh of relief when we pull into a long line of cars waiting for the ferry.

"Okay, Levi, I promise I won't wear the scarf."

He's the relieved one now.

"We aren't responsible for their choices," I say. "We love imperfect people. We can love them and not condone their actions and beliefs."

My brother's lower lip trembles. He seems on the verge of tears. I feel the same way.

"Levi, I don't regret Dana's choice the night of the party on Sugar Island, because it gave me my brother, and I love you."

He smiles as one teardrop falls. I'm filled with hope that we'll get through this mess.

"We could do this, Daunis," he says excitedly. "You and me. We could figure out how to buy out everyone else and run this ourselves. No one would ever suspect us. We would be unstoppable." His expression is absolutely radiant.

My heart tears open, and something leaves. Whatever it is, it stays behind on Sugar Island as Levi claims the last remaining spot on the ferry. I look behind as if I might see a spot of fresh blood on the ground. The hydraulic ramp lifts like a drawbridge. I face forward at the ferry horn.

"Would we be unstoppable because you always get away with stuff?" I ask wearily. "Like when Travis took the blame for the BB gun blinding that lady's eye?"

My brother's face registers shock, fear, guilt, and shame. Then it smooths over into a mask of his own.

Levi digs a flip phone from his coat pocket and dials a number. Instructs someone to meet him at the ferry launch. I listen for Grant's voice, but the person says nothing.

The numbness in my upper arm seems to spread to the rest of my body.

"Put this on," Levi says, handing me a ball cap. When I don't, he adds, "I'll tell Mike."

I comply, and as I do, I think about Jamie alone in a trailer with Mike Edwards.

Assess the problem. Jamie is in danger, and Ron doesn't know where we are.

In the car next to us, Seeney Nimkee stares up at me.

Inventory your resources. One Elder.

My eyes plead. *Help me. Help me. Help me.*

When the reverse thrusters jolt the ferry, I realize there are no barricades or police cars in the mainland parking lot. No one is coming to save me. Which means I won't be able to save Jamie.

The front drawbridge lowers. Cars unload ahead of us.

Levi lays on the horn because the car directly in front of us hasn't started its engine.

"What the hell, Minnie. Start your fucking car!" he shouts to the red Mustang ahead of us.

I look over to Seeney once more. At first, I think she is telling us to get going. But then she mouths the words again, and I understand she is speaking only to me.

Get out.

CHAPTER 50

I have one instant, like when the puck drops, where all is calm and quiet. Enough for one deep breath in and a long, slow release. Then time catches up and sprints ahead.

Levi swears again at Minnie. I grab the door handle and am outside the truck before he's finished his sentence. I'm in the back seat of Seeney's car an instant later.

She puts the car in reverse, backs up, and jolts forward at an angle. Metal scrapes against metal as Seeney blocks Levi from following my exit route.

Minnie hasn't budged. Levi's truck is too close to the back draw-bridge to make any turns. There's nowhere else for him to go except to his left. My view is blocked by the truck.

I grab her flip phone from the drink holder and call Ron's cell phone. He answers.

"Jamie's on Sugar Island," I shout. "In a trailer hidden in between the east shore black rocks, about a hundred feet south of a cave-like opening with a creek along one side. Mike Edwards is going to hurt him." I unlock the right door, leave the car, and sidestep behind the truck to reach its other side.

Jonsy Kewadin's Lincoln Town Car. The one he calls his pony.

Cursing a blue streak from his Navy days, Jonsy sits inside with both feet braced against the open door on his passenger's side. He has created a nearly perpendicular blockade to keep Levi from escaping.

The wind snatches the ball cap from my head. Hair whipping across my face, I rush along the ferry rail until I'm ahead of Minnie's red Mustang. She hasn't moved.

Somehow, these three Elders coordinated a rescue.

Minnie rolls down her window and shouts, "Get in, my girl. Ambe!"

I do as my Elder tells me, and watch Levi's movements from the safety of Minnie's car.

He tries rolling the passenger window down to crawl out. Something must not be working, because Levi thrashes around like a toddler having a tantrum.

Seeney follows my brother's lead, exiting from her passenger side. She runs to the front of the ferry. Instead of continuing down the ramp, she turns to face us on deck.

She points at Levi with one hand, while holding an invisible feather to Creator with the other.

Seeney trills a high-pitched call: "Lee-lee-lee-lee-lee!"

Minnie joins in, laying on her horn. Jonsy adds his horn as well.

At last, Levi gets the window down and rolls over Seeney's car. He runs past Minnie's car, continuing toward the ferry ramp. He speaks into the flip phone he had earlier.

Seeney continues to point and trill at the figure running directly toward her.

I'm out of Minnie's car the instant I realize Levi's not swerving to avoid Seeney. He needs to create a diversion to get away.

Levi plows into her. He continues down the ramp and across the parking lot.

I rush to Seeney, who is flat on her back with her arm still raised overhead. The wind knocked out of her, a pause before she inhales a raspy gulp of air.

What comes out of her makes my heart soar.

She continues her trill. I know it means: *We faced worse than you and we are still here.*

It is our survival song.

While Minnie, Jonsy, the deckhand, and people from waiting cars rush to Seeney, I race after Levi. He reaches the far end of the parking lot and continues toward the golf course down the road. He has too much of a head start. I cannot catch my brother at a full sprint.

Think, Daunis. Think.

I scan the row of cars waiting to board the ferry. I don't see any familiar ones, until a black Range Rover pulls into the line.

Grant's car. He's here to get Levi. Ron needs to know about Grant's involvement. Seeney's cell phone is still in her car.

Before I turn back for it, a car horn grabs my attention. Coach Bobby's BMW pulls up next to me. He can help me.

"Coach Bobby, I need a ride. And your phone. We've gotta follow Levi."

"Of course," he says without hesitation. "Get in."

I do so. He looks at me expectantly, and I realize he's waiting for me to put on my seat belt. It's ridiculous, really. To worry about little things when we are in a crisis.

"Are you serious?" I raise my voice as I comply. "You're gonna be Mr. Safety First?"

Coach Bobby exits the ferry parking lot, turning left toward the golf course. I reach for his cell phone resting in the cup holder. He moves it to his left hand, farther away from me.

I echo my incredulity. "Are you seri—"

Wait. I never told him which way Levi was headed. Coach never asked.

I look back at the cars lined up to board the ferry. Grant's car hasn't moved.

When we were in Green Bay, Coach Bobby said Grant had donated the pucks for the tribal youth program but was keeping it quiet because he didn't want the publicity. But when Grant donated his legal services to set up Robin's foundation, he posed for a photo opportunity splashed across the front page of the *Evening News*.

Grant Edwards has never shied away from publicity.

Coach Bobby lied.

Their partner is a high school business teacher. An entrepreneur. A gambler. Big wins and losses. A starter of many small businesses that never really took off. Until one did.

He says, "Bet you wish you were playing D-one hockey right about now."

CHAPTER 51

B e smart, Daunis. No running," Coach says.
Following Bobby LaFleur's directions feels normal. Muscle memory from the Before.

Coach Bobby always listens to public radio. All those rides home after practice. Returning from away games in the middle of the night.

He looked out for me. Defended me when other high school coaches said no girl should be on a guys' varsity team. *Shut up and treat that player like any other.*

"Once we get you set up outside Raco, middle of nowhere, you'll do everything we say. Forget about your boyfriend. He's done," Coach says with a terrifying calmness.

No. Jamie isn't dead. Mike wouldn't . . .

I am no longer able to assess what people are or are not capable of.

Coach continues, "You'll cook the best meth and your mom stays alive."

Jamie is no longer the incentive. They'll hurt her. I should've called Mom when I had Seeney's phone. I could've warned her.

If they get me to their remote meth lab, I'll never see Mom or

Jamie again. They'll keep threatening people I love to keep me in line. Maybe Auntie and the twins next. One by one.

Coach pulls over at the golf course, near an equipment garage. My brother emerges from it and sprints to the car. In one blink, Levi is in the back seat directly behind me.

He's breathing hard as he reaches around the headrest of my seat to place his hand on my left shoulder. The one he knows always hurts. The one with a bite-shaped bruise. My brother doesn't do anything but rest his hand there. It is a threat and a betrayal.

A low keening comes from deep inside my chest.

Coach shrugs—*too bad, so sad*—as if I've complained about a crap call on the ice.

We can't control the bad calls, Fontaine, but what can we control?

I'd answer, *I can control how I react. Move on. Focus on the next play.*

As Coach gets back on the road, we hear sirens in the distance. Ron and his law-enforcement colleagues arriving at last? Did my tracker bring them? Or are they responding to the ferry captain, who must have reported an assault on an Elder by the Supes' team captain?

Levi turns to look behind us; I only know because his hand pulls away from its resting spot on my shoulder. Coach tilts his head slightly to look in the rearview mirror.

I'm the only one with my eyes ahead, focused on the next play. Which is why I see the tribal cop car approaching from the opposite direction. A massive figure fills the driver's side.

I keep mixing up the bad guys and the good guys.

With lightning speed, I jerk the steering wheel toward me. We instantly leave the road, hitting a tree at an angle with enough force to spin the back end of the car into another tree.

The next thing I know, my face hurts. I piece together what happened.

I raised my arms instinctively as we left the road. The front airbag deployed with enough force that I punched myself in the face with my forearms. Something is dripping over my lips. I taste tangy copper pennies and salt. My nose is bleeding. Both shoulders hurt like hell. The seat belt is tight against my chest. It's only now that I realize how hard it is to breathe. When I manage to undo the seat belt, my lungs expand. My vision comes back. I was on the verge of passing out.

Coach Bobby's door is open. I crawl over the gearshift and his seat to tumble onto the ground. I get away from the car as quickly as possible because the possibility of it exploding from leaking fuel is a rational fear.

A deep voice shouts behind me, "Put your hands on your head and drop to your knees."

I do as TJ orders, landing hard. When I try raising my hands like on television shows, I gasp at the searing pain in both shoulders. My stomach hurts when I twist to look back at him.

TJ's gun is aimed at Coach Bobby, who is frozen exactly like me on the other side of the road. TJ's partner reaches Bobby in a few quick strides.

Once Bobby's arms are secured with handcuffs, TJ runs past me as if I'm invisible.

Wait . . . did I die?

I watch TJ aim at something along the side of the road. I don't remember us hitting a deer. Standing slowly, I announce my movements, so I don't spook TJ or his partner.

"I'm walking over to you. My arms are raised, but my left shoulder can't go any higher. I don't have any weapons on me."

TJ gulps when he looks at my face. He returns his gun to its holster on the black leather belt with all his cop gadgets.

"Paramedics are on their way," he says in his normal voice.

"Wait . . . you know I'm not part of Levi's meth ring?"

"Yes. I know now," TJ says, looking at the deer in the grass. He kneels down to help it.

It's not a deer. I nearly collapse in shock.

Levi is crumpled on his side looking up at us. His leg is bent at an odd angle.

"You and the undercover agent were reported missing and in danger. We know about the FBI investigation. Bobby LaFleur is news to us, but maybe not to the FBI." TJ sounds ticked off. "They aren't telling us everything."

"Help me, Daunis," Levi says. "Tell TJ the truth. Coach forced us to be in his business."

I step back in disbelief.

"I was trying to help you escape," he says.

One more step away from the lies.

"Stay with me, Daunis. Kneel over me like you did when we were little. When you protected me until the ambulance came," he pleads.

It's not that moment I recall, but the one where his hand rested on my shoulder in the car.

"I love you, Levi," I say. Levi brightens with hope. "Enough to do this."

I turn to TJ. "Coach Bobby, Levi, Mike, Stormy, and Dana Firekeeper are part of the meth operations. Maybe Grant Edwards too—I'm not sure. At least one of them was involved in my uncle David's death, and I think they have info about Heather Nodin and Robin Bailey. Dana drugged and kidnapped me. Levi and Mike tasered and drugged Jamie. And . . ."

Jamie.

"I need to go back for Jamie!"

"You need medical attention," TJ says.

"He needs to know I didn't abandon him, Jon!"

It's been almost three years since I called him that. Our middle names whispered to each other. TJ hesitates, then speaks into his walkie-talkie to alert all LEOs that I'm headed to the ferry.

As I take off, my brother shouts after me, "I love you. I'm sorry. I love you. I'm sorry. I love you. I'm sorry."

His voice gets smaller with each repetition until it's no longer in the air.

The ferry hasn't left the mainland. The loading ramp is still extended like a drawbridge.

I run past an ambulance. Seeney pushes away an oxygen mask. Minnie pats her arm.

A line of cop cars waits to board the ferry. An officer drives Levi's rez truck down the ramp.

Ron sprints toward me, but I keep running until I'm on the ferry deck. Jonsy pats the hood of his very good pony. And the door of the tomato-red Mustang is still ajar.

I shout over my shoulder at Minnie that I need to borrow her car. "Miigwech. Miigwech. Miigwech," I add. *For helping Seeney. For slowing Levi down. For safe harbor.*

I turn her car around, into the spot where Levi's truck was just a moment ago. I'm facing the back drawbridge, which will become the front ramp once we reach Sugar Island.

Rolling down my window, I shout at the deckhand for us to go. Instead he waits for Jonsy to exit and the ferry to fill with law enforcement vehicles.

Ron catches up to the car. "Daunis, let me drive," he offers.

I don't budge. He sighs and gets in the passenger side.

"You're hurt," he says calmly.

"Jamie was still alive when I left the trailer." My voice is all cracks and bumps.

The blast of the ferry horn makes me cry out in joy or pain. Or both.

I tell Ron everything as we cross the St. Mary's River. The story spews forth like vomit. There's no time to sequence my thoughts.

It feels like five hours later instead of five minutes when the reverse engine thrusters signal our arrival. The deckhand tosses the thick rope around the dock pilings before pressing the button for the hydraulic ramp.

My patience lasts until the ramp is halfway down. I shift the Mustang into gear and am airborne for an instant before Minnie's tires burn rubber on Sugar Island.

People always tease Minnie about driving ten miles under the speed limit. My foot is heavy on the pedal. The Mustang roars as if to say, *Yes, yes, finally, yes!*

I pass a line of cars waiting to board the ferry.

Ron breaks into my recap to ask about the location. "We've got the Coast Guard headed to Lake George. Is it on the northeast or southeast shoreline? Or more toward the midpoint?"

I shout the east-west road I remember from the way out of the woods. "Ron, it's an overhang in the black rocks. It looks narrow but it angles back. It's wide enough for someone to float a trailer on a barge and wedge it in. It's why Jamie's GPS signal couldn't reach you. He had me wear it around my ankle."

A voice on the other end of the device confirms the Coast Guard is on its way.

It isn't until we are flying across the field that I see the cop cars behind us. Not right on our tail, but still keeping up. They must have been behind me this entire time, lights flashing and sirens blaring. I just hadn't noticed until now.

Strange, how the mind can tune things out.

I pass the stone shaped like a mini madoodiswan and swerve around the fallen birch tree. The road narrows until it's a winding trail. I follow the bread crumbs of tire tracks that zigzag around maple trees until we reach the pine forest. I park in the exact spot where the rez truck was. I don't waste time shutting off the engine or closing the door.

Ron keeps up with me as we hopscotch the rocks to cross the creek. When we run through the cave-tunnel, I get a stitch in my side that takes my breath away. I power through as we run along the shoreline. Ron's in decent shape for an older guy.

We round the sharp corner where the trailer is nestled in the crook of black rocks.

"Don't kill him! We're here. It's all over!" I yell, arms reaching for the door. "I came back for you, Jamie. I didn't abandon you."

I yank it open and rush inside. My legs go rubbery at what I see.

I should not have announced our arrival.

Their backs are to me. Stormy standing and Jamie kneeling in front of the bed.

I scream as Stormy brings an ax down on Jamie's ankle with one powerful heave.

CHAPTER 52

I throw myself onto Stormy's back, knocking him over Jamie and onto the bed. I claw his face and am about to bite his ear, intent on removing chunks of him with my teeth, when Ron pulls me off. Stormy's head is still in my grasp; he is dragged away from the bed with me.

"Daunis." Jamie's voice cuts through my rage. "Daunis, let go."

He spoke. Jamie isn't screaming in agony.

I let go of Stormy, who drops to the floor with his hands at his face. He makes noises like when Auntie was in labor—releasing pain with repeated sounds and deep breaths.

Ron yanks Stormy up and pulls him out of the trailer.

Jamie stands on two feet. I push him back to get a better look, my heart pounding. His black dress boots are scuffed but otherwise undamaged. No blood anywhere. The iron shackle is still around his ankle, but the chain ends abruptly after three links.

Stormy cut Jamie free?

I can't move or speak; every ecstatic thought and feeling envelops me simultaneously.

Jamie's face lights up as he watches my euphoric shock. "Daunis, I'm okay. But we have to get out of here." Taking my hand, he leads me down the trailer steps.

A swarm of law-enforcement officers rounds the black rocks. They arrive in time to escort Stormy back to the mainland for questioning. One guy in a suit stays at his side, a federal agent, most likely. Just before they step out of view, Stormy looks over his shoulder at me.

I don't know why he helped Jamie, but I'm grateful. I put my left hand on my hip even though it hurts my shoulder. My other hand painfully raises an imaginary feather in thanks at the four honor beats I hear in my head. Stormy gives a half-nod acknowledgment before walking beyond the edge of the rocks.

"You did it," Jamie exclaims. "Oh, Daunis, you did it."

Euphoria continues to wash over me. My body starts shivering but I don't mind. Jamie and I are both outside the trailer. Alive.

"What happened?" Jamie asks, looking more closely at my face.

"Car accident with Bobby LaFleur and Levi," I say. "I'm okay. Just punched myself in the nose when the airbag went off."

"Ron, we need medical attention," he calls out.

"Coast Guard coming around the north channel. Should be here any minute," Ron says.

"How did you keep Mike from killing you?" I ask Jamie.

"Mike didn't say anything while we waited. I don't think he thought I was worth the effort. When the deadline passed, I told Mike that no matter what he may have done or known about, he was only seventeen, and with his dad's connections, he had favorable odds in court."

"Why would you try to help him?" I ask incredulously.

"'When you surround an army, leave an outlet free. Do not press a desperate foe too hard,'" Jamie says before grinning. "Mike and his dad aren't the only ones who know Sun Tzu."

"Whoa. That's clever."

"Well, then he took off and left me alone in the trailer with no heat, water, or food. The more time went by, the more I worried something had happened to you."

There is fear and concern in the softness of Jamie's voice.

"I heard someone quietly approach the trailer," he continues. "I didn't know if Mike had changed his mind or if Levi had returned? I never thought it would be Stormy. He peeked in, saw me, saw the chain, and grabbed the hatchet from the woodpile stored under the trailer. I asked what he was going to do, because I really didn't know which way it was gonna go."

"What did he say?" I ask breathlessly.

"Stormy never said a word. The only sound he made was when you went at him."

A scream breaches the cove. We whip our heads around to see Auntie running toward us.

"Oh my God. What happened?" Auntie's eyes are wide with terror.

When she reaches too quickly for my face, I pull back. Auntie bites the back of her hand and tears leak down her face.

"I'm okay," I assure her, and I mean it. I feel light-headed. Like I am giishkwebii, happy and tipsy. Everything surreal and—"Wait." I stare back at Auntie. "What are you doing here?"

"Seeney called from the ferry. Said you looked scared. And Levi was driving. Your mom said you were missing. No one wanted to take it seriously because Jamie was missing too. Everyone tried telling her you ran away together, but she insisted something was wrong." Auntie cautiously inspects my face with gentle fingertips. "TJ came to me . . . he was scared you might become the next

Robin. He told me how widespread meth is, and how certain officers were looking the other way. Judge Firekeeper was letting some people go when TJ knew the case files were solid. He didn't know where to turn."

She continues talking. "I've been meeting with Elders and some traditional healers about the drugs in the community. It all fell into place when Seeney called. I was racing to the ferry when Minnie's car flew past and I saw you behind the wheel being chased by cops. So I followed you."

"She saved me," I tell my aunt. "Seeney boxed Levi in. I don't know how she coordinated it with Minnie and Jonsy."

Auntie grins. "Tribal Youth Council service project. They taught the Elders how to use their cell phones and they set up a group text. Seeney told me she sent a text message for anyone on the ferry to block the truck that Levi was driving."

I love my Elders.

I thought I had no resources on the ferry, except for one lone Elder. But one led to another, and another. A resource I never anticipated during my time of dire need.

I'm reminded that our Elders are our greatest resource, embodying our culture and community. Their stories connect us to our language, medicines, land, clans, songs, and traditions. They are a bridge between the Before and the Now, guiding those of us who will carry on in the Future.

We honor our heritage and our people, those who are alive and those who've passed on. That's important because it keeps the ones we lose with us. My grandparents. Uncle David. Lily. Dad.

I feel giddy as Auntie, Jamie, and I laugh. The sound surrounds us. Echoes off the black rocks and fills the space like an amphitheater. I laugh until I'm dizzy and my stomach hurts. I wince and touch my right side—it feels rock hard and swollen.

Auntie pulls Jamie to her for a half hug. His eyes sparkle. Jamie is alive. It's such an exhilarating feeling that I begin to shiver.

The investigation will wrap up. People will finally learn the truth. There will be justice for those who were taken from us.

I want justice too, for what Grant Edwards did to me. It makes me nauseous to even think about him.

And, just like that, something heavy and dark reaches inside my chest. As if it's not enough that I want to puke, but his name in a thought manifests into a fist squeezing my heart.

I gasp, but it feels like one of these rocks has fallen onto my chest. I cannot breathe.

Jamie's face transforms. His incandescent smile dims in slow motion, before becoming something blank for an instant and then turning into . . . panic.

My legs go out from under me.

I blink and I'm on my back, one arm over my head like Seeney. I cannot catch my breath to mimic her trill.

I see the overhang of black rocks and a beautiful sky beyond. That pretty color the sky gets when the sun is setting and the light has more tricks to reveal. Saving the best colors for that in-between time.

Jamie's face blocks my view. I want to brush him away, but my hand remains against the cold pebbles that make me shiver even harder. Auntie is on her knees next to Jamie. Their faces mouth words to me. She touches my abdomen, but I can't catch my breath to scream. Her eyes are wide with terror.

I don't understand why they're so scared. The pain isn't so bad anymore.

Even my shivering has stopped.

I just want to see the sky. A combination of purple and gray, mixing to become lilac. My mother's favorite color. Her favorite scent. Sweet little flowers that bloom for such a short time. But lilac bushes are hardy, surviving cold temperatures. They can live for over a hundred years.

I want my mom.

She is who I am thinking about—my strong, beautiful mother—when I die.

PART IV

· · · · · · · · ·

KEWAADIN

(NORTH)

**THE JOURNEY INTO THE NORTHERN DIRECTION IS A TIME FOR RESTING
AND REFLECTING IN THE PLACE OF DREAMS, STORIES, AND TRUTH.**

CHAPTER 53

I rest on a large rock, an island of stone surrounded by woods. The rain has only just stopped; heavy drips leak from branches and ping when meeting the forest floor. A breeze rustles the trees, turning them into wind chimes. The last remnants of rain now shower the forest in softer sprinkles. Boulders rumble, low and constant. Sunlight breaks through the forest cover, casting spotlights that hum and awaken sleeping pansies.

A small fire is surrounded by grandfather rocks to my left. East. Its smoke rises, calling out prayers in the melodic cadences of Anishinaabemowin. In front of me, to the south, is another fire with more grandfathers and prayers carried on wisps of gray smoke. To my right, west, the grandfathers wait. There is no fire there yet. Behind me, north, more patient ones.

Pansies sing to me. They surround the rock, dotting the periphery with gently swaying yellow and purple faces. So many voices blending together. I add my own, weaving through the chorus until I find a niche that my voice fills to make the song whole.

This world is beyond any contentment and beauty I have ever known.

We sing more loudly, the pansies and me. Their purple mouths open, faces basking in the sunlight. I do the same, feeling the warmth of the glow as if from within.

A drum joins in. Its steady beat grows louder, fueled by our song.

The pansies grow taller. Leaves become arms outstretched with fluid movements. They dance together with linked hands, as if they have done so, forever.

I want to join them.

I rise, turning to view the panorama. Every pansy has become a singing woman. Their voices have a familiar timbre. Scattered among the faces, I see women who remind me of others. Auntie's eyes. Gramma Pearl's pointed nose. A wide smile I have only seen in a mirror. Women who are neither old nor young.

I am aware of someone on the rock with me as I turn around.

Lily.

As she was and also as something more. She isn't Lily anymore. She is Binesikwe. I want to talk to her. There is so much to say.

Where to begin?

And then I know.

Words are no longer needed. Everything I would say, she already knows. Any question I might ask, I know her answer.

She is part of me and always will be.

The drumbeat continues as everything begins to spin around us. Only Lily and I remain rooted, stone underfoot. The rotation speed increases. The women's linked arms become a braided green circle filled with faces transformed back into pansies. They rise above us, whirling and compacting, until Lily reaches up for the floral necklace. Her touch halts all movement. The drum remains steady.

Lily places the lei of pansies over my head to rest on my shoulders. Her smile is brighter than any star. She kisses me once on each cheek as this world fades.

CHAPTER 54

Everything is loud. Jarring. Heavy darkness. Cold. A rough mixture of sounds. Beeps. Voices. Buzzing. Pain.

I want to go back to the other place. It is so near.

My mother's voice finds me in the chaos.

Her words make no sense, but her voice is a helium balloon lifting me. Each time, I grasp on to it for a little longer. Her voice begins to take shape. She calls to me. Sings. Reads to me. I am so close, sometimes, before I slip back into the darkness.

Daunis, my beautiful girl, come back to me.

Her kiss centers on my forehead. Gentle stroking from the side of her palm to brush hair from my face. A warm washcloth caresses me.

My lips tingle and I cannot make sense of it until I feel the glide of something waxy. It coats my lips. First the upper one, with a dip as she adjusts for the philtrum. Then the lower lip, so full she needs to backtrack.

It falls into place.

Mom is putting lip balm on me. The way we made sure GrandMary started her day with a perfect red lip.

At least . . . I think it is just lip balm.

I hope I'm not lying in this hospital bed with a slash of lipstick. Something pink and cheery. She wouldn't do that. Mom wouldn't dare.

Oh God. She totally would.

I groan and feel the edges of my mouth break into a smile.

CHAPTER 55

When I regain consciousness three days after I nearly died, my brain feels foggy. Mom's eyes are red from crying. Something isn't right. Her voice was upbeat in the darkness.

My first words are "What's wrong?"

"GrandMary passed away this morning," she says.

"I thought she died after a party."

"Sweetie, you're confused and that's okay. The doctor said it's common." Mom kisses my forehead. "GrandMary died in her sleep."

"Can I visit her?" That's not what I meant. "Funeral."

"We are in Ann Arbor. You're in the intensive-care unit at the U of M Medical Center. Aunt Teddie was here, but she went back home to make the arrangements."

"But GrandMary doesn't like any Firekeepers," I say.

"Teddie offered so I could stay here. I'm not leaving you."

"Are you sure GrandMary didn't die after my graduation party?"

"She was in between, I think," Mom says. "Maybe she waited until we weren't there so she could leave us. It's a comforting thought, don't you think?"

"No. It's weird. I'm weird. My brain is fuzzy. I'm sorry, Mom, I'm going back to sleep."

Mom kisses me again. There is healing medicine in those kisses.

"One week ago, I, Daunis Lorenza Fontaine, deliberately grabbed the steering wheel of a BMW to veer off the road, to get the attention of a Tribal Police officer, so I could sprint back to the ferry launch, where I borrowed Minnie Manitou's tomato-red Mustang to lead a high-speed caravan of law-enforcement vehicles to an old aluminum trailer to rescue someone whose name I don't know so his life could not be used as a threat to pressure me into cooking high-quality crystal methamphetamine for a drug operation whose product was distributed via souvenir pucks at hockey games primarily in the Great Lakes states and Ontario."

I take a huge breath and keep going.

"However, when the car hit a tree or two, my liver was torn—probably a grade I or II laceration originally, but exacerbated to a grade IV when I jumped on someone who was helping, but I didn't know that at the time—and I bled internally, undetected, until my blood volume level decreased and I went into hypovolemic shock, which would have killed me if not for the quick actions of my aunt Teddie, who is a registered nurse, and the Coast Guard boat that transported me to the local hospital so I could be stabilized and taken by medical helicopter to the University of Michigan Medical Center in Ann Arbor, where I was unconscious for three days and then monitored for three more days in the intensive-care unit as a precaution against rebleeding and other liver complications, but I am now in a regular room, currently answering your question, which is whether I am aware of my surroundings and the events that led me here."

Dr. Roulain blinks in surprise, then smiles. "Well, Daunis, I'll note in the chart your mental capacity is undiminished. We want to keep you here through next week and monitor you as you increase physical activity. As you stated, we are watching for rebleeding and other complications, such as slow-developing biliary-tract lesions, or infection from sepsis or hepatic abscess. After that, we will transfer your outpatient care to the hepatology clinic."

Mom asks about the time frame for my liver to heal fully.

"The liver is the only internal organ that can regenerate," Dr. Roulain explains. "Even if your daughter's liver had torn completely, it would grow back to its full mass within six months. Since her injury was a laceration, or tear, it should take a few months for her liver to heal." He turns to me. "Now, I hear you're a hockey player. You need to avoid all contact sports, including hockey, for at least six months. To be on the safe side, I'd recommend a year-long hiatus."

I squeeze Mom's hand before answering.

"I gave up hockey because of nerve damage from chronic shoulder instability," I say.

After Dr. Roulain leaves, I pause before I speak. I already alerted my mother that she was going to hear a lot of secrets that might surprise or hurt her.

Protecting my feelings is something you can let go of, Daunis, she said.

Once I stop analyzing and filtering my words, I find I have more energy. It turns out that lies, in whatever form, are exhausting.

I start with the most important secret first.

"Uncle David was helping the FBI as a confidential informant."

Mom's hands fly to her mouth, trapping any gasp or sob. I continue in her silence.

"He was researching mushrooms on Sugar Island that might have been added to crystal meth to cause hallucinations." I add, "He was concerned about Levi and went to talk to Dana about him. That's when Uncle David went missing. I don't know what happened after that."

When my mother moves her hands from her face, her eyes shine with vindication that she had been right about her brother. Uncle David's only defender.

"The FBI might know more by now. Dana could have confessed," I say. "I don't know what details will come out."

"David would only care that you and I know it was foul play. And his students, I think." Mom seems at peace. "He lived his life not caring what the gossips thought."

Auntie brings bundles of medicine when she arrives two days later. She cannot strike a fire to smudge the room, but we know it's there. She has the sage, cedar, sweetgrass, and tobacco nestled in the iridescent bowl of an abalone shell on my bedside table. Next to the raspberry lipstick that gives my mother an inordinate amount of pleasure to put on me every morning.

My aunt has been the dearest friend to my mother for my entire life. She ensured that Mom's wishes were followed. GrandMary wanted to be cremated and her ashes placed with Grandpa Lorenzo after a memorial service that would be scheduled once I was back home. From a place of love and with a good heart, Auntie tended to my grandmother's final journey.

I loved GrandMary and I know she loved me. Correction—I love her, and she loves me. When our loved ones die, the love stays alive in the present.

Ron is my first non-family visitor now that I've been moved from the intensive-care unit to a private room on the regular inpatient floor. My mother bought a white cotton nightgown and a matching robe for me. Although it's more her style than mine, I'm thankful to be wearing something other than the standard issue hospital gown. I sit in a chair flanked by Mom and Auntie. It feels good not to be alone. Ron pulls up a chair across from me.

"Daunis, let me begin by thanking you for helping with the investigation," he says.

Mom interrupts. "You put my daughter in an impossible situation." She squeezes my hand. "It may have been legal, but it was hardly ethical."

Ron accepts her anger, saying nothing to defend himself.

"Who are you?" Auntie asks.

"My name is Ron Cornell. Senior field agent with the FBI."

"Not what you do," she clarifies. "Who are your people? Which community claims you?" Her voice is neither friendly nor hostile; it's her speaking-to-Tribal-Council voice.

He names a tribe from out west. Grew up in Denver.

"Does your family know what you do? Going undercover in tribal communities?"

"They know I work for the FBI," Ron tells her. "My sister thinks it's dangerous. My cousins think I'm a sellout. I do this work because we need good people working at the agencies that help tribes."

Auntie snorts. "Scariest words ever spoken: 'I'm from the federal government and I'm here to help.'" She continues, "Was anyone from our tribal law enforcement involved?"

"This was—is—a federal investigation. We kept the Tribe out of it because there have been investigations on other reservations where people in law enforcement have tipped off family members." He pauses to clear his throat. "I can't speak to more details because the U.S. Attorney's Office is still pursuing charges."

"What can you speak to?" she asks.

Ron focuses his attention on me.

"Levi's been charged with several crimes: kidnapping of a federal officer; possession, manufacture, or distribution of controlled substances; maintaining a drug-involved premises; employment or use of persons under eighteen years of age in drug operations; and conspiracy to defraud the United States. The financial crimes fall under Canadian jurisdiction. You've been implicated in the wire transfers, so you'll need to get an attorney. But it should be fairly straightforward because the evidence will show Levi's activity." He pauses. "When we searched his bedroom, a woman's black platform flip-flop was found in one of the boxes in his closet. It's the same style Heather was seen wearing on Labor Day, and it's her shoe size. Levi is being questioned about her disappearance."

"Ron, I searched every box and bin in that closet looking for my dad's scarf. If the sandal was there before that Sunday, I would've found it. Someone put it there afterward." I meet Auntie's gaze. "Levi is guilty of many things. He may or may not be involved with Heather Nodin's death, but the timing of when the evidence turned up feels . . ." I use Ron's word, "hinky."

"I agree," Ron says.

"I think Mike put Heather's flip-flop in Levi's closet. He's been the mastermind this entire time. Mike had access to Levi's room and could have set up my brother to take the fall."

I can see Ron mulling this over, and I lean forward.

"When you question Levi, watch his face when you tell him about Heather's flip-flop. That's when he will realize he was set up. Levi might turn on Mike at that point." I sigh. "Maybe he won't, though. Levi's choices have been . . . disappointing."

It takes a few beats for Ron to respond.

"Michael Edwards is missing. No one saw him leave Sugar Island. Our best guess is that he crossed into Canada and accessed money and resources there. We've questioned his parents. They were shocked to learn about their son's involvement. Devastated, really."

"Grant Edwards wasn't the person Levi called from the ferry, but he still might be involved," I tell Ron. He nods to acknowledge my suspicion but doesn't confirm or deny.

I envision Mike finding the narrowest passage on the north channel. Swimming the frigid water and struggling not to get pulled under its treacherous current. Regrouping on the other side. Doing post-game analysis and plotting his next move. Basing his strategy on quotes from his dad, Coach Bobby, and Sun Tzu. Starting over somewhere. It seems more likely that Mike would have help from his dad.

"What about Stormy? I still don't know why he freed Jamie," I say. Auntie pats my hand.

"Stormy Nodin hasn't spoken a single word since I led him from that trailer," Ron says. "Since he's a minor for a few more months, his parents have to be with him when he's questioned." Ron looks perplexed. "He hasn't even talked to the attorney his parents hired."

"Maybe Stormy would rather stay quiet than do or say anything to hurt Levi," I say. "What happens if he never talks?"

"Well, there's little if anything that can be done while he's a juvenile," Ron says. "The statute of limitations on federal cases is five years, so once Stormy turns eighteen, the U.S. Attorney's Office can subpoena him into a grand jury. He could be charged with obstruction of justice for failing to provide relevant evidence, and even possibly charged for aiding and abetting if any facts suggest he may have been involved."

"What if he heard or witnessed stuff but told Levi he wouldn't be part of it?" I ask.

"If Stormy wasn't involved, he could still be called to the grand jury and put under oath. Should he refuse to testify, the U.S. Attorney's Office would request a hearing in front of a federal judge to order him to testify." Ron pauses. "If Stormy Nodin never talks, he could be held in contempt and kept in jail until he complies."

I say aloud what I know in my heart with a sinking, nauseating certainty.

"Levi and Stormy are gonna sit in jail, while Mike gets away with everything."

I take Ron's silence as agreement. Auntie reaches for a tissue to wipe her eyes. Mom hugs me, the only comfort she can provide. After a few minutes, Ron begins speaking again.

"I'm sorry, Daunis; I know this is a lot to take in. But I wanted to make sure you heard everything from me. Robert LaFleur was charged with several counts of being part of a conspiracy to distribute methamphetamines on the reservation—aiding and abetting. He had an accomplice at the casino, who wasn't filing currency reports for cash deposits of more than ten thousand dollars. That's how he was able to launder money."

I had ignored the clues: the fancy car, the high-end renovation to his waterfront cabin, gambling trips to Vegas. A lifestyle that exceeded a teacher's salary and modest rental income.

I don't understand how Coach could treat me so well for all those years and then . . .

Over and over, I relive the moment when Coach moved his cell phone away from me and the realization hit me like a slap shot to the throat. *Coach is involved!*

The man who Mom had trusted with my health and safety was

willing to drive me to an isolated house or garage to cook meth for the business he had with Mike . . . and Levi.

My brother was on board with the plan.

Levi's betrayal is a sinking anchor that still hasn't found bottom.

I look at Ron, who is waiting patiently for my attention to return. He continues after I nod.

"Dana Firekeeper has been charged with several counts of aiding and abetting a conspiracy to distribute methamphetamines on the reservation. Those are only the federal charges; the Tribe is expected to file charges against her after finishing an audit of her Tribal Court cases." Ron sounds genuinely shocked. "It looks like, as tough as Judge Firekeeper was on alcohol-related crimes and some drug crimes, a number of meth-related cases were dismissed on technicalities in her court. She protected Levi's operations while taking actions against his competition."

"What about her drugging and kidnapping me?" My voice shakes with fury. "Auntie, wouldn't my blood still have had traces of Rohypnol when I was in the ER in the Sault?"

Before my aunt can answer, Ron clears his throat.

"Daunis, there's something else I need to talk about with you." Ron braces himself, breathing deeply and exhaling loudly.

A chill runs down my spine.

"The trailer is on land the Tribe purchased a few years back and put into federal trust."

I wait for Ron to continue, but he seems unable to go on.

Auntie gasps; I feel her sharp intake within my own lungs. She tells me what Ron cannot.

"You were an enrolled citizen when Dana took you. When a crime takes place on Indian land and the victim is a tribal member, the feds decide whether to press charges." Her words fit between sobs. "They're not going to pursue charges for your kidnapping. Only Jamie's."

Special Agent Ron Cornell doesn't meet my eyes.

"Did Jamie tell you that Grant Edwards raped me in a hotel room at Shagala?" I shout, feeling my mother stiffen next to me. "When Jamie put his GPS watch around my ankle, he said to tell you what Grant did so the U.S. Attorney's Office could seek justice for me."

I shake my head.

"Jamie's naive, isn't he? He thought, after all I did for the FBI, that my case would get more consideration from a federal prosecutor than what's normally given to Native women."

I stare at Ron until he meets my eyes.

"Jamie doesn't know that ten times zero is still zero," I say flatly.

Then something else occurs to me. "I think Grant Edwards planned to rape me as soon as he heard about my enrollment vote. He knew the resort was on tribal land. He counted on the federal government not wasting resources going after non-Native guys like him. They knew the tribal court couldn't touch him."

I am so tired. The weight of my expendability is crushing.

Not everyone gets justice. Least of all Nish kwewag.

Ron seems at a loss for what might be appropriate closure under the circumstances, so I do it for him.

"Please go, Ron." I hold my stare until he breaks away.

As he leaves the room, I collapse against Auntie and my mother. I picture Grant Edwards rolled up in a blanket, in the trunk of a car deep in the woods on Sugar Island. My female cousins lift the heavy roll and drop it on the ground. The muffled groan is an echo of the one in my ear on a hotel bed where the sheets smelled of lavender.

"Blanket party," I tell Auntie. "You'll bring me."

She exhales and closes her eyes. When she opens them and nods, Auntie has aged ten years in one blink.

CHAPTER 56

A little boy visits me. Huge, somber brown eyes gaze up at me. His serious expression reminds me of Grandpa Lorenzo, when he would talk about the old days. This little one approaches everything with an intensity far beyond his few years.

I want to make him smile.

Kneeling in front of him, I say his name. Then I kiss the back of his hand before pretending to lick it and clean his face like a mama cat.

His beautiful lips curve into a smile filling my heart with so much light. Rays of sunlight kiss his tousled hair, brown curls with a few random strands that glimmer copper.

I bask in the gloriousness of that smile. His tiny hand beneath mine is warm.

Then a larger hand is atop mine. A warm thumb caresses the soft pad between my thumb and index finger.

For one perfect instant, my hand is sandwiched between both.

As I open my eyes, the tiny hand fades away and there is only Jamie's touch.

"You're here," I say.

It's been twelve days since he watched me die on Sugar Island. The bruises that made him look like a raccoon in the trailer have faded to a yellowish brown. The bite impression on my left shoulder is about the same color.

"I'm sorry, Daunis. This was the soonest I could come. There were things I needed to take care of with the investigation." He looks at the colorful balloons from the twins. "Ron said you're getting out tomorrow."

I keep my hand beneath his. "I'm moving to an apartment downtown to be near my medical appointments. My mother is staying with me awhile, but then I'll be here on my own."

Jamie looks down at our hands. When he looks back at me, his eyes glisten.

"I'm sorry, Daunis," he says again. "That you were part of this. About Lily. And David Fontaine. For everything that happened to you." His voice cracks. "I am so, so sorry."

He cries. I don't soothe him. He needs to feel this, and I need to hear it. Investigations involve real people. Informants face real risks. Developing real feelings for me doesn't wash away that he was willing to use me, a girl he didn't know, to pursue a case and get a career boost.

Sunlight has changed to an orange dusk outside my window when he wipes tears from his face. At last, I remove my hand from his, so I can trace his scar.

"Jamie, you can't keep doing this. You need to find out where you come from. Stop pretending in other communities, and find yours."

"I wasn't lying about being Cherokee. I am, but that's all I know about it." Jamie closes his eyes against my palm cupping his jaw. "Everything with you was more real than anything in my other life. It didn't feel like pretending, being Jamie Johnson, a guy playing hockey and falling in love with you. It was the realest thing, Daunis." His eyes open. "Don't you see? My life before this? That's what felt fake."

"You are not cut out for undercover work," I tell him. "You cannot wear masks like other agents—it affects you differently. You get sucked in, in a way that Ron doesn't. He can live the lie because he knows it's a lie. But you? You don't know the truth of your life." I grip his hand. "Promise me you'll try to find out?"

Jamie nods before lifting my hand to his lips. He plants kisses that I feel all the way to my toes.

"Let's make plans to be together." There is a frantic edge to his voice. "When you're healed, you pick a school anywhere in the country, and I'll go there. We can meet as strangers, like none of this happened. We can start fresh."

"Oh, Jamie. There you go again, ready to live the lie, but not ready to live the truth."

"I love you, Daunis. You know that part isn't a lie." His voice is low and steady. "I felt something the first time I saw you. At Chi Mukwa. Seeing you in person, not just research in a case file." He reaches for my hand. "You were right in front of me. Beautiful and real."

I want to be with him. Fall asleep to his gentle snoring. Share an apartment. My books and music mixing with his, until we forget whose is whose and there is only *our* stuff. Starting every morning intertwined. Running together. Discovering new things—true things—about each other.

My daydreams must play across my face, because he gets excited.

"I need you, Daunis. Help me find out if there's a plate set out for me at a feast somewhere. I don't think I can do it without you."

Something heavy drops inside me. Into a deep cavern, where Travis's words to Lily bounce off jagged walls.

Tell me what to do and I'll do it.

I can't do it without you.

I need you.

"I can see our life together, Daunis. You can too, right?"

Granny June's voice: *Things end how they start.*

Jamie and me. We started with deception.

I could end it now with a lie. Tell him that I don't see a future for us. Lie about the little boy with the crazy messy hair and dark eyes that observe the world quietly and deeply.

I decide to stand in my truth.

"I love you. Whoever you are. Wherever you came from. Without our names or stories."

I touch the sides of his face—the perfect side and the scar. He closes his eyes, immersing himself in the sensation of my fingertips.

"I love you and I want you to be healthy. To find whatever is missing in your life, so you stop pretending. Stop putting yourself and others in dangerous situations."

Another deep breath. More pain.

"It's *your* journey. You gotta do your work and I gotta do mine." I taste salt from my tears. "Your need scares me. I'm afraid I'll focus on your needs over mine." I clear my throat. Breathe in and out. Steady myself. "I love you . . . and I love myself. I want us to be healthy and strong. On our own. So that no matter what happens, whether we meet again or not . . ." I look him in the eye. "Love means wanting you to have a good life, even if I'm not in it. And your love for me? It should be that strong, so you want that for me, too."

He says nothing, just sits there. Strokes my hand with his thumb. His eyes are sad, as if someone turned out the lights and pulled curtains across.

Finally, he lifts my hand to his lips and gives it a long kiss before setting it gently down on the bed. He leans over and kisses the tip of my bruised nose, smells the top of my head as if committing it to memory. Then he walks to the door. He never looks back.

Only after enough time passes—during which I have imagined his elevator ride, the long walk to a car in a distant parking garage, and his drive away from the city—do I speak.

"We named him Waabun," I say to the space where he was sitting. Telling him about the little boy from my dream. From a Someday in the future. A future in which we are both healthy and independent people. "After the eastern direction."

It dawns on me: I don't even know what our son's last name would have been.

CHAPTER 57

Powwows are not ceremonies, and yet there is something restorative about the gathering of our community. The collective spirit of our tribal nation coming together, sharing songs and fellowship with others. It's our annual powwow, the third weekend in August, and my community needs healing now more than ever.

The recent tribal election included a banishment referendum, heatedly debated during community meetings. Members told heartwrenching stories of loved ones lost to drugs, pleading with Tribal Council to *do something*. Others claimed that the referendum would lead to selective banishments to punish the families of political rivals. Fingers were pointed, and leaders told to "wash your own dirty asses before telling us what stinks."

Last week, my first time voting in a tribal election, the referendum narrowly passed. The day after the election results, a group of members began circulating a petition to recall the Tribal Council members who voiced support for the banishment referendum.

Now, any tribal member convicted of a felony drug crime in any court is subject to a banishment hearing. The length of the banishment, up to five years, depends upon the severity of the crime and whether the individual is in recovery. The intent is to rid the reservation of dealers, while showing compassion to members who are struggling with addiction. Banished individuals are still enrolled citizens but are barred from tribal land and ineligible for any tribal programs, services, or benefits. This includes per capita payments.

Former tribal judge Dana Firekeeper will be the first person to appear at a banishment hearing. She pled guilty in federal court to a single felony count of obstruction of justice in exchange for no prison time. In Tribal Court last week, she was found guilty of ten counts of dereliction of duty for every meth-related mistrial she presided over. She was fined the maximum $5,000 amount for every count but received no jail time. Some think she got off too easy. Others say Dana is being made an example because people enjoy when powerful women are torn down.

On Friday evening of powwow weekend, I pick up Granny June and we head to Sugar Island. When we arrive at Auntie and Art's place, dozens of cars are parked in their front yard. I help Granny from the Jeep and we walk to the clearing overlooking the north channel of the St. Mary's River. I am surprised to see over a hundred women sitting around the fire in concentric circles. Art is nowhere in sight. My aunt motions for us to join her in the innermost circle. We must be the last to arrive, because Auntie welcomes everyone as soon as we sit down.

There was a Nish kwezan who collected pansies with her nokomis all summer long. Each evening she helped separate the flowers by color. She knew the brightest colors would be used to dye the strips of black ash for weaving baskets. Others were for medicines. Her nokomis put all the yellow pansies in one pile. What are the yellow ones for? she asked. Nokomis wouldn't say.

Each summer she collected pansies with her nokomis, who never told her what the yellow pansies were for. The kwezan became a kwe and still helped her nokomis each summer. One day she said nothing as she collected pansies. When her nokomis asked what was wrong, she didn't know how to tell her grandmother that a man had hurt her. She only shrugged. For the rest of the summer, she and her nokomis collected pansies in silence.

At the end of the summer, her grandmother took her into the woods one evening. They were joined by other women, who sat in a circle. She watched as her grandmother's black ash basket was passed around the circle and each woman or girl present took a single yellow pansy. When the basket was in her lap, she took one pansy for herself. One by one each person came to the fire and said a prayer before offering the pansy. Some said their prayers aloud. Others mouthed silent prayers. And others released their prayers through tears. When it was her turn to pray, she understood what the yellow pansies were for. She said a silent prayer and released her pain. The pansy offerings and their prayers were carried in the smoke to Creator and to Grandmother Moon.

As my aunt tells the story, a large basket is passed around the inner circle. I take a yellow pansy and pass the basket to Auntie. I watch as women approach the fire, each one offering a pansy.

As I release the pansy, I think about what Grant Edwards did to me and say my silent prayer. There is comfort in watching the smoke rise to the full moon.

When I return to my seat, Granny June holds my hand.

"Liliban was thankful each year that you weren't here," she says.

"Wait. She was here?" My heart breaks.

"Yes, my girl. Ever since she came to live with me."

I cry for my best friend and the secrets she wanted to protect me from.

On the ferry back to the mainland, I realize that Macy wasn't at the fire. Relief washes over me. Macy wasn't there. When Granny and I do our usual semaa offering midway across the St. Mary's River, I say a silent prayer of profound gratitude for all the Nish kwezanswag and kwewag who weren't at the fire tonight. Chi miigwech.

I spend all of Saturday afternoon walking around the vendor stands, catching up with cousins, Elders, former classmates, and teammates.

A few people pry for details about Levi. My response: Nothing.

I gave Auntie a pouch of semaa and asked her to keep me updated on Levi's case. She doesn't tell me her sources, but I think she stays in contact with Ron.

Levi was deemed a flight risk, even with a busted leg. He remains detained without bond until his trial, to begin in the fall. My brother has refused any plea offerings, but he may change his mind now that the federal prosecution has its star witness.

I am not the star witness. I haven't stepped foot in a courtroom or any law enforcement office since the day I signed my CI agreement. Senior Field Agent Ron Cornell has protected my identity so far. I've had no contact with Levi. He may have tried to reach out but I suspect that Auntie and my mother intercept any messages from him. I know that if I ask Auntie, she will tell me the truth. For now, I am fine with not asking.

Neither is it Stormy Nodin, who has still not uttered a single word in English. Ron's prediction of what would happen once Stormy turned eighteen was spot on. Stormy remained silent before a grand jury and at a hearing in front of a federal judge. Held in contempt of court, he sits in jail.

According to Auntie, when Stormy's parents visit him, they all speak Anishinaabemowin. His parents are there every visiting day;

they moved to a town near the federal detention center where their son is being held. His father parks outside the facility and drums each night.

Nor is it Michael Edwards, who is still at large. There are rumors he is playing hockey for a Swedish pro league under a different name. His parents divorced. Helene moved downstate. Grant still lives in their house. Auntie drove past one night and said the house was dark except for a Sault High hockey game playing on the giant plasma screen.

My nightmares began when Robert LaFleur accepted a plea deal to be the star witness against Levi. It's the same bad dream each time. I jerk the steering wheel of Coach's BMW and nothing happens. Levi grips my bruised shoulder as the Tribal Police car passes by. I scream in pain. TJ never sees me. They drive me to a modular home in the middle of nowhere. I wake up as Mike describes in precise detail what he will do to Jamie if I don't cook meth for them.

On those nights, I light a braid of wiingashk and inhale the sweet smoke. Then I put on my dad's choker and pray for debwewin. To know truth is to accept what cannot be known.

On Sunday, I start my day with a prayer for zaagidiwin. Love. Today is the official end of my traditional one-year mourning period for Lily. I will dance at a powwow for the first time since Uncle David died almost a year and a half ago.

I offer semaa and give thanks for all my loved ones, those in this world and the next.

When it's time to get ready for Grand Entry, my nieces and I sit on the picnic table outside while I braid their hair. I asked Teddie for this time to tell the girls about my college plans. My fingers move quickly through Pauline's hair to get it out of her face, so she will be less likely to chew on it.

"I have some news to tell yous," I say to the back of Pauline's head. "I'm leaving in a few weeks for Hawaii."

"You're going away again?" Perry asks from beside me. She's frowning, and I imagine her sister's face has the same expression.

"The University of Hawaii at Manoa has a great ethnobotany program. That's the study of how people all over the world use plants as medicines. It's got biology and chemistry, but something else, too. They look at things with Indigenous eyes. And every summer, I'm coming back to do an internship with Seeney Nimkee. When I graduate from college, I'll be her apprentice at the Traditional Medicine Program." I can't stop smiling. "I know what I want to be, what I am . . . a traditional medicine practitioner and scientist."

"A traditional scientist?" Perry asks.

My smile grows beyond my face. It reaches my fingers and toes.

"Yeah. That sounds exactly right," I tell her.

I peck a kiss on Pauline's head to let her know I'm done with her hair.

"Yous are gonna visit over Thanksgiving. I'll know my way around by then."

"Can we go to museums?" Pauline turns around, trembling with excitement. She loses herself in museums, absorbing every detail of each exhibit.

"Museums are boring," Perry says, shoving her sister aside to sit in front of my braiding fingers. "I wanna go surfing."

"We'll try different things every day." I spray Perry's head with the setting gel and use a rattail comb to divide her thick, dark hair into sections.

"Is college like a boarding school?" Pauline asks, sitting next to me on the picnic table.

"I guess so. I mean, you sleep in dorms and there are dining halls. Why?"

"Auntie, did you know there were boarding schools for Anish-inaa*bem*?" Pauline asks, overenunciating parts of the Anishinaabe words in her eagerness to pronounce them correctly. "And the government took kids even when moms and dads said no." Her bottom lip trembles. "They didn't give kids back like they promised." She looks up at me with doe-eyed sorrow. "They got punished if they didn't follow the school rules. Will that happen to you?" Before I can respond, Perry turns to me. Her eyes narrow in outrage.

"Kids couldn't speak Anishinaa*be*mowin and they couldn't go to ceremonies." Perry points defiantly at her own chest as she declares, "In*da*nishinaabem."

Auntie and Art must have decided they were old enough for *the talk*.

I am overcome with a mixture of emotions. Sad that their innocent eyes are open to the trauma that still impacts our community today. Angry they must learn these truths in order to be strong Anishinaabeg in a world where Indians are thought of only in the past tense. Proud that they—smart, sturdy, and loved—are the greatest wish our ancestors had, for our nation to survive and flourish.

"College isn't like boarding school in those ways. I take the classes I want. I don't have to stay if I don't want to or if I don't feel safe. I promise I'll come home every summer." I add, "It's good to know our tribal history and what our ancestors went through. It's important to know the truth, even when it makes us feel sad. It's good no one is keeping you from ceremonies." I hug Perry from behind. "And yes, my girl, you do speak our language."

When I finish Perry's hair, both girls stand atop the picnic table. They trill perfect lee-lees as they jump off and run to the RV where their mother waits to dress them for Grand Entry.

I'm wearing the shorts and T-shirt I'll keep on underneath my regalia to help absorb my sweat. I put on my red dress. The top half is plain material, and the skirt has seven rows of gold cone jingles. There are 365 cones, one for each day of the year Auntie spent teaching me about being a strong Nish kwe, when I was fourteen. Gramma Pearl's thick leather belt gives shape to the dress, and I attach the flat beaded bag Teddie gifted me at my berry feast. I lay the black velvet yoke over my shoulders. This summer, Eva beaded it, adding a lei of yellow pansies with purple faces.

My final touches are my dad's bone choker, the blueberry earrings from my mother, and the beaded strawberry bracelet that Jamie gave me. Auntie helps me attach an eagle plume to the back of my head, rising between my two long braids. I look in the mirror and apply Grand-Mary's red lipstick before tucking the gold tube into the high pocket.

I am ready.

Art is snapping pictures of the twins when I emerge from the RV. He calls me over and I pose with them. Then I ask him to take a picture of me with the powwow in the background.

While Art adjusts his camera lens, I think about the envelope that came in the mail yesterday morning. There was no return address, and it was postmarked Milwaukee. Inside were two postcards. The first had a picture of a lake in Minnesota. On the back, someone had written one sentence: *The kids are all right*. The second postcard was of a stately brick building labeled COLLEGE OF LAW, UNIVERSITY OF WISCONSIN, MADISON, WIS. On the back was one word: *Someday*.

"Now, that's a great picture," Art says.

We walk into the arena for Grand Entry. My dance steps are simple. The circle is filled with rows of dancers, no room for big spins or intricate steps. I need to conserve my energy if I'm going to last all day. My dancing muscles have been dormant for a year and a half.

When the drum hits the honor beats of the song, I raise my feather fan in the air. I lead the twins, and Auntie follows behind us. When I glance back, my aunt smiles through happy tears. Niishin. *It is good.*

In the late afternoon, the emcee announces one final special before the contest winners are named for each dance style and age category. Those Jingle dancers who are wearing red regalia are invited to dance. As I make my way to the arena, he tells the story of the jingle dress.

A girl was sick, and her father feared she would not recover. He sought a vision and it came to him: a dress for her, with rows of jingles made from tin cones that clinked melodically when she danced. The more she danced, the more she healed. Once she was all better, she continued to dance, to heal others in her community.

The Jingle Dance represents healing. And the red dress symbolizes our women. So, today's Red Dress Jingle Dance Special is for all the Anishinaabe kwewag and kwezanswag, Indigenous women and girls who are murdered or missing. Their spirits taken too soon, lives cut short. For each one . . . mikwendaagozi. She is remembered.

Everyone rises as seven of us enter the arena. We range in age from around five to fifty years old. Each picks a spot around the dance arena. I find the section on the northern side where Mom, Granny June, Seeney, Auntie, Art, and the twins are standing.

My mother smiles. She is proud of me. Excited for my adventure. Ready to let me go. Understands, at last, that letting me go is not the same as losing me.

As Granny June waves, her words echo from when I told her about my plans to go away to college. *My girl, some boats are made for the river and some for the ocean. And there are some that can go anywhere because they always know the way home.*

When Seeney invited me to become her apprentice, I told her about the ethnobotany program in Hawaii. I gifted her with semaa and asked if it was possible to study both ways. She said, *We Anishinaabeg are not stagnant. We have always adapted to survive.*

I take in a panoramic view of my community: Minnie. Leonard. Jonsy. TJ and Olivia. Macy.

The entire dance arena falls completely silent before the host drum begins the honor song. Every songbird gathers around the drummers to add their voice.

As I dance, I pray for Lily. For Robin. For Heather. And even for myself. For all the girls and women pushed into the abyss of expendability and invisibility. It doesn't matter that my steps are clumsy and heavy. In my mind, my feet move with lightness and speed. I am in the zone, between this world and the next.

I am not dancing in step with the drumbeats.

It is the opposite.

The drumbeats are coming from inside my heart.

Boozhoo, Aaniin Gichimanidoo. Miskwamakwakwe indizhinikaaz. Makwa indoodem. Bahweting indonjiba.

Gizhemanido naadamawishinaam ji-mashkawiziyaang miinawaa naadamaw ikwewag ji-ganawendaagoziwaad, gichi-ayaawag ji-minawaanigoziwaad gaye oniijaanisag ji-inaabandamowaad Anishinaabemong.

Greetings, Creator. I am Red Bear Woman. Bear Clan. From the Place of the Rapids. Keep our community strong. Our women safe. Our men whole. Our Elders laughing. And our children dreaming in the language. Thank you very much for this good life.

When the song ends, I stand at the eastern door. Where all journeys begin.

AHO (THAT IS ALL)

AUTHOR'S NOTE

Ahniin! Angeline Boulley indizhinikaaz. Makwa indoodem. Bahweting indoonjiba. Gimiigwechiwi'in gaa-agindaasoman ndo'mazina'igan. Hello! I'm Angeline Boulley. Bear Clan. From Sault Ste. Marie, the place of the rapids. Thank you for reading my book.

I set out to write *Firekeeper's Daughter* because there are simply too few stories told by and about Native Americans, especially from a contemporary point of view. We exist and have dynamic experiences beyond history books or stories set long ago.

The creative spark for Daunis's story was ignited when I was in high school, and a friend mentioned a new guy at her school who was just my type. Although I never met him, it was later revealed he was actually an undercover narcotics officer. As a teen, I loved reading thrillers, an early favorite being the Nancy Drew series, and I began wondering what would've happened if I'd attended that school. What if I liked the new guy and he liked me? Or, rather, what if he needed my help? The story captured my overactive imagination and stayed with me.

After college, I worked in tribal communities, focusing on Indian education to impact Native students. My career led me back to my own tribe in Sault Ste.

Marie and, eventually, to Washington, DC, when I landed my dream job as director for the Office of Indian Education at the U.S. Department of Education.

Yet every morning, I'd wake early to write for a few hours before going to my "day job." Because that spark of a story—about an Ojibwe Nancy Drew and the new guy in school—had never died, and over the next ten years, it grew into *Firekeeper's Daughter*. When my book sold, I realized it might have a wider impact on Native youth than anything I'd done prior. After all, storytelling is how we share what it means to be Anishinaabe.

Although *Firekeeper's Daughter* is rooted in my tribal community, it is a work of fiction and I have taken a great deal of creative license. Among other changes, I chose to fictionalize a tribe facing issues in the realm of what my actual tribe, the Sault Ste. Marie Tribe of Chippewa Indians, might experience. By no means is it intended to be representative of all 574 federally recognized Indian tribes, bands, and villages. Each has a unique history, culture, and dialect. Even within a community there is a wealth of diverse experiences.

However, one all-too-real aspect of the story is the rampant violence against Native women. More than four in five (84%) Native women have experienced violence in their lifetime and more than half (56%) have experienced sexual violence. Nearly all (97%) of the Native women who have experienced violence had at least one non-Native perpetrator. Although it is a difficult and exhausting narrative, I felt it was important to show the painful reality of these experiences, especially within the specific context of the predatory targeting of Native women and the jurisdictional quagmire on tribal lands.

There's an important distinction between writing about trauma and writing a tragedy. I sought to write about identity, loss, and injustice . . . and also of love, joy, connection, friendship, hope, laughter, and the beauty and strength in my Ojibwe community. It was paramount to share and celebrate what justice and healing looks like in a tribal community: cultural events, language revitalization, ceremonies, traditional teachings, whisper networks, blanket parties, and numerous other ways tribes have shown resilience in the face of adversity.

Growing up, none of the books I'd read featured a Native protagonist. With Daunis, I wanted to give Native teens a hero who looks like them, whose greatest strength is her Ojibwe culture and community. When making decisions for our tribe, we look seven generations ahead, considering the effect on our descendants. My hope is that, in sharing our Anishinaabeg experiences, *Firekeeper's Daughter* will have that impact on future generations.

Mazina'iganan mino-mshkikiiwin aawen.

Books are good medicine!

Angeline Boulley

SOURCES

U.S. Department of the Interior Indian Affairs, "What is a federally recognized tribe?" bia.gov/frequently-asked-questions

Rosay, Andre B., National Institute of Justice, "Violence Against American Indian and Alaska Native Women and Men: 2010 Findings From the National Intimate Partner and Sexual Violence Survey." May 2016. nij.ojp.gov/library/publications/violence-against -american-indian-and-alaska-native-women-and-men-2010-findings

National Institute of Justice, "Estimates of Lifetime Interracial and Intraracial Violence." nij.ojp.gov/media/image/19456

RESOURCES

StrongHearts Native Helpline 1-844-7NATIVE (762-8483) offering culturally-appropriate support and advocacy for American Indians and Alaska Natives experiencing domestic, dating, and sexual violence.
strongheartshelpline.org

National Indigenous Women's Resource Center
niwrc.org/resource-topic/domestic-violence

MIIGWECH

Many people and organizations helped make this book possible.

My children, for inspiring me. Sarah, my first reader-listener, believed in every draft of the story. Ethan, with his superpower of sardonic wit, kept me from taking myself too seriously. Chris was my go-to expert for hockey and shenanigans.

My firekeeper father and my strong, beautiful mother, who told me a never-ending love story. They also shared it with my siblings: Diane, Henry, Allan, and Sarah and Maria, who are telling it in the next world.

Authors Cynthia Leitich Smith and Debby Dahl Edwardson, who organized an unparalleled writing retreat for Native writers, Loon-Song Turtle Island, with editors Arthur Levine, Yolanda Scott, and Cheryl Klein.

Ellen Oh, Dhonielle Clayton, Meg Cannistra, Miranda Paul, and everyone at We Need Diverse Books™, for their work in putting more books featuring diverse characters into the hands of children. Francisco X. Stork, my mentor in the WNDB mentorship program, whose kindness, talent, and generosity changed my life.

Laura Pegram and everyone at Kweli Color of Children's Literature Conference, which will always have a special place in my heart. Beth Phelan, for organizing #DVpit, which was an invaluable part of my search for an agent.

Faye Bender, agent extraordinaire, for her astute guidance, industry reputation, and graciousness that makes her a rock star in the literary world. There is a word in Anishinaabemowin for "beautiful woman" that encompasses the spirit and character of a truly wonderful person. I am beyond blessed to have Faye Bender, Mandaakwe, in my corner. The team at the Book Group, for helping me navigate the business of being an author. The international co-agents, for finding the best publishers to share *Firekeeper's Daughter* around the world. And film agent Brooke Ehrlich at Anonymous Content, for a dream deal.

My editor Tiffany Liao, for scaring me in the best way possible during our first phone call when my manuscript was on submission. I never met anyone who talked so quickly and conveyed such a strong editorial vision for *Firekeeper's Daughter* as Tiff did. She pledged to work with me to Indigenize the YA canon, strengthen the promise of the premise, and protect my voice every step of the way. Mission accomplished!

The team at Henry Holt Books for Young Readers and Macmillan, for fervently believing in *Firekeeper's Daughter* as a publishing game-changer. Jon Yaged, for a moment that Faye and I will never forget. Jean Feiwel, Allison Verost, Molly Ellis, Mariel Dawson, Kathryn Little, Christian Trimmer, Katie Halata, Jennifer Edwards, Mary Van Akin, Katie Quinn, Morgan Rath, Johanna Allen, Allegra Green, Mark Podesta, Kristen Luby, Leigh Ann Higgins, Mandy Veloso, and so many others, for their incredible creativity, hard work, and passion. Macmillan Audio, especially Samantha Mandel and Steve Wagner, and actress Isabella LaBlanc (Dakota/Ojibwe), for bringing Daunis to audio-life.

Creative director Rich Deas, for designing a cover that is so spectacular and truly honors Anishinaabe art. Artist Moses Lunham (Ojibway), for his interpretation of Daunis's journey. I can think of no higher compliment than to say the cover feels purely Nish, and I am grateful to Birchbark Books for hosting a virtual cover reveal event.

Numerous sources helped shape the story. Any errors are solely mine. Those I can thank publicly: Jeff Davis (Chippewa), former assistant U.S. Attorney for the Western District of Michigan; Dr. Aaron Westrick, Associate Professor of Criminal Justice at Lake Superior State University; Walter Lamar (Blackfeet), former FBI agent; and Robert Marchand (Ojibwe), Chief of Police for the Sault Ste. Marie Tribe of Chippewa Indians. Invaluable assistance with Anishinaabemowin was provided by Dr. Margaret Noodin (Anishinaabe) and Michele Wellman-Teeple (Ojibwe). Destany Little Sky Pete (Shoshone-Paiute), for her science fair project on the medicinal properties of chokecherry pudding.

The Alexandria Women of Color Writers Group led by Kat Tennermann, Novuyo Masakhane, and Dr. Cynthia Johnson-Oliver.

Barb Gravelle Smutek, my best friend, for never hesitating to say, "A rez girl wouldn't say that!" My friends, for their love and laughter: Chrissy, Sharon, Leslie, Anne, Laura D., Laura P., Bonnie, Audrey, Mary, Charmaine, Summer, Melissa, Dawn, Stacy, Traci, Carole, Ronalda, Ellen, Lori, Kim, Colleen, Debra-Ann, Elaine, Rachel & Bill, Phillip, Cinda, Stephanie, Dana, Yolanda, Marie, and many others.

Special shout-out to: Sione Aeschliman, for her editorial magic; Alia Jones, for research help; and Bill Matson, for every beautiful chapter in our children's stories.

The readers, listeners, booksellers, educators, librarians, and book bloggers and vloggers, for embracing this debut.

My tribal community, cultural teachers, and ancestors, for being and sharing.

Chi Miigwech.